Bali

Kate Daly
James Lyon

LONELY PLANET PUBLICATIONS
Melbourne • Oakland • London • Paris

BALI

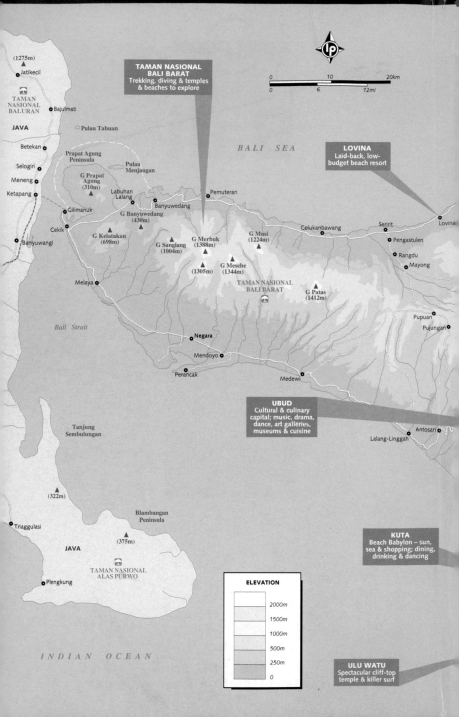

TAMAN NASIONAL BALI BARAT
Trekking, diving & temples & beaches to explore

LOVINA
Laid-back, low-budget beach resort

UBUD
Cultural & culinary capital; music, drama, dance, art galleries, museums & cuisine

KUTA
Beach Babylon – sun, sea & shopping; dining, drinking & dancing

ULU WATU
Spectacular cliff-top temple & killer surf

BALI SEA

Bali Strait

INDIAN OCEAN

JAVA

JAVA

TAMAN NASIONAL BALURAN

TAMAN NASIONAL BALI BARAT

TAMAN NASIONAL ALAS PURWO

Prapat Agung Peninsula

Tanjung Sembulungan

Blambangan Peninsula

Pulau Tabuan

Pulau Menjangan

(1275m)
Jatikecil

Bajulmati

Betekan

Selogiri

Meneng

Ketapang

Gilimanuk

Cekik

Banyuwangi

Melaya

Labuhan Lalang

Banyuwedang

Pemuteran

Celukanbawang

Seririt

Lovina

Pengastulen

Rangdu

Mayong

Pupuan

Pujungan

Antosari

Lalang-Linggah

Negara

Mendoyo

Perancak

Medewi

Triagulasi

Plengkung

G Prapat Agung (310m)

G Banyuwedang (430m)

G Kelatakan (698m)

G Sanglang (1004m)

G Merbuk (1388m)

G Musi (1224m)

G Mesehe (1344m)

(1305m)

G Patas (1412m)

(322m)

(375m)

ELEVATION
2000m
1500m
1000m
500m
250m
0

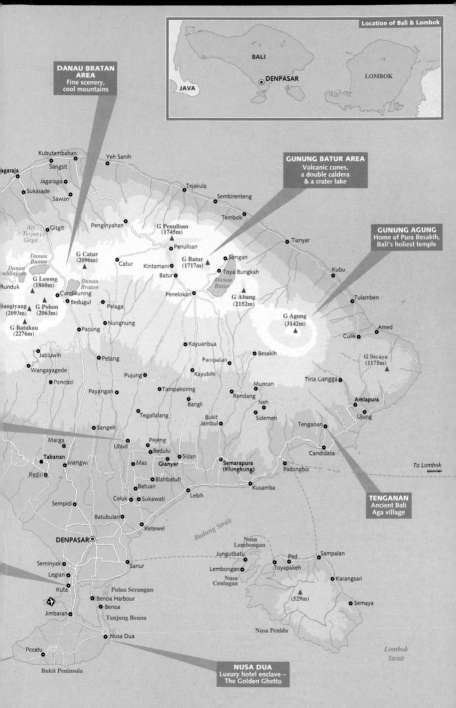

Location of Bali & Lombok

JAVA

BALI

⊙ DENPASAR

LOMBOK

DANAU BRATAN AREA
Fine scenery, cool mountains

GUNUNG BATUR AREA
Volcanic cones, a double caldera & a crater lake

GUNUNG AGUNG
Home of Pura Besakih, Bali's holiest temple

TENGANAN
Ancient Bali Aga village

NUSA DUA
Luxury hotel enclave – The Golden Ghetto

Kubutambahan
Sangsit
agaraja
Jagaraga
Sukasade
Sawan
Yeh Sanih
Tejakula
Sembirenteng
Tembok
Tianyar

Gitgit
Air Terjun Gitgit
Penginyahan
G Penulisan (1745m)
Penulisan
Kubu

Danau Buyan
Danau nblingan
G Catur (2096m)
Catur
Kintamani
Batur
G Batur (1717m)
Songan
Toya Bungkah
Danau Batur
Tulamben

Munduk
G Lesong (1860m)
Danau Bratan
Candikuning
Bedugul
Pelaga
Penelokan
G Abang (2152m)
Culik
Amed

angiyang (2093m)
G Pohon (2063m)
Nungnung
G Agung (3142m)
G Seraya (1175m)

G Batukau (2276m)
Pacung
Kayuanbua
Besakih
Tirta Gangga

Jatiluwih
Petang
Pampatan
Muncan
Amlapura

Wangayagede
Pujung
Kayubihi
Rendang
Iseh
Ujung

Penebel
Payangan
Tampaksiring
Bangli
Sidemen

Sangeh
Tegallalang
Bukit Jambul
Tenganan

Marga
Ubud
Pejeng
Bedulu
Sidan
Candidasa

Tabanan
Mengwi
Mas
Gianyar
Semarapura (Klungkung)
Padangbai
To Lombok

Kediri
Batuan
Blahbatuh
Kusamba

Sempidi
Celuk
Sukawati
Lebih

Batubulan

Ketewel
Badung Strait

DENPASAR
Nusa Lembongan
Jungutbatu
Ped
Sampalan

Seminyak
Sanur
Lembongan
Toyapakeh

Legian
Nusa Ceningan
Karangsari

Kuta
Pulau Serangan
(529m)
Semaya

Jimbaran
Benoa Harbour
Benoa
Tanjung Benoa

Nusa Dua
Nusa Penida
Lombok Strait

Pecatu

Bukit Peninsula

Bali
9th edition – March 2003
First published – January 1984

Published by
Lonely Planet Publications Pty Ltd ABN. 36 005 607 983
90 Maribyrnong St, Footscray, Victoria 3011, Australia

Lonely Planet Offices
Australia Locked Bag 1, Footscray, Victoria 3011
USA 150 Linden St, Oakland, CA 94607
UK 10a Spring Place, London NW5 3BH
France 1 rue du Dahomey, 75011 Paris

Photographs
Many of the images in this guide are available for licensing from
Lonely Planet Images.
W www.lonelyplanetimages.com

Front cover photograph
Flower floating in swimming pool (Mike McQueen, Getty Images)

ISBN 1 74059 346 4

Printed by The Bookmaker International Ltd
Printed in China

Although the authors and Lonely Planet try to make the information as accurate as possible, we accept no responsibility for any loss, injury or inconvenience sustained by anyone using this book.

Contents – Text

Contents – Maps

e Authors

te Daly
rn and bred in Sydney, Kate spent several formative childhood years in the remote country town of Wee Waa, in northwestern New South Wales. She has a BA (Communications) from the University of Technology, Sydney, and has travelled widely in Australia, Asia and Europe. On the work front, she's done it all, from copywriter in Tokyo to editor in Melbourne. She has contributed to Lonely Planet's *Queensland*, *Australia*, *Victoria*, *East Coast Australia*, *Greece* and *Greek Islands* guides.

James Lyon
James is a sceptic by nature and a social scientist by training. He worked for five years as an editor at Lonely Planet's Melbourne office, then 'jumped the fence' to become a researcher and writer. He has since worked on guides to *Mexico*, *Maldives*, *California*, *South America*, and the *USA*, but still finds Bali the most exotic place on earth. His best experiences on Bali and Lombok include temple festivals, Balinese feasts, trekking on volcanoes, taking photos at sunrise and getting lost on backroads. He also likes Balinese gardens, gamelan music, street stall snacks and Bir Bintang.

FROM KATE
Firstly a big thanks to all the Balinese drivers who guided me to out-of-the-way places. Thank you also to the following kind folk for on-the-road tips and much needed help in filling in research gaps. Alan Wilson and staff from Udayana Eco Lodge, Andrew Wellman from Danger Art in Ubud, Barbara Lucas Niggs from Bulan Baru in Senggigi, Hanafi in Kuta, Jero Wijaya from Jero Wijaya Tourist Service in Toya Bungkah, Joanna Witt from Studio Perak in Ubud, Janet De Kneefe from Casa Luna in Ubud, Ketut Suartha from Billibo Seaside Cottages in Lovina, Marcus from Manta Dive in Gili Trawangan, Mark Mickleford and Putu from Pondok Baruna & World Diving in Nusa Lembongan, Meghan Pappenheim from Tegun Galeri in Ubud, Rob Drexhage from Spice Dive in Lovina, Dr Rudiger Krechel and Cilik from Cilik's Beach Garden in Yeh Sanih, Steve from Geko Dive in Candidasa, Sue Mathers from Blue Moon Villas in Amed, Tania Lonker from Lumbung Damuh in Candidasa. Thanks also to Lonely Planet staff for their patience. And the most enormous thank you of all goes to Mikey, for poolside research on the trip (someone had to do it), limitless support at home, and other gooey stuff. Finally, thank you to my little Clem for company in utero…

This Book

This edition of *Bali* is the result of the work of several authors over a number of years. Tony Wheeler first covered the islands as part of his pioneering *South-East Asia on a shoestring* in the mid-1970s. He then expanded and improved the coverage, in concert with Mary Coverton, to create the first edition of *Bali & Lombok* in 1984. Alan Samagalski updated both Bali and Lombok for the 3rd edition and James Lyon assisted him for the 4th. James covered both the islands for the 5th and 6th editions. The 7th edition was updated by Paul Greenway, and James returned to update the 8th edition. Kate Daly updated this 9th edition, *Bali*.

Thanks to Virginia Jealous for the last-minute update following the Kuta bombing in October 2002. The following people contributed material and expertise to previous editions of this book: Michael Slovsky (arts and crafts), Kirk Wilcox (surfing), Haji Radiah (Sasak language), Hunt Kooiker (cycling) and Tony Wheeler (luxury hotels).

FROM THE PUBLISHER

This 9th edition of *Bali* was produced in Lonely Planet's Melbourne office by coordinators Louise McGregor (editorial) and Julie Sheridan (mapping). Cris Gibcus took the book through layout. Julie was assisted by Cris, Kusnandar, Tony Frankhauser and Jacqui Saunders. Louise was assisted by Tony Davidson, Greg Alford and Kristin Odijk. Brendan Dempsey designed the cover, and Julie Rovis prepared the artwork. Kieran Grogan was the project manager, and Mary Neighbour was the commissioning editor. This book was briefed by Jane Thompson and Michael Day. Thanks to Leonie Mugavin for travel information, Quentin Frayne and Emma Koch for the Language chapter, Cathy Viero for the readers' letters, and Kate Daly for her hard work and perseverance!

THANKS
Many thanks to the travellers who used the last edition and wrote to us with helpful hints, advice and interesting anecdotes. Your names appear in the back of this book.

Foreword

ABOUT LONELY PLANET GUIDEBOOKS

The story begins with a classic travel adventure: Tony and Maureen Wheeler's 1972 journey across Europe and Asia to Australia. There was no useful information about the overland trail then, so Tony and Maureen published the first Lonely Planet guidebook to meet a growing need.

From a kitchen table, Lonely Planet has grown to become the largest independent travel publisher in the world, with offices in Melbourne (Australia), Oakland (USA), London (UK) and Paris (France).

Today Lonely Planet guidebooks cover the globe. There is an ever-growing list of books and information in a variety of media. Some things haven't changed. The main aim is still to make it possible for adventurous travellers to get out there – to explore and better understand the world.

At Lonely Planet we believe travellers can make a positive contribution to the countries they visit – if they respect their host communities and spend their money wisely. Since 1986 a percentage of the income from each book has been donated to aid projects and human rights campaigns, and, more recently, to wildlife conservation.

Although inclusion in a guidebook usually implies a recommendation we cannot list every good place. Exclusion does not necessarily imply criticism. In fact there are a number of reasons why we might exclude a place – sometimes it is simply inappropriate to encourage an influx of travellers.

UPDATES & READER FEEDBACK

Things change – prices go up, schedules change, good places go bad and bad places go bankrupt. Nothing stays the same. So, if you find things better or worse, recently opened or long-since closed, please tell us and help make the next edition even more accurate and useful.

Lonely Planet thoroughly updates each guidebook as often as possible – usually every two years, although for some destinations the gap can be longer. Between editions, up-to-date information is available in our free, monthly email bulletin *Comet* (**w** www.lonelyplanet.com/newsletters). You can also check out the *Thorn Tree* bulletin board and *Postcards* section of our website, which carry unverified, but fascinating, reports from travellers.

Tell us about it! We genuinely value your feedback. A well-travelled team at Lonely Planet reads and acknowledges every email and letter we receive and ensures that every morsel of information finds its way to the relevant authors, editors and cartographers.

Everyone who writes to us will find their name listed in the next edition of the appropriate guidebook. The very best contributions will be rewarded with a free guidebook.

We may edit, reproduce and incorporate your comments in Lonely Planet products such as guidebooks, websites and digital products, so let us know if you don't want your comments reproduced or your name acknowledged.

How to contact Lonely Planet:
Online: **e** talk2us@lonelyplanet.com.au, **w** www.lonelyplanet.com
Australia: Locked Bag 1, Footscray, Victoria 3011
UK: 10a Spring Place, London NW5 3BH
USA: 150 Linden St, Oakland, CA 94607

Say 'Bali', and most Westerners think of paradise and rampant tourism. Bali offers plenty of both and much more. The image of Bali as a tropical paradise dates back to Western visitors in the 1930s, and this image has been cultivated by the international tourism industry rather than by the Balinese, who do not even have a word for paradise in their language.

Nevertheless, Bali is a good candidate for paradise – so picturesque it could be a painted backdrop, with rice paddies tripping down hillsides like giant steps, volcanoes rising up through the clouds, lush tropical jungle, long sandy beaches and warm blue water. But Bali's landscape is more than a backdrop; it is imbued with spiritual significance, and forms a part of the rich cultural life of the Balinese, whose natural grace fits the image of how people should live in paradise.

There's no denying that Bali has become a mass tourism destination, and perhaps this is a disappointment to some visitors who not only expect a paradise, but expect it be untouched by the rest of the world. It is still a great place for a tropical island holiday if that's what you're looking for – and lots of people do. There's reasonably priced accommodation at every standard, wonderful food, entertainment, nightlife and excellent shopping. And though the continuing internal political problems of Indonesia are nobody's idea of paradise, their main effect on Bali has been to reduce the growth in tourist numbers, and make the prices more competitive and as a result, the attractions less crowded. The Kuta bombings of October 2002, which shattered the peaceful image of Bali, may have a more profound effect on tourism. It seems inconceivable, though, that tourists will turn their back on this part of the world, given all that it and its people have to offer.

If you want something more than scenery and sunshine, Bali is a place that really rewards the effort to go beyond the tourist experience. Those who complain about commercialism are often those who stay only in tourist areas; a few kilometres away are villages that rarely see a tourist at all, where people live in traditional houses and continue a timeless round of religious rituals and rice cultivation.

In fact, the Balinese seem to cope with tourism better than the tourists. Bali has a long history of absorbing – and profiting from – foreign influences. Six centuries ago, as Islam swept across the islands of

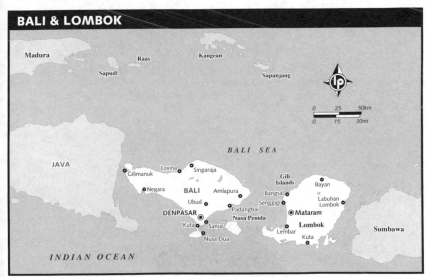

BALI & LOMBOK

Madura
Raas
Kangean
Sapudi
Sapanjang

0   25   50km
0   15   30mi

BALI SEA

JAVA
Lovina
Gilimanuk
Singaraja
Gili Islands
Bayan
Negara
BALI
Amlapura
Bangsal
Labuhan Lombok
Ubud
Senggigi
DENPASAR
Padangbai
Mataram
Kuta
Sanur
Nusa Penida
Lombok
Nusa Dua
Lembar
Kuta
Sumbawa

INDIAN OCEAN

7

Southeast Asia, the last great Hindu dynasty on Java retreated to Bali with an entourage of scholars, artists and intelligentsia. Bali's fertility and the extraordinary productivity of its agriculture has permitted the further development of this culture, with distinctive movements in art, architecture, music and dance; a culture with a vitality that has hardly faltered to this day. Festivals, ceremonies, temple processions, dances and other activities take place almost continuously on Bali – they're easy to enjoy, but so complex that you would need a lifetime to really understand them. It is the great strength of Bali's culture that makes it so much more than just a stereotypical tropical paradise.

The paradise image also sells Bali short, because it denies the reality of its place in the real world – a rapidly developing province in a fast-changing nation in one of the most dynamic regions on earth. Thanks largely to tourism, Bali is now one of the wealthier regions of Indonesia, and prior to the Kuta bombings, its predominantly Hindu population had been spared most of the political and religious violence that has rocked Indonesia.

The island of Lombok, an easy excursion just to the east, is less developed. It has as much natural beauty as Bali, but far fewer tourists. Its beaches are better, its great volcano is larger and more spectacular, and it has a greater variety of landscapes – parts of Lombok drip with water, while pockets are chronically dry, parched and cracked. The culture is rich, but not as colourful or as accessible as on Bali. Its indigenous people, the Sasak, are predominantly Muslim, although some elements of ancient animist beliefs survive, and the Balinese and Bugis communities add to the diversity. Surprisingly, a single, geographically isolated outbreak of sectarian violence in January 2000 continues to impact on Lombok's tourism industry, even though further violence is unlikely to recur.

If you're into outdoor activities, you'll find both islands offer world-class surfing, diving and challenging treks. Whether your idea of paradise is a luxury tourist resort, a deserted beach, an exotic culture or an unspoiled rural landscape, you still have a good chance of finding it on Bali or Lombok. A combination of the two makes for a great travel experience.

Facts about Bali

HISTORY

There are few traces of Stone Age people on Bali, although it's certain that the island was populated very early in prehistoric times – fossilised humanoid remains from neighbouring Java have been dated to as early as 250,000 years ago. The earliest human artefacts found on Bali are stone tools and earthenware vessels dug up near Cekik (western Bali), estimated to be 3000 years old. Other artefacts indicate that the Bronze Age began on Bali before 300 BC.

Little is known of Bali during the period when Indian traders brought Hinduism to the Indonesian archipelago. The earliest written records are inscriptions on a stone pillar near Sanur (southern Bali), dating from around the 9th century AD, and by that time Bali had already developed many similarities to the island you find today. Rice, for example, was grown with the help of a complex irrigation system, probably very like that employed now, and the Balinese had also already begun to develop their rich cultural and artistic traditions.

Hindu Influence

The Hindu state of Java began to spread its influence into Bali during the reign of King Airlangga (1019–42), or perhaps even earlier. At the age of 16, when his uncle lost the throne, Airlangga fled into the forests of western Java. He gradually gained support, won back the kingdom once ruled by his uncle and went on to become one of Java's greatest kings. Airlangga's mother had moved to Bali and remarried shortly after his birth, so when he gained the throne there was an immediate link between Java and Bali. At this time the courtly Javanese language known as Kawi came into use among the royalty of Bali, and the rock-cut memorials seen at Gunung Kawi, near Tampaksiring, are a clear architectural link between Bali and 11th-century Java (see the Tampaksiring section in the Ubud & Around chapter).

After Airlangga's death, Bali retained its semi-independent status until Kertanagara became king of the Singasari dynasty on Java two centuries later. Kertanagara conquered Bali in 1284, but the period of his greatest power lasted a mere eight years, until he was

murdered and his kingdom collapsed. However, the great Majapahit dynasty was founded by his son, Vijaya (or Wiiaya). With Java in turmoil, Bali regained its autonomy, and the Pejeng dynasty, centred near modern-day Ubud, rose to great power. In 1343 the legendary Majapahit chief minister, Gajah Mada, defeated the Pejeng king Dalem Bedaulu and brought Bali back under Javanese influence.

Although Gajah Mada brought much of the Indonesian archipelago under Majapahit control, this was the furthest extent of their power. On Bali, the 'capital' was moved to Gelgel, near modern Semarapura (also known as Klungkung, in eastern Bali), around the late 14th century, and for the next two centuries this was the base for the 'king of Bali', the Dewa Agung. As Islam spread into Java, the Majapahit kingdom collapsed into disputing sultanates. The Gelgel dynasty on Bali, under Dalem Batur Enggong, extended its power eastwards to the neighbouring island of Lombok and even westwards across the strait to Java.

As the Majapahit kingdom fell apart, many of its intelligentsia, including the priest Nirartha, moved to Bali. Nirartha is credited with introducing many of the complexities of Balinese religion to the island, as well as establishing the chain of 'sea temples', which includes Luhur Ulu Watu and Tanah Lot. Artists, dancers, musicians and actors also fled to Bali at this time and the island experienced an explosion of cultural activity. The final great exodus to Bali took place in 1478.

The Portuguese

The Italian explorer Marco Polo was believed to have stopped at the Indonesian archipelago as early as 1292, but the Portuguese were the first Europeans to establish themselves in the region. Vasco da Gama arrived seeking domination of the valuable spice trade in the 'spice islands' of the Moluccas (now Maluku) in 1512, but did not venture as far as Bali. The Spanish and English tried to wrest control of the Moluccas away from the Portuguese, but it was the Dutch who eventually laid the foundations of the Indonesian state.

The Dutch

The first Europeans to set foot on Bali itself were Dutch seamen in 1597. Setting a tradition that has prevailed to the present day, they fell in love with the island and when Cornelius de Houtman, the ship's captain, prepared to set sail from the island, several of his crew refused to come with him. At that time, Balinese prosperity and artistic activity, at least among the royalty, was at a peak, and the king who befriended de Houtman had 200 wives and a chariot pulled by two white buffaloes, not to mention a retinue of 50 dwarfs, whose bodies had been bent to resemble the handle of a kris (traditional dagger). By the early 1600s, the Dutch had established trade treaties with Javanese princes and controlled much of the spice trade, but they were interested in profit, not culture, and barely gave Bali a second glance.

In 1710 the 'capital' of the Gelgel kingdom was shifted to nearby Klungkung (now called Semarapura), but local discontent was growing, lesser rulers were breaking away, and the Dutch began to move in, using the old strategy of divide and conquer. In 1846 the Dutch used Balinese salvage claims over shipwrecks as a pretext to land military forces in northern Bali.

In 1894 the Dutch chose to support the Sasak people of Lombok in a rebellion against their Balinese rajah. The rajah capitulated to the Dutch demands, only to be overruled by his younger princes, who defeated the Dutch forces in a surprise attack. Dutch anger was roused, a larger and more heavily armed force was dispatched and the Balinese were overrun. Balinese power on Lombok finally came to an end – the crown prince was killed and the old rajah was sent into exile.

With the north of Bali long under Dutch control and Lombok now gone, the south was never going to last long. Once again, it was disputes over the ransacking of wrecked ships that gave the Dutch an excuse to move in. In 1904, after a Chinese ship was wrecked off Sanur, Dutch demands that the rajah of Badung pay 3000 silver dollars in damages were rejected, and in 1906 Dutch warships appeared at Sanur.

The Dutch forces landed despite Balinese opposition, and four days later had marched 5km to the outskirts of Denpasar. On 20 September 1906 the Dutch mounted a naval bombardment on Denpasar and then began their final assault. The three princes of Badung realised that they were completely outnumbered and outgunned, and that defeat was inevitable. Surrender and exile, however, would have been the worst imaginable outcome, so they decided to take the honourable path of a suicidal *puputan* (a fight to the death). First the princes burned their palaces, and then, dressed in their finest jewellery and waving ceremonial golden kris, the rajah led the royalty and priests out to face the modern weapons of the Dutch.

The Dutch begged the Balinese to surrender rather than make their hopeless stand, but their pleas went unheeded and wave after wave of the Balinese nobility marched forward to their death. In all, nearly 4000 Balinese died. The Dutch then marched northwest towards Tabanan and took the rajah of Tabanan prisoner, but he also committed suicide rather than face the disgrace of exile.

The kingdoms of Karangasem and Gianyar had already capitulated to the Dutch and were allowed to retain some of their powers, but other kingdoms were defeated and their rulers exiled. Finally, the rajah of Semarapura followed the lead of Badung, and once more the Dutch faced a *puputan*. With this last obstacle disposed of, all of Bali was under Dutch control and became part of the Dutch East Indies. There was little development of an exploitative plantation economy on Bali, and the common people noticed very little difference between Dutch rule and rule under the rajahs.

WWII

In 1942 the Japanese invaded Bali at Sanur, but the Balinese could offer no resistance. The Japanese established headquarters in Denpasar and Singaraja (Buleleng district), and their occupation became increasingly harsh for the Balinese. When the Japanese left in August 1945 after their defeat in WWII, the island was suffering extreme poverty, but the occupation had fostered several paramilitary, nationalist and anti-colonial organisations that were ready to fight the returning Dutch.

Independence

In August 1945, just days after the Japanese surrender, the Indonesian leader Soekarno proclaimed the nation's independence, but it took four years to convince the Dutch that they were not going to get their great colony back. In a virtual repeat of the *puputan* nearly 50 years earlier, a Balinese resistance group called Tentara Keamanan Rakyat (People's Security Force) was wiped out by the Dutch in the battle of Marga on 20 November 1946. (The slain leader of the resistance group, I Ngurah Rai, became a national hero, and Bali's airport is named after him.) The Dutch finally recognised Indonesia's independence in 1949, but Indonesians celebrate 17 August 1945 as Independence Day.

At first, independence was not an easy path for Indonesia to follow, and Soekarno, an inspirational leader during the conflict with the Dutch, proved less adept at governing the nation in peacetime. An ill-advised 'confrontation' with Malaysia in 1963 was just one event that sapped the country's energy.

1965 Coup & Backlash

On 30 September 1965 an attempted coup – blamed on the Partai Komunis Indonesia (PKI, or Communist Party) – led to Soekarno's downfall. General Mohamed Soeharto emerged as the leading figure in the armed forces, displaying great military and political skill in suppressing the coup. The PKI was outlawed and a wave of anticommunist reprisals followed, which escalated into a wholesale massacre of suspected communists throughout the Indonesian archipelago.

On Bali, the events had an added local significance as the main national political organisations, the Partai Nasional Indonesia (PNI, or Nationalist Party) and PKI, crystallised existing differences between traditionalists, who wanted to maintain the old caste system, and radicals, who saw the caste system as repressive and who were urging land reform. After the failed coup, religious traditionalists on Bali led the witch-hunt for the 'godless communists'. Some of the killings were particularly brutal, with numerous people, many of whom were not communists, being rounded up and clubbed to death by fanatical mobs. The Chinese community was particularly victimised. Eventually the military stepped in to control the anticommunist purge, but no-one on Bali was untouched by the killings, estimated at between 50,000 and 100,000 out of a population of about two million.

Soeharto & the New Order

Following the failed coup in 1965 and its aftermath, Soeharto established himself as president and took control of the government, while Soekarno disappeared from the limelight. Under Soeharto's 'New Order' government, Indonesia looked to the West in foreign policy, and Western-educated economists set about balancing budgets, controlling inflation and attracting foreign investment.

Politically, Soeharto ensured that the Golkar party, with strong support from the army (Angkatan Bersenjata Republika Indonesia, or ABRI), became the dominant political force. Under the banner of 'guided democracy', other political parties were banned or crippled by the disqualification of candidates and the disenfranchisement of voters. Regular elections maintained the appearance of a national democracy, but until 1999, Golkar won every election easily. That year, however, Golkar finished a distant second to Megawati Soekarnoputri's Democratic Party of Struggle (PDI-P), with just over half of PDI-P's votes.

On Bali, economic growth has been achieved by a huge expansion in the tourist industry, which has continued to transform the southern part of the island. There have been dramatic improvements in Bali's infrastructure – to roads, telecommunications, electricity and water supply – but also displacement of local populations, sometimes to other Indonesian islands, and disruption of many traditional communities.

The End of the Soeharto Regime

In early 1997 Southeast Asia began to suffer a severe economic crisis, and within the year the Indonesian currency (the rupiah) had all but collapsed and the economy was on the brink of bankruptcy. A year later, 76-year-old Soeharto was re-elected unopposed to a seventh five-year presidential term, much to the anguish of anti-Soeharto and pro-democracy activists. Soeharto's protégé, Dr Bacharuddin Jusuf Habibie, was appointed vice-president.

To help deal with the continuing economic crisis, Soeharto agreed in May 1998 to the International Monetary Fund's (IMF) demand to increase the government-subsidised price of electricity and petrol, resulting in immediate increases in the cost of most public transport. The price of rice and food staples also increased, and the Indonesian-Chinese community, which owns many shops, bore the brunt of riots that broke out across Java, Sumatra and Kalimantan. Fortunately, none of this strife spilled over to Bali.

Unable to stem the protests or address the nation's problems, Soeharto resigned on 21 May 1998, after 32 years in power, and Habibie became president. Habibie made some encouraging moves, including a promise of democratic elections, but he was still regarded as a Soeharto crony, and he failed to have Soeharto's enormous fortune investigated or tackle the issue of corruption.

East Timor

The June 1999 elections saw the first real step towards democracy in post-Soeharto Indonesia, but the country had to wait four months before power transferred to a new president. In the interim, East Timor voted overwhelmingly for independence from Indonesia in a UN-sponsored referendum that the Indonesian government had promised to respect.

Nevertheless, the vote triggered a campaign of burning, looting and killing by Timorese 'militias', while the Indonesian army stood by and watched, if not assisted, in the 'scorched earth' campaign by forces they themselves had armed. Under international pressure, the Indonesian government accepted UN troops, led by Australia, in East Timor. East Timor became an independent nation in May 2002.

Indonesia & Bali Today

In 1999, following the debacle in East Timor, Indonesia's parliament met to elect a new president. The frontrunner was Megawati Soekarnoputri, whose PDI-P party received the largest number of votes (34%) at the election. Megawati is enormously popular on Bali, partly because of family connections (her paternal grandmother was Balinese) and partly because her party is essentially secular (the mostly Hindu Balinese are very concerned about any growth in Muslim fundamentalism). However, Golkar, the party of former president Soeharto, was still a force, and in a surprising development, Abdurrahman Wahid, head of Indonesia's largest Muslim organisation, emerged as president.

Outraged supporters of Megawati took to the streets on Java and Bali. On Bali, the demonstrations were more disruptive than violent – trees were felled to block the main Nusa Dua road, and government buildings were damaged in Denpasar and Singaraja. The election of Megawati as vice-president quickly defused the situation, the demonstrators on Bali helped to clean up, and life returned to normal.

Wahid, commonly known by his nickname Gus Dur, was a moderate, uncharismatic leader who made minor progress on some of Indonesia's serious national problems – surviving the economic crisis, containing the power of the army, and bringing Soeharto and his cronies to account for corruption. He was, however, was less successful in tackling the ethnic, religious and regional conflicts that have plagued Indonesia.

Banking on Bali

As part of the IMF-mandated economic reforms, the Indonesian government closed 66 banks and nationalised another 13. One of the most colourful post-chaos scandals was Bank Bali. All sorts of loans turned bad when the Indonesian economy bit the dust, and when banks started to collapse the Indonesian Bank Restructuring Agency (IBRA) was formed to collect as many outstanding loans as possible. Bank Bali, which later went bankrupt itself, played its part in this debt collection business. However, it was later discovered that Bank Bali had quietly paid out a 'commission' of 546 billion Rp (about US$80 million) to a company called PT Era Giat Prima (EGP) for their assistance in collecting a US$130 million loan.

Somehow the 'commission' never got entered into the books, and when the investigators discovered this minor oversight Indonesia had its own 'Baligate'. One of EGP's executives, it turned out, was not only a high-up representative of Golkar, but also a close friend of the then president Habibie, and it was widely rumoured that the money was intended for Habibie's election campaign. Of course, nothing was ever directly proved, although EGP was forced to repay the money, in the context of a background buzz that this sort of activity was exactly what had caused Indonesia's economic meltdown in the first place.

Tony Wheeler

In July 2001, after a tense standoff during which Gus Dur threatened to impose martial law on the country in order to retain power, Indonesia's parliament finally revoked Gus Dur's presidency in favour of Megawati. The term of Megawati and her vice-president Hamzah Haz runs until 2004.

Ethnic tensions continue to simmer and frequently boil over in some provinces of Indonesia, and corruption remains a widespread problem. Many Indonesians are sceptical as to whether Megawati can make any difference to the social, economic and political problems that Indonesia continues to face.

Bali, like most places, has also been affected by global politics and concerns. In October 2002, two simultaneous bombings in Kuta – targeting an area frequented by tourists – injured or killed more than 500 people. The investigation is continuing as we go to print, but initial findings suggest that the attack came under the umbrella of an international network of radical Islamic terrorists. What long-term emotional and economic effect this will have in Bali remains to be seen, but it's expected that tourism will continue to provide the island's major source of income, despite an inevitable downturn in the industry in the immediate aftermath of the bombings. See also the boxed text 'The Bali Bombings – Paradise Lost?' in the South Bali chapter.

GEOGRAPHY
Bali is a small island, midway along the string of islands that make up the Indonesian archipelago. It's adjacent to Java, the most heavily populated island, and immediately west of the chain of smaller islands comprising Nusa Tenggara. Bali has an area of 5620 sq km, measuring approximately 140km by 80km.

The island is dramatically mountainous – the central mountain chain, a string of volcanoes, includes several peaks around 2000m. Gunung Agung, known as the 'Mother Mountain', is over 3000m high. South and north of the central mountains are Bali's agricultural lands. The southern region is a wide, gently sloping area, where most of Bali's abundant rice crop is grown. The northern coastal strip is narrower, rising rapidly into the foothills of the central range. It receives less rain, but coffee, copra, rice and cattle are farmed there.

Bali also has some arid, less-populated regions. These include the western mountain region, and the eastern and northeastern slopes of Gunung Agung. The Nusa Penida islands are dry, and cannot support intensive wet-rice agriculture. The Bukit peninsula is similarly dry, but with the growth of tourism and other industries, it's becoming more populous.

GEOLOGY
Bali is volcanically active and extremely fertile. The two go hand-in-hand because eruptions contribute to the land's exceptional fertility, and high mountains provide the dependable rainfall that irrigates Bali's complex and amazingly beautiful patchwork of rice terraces. Of course, the volcanoes are a hazard as well – Bali has endured disastrous eruptions in the past and no doubt will again in the future. Apart from the volcanic central range, there are the limestone plateaus that form the Bukit peninsula, in the extreme south of Bali, and the island of Nusa Penida.

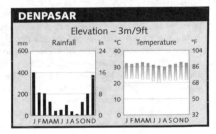

CLIMATE
Just 8° south of the equator, Bali has a tropical climate – the average temperature hovers around 30°C (mid-80s°F) all year. Direct sun feels incredibly hot, especially in the middle of the day. In the wet season, from October to March, the humidity can be very high and oppressive. The almost daily tropical downpours come as a relief, then pass quickly, leaving flooded streets and renewed humidity. The dry season (April to September) is generally sunnier, less humid and, from a weather point of view, the best time to visit, though downpours can occur at any time.

There are marked variations across the island. The coast is hotter, but sea breezes can temper the heat. As you move inland you also move up, so the altitude works to keep things cool – at times it can get chilly up in the highlands, and a warm sweater or light jacket can be a good idea in mountain villages such as Kintamani and Candikuning. The northern slopes of Gunung Batur always seem to be wet and misty, while a few kilometres away, the east coast is nearly always dry and sunny.

Air-con is not really needed on Bali. A cool breeze always seems to spring up in the evening, and the open bamboo windows, so common in Balinese architecture, make the most of the light breezes.

ECOLOGY & ENVIRONMENT

For hundreds of years, Bali has sustained a substantial population with intensive wet-rice cultivation, supported by an elaborate irrigation system that makes careful use of all the surface water. The rice fields are a complete ecological system, home for much more than just rice. In the early morning you'll often see the duck herders leading their flocks out for a day's paddle around a flooded rice field, and at night young boys head out with lights to trap tasty frogs and

Rice

Although the Balinese grow various crops, rice is by far the most important. There are three words for rice in Indonesian – *padi* is the growing rice plant (hence paddy fields); *beras* is the uncooked grain; and *nasi* is cooked rice, as in *nasi goreng* and *nasi putih*. A rice field is called a *sawah*.

The pattern of rice cultivation has changed the natural landscape, yet at the same time made it incredibly beautiful. Terraced rice fields trip down hillsides like steps for a giant, in shades of gold, brown and green as delicately selected as on an artist's palette.

Rice cultivation has also shaped the social landscape – the intricate organisation necessary for growing rice is a large factor in the strength of Bali's community life. The rice growers' association, known as a *subak*, organises community work on water management and irrigation systems, and plans and allocates the use of the water.

The process of growing rice starts with bare, dry and harvested fields. The remaining rice stalks are burnt off and the field is soaked with water and repeatedly ploughed. Nowadays, this may be done with a mechanical, petrol-powered cultivator, but often two bullocks or cattle pulling a wooden plough are still used. Once the field is reduced to the required muddy consistency, a small corner is walled off and the seedling rice is planted there. The rice is grown to a reasonable size and then lifted and replanted, shoot by shoot, in the larger field. After that it's easy living for a while as the rice steadily matures. The walls of the fields have to be kept in working order and the fields weeded, but generally this is a time to practise the gamelan, watch the dancers, do a little woodcarving or just pass the time. Finally, harvest time rolls around and the whole village turns out for a period of solid hard work. Planting the rice is strictly a male occupation but everybody takes part in harvesting it.

Rice production on Bali has increased substantially with the widespread adoption of new high-yield varieties of rice in place of the traditional rice, *padi* Bali. The best-known of these, IR36, was introduced in 1969. The new rice varieties can be harvested sooner (four months after planting instead of five for the traditional variety) and are resistant to many diseases, but there have been problems. The new varieties require the use of more pesticides, and overuse of these chemicals has resulted in ecological changes, such as the depletion of frog and eel populations, which depend on the insects for survival. Rice production actually declined in the early 1980s, because of pests and water distribution problems. These problems are being tackled by more selective use of insecticides using 'integrated pest management' techniques, by breeding varieties that are more insect-resistant, and by reverting to traditional methods of allocating water.

The new rice varieties have led to changes in traditional practices and customs. Because the new rice falls easily from the stalk, it cannot be carried to the village after harvesting and it must be threshed in the fields. The husking is often now done by small mechanical mills, rather than by women pounding it in wooden troughs. A number of songs, rituals and festivals associated with old ways of harvesting and milling rice are dying out, and everyone agrees that the new rice doesn't taste as good as *padi* Bali. New strains now account for more than 90% of the rice planted on Bali, but small areas of *padi* Bali are still planted and harvested in traditional ways to placate the rice goddess Dewi Sri, and there are still temples and offerings to her in every rice field.

eels. Other crops are often grown on the levees between the fields, or planted as a rotation crop after several rice harvests.

It's tempting to paint a picture of an ecologically sustainable island paradise, but it hasn't always been perfect. The periodic volcanic eruptions, which spread essential fertilising ash over much of the island, also cause death and destruction. Droughts, insect plagues and rats have, in the past, ravaged the rice crops and led to famine. The population has been kept at sustainable levels by high infant mortality and short life expectancy. On the other hand, deforestation is hardly an issue on Bali because most of the monsoonal rainforests were cleared long ago to make way for rice cultivation.

Since WWII, improvements in health and nutrition have resulted in increased life expectancy, and a bigger population has put pressure on limited resources. There has been some movement of Balinese people to other islands under the government's *transmigrasi* (transmigration) policy, but mainly it has been family planning that has kept population growth at manageable levels. Against this, Bali's tourist industry has actually attracted people to the island, and there is a rapid growth of urban areas that encroach onto agricultural land.

In order to increase agricultural output, new, high-yield rice varieties were introduced (see the boxed text 'Rice' earlier in this chapter), but these resulted in new problems with insect, viral and fungal pests, and greater needs for irrigation water. The need for high output combined with ecological sustainability has created an ongoing environmental management problem.

There is very little manufacturing industry, so industrial pollution is not a big problem. The most pressing environmental problems on Bali today are water supply and sanitation, solid waste management (what to do with all those plastic bags and bottles?), traffic and vehicle emissions, and the protection of coastal and marine ecosystems.

FLORA & FAUNA

Nearly all of the island is cultivated, and only in the Taman Nasional Bali Barat (West Bali National Park) are there traces of Bali's earliest plant life. The island is geologically young, and virtually all its living things have migrated from elsewhere, so

The Continuing Harvest

Legend relates how a group of Balinese farmers promised to sacrifice a pig if their harvest was good. As the bountiful harvest time approached, no pig could be found and it was reluctantly decided that a child should be sacrificed.

Then one of the farmers had an idea. They had promised the sacrifice after the harvest. If there was always new rice growing, then the harvest would always be about to take place and no sacrifice would be necessary. Since then, the Balinese have always planted one field of rice before harvesting another.

there's really no such thing as 'native' plants and animals. This is not hard to imagine in the heavily populated and extravagantly fertile south of Bali, where the orderly rice terraces are so intensively cultivated they look more like a work of sculpture than a natural landscape.

In fact, rice fields cover only about 20% of the island's surface area, and there is a great variety of other environmental zones: the dry scrub of the northwest, the extreme northeast and the southern peninsula; patches of dense jungle in the river valleys; forests of bamboo; and harsh volcanic regions that are barren rock and volcanic tuff at higher altitudes.

Flora

Trees Like most things on Bali, trees have a spiritual and religious significance, and you'll often see them decorated with scarves and black-and-white check cloths. The *waringin* (banyan) is the holiest Balinese tree and no important temple is complete without a stately one growing within its precincts. The banyan is an extensive, shady tree with an exotic feature: creepers that drop from its branches take root to propagate a new tree. Thus the banyan is said to be 'never-dying', since new offshoots can always take root. Frangipani trees (*jepun*) with their beautiful and sweet-smelling white flowers are also common in temples and family compounds.

Bali has monsoonal rather than tropical rainforest, so it lacks the valuable rainforest hardwoods that require rain year-round. The forestry department is experimenting with new varieties in plantations around the Taman Nasional Bali Barat, but at the moment nearly all the wood used for carving is imported from Sumatra and Kalimantan.

A number of plants have great practical and economic significance. Bamboo *(tiing)* is grown in several varieties and is used for everything from satay sticks and string to rafters and gamelan resonators. The various types of palm provide coconuts, sugar, fuel and fibre.

Flowers & Gardens Balinese gardens are a delight. The soil and climate can support a huge range of plants, and the Balinese love of beauty and the abundance of cheap labour means that every space can be landscaped. The style is generally informal, with curved paths, a rich variety of plants and usually a water feature.

You can find almost every type of flower on Bali, but some are seasonal and others are restricted to the cooler mountain areas. Many of the flowers will be familiar to visitors – hibiscus, bougainvillea, poinsettia, oleander, jasmine, water lily and aster are commonly seen in the southern tourist areas, while roses, begonias and hydrangeas are found mainly in the mountains. Less familiar flowers include: Javanese *ixora* (*soka* or *angsoka*), with round clusters of bright red-orange flowers; *champak* (or *cempaka*), a very fragrant member of the magnolia family; flamboyant, the flower of the royal poinciana flame tree; *manori* (or *maduri*), which has a number of traditional uses; and water convolvulus (*kangkung*), the leaves of which are commonly used as a green vegetable. There are literally thousands of types of orchid.

Flowers can be seen everywhere – in gardens or just by the roadside. Flower fanciers should make a trip to the Danau Bratan area in the central mountains to see the botanical gardens, or visit the plant nurseries along the road between Denpasar and Sanur.

Fauna
Domestic Animals Bali is thick with domestic animals, including ones that wake you up in the morning and others that bark all through the night. Chickens and roosters are kept both for food purposes and as domestic pets. Cockfighting is a popular male activity and a man's fighting bird is his prized possession. Balinese pigs are related to wild boar, and look really gross, with their sway backs and sagging stomachs. They inhabit the family compound, cleaning up all the garbage and eventually end up spit-roasted at a feast – they taste a lot better than they look.

Balinese cattle, by contrast, are delicate and graceful animals that seem more akin to deer than cows. Although the Balinese are Hindus, they do not generally treat cattle as holy animals, yet cows are rarely eaten or milked. They are, however, used to plough rice paddies and fields, and there is a major export market for Balinese cattle to Hong Kong and other parts of Asia.

Ducks are another everyday Balinese domestic animal and a regular dish at feasts. Ducks are kept in a family compound, and are put out to a convenient pond or flooded rice field to feed during the day. They follow a stick with a small flag tied to the end, and the stick is left planted in the field. As sunset approaches the ducks gather around the stick and wait to be led home again. The morning and evening duck parades are one of Bali's small delights.

Wildlife Bali has lots and lots of lizards, and they come in all shapes and sizes. The small ones (onomatopoetically called *cecak*) that hang around light fittings in the evening, waiting for an unwary insect, are a familiar sight. Geckos are fairly large lizards, often heard but less often seen. The loud and regularly repeated two-part cry 'geck-oh' is a nightly background noise that visitors soon become accustomed to, and it is considered lucky if you hear the lizard call seven times.

Bats are quite common, and the little chipmunk-like Balinese squirrels are occasionally seen in the wild, although more often in cages.

Bali's only wilderness area, Taman Nasional Bali Barat, has a number of wild species, including grey and black monkeys (which you will also see around the hills in central Bali), *muncak* (mouse deer), squirrels and iguanas. Bali used to have tigers and, although there are periodic rumours of sightings in the remote northwest of the island, nobody has proof of seeing one for a long time.

Sea Turtles

The green sea turtle and hawksbill turtle both occur in the waters around Bali and throughout Indonesia, and the species are supposedly protected by legislation that prohibits trade in all species of sea turtle. It's also illegal to export any products made from green sea turtles from Indonesia (see the Customs section in the Facts for the Visitor chapter), and in many countries including Australia, the USA, the UK and other EU countries it's illegal to import turtle products without a permit.

On Bali, however, green sea turtle meat is a traditional and very popular delicacy, particularly for Balinese feasts. Bali is the site of the most intensive slaughter of green sea turtles in the world – no reliable figures are available, although in 1999 it was estimated that more than 30,000 are killed annually.

The environmental group World Wide Fund for Nature (W www.wwf.org.id) campaigns to protect Indonesia's sea turtles from illegal trade and slaughter, and actively seeks to bring violations of international treaties to the attention of the government. The organisation appeals to travellers to Indonesia not to eat turtle meat or buy any sea turtle products, including tortoiseshell items, stuffed turtles or turtle-leather goods. A number of individuals and organisations are also involved in protecting the species, including Heinz von Holzen, the owner of Bumbu Bali restaurant in Tanjung Benoa, the Reef Seen Turtle Project at Reef Seen Aquatics in Pemuteran (see the North Bali chapter) and Reefseekers Dive Centre & Turtle Nursery on Gili Air (see the Lombok chapter).

Marine Life There is a rich variety of coral, seaweed, fish and other marine life in the coastal waters. Much of it can be appreciated by snorkellers, but the larger marine animals are only likely to be seen while diving (see Diving & Snorkelling under Activities in the Facts for the Visitor chapter). Turtles are endangered, but can still be seen wild in the waters around Nusa Penida. Dolphins are an attraction at sunrise off Lovina, on the north coast, and also around the Bukit peninsula.

Birds There are more than 300 bird species on Bali, although only one is endemic to the island – the highly endangered Bali starling (see the boxed text 'The Bali Starling' in the West Bali chapter). Other birds have adapted to Bali's intensively cultivated landscape and can be seen near many of the tourist areas.

Endangered Species

Turtle numbers have declined greatly in Indonesian waters, and most tourists are well aware of the problem. Turtle meat dishes have disappeared from tourist menus, and very few tortoiseshell souvenirs are sold. Unfortunately, turtle meat is still considered an important dish at Balinese ceremonial feasts.

Bali's other endangered species is the Bali starling, which has almost disappeared in the wild. It is bred in captivity at Taman Burung Bali Bird Park (see the Ubud & Around chapter), and attempts are being made to reintroduce caged birds to the Taman Nasional Bali Barat (see the West Bali chapter).

National Parks

The only national park on Bali is Taman Nasional Bali Barat (West Bali National Park). It covers 19,000 hectares at the western tip of Bali, plus a substantial area of coastal mangrove and the adjacent marine area, including some fine dive sites (see the West Bali chapter).

GOVERNMENT & POLITICS

Since Indonesian independence, and especially during the three decades of the Soeharto regime, Indonesian government has been centralised and hierarchical – for the last 50 years, all the important strategic decisions regarding Bali's development have been made by the central government in Jakarta. Since the first-ever freely and fairly elected central government took office in 1999, it has been faced with persistent and even violent calls for greater autonomy in Indonesia's *propinsi* (provinces) – some in Aceh and Papua (the former Irian Jaya) are

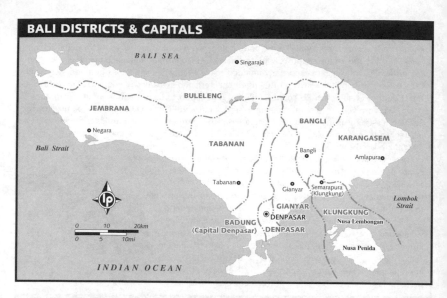

BALI DISTRICTS & CAPITALS

even demanding independence. Former President Wahid made some concessions to these demands, eg, by devolving responsibility for tourism policy to the provinces. The Balinese hope that this devolved power, and the election of Megawati's Democratic Party of Struggle (PDI-P) will result in Bali's tourist development being more sensitive to impacts on Bali's people, culture and environment (see Indonesia & Bali Today in the History section earlier).

Nevertheless, the constitution still places nearly all executive power in the hands of the national president. The legislature, the Dewan Perwakilan Rakyat (DPR, or People's Legislative Assembly) has 500 members, including 38 appointed by the armed forces (until recently, 100 members were from the military), and the rest popularly elected – very few are from Bali, which has only 1.5% of the national population. The DPR forms part of the 700-member Magelis Permusyawaratan Rakyat (MPR, or People's Consultative Assembly), along with 200 other appointed members. The MPR only convenes once every five years, to elect a president.

Under the national government there are 27 propinsi, of which Bali is one. The provincial government does not have the same sort of autonomy as a state would have in a federal system, in countries such as the USA, Australia or Germany. It acts more as a delegate of the central government, and is responsible for implementing national policy in the province. The governor of a province is appointed by the president for a five-year term from a shortlist of candidates nominated by the provincial house of representatives (Dewan Perwakilan Rakyat Daerah). The representatives to the provincial house are elected by popular vote every five years. The current governor is Drs I Dewa Made Beratha; he is Balinese, unlike many of the governors appointed under the Soeharto regime.

Within Bali there are eight kabupaten (districts), which have their origins in the precolonial rajahs' kingdoms, and were the basis of the Dutch administrative regencies. Denpasar was part of the Badung district until 1992, when the city, with Sanur and Tanjung Benoa, became a separate kabupaten kota (city district). Badung's administration is still mostly in Denpasar.

Each kabupaten is headed by a government official known as a bupati. The districts are then further divided into 51 subdistricts headed by a camat; then subdivided further into an official desa, or village (612 at last count), administered by a perbekel; and still further into an enormous number (about 3500) of banjar and dusun, which are the local divisions of a village.

ECONOMY

Bali's economy is principally agricultural. The vast majority of the Balinese work in the fields, and agriculture contributes about 40% of Bali's total economic output, although a much smaller proportion of its export income. Coffee, copra and cattle are major agricultural exports – most of the rice goes to feed Bali's own population. Newer primary industries include aquaculture and seaweed farming.

Economic growth in Indonesia plummeted to -20% in 1998, and is predicted to be around 3% in 2002. Foreign investment, which drove a booming economy up to 1997, has dried up in the face of continuing unrest. Indonesia has a huge debt problem, unemployment remains high, and corruption is ever-present. CPI inflation fell from a 2½-year high of 15.1% in February 2002 to 10.6% in August.

Within the Indonesian economy, Bali is a relatively affluent province, with tourism providing a substantial hard-currency income, along with craft and garment industries. Much of the economic activity is in the noncash sector (subsistence farming and barter), so the figures probably understate the value of Balinese output. Economic problems and unemployment elsewhere in Indonesia have led to an increasing number of people coming to Bali from other islands, hoping for work or for some other way to make money, and this is a continuing source of tension.

The Tourism Industry

Tourism accounts for about one-third of Bali's formal economy. This is achieved through the provision of accommodation, meals, services and souvenirs to visitors. The tourism industry in Indonesia started to

---

Tourism & Environment

The tourism industry, though largely dependent on an attractive environment, does have its negative effects. The growth in tourist numbers levelled off following Indonesia's economic and political problems, but about 1.3 million tourists per year are coming to Bali. The most obvious environmental effect is the conversion of prime agricultural land to make way for hotels and other facilities, including several golf courses. Less obvious is the increased demand for water – with air-con, cleaning, showers, pools and gardens, a top-end hotel requires an average of over 570L of fresh water per day, per room. Much of this water is piped from the central mountains to southern Bali resort areas, sometimes depleting the water sources traditionally used for rice cultivation. In Nusa Dua, some village wells dried up because the big hotels dug their own much deeper, hence lowering the water table.

But much of tourism's environmental impact has been indirect. For example, the huge increase in traffic on Bali is not principally caused by vehicles transporting tourists, but by the massive number of motorcycles and cars purchased with the income from tourism, and the increased use of buses, cars and trucks by a more affluent population. Denpasar has the worst traffic problem, but very few tourists.

Similarly, tourists probably have very little direct impact on the endangered turtle populations (no tourist restaurants offer turtle meat, and turtle-shell souvenirs have virtually disappeared), but increasing numbers of affluent Balinese can afford turtle for ceremonial feasts.

Tourism has had little direct impact on the coastal and marine environment – those who come for diving, snorkelling and fishing actually make a strong case for conservation of coral reefs. The worst damage has resulted from digging up coral reefs for cement and building stone (some of it to make hotels of course), and by large projects such as the expansion of the airport and the abortive resort development on Pulau Serangan. The erosion caused by the development on Pulau Serangan has destroyed the beach at Candidasa and is threatening Sanur's beach as well. This is not what either tourists or the tourist industry want, but the damage has been done.

One risk is the waste management problems caused by the ever-increasing number of water bottles sold to tourists on Bali. Many businesses simply burn discarded bottles, and chemicals carried in the smoke can drift along streets and into homes and hotels. A few towns, such as Padangbai, have started to encourage recycling programmes, with bottles being shipped to Surabaya for processing. In Ubud and other areas a number of outlets provide filtered refills of water bottles for a price that's cheaper than buying a new bottle, in the hope that you'll buy fewer bottles during your stay.

contract in mid-1997 with the well-publicised forest fires in several parts of the country. Since then the Timor crisis, riots and sectarian violence in other parts of Indonesia and political instability have deterred many potential tourists from travelling to Bali. Tourist arrivals were 1.23 million in 1997, declining to 1.18 million in 1998, and recovering to 1.2 million in 1999. In 2000, tourist arrivals reached 1.47 million then they declined again in 2001 to 1.42 million. In fact, the average length of stay in Bali has dipped, to 3.6 days by June 2002.

Though the Balinese generally accepted the idea that Bali must enable its tourist potential to be developed in the national interest, major projects developed in the late '90s were beginning to attract vocal opposition. The collapse of the Soeharto regime and its crony corporations provided a much-needed pause in the breakneck rate of growth. The 1997 decline in tourist numbers and the economic crisis sunk several grandiose schemes, and the Balinese government now has more power to impose and monitor environmental standards.

Manufacturing

The clothing industry has enjoyed spectacular growth from making beachwear for tourists – it now accounts for around half the value of Balinese exports. Furniture is a recent growth industry, with contemporary furniture and reproduction antiques being made from cane, bamboo and tropical timbers. Many pieces are actually made on Java, though they are sent to Bali for final finishing and for marketing – the buyers like to stay on Bali.

POPULATION & PEOPLE

Bali is a densely populated island, with approximately 3.1 million people in an area of 5620 sq km – about 550 people per sq km. The population is almost all Indonesian; 95% are of Balinese Hindu religion and could be described as ethnic Balinese. Most of the other residents are from other parts of Indonesia – particularly Java, but also from Sumatra and Nusa Tenggara; the tourist industry is a real magnet for people seeking jobs and business opportunities. However, quite a few Balinese have moved to more lightly populated islands as part of the *transmigrasi* programme.

The Balinese people are predominantly of the Malay race – descendants of the groups that travelled southeast from China in the migrations of around 3000 BC. Before that time, Bali may have been populated by people related to Australian Aborigines, who appear to have mixed at least a little with the group that displaced them. Other ethnic strands may have come from India, Polynesia and Melanesia, and a diverse range of physical features from all those groups can be seen in Bali's current population.

What defines the people of Bali is cultural rather than racial, and the Balinese culture embraces both the minority Bali Aga groups, whose Hindu traditions predate the arrival of the Majapahit court from Java in the 15th century, and the vast majority of Balinese, whose culture is a legacy of that influx.

Caste System

The caste system derives from Hindu traditions on Java dating back to about 1350, although it is not nearly as strict as the system in India. On Bali, caste determines roles in religious rituals and the form of language to be used in every social situation.

Most aspects of Balinese culture have proved to be adaptable – as Bali becomes more and more a part of Indonesia and the rest of the world – but the question of caste is problematic. There were pressures on and within the caste system even before the Dutch arrived, and the colonial period entrenched a caste structure that suited Dutch interests, rather than those of the Balinese.

During the 1960s the communists opposed the caste system as a feudal relic; a view shared by liberals and intellectuals, at least until the massacres of suspected communists in 1965–66.

Despite the persistence of honorific titles (Ida, Dewa, Gusti etc), the practical importance of one's caste is diminishing, as status becomes more a matter of education, economic success and community influence.

The importance of caste differences in language is mitigated by the use of 'polite' forms of Balinese language, or by using the national Indonesian language (Bahasa Indonesia), itself a sign of some status. In a traditional village, however, caste is still very much a central part of life, and caste concepts are still absolutely essential to all religious practices.

About 90% of Bali's ethnic population belong to the common *sudra* (also known as *wong kesaman*) caste, and the rest belong to the *triwangsa* (three people) caste, also known as *wong menak*. The *triwangsa* is divided into three sub-castes: Brahmana are high priests, with titles of Ida Bagus (male) and Ida Ayu (female); Ksatriyasa (or Satriana) are merchants, with titles of Cokodor (males) and Ana Ayung (females); and Wesia are the main caste of the nobility, with titles of Gusti Ngura or Dewa Gede (male), and Gusti Ayu or Dewa Ayu (female).

Minority Groups

Ethnic minorities on Bali include small Chinese contingents in the larger towns, a few thousand Indian and Arab merchants in Denpasar, plus a number of more or less permanent Western visitors, many of them women married to Balinese men.

In general terms, the island is a model of religious tolerance, with two Christian villages (one Catholic, one Protestant), some Chinese temples, a Buddhist monastery and Javanese and other Muslim communities, particularly around the ports of Gilimanuk, Singaraja and Padangbai.

Population Growth

Population control continues to be a priority of the Indonesian government, and the family planning slogan *dua anak cukup* (two children is enough) is a recurring theme in roadside posters. It seems to be quite successful, as many young families are limiting themselves to two children (or sometimes three), but certainly not the seven or nine children common two or three generations ago.

EDUCATION

In Indonesia, education begins with six years of primary school (*sekolah dasar* or SD), then three years of junior high school (*sekolah menengah pertama* or SMP) and three years of senior high school (*sekolah menengah atas* or SMA), which leads to university. The majority of children on Bali complete primary school, while only a minority complete secondary school. Literacy on Bali, however, is higher than the national average. Going to university is expensive and only a minority can afford it. There are universities in Denpasar, Singaraja and on the Bukit peninsula.

PERFORMING ARTS

Music, dance and drama are closely related on Bali, with Balinese dance the most obvious example of the three elements working together (see the 'Balinese Dance' special section). Nevertheless, Balinese gamelan music is often played in processions, festivals and religious ceremonies, without accompanying dance and drama. *Wayang kulit* (shadow puppet plays) are basically drama performances, though the sound effects and the puppets' movements are part of the show. The *arja* is a sort of dance-drama, comparable to Western opera.

Gamelan

Balinese music is based around an ensemble known as a gamelan, which can comprise from four to as many as 50 or more instruments. It is derived from Javanese gamelan, although the playing style is quite different. Gamelan music is almost completely percussion – apart from the simple *suling* flute and the two-stringed *rebab,* there are virtually no wind or string instruments. Unlike many forms of Asian music, the Balinese gamelan is accessible to ears attuned to Western music. Although it sounds strange at first with its noisy, jangly percussion, it's exciting and enjoyable.

The main instruments of the gamelan are the xylophone-like *gangsa,* which have bronze bars above bamboo resonators. The player hits the keys with their hammer in one hand, while their other hand moves close behind to dampen the sound from each key just after it is struck. Although the *gangsa* make up the majority of the instruments and it is their sound that is most prevalent, the actual tempo and nature of the music is controlled by the two *kendang* drums – one male and one female.

Other instruments are the deep *trompong* drums, the small *kempli* gong and the *cengceng* cymbals used in faster pieces. A gamelan orchestra is also called a *gong*. A *gong gede* (large or big orchestra) is the traditional form, and comprises a complete orchestra, with between 35 and 40 musicians. The *gong kebyar* is the modern, popular form of *gong*, and usually has up to 25 instruments. There are even more ancient forms of the gamelan, such as the gamelan *selunding,* still occasionally played in Bali Aga villages like Tenganan, eastern Bali.

A village's gamelan is usually organised through a *banjar*, which owns the instruments and stores them in the *bale gong*. The musician's club is known as a *seksa,* and the members meet to practise in the *bale banjar* (a large pavilion for meeting, debate, gamelan practise etc). Although gamelan playing is traditionally a male occupation, a gamelan for women has been established in Ubud. The pieces are learned by heart and passed down from father to son – there is little musical notation or recording of individual pieces.

The gamelan is also played on Java, and Javanese gamelan music is held to be more 'formal' and 'classical' than the Balinese. A perhaps more telling point is that Javanese gamelan music is rarely heard, apart from at special performances, whereas on Bali you seem to hear gamelans playing everywhere you go. Gamelan music, in both Balinese and Javanese styles, is available on cassette tapes and the occasional CD. Look in the music shops and bigger department stores in the Kuta region.

The village of Blahbatuh in eastern Bali is a gamelan making centre, where you can see instruments being made, as is Sawan in northern Bali. Giant bamboo gamelan, with deep resonating tones, are made in Jembrana in western Bali. Gamelan instruments are usually made to order, so even at the workshops you might not find anything available for purchase.

Wayang Kulit

The shadow puppet plays known as *wayang kulit* are popular not only on Bali, but throughout the whole archipelago. The plays are far more than mere entertainment, however, for the puppets are believed to have great spiritual power and the *dalang* (the puppet master and storyteller) is an almost mystical figure. He has to be a person of considerable skill and even greater endurance. He not only has to manipulate the puppets and tell the story, but he must also conduct the small gamelan orchestra, the *gender wayang,* and beat time with his chanting – having long run out of hands to do things with, he performs the latter task with a horn held with his toes!

The *dalang's* mystical powers come into play because the *wayang kulit,* like so much of Balinese drama, is another phase of the eternal struggle between good and evil. The endurance factor comes in because a *wayang kulit* performance can last six or more hours, and the performances always seem to start so late that the drama is only finally resolved as the sun peeps up over the horizon.

The intricate lace figures of shadow puppets are made of buffalo hide carefully cut with a sharp, chisel-like stylus and then painted. The figures are completely traditional – there is no deviation from the standard list of characters and their standardised appearance, so there's definitely no mistaking who's who.

Although *wayang kulit* performances are normally held at night, there are sometimes daytime temple performances, where the figures are manipulated without a screen.

At night time performances, the *dalang* sits behind a screen on which the shadows of the puppets are cast, usually by an oil lamp, which gives a far more romantic flickering light than modern electric lighting would do. Traditionally, women and children sit together in front of the screen, while the men sit behind the screen with the *dalang* and his many assistants.

The characters are arrayed to the right and left of the puppet master – goodies to the right, baddies to the left. The characters include nobles, who speak in the high Javanese language Kawi, and common clowns, who speak in everyday Balinese. The *dalang* also has to be a linguist! When the four clowns (Delem and Sangut are the bad ones, Twalen and his son Merdah are the good ones) are on screen, the performance becomes something of a Punch and Judy show, with much rushing back and forth, clouts on the head and comic insults. The noble characters are altogether more refined – they include the terrible Durga and the noble Bima. *Wayang kulit* stories are chiefly derived from the great Hindu epics, the *Mahabharata* and the *Ramayana.*

Wayang kulit puppets are made in the village of Puaya near Sukawati, south of Ubud, and in Peliatan, just east of Ubud, but they're easy to find in craft, antique and souvenir shops.

Arja

An *arja* drama is not unlike *wayang kulit* in its melodramatic plots, its offstage sound effects and its cast of easily identifiable goodies and baddies – represented by the refined *alus* and unrefined *kras* characters, respectively. It's performed outside, on a rectangle of ground, often with a curtain as a backdrop. The setup can represent a room, or other defined space in which the action takes place. Sometimes a small house is built on the stage, and set on fire at the climax of the story!

The story is told by clown characters who describe and explain all the actions of the nobles, so the dialogue uses both high and low Balinese language. The plot is often just a small part of a longer story well known to the Balinese audience. For these reasons, *arja* is very difficult for a foreigner to understand or appreciate, and it is almost never performed for tourists.

LITERATURE

The Balinese language has several forms, but only 'high Balinese' is a written language, and that is a form of Sanskrit used for religious purposes and to recount the great Hindu epics such as the *Ramayana* and the *Mahabharata*. Illustrated versions of these epics inscribed on *lontar* (specially prepared palm leaves) are Bali's earliest books (see the boxed text 'Lontar Books' in the North Bali chapter). The poems and stories of the early Balinese courts, from the 11th to the 19th centuries, were written in Old Javanese or Middle Javanese, and were meant to be sung or recited rather than read. Even the most elaborate drama and dance performances had no real written scripts or choreography, at least until Westerners like Colin McPhee started to produce them in the 1930s.

In the colonial period, education was in Dutch, and a few Indonesians began writing in that language, while Dutch scholars set about documenting traditional Balinese language and literature. In the 1920s and 1930s, the use of Indo-Malay (later called Bahasa Indonesia) became more widespread in the Dutch East Indies. One of the first Balinese writers to be published in that language was Anak Agung Pandji Tisna, from Singaraja in northern Bali. His second novel, *The Rape of Sukreni* (1936) was both a popular and critical success, and notable for its adaptation of the features of Balinese drama – the depiction of good and bad characters, the conflict between good and evil, and the inevitability of karma. Most of the action takes place in a *warung* (food stall), not unlike many small eateries in villages all over Bali today. An

English translation is available at bookshops on Bali, and is highly recommended.

Since Indonesian independence, most modern Balinese literature has been written in Bahasa Indonesia. Short stories have been the preferred genre, and are frequently published in newspapers and magazines, often for literary competitions. Not surprisingly, an important theme has been tradition versus change and modernisation, often elaborated as a tragic love story involving couples of different castes. Politics, money, tourism and relations with foreigners are also explored. Several anthologies of Balinese short stories translated into English are currently in print – see the Books section in the Facts for the Visitor chapter.

ARCHITECTURE

Balinese architecture has a cosmic significance that is much more important than the physical materials, the construction or the decoration. Balinese sculpture and painting were once exclusively used as architectural decoration, and though temples are still heavily decorated, sculpture and painting have developed as separate art forms (see the 'Balinese Arts & Crafts' special section).

A village, a temple, a family compound, an individual structure and even a single part of the structure, must all conform to the Balinese concept of cosmic order. They consist of three parts that represent the three worlds of the cosmos – the world of gods *(swah)*, the world of humans *(bhwah)* and the world of demons *(bhur)*. They also represent a three-part division of a person: the head *(utama)*, the body *(madia)* and the legs *(nista)*. The units of measurement used in traditional buildings are directly based on the anatomical dimensions of the head of the household, ensuring harmony between the dwelling and those that live in it. Traditionally, the designer of the building is a combination architect-priest called an *undagi*.

The basic element of Balinese architecture is the *bale*, a rectangular, open-sided pavilion with a steeply pitched roof of thatch. Both a family compound and a temple will comprise a number of separate *bale* for specific functions, all surrounded by a high wall. The size and proportions of the *bale*, the number of columns, and the position within the compound, are all determined according to tradition and the owner's caste status.

The Family Compound

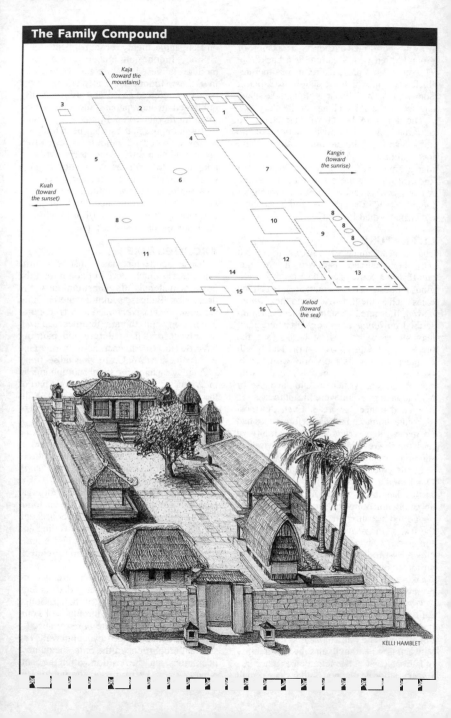

Kaja
(toward the mountains)

Kangin
(toward the sunrise)

Kuah
(toward the sunset)

Kelod
(toward the sea)

KELLI HAMBLET

The Family Compound

1 **Sanggah or Merajan**
   Family Temple
2 **Umah Meten**
   Sleeping pavilion for the family head
3 **Tugu**
   Shrine
4 **Pengijeng**
   Shrine
5 **Bale Tiang Sanga**
   Guest pavilion
6 **Natah**
   Courtyard with frangipani or hibiscus shade tree
7 **Bale Sakenam**
   Working & sleeping pavilion
8 **Fruit trees and coconut palms**
9 **Vegetable garden**
10 **Bale Sakepat**
   Sleeping pavilion for children
11 **Paon**
   Kitchen
12 **Lumbung**
   Rice barn
13 **Rice-threshing area**
14 **Aling Aling**
   Screen wall
15 **Candi Kurung**
   Gate with roof
16 **Apit Lawang or Pelinggah**
   Gate shrines

The focus of a community is a large pavilion, called the *bale banjar*, used for meetings, debates and gamelan practice, among many other activities. You'll find that large, modern buildings such as restaurants and the lobby areas of new hotels are often modelled on the larger *bale*, and they can be airy, spacious and very handsomely proportioned.

During the building process, the pavilions may get beyond a certain size, and tradtional materials cannot be used. In these cases concrete is substituted for timber, and sometimes the roof is tiled rather than thatched. The fancier modern buildings like banks and hotels might also feature decorative carvings derived from traditional temple design. As a result of this, some regard the use of traditional features in modern buildings as pure kitsch, while others see it as a natural and appropriate development of modern Balinese style. Buildings with these features are sometimes described as Baliesque, Bali Baroque, or Bali Rococo if the decoration has become too excessive.

Visitors may be disappointed by Balinese palaces *(puri)*, which prove to be neither large nor imposing. The *puri* are the traditional residences of the Balinese aristocracy, although now they may be used as top-end hotels or as regular family compounds. They prove unimposing as a Balinese palace can never be built more than one storey high. This is because a Balinese noble could not possibly use a ground-floor room if the feet of people on an upper floor were walking above.

The Family Compound
The Balinese house looks inward – the outside is simply a high wall. Inside there will be a garden and a separate small building or *bale* for each function – one for cooking, one for washing and the toilet, and separate buildings for each 'bedroom'. In Bali's mild tropical climate people live outside, so the 'living room' and 'dining room' will be open veranda areas, looking out into the garden. The whole complex is oriented on the *kaja-kelod* axis, between the mountains and the sea.

Many modern Balinese houses, particularly in Denpasar and the larger towns, are arranged much like houses in the west, but there are still a great number of traditional family compounds. For example, in Ubud, nearly every house will follow the same traditional walled design.

Analogous to the human body, there's a head (the family temple with its ancestral shrine), arms (the sleeping and living areas), legs and feet (the kitchen and rice storage building), and even an anus (the garbage pit). There may be an area outside the house compound where fruit trees are grown or a pig may be kept. Usually the house is entered through a gateway backed by a small wall known as the *aling aling*. It serves a practical and a spiritual purpose, both preventing passers-by from seeing in and stopping evil spirits from entering. Evil spirits cannot easily turn corners so the *aling aling* stops them from simply scooting straight in through the gate!

There are several variations on the typical family compound illustrated here. For example, the entrance is commonly on the *kuah,* or sunset side, rather than the *kelod* side as shown (but *never* on the *kangin* or *kaja* side).

Major Temples

Bali has thousands of temples, but some of the most important are listed here, and are shown on the Important Balinese Temples map.

Directional Temples
Some temples are so important they are deemed to belong to the whole island rather than particular communities. There are nine *kahyangan jagat* or directional temples.

Pura Besakih In Besakih, eastern Bali
Pura Goa Lawah Near Padangbai, eastern Bali
Pura Lempuyang Near Tirta Gangga, eastern Bali
Pura Luhur Batukau On Gunung Batukau, central mountains
Pura Luhur Ulu Watu At Ulu Watu, southern Bali
Pura Masceti Near Gianyar, eastern Bali
Pura Sambu On Gunung Agung, eastern Bali

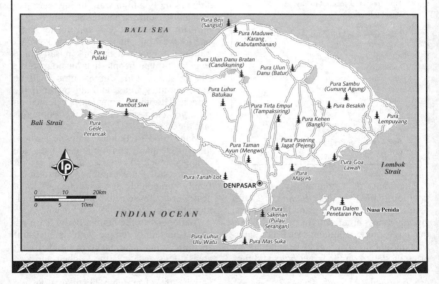

Balinese Temples
Every village on Bali has several temples, and every home has at least a simple house-temple. The Balinese word for temple is *pura*, from a Sanskrit word literally meaning 'a space surrounded by a wall'. Similar to a traditional Balinese home, a temple is walled in – so the shrines you see in rice fields or at 'magical' spots such as old trees are not real temples. Simple shrines or thrones often overlook crossroads, to protect passers-by.

All temples are built on a mountains-sea orientation, not north–south. The direction towards the mountains, *Kaja*, is the end of the temple, where the holiest shrines are

found. The temple's entrance is at the sea end *(kelod)*. The sunrise direction *(kangin)* is more holy than the sunset direction *(kuah)*, so many secondary shrines are on the *kangin* side. *Kaja* may be towards a particular mountain – Pura Besakih in eastern Bali is pointed directly towards Gunung Agung – or towards the mountains in general, which run east–west along the length of Bali.

Temple Types There are three basic temple types, found in most villages. The most important is the *pura puseh* (temple of origin), dedicated to the village founders and at the *kaja* end of the village. In the middle

Major Temples

Pura Ulun Danu Bratan In Candikuning (Danau Bratan), central mountains
Pura Ulun Danu In Batur, central mountains

Most of these are well known and accessible, but some are rarely seen by visitors to Bali. Pura Masceti, on the coast south of Gianyar, is easily reached but seldom visited, and it's a stiff walk to remote Pura Lempuyang.

Sea Temples
The 16th-century Majapahit priest Nirartha founded a chain of temples to honour the sea gods. Each was intended to be within sight of the next, and several have dramatic locations on the south coast. From the west, they include the following.

Pura Gede Perancak Where Nirartha first landed
Pura Rambut Siwi On a wild stretch of the west coast
Pura Tanah Lot The very popular 'sunset temple'
Pura Luhur Ulu Watu A spectacular clifftop position (also one of the nine directionals)
Pura Mas Suka At the very south of the Bukit peninsula
Pura Sakenan On Pulau Serangan
Pura Pulaki Near Pemuteran, in northern Bali

Other Important Temples
Some other temples have particular importance because of their location, spiritual function or architecture. They include the following.

Pura Beji In Sangsit, northern Bali, it is dedicated to the goddess Sri, who looks after irrigated rice fields
Pura Dalem Penetaran Ped On Nusa Penida, dedicated to the demon Jero Gede Macaling, and a place of pilgrimage for those seeking protection from evil
Pura Kehen A fine hillside temple in Bangli, eastern Bali
Pura Maduwe Karang An agricultural temple on the north coast, famous for its spirited bas-relief, including one of a bicycle rider
Pura Pusering Jagat One of the famous temples at Pejeng, near Ubud, it has an enormous bronze drum
Pura Taman Ayun The large and imposing state temple at Mengwi, northwest of Denpasar
Pura Tirta Empul The beautiful temple at Tampaksiring, with springs and bathing pools at the source of Sungai Pakerisan, north of Ubud

of the village is the *pura desa*, for the many spirits that protect the village community in daily life. At the *kelod* end of the village is the *pura dalem*, or temple of the dead. The graveyard is also here, and the temple may include representations of Durga, the terrible side of Shiva's wife Parvati. Both Shiva and Parvati have a creative and destructive side; their destructive powers are honoured in the *pura dalem*.

Other temples include those that are dedicated to the spirits of irrigated agriculture. Rice-growing is so important on Bali, and the division of water for irrigation is handled with the utmost care, that these *pura subak* or *pura ulun suwi* can be of considerable importance. Other temples may also honour dry-field agriculture, as well as the flooded rice paddies.

In addition to these 'local' temples, there are a lesser number of great temples. Each family worships its ancestors in the family temple, the clan worships in its clan temple and the village in the *pura puseh*. Above these are the state temples or temples of royalty, and often a kingdom would have three of these: a main state temple in the heartland of the state (like Pura Taman Ayun in Mengwi, western Bali); a mountain temple (like Pura Besakih, eastern Bali); and a sea temple (like Pura Luhur Ulu Watu, southern Bali).

Every house on Bali has its house temple, which is at the *kaja-kangin* corner of the courtyard. There will be shrines to the Hindu 'trinity' of Brahma, Shiva and Vishnu; to *taksu*, the divine intermediary; and to *tugu*, the lord of the ground.

Temple Design Temple design follows a traditional formula. A temple compound contains a number of *gedong* (shrines) of varying sizes, made from solid brick and stone and heavily decorated with carvings. See the following boxed text for information on temple design.

Temple Decoration Lavishly carved decoration is a very important feature of temple architecture. Ideally, every single square centimetre of a temple gateway should be intricately carved, with a diminishing series of demon faces placed above it as protection. A couple of stone statues act as guardians.

In small or less important temples, there may be little or no sculpture at all. In most others, particularly the exuberant temples of northern Bali, the sculpture may be extremely intricate and beautiful. In some instances a temple is plainly built, and the carving is added when money is available at a later date. Carved stone deteriorates fairly rapidly in Bali's tropical climate, and is restored or sometimes replaced as resources permit. In some cases it's not uncommon to see a temple with old carvings that are barely discernible next to work that has just been finished.

Typical Temple Design

Temple design varies greatly, but the basic elements are shown here.

1. **Candi Bentar** The intricately sculpted temple gateway, like a tower split down the middle and moved apart.
2. **Kulkul Tower** The warning-drum tower, from which a wooden split drum (*kulkul*) is sounded to announce events at the temple or warn of danger.
3. **Bale** A pavilion, usually open-sided, for temporary use or storage. May include a *bale gong* (3A), where the gamelan orchestra plays at festivals; a *paon* (3B) or temporary kitchen to prepare offerings; or a *wantilan* (3C), a stage for dances or cockfights.
4. **Kori Agung or Paduraksa** The gateway to the inner courtyard is an intricately sculpted stone tower. Entry is through a doorway reached by steps in the middle of the tower and left open during festivals.
5. **Raksa or Dwarapala** Statues of fierce guardian figures who protect the doorway and deter evil spirits. Above the door will be the equally fierce face of a *bhoma*, with hands outstretched against unwanted spirits.
6. **Aling Aling** If an evil spirit does get in, this low wall behind the entrance will keep it at bay, as evil spirits find it difficult to make right-angle turns.
7. **Side Gate (Betelan)** Most of the time (except during ceremonies) entry to the inner courtyard is through this side gate, which is always open.
8. **Small Shrines (Gedong)** These usually include shrines to Ngrurah Alit and Ngrurah Gede, who organise things and ensure the correct offerings are made.
9. **Padma** Stone throne for the sun god Surya, placed in the most auspicious *kaja-kangin* corner. It rests on the *badawang* (world turtle), which is held by two *naga* (mythological serpents).
10. **Meru** A multiroofed shrine. Usually there is an 11-roofed *meru* (11A) to Sanghyang Widi, the supreme Balinese deity, and a three-roofed *meru* (11B) to the holy mountain Gunung Agung.
11. **Small Shrines (Gedong)** At the *kaja* (mountain) end of the courtyard, these may include a shrine to the sacred mountain Gunung Batur; a Maospahit shrine to honour Bali's original Hindu settlers (Majapahit); and a shrine to the *taksu*, who acts as an interpreter for the gods. (Trance dancers or mediums may be used to convey the gods' wishes.)
12. **Bale Piasan** Open pavilions used to display temple offerings.
13. **Gedong Pesimpangan** Stone building dedicated to the village founder or a local deity.
14. **Paruman or Pepelik** Open pavilion in the inner courtyard, where the gods are supposed to assemble to watch the ceremonies of a temple festival.

SOCIETY
Traditional Culture

For the average rural Balinese, the working day is not a long one for most of the year. Their expertise at growing rice means that large crops are produced without an enormous labour input, and this leaves time for elaborate cultural events. Every stage of Balinese life, from conception to cremation, is marked by a series of ceremonies and rituals, which are the basis of the rich, varied and active cultural life of the Balinese.

Birth The first ceremony of Balinese life takes place even before birth – when women reach the third month of pregnancy they take part in ceremonies at home and at the village river or spring. A series of offerings is made to ensure the wellbeing of the baby. Another ceremony takes place soon after the birth, during which the afterbirth is buried with appropriate offerings. Women are considered to be *sebel* (unclean) after giving birth and 12 days later they are 'purified' through yet another ceremony. The father is also *sebel*, but only for three days. After 42 days, another ceremony and more offerings are made for the baby's future.

A child goes through 13 celebrations, or *manusa yadnya*, in the formative years. The first ceremony, or *oton*, takes place at 105 days, halfway through the baby's first Balinese year when, for the first time, the baby's feet are allowed to touch the ground. Prior to this time babies are carried continuously, because the ground is believed to be impure,

Typical Temple Design

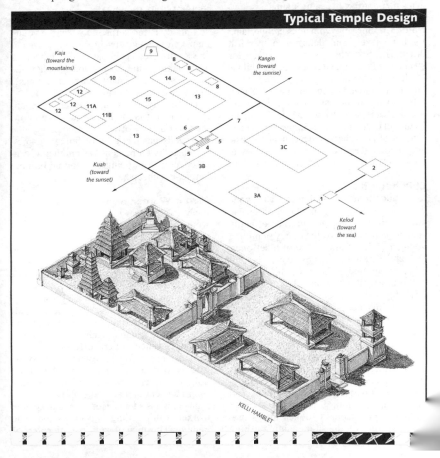

KELLI HAMBLET

and babies, so close to heaven, should not be allowed to come into contact with it. The baby is also ceremonially welcomed to the family at this time. Another ceremony follows at 210 days, at the end of his/her first Balinese year, when the baby is spiritually blessed in the ancestral temple. The first birthday is celebrated in grand style, with huge and expensive feasts for family and other members of the community.

Balinese often regard boy-girl twins as a major calamity. The reasoning is that boy-girl twins are said to have committed a sort of spiritual incest while in the womb and this is dangerous for the whole village. Extensive (and expensive) rituals and ceremonies are performed to purify the children, the parents and the whole village. However, same-sex twins don't attract the same stigma.

Names Balinese given names are the same for both sexes, and determined by birth order. The first child is called Wayan (or sometimes Putu or Gede); the second child is Made (or Kadek or Nengah); the third is Nyoman (or Komang); and the fourth is Ketut. Fifth, sixth, seventh and eighth children re-use the same set (Wayan, Made, Nyoman, Ketut) all over again. The Balinese also have a series of titles that are dependent on caste and gender – see the Caste System entry in the Population & People section earlier.

Childhood If ever there was a people who love children, it's the Balinese – as anyone who has visited Bali with their children can attest. On Bali, coping with a large family is made much easier by the policy of putting younger children in the care of older ones. One child always seems to be carrying another one around on his or her hip.

Balinese children almost always seem remarkably well behaved. Of course, you hear kids crying occasionally, but tantrums, fights, screams and shouts are very infrequent. It's been said that parents achieve this by treating children with respect and teaching them good behaviour by example.

After the ceremonies of babyhood come the ceremonies marking the stages of childhood and puberty, including the important tooth-filing ceremony. The Balinese prize traight, even teeth. Crooked fangs are, ter all, one of the chief distinguishing rks of evil spirits – just have a look at a Rangda mask! A priest files the upper front teeth to produce an aesthetically pleasing straight line. Today the filing is often only symbolic – one pass of the file.

Marriage Every Balinese expects to marry and raise a family, and marriage takes place at a comparatively young age. In general, marriages are not arranged, although there are strict rules that apply to marriages between the castes.

There are two basic forms of marriage on Bali. The respectable form, in which the family of the man visits the family of the woman and politely proposes that the marriage take place, is *mapadik*. The Balinese, however, like their fun and often prefer marriage by elopement *(ngorod)* as the more exciting option.

Of course, the Balinese are also practical, so nobody is too surprised when the young man spirits away his bride-to-be, even if she loudly protests about being kidnapped. The couple go into hiding and somehow the girl's parents, no matter how assiduously they search, never manage to find her.

Eventually the couple re-emerge, announce that it is too late to stop them now, the marriage is officially recognised and everybody has had a lot of fun and games. Marriage by elopement has another advantage: apart from being exciting and mildly heroic, it's cheaper.

Men & Women Social life on Bali is relatively free and easy and, although Balinese women are not kept cloistered, the roles of the sexes are strictly delineated. There are certain tasks clearly to be handled by women, and others that are reserved for men. Running the household is very much the woman's task. In the morning women sweep and clean, and put out the offerings for the gods.

Every household has a shrine or god-throne where offerings must be placed, and areas on the ground, such as at the compound entrance, where offerings for the demons are put. While women are busy attending to these tasks, the men of the household are likely to be looking after the fighting cocks and any other pets.

Shopping is a female job, although at large markets cattle-selling is a man's job. The traditional position of women as preparers of food – and as the buyers and sellers – places them in a very good position to take part in the tourist industry. A successful Balinese restaurant or shop is much more likely to have been established by a woman than a man. In agriculture there's also a division of labour based on sex roles – although everybody turns out in the fields at harvest time, planting the rice is purely a male activity.

In traditional leisure and cultural activities the roles are also gender-based, but things are changing. Both men and women dance, but traditionally only men play in the gamelan, though there is now a women's gamelan group in Peliatan, near Ubud. Painting and carving were once only male pursuits, but women painters in particular are becoming more common.

Community Life The Balinese have an amazingly active and organised village life – you simply can't be a faceless nonentity on Bali. You can't help but get to know your neighbours, as life is so entwined with theirs. Or at least it still is in the small villages that comprise so much of Bali. Even in big towns, the *banjar* ensures that a strong community spirit continues.

Subak

Each individual rice field is known as a *sawah* and each farmer who owns even one *sawah* must be a member of their local *subak* (rice growers' association). The rice paddies must have a steady supply of water and it is the *subak's* job to ensure that the water gets to everybody.

The head of the local *subak* will often be the farmer whose rice fields are at the bottom of the hill, for he will make quite certain that the water gets all the way down to his fields, passing through everybody else's on the way!

Of course, the *subak* has far more to do than share out the water and ensure that the water channels, dikes and so forth are in good order. Each *subak* will have a small temple out among the rice fields, where offerings to the spirits of agriculture are made and regular meetings are held for the *subak* members. Like every temple on Bali there are regular festivals and ceremonies to observe. Even individual *sawahs* may have small altars. Rice growing is a spiritual as well as an agricultural task.

In the centre of a village, usually at the crossroads of the two major streets, there will be the open meeting space known as the *alun alun*. It's actually more than just a meeting space, because you will also find temples, the town market or even the former prince's home. The *kulkul* tower will be here and quite likely a big banyan tree.

Each *desa* is further subdivided into different *banjar*, which each adult male joins when he marries. It is the *banjar* that organises village festivals, marriage ceremonies and cremations. Its headquarters is the open-sided *bale banjar*, which serves a multitude of purposes, from a local meeting place, to a storage room for the *banjar's* musical equipment and dance costumes. Gamelan orchestras are organised at the *banjar* level and a glance in a *bale banjar* at any time might reveal a gamelan practice, a meeting, food being prepared for a feast, or even a group of men getting their roosters together, in preparation for the next round of cockfights.

Death & Cremation There are ceremonies for every stage of Balinese life, but often the last ceremony – the cremation or *pitra yadna* – is the biggest. A Balinese cremation can be an amazing, spectacular, colourful, noisy and exciting event. In fact, it often takes so long to organise a cremation that years have passed since the death; during that time the body is temporarily buried.

Of course, an auspicious day must be chosen for the cremation and, since a big cremation can be a very expensive business, many people may take the opportunity of joining in at a larger cremation and sending their dead on their way at the same time. Brahmanas, however, must be cremated immediately.

A cremation ceremony is a fine opportunity to observe the incredible energy the Balinese put into creating real works of art that are totally ephemeral. The body is carried from the burial ground (or from the deceased's home if it's an 'immediate' cremation) to the cremation ground in a high, multitiered tower made of bamboo, paper, string, tinsel, silk, cloth, mirrors, flowers and anything else bright and colourful they can think of.

The tower is carried on the shoulders of a group of men, the size of the group depending on the importance of the deceased and hence the size of the tower (although in modern times the size of the towers has been limited by the presence of overhead power lines). The funeral of a former rajah or high priest may require hundreds of men to tote the tower.

Along the way to the cremation ground, certain precautions must be taken to ensure that the deceased's spirit does not find its way back home, eg, getting the spirits confused about their whereabouts, by shaking the tower, running it around in circles, spinning it around, throwing water at it, generally making the trip to the cremation ground anything but a stately and funereal crawl.

Meanwhile, there's likely to be a priest halfway up the tower, hanging on grimly as it sways back and forth, and doing his best to soak bystanders with holy water. A gamelan sprints along behind, providing a suitably exciting musical accompaniment to the procession.

At the cremation ground the body is transferred to a funeral sarcophagus – this should be in the shape of a bull for a Brahmana, a winged lion for a Ksatriyasa, and an elephant-fish for a Sudra. Almost anybody from the higher castes will use a bull – a black bull for Brahmanas or a white bull for priests. Finally, up it all goes in flames – funeral tower, sarcophagus and body. The eldest son does his duty by raking through the ashes to ensure that the entire body is burnt.

And where does your soul go after cremation? Why, to a heaven that is just like Bali!

Avoiding Offence

All sorts of behaviour is tolerated in tourist areas, especially Kuta, but it may still be insensitive and disrespectful. In other parts of the island – particularly the more traditional rural villages and religious sites – visitors should be aware and respectful of local sensibilities, and dress and act appropriately.

Dress In much of Asia, including Bali, shorts are not considered polite attire for men or women. Similarly, sleeveless singlet tops are not considered respectable – you're supposed to cover your knees, shoulders and armpits. At Kuta, and the all other beach resorts, shorts and singlets have become a part of everyday life, however, and in any case tourists are considered a little strange and their clothing habits are expected to be

somewhat eccentric. Many women go topless on Bali's tourist beaches, but bring a bikini top for less touristy beaches (definitely if you're going to Lombok).

In temples and government offices, you're expected to be 'properly' dressed, and shorts and singlets don't fulfil that expectation. Thongs (flip-flops) are acceptable in temples if you're otherwise well dressed, but not for government offices. If you want to renew a visa, or even get a local driving licence, ask yourself how you'd dress in a similar situation back home.

It is customary to take off your shoes before entering someone's house. Always remember to remove your footwear before entering a mosque.

Behaviour People within many Asian cultures resent being touched on the head – the head is regarded as the abode of the soul and is therefore sacred.

When handing over or receiving things, it's polite to use the right hand – the left hand is used as a substitute for toilet paper. To show great respect to a high-ranking or elderly person, give something to them using both hands.

Talking to someone with your hands on your hips is impolite and is considered a sign of contempt, anger or aggressiveness – it's the same stance taken by characters in traditional dance and operas to signal these feelings to the audience.

Handshaking is customary for both men and women on introduction and greeting.

The correct way to beckon to someone is with the hand extended and a downward waving motion of all the fingers (except the thumb). The Western method of beckoning, with the index finger crooked upward, won't be understood and is considered very rude.

Small Talk Chances are you'll be asked quite a few questions while you're on Bali. These questions may range from the general, to the personal. If you're not comfortable telling a stranger where you're staying, give some vague reply like 'in a cheap *losmen* (basic accommodation) at the other end of town. I can't remember the exact name, but it's run by a guy called Wayan'.

The question about marriage should be treated very carefully. Indonesians find it absurd that anyone would not want to be

Gunung Agung dominates the horizon behind Padangbai Beach

Rice terraces trip down a hillside near Ubud

The spectacular Gitgit Multi-tier Waterfalls

The mythological lion creature Barong dances his way to the temple on Galungan Day

A colourful array of flowers at the market

Hindus deep in prayer at Pura Ulun Danu Batur

A mesmerising Kecak (Monkey Dance) performance at sunset

Cockfights

Cockfights are a regular feature of temple ceremonies – a combination of sacrifice, sport and gambling. Men keep fighting cocks as prized pets. Carefully groomed and cared for, they are lovingly prepared for their brief moment of glory or defeat. On quiet afternoons men will often meet to compare their roosters, spar them against one another and line up the odds for the next big bout.

You'll often see the roosters by the roadside in their bell-shaped cane baskets – they're placed there to be entertained by passing activity. When the festivals take place, the cocks are matched one against another, a lethally sharp metal spur is tied to one leg, then there's a crescendo of shouting and betting, the birds are pushed against each other to stir them up, then they're released and the feathers fly. It's usually over in seconds – a slash of the spur and one rooster is down and dying. Occasionally a rooster turns and flees, but in that case both roosters are put in a covered basket where they can't avoid fighting. After the bout, the successful gamblers collect their pay-offs and the winning owner takes the dead rooster home for his cooking pot.

married, and being divorced is a great shame. Your social relations will go more smoothly if you say you are 'already married' *(sudah kawin)* or 'not yet married' *(belum kawin)*.

If you are over 30 years in age, it's better to be 'married', or else people will assume there must be some serious defect in your personality. If you really can't handle pretending to be married, you could say your spouse is dead, which is considered less of a tragedy than being divorced. If you are a woman and don't want a lot of attention from local guys, it's easier to be 'married' than single.

Be careful about the religion question. Many Indonesians presume that Westerners are Christian. If you're an atheist you'll be better off not telling them at all; in Indonesia the logic is that communists are atheists, and therefore if you're an atheist you must be a communist.

In all cases, try not to get annoyed by the questions and ask some of your own to show a polite interest in the other person. This is a great way to deflect attention from your personal business and learn something about the local people.

For detailed information on Bahasa Bali, Bahasa Indonesia and Sasak languages, see the Language chapter at the end of this book.

Treatment of Animals

Bull races are a regular and traditional event in northern and western Bali, and are sometimes promoted as a tourist attraction. The animals do not seem to be severely mistreated and they probably fare no worse than racehorses in most Western countries.

Cockfighting is a long-standing, popular and culturally important activity for Balinese men. Gambling is a big part of the attraction, and gambling is illegal, so cockfights are not widely publicised or promoted as a tourist attraction, but are commonly encountered on festive occasions in many villages. Cockfights are mercifully brief, and unquestionably cruel.

RELIGION
Hinduism

The Balinese are nominally Hindus, but Balinese Hinduism is a world away from that practised in India. At one time, Hinduism was the predominant religion in Indonesia (as evidenced by the many remarkable Hindu monuments on Java), but it died out with the spread of Islam through the archipelago. The final great Hindu kingdom, the Majapahit, virtually evacuated to Bali, taking not only their religion and its rituals, but also their art, literature, music and culture. To a large extent, the new influences were simply overlaid on top of existing religious beliefs, which were basically animist – hence the peculiar Balinese interpretation of Hinduism.

Basically, the Balinese worship the same gods as the Hindus of India – the trinity of Brahma, Shiva and Vishnu – although the Balinese have a supreme god, Sanghyang Widi. This basic threesome is always alluded to, but never seen, on Bali – a vacant shrine or empty throne tells all. The interpretation of the Hindu pantheon as being many manifestations of a single god makes the religion consistent with the first of the five national principles of Pancasila: a belief in one God.

To the Balinese, spirits are everywhere; it's a reminder that animism is the basis of much of Balinese religion. The offerings put out every morning are there to pay homage to the good spirits and to placate the bad ones – the Balinese take no chances! And if the offerings thrown on the ground are immediately consumed by dogs? Well, so it goes – you'll find that everybody is suspicious of dogs anyway!

You can't get away from religion on Bali: there are temples in every village; shrines in every field; and offerings made at every corner. Balinese also feel that their religion should be an enjoyable thing, for mortals as well as the gods. It's summed up well in their attitude to offerings – you make up a lot of fancy food for offerings, but once the gods have eaten the 'essence' of the food, you've got enough 'substance' left over for a fine feast. For more information on offerings, see Offerings & Ephemera in the 'Balinese Arts & Crafts' special section.

Balinese temples are deserted much of the time, but they come to life at the regular and colourful temple festivals. See the earlier boxed text 'Major Temples', and 'Temple Etiquette' on this page for more information.

Islam

Islam is a minority religion on Bali, though some Muslims have been here for many generations, particularly the descendants of seafaring people from Sulawesi. Mosques are most often seen at seaports and fishing villages. The number of Muslims is increasing, due to recent immigration from Java, Sumatra, Lombok and other parts of the country. Lombok is predominantly of Islamic faith – see the Lombok chapter for more on Islam.

Temple Etiquette

Foreigners can enter most temple complexes, except perhaps during a major festival, but some are restricted to practising Hindus. You don't have to go barefoot (as in many Buddhist shrines), but you are expected to be properly dressed. You have to wear a sarong, but long trousers or a skirt may be acceptable. You may also need a temple scarf (*selandong*) to tie around your waist. Some temples have sarongs and scarfs for hire (for around 2000Rp, or a donation), but it's worth buying your own.

Priests should be shown respect, particularly at festivals. They are the most important people and should be on a higher level at the temple – don't put yourself higher than them, eg, by climbing up on a wall to take photos.

Usually there's a sign at temple entrances warning you to be well dressed and respectful, and also asking that women don't enter the temple if menstruating. Menstruating women are thought to be *sebel* 'ritually unclean', as are people with cuts, pregnant women and those who have recently given birth, and anyone who has been recently bereaved.

Facts for the Visitor

SUGGESTED ITINERARIES

If you're based in southern Bali, you can see most of the island on day trips and be back in your hotel every night. You can take organised tours (see the Getting Around chapter for more information); alternatively, you can rent a vehicle, or charter a vehicle and driver, to visit the sights independently. It's more difficult and time-consuming on public transport – because it's slow and services become infrequent in the afternoon – but it's certainly a cheaper and more interesting way to get around. Your itinerary will depend on your interests, time and energy.

Short Trips

Here are some trips that can be done in less than a day from the main tourist areas, especially if you rent or charter a vehicle.

Bukit Peninsula Check out the luxury enclave at Nusa Dua – make a beeline for one of the beachside bars at a five-star resort. Go to Tanjung Benoa for water sports and lunch on traditional Balinese cuisine at Bumbu Bali restaurant. Then visit the clifftop temple at Ulu Watu, stop at Jimbaran for a swim at the beautiful beach and finish with a seafood dinner as the sun goes down.

Ubud Area If you come on a day trip, stop for lunch in one of Ubud's excellent restaurants, and visit at least one of the museums. There's an almost unbroken stretch of villages selling handicrafts between Denpasar and Ubud. Other attractions include the temple at Mengwi, Goa Gajah cave, and the impressive Gunung Kawi.

East Bali A most pleasant trip is a circuit from Rendang, around the slopes of Gunung Agung to Amlapura, then following the coast back to southern Bali via Candidasa. You can also do the trip via Bangli, taking the scenic back road from there to Rendang. Possible detours are to Besakih; the southern road through Sidemen and Iseh; and to Tenganan or Padangbai. Putung, Tirta Gangga and Semarapura (Klungkung) are all worth a stop.

Tabanan In a day trip northwest of Denpasar with your own transport, you can visit the temple at Mengwi, Sangeh monkey forest, the Bali Butterfly Park, the memorial at Marga, the Subak Museum at Tabanan and sunset at Tanah Lot (see the West Bali chapter for more information).

Gunung Batur There are several routes up to Gunung Batur from southern Bali, each with its own attractions. From Ubud you can go via Tampaksiring (stopping at Gunung Kawi and/or Tirta Empul) or via Tegallalang (through craft villages using scenic roads). Further east, there are routes through Bangli or Rendang (with a possible detour to Besakih temple). Another route, northwest of Ubud via Payangan, is longer, little used and lovely. You can go up to the crater rim by one route and return by another.

North Bali & the Central Mountains

The circuit via Gunung Batur to the north coast and back via Danau Bratan is possible in a single day with your own transport, but it's a long day. Start early to see Gunung Batur before the crater is covered in mist. Descend to the north coast and check out some of the elaborately carved temples on your way to Singaraja. Detour to Lovina for a swim and lunch, and maybe stop at the Gitgit waterfalls on the way up to Danau Bratan, where Pura Ulun Danu Bratan is the main attraction. From there you might make it to Tanah Lot for the sunset.

Longer Trips

Most of the trips previously mentioned can be combined and/or extended to several days or even weeks, if you want to explore in depth. There's basic accommodation in or near most of the places mentioned, and if you want Western comforts, you'll find quite a few mid-range and top-end hotels in out-of-the-way locations, as well as in all the main tourist areas.

Around the Coast Roads run all the way around the coast of Bali, except for the Bukit peninsula in the far south. There are many places to stop for the night – or longer – and a round-the-island trip can be done entirely on public transport or by bicycle. Allow at least five days by car, or longer if you plan to stop to relax, sightsee, snorkel or whatever. Going anticlockwise, you could visit Semarapura (Klungkung), Padangbai, Candidasa, Tirta Gangga, Amed, Tulamben, Singaraja, Lovina, Gilimanuk (the jump-off point for Taman Nasional Bali Barat – West Bali National Park), Medewi and several places around Tabanan.

East Bali This area can be covered in one day, but it's well worth spending more time here. You could spend two to three days in each of Sidemen, Padangbai, Candidasa, Tirta Gangga, Amed and/or Tulamben – allow plenty of time to move between each town by public *bemo* (small pick-up truck). Attractions include beautiful scenery, traditional villages, some important temples and a climb up Gunung Agung.

West Bali While you can see most of the sights around Tabanan in a day trip, it's worth spending a few days in the area. You can spend a few more days exploring further west and criss-crossing from north to south. From Tabanan, go north to Danau Bratan and across to Munduk, then down to the coast at Seririt. Stay at Lovina, then head back to Seririt and south across the mountains via Pupuan. There are three routes

south of Pupuan – they're all scenic, but take the westernmost one, and stay the night at Medewi or Negara.

Heading west again, the Christian villages of Palasari and Belimbingsari make an interesting detour. At Cekik, you can arrange a trek to the national park, then stay in Gilimanuk before returning via the north coast, with a side trip to Pulau Menjangan. Return to southern Bali, via Danau Batur or via the scenic Seririt–Pupuan–Antosari–Tabanan road.

Central Mountains Many people stay only a single night in Toya Bungkah and climb Gunung Batur for the sunrise. (People might like to stay longer but given the stranglehold that the HPPGB, the 'official' organisation of guides, has on the area it is difficult to explore the various volcanic features without being hassled.) From Toya Bungkah go down to the north coast, staying in Yeh Sanih or Lovina. You can take the main road south of Singaraja via the Gitgit waterfalls to Danau Bratan, or the more scenic route via Munduk. Allow more time to hike around Munduk. Another possible detour is to Jatiluwih and the sacred temple on the southern slopes of Gunung Batukau.

Bali's Best...

Beaches
Jimbaran, southern Bali White sand, seafood, sea breezes and sunsets
Sanur, southern Bali Restaurants and bars on a lovely beachfront promenade
Mushroom Bay, Nusa Lembongan A perfect little bay
Kuta Beach, southern Bali The widest beach with the easiest surfing, and that famous Kuta sunset

Museums
Neka Museum, Ubud A veritable history of Balinese art
Agung Rai Museum of Art (ARMA), Ubud A fine art collection set in gorgeous gardens
Museum Negeri Propinsi Bali, Denpasar Prehistoric artefacts, traditional tools, textiles, masks and costumes

Outdoor Activities
Walking Take a trip through the rice fields around Ubud, Tabanan or Tirta Gangga, or try trekking up the two great volcanoes, Gunung Batur and Gunung Agung
Rafting For fun, excitement and a different perspective on beautiful Bali
Surfing Ulu Watu is killer, but crowded; there are plenty more surf spots around southern Bali and Nusa Lembongan
Diving & Snorkelling The Tulamben wreck and Pulau Menjangan are Bali's must-do dives; there's safe snorkelling at Amed and demanding drift dives round Nusa Penida

PLANNING
When to Go
The best time to visit Bali, in terms of the weather, is during the dry season (April to October). The rest of the year is more humid, cloudier and has more rainstorms, but you can still enjoy a holiday.

There are also distinct tourist seasons that affect the picture. The European and Japanese summer holidays bring the biggest crowds – July, August and early September are busy. Accommodation can be very tight in these months and prices are higher. Many Australians arrive between Christmas and early January, when air fares to/from Australia are higher and flights can be booked solid. The school holidays in early April, late June to early July and late September also see more Australians, most of them on package tours to resort areas in southern Bali. Many Indonesians visit Bali around the end of December and during some Indonesian holidays. Outside these times Bali has surprisingly few tourists and there are empty rooms and restaurants everywhere.

Balinese festivals, holidays and special celebrations occur all the time, and most of them are not scheduled according to Western calendars, so don't worry too much about timing your visit to coincide with local events (see the Public Holidays & Special Events section later in this chapter).

Maps
For tourist resorts and towns, the maps in this guidebook are as good as you'll get. If you need a more detailed road map of the island, there are some good sheet maps available. Some may be available in your home country, but others can only be found on Bali; the Bookshops section later in this chapter mentions the best places to find maps. Because Bali is so humid, paper gets damp and maps start falling to pieces after a few days' use; bring some adhesive plastic film and cover the whole map with it. The following are examples of good maps that are available.

- Bali Pathfinder has a good map that includes the provincial capitals, Ubud and southern Bali, but has nothing for Sanur, Nusa Dua or Kuta. It is mainly available in Ubud.
- *Insight Map Bali* (1:225,000) has the great advantage of being laminated in plastic, and it's quite detailed and up to date, albeit expensive.
- Nelles' full-colour *Bali* map (1:180,000) is excellent for topography and roads, although the maps of Kuta, Denpasar and Ubud aren't particularly good.
- Periplus Travel Maps has a decent contour map (1:250,000), with a detailed section on southern Bali, plus maps of the main towns areas.

Bali's Best...

Scenery
Penelokan, central mountains Great volcanic views, with steaming caldera, craters, lakes and lava flows

Tirta Gangga, eastern Bali Classic, contoured rice fields step down steep hillsides in stunning shades of green

Jatiluwih, central mountains More luscious rice fields on the southern slopes of Gunung Batukau

Amlapura, eastern Bali A winding road passes pretty villages, with tall bamboos and beautiful distant sea views

Sidemen, eastern Bali Valley views have a spectacular mountain backdrop along the Duda–Semarapura road

Temples & Monuments
Gunung Kawi, Tampaksiring Strange shrines cut into cliffs along a lush river valley

Pura Besakih, eastern Bali Bali's 'Mother Temple' is wonderful to see during the frequent festivals

Pura Luhur Ulu Watu, southern Bali An incredible clifftop temple

Pura Rambut Siwi, western Bali Another clifftop temple, with a great outlook over rugged coastline

Villages
Padangbai, eastern Bali A busy little port on a pretty bay

Tenganan, eastern Bali See traditional Bali Aga architecture

Tejakula, northeast coast An isolated, untouristed town with unusual baths

What to Bring

'Bring as little as possible' is the golden rule of good travelling. It's better to leave something behind and get a replacement when you're there than bring too much and have to lug unwanted items around. Also, you can buy just about anything you need on Bali.

You should bring lightweight clothes – short-sleeved shirts or blouses, T-shirts and light trousers. A sweater is a good idea for cool evenings, particularly if you're going up into the central mountains, which can get quite cold. You'll also need more protective clothing if you're going to travel by motorcycle. A hat and sunglasses are important protection from tropical sun. An umbrella will help protect you against short, sharp rain showers at any time of the year.

Men should bring at least one pair of long trousers and a collared shirt, and women a long skirt, dress or trousers, for occasions when they may have to look respectable, such as visiting temples. (See the Avoiding Offence section in the Facts about Bali chapter for more information.)

VISAS & DOCUMENTS
Passport

Your passport must be valid for at least six months from the date of your arrival. If it's not, you will probably be sent home on the next available flight.

Visas & Tourist Cards

Visa regulations changed on 1 February 2004 – it is worth checking the current situation with an Indonesian embassy before you travel. Visitors from Australia, Japan, New Zealand, the UK, the USA, Canada, Taiwan and much of Western Europe need a visa to enter Indonesia. However, this can be obtained on arrival, at the usual ports of entry. Provided you have a ticket out of the country, on payment of the US$25 fee you'll be issued with a visa valid for a 30-day stay. Keep the tourist card with your passport, as you'll have to hand it back when you leave the country. Remember the visa is good for 30 days, not one month - the fine for overstaying - even by a couple of days - is US$20 per day.

Citizens of 11 countries (including Malaysia, Singapore and Thailand) are is-sued with free 30-day visas on arrival. Citizens of countries not on the visa-free or the visa-on-arrival list, as well as those wishing to stay in Indonesia for longer than 30 days, must obtain the appropriate visa in advance from any Indonesian embassy or consulate.

Tourist, Social & Business Visas

A single-entry 60-day tourist visa is available from Indonesian embassies and consulates. If you have a good reason for staying longer (eg, study or family reasons), you can apply for a 'social/ cultural' *(sosial/budaya)* visa. You will need an application form from an Indonesian embassy or consulate, and a letter of introduction or promise of sponsorship from a reputable person or school in Indonesia. It's initially valid for three months, but it can be extended for one month at a time at an immigration office within Indonesia for a maximum of six months. There are fees for the application and for extending the visa too.

Limited-stay visas (Kartu Izin Tinggal Terbatas, or KITAS), valid for one-year periods, are also issued, usually for those who have permission to run a business or to work. In the latter case, a work permit must be obtained first from the Ministry of Manpower and should be arranged by your employer. Those granted limited stay are issued with a KITAS card, often referred to as a KIMS card. It's sometimes easier, and even cheaper, to leave the country every two months and get a new tourist card than to get a visa and update it every month.

Extensions

It's not possible to extend a 30-day on-arrival visa or a 60-day tourist visa, unless there's a medical emergency or you have to answer legal charges. If you want to spend more time in Indonesia you have to leave the country and then re-enter - some long-term foreign residents have been doing this for years.

Immigration Offices

There are two main **immigration offices** *(kantor imigrasi)*. The office in Denpasar (☎ 0361-227828; open 8am-2pm Mon-Thur, 8am-11am

Fri & 8am-noon Sat) is just up the street from the main post office in Renon. The other office (☎ 0361-751038) is at the international airport. If you have to apply for changes to your visa, make sure you're neatly dressed.

Onward Tickets

Officially, an onward/return ticket is a requirement for a tourist card (and normal visa), and visitors are frequently asked to show their ticket on arrival. If you look scruffy or broke, you may also be asked to present evidence of sufficient funds to support yourself during your stay – US$1000 in cash or travellers cheques (or the equivalent in other currencies) should be sufficient. A credit card in lieu of cash or travellers cheques may not satisfy these requirements.

Travel Insurance

You should definitely take out travel insurance – bring a copy of the policy as evidence that you're covered. Get a policy that pays for medical evacuation if necessary.

Some companies offer a range of medical expense options; the higher ones are chiefly for countries such as the USA, which have extremely high medical costs. There is a wide variety of policies available, so check the small print.

Some policies also specifically exclude 'dangerous activities', which can include scuba diving, renting a local motorcycle and even trekking. Be aware that a locally acquired motorcycle licence is not valid under some policies.

You may prefer a policy that pays doctors or hospitals directly rather than you having to pay on the spot and claim later. If you have to claim later, make sure you keep all documentation. Some policies ask you to call back (reverse charges) to a centre in your home country, or a nearby country, where an immediate assessment of your problems is made. Check that the policy covers ambulances and an emergency flight home.

Driving Licence & Permits

If you plan to drive a car, you *must* have an International Driving Permit (IDP). It's easy to obtain one from your national motoring organisation if you have a normal driving licence. If you also have a motorcycle licence at home, get your IDP endorsed for motorcycles too (see the Getting Around chapter for details about local licences on Bali). Bring your home licence as well – it's supposed to be carried in conjunction with the IDP.

Student, Youth & Seniors Cards

The International Student Identity Card (ISIC) can get you a discount on domestic flights (a maximum age limit of 26 years applies). There are virtually no discounts or special deals for senior citizens.

Copies

All important documents (passport data page and visa page, credit cards, travel insurance policy, air/bus/train tickets, driving licence etc) should be photocopied before you leave home. Leave one copy with someone at home and keep another with you, separate from the originals.

It's also a good idea to store details of your vital travel documents in Lonely Planet's free online Travel Vault in case you lose the photocopies or can't be bothered with them. Your password-protected Travel Vault is accessible online anywhere in the world; create it at ⓦ www.ekno.lonelyplanet.com.

EMBASSIES & CONSULATES
Indonesian Embassies & Consulates

Countries in which Indonesia has diplomatic representation include the following.

Australia
Embassy: (☎ 02-6250 8600, fax 6273 6017) 8 Darwin Ave, Yarralumla, ACT 2600
Consulates: Adelaide, Darwin, Brisbane, Perth and Sydney

Canada
Embassy: (☎ 613-724 1100, fax 724 1105) 55 Parkdale Ave, Ottawa, Ontario K1Y 1E5
Consulates: Toronto and Vancouver

East Timor
Representative: (☎ 670-312 333, fax 312 332) Kompleks Pertamina, Pantai Kelapa, Correios Timor Leste, Dili

France
Embassy: (☎ 01 45 03 07 60, fax 01 45 04 50 32) 47-49 Rue Cortambert 75116, Paris
Consulate: Marseilles

Germany
Embassy: (☎ 030-445 9210, fax 4473 7142) Lehrterstrasse 16-17, 10557 Berlin
Consulates: Bonn, Bremen, Dusseldorf, Hamburg, Hannover, Kiel, Munich and Stuttgart

Malaysia
Embassy: (☎ 03-245 2011, fax 241 7908) 233 Jl Tun Razak, 50400 Kuala Lumpur
Consulates: Johor Bahru, Penang, Kota Kinabalu

Netherlands
Embassy: (☎ 070-310 8100, fax 364 3331)
Tobias Asserlaan 8, 2517 KC, The Hague
New Zealand
Embassy: (☎ 04-475 8697, fax 475 9374)
70 Glen Rd, Kelburn, Wellington
Consulate: Auckland
Papua New Guinea
Embassy: (☎ 675-325 3116, fax 325 0535)
1+2/410 Kiroki St, Sir John Guise Drive,
Waigani, Port Moresby
Consulate: Vanimo
Philippines
Embassy: (☎ 02-892 5061/7, fax 818 4441)
185 Salcedo St, Legaspi Village, Makati, Manila
Consulate: Davao
Singapore
Embassy: (☎ 737 7422, fax 737 5037)
7 Chatsworth Rd
Thailand
Embassy: (☎ 022 523 135, fax 022 551 267)
600-602 Thanon Phetburi, Phyathai, Bangkok
10400
Consulate: Songkhla
UK
Embassy: (☎ 020-7499 7661, fax 7491 4993)
38 Grosvenor Square, London W1X 9AD
USA
Embassy: (☎ 202-775 5200, fax 775 5365)
2020 Massachusetts Ave NW, Washington DC
20036
Consulates: Chicago, Houston, Los Angeles,
New York and San Francisco

Embassies & Consulates in Indonesia

Foreign embassies are in Jakarta, the national capital. Most of the foreign representatives on Bali are consular agents (or honorary consuls) who can't offer the same services as a full consulate or embassy. For many nationalities this means a long trek to Jakarta in the event of a lost passport.

Bali Only Australia and Japan (which together make up nearly half of all visitors) have formal consulates on Bali. The following offices are open from about 8.30am to noon Monday to Friday, and some also open in the afternoon. All telephone area codes are ☎ 0361.

Australia (☎ 235092, fax 231990) Jl Mochammad Yamin 4, Renon, Denpasar. The Australian consulate has a consular sharing agreement with Canada, and may also be able to help citizens of New Zealand, Ireland and Papua New Guinea

France (☎/fax 285485) Jl Bypass Ngurah Rai 35, Sanur
Germany (☎ 288535, fax 288826) Jl Pantai Karang 17, Batujimbar, Sanur
Japan (☎ 227628, fax 231308) Jl Raya Puputan 170, Renon, Denpasar
Netherlands (☎ 751517, fax 752777) Jl Raya Kuta 127, Kuta
Switzerland & Austria (☎ 751735, fax 754457) Swiss Restaurant, Jl Pura Bagus Taruna, Legian
USA (☎ 233605 ext 3575, fax 222426) Jl Hayam Wuruk 188, Renon, Denpasar

Jakarta Indonesia is a big country, and is important in the Asian region. Most nations have an embassy in Jakarta (area code ☎ 021), including the following.

Australia (☎ 2550 5555; W www.austembjak .or.id) Jl H.R. Rasuna Said, Kav. C 15-16, Kuningan
Brunei Darussalam (☎ 574 1437) Wisma GKBI, Jl Jenderal Sudirman 28
Canada (☎ 525 0709) 5th floor, Wisma Metropolitan I, Jl Jenderal Sudirman, Kav. 29
France (☎ 314 2807) Jl M.H. Thamrin 20
Germany (☎ 390 1750) Jl M.H. Thamrin 1
Malaysia (☎ 522 4947) Jl H.R. Rasuna Said, Kav. X/6 No 1-3
Myanmar (Burma; ☎ 314 0440) Jl Haji Agus Salim 109
Netherlands (☎ 525 1515) Jl H.R. Rasuna Said, Kav. S-3
New Zealand (☎ 570 9460) BRI II Building, 23rd floor, Jl Jenderal Sudirman, Kav. 44-46
Papua New Guinea (☎ 725 1218) 6th floor, Panin Bank Centre, Jl Jenderal Sudirman 1
Philippines (☎ 315 5118) Jl Imam Bonjol 6-8
Thailand (☎ 390 4052) Jl Imam Bonjol 74
UK (☎ 315 6264) Jl M.H. Thamrin 75
USA (☎ 344 2211) Jl Medan Merdeka Selatan 5

CUSTOMS

Indonesia has the usual list of prohibited imports, including drugs, weapons and anything remotely pornographic. In addition, TV sets, radio receivers, fresh fruit, Chinese medicines and printed matter containing Chinese characters are prohibited.

Each adult can bring in 200 cigarettes (or 50 cigars or 100g of tobacco), a 'reasonable amount' of perfume and 1L of alcohol.

Officially, photographic equipment (both still and video cameras), computers, typewriters and tape recorders must be declared to customs on entry, and you must take them with you when you leave. In practice, customs officials rarely worry about the usual gear tourists bring into Bali. Surfers with more than two or three boards may be charged a 'fee', and this could apply to other items if the officials suspect that you aim to sell them in Indonesia. If you have nothing to declare, customs clearance is quick and painless.

There is no restriction on foreign currency, but the import or export of rupiah is limited to 5,000,000Rp. Amounts greater than that must be declared.

Indonesia is a signatory to the Convention on International Trade in Endangered Species (CITES) and as such bans the import and export of products made from endangered species. In particular, it is forbidden to export any product made from green sea turtles or turtle shells. In the interests of conservation, as well as conformity to customs laws, please don't buy turtle shell products. There may also be some ivory artefacts for sale on Bali, and the import and export of these is also banned in most countries.

It's also forbidden to export antiquities, ancient artefacts or other cultural treasures, so if someone tries to sell you an 'ancient' bronze statue, remind them of this law and they may decide it's not so old after all!

MONEY

The economic crisis that started in early 1997 hit Indonesia very hard, and the value of the currency fluctuated wildly. Since 1998, International Monetary Fund (IMF) support has kept the currency reasonably stable, though it is declining in value because of domestic inflation. Many mid-range hotels and all top-end hotels, along with many tourist attractions and tour companies, list their prices in US dollars, though you can usually pay in rupiah at a poorer exchange rate (but the rupiah price will reflect the effectiveness of your bargaining as much as the current exchange rate).

Currency

Indonesia's unit of currency is the rupiah (Rp). There are coins worth 50, 100, 500 and 1000Rp. Notes come in denominations of 100Rp, 500Rp, 1000Rp, 5000Rp, 10,000Rp, 20,000Rp, 50,000Rp and 100,000Rp.

Exchange Rates

The Bank of Indonesia (BoI) has an official exchange rate, but it is not legally set – it's a more-or-less free-market rate. There's no black market.

country	unit		rupiah
Australia	A$1	=	5100Rp
Canada	C$1	=	5750Rp
euro zone	€1	=	9100Rp
Japan	¥100	=	7600Rp
New Zealand	NZ$1	=	4500Rp
UK	UK£1	=	14,400Rp
USA	US$1	=	9050Rp

Exchanging Money

Changing money on Bali is easy. The rates offered for travellers cheques are sometimes a little less than for cash, and small denominations usually get a lower rate, sometimes much lower. Bring travellers cheques in denominations of US$100 or equivalent. The best cash rates are for US$100 dollar notes in the new design (they're called 'big heads' on Bali) and in mint condition. Damaged banknotes, with any tears, holes or writing on them, may be unacceptable. Rates offered by banks and moneychangers fluctuate every day, sometimes several times a day, and are usually better in the main budget tourist centres like Kuta or Ubud.

If you're in a remote area, it can be hard to change big notes – breaking a 50,000Rp note in an out-of-the-way location can be a major hassle. Sometimes notes stay in circulation a long time and get very tatty – when they're too dog-eared, people won't accept them. For small purchases and public transport fares, always make sure you have a good stock of 500Rp and 1000Rp notes or coins.

Banks Several major banks have branches in the main tourist centres (particularly Kuta, Sanur and Ubud) and provincial capitals. Smaller towns may not have banks at all, and those that exist may not change foreign currency, and those that do may have woeful rates. Banking hours are generally from 8am to 2pm Monday to Thursday, from 8am to noon Friday and from 8am to about 11am Saturday. The banks enjoy many public holidays. Changing money at a bank can involve a fair amount of waiting, form-filling and paper-shuffling.

Moneychangers Exchange rates offered by moneychangers are normally better than the banks, plus they offer quicker service and keep much longer hours. The exchange rates are advertised on boards along the footpaths or on windows outside the shops. It's worth looking around because rates vary a little, but beware of places advertising exceptionally high rates – they may make their profit by shortchanging their customers. Cheating moneychangers are very common in Kuta – see the Kuta section of the South Bali chapter for specifics, and also the Dangers & Annoyances section later in this chapter. In upmarket hotels and modern shopping centres, the rates can be up to 20% less than a street moneychanger.

ATMs There are ATMs all over Bali. Most accept Visa, MasterCard, Cirrus, Plus and Alto cards, though some ATMs are only for local bank account holders. The exchange rates for ATM withdrawals are usually quite good, but your home bank may charge a hefty fixed fee, and that's the catch. Most ATMs on Bali allow a maximum withdrawal of only 600,000Rp.

Credit Cards Visa, MasterCard and American Express (AmEx) are accepted by most of the bigger businesses that cater to tourists. You sign for the amount in rupiah and the bill is converted into your domestic currency. The conversion is at the interbank rate and is usually quite good, though some banks add a foreign exchange transaction fee that may be higher than the 1% commission on travellers cheques.

You can also get cash advances on major credit cards over the counter, or at an ATM. Cash advances over the counter attract a commission, so ask about this – it's often a fixed charge.

International Transfers Western Union is a reliable option. It transfers funds via **Bank International Indonesia** (☎ 0362-21234, Jl Diponegoro 93B, Denpasar). A cash advance on your credit card, however, will be quicker, easier and cheaper than having money sent.

Security
Carrying a credit card for cash advances, major purchases and as an emergency backup is a good idea. Bring a portion of your funds in travellers cheques for security and convenience, although cash normally receives a better exchange rate.

US dollars are the most negotiable currency, particularly in more remote areas. British, Canadian, Japanese and Australian cash and travellers cheques are negotiable at competitive rates in tourist areas, and can be changed in most major towns.

If you're heading into more remote regions, change money in one of the resort areas first and take a good supply of rupiah in small denominations with you.

Costs
On Bali, you can spend as much as you want – there are hotels where a double can be US$500 or more a night, where lunch can cost more than US$75 per person, and a helicopter can be arranged for US$250 if you're desperate to see Bali fast. At the other extreme, you can find decent budget singles/doubles for as little as 35,000/50,000Rp and enjoy a filling meal from a *warung* (food stall) for about 7000Rp. In short, Bali is a bargain for budget travellers, and offers excellent value for those seeking first-class comforts.

In general, travellers who don't need aircon and hot water will discover they can get good rooms almost anywhere on Bali for under US$10. You can have an excellent three-course meal for US$5, including a large bottle of beer, at many tourist restaurants, while US$10 will get you a gourmet delight at some of the finest restaurants around.

Transport is equally affordable – remember that Bali is a small island. Public minibuses, buses and bemos are the local form of public transport and they're very cheap. A rental motorcycle costs around US$3.50 per day and a small Suzuki jeep is about US$8 per day. You can charter a car *and* a driver for around US$15 per day.

Entry Charges Nearly every museum, major temple or tourist site has an entry charge of about 3000/1500Rp per adult/child – it's a trifling amount. Government-run tourist attractions also charge an insurance premium of 100Rp on top of the admission price, which supposedly covers you against accident or injury while you're there, or maybe it just covers the management against you suing them. You may also have to pay another few thousand rupiah to rent a sarong and/or sash when you visit a temple, and vehicle parking is usually a little extra – around 500Rp to 1000Rp. If there is no fixed charge a donation is sometimes requested – anything from 5000Rp to 10,000Rp is acceptable, but you may be encouraged to contribute a lot more. Commercial attractions, like the Taman Burung Bali Bird Park, are considerably more expensive.

Tipping

Tipping a set percentage is not expected on Bali, but restaurant workers are poorly paid; if the service is good, it's appropriate to leave 4000Rp or so. Most mid-range hotels and restaurants and all top-end hotels and restaurants add 21% to the bill for tax and service (known as 'plus plus'). This service component is distributed among hotel staff (one hopes), so you needn't tip under these circumstances.

Bargaining

Many everyday purchases on Bali require bargaining ('discussing the price' is a more polite term). This particularly applies to clothing, arts and crafts (see the boxed text 'The Art of Bargaining'). Accommodation has a set price, but this is usually negotiable in the low season, or if you are staying at the hotel for several days. This applies particularly in places like Kuta, Lovina, Ubud and Candidasa, where there's lots of competition. On the other hand, many *losmen* (basic accommodation) will charge more than their usual price if they have to pay a commission to a taxi driver, or if they think you look so tired or disoriented that you won't make it to the place next door.

If a local accompanies you, it may be harder to bargain the price down. Even if your companion is not on a commission, they will tend to feel very uncomfortable seeing a fellow Balinese being 'beaten down' by a foreigner. It reflects on both the guide and the shopkeeper, and each loses face. The advantage of finding things more easily and quickly is often outweighed by this local loyalty.

The best buy is said to be at the 'morning price'. The seller feels that making a sale to the first customer will ensure good sales for the rest of the day, so is more likely to lower the price for an early-morning customer.

In most instances, locals will pay less than foreigners. The Balinese consider this to be eminently fair, as in their eyes, all Westerners are wealthy, as are any Javanese who can afford to travel. Remember that, on balance, Bali offers great value for money.

The Art of Bargaining

In an everyday bargaining situation the first step is to establish a starting price – it's usually better to ask the seller for their price rather than make an initial offer. Then ask if that is the 'best price' and you may get an immediate reduction. To bargain effectively you have to have an idea of what you consider is a fair price for the article, and not just try to get it for less than the first asking price.

Your 'first price' should be a worthwhile notch below what you're willing to pay, but not so low as to be ludicrous. A silly offer suggests that the customer hasn't any idea of what the price should be, and is therefore a target for some serious overcharging. Of course, lots of people have bought things they didn't want because their paltry first offer was accepted.

As a rule of thumb, your first price could be anything from one-third to two-thirds of the asking price – assuming that the asking price is not completely over the top (which it sometimes is!). Then, with offer and counter offer, you move closer to an acceptable price – for example, the seller asks 60,000Rp for the handicraft, you offer 30,000Rp and so on, until eventually you both agree at somewhere around 45,000Rp.

Along the way you can plead end-of-trip poverty or claim that Ketut down the road is likely to be even cheaper. The seller is likely to point out the exceptional quality of the item and plead poverty too. An aura of only mild interest helps – if you're obviously desperate or pressed for time, vendors will not be in a hurry to drop their price. If you don't get to an acceptable price you're quite entitled to walk away – the vendor may even call you back with a lower price.

When you name a price, you're committed – you have to buy if your offer is accepted. Remember it's not a matter of life or death. Bargaining should be an enjoyable part of shopping on Bali, so maintain your sense of humour and keep things in perspective.

Taxes

Throughout Bali in many mid-range and all top-end hotels and restaurants there's a 21% tax on rooms and meals. At mid-range places the tax may or may not be included, so always ask (or check the menu) and avoid nasty surprises. At budget lodgings and cheap food stalls, the tax is usually included in the stated price.

Plus Plus

The top-end hotels and restaurants add a 10% service charge as well as 10% tax, so with a percentage of a percentage added on, that's 21% extra on your bill – it's called 'plus plus' locally. Tax and service charges are a factor when you're 'discussing the price' of a hotel room. If a room has a published rate of US$50 plus plus, and you're offered a 'special price' of US$40 net, that's a big discount – it will save you US$20, or 33% of the full rate. Prices quoted in this book for mid-range and top-end hotels *do not* include tax and service charges.

POST & COMMUNICATIONS
Postal Rates

Sending postcards and normal-sized letters (ie, under 20g) by airmail costs 4000Rp to Australia and New Zealand, 6000Rp to Europe, and 8000Rp to the USA and Canada. Delivery takes seven to 10 days, but 'express service' (ie, delivery in five to seven days) is available to 46 countries for 2000Rp extra. For anything over 20g, the charge is based on weight. Sending large parcels is quite expensive, but at least you can get them properly wrapped and sealed at any post office.

Sending Mail

Every substantial town has a post office *(kantor pos)*, open from about 8am to 2pm Monday to Thursday and 8am to noon Friday. In the larger tourist centres, the main post offices are often open to noon on weekends. In small towns, and dotted around the tourist centres, there are also postal agencies called *warpostels* or *warparpostels*. They provide normal postal and telephone services – often for slightly higher rates – and are sometimes open for extended hours.

Receiving Mail

There are poste restante services at the various post offices around Bali. The Denpasar post office is inconveniently located, so you're better off having mail sent to you via the post offices at Kuta, Ubud or Singaraja. Mail should be addressed to you with your surname underlined and in capital letters, then 'Kantor Pos', the name of the town, and then 'Bali, Indonesia'. You can also have mail sent to your hotel.

Courier Companies

For a reliable, fast and expensive service, call **DHL** (☎ *0361-762138*), **FedEx** (☎ *0361-701727*), **TNT** (☎ *0361-703519*) or **UPS** (☎ *0361-481370*) – they all pick up.

Telephone

The telecommunications service within Indonesia is provided by Telkom, a government monopoly. All of Indonesia is covered by a domestic satellite telecommunications network. To call any country direct from Indonesia dial ☎ 001 + country code + area code + number, or make a call via the international operator (☎ 101).

Telephone Area Codes The country code for Indonesia is ☎ 62. The area code for Jakarta is ☎ 021 and for Lombok it's ☎ 0370. Bali has six telephone area codes, listed here according to the relevant chapters in this book.

Central Mountains ☎ 0361: Pelaga, Petang; ☎ 0362: Munduk, Pancasari; ☎ 0366: Buahan, Kedisan, Kintamani, Penelokan, Toya Bungkah; ☎ 0368: Bedugul, Candikuning, Pacung

East Bali ☎ 0361: Gianyar; ☎ 0363: Amlapura, Buitan (Balina), Candidasa, Padangbai, Tirta Gangga; ☎ 0366: Bangli, Besakih, Manggis, Mendira, Putung, Semarapura (Klungkung), Sidemen

North Bali ☎ 0362: Banjar, Celukanbawang, Gitgit, Jagaraga, Kubutambahan, Lovina, Sangsit, Sawan, Seririt, Singaraja, Yeh Sanih

South Bali ☎ 0361: Berewa, Bukit peninsula, Canggu, Denpasar, Jimbaran, Kuta, Legian, Seminyak, Nusa Dua, Benoa harbour, Sanur, Sidakarya, Tanjung Benoa, Tuban

Ubud & Around ☎ 0361: Batuan, Batubulan, Bedulu, Bona, Celuk, Kutri, Mas, Pejeng, Singapadu, Sukawati, Tampaksiring, Ubud

West Bali ☎ 0361: Dukuh, Lalang-Linggah, Mengwi, Penatahan, Tabanan, Tanah Lot, Wanasari; ☎ 0362: Pemuteran, Pulaki; ☎ 0365: Belayu, Cekik, Gilimanuk, Medewi, Negara, Perancak

Telephone Numbers Periodically, the telephone numbers in an area will change. If you dial an old number you should get a recorded message telling you how to convert it to a new number – don't hang up too quickly because the message is repeated in English after the Indonesian version.

Phone books can be a little hard to find, but the local directory assistance operators (☎ 108) are very helpful and some of them speak English. If you call directory assistance and have to spell out a name, try to use the Alpha, Bravo, Charlie system of saying the letters; otherwise just use simple, common English words to help the operators identify the letters.

Useful Telephone Numbers The following numbers work throughout Indonesia.

Ambulance	☎ 118
Directory assistance, international	☎ 102
Directory assistance, local	☎ 108
Directory assistance, long-distance	☎ 106
Fire Brigade	☎ 113
Operator-assisted international calls	☎ 101
Operator-assisted local calls	☎ 100
Police	☎ 110
Postal Service Information	☎ 161

Telephone Offices A *kantor telekomunikasi* (telecommunications office) is a main telephone office operated by Telkom, usually only found in bigger towns. *Wartel* (public telephone office) are sometimes run by Telkom, but the vast majority are private, and there's a lot of them. You can make local, long-distance *(inter-lokal)* and international calls from any wartel.

The charge for international calls is the same from all parts of Bali, but may be cheaper in Telkom offices than private ones. In the few areas that still don't have a computerised, automatic exchange, there is a three-minute minimum and increments of one minute thereafter. When you book the call, you may be asked how long you want to talk for, and will be cut off as soon as the time you requested is up. In areas with modern exchanges you dial the number yourself, and the cost increases in *pulsa* – a unit of time that varies according to the destination. The number of pulsa is shown on a display in the phone booth. This display also shows the price, sometimes including the 10% tax, sometimes not.

The official Telkom price of a one-minute call is 9100Rp to Australia, New Zealand, the USA and Canada; 10,300Rp to Japan and the UK; and 11,700Rp to most of Western Europe. Most wartels, however, will charge higher per-minute rates. You're supposed to get discounts of 25% to 50% for calls in the evenings and on Sunday, but very few private wartels actually discount the price.

You can sometimes make reverse-charge (collect) calls from Telkom wartels, though most private ones don't allow it and those that do will charge a set fee. Very few private wartels will let you receive an incoming call.

Public Telephones The vast majority of public phones are card phones. The more common one uses the regular *kartu telepon* (phonecard) with a magnetic strip. The newer one uses a *kartu chip*, which has an electronic chip embedded in it. You can buy phonecards in denominations of 5000Rp, 10,000Rp, 25,000Rp, 50,000Rp and 100,000Rp at wartels, moneychangers, post offices and many shops. An international call from a card phone costs about the same per minute as a call from a wartel.

Mobile Telephones The cellular service in Indonesia is GSM. Major Indonesian service providers are Telkomsel, Satelindo and XL Ritel. If your phone company offers international 'roaming' in Indonesia, you can use your own mobile telephone on Bali – check first with the company to find out how much they charge (SMS messaging is generally the cheapest mobile option to use). Alternatively, a mobile telephone (called a handphone in Indonesia) using the GSM system can be used more cheaply if you purchase a prepaid SIM card with a chip that you insert into your phone – check with your mobile telephone company. Long-distance and international calls from a mobile can be less expensive than through the regular phone system.

Foreign Phonecards Some foreign telephone companies issue cards that enable you to make calls from Indonesian phones and have the cost billed to your home phone account. You dial a toll-free number to access an operator with your home phone company, then key in (or quote) your card number and a personal identification number (PIN), then you dial the number you want (long-distance or international). You must arrange this before you leave home, and get the card, PIN and a list of toll-free access numbers for the various countries (ie, Indonesia) – prices will be pretty much what you'd pay if you made the call from home. The catch is that most public telephones, wartels and hotels won't allow you to call the toll-free ☎ 008 or ☎ 001 access numbers, and the few hotels and wartels that do permit it charge a fee for doing so. Your best chance is at a Telkom office.

Lonely Planet's eKno global communication service provides low-cost international calls – for local calls you're usually better off with a local phonecard. It also offers free messaging services, email, travel information and an online travel vault, where you can securely store all your important documents. You can join online at w www.ekno .lonelyplanet.com, or by phone from Bali and Lombok by dialling ☎ 0018-030-112-722 or ☎ 008-800-105-346.

Fax
Fax services are available at most wartels. At some of them you can arrange to receive a fax or even have it delivered to a specified address – for a fee. The cost of sending an international fax is timed at the same rate as an international telephone call, although sometimes there's a set charge.

Email & Internet Access
Internet centres have mushroomed in all Bali's main tourist areas, especially in Kuta-Legian, Ubud and Lovina, where rates are very competitive – about 300Rp to 500Rp per minute – but access speeds are sometimes frustratingly slow. Most open from around 8am to 9pm daily. *Warnet* (warung Internet) are sometimes attached to post offices in provincial capitals, but access speeds are no better than at regular Internet centres.

INTERNET RESOURCES
The World Wide Web is a rich resource for travellers. You can hunt down bargain air fares, book hotels, check weather conditions or chat with locals and other travellers about the best places to visit (or avoid!).

There's no better place to start your web explorations than the Lonely Planet website (w www.lonelyplanet.com). Here you'll find succinct summaries on travelling to most places on Earth, postcards from other travellers and the Thorn Tree bulletin board, where you can ask questions before you go or dispense advice when you get back. You can also find travel news and updates to many of our most popular guidebooks, and the subwwway section links you to the most useful travel resources elsewhere on the web.

Bali is well represented on the World Wide Web. You can check the latest political situation, get background information and book tours and hotels. Sites worth investigating include the following.

Australian Department of Foreign Affairs & Trade (w www.dfat.gov.au) Up-to-date travel advice and warnings for all of Indonesia, including Bali

Bali & Beyond (w www.baliandbeyond.co.id) Online version of a tourism magazine, with interesting articles and useful information

Bali Portal (w www.bali-portal.com) Lots of links to hotel-booking sites, cultural information, weather and more

Bali Travel Forum (w www.balitravelforum.com) Useful travellers site with an archive allowing a full search of previous entries

Living in Indonesia (w www.expat.or.id) Information and advice for the expatriate community, including links and contacts for groups of expats

TEMPO Interactif (w www.tempo.co.id/index,uk.asp) Indonesian news and current affairs magazine

BOOKS
It is striking how much has been published about Bali in the Western world, and (until recently) how little of it has been written by Balinese – it says a lot about the Western fascination with Bali. Various Indonesian journals regularly have articles about aspects of Bali – its geography, economy, history and so on – and though many are written in English, few are appealing to a general audience.

Unless otherwise stated, most of the following books should be available on Bali, though you may have to look hard. Those that are long out of print may still be available in libraries.

Lonely Planet
If you're also planning to visit other parts of Indonesia, you can buy other Lonely Planet guidebooks. *Indonesia* covers the entire archipelago and food lovers should take a copy of *World Food Indonesia* with them.

Other guidebooks include *Southeast Asia on a shoestring*, *Papua New Guinea* and

Malaysia, Singapore & Brunei, as well as the Singapore city and condensed guides. LP's *Indonesian phrasebook* is a concise and handy introduction to Bahasa Indonesia. You can pick up these guidebooks at major bookshops in Kuta, Denpasar and Ubud (see the Bookshops entry later in this section).

Diving & Snorkeling Bali & Lombok, by Tim Rock and Susanna Hinderks, is part of LP's series of diving and snorkelling guides, and is a must buy. This colourful and informative book details 59 spectacular diving and snorkelling sites around Bali, Lombok and other nearby islands.

Guidebooks
Guides about diving and surfing are listed under the relevant sections later in the chapter.

Art & Culture
For information on Bali's complex and colourful artistic and cultural heritage *The Art & Culture of Bali* by Urs Ramseyer is one of the best published sources. *Artists on Bali* by Ruud Spruit is a well-illustrated description of the work of six European artists on Bali and follows their influence on Balinese styles.

The design of *Balinese Architecture – Towards an Encyclopaedia,* by Made Wijaya, resembles a scrapbook, but is full of information and illustrations of traditional, colonial and contemporary Balinese architecture. It is available on Bali. Another architecture guide that's worth seeking out is *Balinese Architecture* by Julian Davison, a small well-illustrated book on the philosophy and structure of Balinese building. Also by Julian Davison is *Balinese Temples,* which explains and illustrates the form of a Balinese temple as a model of the universe.

Balinese Music by Michael Tenzer is a readable treatment of all types of music throughout Bali.

Balinese Paintings by Balinese author Anak Agung Made Djelantik offers a concise and handy overview of the field.

Balinese Textiles by Brigitta Hauser, Marie-Louise Nabholz-Kartaschoff & Urs Ramseyer is a large and lavishly illustrated guide detailing weaving styles and their significance.

Bali the Imaginary Museum: The Photographs of Walter Spies and Beryl de Zoete by Lucy Norris is an expensive hardcover publication of superb photos from the 1930s.

Dance & Drama in Bali by Beryl de Zoete & Walter Spies was published in 1938 and is now difficult to find. It draws from Spies' deep appreciation and understanding of Bali's arts and culture.

Miguel Covarrubias, a Mexican artist, wrote *Island of Bali* in 1937, and it is still widely available today. It's a readable yet learned book that is incredibly detailed yet always interesting. The closing speculation that tourism may spoil Bali is thought-provoking, but it's also a real pleasure to discover how some aspects of Bali remain exactly as Covarrubias describes them.

Keris Bali/Balinese Keris by IB Dibia is an illustrated and informative book on the kris (or *keris*), the legendary Indonesian dagger, its manufacture, decoration and mystic power.

Perceptions of Paradise: Images of Bali in the Arts is published by the Neka Museum in Ubud, as is *The Development of Painting in Bali,* which covers the various schools of painting and has short biographies of well-known artists, including many relevant Western artists.

Pre-War Balinese Modernists 1928–1942 by F Haks et al. is a beautiful book on the work of some brilliant but long-neglected Balinese artists.

History & Anthropology
Bali – Cultural Tourism or Touristic Culture by Michel Picard is a thoughtful analysis of the symbiotic (or mutually destructive) relationship between Bali's culture and the tourist industry.

Bali – A Paradise Created by Adrian Vickers traces Balinese history and development by concentrating on the island's image in the West.

Bali in the 19th Century by Ide Anak Agung Gede is a rare book covering the early colonial period and the ritual capitulation of the Balinese nobility.

Balinese Character – a Photographic Analysis by the anthropologists Margaret Mead & Gregory Bateson is available in many libraries. The study, written in 1942, has been heavily discussed and criticised. For example, a passivity that they observed in children, and explained in cultural terms, was more probably attributable to malnutrition.

Bali – Sekala & Niskala; Vol I: Essays on Religion, Ritual & Art and *Bali – Sekala & Niskala; Vol II: Essays on Society, Tradition & Craft* by Fred Eiseman are anthologies of essays that cover aspects of Balinese life.

The Balinese People – A Reinvestigation of Character by GD Jensen & LK Suryani is a critique of the Mead-Bateson book, *Balinese Character – a Photographic Analysis*.

Monumental Bali by AJ Bernet Kempers is hard to find, but offers the best descriptions and illustrations of the ancient sites of Bali, with text that places them in their historical and cultural context.

To Change Bali edited by Adrian Vickers & I Nyoman Darma Putra is a contemporary collection of essays on social and cultural change on Bali.

Western Visitors in the 1930s

Modern tourism started on Bali in the late 1960s, but the island had an earlier, and in many ways much more intriguing, tourist boom in the 1930s. A prime source of inspiration for these interwar visitors was Gregor Krause's book *The Island of Bali*, published in 1920. Krause had worked in Bangli as a doctor between 1912 and 1914, and his photographs of an uninhibited lifestyle in a lush, tropical environment aroused Western interest in Bali.

By the early 1930s, about 100 tourists a month were visiting the island and the first concerns were already being raised about whether Balinese culture could withstand such a massive onslaught! Visitors included some talented and very interesting individuals, who aided the rejuvenation of many dormant Balinese arts, and played a great part in creating the image of Bali that exists today.

Miguel Covarrubias

Island of Bali, written by this Mexican artist (1904–57), is still the classic introduction to the island and its culture. Covarrubias visited Bali twice in the early 1930s and, like many visitors at that time, the artist Walter Spies was his introduction to the island and its people. He was also involved in theatre design and printmaking.

Walter Spies

Spies (1895–1942) was the father-figure for the cast of 1930s visitors, and in many ways played the largest part in interpreting Bali for them and establishing the image of Bali that prevails today. Spies first visited Bali in 1925 and two years later moved there permanently.

Befriended by the important Sukawati family, he built a house at the confluence of two rivers at Campuan, west of Ubud. His home soon became the prime gathering point for the most famous visitors of the 1930s and Spies, who involved himself in every aspect of Balinese art and culture, was an important influence on its renaissance.

In 1932 he became curator of the museum in Denpasar, and with Rudolf Bonnet and Cokorda Gede Agung Sukawati, their Balinese patron, he founded the Pita Maha artists' cooperative in 1936. He co-authored *Dance & Drama in Bali*, which was published in 1938, and he recreated the Kecak dance for a visiting German film crew. In 1937 he moved to the remote village of Iseh in eastern Bali.

In 1938 a puritan clampdown in the Netherlands spread to the Dutch colony and Spies was arrested for homosexual activities with minors. He was imprisoned in Denpasar, and later jailed in Surabaya for eight months. He was no sooner released than WWII began and, when the Germans invaded Holland in 1940, he was arrested again by the Dutch, this time as an enemy alien, and held in Sumatra until the Pacific War began. On 18 January 1942 Spies, along with other prisoners of war, was shipped out of Sumatra bound for Ceylon (now Sri Lanka). The following day the ship was bombed by Japanese aircraft and sank near the island of Nias. Spies drowned.

Colin McPhee

A chance hearing of a record of gamelan music compelled Canadian musician Colin McPhee (1900–65) to join the stream of talented 1930s visitors. His book, *A House in Bali*, was not published until 1944, long after his departure from the island, but it remains one of the best written of the Bali accounts, and his tales of music and house building are often highly amusing. After WWII,

WOJ Nieuwenkamp: First Artist of Bali by Bruce Carpenter is a fascinating depiction of Bali from 1904, when the Dutch artist Nieuwenkamp first arrived.

Natural History & Environment

Birds of Bali by Victor Mason & Frank Jarvis is enhanced by lovely watercolour illustrations.

Field Guide to the Birds of Java & Bali by John Mackinnon is probably the best field guide for birdwatchers on Bali.

Flowers of Bali and *Fruits of Bali* by Fred & Margaret Wiseman are nicely illustrated books that will tell you what you're admiring or eating.

The Malay Archipelago by Alfred Wallace is a recently republished natural history

Western Visitors in the 1930s

McPhee taught music at UCLA and played an important role in introducing Balinese music to the West, and encouraging gamelan orchestras to visit the US.

Rudolf Bonnet

Bonnet (1895–1978) was a Dutch artist who, along with Walter Spies, played a major role in the development of Balinese art in the mid-1930s. Bonnet arrived on Bali in 1929, two years after Spies moved there, and immediately contacted him. In 1936 he was one of the principal forces behind the foundation of the Pita Maha artists' cooperative. Bonnet's work concentrated on the human form and everyday Balinese life. To this day, the numerous classical Balinese paintings with their themes of markets, cockfights and other aspects of day-to-day existence are indebted to Bonnet.

Bonnet was imprisoned in Sulawesi by the Japanese during WWII and returned to Bali in the 1950s to plan the Museum Puri Lukisan in Ubud. He left the island, but returned in 1973 to help establish the museum's permanent collection. He died in 1978 on a brief return visit to Holland.

K'tut Tantri

A woman of many aliases, K'tut Tantri was named Vannine Walker, or perhaps it was Muriel Pearson, when she breezed in from Hollywood in 1932. The film *Bali, The Last Paradise* was her inspiration to visit Bali, where she dyed her red hair black (on Bali, only demons have red hair) and was befriended by the prince of the Bangli kingdom.

She teamed up with Robert Koke to open the first hotel at Kuta Beach (the Kuta Beach Hotel) in 1936. Later she fell out with the Kokes and established her own hotel. She stayed on when war swept into the archipelago, was imprisoned by the Japanese, and then worked for the Indonesian Republicans in their postwar struggle against the Dutch. As Surabaya Sue, she broadcast from Surabaya in support of their cause. Her book *Revolt in Paradise* (written as K'tut Tantri) was published in 1960.

Robert & Louise Koke

In 1936 Americans Robert Koke and Louise Garret arrived on Bali as part of a long trip through Southeast Asia. They fell in love with the island and Kuta Beach, and soon established the Kuta Beach Hotel, at first in partnership with K'tut Tantri, although their accounts of the hotel differ widely.

While the Dutch insisted that the hotel was nothing more than a few 'dirty native huts', it was an instant hit and Bali's 1930s tourist boom ensured that it was always full. Robert Koke, who learned to surf in Hawaii, can also claim the honour of introducing surfing to Bali.

The Kokes' success continued until the Japanese entry into WWII. The pair made a last-minute escape from Bali, and when Robert Koke visited Bali just after the war, only traces of the hotel's foundations remained. In 1987 Louise Koke's long-forgotten story of their hotel was published as *Our Hotel in Bali*, illustrated with her incisive sketches and her husband's photographs.

Other Western Visitors

Others played their part in chronicling the period, such as writers Hickman Powell, whose book *The Last Paradise* was published in 1930, and German author Vicki Baum, whose book *A Tale from Bali*, a fictionalised account of the 1906 *puputan*, is still in print.

classic by the great 19th-century biogeographer, who postulated that the Lombok Strait was the dividing line between Asia and Australia.

Contemporary Bali

A Little Bit of One O'Clock by William Ingram is widely available in Bali, and relates an American's life with a Balinese family, exploring issues of culture and tradition.

Bali Style by Rio Helmi & Barbara Walker is a superbly illustrated book, which covers architecture, landscaping and decoration on contemporary Bali.

Bali, The Ultimate Island by Leonard Leuras & R Ian Lloyd is the ultimate coffeetable book on Bali. It's a heavyweight volume with superb photographs, both old and new, together with interesting text.

The Balinese by Hugh Mabbett is a readable collection of anecdotes, observations and impressions of Bali and its people. If you have a real interest in Kuta, read Mabbett's *In Praise of Kuta*. It recounts Kuta's early history and its frenetic modern development.

Balinese Gardens by William Warren & Invernizzi Tettoni offers handsome coverage of the wonders of Balinese gardens and landscapes.

Food of Bali by Heinz von Holzen, Lothar Arsana & Wendy Hutton is a mouth-watering book that not only explains the cultural context of Balinese food, but also describes ingredients, recipes and techniques.

Stranger in Paradise by Made Wijaya, also known as Michael White, is an expat classic offering a personal account of Bali's post-WWII emergence as a hot spot for cross-cultural exchange.

Literature

The post-WWII period has seen the emergence of modern Balinese writing in Indonesian. This work has only recently begun appearing in English translations.

The Birthmark – Memoirs of a Balinese Prince by Dr AAM Djelantik is the autobiography of a Balinese prince who became a medical doctor. It details his life and work spanning the old aristocracy, the Dutch administration and the modernisation of Bali.

The Butterflies of Bali by Victor Mason, a long-term expatriate and bird lover, has nothing to do with butterflies, but it's a good story, with perceptive details of village life.

Bali Behind the Seen, translated by Vern Cork, is a collection of recent fiction by contemporary Balinese writers, and conveys much of the tension between deeply rooted traditions and the irresistible pressure of modernisation.

Bali – The Morning After, translated by Vern Cork, is a collection of work by current Balinese poets, many of them women. Responses to foreign influences and traditional gender roles are a recurrent theme.

Folk Tales from Bali & Lombok by Margaret Muth Alibasah is a collection of tales retold in English.

The Rape of Sukreni by Anak Agung Pandji Tisna, translated by George Quinn, is the second novel (1936) of this pioneering Balinese writer – a classic good-versus-evil story set in colonial times, which has familiar elements even today.

The Seat of Tears by Putu Oka Sukanta, translated by Vern Cork, is an anthology of short stories about Balinese women and the changes they are confronting.

Bookshops

Bali has a few good bookshops that carry a selection of books on Bali and Indonesia, plus travel guides, maps, local and international newspapers and magazines. The best of them are: Gramedia Book Shop in Matahari department store, Denpasar; M-Media, in Matahari department store at Kuta Square; and Ganesha and Ary's bookshops in Ubud.

Second-hand bookshops and book exchanges in the tourist centres mostly sell paperback novels in many of the major European languages.

NEWSPAPERS & MAGAZINES

The *Jakarta Post,* the English-language daily, is published in Jakarta and available in Bali. Current issues can be bought from shops in Kuta-Legian, Sanur and Ubud, as well as from young streetsellers who charge marginally more than newsstands. Indonesian readers can enjoy the daily *Bali Post*, which also has an online version (w www.balipost.co.id). Current editions of *Time*, *Newsweek* and the *Economist* and daily editions of the *International Herald Tribune* are also available in the tourist areas. Recent Australian, US and European newspapers are available only one or two days after publication date, mainly from streetsellers.

Several tourist-oriented magazines and newspapers are available on Bali – and all are free, including the *Bali Advertiser*, which has an eco-bent section featuring stories and advertisements on topics such as yoga and sustainable living. Its target reader is the expat community, so it's a good place to source community events, house rentals, work, discounted travel or accommodation. You can contact them on ☎/fax 0361-755392. *Bali Travel News* is a free broadsheet featuring a colourful, readable jumble of local news, entertainment and information, aimed at both tourists and the local tourist industry. *Bali & Beyond* is a new monthly tourist magazine, which has an excellent parallel online edition. *The Beat* is a free entertainment gig guide, covering both Bali and Jakarta, and is well worth picking up for the lowdown on nightlife in Kuta and Seminyak. It's available from cafés, bars and restaurants.

Magic Wave is a new surf-community newspaper. It publishes a tide chart, reviews of surf spots, the lowdown on the local surf scene and places to party. You can contact them by email at [e] bugdesign@yahoo.com

Latitudes is a monthly colour magazine covering all of Indonesia, which focuses on intelligent feature stories. It's highly recommended.

RADIO

The government radio station, Radio Republic Indonesia (RRI; 93.5FM), broadcasts 24 hours, and has an English-language news service twice daily. It also transmits Kang Guru, an English-language radio programme produced by the Indonesia Australia Language Foundation and funded by AusAID. There are several other stations on Bali. Hard Rock Radio (87.6FM) has some English programming and a playlist featuring Indonesian and Western hits, while Radio Plus FM (106.5FM) and Kuta FM (96.4FM) feature contemporary Western pop, with English-speaking DJs. Bali FM (100.9FM) is a tourist-oriented radio station that broadcasts in English and Indonesian over most of southern Bali. It plays some contemporary rock and lots of oldies, and has a regular news service.

Short-wave broadcasts, such as Voice of America and the BBC World Service, can be picked up on Bali.

TV

Several public and private TV stations broadcast a range of foreign movies, mostly with Indonesian subtitles, plus bizarre Indonesian quiz shows, soap operas from all over the world (with Indonesian subtitles) and sports – mainly basketball from the US and soccer from Europe. There are also English-language news services on the government-run TVRI at 7.30pm. Private networks SCTV and RCTI also have news services. The daily *Jakarta Post* includes a list of programmes for each channel (but at Jakarta time).

Places with the necessary satellite dish (*parabola* is the local term) pick up international networks like CNN. Satellite TV is a popular feature in top-end hotels.

VIDEO SYSTEMS

Indonesia subscribes to the PAL broadcasting standard, the same as Australia, New Zealand, the UK and most of Europe.

PHOTOGRAPHY & VIDEO

Bali is one of the most photogenic places on Earth, so make sure that you take plenty of film with you!

Film & Equipment

A good variety of film is widely available at reasonable prices. It pays to shop around if you want to buy a lot of film, or if you have special requirements – always check the expiry date before handing over your cash.

Developing and printing is also widely available, very cheap and of reasonably good quality. You can get colour print film done very cheaply in a few hours at one of the innumerable photographic shops in the tourist centres and major towns. Slide film is generally sent to Jakarta for processing, takes three or four days to develop, and costs more.

Technical Tips

Shoot early in the day – after about 10am the sun is intense and straight overhead, so you're likely to get a bluish, washed-out look to your pictures. In the late afternoon, the sky is often overcast or hazy, and it's hard to get really clear, sharp images. If you do shoot in the middle of the day, a skylight filter will cut out some of the haze. When the sun is low in the sky, a lens hood can help reduce problems with reflection or direct sunlight on the lens.

Those picturesque, green rice fields come up best if backlit by the sun. For the oh-so-popular sunset shots at Kuta, Lovina and Tanah Lot, set your exposure on the sky without the sun making an appearance – then shoot at the sun.

It's surprisingly dark in the shade of the trees, so you might find it difficult to take photos of lush gorges or forests without a flash. Faster film (400 ASA) can be useful.

For more information, see Lonely Planet's *Travel Photography: A Guide To Taking Better Pictures* by Richard I'Anson.

Video

Blank video tapes are available in some of the bigger stores in Denpasar and the main tourist areas. They're not particularly cheap and the range is limited, so it would probably be better to bring plenty of tapes with you. Bring them in sealed packages – customs authorities may insist on viewing tapes they suspect may contain prohibited material. Also bring some spare parts and batteries.

Restrictions

Military installations are not widespread on Bali, but you should be aware that these are sensitive subjects – if in doubt, ask before you shoot. You are usually welcome to take photos of ceremonies in the villages and temples, but try not to be intrusive. Ask before taking photos inside a temple.

There's one place where you must not take photographs at all – public bathing places. Just because the Balinese bathe in streams, rivers, lakes or other open places doesn't mean they don't think of them as private. Balinese simply do not 'see' one another when they're bathing, and to intrude with a camera is like sneaking up to someone's bathroom window and pointing your camera through it.

Photographing People

Photograph with discretion and manners. It's always polite to ask first, and if they say no, then don't. A gesture, smile and nod are all that is usually necessary. Often people will ask you to take their photo, and you more-or-less have to – the problem is getting them in a natural pose. If you promise to send someone a copy of a photo, do so. And don't be surprised if you're asked to be in a few snaps taken by domestic tourists from other parts of Indonesia, especially the Javanese.

TIME

Bali, Lombok and the islands of Nusa Tenggara to the east are all on Central Indonesian Standard Time *(Waktu Indonesian Tengah* or WIT*)*, which is eight hours ahead of GMT/UTC or two hours behind Australian Eastern Standard Time. Java is another hour behind Bali/Lombok.

Not allowing for variations due to daylight-saving time in foreign countries, when it's noon on Bali and Lombok, it's 11pm the previous day in New York and 8pm in Los Angeles, 4am in London, 5am in Paris and Amsterdam, noon in Perth, 1pm in Tokyo, and 2pm in Sydney and Melbourne.

As Bali is close to the equator, days and nights are approximately equal in length. The sun pops up over the horizon at about 6am and drops down in the west at about 6pm. The sunsets are often orange-fire spectaculars, but don't expect to enjoy a pleasant twilight – it gets dark almost immediately.

'Bali time' is an expression that refers to the Balinese reluctance to be obsessed by punctuality. It is equivalent to *jam karet*, the 'rubber time' found in other parts of Indonesia, but even more elastic.

ELECTRICITY

Electricity is usually 220–240V AC in Bali. In some smaller villages it's still 110V (if they have electricity at all), so check first. Wall plugs are the standard European variety – round with two pins. Electricity is usually fairly reliable and blackouts are not common, although the electricity grid is always running at its maximum capacity. In many small towns, and even in parts of larger towns, electricity is a recent innovation – if you travel around a lot you're likely to stay in the odd losmen where lighting is provided with oil lamps.

Even where there is electricity, the lighting can be very dim. Lots of losmen seem to have light bulbs of such low wattage that you can almost see the electricity crawling around the filaments. Street lighting can also be a problem – there often isn't any. If stumbling back to your losmen down dark alleys in Kuta or through the rice fields in Ubud doesn't appeal, a strong flashlight can be very useful. Indonesian batteries are pretty poor, so bring some long-life ones with you – and take dead batteries home, as there's a disposal problem on Bali.

WEIGHTS & MEASURES

Indonesia follows the metric system. For people accustomed to the imperial system, there is a conversion table at the back of this guidebook.

LAUNDRY

All the fancier hotels advertise laundry services, and charge quite steeply for them. The cheaper places don't advertise the fact, but will normally wash and iron your clothes for a pretty reasonable price. The family-run laundry services in the backstreets of the tourist centres are the cheapest (but aren't always reliable). In Kuta, for example, a shirt, skirt or jeans costs as little as 1500Rp to wash, dry and fold. Allow 24 hours, or a bit longer if it is raining.

TOILETS

You'll still encounter Asian-style toilets in cheaper losmen around Bali (particularly in the far west). These toilets have two footrests and a hole in the floor – you squat down and aim. In most places catering for tourists, Western-style sit-down toilets are the norm. At some tourist attractions on Bali, there are public toilets that cost about 500Rp per visit.

Apart from tourist cafés and restaurants, and mid-range and top-end accommodation, you won't find toilet paper, so bring your own. If there is a bin next to the toilet, it's for toilet paper – the sewerage system may not be able to cope with toilet paper. To locate a toilet ask for the *kamar mandi* (bathroom), *kamar kecil* (little room) or 'WC' (pronounced 'waysay').

HEALTH

Travel health depends on your predeparture preparations, your daily health care while travelling and how you handle any medical problem that develops. While the potential dangers can seem quite frightening, in reality few travellers experience anything more than an upset stomach on Bali. The greatest risk is accidental injury, particularly from traffic accidents.

Predeparture Planning

Immunisations Plan ahead for getting your vaccinations: some of them require more than one injection, while some vaccinations should not be given together. Note that some vaccinations should not be given

Medical Kit Check List

Following is a list of items you should consider including in your medical kit – consult your pharmacist for brands available in your country.

☐ **Aspirin or paracetamol (acetaminophen in the USA)** – for pain or fever

☐ **Antihistamine** – for allergies, eg, hay fever; to ease the itch from insect bites or stings; and to prevent motion sickness

☐ **Cold and flu tablets, throat lozenges and nasal decongestant**

☐ **Multivitamins** – consider for long trips, when dietary vitamin intake may be inadequate

☐ **Antibiotics** – consider including these if you're travelling well off the beaten track; see your doctor, as they must be prescribed, and carry the prescription with you

☐ **Loperamide or diphenoxylate** –'blockers' for diarrhoea

☐ **Prochlorperazine or metaclopramide** – for nausea and vomiting

☐ **Rehydration mixture** – to prevent dehydration, which may occur, for example, during bouts of diarrhoea; particularly important when travelling with children

☐ **Insect repellent, sunscreen, lip balm and eye drops**

☐ **Calamine lotion, sting relief spray or aloe vera** – to ease irritation from sunburn and insect bites or stings

☐ **Antifungal cream or powder** – for fungal skin infections and thrush

☐ **Antiseptic (such as povidone-iodine)** – for cuts and grazes

☐ **Bandages, Band-Aids (plasters) and other wound dressings**

☐ **Water purification tablets or iodine**

☐ **Scissors, tweezers and a thermometer** – note that mercury thermometers are prohibited by airlines

☐ **Sterile kit** – in case you need injections in a country with medical hygiene problems; discuss with your doctor

during pregnancy or to people with allergies, and there is often a greater risk of disease with children and during pregnancy. Discuss your requirements with your doctor.

There are no health entry requirements for Indonesia, but if you have been to Africa or South America in the previous six days, you may need a vaccination for yellow fever.

Record all vaccinations on an International Certificate of Vaccination, available from your doctor or national health department.

Discuss your personal requirements with your doctor, but vaccinations you should consider for this trip include the following (for more details about the diseases themselves, see the individual disease entries later in this section).

Diphtheria & Tetanus Vaccinations for these two diseases are usually combined and are recommended for everyone. After an initial course of three injections (usually given in childhood), boosters are necessary every 10 years.

Hepatitis A Hepatitis A vaccine (eg, Avaxim, Havrix 1440 or VAQTA) provides long-term immunity (possibly more than 10 years) after an initial injection and a booster at six to 12 months. Alternatively, an injection of gamma globulin can provide short-term protection against hepatitis A – two to six months, depending on the dose given. It is not a vaccine, but is a ready-made antibody collected from blood donations. It is reasonably effective and, unlike the vaccine, it is protective immediately, but because it is a blood product, there are current concerns about its long-term safety. Hepatitis A vaccine is also available in a combined form, Twinrix, with hepatitis B vaccine. Three injections over a six-month period are required, the first two providing substantial protection against hepatitis A.

Hepatitis B Travellers who should consider vaccination against hepatitis B include those on a long trip, as well as those visiting countries where there are high levels of hepatitis B infection, where blood transfusions may not be adequately screened or where sexual contact or needle sharing is a possibility. Vaccination involves three injections, with a booster at 12 months. More rapid courses are available if necessary.

Japanese B Encephalitis Consider vaccination against this disease if spending a month or longer in a high-risk area (parts of Asia), making repeated trips to a risk area or visiting during an epidemic. It involves three injections over 30 days.

Polio Everyone should keep up to date with this vaccination, which is normally given in childhood. A booster every 10 years maintains immunity.

Tuberculosis The risk of TB to travellers is usually very low, unless you will be living with or associating closely with local people in high-risk areas such as Asia, Africa and some parts of the Americas and Pacific. Vaccination against TB (BCG) is recommended for children and young adults living on Bali or Lombok for three months or more.

Typhoid Vaccination against typhoid may be required if you are travelling for more than a couple of weeks in most parts of Asia, Africa, Central and South America and Central and Eastern Europe. It is now available either as an injection or as capsules to be taken orally.

Malaria Medication Antimalarial drugs do not prevent you from being infected, but kill the malaria parasites at an early stage in their development and significantly reduce the risk of becoming very ill or dying. Expert advice on medication should be sought, as there are many factors to consider, including the area to be visited, the risk of exposure to malaria-carrying mosquitoes, the side effects of medication, your medical history and whether you are a child or are pregnant. The risk of contracting malaria on Bali is extremely low, but Lombok is viewed as a malaria risk area.

Health Insurance Make sure that you have adequate health insurance. For details see the Travel Insurance section under Visas & Documents earlier in this chapter.

Travel Health Guides Lonely Planet's *Healthy Travel Asia & India* is a handy pocket size and is packed with useful information, including pretrip planning, emergency first aid, immunisation and disease information and what to do if you get sick on the road. *Travel with Children* from LP also includes advice on travel health for younger children.

There are also a number of excellent travel-health sites on the Internet. From the Lonely Planet home page there are links at ⓦ www.lonelyplanet.com/weblinks/wlheal .htm to the World Health Organization and the US Center for Disease Control and Prevention.

Other Preparations Make sure you're healthy before you start travelling. If you are going on a long trip make sure your teeth are OK – it's not hard to find a dentist *(dokter gigi)* on Bali, but it's not really how you want to spend your holiday. If you wear glasses, take a spare pair and your prescription. You can get new glasses reasonably cheaply in the main towns, but it can take a few days, as the lenses are made on Java.

If you require a particular medication take an adequate supply, as it may not be available locally. Take part of the packaging showing the generic name rather than the brand, which will make getting replacements easier. It's a good idea to have a prescription or letter from your doctor to show that you legally use the medication to avoid any problems. It's also a good idea to bring a supply of condoms from home, though local brands are available.

Basic Rules

Food There is an old adage that says: 'If you can cook it, boil it or peel it you can eat it…otherwise forget it.' Vegetables and fruit should be washed with purified water or peeled where possible. Beware of ice cream that is sold in the street (or anywhere else for that matter!) It may have melted and consequently refrozen; if there's any doubt (eg, a power cut in the last day or two), steer well clear. Shellfish such as mussels, oysters and clams should be avoided, as well as undercooked meat, particularly in the form of mince. Steaming does not make shellfish safe for eating.

If a place looks clean and well run and the vendor also looks clean and healthy, then the food is probably safe. In general, places that are packed with travellers or locals will be fine, while empty restaurants are questionable. The food in busy restaurants is cooked and eaten quite quickly with little standing around and is probably not reheated.

Water The number one rule is *be careful of the water* and especially ice. If you don't know for certain that the water is safe, assume the worst. Reputable brands of bottled water or soft drinks are generally fine. Only use water from containers with a serrated seal – not tops or corks. Take care with fruit juice, particularly if you think water has been added. Most milk available on Bali and Lombok is UHT pasteurised, and should be fine if it is kept hygienically after opening. Tea or coffee should also be OK, since the water should have been boiled.

Bottled water is available almost everywhere on Bali, but if you do need to purify water, the simplest way is to boil it thoroughly. Chlorine tablets will kill many pathogens, but not some parasites like giardia and amoebic cysts. Iodine is more effective in purifying water and is available in tablet form. Follow the directions carefully and remember that too much iodine can be harmful.

Medical Problems & Treatment

Self-diagnosis and treatment can be risky, so you should always seek medical help. A consulate or a top-end hotel can usually recommend a local doctor or clinic. Although we do give drug dosages in this section, they are for emergency use only. Correct diagnosis is vital. In this section we have used the generic names for medications – check with a pharmacist for brands available locally.

Note that antibiotics should ideally be administered only under medical supervision. Take only the recommended dose at the prescribed intervals and finish the course, even if the illness seems to be cured earlier. Stop immediately if there are any serious reactions and don't use the antibiotic at all if you are unsure that you have the correct one. Some people are allergic to commonly prescribed antibiotics such as penicillin; carry this information (eg, on a bracelet) when travelling.

Medical Services

Bali's best public hospitals are in Denpasar and Singaraja. In the first instance, foreigners would be best served in one of the private clinics that cater mainly to tourists, in Kuta-Legian, Nusa Dua, Tanjung Benoa and Ubud. The best one is probably **BIMC** (☎ 0361-761263; w www.bimcbali.com; Jl Ngurah Rai 100X, Kuta), on the bypass road just east of Kuta, and accessible from most of southern Bali. It's a modern Australian-run clinic that can do blood tests, hotel visits and arrange medical evacuation. It's expensive (US$60 minimum consultation), but your travel insurance will cover it. If you need to be hospitalised, a good clinic will arrange transport and make sure your needs are understood.

In more remote areas, facilities are basic; generally a small public hospital, doctor's surgery or community health care centre (*puskesmas*). Specialist facilities for neurosurgery and heart surgery are nonexistent, and the range of available drugs (including painkillers) is limited. Your hotel should be able to recommend a local English-speaking doctor, or you could call one of the upmarket hotels and ask them. Travel insurance policies often have an emergency assistance phone number, which might be able to recommend a doctor or clinic, or use its contacts to find one in a remote area.

Health care is not free on Bali, and you will get more prompt attention if you can pay cash up-front for treatment, drugs, surgical equipment, drinking water, food and so on. Try to get receipts and paperwork so you can claim it all later on your travel insurance. Services such as meals, washing and clean clothing, are normally provided by the patient's family. If you are unfortunate enough to be on your own in a Bali hospital, contact your consulate – you need help.

Pharmacies

There are plenty of pharmacies (drugstores) – called *apotik* or *apotek* – in the tourist centres, and usually a few in the major towns, often located near the main hospital or a doctor's surgery. Always double-check the expiry date before you buy any medicines.

The asking price for drugs and medicines may be exorbitant – you could ask to see the official price list, but you may not be in a strong bargaining position. Get receipts for your insurance claim.

Environmental Hazards

Heat Exhaustion Dehydration and salt deficiency can cause heat exhaustion. Take time to acclimatise to high temperatures, drink sufficient liquids and do not do anything too physically demanding.

Anhidrotic heat exhaustion is a rare form of heat exhaustion that is caused by an inability to sweat. It tends to affect people who have been in a hot climate for some time, rather than newcomers. It can progress to heatstroke. Treatment involves removal to a cooler climate.

Heatstroke This serious, occasionally fatal condition can occur if the body's heat-regulating mechanism breaks down and the body temperature rises to dangerous levels. Long, continuous periods of exposure to high temperatures and insufficient fluids can leave you vulnerable to heatstroke.

The symptoms are feeling unwell, not sweating very much (or at all) and a high body temperature (40°C or 104°F). Where sweating has ceased, the skin becomes flushed and red. Severe, throbbing headaches and lack of coordination will also occur, and the sufferer may be confused or aggressive. Eventually the victim will become delirious or convulse. Hospitalisation is essential, but in the interim, get the victim out of the sun, remove their clothing, cover them with a wet sheet or towel and then fan continually. Give fluids if they are conscious.

Prickly Heat This is an itchy rash caused by excessive perspiration trapped under the skin. It usually strikes people who have just arrived in a hot climate. Keeping cool (resorting to air-conditioning), bathing often, drying the skin and using a mild talcum or prickly heat powder may help.

Sunburn On Bali, you can get sunburnt very quickly, even through cloud, and especially while rafting, trekking, swimming, surfing, snorkelling or diving. Use a maximum-strength sunblock (readily available); protect your eyes with good-quality sunglasses, particularly if you are near water or sand; and take extra care with areas that don't normally see sun, like your feet. A broad-rimmed hat provides good protection, but you should also put sunblock on your nose, lips and ears. Even good sunblocks wash off with heavy sweating and swimming, so reapply every two or three hours. For surfers, a helmet protects your head against the sun as well as coral. Calamine lotion or aloe vera provide some relief from mild sunburn.

Jet Lag This is experienced when a person travels by air across more than three time zones (each time zone usually represents a one-hour time difference). It occurs because many of the functions of the human body (such as temperature, pulse rate and emptying of the bladder and bowels) are regulated by internal 24-hour cycles. When we travel long-distances rapidly, our bodies take time to adjust to the 'new time' of our destination, and we may experience fatigue, disorientation, insomnia, anxiety, impaired concentration and loss of appetite. These effects will usually be gone within three days of arrival, but to minimise the impact of jet lag the following points will help.

- Rest for a couple of days prior to departure.
- Try to select flight schedules that minimise sleep deprivation; arriving late in the day means you can go to sleep soon after you arrive. For very long flights, try to organise a stopover.
- Avoid excessive eating (which bloats the stomach) and alcohol (which causes dehydration) during the flight. Instead, drink plenty of non-carbonated, nonalcoholic drinks such as fruit juice or water.

• Avoid smoking.
• Make yourself comfortable by wearing loose-fitting clothes and perhaps bringing an eye mask and ear plugs to help you sleep.
• Try to sleep at the appropriate time for the time zone you are travelling to.

Motion Sickness Eating lightly before and during a trip will reduce the chances of motion sickness. If you are prone to motion sickness try to find a place that minimises movement – near the wing on aircraft, close to midships on boats, near the centre on buses. Fresh air usually helps; reading and cigarette smoke don't. Commercial motion-sickness preparations, which can cause drowsiness, have to be taken before the trip commences. Ginger (available in capsule form) and peppermint (including mint-flavoured sweets) are believed by some to be natural preventatives, though there is no medical evidence to support this.

Infectious Diseases

Diarrhoea Simple things like a change of water, food or climate can all cause a mild bout of diarrhoea, but a few rushed toilet trips with no other symptoms is not indicative of a major problem.

Dehydration is the main danger with any diarrhoea, particularly in children or the elderly, as dehydration can occur quite quickly. Under all circumstances *fluid replacement* (at least equal to the volume being lost) is the most important thing to remember. Weak black tea with a little sugar, soda water, or soft drinks allowed to go flat and diluted 50% with clean water are all good. With severe diarrhoea a rehydrating solution is preferable to replace minerals and salts lost. Commercially available oral rehydration salts (ORS) are very useful; add them to boiled or bottled water. In an emergency you can make up a solution of six teaspoons of sugar and half a teaspoon of salt to a litre of boiled or bottled water. You need to drink at least the same volume of fluid that you are losing in bowel movements and vomiting. Urine is the best guide to the adequacy of replacement – if you have small amounts of concentrated urine, you need to drink more. Keep drinking small amounts often. Stick to a bland diet as you recover.

Gut-paralysing drugs such as loperamide or diphenoxylate can be used to bring relief, but they do not actually cure the problem.

Only use these drugs if you don't have access to toilets, eg, if you *must* travel. Note that these drugs are not recommended for children under 12 years.

In certain situations antibiotics may be required: diarrhoea with blood or mucus (dysentery), any diarrhoea with fever, profuse watery diarrhoea, persistent diarrhoea not improving after 48 hours and severe diarrhoea. These suggest a more serious cause of diarrhoea and in these situations gut-paralysing drugs should be avoided.

In these situations, a stool test may be necessary to diagnose what bug is causing your diarrhoea, so you should seek medical help urgently. Where this is not possible the recommended drugs for bacterial diarrhoea (the most likely cause of severe diarrhoea in travellers) are norfloxacin 400mg twice daily for three days or ciprofloxacin 500mg twice daily for five days. These are not recommended for children or pregnant women. The drug of choice for children would be co-trimoxazole with dosage dependent on weight. A five-day course is given. Ampicillin or amoxycillin may be given in pregnancy, but medical care is necessary.

Two other causes of persistent diarrhoea in travellers are giardiasis and amoebic dysentery.

Giardiasis Caused by a common parasite, *Giardia lamblia*, the symptoms include stomach cramps, nausea, a bloated stomach, watery foul-smelling diarrhoea and frequent gas. Giardiasis can appear several weeks after you have been exposed to the parasite. The symptoms may disappear for a few days and then return; this can go on for several weeks.

Amoebic Dysentery Caused by the protozoan *Entamoeba histolytica,* amoebic dysentery is characterised by a gradual onset of low-grade diarrhoea, often with blood and mucus. Cramping abdominal pain and vomiting are less likely than in other types of diarrhoea, and fever may not be present. It will persist until treated and can recur and cause other health problems.

You should always seek medical advice if you think you have giardiasis or amoebic dysentery (especially during pregnancy), but where this is not possible, tinidazole or metronidazole are the recommended drugs.

Treatment is a 2g single dose of tinidazole or 250mg of metronidazole three times daily for five to 10 days.

Fungal Infections These occur more commonly in hot weather and are usually found on the scalp, between the toes (athlete's foot) or fingers, in the groin and on the body (ringworm). You get ringworm (which is a fungal infection, not a worm) from infected animals or other people. Moisture encourages these infections.

To prevent fungal infections wear loose, comfortable clothes, avoid artificial fibres, wash frequently and dry yourself carefully. If you do get an infection, wash the infected area at least daily with a disinfectant or medicated soap and water, and rinse and dry well. Apply an antifungal cream or powder like tolnaftate. Try to expose the infected area to air or sunlight as much as possible and wash all towels and underwear in hot water, change them often and let them dry in the sun.

Intestinal Worms These parasites are most common in rural, tropical areas. The different worms have different ways of causing infecting. Some may be ingested on food like undercooked meat (eg, tapeworms) and some enter through your skin (eg, hookworms). Infestations may not show up for some time, and although they are generally not serious, if left untreated some can cause severe health problems later. Consider having a stool test when you get home to check for these and determine the appropriate treatment.

Typhoid Typhoid fever is a dangerous gut infection caused by contaminated water and food. Medical help must be sought. In its early stages sufferers may feel they have a bad cold or flu on the way, as early symptoms are a headache, body aches and a fever that rises a little each day until it is around 40°C (104°F) or more. The victim's pulse is often slow relative to the degree of fever present – unlike a normal fever where the pulse increases. There may also be vomiting, abdominal pain, diarrhoea or constipation.

In the second week the high fever and slow pulse continue and a few pink spots may appear on the body; trembling, delirium, weakness, weight loss and dehydration may occur. Complications such as pneumonia, perforated bowel or meningitis may occur.

Hepatitis This is a general term for inflammation of the liver. It is a common disease worldwide. There are several different viruses that cause hepatitis, and they differ in the way that they are transmitted. The symptoms are similar in all forms of the illness, and include fever, chills, headache, fatigue, feelings of weakness and aches and pains, followed by loss of appetite, nausea, vomiting, abdominal pain, dark urine, light-coloured faeces, jaundiced (yellow) skin and yellowing of the whites of the eyes. People who have had hepatitis should avoid alcohol for some time after the illness, as the liver needs time to recover.

Hepatitis A is transmitted by contaminated food and drinking water. You should seek medical advice, but there is not much you can do apart from resting, drinking lots of fluids, eating lightly and avoiding fatty foods. Hepatitis E is transmitted in the same way as hepatitis A; it can be particularly serious in pregnant women.

There are almost 300 million chronic carriers of hepatitis B in the world. It is spread through contact with infected blood, blood products or body fluids, eg, through sexual contact, unsterilised needles and blood transfusions, or contact with blood via small breaks in the skin. Other risk situations include having a shave, tattoo or body piercing with contaminated equipment. The symptoms of hepatitis B may be more severe than type A and the disease can lead to long-term problems such as chronic liver damage, liver cancer or a long-term carrier state. Hepatitis C and D are spread in the same way as hepatitis B and can also lead to long-term complications.

There are vaccines against hepatitis A and B, but there are currently no vaccines against the other types of hepatitis. Following the basic rules about food and water (hepatitis A and E) and avoiding risk situations (hepatitis B, C and D) are important preventative measures.

HIV & AIDS Infection with the human immunodeficiency virus (HIV) may lead to acquired immune deficiency syndrome (AIDS), which is a fatal disease. HIV is a major problem in many Asian countries, and Bali has one of the highest rates of HIV infection in Indonesia. Official HIV figures in Indonesia are unrealistically low and it's believed the incidence of the disease will increase significantly unless hospital procedures are improved and safe sex is promoted. The main risk for most travellers is sexual contact with local men, prostitutes and other travellers – in Indonesia the spread of HIV is primarily through heterosexual activity.

The risk of sexual transmission of the HIV virus can be dramatically reduced by the use of a condom (*kondom*). These are available from supermarkets, street stalls and drugstores in tourist areas, and from the pharmacy (*apotik*) in almost any town (from about 1500Rp to 3000Rp each – it's worth getting the more expensive brands).

HIV/AIDS can also be spread through infected blood transfusions – blood products on Bali and Lombok are screened for HIV/AIDS, but are usually in short supply. If you need a transfusion, you may have to find a donor yourself, in which case you need to be confident they are HIV negative. It helps to know what your blood group is. If you do need an injection, ask to see the syringe unwrapped in front of you, or take a needle and syringe pack with you.

Fear of obtaining a HIV infection should never preclude treatment for serious medical conditions.

Sexually Transmitted Infections (STIs)

HIV/AIDS and hepatitis B can be transmitted through sexual contact – see the relevant sections earlier for more details. Other STIs include gonorrhoea, herpes and syphilis; sores, blisters or rashes around the genitals and discharges or pain when urinating are common symptoms. In some STIs, such as wart virus or chlamydia, symptoms may be less marked or not observed at all, especially in women. Chlamydia infection can cause infertility in men and women before any symptoms have been noticed. Syphilis symptoms eventually disappear completely, but the disease remains and can cause severe problems in later years.

While abstinence from sexual contact is the only 100% effective prevention, using condoms is also effective. The treatment of gonorrhoea and syphilis is with antibiotics. The different sexually transmitted infections each require specific antibiotics. Strains of drug-resistant STIs, notably gonorrhoea, are present on Bali, so prevention is definitely better than cure.

Scabies, a contagious skin infection caused by mites, is also present on Bali, and is acquired from close personal contact. It can be treated in adults with gamma benzene hexachloride, permethrin or benzyl benzoate. Gamma benzene hexachloride is sold under the brand name Scabecid in some countries.

Insect-Borne Diseases

Malaria This serious and potentially fatal disease is spread by mosquito bites. During and just after the wet season (October to March), there is a very low risk of malaria in northern Bali, and a slightly higher risk in far western Bali, particularly in and around Gilimanuk. So, if you are staying in budget accommodation anywhere outside of southern Bali, or trekking in northern or western Bali during, or just after, the rainy season, you should consider taking antimalarial drugs and seek medical advice about this. However, it is not currently considered necessary to take antimalarial drugs if you are sticking to the tourist centres in southern Bali, regardless of the season – but confirm this with your doctor prior to departure.

Lombok is an area of malaria risk, and if you are going there, or further afield in Indonesia, you should take preventative measures. It is extremely important to avoid mosquito bites and to take tablets to prevent this disease. See your doctor at least a month before departure and discuss the most appropriate antimalarial drugs, and make sure you understand when they should be taken.

Malaria symptoms range from fever, chills and sweating, headache, diarrhoea and abdominal pains to a vague feeling of ill-health. Seek medical help immediately if malaria is suspected. Without treatment, malaria can rapidly become more serious and can be fatal.

If medical care is not available, malaria tablets can be used for treatment. You need to use a malaria tablet that is different from the one you were taking when you contracted malaria. The standard treatment dose of mefloquine is two 250mg tablets and a further two tablets six hours later. For Fansidar, it's a single dose of three tablets. If you were previously taking mefloquine and cannot obtain Fansidar, then other alternatives are Malarone (atovaquone-proguanil; four tablets once daily for three days), halofantrine (three doses of two 250mg tablets every six hours) or quinine sulphate (600mg every six hours).

There is a greater risk of side effects with these dosages than in normal use if used with mefloquine, so medical advice is preferable. Be aware also that halofantrine is no longer recommended by the WHO as emergency standby treatment, because of side effects, and should only be used if no other drugs are available.

Travellers are advised to guard against mosquito bites at all times. The following points are important.

- Wear light-coloured clothing.
- Wear long trousers and long-sleeved shirts.
- Use mosquito repellents containing the compound DEET on exposed areas (prolonged overuse of DEET may be harmful, especially to children, but its use is considered preferable to being bitten by disease-transmitting mosquitoes).
- Avoid perfumes or aftershave.
- Use a mosquito net impregnated with mosquito repellent (permethrin) – these are available on Bali, but it may be worth taking your own.
- Light a mosquito coil in your room an hour before going to bed – coils are widely available and are provided by many hotels and lodgings.
- Impregnating clothes with permethrin effectively deters mosquitoes and other insects.

Dengue Fever This viral disease is transmitted by mosquitoes and is fast becoming one of the top public health problems in the tropical world. Unlike the malarial mosquito, the *Aedes aegypti* mosquito, which transmits the dengue virus, is most active during the day, and is found mainly in urban areas, in and around human dwellings. There was an outbreak of dengue fever in the Denpasar area in 2002, but it more commonly occurs on Java and in Nusa Tenggara.

Signs and symptoms of dengue fever include a sudden onset of high fever, headache, joint and muscle pains (hence its old name, 'breakbone fever'), nausea and vomiting. A rash of small red spots sometimes appears three to four days after the onset of fever. In the early phase of illness, dengue may be mistaken for other infectious diseases, including malaria and influenza. Minor bleeding, such as nose bleeds, may occur in the course of the illness, but this does not necessarily mean that you have progressed to the potentially fatal dengue haemorrhagic fever (DHF). This is a severe illness, characterised by heavy bleeding, which is thought to be a result of second infection due to a different strain (there are four major strains) and usually affects residents of the country rather than travellers. Recovery even from simple dengue fever may be prolonged, with tiredness lasting for several weeks.

You should seek medical attention as soon as possible if you think you may be infected. A blood test can exclude malaria and indicate the possibility of dengue fever. There is no specific treatment for dengue. Aspirin should be avoided, as it increases the risk of haemorrhaging. There is no vaccine against dengue fever. The best prevention is to avoid mosquito bites at all times by covering up, using insect repellents containing the compound DEET and mosquito nets – see the Malaria section earlier for more advice on avoiding mosquito bites.

Japanese B Encephalitis This viral infection of the brain is transmitted by mosquitoes. Most cases occur in rural areas as the virus exists in pigs and wading birds. Symptoms include fever, headache and alteration in consciousness. Hospitalisation is needed for correct diagnosis and treatment. There is a high mortality rate among those who have symptoms; of those who survive, many are intellectually disabled. While extremely rare on Bali, there have been instances during the rainy season. You might consider the vaccination if you are spending a month or longer in rural areas of Bali or Lombok, especially during the wet season, but it is not generally recommended.

Cuts, Bites & Stings

See Less Common Diseases later for information on rabies, which is passed through animal bites.

Cuts & Scratches Wash well and treat any cut with an antiseptic such as povidone-iodine. Where possible, avoid bandages and Band-Aids, which can keep wounds wet. Coral cuts are notoriously slow to heal and if they are not adequately cleaned, small pieces of coral can become embedded in the wound. For conservation reasons you should avoid walking on or touching coral reefs, but if it's unavoidable, wear shoes or sandals. Clean any cut thoroughly with hydrogen peroxide if available. A good dressing is a Chinese preparation called Tieh Ta Yao Gin, which may sting a little, but will dry and heal coral cuts in the warm tropical climate.

Bedbugs & Lice Bedbugs live in various places, but particularly in dirty mattresses and bedding, evidenced by spots of blood on bedclothes or on the wall. Bedbugs leave itchy bites in neat rows. Calamine lotion or a sting relief spray may help.

All lice cause itching and discomfort. They make themselves at home in your hair (head lice), your clothing (body lice) or in your pubic hair (crabs). You catch lice through direct contact with infected people or by sharing combs, clothing and the like. Powder or shampoo treatment will kill the lice, and infected clothing should then be washed in very hot, soapy water and left in the sun to dry.

Bites & Stings Bee and wasp stings are usually painful rather than dangerous. However, in people who are allergic to them severe breathing difficulties may occur and require urgent medical care. Calamine lotion or a sting relief spray will give relief and ice packs will reduce the pain and swelling.

Jellyfish Some jellyfish, including the Portuguese man-of-war, occur on the north coast of Bali, especially in July and August, and also between the Gili islands and Lombok. The sting is extremely painful but rarely fatal. Dousing in vinegar will deactivate any stingers that have not yet 'fired'. Calamine lotion, antihistamine and analgesics may reduce the reaction and relieve the pain. Local advice is the best way of avoiding contact with these sea creatures.

Leeches & Ticks Leeches may be present in damp rainforest conditions; they attach themselves to your skin to suck your blood. Trekkers often get them on their legs or in their boots. Salt or a lighted cigarette end will make them fall off. Do not pull them off, as the bite is then more likely to become infected. Clean and apply pressure if the point of attachment is bleeding. An insect repellent may keep them away.

You should always check all over your body if you have been walking through a potentially tick-infested area, as ticks can cause skin infections and other, more serious diseases. If a tick is found attached, press down around the tick's head with tweezers, grab the head and gently pull upwards. Avoid pulling the rear of the body, as this may increase the risk of infection and disease. Smearing chemicals on the tick will not make it let go and is not recommended.

Snakes Indonesia has several venomous snakes, the most famous being the cobra *(ular sendok)*, but you are most unlikely to encounter any of them on Bali. Sea snakes are venomous and may be encountered in coastal waters.

Snake bites do not cause instantaneous death and antivenenes are usually available. Immediately wrap the bitten limb tightly, as you would for a sprained ankle, and then attach a splint to immobilise it. Keep the victim still and seek medical help, if possible with the dead snake for identification. Don't attempt to catch the snake if there is a possibility of being bitten again. Tourniquets and sucking out the poison are now comprehensively discredited.

Less Common Diseases

The following diseases pose a small risk to travellers, and so are only mentioned in passing. Seek medical advice if you think you may have any of these diseases.

Cholera This is the worst of the watery diarrhoeas and medical help should be sought. Outbreaks of cholera are generally widely reported, so you can avoid problem areas. Cholera shots offer poor protection and have many side effects, and are not generally recommended for travellers.

Lyme Disease This is a tick-transmitted infection that may be acquired throughout North America, Europe and Asia. The illness usually begins with a spreading rash at the site of the tick bite and is accompanied by fever, headache, extreme fatigue, aching joints and muscles and mild neck stiffness. If untreated, these symptoms usually resolve over several weeks but over subsequent weeks or months disorders of the nervous system, heart and joints may develop. Treatment works best early in the illness. Medical help should be sought.

Rabies This fatal viral infection is found in many countries. Many animals can be infected, including dogs, cats, bats and monkeys, however there is currently no risk of rabies on Bali. It is the animal's saliva that is infectious, and any bite, scratch or even lick should be cleaned immediately and thoroughly. Scrub with soap and running water, and then apply alcohol or iodine solution. Medical help should be sought promptly to receive a course of injections to prevent the onset of symptoms and death.

Tetanus This disease is caused by a germ that lives in soil and in the faeces of horses and other animals. It enters the body via breaks in the skin. The first symptom may be discomfort in swallowing, or stiffening of the jaw and neck; this is followed by painful convulsions of the jaw and whole body. The disease can be fatal. It can be prevented by vaccination.

Tuberculosis (TB) Tuberculosis is a bacterial infection usually transmitted from person to person by coughing, but may be transmitted through consumption of unpasteurised milk. Bolied milk is usually safe to drink, and the souring of milk to make yoghurt or cheese also kills the bacilli. Travellers are usually not at great risk, as close contact with the infected person is usually required before it's passed on. You may need to have a TB test before you travel, as this can help diagnose the disease later if you become ill.

Typhus Ticks, mites or lice spread this disease. It begins with fever, chills, headache and muscle pains followed a few days later by a body rash. There is often a large painful sore at the site of the bite and nearby lymph nodes are swollen and painful. Typhus can be treated under medical supervision. Seek local advice on areas where ticks pose a danger and always check your skin carefully for ticks after walking in a danger area such as a tropical forest. An insect repellent can help, and walkers in tick-infested areas should consider having their boots and trousers impregnated with benzyl benzoate and dibutylphthalate.

Women's Health

Tampons and pads are widely available in supermarkets in the tourist areas on Bali. If you're travelling to more remote parts of Bali, take a supply with you.

Gynaecological Problems Antibiotic use, synthetic underwear, sweating and contraceptive pills can lead to fungal vaginal infections, especially when travelling in hot climates. Fungal infections are characterised by a rash, itch and discharge and can be treated with a vinegar or lemon-juice douche, or with yoghurt. Nystatin, miconazole or clotrimazole pessaries or vaginal cream are the usual treatment. Maintaining good personal hygiene and wearing loose-fitting clothes and cotton underwear may help prevent these infections.

Sexually transmitted infections are a major cause of vaginal problems. Symptoms include a smelly discharge, painful intercourse and sometimes a burning sensation when urinating. Medical attention should be sought and male sexual partners must also be treated. For more details see the section on Sexually Transmitted Infections earlier. Besides abstinence, the best thing is to practise safer sex using condoms.

Pregnancy It is not advisable to travel to some places while pregnant, as some vaccinations normally used to prevent serious diseases are not advisable during pregnancy (eg, yellow fever). In addition, some diseases are much more serious for a pregnant woman, and may increase the risk of a stillborn child (eg, malaria).

Most miscarriages occur during the first three months of pregnancy. Miscarriage is not uncommon and can occasionally lead to severe bleeding. The last three months should also be spent within reasonable distance of good medical care. A baby born as early as 24 weeks stands a chance of survival, but only in a modern hospital. Pregnant women should avoid all unnecessary medication, although vaccinations and malarial prophylactics should still be taken where needed.

WOMEN TRAVELLERS

Women travelling solo on Bali will get a lot of attention from Balinese guys, but Balinese men are, on the whole, fairly benign. On the whole, Bali is safer for women than most areas of the world and, with the usual care, women should feel secure travelling alone.

Some precautions are simply the same for any traveller, but women should take extra care not to find themselves alone on empty beaches, down dark streets or in other situations where help might not be available. Late at night in the tourist centres, solo women should take a taxi, and sit in the back.

Kuta Cowboys

In tourist areas of Bali and Lombok, you'll encounter young men who are keen to spend time with visiting women. Commonly called Kuta Cowboys, beach boys, bad boys, guides or gigolos, these guys think they're super cool, with long hair, lean bodies, tight jeans and lots of tattoos. While they don't usually work a straight sex-for-money deal, the visiting woman pays for the meals, drinks and accommodation, and commonly buys the guy presents.

It's not uncommon for them to form long-term relationships, with the guy hopeful of finding a new and better life with his partner in Europe, Japan, Australia or the USA. While most of these guys around Bali are genuinely friendly and quite charming, some are predatory con-artists who practise elaborate deceits. Many of them now come from outside Bali, and have a long succession of foreign lovers. Be healthily sceptical about what they tell you, particularly if it comes down to them needing money. Always insist on using condoms.

Women on Bali

Balinese society has well-defined gender roles, but females are not at all segregated from daily life (see Society in the Facts about Bali chapter). Women are particularly active in the tourist industry, and visiting women will have no trouble meeting and communicating with them.

GAY & LESBIAN TRAVELLERS

Gay travellers on Bali will experience few problems, and many of the island's most influential expatriate artists have been more-or-less openly gay. Physical contact between same-sex couples is quite acceptable and friends of the same sex often hold hands, though this does not indicate homosexuality. However, a male and female holding hands is regarded as improper in most of Indonesia, although it's becoming more common among young heterosexual couples on Bali.

There are several venues where gay men congregate, mostly in Kuta. There's nowhere that's exclusively gay, and nowhere that's even inconspicuously a lesbian scene. Hotels are happy to rent a room with a double bed to any couple, although most hotels won't expect guests in your room if you've booked a single room. Homosexual behaviour is not

Waria

Indonesia, and particularly Java, has a long tradition of female impersonators, often working as entertainers, hostesses or prostitutes. They may be transsexual, but are mostly transvestite. They were customarily known as *banci*, but the term *waria* is now more polite and acceptable – it's a combination of the words *wanita* (female) and *pria* (male).

illegal, and the age of consent for sexual activity is 16 years. Immigration officials may restrict entry to people who reveal HIV-positive status. Gay men in Indonesia are referred to as *homo*, or more recently, *gay*, and are quite distinct from the female impersonators called waria (see the boxed text 'Waria').

Gay Balinese experience difficulties not so much because of their sexual preferences, but because they are expected to become parents and participate in the family and community life, which is so important in Balinese culture. For this reason, many gays feel compelled to leave Bali and live in other parts of Indonesia. Paradoxically, many gays from other parts of the country come to live on Bali, as it is more tolerant, and also because it offers opportunities to meet foreign partners.

Gay prostitutes are mostly from Java, and some have been known to rip off their foreign clients. Gay Balinese men are usually just looking for nothing more than some adventures, though there is an expectation that the (relatively) wealthy foreign guy will pay for meals, drinks, hotels etc. Hanafi (see the Organisations entry, following) has cleverly coined the term of BCA boys for young hustlers who also expect cash (after the BCA Bank), with the abbreviation standing for 'bills come after' – after you leave Bali, they'll have to pay their way somehow.

Organisations

Gaya Nusantara (W *www.welcome.to/gaya*) is a national gay organisation that provides counselling, promotes gay awareness, coordinates other gay organisations, and publishes the monthly *Gaya Nusantara* magazine. The local gay organisation on Bali is **Gaya Dewata** (☎ *0361-264926; Jl Teuku Umar, Gang Maruti/Merpati 17, Denpasar*). One of the best Asian gay websites is **Utopia Asia** (W *www.utopia-asia.com*); although it's not specific to Bali, it does include information about the Bali gay scene.

For gay women, the **Indonesian Lesbians' Homepage** (w *www.geocities.com/WestHolly wood/Heights/5855/*), might be a good place to start. **Lembayung Dewata** *(PO Box 269, Singaraja)* is a local lesbian organisation.

Utopia Tours (e *info@utopia-tours.com;* w *www.utopia-tours.com*) organises tours for gay and lesbian travellers. **Hanafi** (☎ *0362-756454, fax 752561;* e *hanafi@con sultant.com; Poppies Gang I 77, Kuta*) is a gay-friendly tour operator and guide, who can also book accommodation. It's worth stopping by Hanafi's just for a friendly chat to get the lowdown on the local scene.

DISABLED TRAVELLERS

Bali is a difficult destination for those with limited mobility. While some of the airlines flying to Bali have a good reputation for accommodating people with disabilities, the airport in Denpasar is not well set up. Contact the airlines, and ask them if they provide sky-chairs, and what arrangements can be made for disembarking and boarding at Denpasar.

The bemos, minibuses and buses that provide public transport all over the islands are certainly not made for very large, tall or physically disabled people, nor for wheelchairs. The minibuses used by tourist shuttle bus and tour companies are similar. Upmarket hotels often have steps, but lack ramps for wheelchairs, while the cheaper places usually have more accessible bungalows on ground level. Out on the street, the footpaths, where they exist at all, tend to be narrow, uneven, pot-holed and frequently obstructed.

The only hotels likely to be set up at all for disabled travellers are the big international chains like the Hyatt (at Nusa Dua and Sanur), Sheraton (Nusa Dua, Senggigi and Kuta) and the Hilton (Nusa Dua). If you're keen to see Bali, your best bet is to contact these corporations in your home city and ask them what facilities they have for disabled guests in their Bali hotels. The website **Bali Paradise** (w *www.bali-paradise.com/special -needs-traveler*) also has an entry on hotels that provide disabled facilities.

Bali is an enormously rewarding destination for unsighted people or for those with limited vision. Balinese music is heard everywhere, and the languages are fascinating to listen to. The smells of incense, spices, tropical fruit and flowers pervade the island, and are as exotic as you could wish for. With a sighted companion, most places should be reasonably accessible.

SENIOR TRAVELLERS

If you have trouble climbing stairs or walking on rough ground, you will find it difficult to get around Bali. However, as in many Asian cultures, older people are treated with great respect. Senior travellers are probably better off staying in better hotels and travelling on organised tours.

Take all the medication, equipment and prescriptions that you need, and don't expect much from the hospitals on the islands. There are no special deals for senior travellers on Bali or Lombok, but they are inexpensive destinations so this is not a real problem.

TRAVEL WITH CHILDREN

Travelling with children *(anak-anak)* anywhere requires energy and organisation (see Lonely Planet's *Travel with Children* by Cathy Lanigan), but on Bali the problems are somewhat lessened by the Balinese affection for children. They believe that children come straight from God, and the younger they are, the closer they are to God. To the Balinese, children are considered part of the community and everyone, not just the parents, has a responsibility towards them. If a young child cries, the Balinese get most upset and insist on finding a parent and handing the child over with a reproachful look. Sometimes they despair of uncaring Western parents, and the child will be whisked off to a place where it can be cuddled, cosseted and fed. In tourist areas this is less likely, but it's still common in a more traditional environment. A toddler may even get too much attention!

Children are a social asset when you travel on Bali, and people will display great interest in any Western child they meet. You will have to learn their ages and sex in Bahasa Indonesia – *bulan* (month), *tahun* (year), *laki-laki* (boy) and *perempuan* (girl). You should also make polite inquiries about their children, present or absent.

What to Bring

Apart from those items already mentioned in the earlier Health section, bring some infant analgesic, anti-lice shampoo, a medicine measure and a thermometer.

Surf's up at Kuta Beach

Parasailing through blue skies

Diving through a spiral of friendly fish

Danger flag for strong swells and rips on Legian

Up close to a white-tip reef shark

JOHN BANAGAN

NICHOLAS REUSS

JOHN BORTHWICK

MICHAEL AW

TIM ROCK

Spice up your life at Candikuning

A melee of food stalls at Denpasar market

A feast honouring seven months of pregnancy

Babi guling (spit-roasted pig), just for starters!

Traditional nasi (rice) dishes to take away

You can take disposable nappies (diapers) with you, but they're widely available on Bali. Cloth nappies are more environmentally friendly, and not too much trouble – just rinse them in the bath with the hand-held shower head, soak them in a plastic bucket (always available) and wash them in the bucket when you can.

For small children, bring a folding stroller or pusher, or you will be condemned to having them on your knee constantly, at meals and everywhere else. However, it won't be much use for strolling, as there are few paved footpaths that are wide and smooth enough. A papoose or a backpack carrier is a much easier way to move around with children.

Some equipment, such as snorkelling gear and boogie boards, can be rented easily in the tourist centres. A simple camera, or a couple of the throwaway ones, will help your child feel like a real tourist. A pair of binoculars can make looking at things more fun, and bring a few books for older children, and a scrapbook for their cuttings and drawings.

Accommodation

A package tour in a hotel with a swimming pool, air-con and a beachfront location is fun for kids, very convenient and provides a good break for the parents, but you won't see much of Bali unless you make a real effort to get out. A beachfront place in Sanur or Lovina, or a place with a pool in Ubud, would be the best choices for a package holiday with kids. The Kuta-Legian area has very heavy traffic and the surf can be rough.

If you travel independently, you can stay in losmen or budget hotels, in smaller, quieter areas with minimal traffic and few tourists. You will have much closer contact with the Balinese, and your children will be secure with the losmen owner's family watching over them.

Most places, at whatever price level, have a 'family plan', which means that children up to about 12 years old can share a room with their parents free of charge. The catch is that hotels charge for extra beds. If you need more space, just rent a separate room for the kids. You can usually negotiate a cheaper price for the second room (single room rate is a common deal). Another idea is to bring an inflatable air mattress or two from home, and place it on the floor of your room for the kids – hotels rarely charge extra for this.

Several top-end hotels offer special programmes or supervised activities for kids, and where this isn't the case, most hotels can arrange a baby-sitter.

Food

The same rules apply as for adults – kids should drink only clean water, eat only well-cooked food or fruit that you have peeled yourself. If you're travelling with a young baby, breast-feeding is much easier than bottles. For older babies, mashed bananas, eggs, peelable fruit and *bubur* (rice cooked to a mush in chicken stock) are all generally available. In tourist areas, supermarkets sell jars of Western baby food and packaged UHT milk and fruit juice. Bottled drinking water is available everywhere. Bring plastic bowls, plates, cups and spoons for do-it-yourself meals.

Health

If your child develops stomach trouble, it may be no more than 'Baby Bali Belly'. If there is no pain or stomach cramps, put the child on a light, bland diet and make sure the fluid intake is kept high. The major danger is dehydration, so it's a good idea to carry an electrolyte mixture with you for such cases. Ask your doctor to recommend a kaolin mixture for your child; Pepto-Bismol is very good. If the child has a fever, the stools contain blood or mucus, or diarrhoea persists for more than two days, you should continue the fluid replacement treatment and find a doctor quickly.

Bali is officially in a malarial zone, but the risk in most tourist areas is so slight that it is probably not worth a child taking anti-malarial drugs (but confirm this with your own doctor before you go). In any case, the first defence against malaria is to protect your child from mosquito bites. If you're going to Lombok, however, a course of antimalarials is generally required – refer to the Health section earlier in this chapter.

Never let your child run around in bare feet, as worms and other parasites can enter through the feet. Any cut or scratch should be washed immediately and treated with Betadine. Head lice are common on Bali; lice shampoo will get rid of them.

Tropical sun is a very real hazard. Use a total sunblock (SPF30+) on all exposed skin, whenever they are out, and reapply it every few hours, especially if they have been swimming. Hats, shirts and shorts should always be worn in the sun. The lightweight Lycra T-shirts that kids can wear while swimming are excellent. If your child does get sunburnt, apply Caladryl.

Safety Precautions
The main danger is traffic, so try to stay in less busy areas. If your children can't look after themselves in the water then they must be supervised – don't expect local people to act as lifesavers. Steep stairways and unfenced drops are other common hazards.

On Bali, the sorts of facilities, safeguards and services that Western parents regard as basic may not be present. Here, children are part of a small community and they share the same furniture, food, transport and entertainment as everyone else. Not many restaurants provide a highchair; many places with great views have nothing to stop your kids falling over the edge; shops often have breakable things at kiddie height; and violent videos are sometimes shown in circumstances (and at volumes) in which they can't be ignored.

Hotel and restaurant staff are usually very willing to help and improvise, so always ask if you need something for your children. The situation is improving as more young kids come to Bali and more parents make their wishes known.

Baby-Sitting & Child Care
Most expensive hotels advertise a baby-sitting service (sometimes written as a 'baby sister'). The price is proportional to the cost of the hotel and can be quite expensive by local standards. It's fine for a few hours in the evening, but the baby-sitter may not be willing or experienced enough to entertain and supervise active kids for a whole afternoon. In small, family-style losmen, you'll always find someone to look after your children – often the owners' daughters, sisters or nieces. They will be much more comfortable looking after your child in their own family compound or village. Generally speaking, most Balinese over the age of 14 will be responsible child minders.

For more regular child care, you'll need a *pembantu*, which roughly translates as a nanny. Ask around to find a good one. They generally prefer to look after kids at their own place rather than yours – about 60,000Rp for two children for one day is a reasonable fee.

Activities
Many of the things that adults want to do on Bali will not interest their children. Have days when you do what they want, to offset the times you drag them to shops or temples. Encourage them to learn about the islands so they can understand and enjoy more of what they see.

Water play is always fun – you can often use a hotel pool, even if you're not staying there. Waterbom Park in Kuta is a big hit with most kids. If your kids can swim a little, they can have a lot of fun with a mask and snorkel. Chartering a boat for a few hours sailing and snorkelling is good value. Hiring paddle boards is OK for a while, but can get pretty expensive. You can buy a model *prahu* (small boat) and try sailing it on a quiet beach. Colourful kites are sold in many shops and market stalls; get some string at a supermarket. For some more tips about where to take the kids, refer to Activities later in this chapter.

In Ubud there are a number of craft courses on woodcarving and batik. Older children may like to see some Balinese dances – the Kecak dance is probably the most entertaining for kids. Some restaurants have video movies for kids in the early evening; the ones shown later in the evening are inevitably loud and violent. TV stations often show cartoons in the afternoon, in English with Indonesian subtitles.

USEFUL ORGANISATIONS
A few useful organisations are mentioned in the relevant places throughout the book, but the following may be of interest.

Bali International Women's Association (BIWA; ☎ 0361-287482; e biwabali@yahoo.com) BIWA was established by expats to 'foster friendship and mutual understanding' and meets monthly to organise support for local charities.
Rotary Club (☎ 0361-758635, fax 757125; w www.rotarybali.org; e president@rotarybali .org) PO Box 48, Nusa Dua. This international organisation meets at 12.30pm on Thursdays at the Nusa Dua Beach Hotel.

DANGERS & ANNOYANCES
Theft

Violent crime is relatively uncommon, but there is some bag-snatching, pickpocketing and theft from losmen rooms and parked cars in the tourist centres. Don't leave anything on the back seat of a rented vehicle.

Snatchers sometimes work in pairs from a motorcycle. Here is how the scam works: they pull up next to someone in a busy area, then the guy on the back grabs the bag and slashes the strap, the guy on the front hits the throttle and they're gone within half a second. Money belts, or bum bags, worn *outside* the clothes are particularly vulnerable. Always carry money belts inside your clothes; and bags over your neck (not shoulder). Be sure to put all your money in your money belt *before* you leave the bank or moneychanger.

Pickpockets on bemos are also something to be aware of. The usual routine is for somebody to start a conversation to distract you, while an accomplice steals your wallet or purse. Bemos are always tightly packed, and a painting, large parcel, basket or the like can serve as a cover. The thieves can be very cunning, charming and skilful – so be extra careful.

Losmen rooms are often not secure. Don't leave valuables in your room, and beware of people who wander in and out of losmen; always keep your room locked if you're not actually in it. Thieves will often enter through open-air bathrooms, so be sure to fasten the bathroom door. Keep your valuables at more than an arm's length from any unsecured window. Many people lose things simply by leaving them on the beach while they go swimming. You can usually leave airline tickets or other valuables in safe deposit boxes, which are available in most hotels.

Rip-Offs & Scams

Bali has such a relaxed atmosphere, and the people are so friendly, that you may not be on the lookout for scams. It's hard to say when an 'accepted' practice like overcharging becomes an unacceptable rip-off, but be warned that there are some people on Bali (not always Balinese) who will engage in a practised deceit in order to get money from a visitor. Here is a rundown of the most common scams.

Excuse me – there's something wrong with your car Friendly locals (often working in pairs) discover a 'serious problem' with your car or motorcycle – it's blowing smoke, leaking oil or petrol, or a wheel is wobbling badly (problems that one of the pair creates while the other distracts you). Coincidentally, he has a brother/cousin/friend nearby who can help, and before you know it they've put some oil in the sump, or changed the wheel, and are demanding an outrageous sum for their trouble. The con relies on creating a sense of urgency, so beware of anyone who tries to rush you into something without mentioning a price.

Come and see my village A Balinese guy takes a foreign friend to see 'his' poor village – usually it's not the guy's own village but the friend doesn't know that. The visitor is shocked by the poor circumstances of their Balinese friend, who concocts a hard-luck story about a sick mother who can't pay for an operation, a brother who needs money for his education or an important religious ceremony that his family can't afford. Visitors have been persuaded to hand over large sums of money on such a pretext. A healthy scepticism is your best defence.

Do you want to win some money? Friendly locals will convince a visitor that easy money can be made in a card game. They're taken to some obscure place, and do well at first. Then, after a few drinks and a spell of bad luck, they find themselves being escorted to a bank, where they need a large cash advance on their credit card to pay off the debt. Gambling is totally illegal in Indonesia, so the victim has no recourse to the law.

High rates – no commission In the Kuta and Sanur area especially, many travellers are ripped off by moneychangers, who use sleight of hand and rigged calculators. The moneychangers who offer the highest rates are usually the cheats. Always count your money at least twice in front of the moneychanger, and don't let him touch the money again after you've finally counted it. Try to change even amounts, eg, US$100, which are easier to convert to rupiah, or bring your own pocket calculator.

Most Balinese would never perpetrate a rip-off, but it seems that very few would warn a foreigner when one is happening. Not many people would pick your pocket on a bemo, but neither would they say anything if they saw his fingers in your bag. Bystanders will watch someone put oil in your car unnecessarily for a rip-off price, and they may look uncomfortable and embarrassed about it, but they won't tell you what the right price is. Be suspicious if you notice that bystanders are uncommunicative and perhaps uneasy, and one guy is doing all the talking.

Hawkers, Pedlars & Touts

Many visitors regard the persistent attentions of people trying to sell as *the* No 1 annoyance on Bali. These activities are now officially restricted in many areas, including the grounds of just about any decent hotel or restaurant (but hawkers will still work just outside the fenceline). Elsewhere, especially around many tourist attractions, visitors are frequently, and often constantly, hassled to buy things.

Some hawkers display a superb grasp of sales techniques in several languages, and have a persistence that's as impressive as it is infuriating. Some of Bali's most successful tourist businesses are run by people who started by selling postcards to tourists.

The best way to deal with hawkers is to completely ignore them from the first instance. Eye contact is crucial – don't make any! Even a polite '*tidak*' (no) seems to encourage them. Never ask the price or comment on the quality unless you're interested in buying, or you want to spend half an hour haggling. It may seem very rude to ignore people who smile and greet you so cheerfully, but you might have to be a lot ruder to get rid of a hawker after you've spent a few minutes politely discussing his/her watches, rings and prices. In many Asian cultures, it is impolite to say 'no' anyway – it's better form to firmly change the subject to anything other than what is for sale. Keep in mind though, that ultimately they're just people trying to make an honest living.

Begging

You may be approached by the occasional beggar on the streets of Kuta – typically a woman with a young child. Begging has no place in traditional Balinese society, so it's likely that most of the beggars come from elsewhere. (In Ubud, beggars from the central mountains Bali Aga village of Trunyan often walk the streets.)

Children often ask for sweets, pens, cigarettes etc. Please do not encourage this. If you want to contribute to a kid's education, with pens, books or whatever, give them to their teacher or parent.

Traffic

Apart from the dangers of driving on Bali (see the Getting Around chapter), the traffic in most tourist areas is often annoying, and frequently dangerous to pedestrians. Footpaths can be rough, even unusable, so you often have to walk on the road. Zebra stripes across the road are mainly decorative – never expect traffic to stop because you think you're on a pedestrian crossing.

Swimming

The beaches at Kuta and Legian are subject to heavy surf and strong currents – always swim between the flags. Trained lifeguards operate only at Kuta-Legian, Nusa Dua, Sanur and (sometimes) Senggigi. Most other beaches are protected by coral reefs, so they don't have big waves, but the currents can still be treacherous.

Be careful when swimming over coral, and never walk on it at all. It can be very sharp and coral cuts are easily infected.

Drugs

You may be offered dope on the street, particularly in the Kuta region and tablets purported to be Ecstasy are sometimes sold on the street and at some nightclubs, but they could contain just about anything. In all cases, entrapment by police and informers is a real possibility.

The authorities take a dim view of recreational drug use, and losmen owners can be quick to turn you in. It is an offence not to report someone whom you know to be using drugs, and there are not many places on Bali where you could light up a joint without someone getting a whiff of it.

Bali's famed magic mushrooms (*oong*) come out during the wet season. They are usually mixed with food, such as an omelette, or in a drink – if a barman offers you an 'umbrella cocktail' you may get more than you bargained for. The mushrooms contain psylocibin, which is a powerful hallucinogen, but the dosage in a mushroom omelette is pretty inexact and the effect is very variable. Psylocibin may give you a stratospheric high, but it may also result in paranoid or psychotic reactions that can be extremely unpleasant. The likely response of the authorities to this form of recreation is also unpredictable, so it really can't be recommended. Mushrooms are most common in low-budget beach resorts like Lovina or Lombok's Gili islands.

One drug that is very popular among visitors is alcohol. There are lots of bars and pubs around, and an awful lot of beer bottles being recycled. The local firewater, *arak*, is distilled from rice wine and can be very strong. Overdosing on this stuff has probably caused more foreigners to freak out than all the other drugs on Bali combined. Nicotine is also worth mentioning – those sweet smelling clove cigarettes (*kretek*) may be tempting, but they are high in tar and nicotine and very addictive.

Other Issues

Following the October 2002 Kuta bombings (see History in the Facts about Bali chapter) there was an immediate increase in security in public places. By the time you travel you may still find yourself being asked for personal identification, and may be asked to comply with bag searches. Needless to say, it's in everyone's interests to accept this with good grace.

Be careful, not paranoid. The likelihood of further attacks is widely thought to be minimal, but on Bali you now need to be aware of the same sort of issues faced in most countries. As for all destinations, you might want to check your government's travel advisories before you depart, and listen to local advice when you arrive.

LEGAL MATTERS

Gambling is illegal (although it is carried out in some of the rural areas), as is pornography. The Indonesian government takes the smuggling, using and selling of drugs very, *very* seriously. Once you have been caught, and then put in jail, there is very little that your consulate on Bali (if you have one) can do for you. You may have to wait for up to six months in jail before you even go to trial. It is also an offence for a visitor with a tourist card to engage in paid work or to stay in the country for more than the designated 60 days.

Generally, you are unlikely to have any encounters with the police unless you are driving a rented car or motorcycle (see the Getting Around chapter). Drinking and driving is never clever, and an accident whilst under the influence of alcohol or any drug may invalidate your car/motorcycle insurance, and it possibly may even effect your travel insurance policy.

Some governments (including the Australian government) have laws making it illegal for their citizens to use child prostitutes or engage in other paedophiliac activities anywhere in the world.

There are police stations in all district capitals. If you have to report a crime or have other business at a police station, expect a lengthy and bureaucratic encounter. You should dress as respectably as possible, bring a fluent Indonesian-speaking friend for interpretation and moral support, arrive early and be very polite.

Police officers frequently expect to receive bribes, either to overlook some crime, misdemeanour or traffic infringement, or to provide a service that they should provide anyway. Generally, it's easiest to pay up – and the sooner you do it and the less fuss you make, the less it will cost.

If you're in trouble, contact your consulate as soon as you can – they can't get you out, but they can recommend English-speaking lawyers and may have useful contacts.

BUSINESS HOURS

Government office and bank hours on Bali are roughly from 8am to 3pm Monday to Thursday and from 8am to noon on Friday, but they are not completely standardised. Postal agencies will often keep longer hours, and the main post offices are open every day.

Most commercial businesses are open from 8am to 4pm Monday to Friday, and also on Saturday morning, often closing for an hour or so at lunch time.

Moneychangers, travel agents and shops catering to tourists keep longer hours and are normally open every day.

PUBLIC HOLIDAYS & SPECIAL EVENTS

Apart from the usual Western calendar, the Balinese also use two local calendars.

Wuku Calendar

The *wuku* calendar is used to determine festival dates. The calendar uses 10 different types of weeks between one and 10 days long, which all run simultaneously. The intersection of the various weeks determines auspicious days. The seven- and five-day weeks are of particular importance. A full year is made up of 30 individually named seven-day weeks (210 days).

Galungan, which celebrates the death of a legendary tyrant called Mayadenawa, is one of Bali's major festivals. During this 10-day period, held every 210 days, all the gods, including the supreme deity Sanghyang Widi, come down to earth for the festivities. Barong (mythical lion-dog creatures) prance from temple to temple and village to village, and locals rejoice with feasts and visits to families. You'll notice the bamboo poles called *penjor*, which line the village streets, laden with gifts to the gods. The celebrations culminate with the Kuningan festival, when the Balinese say thanks and goodbye to the gods.

Every village on Bali will celebrate Galungan and Kuningan in grand style. Particularly colourful festivals are held at the temple on Pulau Serangan, just off Sanur, and all around Ubud. Forthcoming dates are the following.

Year	Galungan	Kuningan
2003	18 June	28 June
2004	14 January	24 January
2004	11 August	21 August
2005	9 March	19 March
2005	5 October	15 October

Saka Calendar

The Hindu *saka* (or *caka*) calendar is a lunar cycle that more closely follows the Western calendar in terms of the length of the year (eg, in 1998, the *saka* year was 1920). Nyepi is the major festival of the *saka* year – it's the last day of the year, ie, the day after the new moon of the ninth month.

Certain major temples celebrate their festivals by the *saka* calendar. This makes the actual date difficult to determine from our calendar, since the lunar *saka* calendar does

Nyepi – The Day of Silence

The major festival for the Hindu Balinese is Nyepi, usually falling around the end of March or early April. It celebrates the end of the old year and the start of the new one, according to the *saka* calendar, and usually coincides with the end of the rainy season. The celebrations are great to see, but the lack of public transport can cause interruptions to travel plans.

Out with the Old Year...

In the weeks before Nyepi, much work goes into the making of *ogoh-ogoh* – huge monster dolls with menacing fingers and frightening faces – and into the preparation of offerings and rituals that will purify the island in readiness for the new year. The day before Nyepi, Tawur Agung Kesanga is the 'Day of Great Sacrifices', with ceremonies held at town squares and sports grounds throughout the island. At about 4pm, the villagers, all dressed up in traditional garb, gather in the centre of town, playing music and offering gifts of food and flowers to the *ogoh-ogoh*. Then comes the *ngrupuk* – the great procession where the *ogoh-ogoh* figures are lifted on bamboo poles and carried through the streets, to frighten away all the evil spirits. This is followed by prayers and speeches and then, with flaming torches and bonfires, the *ogoh-ogoh* are burnt, and much revelry ensues. The biggest *ngrupuk* procession is in Denpasar, but any large town will have a pretty impressive parade.

...And In with the New

The day of Nyepi itself officially lasts for 24 hours from sunrise, and is one of complete inactivity, so when the evil spirits descend they decide that Bali is uninhabited and leave the island alone for another year. All human activity stops – all shops, bars and restaurants close, no-one is allowed to leave their home and foreigners must stay in their hotels, and even Bali's international airport is closed down. No fires are permitted and at night all buildings must be blacked out – only emergency services are exempt.

Government offices, banks and many shops close the day before Nyepi, and some shops remain closed the day after. For visitors, Nyepi is a day for catching up on sleep, writing letters or washing. Most hotels with a restaurant will arrange for simple buffet meals to be served for guests. Otherwise, stock up on snacks for the day. You could make a side-trip to Lombok, which is predominantly Muslim, and won't close for the day, but you'd miss out on the festivities prior to Nyepi. While some may resent this interruption to their travel plans, the Balinese ask that you respect their customs for this short time.

not follow a fixed number of days (like the *wuku* calendar).

Public Holidays
The following holidays are celebrated throughout Indonesia. Many of these dates change according to the phase of the moon (not by month), and are estimates.

Tahun Baru Masehi (New Year's Day) 1 January
Idul Adha (Muslim festival of sacrifice) February
Muharram (Islamic New Year) February/March
Nyepi (Hindu New Year) March/April
Hari Paskah (Good Friday) April
Ascension of Christ April/May
Hari Waisak (Buddha's birth, enlightenment and death) April/May
Maulud Nabi Mohammed or Hari Natal (Prophet Mohammed's birthday) May
Hari Proklamasi Kemerdekaan (Indonesian Independence Day) 17 August
Isra Miraj Nabi Mohammed (ascension of the Prophet Mohammed) September
Idul Fitri (the end of Ramadan) November/December
Hari Natal (Christmas Day) 25 December

The Muslim population on Bali observes Islamic festivals and holidays, including Ramadan. See the Lombok chapter for more information.

Temple Festivals
Temple festivals on Bali are quite amazing, and you'll often come across them unexpectedly, even in remote corners of the island. The annual 'temple birthday' is known as an *odalan* and is celebrated once every Balinese year of 210 days. Since most villages have at least three temples, you're assured of at least five or six annual festivals in every village. In addition, there can be special festival days common throughout Bali, festivals for certain important temples and festivals for certain gods. The full moons which fall around the end of September to the beginning of October, or from early to mid-April, are often times for important temple festivals.

The most obvious sign of a temple festival is a long line of women in gorgeous traditional costume, walking gracefully to the temple with beautifully arranged offerings of food, fruit and flowers artistically piled in huge pyramids which they carry on their heads. Outside the temple, warung and other stalls selling toys and trinkets are set up, while in the outer courtyard a gamelan

Bali Arts Festival
The annual Bali Arts Festival is based at the Taman Wedhi Budaya arts centre in Denpasar, and lasts for about one month over June and July. It's a great time to be on Bali, and the festival is an easy way to see an enormous variety of traditional dance, music and crafts from all over the island. The productions of the Ramayana and Mahabharata ballets are grand, and the opening ceremony and parade in Denpasar are particularly colourful.

provides further amusement. Nearby, a cockfight might be underway, both as a form of sacrifice and an extra source of excitement.

While all this activity is going on in and around the temple, the various *pemangku* (temple guardians and priests for temple rituals) suggest to the gods that they should come down for a visit. That's what those little thrones are for in the temple shrines – they are symbolic seats for the gods to occupy during festivals. Sometimes small images known as *pratima* are placed on the thrones to represent gods. Women dance the stately Pendet, an offering dance for the gods.

All night long there's activity, music and dancing – it's like a country fair, with food, amusements, games, stalls, gambling, noise, colour and confusion. Finally, as dawn approaches, the entertainment fades away, the women perform the last Pendet, the *pemangkus* suggest to the gods that maybe it's time they made their way back to heaven and the people wend their weary way back to their homes.

When you first arrive, it's well worth visiting a tourist office and asking what festivals will be held during your stay. The biggest temple festivals are all listed on a calendar of events, and seeing one will be a highlight of your stay. Foreigners are welcome to watch the festivities and take photographs, but please be unobtrusive and dress modestly.

Special Events
Try to beg, borrow or steal a *Calendar of Events* booklet – several versions are published by several levels of government. It lists every temple ceremony and village festival on Bali for the current (Western) year. Check out w www.indo.com/active/events.html for more information.

ACTIVITIES

Surfing, diving and snorkelling are major activities on Bali, but there are lots of other activities available, too, ranging from adventure activities for tourists seeking a day's diversion to indulgent hours spent at massage spas. For information on recommended spas, see the relevant destination chapters.

Most outdoor activities operators include pick-up from hotels in the southern Bali resorts, and will drop off at the end of the day. The most comprehensive programme is offered by **Bali Adventure Tours** (☎ 0361-721480; W www.baliadventuretours.com), which offers a choice of elephant rides, rafting, mountain biking, tandem parachuting, tandem paragliding and helicopter tours. **Sobek** (☎ 0361-287059; W www.sobekbali .com) is another multi-option agency, offering rafting, trekking and mountain biking tours.

Other general activities include birdwatching and elephant rides around Ubud, cruises and boat trips to Nusa Lembongan, snorkelling and fishing trips from most seaside destinations, dolphin watching at Lovina (although we don't recommend it), golf at Danau Bratan and Sanur, and water sports particularly at Sanur and Tanjung Benoa.

Surfing

In recent years, the number of surfers on Bali has increased enormously, and good breaks can get very crowded. Many Balinese have taken to surfing, and the grace of traditional dancing is said to influence their style. The surfing competitions on Bali are a major local event. Facilities for surfers have improved, and surf shops in Kuta will sell just about everything you need. For information on surfing courses, see Courses later in this chapter.

Information A long-running place, **Tubes Surf Bar & Restaurant** (*Poppies Gang II*) is a popular centre for anything to do with surfing – the Tubes tide chart is widely available.

Indo Surf & Lingo by Peter Neely (W www .indosurf.com.au) tells surfers where and when to find good waves around Bali and other Indonesian islands. The book also has a language guide with Indonesian translations of useful words. It's available at surf shops in the Kuta region. *Surfing Indonesia* by Leonard & Lorca Lueras is a more professional publication, with about 80 pages on

Bali. It has great photos, a comprehensive coverage of the waves, and some good surfing background.

Equipment A small board is usually adequate for the smaller breaks, but a few extra inches on your usual board length won't go astray. For the bigger waves – 8 feet and upwards – you will need a gun. For a surfer of average height and build, a board around the 7-foot mark is perfect.

You can bring a couple of boards, but if you have more than two or three, customs officials may object, suggesting that you intend to sell them. They sometimes ask you to pay a 'fee' for the extra boards, although it's not clear whether this is an official charge or not.

To get your boards to Bali in reasonable condition, you need a good board cover. Bali-bound airlines are used to carrying boards, but fins still get broken. Long hikes with your board are difficult unless you have a board-strap – add some foam padding to the shoulder. Take a good pair of running shoes for walking down steep, rocky paths on cliff faces. When you book any long-distance buses, find out if they take surfboards – some don't, or will charge extra. Perama charges a small fee to carry a board. Bring a soft roof-rack to secure your boards to a car or taxi.

Wax is available locally, but take your own anyway if you use it – in the tepid water and the hot sun a sticky wax is best. Board repairs and materials are readily available in Kuta, but it's always advisable to have your own, especially if you're going to more remote spots. You can carry resin in a well-sealed container, but don't carry hardener or acetone on a plane.

To protect your feet take a pair of wetsuit booties or reef boots. A wetsuit vest is also very handy for chilly, windy overcast days, and it also protects your back and chest from sunburn, and from being ground into the reefs. If you are a real tube maniac and will drive into anything no matter what the consequences, you are advised to take a short-sleeved spring-suit. A Lycra swimshirt or rash vest is good protection against chills and sunburn.

Bring surgical spirit, and cotton buds to put it on your cuts each night. Also bring a needle and pointed tweezers to remove sea urchin spines. Adhesive bandages that won't come off in the water are also necessary – Elastoplast is excellent. The pharmacies on Bali are fairly well stocked, but it's easier to take your own.

A surfing helmet is a good idea, not just for protection from the reefs, but also to keep the sun off while you wait in the line-up. And it will probably give you better protection in a motorcycle accident than the helmets that come with rented bikes.

Rental There are surfboards and boogie boards for rent on Kuta Beach and on Poppies Gang, with very variable quality and prices. Some of the warung at Ulu Watu also rent boards.

Surviving Surfing Wear a shirt when surfing and take ample supplies of a good sunblock, or you will miss out on good surf because you're too burnt to move. Riding a motorcycle with a surfboard can be deadly, although you can rent them with board brackets on the side, which some surfers think are safer. Renting a car between a few surfers is just as cheap, and a lot more sensible. Brush up on basic mouth-to-mouth resuscitation – you might be called upon to use it, especially around the beach breaks of Kuta, where people often get into trouble.

If you write yourself off severely while surfing, or on the way to surf, head to the top-end hotels, which have access to the best doctors. The medical centres at Kuta, Tanjung Benoa and Nusa Dua are modern and well equipped, and handy to the surfing areas around Bukit peninsula. If you have a serious accident, get the next plane home.

Where to Surf The swells come from the Indian Ocean, so the surf is on the southern side of the island and, strangely, on the north-west coast of Nusa Lembongan, where the swell funnels into the strait between there and the Bali coast.

In the dry season (around April to September), the west coast has the best breaks, with the trade winds coming in from the southeast; this is also when Nusa Lembongan works best. In the wet season, surf the eastern side of the island, from Nusa Dua around to Padangbai. If there's a north wind – or no wind at all – there are also a couple of breaks on the south coast of Bukit peninsula. There

are lots of places to stay around Kuta, but just a few places appearing near the breaks on the Bukit peninsula. No matter where you stay, you'll probably need transport at least some of the time.

The most well-known breaks are listed in this section, but there are other places that you can find. As you learn more about the weather and the ocean conditions you'll know where to look. No-one is giving away any 'secret spots'. Most of the main surf breaks are shown on the South Bali map at the start of that chapter.

Kuta & Legian For your first plunge into the warm Indian Ocean, try the beach breaks at **Kuta Beach**; on full tide go out near the life-saving club at the southern end of the beach road. At low tide, try the tubes around **Halfway Kuta**, probably the best place on Bali for beginners to practise. Start at the beach breaks if you are a bit rusty. The sand here is fine and packed hard, so it can hurt when you hit it. Treat even these breaks with respect. They provide zippering left and right barrels over shallow banks and can be quite a lot of fun.

Further north, the breaks at **Legian Beach** can be pretty powerful, with lefts and rights on the sand bars off Jl Melasti and Jl Padma. At Kuta and Legian you will encounter most of the local Balinese surfers. Over the years their surfing standard has improved enormously and because of this, and also because it is their island, treat them with respect. By and large, they're usually quite amenable in the water; give them the benefit of the doubt on a wave, and avoid getting into disputes.

Further north again, there are more beach breaks off Seminyak, such as the **Oberoi**, near the hotel of the same name. The sea here is fickle and can have dangerous rip tides – take a friend and take good care.

For more serious stuff, go to the reefs south of the beach breaks, about 1km out to sea. **Kuta Reef**, a vast stretch of coral, provides a variety of waves. You can paddle out in around 20 minutes, but the easiest way is by outrigger. You will be dropped out there and brought back in for a fee. The main break is a classic left-hander, best at mid- to high tide with a 5- to 6-foot swell, when it peels across the reef and has a beautiful inside tube section; the first part is a good workable wave. Over 7 feet it tends to double up and section.

The reef is well suited for backhand surfing. It's not surfable at dead-low tide, but you can get out there not long after the tide turns. The boys on the boats can advise you if necessary. It gets very crowded here, but if conditions are good there's another, shorter left, 50m further south along the reef, which usually has fewer surfers. This wave is more of a peak and provides a short, intense ride. On bigger days, check out breaks on the outer part of the reef, 150m further out.

South of Kuta Reef there are some good breaks around the end of the airport runway. Offshore from Hotel Patra Jasa Bali a reef break called **Airport Lefts**, with a workable wave at mid- to high tide. On the southern side of the runway, **Airport Rights** has three right-handers that can be a bit fickle, and are shallow and dangerous at low tide – they're best for good surfers at mid- to high tide with a strong swell. Get there by outrigger from Kuta or Jimbaran.

Ulu Watu When Kuta Reef is 5 to 6 feet, Ulu Watu, the most famous surfing break on Bali, will be 6 to 8 feet with bigger sets. Kuta and Legian sit on a huge bay – Ulu Watu is way out on the southern extremity of the bay, and consequently picks up more swell than Kuta. It's about a half-hour journey from downtown Kuta by private transport; some surf shops near Tubes Bar have handy shuttle bus services.

Just before the temple, a sign points to Suluban surf beach. You can now drive a car in to within a few hundred metres of the spot – a board-strap and small backpack are still useful. A concrete stairway leads into the Ulu Gorge and in front of you is a sight you will never forget, especially if a decent swell is running. The various thatched warung are set on one side of the gorge, above the cave; one warung is right on the edge of the cliff. The Ulu Watu bay stretches out in front of you. In the shade you can eat, drink, rest and even stay overnight. It's a great setup for surfers – local boys will wax your board, get drinks for you and carry the board down into the cave, which is the usual access to the wave. A new road goes round to the cliff top above the Ulu Gorge, and is a bit closer.

Ulu Watu has about seven different breaks. If it's your first trip here, sit for a while in the shade and survey the situation. See where other surfers are sitting in the line-up and watch where they flick off. **The Corner** is straight in front of you to the right. It's a fast-breaking, hollow left that holds about 6 feet. The reef shelf under this break is extremely shallow, so try to avoid falling head-first. At high tide, **The Peak** starts to work. This is good from 5 to 8 feet, with bigger waves occasionally right on the Peak itself. You can take off from this inside part or further down the line. A great wave. At low tide, if the swell isn't huge, go further south to **The Racetrack**, a whole series of bowls.

At low tide when the swell is bigger, **Outside Corner** starts operating, further out from The Racetrack. This is a tremendous break and on a good day you can surf one wave for hundreds of metres. The wall here on a 10-foot wave jacks up with a big drop and bottom turn, then the bowl section. After this it becomes a big workable face. You can usually get tubed only in the first section. When surfing this break you need a board with length, otherwise you won't be getting down the face of any of the amazing waves.

Another left runs off the cliff that forms the southern flank of the bay. It breaks outside this in bigger swells, and once it's 7 feet, a left-hander pitches right out in front of a temple on the southern extremity. Out behind The Peak, when it's big, is a bombora (submerged reef) appropriately called **The Bommie**. This is another big left-hander and it doesn't start operating until the swell is about 10 feet. On a normal 5- to 8-foot day there are also breaks south of The Peak. One is a very fast left, and is also very hollow, usually only ridden by goofy-footers, due to its speed.

Observe where other surfers paddle out and follow them. If you are in doubt, ask someone. It is better having some knowledge than none at all. Climb down into the cave and paddle out from there. When the swell is bigger you will be swept to your right. Don't panic, it is an easy matter to paddle around the whitewater from down along the cliff. Coming back in you have to aim for the cave. When the swell is bigger, come from the southern side of the cave as the current runs to the north. If you miss the cave, paddle out again and repeat the procedure. If you get into trouble ask for help from a fellow surfer.

Padang Padang Just Padang for short, this super shallow, left-hand reef break is just north of Ulu Watu towards Kuta – the new road round the coast makes it easy to get to. Again, check this place carefully before venturing out. It's a very demanding break that only works over about 6 feet from mid- to high tide – it's a great place to watch from the cliff top.

If you can't surf tubes, backhand or forehand, don't go out: **Padang** is a tube. After a ledgey take-off, you power along the bottom before pulling up into the barrel. So far so good, now for the tricky part. The last section turns inside out like a washing machine on fast-forward. You have to drive high through this section, all the time while in the tube. Don't worry if you fail to negotiate this trap, plenty of other surfers have been caught too. After this, the wave fills up and you flick off. Not a wave for the faint-hearted and definitely not a wave to surf when there's a crowd.

Impossibles Just north of Padang, this outside reef break has three shifting peaks with fast left-hand tube sections that can join up if the conditions are perfect (low tide, 5-foot swell), but don't stay on for too long, or you'll run out of water.

Bingin North of Padang and accessible by road, this once-secret spot can now get crowded. It's best at mid-tide with a 6-foot swell, when it manufactures short but perfect left-hand barrels.

Dreamland You have to go through the abortive Pecatu Indah resort to reach this spot, which can also get crowded now that the road is better. At low tide with a 5-foot swell, this solid peak offers a short, sharp right and a longer, more tubular left.

Balangan Go through Pecatu Indah resort and follow the 'alternative' road around to the right to reach the Balangan warung. Balangan is a fast left over a shallow reef, unsurfable at low tide, good at mid-tide with anything over a 4-foot swell; with an 8-foot swell, this can be a classic wave.

Canggu North of Kuta-Legian-Seminyak, on the northern extremity of the bay, Canggu has a nice white beach, a warung, a very expensive hotel and a few surfers. The peak breaks over a 'soft' rock ledge – well, it's softer than coral. Five to 6 feet is an optimum size for Canggu. There's a good right-hander that you can really hook into, which works at full tide, and what the surf writer Peter Neely calls 'a sucky left ledge that tubes like Ulu but without the coral cuts', which works from mid-tide. A driveable track goes right to the beach – get there early, before the crowds and the wind.

Nusa Dua During the wet season you should surf on the east side of the island, where there are some very fine reef breaks. The reef off the expensive resort area of Nusa Dua has very consistent swells. There's nowhere cheap to stay in Nusa Dua, so go to nearby Tanjung Benoa. The main break is 1km off the beach to the south of Nusa Dua – go past the golf course, and look for the small handwritten sign that tells you where to park. There's a whole row of warung and some boats to take you out. There are lefts and rights that work well on a small swell at low to mid-tide. On bigger days, take a longer board and go further out, where powerful peaks offer long-rides, fat tubes and lots of variety. Further north, in front of the Club Med, is a fast, barrelling, right reef break called **Sri Lanka**, which works best at mid-tide and can handle swells from 6 to 10 feet.

Serangan The abortive development at Pulau Serangan entailed huge earthworks at the southern and eastern sides of the island, and this has made the surf here much more consistent, though the landfill looks like a disaster. The new causeway has made the island much more accessible, and a dozen or so warung face the water, where waves break right and left in anything over a 3-foot swell.

Sanur Sanur reef has a hollow wave with excellent barrels. It's fickle, and doesn't even start till you get a 6-foot swell, but anything over 8 feet will be world-class, and anything over 10 feet will be brown board-shorts material. There are other reefs further offshore and most of them are surfable.

Hyatt Reef, over 2km from shore, has a shifty right peak that can give a great ride at full tide. Closer in, opposite the Sanur Beach Market, **Tanjung Sari** gives long left rides at low tide with a big swell, while **Tanjung Right** can be a very speedy wall on a big swell. The classic right is off the Grand Bali Beach Hotel. A couple of kilometres north, **Padang Galak** is a beach break at high tide on a small to medium swell, but it can be very dirty.

Ketewel & Lebih These two beaches are northeast of Sanur, and access is easy from the new, but incomplete, coastal road. They're both right-hand beach breaks, which are dodgy at low tide and close out over 6 feet. There are probably other breaks along this coast all the way to Padangbai, but there needs to be a big swell to make them work.

Jasri Further east, where the main road swings inland to Amlapura, a side road goes to this scarcely developed black-sand beach with a modest but uncrowded right-hand beach break.

Balian There are a few peaks near the mouth of Sungai Balian (Balian River) in western Bali – sea water here is often murky because the river can carry a lot of pollution. Look for the Taman Rekreasi Indah Soka, along the main road, just west of Lalang-Linggah. You'll be charged a few hundred rupiah to get in; park at the beach end of the track. There are a few warung. The best break here is an enjoyable and consistent left-hander that works well at mid- to high tide if there's no wind.

Medewi Further along the south coast of western Bali is a softer left called Medewi – it's a point break that can give a long ride right into the river mouth. This wave has a big drop, which fills up then runs into a workable inside section. It's worth surfing if you feel like something different, but to catch it you need to get up early, because it gets blown out as the wind picks up. It works best at mid- to high tide with a 6-foot swell, but it depends on the direction. There are several places to stay and eat at Medewi, and it's easily accessible by public transport (see the West Bali chapter for more details).

Nusa Lembongan In the Nusa Penida group, this island is separated from the southeast coast of Bali by the Selat Badung (Badung Strait). You can easily get there by public or shuttle boat from Sanur, and there are plenty of good budget hotels on the island (see the Nusa Penida chapter for details).

The strait is very deep and generates huge swells that break over the reefs off the northwest coast of Lembongan. **Shipwreck**, clearly visible from the beach, is the most popular break, a longish right that gets a good barrel at mid-tide with a 5-foot swell.

A bit to the south, **Lacerations** is a very fast, hollow right breaking over a very shallow reef – hence the name. Still further south is a smaller, more user-friendly left-hander called **Playground**.

There's also a break off **Nusa Ceningan**, the middle island of the group, but it's very exposed and only surfable when it's too small for the other breaks. Remember that Lembongan is best with an easterly wind, like Kuta and Ulu Watu, so it's dry-season surfing.

South Coast The extreme south coast, around the end of Bukit peninsula, can be surfed any time of the year provided there is a northerly wind, or no wind at all – get there very early to avoid onshore winds. The peninsula is fringed with reefs and gets big swells, but access is a problem. There are a few roads, but the shoreline is all cliff. If you want to explore it, charter a boat on a day with no wind and a small swell.

Nyang Nyang is a right-hand reef break, reached by a steep track down the cliff. **Green Ball** is another right, which works well on a small to medium swell, ie, when it's almost flat everywhere else. Take the road to the Bali Cliffs Resort, fork left just before you get there and take the steps down the cliff. The south coast has few facilities and tricky currents, and it would be a bad place to get into trouble – be very careful on the cliff tracks and in the water.

Surf Trips from Bali Charter boats take groups of surfers for day trips around various local reefs, or for one-week 'surfaris' to great breaks on eastern Java (Grajagan, also known as G-Land), Nusa Lembongan, Lombok and Sumbawa, some of which cannot be reached by land. These are especially popular with those who find that the waves on Bali are too crowded. You'll see them advertised in numerous agents and surf shops in Kuta. Prices start at around 300,000Rp per person per week (seven days/six nights), including food. The most basic boats are converted Indonesian fishing boats with minimal comforts and safety equipment – the best ones are purpose built and fully equipped with TV, sound system, VHF radio, fridge, freezer etc.

Surf Travel Online (☎/fax 0361-750550; W www.surftravelonline.com) has two locations, one on Gang Sorga, off Poppies Gang II, and the other on the 1st floor of the Quiksilver/Surfer Girl building, Jl Legian 138 in Kuta. The Gang Sorga office has information on daily surfing tours, while the Jl Legian office has information on surf camps, boat charters and package deals for surf trips to remote Indonesian locations, as well as Nusa Lembongan.

Wanasari Wisata (☎ 0361-755588, fax 755690; W www.grajagan.com; Jl Pantai Kuta 8B) is one of the most established operators. For a seven-day/six-night G-Land surf camp it charges 300,000/400,000/650,000Rp for an economy/standard/exclusive package (prices are dependent upon the type of accommodation). Economy is a shared room with cold water.

International Surf Travel Agents If you want everything organised in advance, several companies will arrange package tours for surfers, including boat trips to other islands. Check out the following companies.

Surf Travel Company (☎ 02-9527 4722; W www.surftravel.com.au) 2/25 Cronulla St, Cronulla Beach, NSW 2230, Australia
Waterways (☎ 800-669 7873, fax 310-456 7755; W www.waterwaytravel.com) Suite 1, 21625 Prairie St, Chatsworth, CA 91311, USA

Diving & Snorkelling

With its warm water, extensive coral reefs and abundant marine life, Bali offers excellent diving and snorkelling possibilities. Reliable dive schools and operators all around Bali's coast can train complete beginners or arrange challenging trips that will satisfy the most experienced divers. The best sites can all be accessed in a day trip from the southern Bali resorts, though the more distant ones will involve several hours of travelling

time (think of it as a chance to see some untouristed parts of Bali). Snorkelling gear is available near all the most accessible spots, but if you're keen, it's definitely worthwhile to bring your own, and to check out some of the less visited parts of the coast.

During the wet season storms tend to reduce visibility at times, although Pulau Menjangan and Nusa Penida can still be good. Some coral bleaching occurred during the 1998 El Niño event, with a lot of the shallow-water coral on the north and northeast coast being killed, but there are still plenty of fish to see, and most of the coral deeper than 10m is still OK.

Information For a detailed guide to Bali's underwater possibilities, get a copy of Lonely Planet's *Diving & Snorkeling Bali & Lombok* by Tim Rock and Susanna Hinderks. Most of the dive operators mentioned in this guide have websites with excellent information about dive sites and conditions. For information on diving courses, see Courses later in this chapter.

When heading out on a dive, it's best to leave your valuables at your hotel, or at the dive operators' headquarters, rather than on the boat.

Dive Costs On a local trip, count on US$40 to US$75 per person for two dives, which includes all equipment. A trip to remote areas like Pulau Menjangan from southern Bali will cost more. Like most prices on Bali, the cost of diving might be discounted during quiet times and in areas where several dive operators compete for business, so you should shop around. But remember – quality equipment is not cheap, and professional instructors don't work for nothing, so a super-cheap price might mean that corners have been cut somewhere.

Equipment All the equipment you need is available on Bali, but you may not be able to get exactly what you want in the size you need, and the quality is variable – some operators use equipment right to the end of its service life. Most dive operators on Bali include the cost of equipment in the cost of the dive, but if you have your own equipment (excluding mask, snorkel and fins), you'll receive a discounted rate. Tanks and weight belt – as well as lunch, drinking water, transport, guides and insurance – are generally included in dive trips.

The basic equipment to bring is a mask, snorkel and fins – you know they'll fit and they're not too difficult to carry. At any area with coral and tourists you will be able to rent snorkelling gear for around 20,000Rp per day, but check the condition of the equipment before you take it away.

Also worth bringing if you plan to do a lot of diving is a thin, full-length wetsuit, which is important for protection against stinging animals and coral abrasions. A thicker one (3mm) would be preferable if you plan frequent diving, deep dives or a night dive – the water can be cold, especially deeper down. Some small, easy-to-carry things to bring from home include protective gloves, spare straps, silicone lubricant and extra globes for your torch (flashlight). Most dive operators can rent good-quality regulators (about US$5 per day) and BCVs (aka BCDs; about US$5), but if you bring your own you'll save money, and it's a good idea if you're planning to dive in more remote locations than Bali, where the rental equipment may not be as good.

Dive Operators Dive operators in the southern and eastern tourist centres can arrange trips to the main dive sites all around the island. However, you'd have to start early to travel from (say) Sanur to Pulau Menjangan, do two dives and drive back that day.

Another option is to get yourself to an area near where you want to dive, and contact a local dive operation. This gives you a chance to travel around some of Bali at your own speed, and dives will be cheaper because you're not paying extra to transport you and your equipment. Recommended dive operators are listed under destination sections in the relevant chapters.

Dive Sites Some of Bali's main dive sites are listed in this section, roughly in order of their accessibility from southern Bali. For more details on local dive operators, accommodation, food and getting to these places, see the entries in the relevant chapters.

Responsible Diving

The popularity of diving is placing immense pressure on many sites. Please consider the following tips when diving and help preserve the ecology and beauty of reefs.

- Do not use anchors on the reef, and take care not to ground boats on coral. Encourage dive operators to use permanent moorings at popular dive sites.
- Avoid touching living marine organisms with your body or dragging equipment across the reef. Polyps can be damaged by even the gentlest contact. Never stand on corals, even if they look solid and robust. If you must hold on to the reef, only touch exposed rock or dead coral.
- Be conscious of your fins. Even without contact, the surge from heavy fin strokes near the reef can damage delicate organisms. When treading water in shallow reef areas, take care not to kick up clouds of sand. Settling sand can easily smother the delicate organisms of the reef.
- Practise and maintain proper buoyancy control. Major damage can be done by divers descending too fast and colliding with the reef. Make sure you are correctly weighted and that your weight belt is positioned so that you stay horizontal. Be aware that buoyancy can change over the period of an extended trip: Initially you may breathe harder and need more weight; a few days later you may breathe more easily and need less weight.
- Take great care in underwater caves. Spend as little time within them as possible as your air bubbles may be caught within the roof and thereby leave previously submerged organisms high and dry. Taking turns to inspect the interior of a small cave will lessen the chances of damaging contact.
- Don't buy coral or shell souvenirs. Aside from the ecological damage, taking home marine souvenirs depletes the beauty of a site and spoils the enjoyment of others. The same goes for marine shipwreck sites – respect their integrity.
- Ensure that you take home all your rubbish and any litter you may find as well. Plastics in particular are a serious threat to marine life. Turtles can mistake plastic for jellyfish and eat it.
- Don't feed fish. You may disturb their normal eating habits, encourage aggressive behaviour or feed them food that is detrimental to their health.
- Minimise your disturbance of marine animals. In particular, do not ride on the backs of turtles, as this causes them great anxiety.

If you just want to do a little snorkelling, try the reefs off Nusa Dua, Padangbai, Candidasa (boats will take you out), Tulamben (you can enjoy the wreck just snorkelling), Amed and various points along the northeast coast.

Nusa Dua The beach is nice and gently sloping, but for the best diving, take a boat out to the reef. There's a drop-off, and colourful corals are seen between 3m and 20m (beware of currents).

Padangbai This beautiful bay is becoming more popular with tourists – you can dive from the beach, or get an outrigger canoe to the best sites, especially the Blue Lagoon, with lots of fish and colder water than southern Bali.

Candidasa There are quite a few dive sites on the reefs and islands around Candidasa, and it's a comfortable base for diving trips to the east coast. The fish life here is particularly rich and varied, and is said to include sharks. The currents on this coast are strong and unpredictable – it's recommended for experienced divers only. The **Canyon** at Tepekong is a particularly challenging dive.

Tulamben The big diving attraction is the wreck of the USAT *Liberty*, which is spectacular but eerie, encrusted with marine flora and inhabited by thousands of tropical fish. It's close to the shore and can easily be appreciated by snorkellers, but divers will find it even more interesting. Depths are less than 30m. There's also the **Tulamben Drop-Off**, a 60m drop-off into Lombok Strait. The wreck is a very popular dive, so to avoid other groups you can stay at Tulamben, where there are several dive operators and hotels, and dive early or late in the day.

Amed Dives at Amed take place off the black-sand beach of Jemeluk, which slopes gently then drops off to about 35m, with a spectacular wall. There are lots of fish, and a great variety of coral.

Lovina The beaches west of Singaraja have extensive coral reef, though much has been killed by coral bleaching. Diving at lower depths and night diving is recommended.

Safe Diving

Observe these points to ensure a safe and enjoyable diving or snorkelling experience:

- Possess a current diving certification card from a recognised scuba diving instructional agency (if scuba diving).
- Be sure you are healthy and feel comfortable diving.
- Obtain reliable information about physical and environmental conditions at the dive site (from a reputable local dive operation).
- Be aware of local laws, rules and etiquette about marine life and the environment.
- Dive only at sites within your realm of experience; if available, engage the services of a competent, professionally trained dive instructor or dive master.
- Be aware that underwater conditions vary significantly from one region, or even site, to another. Seasonal changes can significantly alter any site and dive conditions. These differences influence the way divers dress for a dive and what diving techniques they use.
- Ask about the environmental characteristics that can affect your diving and how local, trained divers deal with these considerations.

Pulau Menjangan 'Deer Island' is in the Taman Nasional Bali Barat (West Bali National Park), and is accessible by boat from Labuhan Lalang. It has superb, unspoilt coral (partly because of the absence of human development in the area), lots of sponges and fish, great visibility and a spectacular drop-off. It's regarded as the best diving on Bali. Transport to the remote location and boat rental can make this a more expensive dive, but it's definitely worth it. There are dive operators in Lovina and Pemuteran. The dive shop that you choose to go with will arrange for your boat trip and a dive pass.

Nusa Penida & Nusa Lembongan There are dive sites all around Nusa Penida and Nusa Lembongan. At Lembongan you enter from the white-sand beach, which slopes gently out to the reef, where diving is from 5m to 20m down.

Dives around Nusa Penida are more demanding, with big swells, strong and fickle currents, and cold water. There are some impressive underwater grottoes in the area, and the amount of large marine life, including manta rays, sharks and turtles, is impressive.

Trekking

Bali is not usually thought of as a trekking destination, but so many people climb Gunung Batur to see the sunrise that it can get crowded up there some mornings. There are numerous other possibilities for treks in the Batur area, around the volcanoes near Bedugul and in Taman Nasional Bali Barat in western Bali. The biggest challenge is a climb of the 3142m Gunung Agung.

Bali does not offer remote 'wilderness treks'; it's simply too densely populated. For the most part, you make day trips from the closest village, often leaving before dawn to avoid the clouds that usually blanket the peaks by mid-morning – for most treks, you won't need a tent, sleeping bag or stove. However, waterproof clothing and a sweater are essential for trekking in the central mountains. Treks in the national park must be accompanied by a guide, which can be arranged at the park office at Cekik. A few guides are available for climbs on Gunung Agung, and you won't be able to ignore the infamous guiding business on Gunung Batur.

Walking is also a good way to explore the backblocks of Bali – you can walk from village to village on small tracks and between the rice paddies. You can easily go on short hikes, without guides, around Tirta Gangga; to villages near Ubud; around Tamblingan, Buyan and Bratan lakes and Munduk; and in the hills north of Padangbai and Candidasa.

Several agencies offer organised hiking trips, commonly following rice-field routes and visiting remote villages. For information on walks, guide services and organised hiking trips, see the Around Tirta Gangga section in the East Bali chapter; the Walks Around Ubud section in the Ubud & Around chapter; and the Munduk and Trekking sections of the Central Mountains chapter. Reputable trekking companies include the following.

Jero Wijaya Tourist Service (☎ 0366-51249, fax 51250; W www.balitrekking.com), based in Toya Bungkah at the foothills of Gunung Batur, charges US$30 per person (minimum of five people) for the sunrise climb of Batur. It also offers treks up Gunung Agung (US$75) and trekking in nearby Taman Nasional Bali Barat (US$90).

Trio Pesona Perkasa Tours & Travel (☎ 0361-722706, fax 726905; W www.baliagency.com) organises trekking in Gunung Batur, including transportation and overnight accommodation for US$129 per person.

Safety Guidelines for Walking

When you go on a walking trip, carefully consider the following points to ensure a safe and enjoyable experience.

- Pay any fees and possess any permits required by local authorities.
- Remember that many Balinese mountains are sacred, and at times it is taboo to climb on them.
- Be sure you are healthy and feel comfortable walking for a sustained period.
- Ask before you set out about the environmental characteristics that can affect your walk and how local, experienced walkers deal with these considerations. Regardless of location, there may be special requirements for walking in that area.
- Obtain reliable information about physical and environmental conditions along the route you intend to take (eg, from park authorities or a reputable local guiding operation).
- Make yourself aware of local laws, regulations and etiquette about wildlife and the environment.
- Walk only in regions, and on tracks or trails, within your realm of experience; if available, engage a competent, professionally trained guide.
- Seasonal changes can significantly alter any track or trail. These differences influence the way walkers dress and the equipment they carry, and may warrant a decision not to undertake a walk at a given time.

Rafting

Rafting is very popular, usually as a day trip from Kuta, Sanur, Nusa Dua or Ubud (Ubud is closest to the best rapids). Operators pick you up from your hotel, take you to the put-in point, provide all the equipment and guides, and return you to your hotel at the end of the day. The best time is during the wet season (October to March), or just after; by the middle of the dry season (April to September), the best river rapids may just be a dribble.

Most operators use the Sungai Ayung, near Ubud, where there are between 19 and 25 Class II to III rapids (ie, exciting but not perilous). During the rare bits of calm water, you can admire the stunning gorges and rice paddies from the boat. Other outfits plunge down the very scenic Sungai Telaga Waja, or Sungai Unda, which supposedly has the hairiest rapids.

Bring shorts, shirt, sandshoes (sneakers) and sunblock. Afterwards, you'll need a full change of clothes and a towel (although this may be supplied for you). The operator should provide plastic bags for cameras and any other item that may be damaged by water. Prices include all transport, equipment and insurance, and lunch at the end of the day. You can book any trip directly, or you can go through a travel agent or one of the hotels in the tourist centres.

Advertised prices run from around US$40 to US$70, but those with high published rates will often discount. Like scuba diving, however, it is worth paying more for a reputable operator, with reliable equipment and experienced guides, such as the following.

Bali Adventure Tours (☎ 0361-721480, fax 721 481; W www.baliadventuretours.com) This large, professional operator offers trips down Sungai Ayung from US$42 to US$66, and can combine rafting with a big choice of other outdoor activities.

Sobek (☎ 0361-287059, fax 289448; W www.so bekbali.com) This well-established agency runs trips on Sungai Ayung or Telaga Waja for US$68/45 per adult/child.

4WD Touring

Sobek (☎ 0361-287059, fax 289448; W www .sobekbali.com) runs a 4WD tour of eastern Bali, starting in Bangli and heading off-road to small villages in the area and south to Semarapura for US$78/45 per adult/child. Lunch is included.

Trio Pesona Perkasa Tours & Travel (☎ 0361-722706, fax 726905; W www.bali agency.com) runs reputable 4WD trips around the Gunung Batur crater for US$50/27/19 for one/two–three/four–six persons. Trico also runs combined 4WD cooking tours, beginning with a market trip to Gianyar, cooking in a small village and a tour of the Sidemen area.

Mountain Biking

Sobek runs a mountain bike trip, which starts in Kintamani and heads downhill to Ubud on little-used back roads through luscious scenery, for $55/45 per adult/child, including lunch. Sobek also runs a cycle trip in the Batukau valley area, which combines road and off-road riding for US$55/45 per adult/child.

Horse Riding

Umalas Stables (☎ 0361-731402; W www .99bali.com) in Kerobokan, near Kuta, has a stable of 30 horses and ponies, and offers one-hour rice field tours for US$30, and two/three-hour beach rides for US$50/70. Lessons in equestrian events such as dressage and showjumping can also be arranged.

Matangi Tours (☎ 0361-731402; e matangi @idola.net.id) offers horseriding day tours that include a two-hour horseback ride through Umulas Stables, a swim in the pool at Umulas Stables, a traditional Balinese massage and a vehicle tour of the Balinese countryside for US$99.

Island Cruising

Sea Trek (Anasia Cruises) (☎ 0361-283192, fax 285440; W www.anasia-cruise.com; Jl Danau Tamblingan 77, Sanur) is a highly reputable cruising company, delivering high-quality cruises to eastern Indonesia. Its vessels are extremely comfortable and all catering is organised, including the services of a four-star chef. Prices start at around US$185 per day.

COURSES

More and more people find it rewarding to take one of the various courses available on Bali. For an overview of diving courses, see the relevant sections later in this chapter, or the relevant destination entries. Courses are often advertised on notices at cafés, particularly in Ubud, and sometimes also in local newspapers. Most courses are small group sessions.

Arts & Crafts

The Ubud area is the best place for art courses, some of which are advertised in **Pondok Pecak Library & Learning Centre**. A wide range of courses is available including batik, jewellery making and painting.

Based at the museum, **Art & Cultural Workshops** (☎ 0361-971159, fax 975136; W www.dwibhumi.com; Museum Puri Lukisan, Ubud) offer courses including; the art of making offerings, Kecak singing, kite making, woodcarving, mask painting and Balinese dance. Costs range, for example, from 65,000Rp for a 90-minute gamelan class to a full-day woodcarving class at 235,000Rp.

Nirwana Batik Course (Nirwana Pension & Gallery; ☎/fax 0361-975415; Jl Goutama

10, Ubud) holds batik classes every Monday, Wednesday and Saturday from 10am to 3pm. One-day courses are $35, two/three day courses are $30 per day, and four/five day courses are $25 per day.

Nyoman Warta Batik Lessons *(Jl Goutama 12, Ubud)*, next door to Nirwana, offers batik and painting courses that come well recommended. A full-day course, where you'll produce a finished piece, costs 210,000Rp. Longer courses are also available.

Pondok Pecak Library & Learning Centre *(☎ 0361-976194; e pondok@indo.net.id; Monkey Forest Rd, Ubud; open 9am-9pm Mon-Sat, noon-5pm Sun)* runs dance classes three times weekly for children on Wednesday, Saturday and Sunday at 3pm for 35,000Rp per hour. Gamelan, woodcarving and painting classes are also available course options.

Santra Putra *(☎ 0361-977810, fax 977321; e karjabali@yahoo.com, Penestan, Ubud)* provides intensive painting and drawing classes run by abstract artist I Wayan Karja, whose studio is also onsite. The classes cost 50,000Rp per hour. Accommodation is also available.

Studio Perak *(☎ 08123651809; e studioperak@yahoo.ca; Jl Goutama, Ubud)* has a friendly atmosphere and it specialises in Balinese-style silversmithing courses. A three-hour/full-day lesson, where you'll make a finished piece, costs 100,000/120,000Rp.

Taman Harum Cottages *(☎ 0361-975567, fax 975149; Mas)*, at the centre of Bali's woodcarving district, offers carving and painting courses.

Threads of Life Indonesian Textile Arts Center *(☎ 0361-972187, fax 976582; w www .threadsoflife.com; Jl Kajeng 24, Ubud)* runs textile appreciation courses in their gallery and educational studio. Introducing the Textiles of Bali and Indonesia is held every Tuesday (10.30am–noon) for 50,000Rp. It covers the basics of the weaving process and natural weaving techniques. Textiles and their Place in Indonesian Culture is held every Thursday (10am–noon) for 70,000Rp and looks at the history and uses of textiles.

Tenun Ikat Setia Cili *(☎/fax 0363-943409; e yunpande@yahoo.com; Gianyar; open 9am-5pm)* is a weaving factory running textile courses on demand, including ikat weaving and batik, ranging from two-hour to six-month courses.

Music & Dance

The most visitor-friendly courses are in Ubud, where private teachers advertise instruction in various Balinese/Indonesian instruments. A well-recommended teacher of Balinese music is **Wayan Pasek Sucipta** *(Eka's Homestay, Jl Sriwedari 8, Ubud)*, who charges 50,000Rp for one hour, or lower rates for longer lessons.

Ganesha Bookshop & Music *(☎ 0361-970320; w www.ganeshabooksbali.com)* conducts informal music workshops for US$8 every Tuesday at 6pm, where you can learn about and play Balinese instruments.

In Denpasar, **Sekolah Tinggi Seni Indonesia** *(STSI; ☎ 0361-227316, fax 233100)*, just off Jl Nusa Indah, is a government-run college for Balinese and Indonesian music, theatre and dance. Some of its courses may admit qualified visitors; contact them in advance of your trip.

Language

The best place for courses in Bahasa Indonesia is the **Indonesia Australia Language Foundation** *(IALF; ☎ 0361-221782, fax 263 509; w www.ialf.edu; Jl Kapten Agung 17, Denpasar)*, which has a language lab, library, and well-run four-week courses for A$850 for the language and cultural component; and an extra A$280 for a local homestay.

In Ubud, **Pondok Pecak Library & Learning Centre** *(☎ 976194; e pondok@indo.net.id; Monkey Forest Rd)* offers an inexpensive 20-hour course spread over one month, and its noticeboard has ads for the private tutors and teachers who offer courses on an ad hoc basis in both Bahasa Indonesia and the Balinese language.

Meditation & Spiritual Interests

For the Balinese, everything on the island is imbued with spiritual significance, and this ambience is an attraction for travellers looking for an alternative holiday experience. In Ubud, **Ubud Sari Health Resort** *(☎ 0361-974393; w www.ubudsari.com)* offers private guided meditation, as well as spa treatments; while the **Meditation Shop** *(☎ 0361-976206; Monkey Forest Rd)*, part of the Brahma Kumaris Society, offers silent meditation practice between 6pm and 7pm daily, and five-day meditation courses.

In eastern Bali **Nirarta (Centre for Living Awareness)** *(☎ 0366-24122, fax 21444;*

W *www.awareness-bali.com; Br Tabola, Sidemen)* conducts a variety of programmes for personal and spiritual development, including meditation intensives.

Cooking

Several places offer cooking courses, with an emphasis on Balinese cuisine. In Ubud, Bali's culinary capital, Janet de Neefe was the pioneer in this field and she runs regular **Balinese Cooking Courses** *(☎ 0361-973283, fax 973282;* **W** *www.casalunabali.com; Honeymoon Guesthouse, Jl Bisma, Ubud).* Well-recommended half-day courses (150,000Rp) are held five days per week and cover ingredients, cooking techniques and the cultural background of the Balinese kitchen. Weekend gourmet tours are also held.

Bumbu Restaurant *(☎/fax 0361-974217; Jl Suweta)* in Ubud also offers a Balinese cooking course, with Indian cuisine also a possibility. Courses cost 120,000Rp for the first day and 80,000Rp thereafter.

In Tanjung Benoa near Nusa Dua, Heinz von Holzen, one-time executive chef of the Grand Hyatt Hotel and author of The Food of Bali, runs the brilliant restaurant **Bumbu Bali** *(☎ 0361-774502)* and leads a cooking course in classic Balinese cuisine, which includes an early morning visit to Jimbaran fish market.

Just outside Candidasa, an upmarket option is the cooking course at the top-end hotel, **The Serai** *(☎ 0363-41011;* **e** *serai manggis@ghmhotels.com).* Classes focus on the cultural side of cooking and include market visits to Semarapura or Amlapura markets, as well as visits to small villages, which are known for their local specialities. A half-day/two-day/five-day course costs US$75/220/550.

Sacred Mountain Sanctuary *(☎ 0366-24330;* **W** *www.sacredmountainbali.com),* in the Sidemen area of eastern Bali, offers Indonesian and Thai cooking courses, although these are generally for guests.

Trio Pesona Perkasa Tours & Travel *(☎ 0361-722706, fax 726905;* **W** *www.bali agency.com)* runs reputable 4WD cooking tours (rather than courses), beginning with a trip to Gianyar market, a lunch time cooking session in Muncan and a tour of the Sidemen area for US$49 per person.

Surfing

A few places at Kuta offer courses for beginner surfers. The reputable **Cheyne Horan School of Surf** *(☎ 0361-735858;* **W** *www .schoolofsurf.com; Legian Kaja, Kuta)* offers half-day ($35), full-day ($65), and three-day courses ($165), plus surf clinics ($25 per hour) for intermediate and advanced surfers.

Do-It-Yourself Gado Gado

If you enjoy authentic Balinese food you'll love the cooking classes led by the enthusiastic Australian Janet de Neefe, who lives in Ubud with her Balinese husband. Together they live in and run Honeymoon Guesthouse, where the classes are held, as well as the local restaurants, Casa Luna and Indus.

Janet introduces participants to the smell and tastes of the raw forms of spices, roots, herbs, fruits and other ingredients of Balinese cooking. Colours and shapes that you might never have associated with turmeric or torch ginger can be touched and seen on the table in front of you. The uses and significance of each ingredient in cuisine, culture and family life are explained. In this way you will learn about what makes Balinese food distinctive from Indonesian food, while you taste dishes at the various stages they go through to finish as chicken satay, *gado gado*, beans in coconut milk, jackfruit salad, *nasi kuning* with turmeric rice and so on.

You could even get involved by stir-frying a sacred-spice mix until it's fragrant just before throwing some chicken in the wok to make the ceremonial dish *lawar buncis*, or by grinding just the right amount of chilli with a mortar and pestle to create the perfect sambal.

You'll sit at a table in Janet's family compound under the large roof of an open-sided bale surrounded by the kids, friends and employees of the family and your fellow travellers.

Best of all, the food you've watched being prepared and helped cook becomes lunch – a grand spread of eight to 10 dishes, all delicious in their colour, smell, freshness and authenticity.

Recipes are provided to help you recreate the taste when you get home. Classes run five days a week, and on some days include a tour of the Ubud market to seek out the freshest seasonal ingredients.

The **Hard Rock Hotel** *(☎ 0361-761869; Jl Pantai Kuta)* in Kuta also offers surf lessons.

Diving

There are many dive operators who are licensed to take out certified divers (ie, those with recognised open-water qualifications), but only a few of them have qualified instructors who can train a beginner to this level. If you're not a qualified diver, and you want to try some scuba diving on Bali, you have three options.

First, nearly all the operators offer an 'introductory', 'orientation' or 'initial' dive for beginners, usually after some classroom training and shallow-water practice. These courses are reasonably cheap (from around US$60 for one dive), but can be nasty. Some of the less professional outfits conduct these 'introductory' dives with unqualified, or even inexperienced, dive masters and minimal back-up, in sometimes difficult conditions, to depths as low as 20m. Novices would be well advised to stick with well-known and reputable operators, and ensure that the people actually conducting the dive (not the ones who sign you up, or the owners of the company) are properly qualified instructors.

Secondly, some of the larger hotels and diving agencies offer four- or five-day 'resort courses' that certify you for basic dives in the location where you do the course. A resort course will give you a better standard of training than just an introductory dive, but it doesn't make you a qualified diver. These courses cost about US$300, which is about the same cost as a full course on Bali.

Finally, if you are serious about diving, the best option is to enrol in a full open-water diving course, which gives you an internationally recognised qualification. A four-day open-water course, to PADI standards, with a qualified instructor, manual, dive table and certification, will cost about US$280 to US$360. Experienced divers can also upgrade their skills with advanced open-water courses in night, wreck and deep diving etc, from around US$200 for a three-day course, depending on the course and the operator.

WORK

Quite a lot of foreigners own businesses on Bali – mostly hotels, restaurants and tour agencies. To do so legally, foreigners need the appropriate work or business visa, which requires sponsorship from an employer, or evidence of a business that brings investment to Indonesia. Many foreigners are engaged in buying and exporting clothing, handicrafts or furniture, and stay for short periods – within the limits of the 60-day tourist card. It's illegal to work if you've entered Indonesia on a tourist card, and you'll have to leave the country to change your visa status. Even if you do get work, typically teaching English, payment is often in rupiah, which doesn't convert into a lot of foreign currency.

Volunteer & Aid Work

Anyone seeking long-term paid or volunteer work in Bali may want to contact one of the following agencies.

Australian Volunteers International (☎ 03-9279 1788, fax 9419 4280; **W** www.ozvol.org.au) PO Box 350, Fitzroy, Vic 3065. This organisation organises professional contracts for Australians.

Global Volunteers (☎ 800 487 1074, fax 651-482 0915; **W** www.globalvolunteers.org) 375 E Little Canada Rd, St Paul, MN 55117-1628, USA. This organisation arranges professional and paid volunteer work for US citizens

Lisle Fellowship Inc (☎ 800 477 1538, fax 512-259 0392; **W** www.lisleinternational.org) 900 Country Road 269, Leader, TX 78641, USA. This nonprofit intercultural education organisation arranges short community programmes on Bali for any nationality, although there are costs for the 'volunteers'

Volunteer Service Abroad (☎ 04-472 5759, fax 472 5052; **W** www.vsa.org.nz) PO Box 12-246, Wellington 1, New Zealand. This group organises professional contracts for New Zealanders

Voluntary Service Overseas (VSO; ☎ 020-8780 7200; **W** www.vso.org.uk) 317 Putney Bridge Rd, London SW15 2PN. This British overseas volunteer programme also accepts qualified volunteers from other countries. VSO also has branches in Canada (**W** www.vsocanada.org) and the Netherlands (**W** www.vso.nl).

ACCOMMODATION

All accommodation attracts a combined tax and service ('plus plus') charge of 21%. In the budget places, this is generally included in the price, but check first. Many mid-range (but not all) and top-end places will add it on, which can add substantially to your bill. In this guide, the rates quoted are the peak season published rates – prices for

Continued on page 90

Luxurious Bali

Travellers head to Bali not just for the beach, the great shopping, the vistas of terraced paddy fields or the spirituality of the Balinese, but to be blissfully indulged in exotic, lush settings and experiences. Be it hotel, restaurant or spa, luxury is easy to attain here, and it doesn't necessarily have an upscale price tag.

HOTELS

Balinese hotels have always had style. Overland travellers who first stumbled onto Bali in the late 1960s and early 1970s were amazed to find that 'cheap' and 'stylish' were words that could be combined in the same sentence. The crumbling, box-like rooms that they'd encountered elsewhere in Asia were suddenly exchanged for pretty little rooms overlooking immaculately kept gardens, dotted with exotic stone sculptures. At the other end of the price scale, as holidaymakers discovered Bali in the 1980s and 1990s, Kuta and Sanur became filled with beautifully designed hotels and boutique resorts, blending Western luxury and Balinese design. Today, Ubud is Bali's luxury epicentre.

Typically, luxury Balinese hotels have rooms that face inwards to a lush, landscaped garden, in a layout that has its origins in a traditional family compound (*pekarangan*). Bathrooms are small flowering gardens, open to the sky; while the swimming pool design is always arresting in combination with the adjacent paddy fields or ocean vistas. The hotel lobby is usually styled on a *bale banjar* (the meeting hall of a community or village), and rooms and public areas are often decorated with Balinese paintings, ikat textiles, woodcarvings and stone work of the highest quality.

Beyond obvious five-star luxury, there are many hotels on a much smaller and humbler scale that are just as inviting and, when compared to hotels worldwide, refreshingly exotic and luxurious. Most of those listed below offer a little bit of luxury at a palatable price. (The hotels described are also listed, with contact details, in the corresponding regional chapters.)

TONY WHEELER

Previous page: Facilities at the Amankila Resort in Manggis (Photograph by Tony Wheeler)

Left: Facilities available at the Amandari Resort, Ubud

South Bali

Bali Matahari Hotel in Kuta features impressive contemporary architecture and rooms that are just a step away from the pool. **Flashbacks** in Sanur is a delightfully stylish little haven.

Ubud & Around

Perched on the edge of the valley of the Sungai Ayung (Ayung River), just to the west of Ubud, the **Amandari** was the first of Bali's super-luxury small hotels. It set the standard and its style and features are echoed in many top-end and mid-range Balinese hotels. Amandari's reception area is designed like a *bale banjar*, while each of the rooms imitates a Balinese house, so that the room is in a garden within a walled compound, with a separate outdoor sitting or eating area, with its own private pool. One of the rooms even has its own small temple. The hotel's open-air restaurant looks out over the swimming pool, the 'infinity edge' seemingly spilling straight into the paddy fields that terrace down to the river. A small *bale* (pavilion) shelters melodic gamelan players at night. At the river's edge, moss-coated statues are sculpted directly in the rock cluster around a holy spring, still used by the villagers for ceremonies. It's a decidedly magical place.

One of Ubud's many charming smaller hotels is **Ketut's Place**. Once a simple *losmen* (basic accommodation), it still has a quiet family atmosphere, but rooms have gone upmarket and it now has its very own stunning swimming pool overlooking the river valley below. Its tariff, though, is a fraction of the price of a 'luxury' hotel, proving the point that a little bit of luxury in Bali is within anyone's reach.

East Bali

Lumbung Damuh, in Buitan, has gorgeous traditional rice-barn dwellings on a small plot of land by the ocean. **Grand Natia** in Candidasa is a swish place resembling a modern water palace, with the luxury must-have – an 'infinity edge' pool that drops away to ocean views. The exclusive **Amankila Resort**, near Manggis, has a classic design, and three pools stepping down to the sea. **Jukung Bali Inn** in Amed features indulgent day beds on its ocean-facing balconies, smart design and lush open-air bathrooms. **Apa Kabar** in Jemuluk and **Blue Moon Villas** in Selang, both in the Amed area, celebrate stylish lounging indoors and by the pool.

Central Mountains

Prana Dewi Mountain Resort in Wangayagede sits at the foothill of Gunung Batukau. It is set amongst paddy fields, and has rustic, beautifully furnished bungalows with expansive views.

North Bali

Kubu Lalang in the Anturan area of Lovina, edged in between paddy fields and perfect for a romantic retreat, has exotically decorated thatched-roof bungalows.

West Bali

For some authentic Balinese luxury, head to **Puri Anyar Kerambitan**, south of Tabanan. It's a lively palace compound featuring traditional accommodation and gracious hosts.

SPA TREATMENTS

Whether it's a total fix for the mind, body and spirit, or simply the desire for some quick-fix serenity, lots of travellers in Bali are spending hours and days being massaged, scrubbed, perfumed, pampered, bathed and blissed-out. Every upmarket hotel worth its stars has spa facilities (which are generally open to non-guests) offering health, beauty and relaxation treatments. Day spas are also common in all the tourist centres, particularly Ubud, and are usually priced in rupiah rather than US dollars, making them far more accessible to the average traveller in search of a little peaceful indulgence.

Where to Relax

Expect a calm, fragrant and sunlit-filled atmosphere in most Balinese spas, which range from the dazzling **Matahari Beach Resort** spa in Pemuteran, northern Bali, which resembles a grand water palace, to the equally charming **Indiana Massage**, a tiny open-air pavilion on the beach in Lovina. In the main tourist centres, luxury spa options worth treating yourself to include **Jamu Spa** in the Alam Kul Kul hotel in Kuta and **Spa Me** in the Bali Mandira Hotel in Legian, both redolent with Balinese style, and **Hotel Tjampuhan Spa** in Ubud, which is in a fairytale grotto setting. See the regional chapters for more details and other recommendations.

TONY WHEELER

Left: The Amandari Resort in Ubud

Massage, Scrub & Soak

Massage and herbal body scrubs have an important place in Balinese family life. From birth, parents massage their children, and as soon as children are able it's normal for them to reciprocate. Anyone with an ailment receives a specially formulated scrub, and men provide and receive massage as much as women. The Balinese massage techniques of stretching, long strokes, skin rolling and palm and thumb pressure result in a lowering of tension, improved blood flow and circulation, and an all-over feeling of calm.

So what can you expect in a spa? It's basically a three-stage process – the massage, the scrub and the soak. Therapists are often female, although top-end spas may have male therapists. Many massage rooms are also set up with two massage beds, so you can have a massage alongside your partner or friend.

A basic therapeutic massage is a one-hour, top-to-toe, deep-tissue massage to relax the muscles, tone the skin and eliminate stress, while aromatherapy massages feature a choice of essential oils, such as ginger, nutmeg, coconut and sandalwood. Commonly offered massage options also include Shiatsu, Thai and Swedish massage and reflexology (concentrating on pressure points of the feet). For something special, the 'four-hands' massage, where two therapists will treat you, is also an option at many spas.

Based on traditional herbal treatments, popular spa options include the *mandi rempah* (spice bath) and the *mandi susu* (milk bath). The *mandi rempah* begins with a massage, followed by a body scrub with a paste made from assorted spices, and ending with a herbal-and-spice hot bath. The *mandi susu* begins with a massage, followed by a herbal scrub and a milk-and-yoghurt body mask. The treatment ends with a soak in a milk bath.

The most popular treatment though, is the Javanese *mandi lulur* body scrub. Based on a centuries-old Javanese palace ritual, the *mandi lulur* takes almost two hours but it feels longer as all sense of time is lost during the deep-tissue massage (ask for strong treatment if you dare). The massage is followed by a full body rub made from a vibrant yellow paste of turmeric, sandlewood and rice powder. This is allowed to dry and then gently rubbed off, exfoliating and polishing the skin. Next, a mixture of yoghurt and honey is smoothed on, to moisturise and feed the skin and restore the perfect pH balance. After a quick rinsing shower, the highlight follows – a long and lovely bath in fragrant essential oils amid pale, floating frangipani petals. Refreshing hot ginger tea is normally served during the calming recovery time following the bath, when you'll feel so good you'll be dreamily planning another two hours of luxurious bliss.

Continued from page 84

budget accommodation include tax and service and prices for mid-range and top-end accommodation exclude tax and service charges unless otherwise stated.

The published rate is always negotiable, especially outside the main peak season, and if you are staying for a few days (or longer) at mid-range or top-end places, you should always seek a discount. In the low season, discounts between 30% and 50% are not uncommon in many mid-range and top-end hotels. Note that a high-season surcharge applies in many top-end hotels from 27 December to 3 January.

Many mid-range and most top-end places can now be booked over the Internet, at discounted rates.

In this guide, when we refer to accommodation rates as 'rooms' rather than singles/doubles, it means that the same price applies whether the room is occupied by one or two people.

Camping

The only campground on the whole island is at the headquarters of the Taman Nasional Bali Barat at Cekik in western Bali. It is only useful if you want to trek in the national park, and you will have to bring your camping and cooking equipment.

Even if you're trekking in the central mountains, or in the national park, you will rarely find use for a tent – there are usually shelters of some sort, and most hikes can be completed in one day anyway.

Hotels

Budget Hotels The cheapest accommodation on Bali is in small places that are simple, but clean and comfortable. The best of them are in interesting locations with friendly, helpful staff who can really make your stay a pleasure. A losmen is a small hotel, often family-run, which rarely has more than about 10 rooms; names usually include the word 'losmen', 'homestay' or 'inn'. (The word *losmen* is a corruption of the Dutch *logement*.) Losmen are often built in the style of a Balinese home, ie, a compound with an outer wall and separate buildings around an inner garden. On Bali, you usually live outside – the 'living room' is an open veranda. It's pleasant sitting out in the garden, and you're out there with all the other travellers, not locked away inside a room.

There are losmen all over Bali, and they vary widely in standards and price. In a few places you'll find a room for as little as 35,000Rp, but generally they're in the 50,000Rp to 100,000Rp range. Bigger and better rooms in popular locations can rise to 150,000Rp, but can still be very good value. Some of the cheap rooms are definitely on the dull and dismal side, but others are attractive, well kept and excellent value for money. A lush garden can be one of the most attractive features, even in very cheap places. The price usually includes a light breakfast, and rooms have an attached bathroom with a shower (cold water only), basin and generally a Western-style toilet. All but the cheapest rooms will have a ceiling fan (*kipas*).

Some mid-range hotels have cheaper 'economy' rooms, which means you can enjoy the gardens, service and pool of a mid-range hotel, while paying for a budget-priced room. Also, don't be afraid to check out a mid-range hotel, and ask for a discount if you are staying a few days, or if it's the low season.

Mid-Range Hotels Mid-range hotels are often constructed in Balinese bungalow-style and set on spacious grounds with a pool. In the less expensive mid-range hotels, rooms are priced from about 160,000Rp to 300,000Rp, which includes breakfast and a private bathroom. Mid-range hotels may have a variety of rooms and prices, with the main difference being air-conditioning and hot water versus a fan and cold water.

Upper mid-range hotels normally give their price in US dollars. Prices range from US$30 to US$75, and should include hot water, air-conditioning, colour TV (with satellite TV if you're lucky but more likely local programmes only). Rooms at the top price end are likely to have a sunken bar in the swimming pool (sometimes unattended, but it looks good on the brochure) and a colour satellite TV, fridge and telephone.

Top-End Hotels The top of the top-end on Bali is world-class. The biggest concentration of super-luxury five-star hotels is at Nusa Dua, but various hotels at Sanur, Kuta, Legian, Seminyak and Ubud are not far behind, while some of the very best ones are at secluded, isolated points around the coast or in the countryside. For this guidebook, top end usually means any place where the cheapest room costs from US$75 a double, but many top-end places have published rates at least two or three times this amount. Remember: you are far more likely to get a good deal on upmarket accommodation by buying a package tour (ie, air fare and accommodation) from home, rather than booking accommodation yourself, or just turning up at the hotel.

Palaces
A number of palaces accept guests in traditional accommodation within the palace compound, offering a unique experience. Palaces include Puri Anyar Kerambitan (see the South of Tabanan section in the West Bali chapter) and Puri Saren Agung in Ubud (see Places to Stay – Mid-Range in the Ubud & Around chapter).

Remote Areas
In remote villages, you can often find a place to stay by asking the village chief or headman, the *kepala desa*, and it will usually be a case of sleeping in a pavilion in a family compound. The price is negotiable, maybe about 25,000Rp per person per night. Your hosts may not even ask for payment, and in these cases you should definitely offer some gifts, like bottled water, sweets or fruit. If they give you a meal, it is even more important to make an offer of payment or gifts. It's a very good idea to take a Balinese friend or guide to help facilitate introductions, and to ensure that you make as few cultural faux pas as possible.

FOOD
You will eat well on Bali: the dining possibilities are endless, the prices pleasantly low and the taste, aroma and presentation will more than satisfy. Ubud is the gourmet highlight of Bali, with a wonderful choice of Balinese, Indonesian, Asian, European and fusion cuisine. The Kuta area is not far behind, and there are excellent restaurants in Sanur, Candidasa and Lovina.

Balinese Food
Although Bali does have its own cuisine, it's not readily adaptable to a restaurant menu. The everyday Balinese diet at home

---

Seafood Cooked Just Right
Fantastically fresh fish, prawns, squid and other seafood is available round much of Bali's coastline – Jimbaran Bay has a major seafood scene every evening.

Tragically, much of this seafood is overcooked, dry and rubbery. Perhaps this is understandable, as Balinese traditionally eat their fish well done, desiccated or mashed up with other ingredients – the fresh, juicy, succulent whole fish beloved of Western seafood aficionados is foreign to local cooks.

You can do your bit to end this tragedy by always asking politely that your fish not be overcooked. In Indonesian that's *'jangan terlalu matang'*.

---

is a couple of meals and a few snacks of cold steamed rice, with some vegetables, some crunchy stuff like nuts or *krupuk* (prawn crackers), and a little chicken, pork or fish. The food is prepared in the morning and people help themselves throughout the day. Dedicated Balinese cuisine is reserved for the elaborate food offerings made to the gods and sumptuous feasts to celebrate important occasions.

The dishes for a traditional Balinese feast require some time to cook, and the elaborate preparations and ritual are a major community exercise. Two of the great feast dishes, *babi guling* (spit-roasted suckling pig) and *betutu bebek* (duck roasted in banana leaves), are the only truly Balinese dishes you'll see with any regularity in restaurants, and they usually have to be ordered at least day in advance. The best places to try authentic Balinese feast dishes are in Gianyar and Ubud, and at Bumbu Bali restaurant in Tanjung Benoa. Upmarket tourist hotels do offer elaborate recreations of the traditional Balinese feast, but the ambience at these places can be more like a suburban barbecue.

Warung & Food Carts
Food in Indonesia generally is Chinese-influenced, although there are a number of purely Indonesian dishes.

Balinese like to eat snacks throughout the day, and when they're away from home, they go to a warung, or cart (often called

Snack Time Takeaways

When the Balinese wants a snack, and can't wait long enough for a warung or a food-cart meal, it's time for a takeaway – *nasi bungkus*. Literally 'rice in a packet', it consists of white rice, a little meat, chicken or fish, and some spicy sauce, wrapped in a piece of banana leaf called *tekoran*, which is cheap, leak-proof and disposable. These days the conical package is as likely to be waxed brown paper as banana leaf – it's just as cheap, but not quite as disposable, as it takes a little longer to biodegrade.

Street-stall satay is basically Javanese, but very popular on Bali too. Tiny pieces of chicken or beef are skewered on bamboo sticks, cooked over a fire of coconut husks, coated with a delectable sauce of peanut paste, garlic, lemon juice, soy sauce, ginger and spices, and served on a piece of folded banana leaf. You can eat at the stall, or take away.

Another popular takeaway is called *lupis* – some sweet, sticky rice with grated coconut and palm sugar syrup. This sweet snack is also wrapped in banana leaf or waxed paper, folded in a sort of tetrahedron shape, and secured with bamboo pins called *cemat*.

kaki lima, or 'five legs') parked along the side of the road, which often serve Javanese, Chinese or even Sumatran (ie, Padang) food. The most common is *bakso*, a soup with noodles and meatballs; *bakso ayam* is chicken soup. *Nasi campur* is the most authentic Balinese-style dish served in a warung. Most budget tourist restaurants do Chinese-Indonesian-style food, with the standard dishes being *nasi goreng*, *nasi campur*, *cap cai* and *gado gado*.

The great paradox of eating on Bali is that the cheaper the place, the tastier the food. The really inexpensive places are for the locals, and they serve the genuine Balinese article. At a street cart, for about 5000Rp you can get a *nasi goreng* that is simply out of this world – hot and spicy, with fresh ingredients that are cooked while you wait. Of course, the trade-off is that you might have to sit on the kerb to eat it, and the plate may not be as carefully washed as you would like. At a tourist restaurant around the corner, a *nasi goreng* costs around 12,000Rp, but it might not be freshly cooked and it won't have the same spicy taste.

Fried noodles (*mie goreng*), satay and soup (*soto*) are other cheap staples that taste better and cost less at a warung or *kaki lima*.

Fruit

It's almost worth making a trip to Bali just to sample the tropical fruit. If you've never gone beyond apples, oranges and bananas you've got some rare treats in store when you discover rambutans, mangosteens, *salaks* or *sirsaks*.

Foreign Food & Tourist Restaurants

There are a growing number of very good restaurants in tourist areas serving what can only be described as 'modern international' cuisine. They serve excellent meals for a fraction of what you'd pay in Europe, the US or Australia, and they are usually spacious, ambient, open-air places with friendly and efficient service. Many of the top-end hotels also have first-class kitchens, but the cost will not be much less than back home. Most tourist restaurants will have token Indonesian dishes on the menu, including *rijstaffel*.

Also readily available are Western dishes such as omelettes, pancakes and waffles for breakfast. For lunch and dinner, you can find steaks, spaghetti, hamburgers or pizza, and nachos and guacamole dips for starters – and they are usually well made, with fresh ingredients.

And for those who can't live without something from their favourite chain of fast-food restaurants, there are plenty of options in the Kuta and Denpasar regions.

DRINKS
Nonalcoholic Drinks
Drinking Water Plastic bottles of drinking water are widely available. A 500mL bottle costs about 2500Rp; a 1.5L bottle is around 3000Rp at a supermarket or a local shop, but more in a tourist restaurant or hotel. Plastic water bottles are now a major litter problem, so it's a good idea to have your bottle refilled from a bulk container – some environmentally friendly shops offer

this service, and it's cheaper than buying a new bottle.

Soft Drinks The usual brands are available. Soda water is bottled in a Fanta bottle and called Fanta Soda.

Juice & Milk Fruit juice and UHT milk (flavoured if you like) are available in sealed cartons from supermarkets and most small shops.

Coffee Locally produced coffee is called *kopi Bali*. It is grown around volcanic areas near Kintamani, on the hills around Pupuan in central Bali, and along the north coast, not far from Singaraja. It's served strong, black and thick. In most of the tourist areas, you can usually hunt down a decent espresso at an upmarket café.

Alcoholic Drinks

Beer *Bir* is expensive compared to other things on Bali, but served cold in a bar or restaurant it's still cheaper than in most Western countries. Some places offer happy hours where a beer, and other drinks, are a few thousand rupiah cheaper for an hour or two after about 6pm. The most common brands of beer are Bintang, Bali Hai, Anker and San Miguel. Bintang is the best; Bali Hai is not as good, but is often cheaper. Prices for a large bottle (620mL) range enormously, from about 8500Rp during a happy hour to over 20,000Rp in a top-end restaurant.

Wine Wine is expensive on Bali, but becoming more widely available as people crave a drop with the excellent food. Hatten wine is a locally produced, somewhat pricey rosé that needs to be served very cold to be palatable. The quality is uneven, from pleasantly drinkable to bloody awful – apparently it doesn't keep well. Imported wines cost around 200,000Rp to 400,000Rp for an indifferent French or Australian bottle. It's worth bringing in a couple of bottles duty free, but you'll have to pay for corkage in top-end restaurants.

Local Drinks

For a list of popular Indonesian and Balinese drinks, both alcoholic and nonalcoholic, see the Glossary at the end of this book.

ENTERTAINMENT

The best way to find out about current exhibitions, music, dance and film in the Kuta-Seminyak area is to get hold of a copy of *The Beat*, a free fortnightly palm-sized colour magazine. Other tourist magazines will also feature information on more traditional entertainment, such as Balinese dance performances, but the best place for information on dance is the Ubud Tourist Office.

Bars & Clubs

Kuta, Legian and Seminyak are the nightlife hubs of Bali. Bars and nightclubs in Kuta-Legian cater to package tourists keen to wake with a hangover, which is easily aided by *arak*-laced 'jam jar' happy hours, when drink prices are reduced. The music played is generally cringeworthy.

Nearby, in Seminyak, there's not a jam jar in sight and the mood is definitely less desperate, with chic and sexy nightclub interiors, fine tunes played by DJs and a more discerning band of clubbers, including the gay contingent. Bars and nightclubs in Seminyak generally don't get going until well after midnight. A short drive away, Sanur has a number of jazz cafés, as well as a genuine pub popular among expats.

Outside the Kuta zone, other popular destinations such as Candidasa, Ubud and Lovina have fairly low-key nightlife options. Each has a few bars and travellers cafés that fill up after dark and often feature live music, such as reggae or acoustic guitar.

Bars and nightclubs are generally free to enter, and often have special drink promotions and 'happy hours'. During the low season, when tourist numbers are down, you might have to visit quite a few venues to find one with any action.

Sports Bars A number of bars and pubs in the main tourist centres show exclusively sports telecasts including, for example, live crossovers to Australian Football League (AFL) games.

Cinema & Video

A cinema has opened at the **Galeria Kuta** (☎ 0361-767 021), which shows recently released films. There's also a modern multi-screen place in Denpasar, which shows B-grade adventure epics. In all the tourist centres, recently released films are shown in bars and restaurants, sometimes on small TVs and at the more established places on a big screen.

Cultural Performances

Balinese dance performances and shadow puppet plays are popular entertainment for tourists, but of course they're much more than that. For details, see the Performing Arts section in the Facts about Bali chapter, and the 'Balinese Dance' special section. Ubud is the place to go to for traditional dance, whereas the Kecak dance is performed in the grounds of Ulu Watu temple.

SHOPPING

Many people come to Bali to 'shop 'til they drop', and everyone else will probably end up buying quite a few things anyway. The growing number of Western-style department stores and shopping centres in Denpasar, Kuta, Sanur and Nusa Dua sell a large variety of clothing, shoes, leathergoods, sports gear and toys. There's a huge range, the service is generally good, and prices are mostly very good because of the low value of the rupiah.

Sculpture

Balinese stone is surprisingly light and it's not at all out of the realms of possibility to bring a friendly stone demon back with you in your airline baggage. A typical temple door guardian weighs around 10kg. The stone, however, is very fragile so packing must be done carefully if you're going to get it home without damage. Some of the Batubulan workshops will pack figures quickly and expertly, often suspending the piece in the middle of a wooden framework and packing around it with shredded paper. There are also many capable packing and forwarding agents, though the shipping costs will almost certainly be more than the cost of the article.

Batubulan, on the main highway from Denpasar to Ubud, is a major stone-carving centre. Stone figures from 25cm to 2m tall line both sides of the road, and stone carvers can be seen in action in the many workshops here.

Paintings

There are a relatively small number of creative original painters on Bali today, and an enormous number of imitators who produce copies, or near copies, in well-established styles. Many of these imitative works are nevertheless very well executed and attractive pieces. Originality is not considered as important in Balinese art as it is in the West. A painting is esteemed not for being new and unique but for taking a well-worn and popular idea and making a good reproduction of it. Some renowned artists will simply draw out the design, decide the colours and then employ apprentices to actually apply the paint. This leads to the mass production of similar works that is so characteristic of Balinese art.

Unfortunately, much of the painting today is churned out for the tourist market and much of that market is extremely undiscriminating about what it buys. Thus the shops are packed full of paintings in the various popular styles – some of them quite good, a few of them really excellent, many of them uniformly alike and uniformly poor in quality. It's rare to see anything really new – most painters aim for safety and that means painting what tourists will buy.

Before making a purchase, visit the Neka Museum and Museum Puri Lukisan in Ubud to see the best of Balinese art and some of the European influences that have shaped it. Then visit some of the better commercial galleries like the Neka Gallery near Ubud and the Agung Rai Gallery to view high-quality work and get an idea of prices.

Paintings can be transported in cardboard or plastic tubes (available from hardware stores). If you do buy a painting, and can afford the additional weight, consider taking a frame back as well. These are often elaborately carved works of art in themselves, and are much cheaper than framing costs in the West.

Woodcarvings

As with paintings, try to see some of the best quality woodcarvings in museums and galleries before you consider buying. Again, many standard pieces are produced in the same basic designs, and craft shops are full of them. Even with a basic lizard, hand or fisherman design, some are much better than others. Look for quality first, then look at the price – you may see the same article vary in price by anything from 10% to 1000%!

Apart from the retail mark-up and your bargaining skills, many factors determine costs, including the artist, the type of wood used, the originality of the item and the size. The simplest small carvings start at around 15,000Rp, while many fine pieces can be found for under 100,000Rp, and there's no upper limit.

Wooden articles may have an excess of moisture from Bali's tropical climate and the wood may shrink and crack in drier environments. It may be possible to avoid this by placing the carving(s) in a plastic bag at home, and then letting some air in for about one week every month (for a total of three to four months), so the wood can get used to the drier air.

Fabrics & Weaving

Gianyar, in eastern Bali, is a major textile centre with a number of factories where you can watch *ikat* sarongs being woven on a hand-and-foot powered loom; a complete sarong takes about six hours to make. You can buy direct from the factories, although prices can be inflated in the tourist season. Any market will have a good range of textiles – those in Denpasar have a good range.

In the Bali Aga village of Tenganan, in eastern Bali, a double ikat process called *gringsing* is used, in which both the warp and weft are predyed – this is time consuming and expensive. Belayu, a small village in south-western Bali between Mengwi and Marga, is a centre for *songket* weaving. *Songket* is also woven near Singaraja. For *prada*, have a look at shops in Sukawati, south of Gianyar.

Ceramics

If you wish to see potters at work, visit the village of Pataen near Tanah Lot. Ubung and Kapal, north and west of Denpasar, respectively, are also pottery centres. Nearly all local pottery is made from low-fired terracotta. Most styles are very ornate, even for functional items such as vases, flasks, ashtrays and lamp bases. Pejaten near Tabanan also has a number of pottery workshops producing small ceramic figures and glazed ornamental roof tiles. Some excellent, contemporary glazed ceramics are produced in Jimbaran, south of Kuta.

Jewellery

Celuk has always been the village associated with silversmithing. The large shops that line the road into Celuk have imposing, bus-sized driveways and slick credit-card facilities. If you want to see the 'real' Celuk, walk about 1km east of the road to visit family workshops. Other silverwork centres include Kamasan, near Semarapura in eastern Bali, and Beratan, south of Singaraja in northern Bali.

Jewellery can be purchased ready-made or made-to-order – there's a wide range of earrings, bracelets and rings available, some using gemstones, which are imported from all over the world. Different design influences can be detected, from African patterning to the New Age preoccupation with dolphins and healing crystals.

You'll find many jewellery workshops in other areas around Ubud. Tampaksiring, northeast of Ubud, has long been a centre for cheaper styles of fashion jewellery. Brightly painted, carved wooden earrings are popular and cheap.

Gamelan

If you are interested in seeing gamelan instruments being made, visit the village of Blahbatuh, on the main road between Denpasar and Gianyar, and ask for Gablar Gamelan.

In northern Bali, Sawan, a small village southeast of Singaraja, is also a centre for the manufacture of gamelan instruments. Jembrana near Negara, in western Bali, makes giant gamelan instruments with deep resonating tones.

Wayang Kulit

Wayang kulit puppets are made in the village of Puaya near Sukawati, south of Ubud, and in Peliatan near Ubud.

Clothing

All sorts of clothing is made locally, and sold in hundreds of small shops in all tourist centres, especially Kuta-Legian and Seminyak. It's mostly pretty casual, but it's not just beachwear – you can get just about anything you want including tailor-made clothing. Leatherwear is quite cheap and popular.

Music

CDs featuring Western artists are good value at around 80,000–90,000Rp. Cassettes cost about 35,000Rp. The costs of cassettes and CDs featuring Balinese and Indonesian artists is generally lower. Kuta and Ubud have the best selection.

Furniture

Since the mid-1990s, timber furniture has been a huge growth industry, though much of the furniture is actually made on Java and sent to Bali for finishing and sale. Much of it is purchased by wholesale buyers for export, but tourists are also tempted by contemporary designs and reproduction antiques at much lower prices than they'd find at home. Some of the most attractive pieces are tropical-style cane and bamboo chairs, sofas and coffee tables. There are also outdoor settings of teak, mahogany and other rainforest timbers. (Harvesting timber for the local furniture industry and furniture manufacturing involves a high local value-added content and probably has a lesser impact on rainforests than large-scale clearing for export of logs and wood-chips, which are much more significant causes of deforestation, and generate a lot less local employment.)

The best places to look for furniture are the stores/warehouses along Jl Bypass Ngurah Rai around Kuta and Jimbaran, and also in Mas, south of Ubud. Many of these places will offer to make furniture to order, but if you're a one-off buyer on a short visit it's best to stick to items that are in stock, so you can see what you're getting. It might just be feasible to carry home a few small folding chairs, but generally, if you buy furniture you'll need to have it shipped home. For items that are shipped, you'll pay a 40% or 50% deposit and the balance (plus any taxes or import duties) when you collect the items at home. If possible, arrange for delivery to your door – if you have to pick the items up from the nearest port or freight depot you may be up for extra port charges.

Most places selling furniture can arrange packing, shipping and insurance, but it might be better to make arrangements yourself with a reputable shipping company. Shipping costs for volumes less than a full container load vary greatly according to the company, destination and quantity – think in terms of around US$150 plus per cubic metre. Be aware that packing costs, insurance, fumigation and so on are included in some companies' prices but are charged as extras by others.

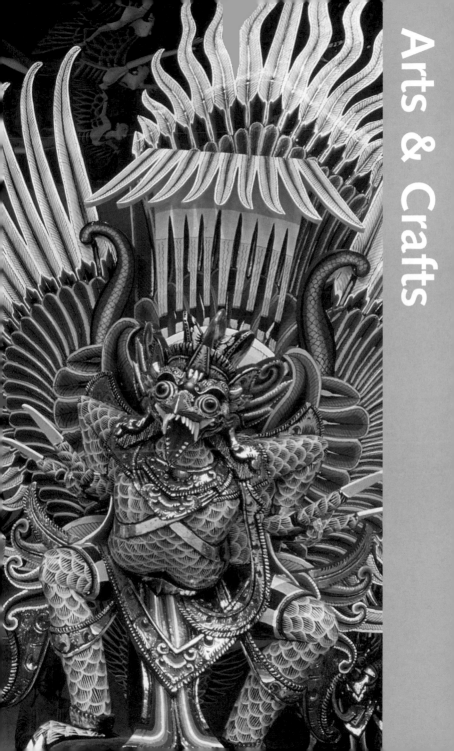

GREGORY ADAMS

RICHARD I'ANSON

RICHARD I'ANSON

JAMES LYON

JAMES LYON

JAMES LYON

Previous page: A ghoul ish burst of carved colour on show in Ubud (Photograph by John Banagan)

Top: A Balinese woman appraising banten tegeh (temple offerings)

Middle Top: Classical Balinese paintings line the roof of the Kertha Gosa, Semerapura

Middle Bottom: Ornate door detail, Ubud, southern Bali

Bottom Left: Ikat weaving in a gringseng design

Bottom Middle: Endek weaving

Bottom Right: The silky sheen of songket.

The richness of Bali's arts and crafts has its origin in the fertility of the land and the extraordinary productivity of its agriculture. Food can be produced in abundance with a small input of labour, allowing plenty of time for cultural activities. Aptly, the purest forms of Balinese art are the depictions of Dewi Sri, the rice goddess, intricately made from dried and folded strips of palm leaf. These are used as offerings ensuring that the fertility of the rice fields continues.

Up until the tourist invasion, painting or carving was simply an everyday part of life for the Balinese – what was produced went into temples or was used for their many festivals. It is a different story today, with hundreds, even thousands, of galleries and craft shops in every possible place that a tourist might pass. You can't turn around without tripping over more stone- or woodcarvings, and in the galleries the paintings are stacked up in piles on the floor. This is unfortunate, as much of this work is churned out quickly for people who want to buy a cheap souvenir to take home, but you will still find a great deal of beautiful work.

Inset: Beautifully hand-crafted ornaments were once regular temple offerings, particulary to Dewi Sri, the rice goddess (Illustration by Jenny Bowman)

BALI ARTS & CRAFTS

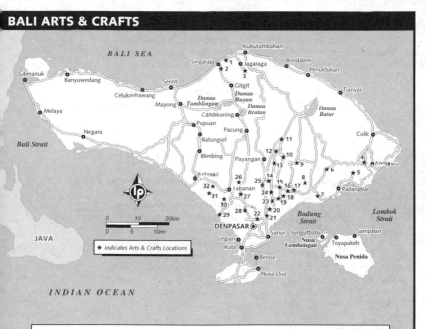

1 Banyuning – Pottery
2 Beratan – Silverwork & Weaving (Songket)
3 Sawan – Gamelan Instruments
4 Budakaling – Silver & Gold Work
5 Tenganan – Double Ikat Weaving (Gringsing)
6 Sideman – Weaving
7 Kamasan – Classical Painting
8 Tihingan – Gongs & Gamelan
9 Bangli – Coconut & Bone Carving, Silverwork
10 Tampaksiring – Coconut & Bone Carving, Jewellery
11 Jati – Woodcarving
12 Pujung – Woodcarving
13 Tegallalang – Woodcarving
14 Ubud – Painting & Woodcarving
15 Bedulu – Painting (Classical Calendars)
16 Gianyar – Weaving
17 Bona – Basketware & Bamboo Work
18 Blahbatuh – Gongs & Gamelan
19 Puaya – Mask Carving & Puppet Making
20 Celuk – Silver & Gold Work
21 Batubulan – Stonecarving & Furniture
22 Ubung – Pottery
23 Batuan – Basketware & Painting
24 Mas – Wood & Mask Carving
25 Tohpati – Painting
26 Belayu – Weaving (Songket)
27 Mengwi – Weaving
28 Sempidi – Ceramics & Tiles
29 Pataen – Pottery
30 Pejaten – Pottery
31 Penarukun – Carving
32 Krambitan – Painting

THE INTER-ISLAND CONNECTION

The cultural and trading relationship between Java and Bali has always been strong, and much of Bali's craft traditions come directly from Java. The ceremonial dagger (kris), so important in a Balinese family, will often have been made on Java. Most of the batik sarongs that are worn for important ceremonies are made in central Java. Similarly, Java is the main supplier of puppets and metalwork items, including sacred images.

In many ways, Bali is a showroom for all the crafts of Indonesia. A typical tourist shop will sell puppets and batiks from Java, ikat garments from Sumba, Sumbawa and Flores, and textiles and woodcarvings from Bali, Lombok and Kalimantan.

OFFERINGS & EPHEMERA

Traditionally, many of Bali's most elaborate crafts have been religious offerings and ceremonial decorations that are not intended to last. Just take a look at those little offering trays placed on the ground for the spirits every morning – each one is a throwaway work of art. Look at the temple offerings, the artistically stacked pyramids of fruit, rice cakes and flowers (baten tegeh) or other beautifully decorated foods. Look for the lamak, long woven palm-leaf strips used as decorations in festivals and celebrations, or the stylised female figures known as cili, which are representations of Dewi Sri. See the intricately carved coconut-shell wall hangings, or simply marvel at the care and energy that goes into constructing huge funeral towers and exotic sarcophagi, all of which will soon go up in flames.

STONE CARVING & SCULPTURE

JENNY BOWMAN

Traditionally, stone carving was employed almost exclusively for the adornment of temples. Unlike other Balinese arts, architecture and sculpture have been little affected by foreign influences, mainly because your average stone statue is too big and heavy to make a convenient souvenir. Stone carving is also Bali's most durable art form, and, though it is soon covered in moss, mould or lichen, it outlasts woodcarvings and paintings, which deteriorate quickly in the hot, humid atmosphere.

Stone carving appears in a number of set places in temples, depicting the character, deity or decorative theme appropriate for that position. Door guardians are usually legendary figures like Arjuna, or some other protective personality. Above the main entrance, Kala's monstrous face often peers out, sometimes a number of times, his hands reaching out beside his head to catch any evil spirits. The side walls of a pura dalem (temple of the dead) might feature sculpted panels that show the horrors that await evildoers in the afterlife.

Left: Intricate stone carvings are an integral part of Balinese architecture, particulary at temples

PAUL BEINSSEN

Even when decorating a modern building, like a hotel or bank, stone carvers tend to stick to the tried and trusted – patterned friezes, floral decoration or bas-reliefs depicting scenes from the *Ramayana*. Nevertheless, many modern trends can still be seen and many sculptors are happy to work on nontraditional themes, like Japanese-style stone lanterns or McDonalds' characters outside its Kuta franchise. Classic or kitsch? You be the judge.

Much of the local work is made from a soft, grey volcanic stone called *paras*. It's a little like pumice, not particularly strong or dense, and so soft it can be scratched with a fingernail. When newly worked, it can be mistaken for cast cement, but with age and exposure to the elements, the outer surface becomes tougher and darker. Soft sandstone is also used, and sometimes has attractive colouring.

PAINTING

Of the various art forms popular on Bali, painting is probably the one most influenced by Western ideas and Western demand. Traditionally, painting was for temple and palace decoration. When Western artists first arrived in the 1920s and 1930s, they introduced the novel concept that paintings could be seen as artistic creations in their own right, and moreover, creations that could be sold for money. The range of themes, techniques and styles expanded enormously, and Balinese artists gained access to completely new media and materials to work with.

Balinese paintings have been classified into several styles, but there is some overlap between them, and there are some artists whose work does not really fit into any of the main styles. The best place to see fine examples of every style is the Neka Museum in Ubud.

First, there are the classical, or Kamasan, paintings, named for the village of Kamasan near Semarapura (Klungkung) – these are also called Wayang style. The Ubud style of painting developed in the 1930s, with the influence of the Pita Maha artists' cooperative. The similar Batuan style started at the same time in a nearby village. The postwar Young Artists' style developed in the 1960s, influenced by Dutch artist Arie Smit. Finally, the modern, or 'academic', style can be loosely defined as anything that doesn't fall into the main Balinese categories – it shows influences of everything from the postimpressionists to Rothko.

Top: The fierce, defensive face of a Raksas (nocturnal demon) carved in stone, Batubulan

Classical Painting

Until the arrival of Western artists in the 1920s and 1930s, Balinese painting was strictly limited to three basic types – *langse, iders-iders* and calendars. *Langse* are large rectangular decorative hangings used in palaces or temples. *Iders-iders* are scroll paintings hung along the eaves of temples. These styles can be traced back to 9th-century Javanese sculpture – the 14th-century temple complex at Panataran in eastern Java has relief sculptures that display *wayang* figures, rich floral designs and flame-and-mountain motifs characteristic of classical Balinese painting.

Balinese calendars are still used to set dates and predict the future, although today most of them are painted for tourists. There are two types – the simpler yellow-coloured calendars from Bedulu, near Ubud, and the more complex classical calendars from Semarapura and Kamasan. The style has also been adapted to create large versions of the zodiacal and lunar calendar, especially the 210-day *wuku* calendar, which still regulates the timing of Balinese festivals.

Langse paintings were prized by local rulers and given as gifts between rival royal households. The paintings also helped fulfil the important act of imparting ethical values and customs *(adat)* to the ordinary people, in much the same way as traditional dance and *wayang kulit* puppetry.

In fact, it's from the Wayang tradition that Kamasan painting takes its essential characteristics – the stylisation of human figures shown in profile or three-quarter view, their symbolic gestures, the depiction of divine and heroic characters as refined, and of evil ones as vulgar and crude. The paintings were in a narrative sequence, rather like a comic strip, with a series of panels telling a story. The definitive example of this style is the painted ceilings of the Kertha Gosa (Hall of Justice) in Semarapura.

Classical paintings may still show action in comic-strip style, and commonly depict scenes from ancient Hindu epics, the *Ramayana* and *Mahabharata*. Other themes are the Kakawins poems, written in the archaic Javanese language of Kawi, and indigenous Balinese folklore with its pre-Hindu/pre-Buddhist beliefs in demonic spirit forces.

Traditionally, the style is essentially linear, with the skill of the artist apparent in the overall composition and sensitivity of the line work. The colouring was of secondary importance and left to apprentices, usually the artist's children. Natural colours were made from soot, clay, pig's bones and other such ingredients, and artists were strictly limited to a set list of shades. Today, modern oils and acrylics are used, but the style is still restricted to a limited range of colours. A final burnishing gives an aged look even to new paint, and these pictures are known as *lukisan antik* (antique paintings).

The Pita Maha

Walter Spies and Rudolf Bonnet were the Western artists who turned Balinese artists around in the 1930s (see the boxed text 'Western Visitors in the 1930s' in the Facts for the Visitor chapter). At that time painting was in a serious decline: painting styles had become stagnant, and since few commissions were forthcoming from palaces and temples, painting was virtually dying out as an art form.

Bonnet and Spies, with their patron Cokorda Gede Agung Sukawati, formed the Pita Maha (literally, 'Great Vitality') to encourage painting as an art form and find a market for the best paintings. The group had more than 100 members at its peak in the 1930s.

The changes Bonnet and Spies inspired were revolutionary – suddenly Balinese artists started painting single scenes instead of narrative tales and using everyday life rather than romantic legends as their themes. Paintings influenced by the Pita Maha association typically depict a scene from everyday life – harvesting rice, bartering at the market, watching a cockfight, presenting offerings at a temple or preparing a cremation. These paintings came to be known as the 'Ubud style'.

Batuan is a noted painting centre that came under the influence of the Pita Maha at an early stage, but retained many features of classical painting. Batuan painters also started to depict scenes from daily life, but included many scenes in each painting – a market, a dance, a rice harvest and other scenes might all appear in a single work. The Batuan style is also noted for its inclusion of some very modern elements, such as sea scenes with the odd windsurfer.

The themes not only changed, the actual way of painting also altered. Modern paint and materials were used and the stiff formal poses of old gave way to realistic three-dimensional representations. Even more importantly, pictures were painted for their own sake – not as something to cover a space in a palace or temple.

In one way, however, the style remained unchanged – Balinese paintings were packed with detail; every spare corner of the picture was filled in. A painted Balinese forest has branches and leaves reaching out to fill every tiny space and is inhabited by a whole zoo of creatures. You can see fine examples of these new styles at the Museum Puri Lukisan in Ubud and, of course, in all the galleries and art shops.

The new artistic enthusiasm was short-lived, however, for WWII interrupted and later in the 1950s and 1960s Indonesia was wracked by internal turmoil and confusion. The new styles degenerated into stale copies of the few original spirits, with one exception: the development of the Young Artists' style.

The Young Artists

Dutch painter Arie Smit survived imprisonment by the Japanese during WWII and arrived on Bali in 1956. One day while painting in Penestanan, just outside Ubud, he noticed a young boy drawing in the dirt and wondered what he would produce if he had proper equipment to paint with. The story is regularly told of how the lad's father would not allow him to take up painting until Smit offered to pay somebody else to watch the family's flock of ducks.

Other 'young artists' from Penestanan soon joined that first pupil, I Nyoman Cakra, but Arie Smit did not actively teach them. He simply provided the equipment and the encouragement, and unleashed what was clearly a strong natural talent. An engaging new 'naive' style quickly developed, as typically Balinese rural scenes were painted in brilliant technicolour.

The style quickly caught on and is today one of the staples of Balinese tourist art. Of course, not all the artists are young boys anymore,

ARTS & CRAFTS

BERNARD NAPTHINE

and the style is also known as work by 'peasant painters'. I Nyoman Cakra, the original Young Artist, still lives in Penestanan, still paints and cheerfully admits that he owes it all to Smit.

Other Styles

There are some other variants of the main Ubud and Young Artists' styles. The depiction of forests, flowers, butterflies, birds and other naturalistic themes, sometimes called Pengosekan style, became popular in the 1960s, but can probably be traced back to Henri Rousseau, who was a significant influence on Walter Spies. An interesting development of this style is the depiction of underwater scenes, with colourful fish, coral gardens and some (largely imaginary) sea creatures. Somewhere between the Pengosekan and Ubud styles are the miniature landscape paintings that are a popular commercial offering.

Though many of the Pita Maha artists turned to the hitherto unexplored themes of daily life, the new techniques were also used to depict some traditional subjects. There were radically new versions of Rangda, Barong, Hanuman and the *Ramayana* characters, and other figures from Balinese and Hindu mythology. Scenes from folk tales and stories also appeared, in many cases featuring dancers, nymphs and love stories, with an understated erotic appeal.

Academic Painting

A small but growing number of Balinese artists receive formal art training, often in schools in Yogya Karta or overseas. Others are influenced by Western or Asian artists who visit and work on Bali for various periods. Basically, any painting that does not depict a recognisably Balinese subject or does not follow one of the well-established Balinese styles can be called 'academic', and is very likely to be the work of someone who has had formal art training.

Top: Balinese painting b I Ketat Tagen, Neka Museum, Ubud

WOODCARVING

Woodcarving has undergone a major transformation over the past 70 years, from being a decorative craft to something done for its own sake. Prior to this change, woodcarving was chiefly used for architectural decoration, such as carved doors or columns, or of figures such as Garudas, or demons with a symbolic nature. There were also decorative carvings on minor functional objects, such as bottle tops, and the carved wooden masks used in Balinese dance. Yet, as with painting, it was the same demand from outside that inspired new carving subjects and styles. It was also some of the same Western artists who served as the inspiration.

As with painting, Ubud was a centre for the revolution in woodcarving. Some carvers started producing highly stylised figures, and the wood was sometimes left with its natural finish and not painted. Others carved delightful animal figures, some realistic, some complete caricatures. More styles and trends developed: whole tree trunks carved into ghostly, intertwined 'totem poles', and curiously exaggerated and distorted figures.

Any visitor to Bali will be exposed to woodcarving in all its forms, whether it be the traditional ornately carved double-doors seen in houses, the carved figures of gods carried in processions and seen in temples, or the carved items in shops. Almost all carving is of local woods, including *belalu*, a quick-growing light wood, and the stronger fruit timbers such as jackfruit wood. Ebony from Sulawesi is also used. Sandalwood, with its delightful fragrance, is expensive, soft and used for some small, very detailed pieces.

Tegallalang and Jati, on the road north from Ubud to Batur, are noted woodcarving centres. Many workshops line the road east of Peliatan, near Ubud, to Goa Gajah (Elephant Cave). The route from Mas, through Peliatan, Petulu and up the scenic slope to Pujung is also a centre for family-based workshops; listen for the tapping sound of the carvers' mallets.

An attempt to separate traditional and foreign influences is difficult. The Balinese have always incorporated and adapted foreign themes in their work. Balinese carvings of religious figures may be based on Hindu mythology, but are very different from the same figures made in India.

Carving, however, suffers from similar problems to painting, in that there's an overwhelming emphasis on what sells, with the successful subjects mimicked by every other carver. Still, there's always something to see, the technical skill is high and the Balinese sense of humour often shines through – a frog clutching a large leaf as an umbrella, or a weird demon on the side of a wooden bell clasping his hands over his ears.

Mask Carving

Mask making is a specialised form of woodcarving, and only experts carve the masks used in many of Bali's theatre and dance performances. A particularly high level of skill is needed to create the 30 or 40 masks used in the Topeng dance. The mask maker must know the movements that each Topeng performer uses, so that the character can be shown by the mask.

Other Balinese masks, such as the Barong & Rangda, are brightly painted and decorated with real hair, enormous teeth and bulging eyes.

Mas is recognised as the mask-carving centre of Bali. The small village of Puaya, near Sukawati, also specialises in the art of mask making. The

Middle: *Wayang kulit* puppet

JENNY BOWMAN

ARTS & CRAFTS

TAMSIN WILSON

Museum Negeri Propinsi Bali in Denpasar has an extensive mask collection and is a great place to get an idea of different styles before buying anything from the craft shops. Or you could check out the masks at Balinese dance performances (see the 'Balinese Dance' special section later).

TEXTILES & WEAVING

The sarong is an attractive, versatile workaday item – a comfortable article of clothing, which can serve as a sheet or towel and has a multitude of other uses. The cheapest ones are plain or printed cotton, while more elegant batik designs are a little more expensive. The more elegant fabrics, like *endek* and *songket*, are necessary for special occasions – it is a religious obligation to look one's best at a temple ceremony. Dress for these occasions is a simple shirt or blouse, a sarong and a *kain,* a separate length of cloth wound tightly around the hips, over the sarong.

For more formal occasions, the blouse is replaced by a length of songket wrapped around the chest. These chest cloths are called *kamben*. The styles of wearing the sarong are different for men and women.

Batik

Traditional batik sarongs are handmade in central Java. The dyeing process has been adapted by the Balinese to produce brightly coloured and patterned fabrics for clothing etc, although batik is not an indigenous Balinese technique.

Watch out for 'batik' fabric that has actually been screen printed in factories. The colours will be washed out compared to the rich colour of real batik cloth, and the pattern is often only on one side (in true batik cloth, the dye penetrates to colour both sides).

Ikat

In various places in Indonesia you'll find material woven by the complex *ikat* process, where the pattern is dyed into the threads before the material is woven. *Ikat* usually involves predyeing either the warp threads (those stretched on the loom), or the weft threads (those woven across the warp). The usual Balinese technique, in which the weft threads are predyed, is known as *endek*. The resulting pattern is geometric and slightly wavy, like a badly tuned TV. Its beauty depends on the complexity of the pattern and the harmonious blending of colours. Typically the pattern is made in colours of similar tone – blues and greens; reds and browns; or yellows, reds and oranges. *Ikat* sarongs and *kain* are not everyday wear, but they are not for strictly formal occasions either.

Top: Woodcarved Topeng masks used Balinese dancers

Gringsing

In the Bali Aga village of Tenganan, in eastern Bali, a double *ikat* process is used, in which both the warp and weft threads are predyed. Called *gringsing* (or *geringsing*), this complex and time-consuming process is practised nowhere else in Indonesia. Typical colours are red, brown, yellow and deep purple. The dyes used are obtained from natural sources, and some of the colours can take years to mix and age. The dyes also weaken the cotton fabric, so old examples of *gringsing* are extremely rare.

Songket

A more elaborate material, for ceremonial and other important uses, *songket* cloth has gold or silver threads woven into the tapestry-like material, and motifs include birds, butterflies, leaves and flowers. *Songket* material is used for *kamben*, *kain* and sarongs worn exclusively for ceremonial occasions.

Prada

Another tnique for producing very decorative fabrics for special occasions, *prada* involves the application of gold leaf, or gold or silver paint or thread to the surface of a finished material. Motifs are similar to those used In *songket*. The result is not washable, so *prada* is reserved for *kain*, which are worn over the top of a sarong, and also used for decorative wraps on offerings and for temple umbrellas.

JEWELLERY

Silversmiths and goldsmiths are traditionally members of the *pande* caste, which also incudes blacksmiths and other metalworkers. Bali is a major producer of fashion jewellery, along with Thailand and Mexico, and produces variations on the same currently fashionable designs.

Very fine filigree work is a Balinese speciality, as is the use of tiny spots of silver to form a pattern or decorative texture – this is considered a very skilled technique, as the heat must be perfectly controlled to weld the delicate wire or silver spots to the underlying silver without damaging it. Balinese work is nearly always handmade, rarely involving casting techniques. Most silver is imported, though some Balinese silver is mined near Singaraja in northern Bali.

KRIS

Often with an ornate, jewel-studded handle and sinister-looking wavy blade, the kris is the traditional and ceremonial dagger of Bali and Indonesia. Although a Balinese-made kris is slightly larger and more elaborate than one from Java, it is almost exactly the same shape. A kris can be the most important of family heirlooms, a symbol of prestige and honour. It is supposed to have great spiritual power, and an important kris is thought to send out magical energy waves, thus requiring great care in its handling and use. Even making a kris requires careful preparation, as does anything on Bali that involves working with the forces of magic.

Getting There & Away

Most international visitors to Bali will arrive by air, either directly or via Jakarta. For island-hoppers, there are frequent ferries between eastern Java and Bali, and between Bali and Lombok, as well as domestic flights between the islands. Lombok is usually visited as a side trip from Bali, by plane, ferry or fast catamaran.

AIR
Although Jakarta, the national capital, is the gateway airport to Indonesia, there are also many direct international flights to Denpasar. If you fly to Jakarta first, take one of the very frequent domestic flights to Denpasar, or travel overland through Java to Bali.

Ngurah Rai Airport
The only airport on Bali, Ngurah Rai is just south of Kuta, although it is referred to internationally as just Denpasar (airline code DPS). The **domestic terminal** (☎ 0361-751011) and **international terminal** (☎ 0361-751011) are a few hundred metres apart.

Arrival procedures at the international airport are fairly painless, although it can take some time for a whole planeload of visitors to clear immigration. At the baggage claim area, porters are keen to help get your luggage to the customs tables and beyond, and they've been known to ask up to US$20 for

their services – if you want help with your bags, agree on a price beforehand. The formal price is a paltry 1500Rp per piece.

Once through customs, you're out with the tour operators, touts and taxi drivers. The touts will be working hard to convince you to come and stay at some place in the Kuta area. Most have contacts at a few places, and if you're not sure where you intend to stay, they may be worth considering, but you'll pay more for accommodation if a tout or a taxi driver takes you there.

See the Getting Around chapter for information on transport to/from the airport.

Money The rates offered at the exchange counters at the international and domestic terminals are competitive, and as good as the moneychangers in Kuta and the tourist centres. Check the rates at a few of them – those further away from the customs area may have better rates. There are several ATMs that take Visa, MasterCard, Cirrus and Alto cards.

Luggage The left-luggage room is in the international terminal, behind a café near the departures area. It's open 24 hours and charges 15,000Rp per piece per day, or part thereof.

Airlines
International Airlines These offices are at the airport, unless stated otherwise. All telephone and fax numbers are in ☎ 0361 area code.

Air New Zealand (☎ 758686, fax 752518)
Jl Bypass Ngurah Rai 12, Denpasar
Cathay Pacific Airways (☎ 766931, fax 766935, w www.cathaypacific.com)
Continental Micronesia (☎ 768358, w www .continental.com)
Japan Airlines (JAL; ☎ 757077, fax 757082, airport ☎ 287577, fax 287460) Jl Raya Kuta 100X, Tuban
Lauda Air (☎ 758686, fax 752518, e mustikad@ laudaair.co.id) Gedung Paj Travel, Jl Bypass Ngurah Rai 12, Kuta
Malaysia Airlines (☎ 764995, fax 764996)
NorthWest Airlines (☎ 287841, fax 287840) Garden Wing Room 1115, Grand Bali Beach Hotel, Sanur

Warning

The information in this chapter is particularly vulnerable to change: Prices for international travel are volatile, routes are introduced and cancelled, schedules change, special deals come and go, and rules and visa requirements are amended. You should check directly with the airline or a travel agent to make sure you understand how a fare (and ticket you may buy) works and be aware of the security requirements for international travel.

The upshot of this is that you should get opinions, quotes and advice from as many airlines and travel agents as possible before you part with your hard-earned cash. The details given in this chapter should be regarded as pointers and are not a substitute for your own careful, up-to-date research.

Qantas Airways (☎ 288331, fax 287331) Grand Bali Beach Hotel, Sanur; open 8.30am to 4.30pm Monday to Friday, 8.30am to 12.30pm Saturday, closed Sunday. There is also an office at the airport, which only opens at flight arrival/departure time.

Singapore Airlines (☎ 768388, fax 768383, [W] www.singaporeair.com.sg)

Thai Airways International (THAI; ☎ 288141, fax 288063, airport ☎ 755063, [e] thaidps@indosat.net.id) Grand Bali Beach Hotel, Sanur; open 8am to 5pm Monday to Friday, 8am to 1pm Saturday; closed Sunday.

Indonesian Airlines Garuda Indonesia is the main carrier.

Bouraq (☎ 241396, fax 241390, airport ☎ 755696, fax 755696) Natour Bali Hotel, Jl Sudirman 7A, Denpasar

Garuda Indonesia (☎ 241688/287915, airport ☎ 751177) Jl Melati 61, Denpasar

Merpati Nusantara Airlines (☎ 235358, fax 242 868, airport ☎/fax 758696; [e] bali@merpati .co.id; [W] www.merpati.co.id) Jl Melati 51, Denpasar; open 8am to 5pm daily

Buying Tickets

With a bit of research – ringing around travel agents, checking Internet sites, perusing the travel ads in newspapers – you can often get yourself a good travel deal. Start early as some of the cheapest tickets need to be bought well in advance and popular flights can sell out.

Full-time students and people under 26 years (under 30 in some countries) have access to better deals than other travellers. You have to show a document proving your date of birth or a valid International Student Identity Card (ISIC) when buying your ticket and boarding the plane.

Generally, there is nothing to be gained by buying a ticket direct from the airline. Discounted tickets are released to selected travel agents and specialist discount agencies, and these are usually the cheapest deals going.

One exception to this rule is the expanding number of 'no-frills' carriers, which mostly sell only direct to travellers. Unlike the 'full-service' airlines, no-frills carriers often make one-way tickets available at around half the return fare, meaning that it is easy to put together an open-jaw ticket when you fly to one place but leave from another.

The other exception would be to book on the Internet. Many airlines, full-service and no-frills, offer some excellent fares to Web surfers. They may sell seats by auction or simply cut prices to reflect the reduced cost of electronic selling.

Many travel agencies around the world have websites, which can make the Internet a quick and easy way to compare prices. There's also an increasing number of on-line agents which operate only on the Internet.

On-line ticket sales work well if you are doing a simple one-way or return trip on specified dates. However, on-line super-fast fare generators are no substitute for a travel agent who knows all about special deals, has many strategies for avoiding layovers and can offer advice on everything from which airline has the best vegetarian food to the best travel insurance to bundle with your ticket.

You may find the cheapest flights are advertised by obscure agencies. Most of these firms are honest and solvent, but there are some rogue fly-by-night outfits around. Paying by credit card generally offers protection, as most card issuers provide refunds if you can prove you didn't get what you paid for. Similar protection can be obtained by buying a ticket from a bonded agent, such as one covered by the Air Travel Organiser's Licence (ATOL) scheme in the UK. Agents who accept only cash should hand over the tickets straight away and not tell you to 'come back tomorrow'.

After you've made a booking or paid your deposit, call the airline and confirm that the booking was made. It's generally not advisable to send money (even cheques) through the post unless the agent is very well established – some travellers have reported being ripped off by fly-by-night mail-order ticket agents.

If you purchase a ticket and later want to make changes to your route or get a refund, you need to contact the original travel agent. Airlines issue refunds only to the purchaser of a ticket – usually the travel agent who bought the ticket on your behalf. Many travellers change their routes halfway through their trips, so think carefully before you buy a ticket which is not easily refunded.

Types of Tickets

For those visiting Bali as part of a longer trip, many discount and regular tickets are valid for 12 months, allowing multiple stopovers with open dates. However, most visitors who are travelling only to Bali, Lombok or other parts of Indonesia will be limited to the 60-day stay allowed by a tourist visa, and will be able to take advantage of many short-term packages and promotional offers. These must usually be booked at least a few weeks in advance, and may prohibit (or charge extra for) changes to the departure or return dates.

Round-the-World Tickets Round-the-world (RTW) tickets that include Bali are usually offered by an alliance of several airlines, and give you a year in which to circumnavigate the globe. Because Bali is a long way from Europe, and almost on the other side of the world from North America, RTW tickets can be a great deal – you might be able to visit several places in Asia, Australia, Europe and North America for about the same cost as a simple return flight to Bali. Denpasar has a variety of connections to the east (Hong Kong, Japan, Australia, New Zealand) and west (Jakarta, Singapore, Kuala Lumpur, Bangkok), so it can fit in well with many RTW itineraries.

Departure Tax
The departure tax for all domestic flights from Bali is 11,000Rp, and 100,000Rp for all international flights. Only children under two years of age are exempt.

Travellers with Specific Needs

If they're warned early enough, airlines can often make special arrangements for travellers such as wheelchair assistance at airports or vegetarian meals on the flight. Children under two years travel for 10% of the standard fare (or free on some airlines) as long as they don't occupy a seat. They don't get a baggage allowance. 'Skycots', baby food and nappies should be provided by the airline if requested in advance. Children aged between two and 12 can usually occupy a seat for around two-thirds of the full fare, and do get a baggage allowance.

The disability-friendly website [W] www .everybody.co.uk has an airline directory that provides information on the facilities offered by various airlines.

The USA
Discount travel agents in the USA are known as consolidators (although you won't see a sign on the door saying 'Consolidator'). San Francisco is the ticket consolidator capital of America, although some good deals can be found in Los Angeles, New York and other big cities.

STA Travel (☎ 800-781-4040; [W] www.sta travel.com) has offices in Boston, Chicago, Miami, New York, Philadelphia, San Francisco and other major cities. Call the toll-free 800 number for office locations.

Bali is a long way from the USA and there are no direct flights. From the US west coast, typical connections are: Singapore Airlines, via Singapore; NorthWest Airlines, via Singapore or Tokyo; United Airlines and Garuda, via Bangkok; JAL, via Tokyo; China Airlines and Garuda, via Taipei; Continental Airlines, via Hawaii and Guam. From the US east coast you could go via Europe: KLM and Garuda, via Amsterdam and Singapore; or Singapore Airlines, via Frankfurt and Singapore.

If you are visiting other parts of Asia, some good deals can be put together. For example, there are cheap tickets between the US west coast and Singapore, with stopovers in Bangkok for a little extra, but bookings can be very heavy during July and August and Chinese New Year.

There are good open tickets that remain valid for six months or one year, but don't lock you into fixed dates. Cheap package deals are also available from as little as US$1400 for seven nights and return air fares from the west coast.

Canada
Canadian discount air ticket sellers are also known as consolidators and their air fares tend to be about 10% higher than those sold in the USA.

Travel CUTS (☎ 800-667-2887; [W] www .travelcuts.com) is Canada's national student travel agency and has offices in all major cities.

From western Canada, go via Asia (Tokyo, Taipei, Hong Kong, Bangkok or Singapore) to Denpasar. From eastern Canada, go via Europe (London, Frankfurt or Amsterdam) and either Singapore, Bangkok or Jakarta to Denpasar. Routes via Europe involve extra connections, but may be cheaper.

Australia

Quite a few travel offices specialise in discount air tickets. Some travel agents, particularly smaller ones, advertise cheap air fares in the travel sections of weekend newspapers.

Two well-known agents for cheap fares are STA Travel and Flight Centre. STA Travel has offices in major cities and on many university campuses. Call **STA Travel** (☎ 1300 733 035; W www.statravel.com.au) for the location of your nearest branch or visit its website. **Flight Centre** (☎ 131600; W www.flightcentre.com.au) has dozens of offices throughout Australia.

You can fly directly from the larger capital cities most days, but from the smaller cities there are only direct flights a few days per week – on other days you must go via one or two of the other cities. **Qantas** (☎ 131313; W www.qantas.com.au) has direct flights from Sydney, Melbourne, Perth and Darwin. **Garuda** (☎ 1300 365 330; W www.garuda -indonesia.com) has direct flights from these cities, plus Adelaide and Brisbane.

At the time of writing **Air Paradise** (W www.airparadise.com.au) was about to commence discounted flights between Bali and several Australian cities.

Fares There are three types of discount fares available between Australia and Bali – Inclusive Tour (IT) fares, only available when purchased as part of a package tour holiday; excursion fares allowing a stay of five to 35 days; and excursion fares with a maximum stay of up to one year.

There are three pricing periods. Roughly speaking, the high season is around Christmas, shoulder season is on and around any school holidays, and the basic season is the rest of the year. Flights to/from Australia are very heavily booked in the high and shoulder seasons, so you must plan well ahead.

Current 35-day Qantas return excursion fares to Denpasar are A$1189/1297/1525 excluding taxes in basic/shoulder/peak season from Sydney, Melbourne, Adelaide, Brisbane and Cairns (these cities are 'common rated'); A$952/1027/1222 from Perth; and A$883/938/1103 from Darwin. A 12-month excursion ticket is about A$100 dearer for all these fares. Garuda's fares are generally A$100 to A$200 cheaper than those of Qantas.

A full-price return economy air fare is about A$3288 from Sydney, Melbourne, Adelaide, Brisbane and Cairns; A$2600 from Perth; and A$2184 from Darwin. Qantas one-way fares are all charged at full price but vary by season. From Sydney, Melbourne, Adelaide, Brisbane and Cairns the fare is A$843/914/1062 excluding taxes in basic/shoulder/peak season; from Perth it's A$682/732/858; and from Darwin it's A$653/696/805.

Package Tours To get the Inclusive Tour (IT) fare, you must purchase the air fare as part of a package that includes some prepaid accommodation, which can mean as little as four nights' accommodation prebooked. IT fares permit a maximum stay of 28 or 35 days, and on some fares you can stay longer than the period for which you have prepaid accommodation. This requires a fee, so you can get the lower fare, a few cheap nights in a resort hotel and still be able to do some independent travelling staying at cheaper places. Make sure you check with the airline or travel agent about this option. You can often get a package tour, including accommodation, for less than a 35-day excursion fare. The flights each way are on fixed dates, and there are penalties if you want to change.

For example, package tours from the east coast of Australia, including return air fares, airport transfers and four nights' accommodation, are advertised from as low as A$1130 per person twin share in the low season. Children between two and 11 are usually charged 67% to 75% of the adult air fare, and their accommodation is charged as an addition to the adult price, although sometimes one or two kids are included in a family package fare. If you travel as a single, you will usually have to pay a 'single supplement', which offsets much of the potential savings.

The price of a package varies depending on when you go, how long you stay, and what class of hotel you stay in. Most package tour hotels are in the Kuta area, Sanur and Nusa Dua, but an increasing number of packages offer accommodation in Ubud, Candidasa, Lovina, Nusa Lembongan and other coastal areas. Costs vary from one operator to another, even on packages using the same hotels.

New Zealand

Flight Centre (☎ 0800 243 544; w www .flightcentre.co.nz) has an office in Auckland and many branches throughout the country. **STA Travel** (☎ 0800 874 773; w www.sta travel.com.nz) has offices in Auckland as well as in Hamilton, Palmerston North, Wellington, Christchurch and Dunedin.

Garuda, Qantas and Air New Zealand regularly fly between Auckland or Wellington and Denpasar, via Melbourne, Brisbane or Sydney. Christmas is the high season, school holidays are shoulder season, and other times are low season (some fares only have two seasons, with all school holidays and Christmas as high season).

As an example, the Garuda six-month return fare from Auckland to Denpasar, via Brisbane, is about NZ$1549/1349 in high/ low season. The other airlines are a little more expensive. Malaysia Airlines does similar fares with a Kuala Lumpur stopover. Fares for Wellington and Christchurch are the same as for Auckland. Ask your travel agent about holiday package tours – from as little as NZ$1149 for six nights and return air fares.

The UK & Ireland

Discount air travel is big business in London. Advertisements for many travel agencies appear in the travel pages of the weekend broadsheet newspapers, in *Time Out*, the *Evening Standard* and in the free magazine *TNT*. Discount return fares to Bali are around UK£700 in the high season, and around UK£450 in the low season.

Though London is the travel-discount capital of Europe, there are several other cities where you will find a range of good deals. Generally there is not much variation in air fare prices from the main European cities. The major airlines and travel agents generally have a number of deals on offer, so shop around.

For students or travellers under 26 years of age, a popular travel agent in the UK is **STA Travel** (☎ 0870 160 0599; w www.statravel .co.uk), which has branches across the country. STA sells tickets to all travellers but caters especially to young people and students.

Other recommended travel agents include: **Trailfinders** (☎ 020-7938 3939; w www.trail finders.co.uk), with offices throughout the UK and Ireland; **Bridge the World** (☎ 0870 444 7474; w www.bridgetheworld.com); and

Flightbookers (☎ 020-7757 2444; w www .flightbookers.co.uk).

From the UK regional airports or Ireland, you have to get a connection through London, or possibly through Amsterdam, or Paris, then via Singapore or Bangkok.

There are no direct flights from the UK to Bali. The most convenient connections from London are with Singapore Airlines or Qantas via Singapore; with Garuda via Jakarta; with Malaysia Airlines via Kuala Lumpur; with THAI via Bangkok; and with KLM via Amsterdam and Singapore. Another option is to fly from London to Singapore on any cheap ticket, and make your own way to Bali by sea and land. If you're going on to Australia, it's best to get a through ticket with a stopover in Indonesia. Bali and other Indonesian cities can also be included in RTW fares.

Continental Europe

Fares from European cities are often higher than from London; it may be cheaper to get to the UK and travel from there. Most European airlines will get you to either Singapore, Kuala Lumpur, Bangkok or Jakarta, and you'll need a connection with Singapore Airlines, Malaysia Airlines, THAI or Garuda to Denpasar – this isn't an expensive add-on, and there are frequent connections. Lauda Air has about the only direct flight from Europe – one weekly from Vienna to Denpasar via Bangkok for US$848/1074 one way/return.

From Europe, the high season is July, August, and the Christmas/New Year period.

France France has a network of student travel agents that supply discount tickets to travellers of all ages. **OTU Voyages** (☎ 0820 817 817; w www.otu.fr) has 42 offices around the country.

General travel agents in Paris that offer some of the best services and deals include **Nouvelles Frontières** (☎ 08 825 000 825; w www.nouvelles-frontieres.fr; 13 Ave de l'Opéra, 1er), and **Voyageurs du Monde** (☎ 01 42 86 16 40; w www.vdm.com; 55 rue Sainte Anne, 2e).

Germany One possibility for a discount fare from Germany is **STA Travel** (☎ 01805- 456 422; w www.statravel.de; Hardenberg- strasse 9, 10623 Berlin), which has offices throughout the country.

Lufthansa flies from Frankfurt to Jakarta every day, with connections to Bali on Garuda. Direct flights leave every day in the high season but four days a week at other times. Daily services stop in Singapore throughout the year. Garuda also flies from Frankfurt to Denpasar with frequencies varying with the season.

Netherlands KLM flies regularly from Amsterdam to Jakarta, sometimes via Singapore or Kuala Lumpur. Garuda also flies Amsterdam–Singapore–Jakarta, and Amsterdam–Singapore–Denpasar. **NBBS Reizen** (☎ 0900-10 20 300; Linnaeusstraat 28) is the official student travel agency. You can find it in Amsterdam, and there are several other agencies around the city and throughout the Netherlands.

Italy In Italy, **CTS Viaggi** (☎ 840 501 150; W www.cts.it) is a student and youth specialist with branches in major cities.

Spain In Spain, a recommended agency is **Barcelo Viajes** (☎ 902 116 226; W www .barcelo-viajes.es), which has branches in all the major cities.

Asia

Most Asian countries offer fairly competitive air fare deals; Bangkok, Singapore and Hong Kong are the best places to shop around for discount tickets. Hong Kong's travel market can be unpredictable, but some excellent bargains are available if you are lucky.

Khao San Road in Bangkok is the budget travellers headquarters. Bangkok has a number of excellent travel agents, but there are also some suspect ones; you should ask the advice of other travellers before handing over your cash. **STA Travel** (☎ 02-236 0262; 33 Surawong Rd) is a good and reliable place to start.

In Singapore, **STA Travel** (☎ 65-737 7188; W www.statravel.com.sg; 35a Cuppage Rd, Cuppage Terrace) offers competitive discount fares for Asian destinations and beyond. Singapore, like Bangkok, has hundreds of travel agents, so you can compare prices on flights. Chinatown Point shopping centre on New Bridge Road has a good selection of travel agents.

Hong Kong has a number of really excellent, reliable travel agencies and some

not-so-reliable ones. A good way to check up on a travel agent is to look it up in the phone book. Fly-by-night operators don't usually stay around long enough to get listed. **Phoenix Services** (☎ 2722 7378, fax 2369 8884; Room B, 6th floor, Milton Mansion, 96 Nathan Rd, Tsimshatsui) is recommended. Other agencies to try include **Shoestring Travel** (☎ 2723 2306; Flat A, 4th floor, Alpha House, 27-33 Nathan Rd, Tsimshatsui) and **Traveller Services** (☎ 2375 2222; Room 1012, Silvercord Tower 1, 30 Canton Rd, Tsimshatsui).

The following are standard one-way fares to Denpasar from other Asian cities. A standard return excursion fare may be 50% more than the one-way fare, but big discounts are possible if you shop around.

East Timor Merpati flies daily to Dili

Hong Kong Cathay Pacific and Garuda have frequent flights for around US$431 one way

Japan JAL flies every day from Tokyo and Garuda flies from Tokyo, Nagoya and Osaka, for around US$1151 one way

Malaysia Malaysia Airlines and Garuda fly from Kuala Lumpur daily for around US$296 one way

Singapore Look around for very cheap one-way Singapore–Jakarta flights; from Jakarta you can then continue overland or by domestic flight to Bali. Garuda flies from Singapore for around US$296 one way. Qantas flies three times weekly from Singapore for US$239 return.

Thailand THAI flies daily from Bangkok for US$335 return

Other Indonesian Islands

Bali is well-connected to almost all of the Indonesian archipelago. The main carrier is Merpati and Garuda flies daily to Jakarta. Bouraq also has regular flights to Surabaya and Jakarta (Java); Banjarmasin (Kalimantan); and Makasar, Manado and Palu (Sulawesi). Return fares are usually work out at twice the one-way fare, and are about the same for all airlines. The following are one-way fares.

Java Jakarta (805,700Rp), Surabaya (329,000Rp) and Yogyakarta (429,700Rp)

Nusa Tenggara Bima (572,000Rp, sometimes via Mataram), Maumere (650,000Rp) and Kupang (728,000Rp)

Sulawesi Makasar (formerly Ujung Pandang; 559,000Rp) and Manado (1,205,500Rp)

SEA
Java
When visiting Java from Bali and Lombok, some land travel is necessary.

Ferry Frequent ferries cross the Bali Strait between Gilimanuk in western Bali and Ketapang (Java) every 15 to 30 minutes, 24 hours per day. The actual crossing takes under 30 minutes, but you'll spend longer than this loading, unloading and waiting around. The fare is 2000/1300Rp per adult/child. Fares for bicycles are 3000Rp, motorcycles 5000Rp, and cars or jeeps 25,000Rp. Car rental contracts usually prohibit rental vehicles being taken out of Bali, but it may be possible to take a rented motorcycle across, by arrangement with the owner.

From Ketapang, *bemos* (small pick-up truck) travel 4km north to the terminal, where buses leave for Baluran, Probolingo (for Gunung Bromo), Surabaya, Yogyakarta and Jakarta. There's a train station near the ferry port, with trains to Probolingo, Surabaya and Yogyakarta. The larger town of Banyuwangi is 8km south, and has another bus terminal with transport to destinations in southeastern Java.

Public Bus The ferry crossing is included in the services to/from Ubung terminal in Denpasar offered by numerous bus companies. Many of them travel overnight, and they can arrive at an uncomfortably early hour in the morning. If you just turn up at Ubung terminal, you will probably get on a bus within an hour or so, but it's advisable to buy your ticket at least one day in advance, at travel agents in all the tourist centres, or directly from the Ubung terminal.

Fares vary between operators, and depend on what sort of comfort you want – it's worth paying extra for a decent seat and air-conditioning. For a comfortable bus ride, typical fares and travel times are Surabaya (59,500Rp, 10 to 12 hours), Yogyakarta (111,500Rp, 15 to 16 hours) and Jakarta (185,000Rp, 26 to 30 hours). Some companies travel directly between Java and Singaraja, via Lovina, on the north coast of Bali. Prices are similar to those from Denpasar, and travel times are slightly shorter (see Lovina in the North Bali chapter for more information).

Tourist Shuttle Bus Tourist shuttle companies such as Perama offer services between Bali and Java – usually this is a shuttle bus service to Ubung terminal in Denpasar, and then a 'tourist' bus travelling the rest of the way to Java. Daily services run from Kuta, Sanur or Ubud to Surabaya (60,000Rp), Yogyakarta (110,000Rp) and Jakarta (170,500Rp).

Bus & Train There are no trains on Bali, but you can purchase a ticket from Denpasar to Banyuwangi (Java) by bus and ferry, which connects with daily eastbound trains on the Java rail system, heading to Probolingo (78,000/58,000Rp executive/business class), Surabaya (78,000/58,000Rp executive/business class), Yogyakarta (60,000Rp) and Jakarta (328,500Rp for executive class). Contact the **Train Information Service** (☎ 0361-227131) for more information.

Other Indonesian Islands
For information on getting to Lombok by boat, see the Boat section in the Getting Around chapter.

Four ships from the national shipping line, Pelni, stop at Benoa harbour (Bali) as part of their regular loops throughout Indonesia. *Tatamailau* links Bali with Nusa Tenggara, Maluku and southern Papua; *Dobonsolo* with Java, Nusa Tenggara, Maluku and northern Papua; and *Awu* and *Tilongkabila* with Nusa Tenggara and southern Sulawesi. Prices are dependent on the route and the class of travel, and this can range from extremely cheap to quite expensive. The main **Pelni office** (☎ 0361-723483; ⃰ www.pelni.co.id; open 9am-3pm Mon-Fri, 9am-noon Sat) is located at Benoa harbour, and there is also another office in Tuban (☎ 0361-720962, fax 763763; 299 Jl Raya Tuban) and an agent in Denpasar (☎ 0361-234680; Jl Diponegoro 165; open 8am-4pm Mon-Sat).

ORGANISED TOURS
The numerous package tours to Bali can offer great value for a short holiday. You can sign up for sightseeing tours as part of the package, but it's easy and less expensive to arrange tours in Bali. For specific activities such as diving, surfing or cycling, specialist tours are available (see the Facts for the Visitor chapter).

There are a few options for tours from Bali to other destinations within Indonesia.

Java

Several companies offer organised tours from Bali to Java, with Gunung Bromo and Borobodur temple near Yogyakarta as the main attractions. **Semara Tours** *(☎/fax 0361-975576;* e *semara@indo.net.id; Jl Hanoman 27A, Ubud)* runs overnight Borobodur tours for US$230, including Yogyakarta air fare.

Nusa Tenggara

Cheap boat trips to Sumbawa, Komodo and Flores are also available but are not recommended. For a more upmarket and reputable Komodo experience, contact **Grand Komodo Tours and Travel** *(☎ 0361-287166, fax 287165; Jl Hang Tuah 26, Sanur).*

Other Indonesian Islands

Nominasi Chandra Wisata *(☎ 0361-975067, fax 977500;* e *nominasi@indosat.net.id; open 9am-10pm Mon-Sat, 10am-2pm Sun)*, based in Ubud, offers a range of tours throughout Indonesia.

Sea Trek (Anasia Cruises) *(☎ 0361-283192;* w *www.anasia-cruise.com; Jl Danau Tamblingan 77, Sanur)* is a reputable set-up that offers a wide range of luxury cruises throughout the eastern islands at an average cost of US$185 per day.

Getting Around

The main forms of public transport on Bali are the cheap buses, minibuses and *bemos* (small pick-up trucks) that run on more or less set routes within or between towns. If you want your own transport, you can charter a bemo or rent a car, motorcycle or bicycle. Tourist shuttle buses, running between the major tourist centres, are more expensive than public transport, but are more comfortable and convenient.

AIR
Ngurah Rai airport, Bali's only airport, is just south of Kuta, although it is known as Denpasar airport. The **domestic terminal** (☎ 0361-751011) is just a few hundred metres from the international terminal. Most travellers use land transport around Bali, but flying to Lombok is an option.

Lombok
Merpati and Garuda have several flights daily between Denpasar and Mataram on Lombok (225,500Rp, including local taxes, 25 minutes). The flight is cheaper than the fast catamaran boat services.

BUS
Larger minibuses and full-size buses ply the longer routes, particularly between Denpasar and Singaraja, and on to Gilimanuk along the northern coastal route. They operate out of the same terminals as the bemos. Buses are faster than bemos because they do not make as many stops along the way. A bus is also often slightly cheaper than a bemo if you take it for the full trip (eg, Singaraja to Denpasar), but it is more expensive if you want to get off halfway, as only a set fare is available.

TOURIST SHUTTLE BUS
Tourist shuttle buses travel between the main tourist centres on Bali and connect to destinations on Lombok. Shuttle buses are quicker, more comfortable and more convenient than public transport, and though considerably more expensive, they are very popular with budget, and increasingly midrange, travellers. If you're with a group of three or more people (or sometimes even two), it will probably be cheaper to charter a vehicle, however.

Several shuttle bus companies operate out of Kuta-Legian, and other smaller outfits in other tourist areas provide more limited services. For example, in Ubud dozens of travel agents advertise transport to most tourist destinations at competitive prices. The most established company with the widest network is **Perama**, with its **head office** (☎ 0361-751551, fax 751170; Jl Legian 39) based in Kuta. It also has offices (or agents) at all of its destinations; office hours are 7am to 10pm. Taking one trip with Perama entitles you to join the Perama Travel Club and get a 5% discount on any future ticket purchase. You may be charged extra for a surfboard, bicycle or other bulky item.

Always try to book a ticket at least one day before you want to leave, at any of the hundreds of travel agents in the tourist centres. Fares are set by the companies, and are not negotiable. Fares do vary a little between companies, but the main reason to shop around is to find the travel times that suit you best.

Shuttle buses will normally pick you up outside the travel agent where you booked, or at some other predetermined spot. Perama will do a hotel pick-up for an extra 5000Rp. In some places (notably Ubud and Lovina) the Perama shuttle bus arrival points are not convenient to the centre of town or to any hotels (although drop-off can be arranged for another 5000Rp). Check this when you book – some companies may have a better-located terminal, while others may take you right to your hotel.

Note that shuttle buses often do not provide a direct service – those from Kuta to Candidasa will stop en route at Sanur, Ubud and Padangbai, and maybe other towns on request.

BEMO
The main form of public transport on Bali is the bemo. A generic term for any vehicle used as public transport, it's normally a minibus or van with a row of low seats down each side. The word 'bemo' is a contraction of *becak* (bicycle rickshaw) and *mobil* (car), but bemos no longer resemble a motorised rickshaw. Apart from the driver, the bemo sometimes has a young guy (let's call him a

bemo jockey) who touts for passengers, handles the luggage, collects the fare and makes sure the stereo is working (loudly). However, jockeys are being phased out in the more populated areas of Bali.

See the Dangers & Annoyances section in the Facts for the Visitor chapter for information on pickpocketing on public bemos.

Fares

Fares for public bemos are fixed by the government, but they are subject to change (especially with the rise and fall of petrol prices), and visitors from overseas and even from other parts of Indonesia are often charged higher prices. The official prices are sometimes displayed at offices at the major terminals, but the notice can be out of date. If you're overcharged a little, don't overreact.

Bemos operate on a standard route for a set (but unwritten) fare. Unless you get on at a regular starting point, and get off at a regular finishing point, the fares are likely to be fuzzy. The cost per kilometre is pretty variable, but is cheaper on longer trips. The minimum fare is about 1000Rp. The fares listed in this book were correct at the time of writing, but are likely to increase by the time you clamber onto the bemo, and a higher 'tourist price' (harga turis) is well established on some routes.

If you've just arrived at Ngurah Rai airport, are on a tight budget and can't afford a taxi, walk across the airport car park northeast to Jl Raya Tuban, which is on the route for the S1 bemos which loop back to Kuta (about 2000Rp) and continue to Denpasar. The bemos are infrequent after 4pm and don't run at all late at night.

Bemos are justly famous for overcharging tourists, and finding out the 'correct' fare (harga biasa) requires local knowledge and subtlety. The best procedure is to hand over the correct fare as you get off, as the locals do, no questions asked. To find out the correct fare, consult a trusted local before you get on – if you're staying at a cheap losmen (basic accommodation), the owner will usually be helpful (at an expensive hotel they'll discourage you from using bemos and offer to charter transport for you). Note what other passengers pay when they get off, bearing in mind that school children and the driver's friends pay less. If you speak Bahasa Indonesia, you can ask your fellow passengers, but in a dispute they will probably support the bemo jockey.

The whole business of overcharging tourists is a bit of a game; bemo drivers and jockeys are usually good-humoured about it, but some tourists take it very seriously and have unpleasant arguments over a few hundred rupiah. Sometimes you will be charged extra (perhaps double the passenger price) if you have a big bag.

Make sure you know where you're going, and accept that the bemo normally won't leave until it's full and will usually take a roundabout route to collect and deliver as many passengers as possible. One way to hurry up a departure, and make yourself instantly popular with other frustrated passengers, is to fork out a few extra thousand rupiah and pay for the one or more fares that you seem to be waiting all day for. If you get into an empty bemo, always make it clear that you do not want to charter it. (The word 'charter' is understood by all drivers.)

Terminals & Routes

Every town has at least one terminal (terminal bis) for all forms of public transport. There are often several terminals in larger towns, according to the direction the bus or bemo is heading. For example, Denpasar, the hub of Bali's transport system has four main bus/bemo terminals and three minor ones. Terminals can be confusing, but most bemos and buses have signs and, if in doubt, you will be told where to go by a bemo jockey or driver anyway.

To go from one part of Bali to another, it is often necessary to go via one or more of the terminals in Denpasar, or via a terminal in one of the other larger regional towns. For example, to get from Sanur to Ubud by public bemo, you go to the Kereneng terminal in Denpasar, transfer to the Batubulan terminal, and then take a third bemo to Ubud. This is circuitous and time consuming, so many visitors prefer the tourist shuttle buses.

CAR & MOTORCYCLE
Road Rules & Risks

Visiting drivers commonly complain about crazy Balinese drivers, but often it's because the visitors don't understand the local conventions of road use. The following rules are very useful.

Road Distances (km)

	Amed	Bangli	Bedugul	Candidasa	Denpasar	Gilimanuk	Kintamani	Kuta	Lovina	Negara	Nusa Dua	Padangbai	Sanur	Semarapura	Singaraja	Tirtagangga	Ubud
Amed	---																
Bangli	59	---															
Bedugul	144	97	---														
Candidasa	32	52	88	---													
Denpasar	98	47	78	72	---												
Gilimanuk	238	181	148	206	134	---											
Kintamani	108	20	89	71	67	135	---										
Kuta	114	57	57	82	10	219	77	---									
Lovina	89	86	41	139	89	79	70	99	---								
Negara	202	135	115	167	95	33	163	104	107	---							
Nusa Dua	122	81	102	96	24	158	91	14	113	109	---						
Padangbai	45	39	75	13	59	219	58	69	126	154	83	---					
Sanur	105	40	85	79	7	141	78	15	96	102	22	78	---				
Semarapura	37	26	61	27	47	181	46	57	112	124	71	14	52	---			
Singaraja	78	75	30	128	78	90	59	88	11	118	92	115	85	105	---		
Tirtagangga	14	65	101	13	84	212	85	95	112	179	108	26	91	44	142	---	
Ubud	68	29	35	54	23	157	29	33	40	120	47	41	30	29	95	67	---

- The main thing to remember is the 'watch your front' rule – it's your responsibility to avoid anything that gets in front of your vehicle. A car, motorcycle or anything else pulling out in front of you, in effect, has the right of way. Often drivers won't even look to see what's coming when they turn left at a junction – they listen for the horn.
- The second rule is: use your horn to warn anything in front that you're there, especially if you're about to overtake.
- The third rule is: drive on the left side of the road, although it's often a case of driving on whatever side of the road is available, after avoiding the road works, livestock and other vehicles.

Avoid driving at night or at dusk. Many bicycles, carts and horse-drawn vehicles do not have proper lights, and street lighting is limited. Motorcycling at dusk offers the unique sensation of numerous insects, large and small, hitting your face at 60 km/hour – at least you won't fall asleep!

Roads

Once you've cleared the southern Bali traffic tangle, the roads are relatively uncrowded. The traffic can be horrendous around Kuta, Denpasar and from Batubulan to Ubud, and is usually quite heavy as far as Padangbai to the east and Tabanan to the west. Finding your way around the main tourist sites is not difficult: roads are well signposted and maps are easy to find. Off the main routes, roads are often very potholed, but they are usually surfaced – there are few dirt roads on Bali. Driving is most difficult in the large towns, where streets are congested, traffic can be terrifying, and one-way streets are infuriating.

Police

Police will stop drivers on some very slender pretexts, and it's fair to say that they're not motivated by a desire to enhance road safety. If a cop sees your front wheel half an inch over the faded line at a stop sign, if the chin strap of your helmet isn't fastened, or if you don't observe one of the ever-changing and poorly signposted one-way traffic restrictions, you may be waved down. They also do spot checks of licences and vehicle registrations, especially before major holiday periods.

The cop will ask to see your licence and the vehicle's registration papers, and he will also tell you what a serious offence you've committed. He may start talking about court appearances, heavy fines and long delays. Stay cool and don't argue. Don't offer him a bribe. Eventually he'll suggest that you can pay him some amount of money to deal with the matter. If it's a very large amount, tell him politely that you don't have that much. These matters can be settled for something between 40,000Rp and 60,000Rp; although it will be more like 100,000Rp if you don't have an IDP or if you argue. Always make sure you have the correct papers, and don't have too much visible cash in your wallet.

Car Rental

By far the most popular rental vehicle is the small Suzuki Katana or Jimny – they're compact, have good ground clearance and the low gear ratio is well suited to exploring Bali's back roads, although the bench seats at the back are uncomfortable on a long trip. The main alternative is the larger Toyota Kijang, which seats six but is still economical and lightweight. Automatic transmission is uncommon in rental cars.

Big international rental operators have a token presence and are worth investigating if you're not travelling on a budget – vehicle quality and safety is likely to be of a much higher standard than most vehicles available from smaller operators. Typical rates for a Toyota Kijang are 450,000/2,700,000Rp per day/week and for a Toyota Soluna 430,000/2,580,000Rp.

Rental outlets include large companies such as **Avis Rent a Car** (☎/fax 0361-701770; ⓦ www.avis.com; Jl Raya Uluwatu 8A, Jimbaran) and **Thrifty** (☎ 0361-701621, fax 701628; Jl Bypass Nusa Dua 4, Jimbaran).

Rental and travel agencies at all tourist centres advertise cars for rent. A Suzuki Jimny jeep costs about 80,000Rp per day, with unlimited kilometres and very limited insurance – maybe less per day for longer rentals. A Toyota Kijang costs from around 120,000Rp per day. These costs will vary considerably according to demand, the condition of the vehicle, length of hire and your bargaining talents.

There's no reason to book rental cars in advance over the Internet or with a tour package, and it will almost certainly cost more than arranging it locally. Shop around for a good deal, and check the car carefully

Accidents

If you are involved in an accident, unfortunately it will be considered your fault. The logic behind this is Asian and impeccable: 'I was involved in an accident with you. I belong here, you don't. If you hadn't been here, there would not have been an accident. Therefore it is your fault.'

It is not unusual for a foreign driver to be roughed up by aggrieved locals after an accident, or for them to demand immediate promises of compensation. In these circumstances it is essential to keep a cool head and avoid being pressured into an admission or commitment.

If you are involved in a serious accident (such as one involving death or injury), insist that the police come as soon as possible and have someone you trust contact your consulate. If you concede liability, it could invalidate both your travel insurance policy and the policy you took out when you rented the vehicle. If your vehicle is still going, it may be advisable to drive it straight to the nearest police station, rather than stopping at the scene and risking a violent confrontation. The police are unlikely to take your side, but at least they will ensure that formalities are complied with and excessive reactions are moderated. It is likely that they will impound your vehicle, and they may even detain you in jail until the matter is sorted out. You will be safe there, and any settlement should be official enough to satisfy your insurance company.

With evidence of insurance, your consulate can usually persuade the police that the insurance company will provide restitution, the driver can be released from jail and the details can be sorted out later with the insurance company. Without insurance, there will probably have to be some agreement and payment before they let you go.

If it's a minor accident (property damage only), it may be better to negotiate a settlement directly, rather than spend days hassling with police, lawyers, insurance companies and so on. Try to delay matters a little, so you can recover from the shock, get someone with local knowledge that you trust to advise you, and perhaps contact your consulate and/or a lawyer.

before you sign up – it's unusual to find a car that has everything working. Don't wait until you really need the horn, wipers, lights, spare tyre or registration papers before you find that they're not there. Rental cars usually have to be returned to the place from where they are rented – you can't do a one-way rental, but some operators will let you leave a car at the airport.

You must have an International Driving Permit (IDP) – get this from a motoring organisation in your home country. The rental company will probably insist, and driving without a licence could incur a 2,000,000Rp fine plus a *lot* of bureaucratic hassles.

Costs & Benefits Bali has about the cheapest rental cars and the cheapest petrol in the world, but consider the drawbacks before you launch yourself into Bali's frenetic traffic. Remember that driving on Bali can be stressful. It's potentially very hazardous, and the consequences of an accident can be serious. And do consider the effect on the environment – do the roads of Bali really need another vehicle? Hiring a vehicle is only really useful if you really want to get off the beaten track, in areas like western Bali.

If you want to see a lot of Bali, stopping for a day or so in a number of places, then you'd be better off on tourist shuttle buses (for convenience) or public bemos and buses (for value and lots of local contact). If you have a few people travelling together who want to do some day trips with the convenience of a car but without the risks, consider chartering a vehicle with a driver.

Taking Rental Cars off Bali Few, if any, agencies on Bali will allow you to take their rental cars to Lombok or Java – the regulations were tightened in 1998, and the regular vehicle insurance is not valid outside Bali.

Motorcycle Rental

Motorcycles are a popular way of getting around Bali, especially with Balinese, who ride pillion on a *sepeda motor* almost from birth. Motorcycling is just as convenient and flexible as driving, the environmental impact and the cost are much less, but it's potentially even more dangerous. Every year a number of visitors go home in a wheelchair, or in a box – Bali is no place to learn to ride a motorcycle.

Finding a Motorcycle Motorcycles for rent on Bali are almost all between 90cc and 200cc, with 100cc the usual size. You really don't need anything bigger, as the distances are short and the roads are rarely suitable for travelling fast.

Rental charges vary with the motorcycle and the period of rental – bigger, newer motorcycles cost more, while longer rental periods attract lower rates. A newish 125cc Honda Astrea in good condition might cost 30,000Rp a day, but for a week or more you might get the same cycle for as little as 25,000Rp per day. This should include minimal insurance for the motorcycle (probably with a US$100 excess), but not for any other person or property.

Individual owners rent out the majority of motorcycles. A few places around Kuta-Legian seem to specialise in motorcycle rental, but generally it's travel agencies, restaurants, losmen or shops with a sign advertising 'motorcycle for rent'. Kuta-Legian is the easiest and cheapest place to rent a motorcycle, but you'll have no trouble finding one in Ubud, Sanur, Candidasa or Lovina. Check the motorcycle over before riding off – some are in very bad condition.

Motorcycle Licence If you have an IDP endorsed for motorcycles you will have no problems. If not, you should obtain a local licence, which is valid for one month on Bali only. It's not worth getting a motorcycle licence for a day or two – rent or charter a car or minibus instead.

The person renting the bike may not check your licence or IDP, and the cop who stops you may be happy with a nonendorsed IDP or bribe. You might get away without a motorcycle endorsement, but you *must* have an IDP. Officially there's a 2,000,000Rp fine for riding without a proper licence, and the motorcycle can be impounded – unofficially, the cop may expect a substantial 'on-the-spot' payment. And if you have an accident without a proper licence, your insurance company might well disown you.

To get a local motorcycle licence, go independently (or have the rental agency/owner take you) to the Denpasar Police Office for a Temporary Permit, which is valid for 30 days, and will cost 100,000Rp. Take along your passport, three passport photos and your IDP. Remember to dress properly.

Other Essentials You must carry the motorcycle's registration papers with you while riding. Make sure the agency/owner gives them to you before you ride off.

Helmets are compulsory and this requirement is enforced in tourist areas, but less so in the countryside. You can even be stopped for not having the chin-strap fastened – a favourite of policemen on the lookout for some extra cash. The standard helmets you get with rental bikes are pretty lightweight. If you value your skull, bring a solid helmet from home (but don't leave it lying around because it'll get pinched).

Despite the tropical climate, it's still wise to dress properly for motorcycling. Thongs, shorts and a T-shirt are not going to protect your skin from being ground off as you slide along the pavement. As well as protection against a spill, be prepared for the weather. It can get pretty cold on a cloudy day in the mountains. Coming over the top of Gunung Batur you might wish you were wearing gloves. And when it rains on Bali, it really rains, so be ready for that as well. A poncho is handy, but it's best to get off the road and sit out the storm. Your hands, arms and face can get sunburned quickly when riding, so cover up and use sunblock.

Insurance

Rental agencies and owners usually insist that the vehicle itself is insured, and minimal insurance should be included in the basic rental deal – often with an excess of as much as US$100 for a motorcycle and US$500 for a car (ie, the customer pays the first US$100/500 of any claim). The more formal motorcycle and car rental agencies may offer additional insurance to reduce the level of the excess, and cover damage to other people or their property, ie, 'third-party' or 'liability' cover. A private owner renting a motorcycle may not offer any insurance at all. Full insurance for rental cars is very expensive for the first few days, but for a week or more it doesn't add much to the total cost.

Especially with cars, the owner's main concern is insuring the vehicle. In some cases, a policy might cover the car for 30 million Rp, but provide for only 10 million Rp third-party cover. Your travel insurance may provide some additional protection, although liability for motor accidents is specifically excluded from many policies. The third-party cover might seem inadequate, but if you do cause damage or injury, it's usually enough for your consulate to get you out of jail (see the boxed text 'Accidents' earlier in this section).

Ensure that your personal travel insurance covers injuries incurred while driving or motorcycling. Some policies specifically exclude coverage for motorcycle riding, or have special conditions.

Fuel

Petrol *(bensin)* is sold by the government-owned Pertamina company, and currently costs around 1750Rp per litre. Bali now has numerous petrol stations, but they are sometimes out of petrol. In that case, look for the little roadside fuel shops that fill your tank from a plastic container with a funnel for a similar price per litre. Petrol pumps usually have a meter, which records the litres and a table that shows how much to pay for various amounts, but cheating does occur. Make sure to check that the pump is reset to zero before the attendant starts to put petrol in your vehicle, and check the total amount that goes in before the pump is reset for the next customer. Ensure the amount you are charged is consistent with the capacity of your tank and that the arithmetic is accurate.

CHARTERING A VEHICLE & DRIVER

An excellent way for a group or family to travel anywhere around Bali is by chartered vehicle. For example, as an alternative to the Sanur–Ubud bemo trip described earlier, you can, with some negotiating, charter a bemo directly to Ubud from Sanur for around 100,000Rp. The advantages of chartering a bemo (as opposed to renting a vehicle) are that you don't have to worry about a licence or insurance; the driver can be a real asset, particularly if he speaks some English; and you don't have to worry about the horrific traffic.

It's easy to arrange a charter: just listen for one of the frequent offers of 'transport?' in the streets around the tourist centres; approach a driver yourself; or ask at your hotel. Chartering a vehicle costs about 100,000Rp to 170,000Rp – although this depends greatly on the distance and, more importantly, your negotiating skills. If you are planning to start early, finish late and cover an awful lot of territory, then you will have to pay more. Sometimes you will be given a lower rate if you agree to pay for petrol, but this can be difficult to arrange on a fair basis, so it's better to negotiate a fixed price. Although a driver may reasonably ask for an advance for petrol, never pay the full fare until you have returned. For day trips, you will be expected to buy meals for the driver (*nasi campur* and water is the standard), particularly if you stop to eat yourself. Tipping for a job well done is also expected.

Drivers that hang around obvious tourist spots and upmarket hotels will tend to overcharge and are rarely interested in negotiating. Beware of tactics like claiming you must hire the vehicle for a minimum of five hours, or assertions that your destination is 'very far' or that 'the roads are very rough'. Agree clearly on a route beforehand.

TAXI

Metered taxis are common in Denpasar and the tourist areas of southern Bali. They're often a lot less hassle than haggling with bemo jockeys and charter drivers. It's best to order a taxi by phone, especially at night. The most reputable taxi agency is **Bali Taxi** (☎ 0361-701111), which uses distinctive blue vehicles. Drivers often speak reasonable English and won't argue about putting on the meter. Other taxis are **Praja Taxi** (☎ 0361-289090), or **Ngurah Rai Airport Taxi** (☎ 0361-724724). You'll hear them beep their horns at you if you walk anywhere around a tourist centre.

The usual rate for a taxi is 4000Rp flag fall and 1500Rp per kilometre, but the rate is higher in the evening, and much higher later at night, when drivers will often refuse to use the meter. During the day, you should always insist on using the meter – if the driver tells you it isn't working, then get another taxi.

The total is usually rounded to the nearest 1000Rp, and if you're happy with the service a 10% tip is not uncommon.

To/From the Airport

From the official counters, just outside the international and domestic terminals, the cost of prepaid airport taxis costs the following.

destination	fare (Rp)
Candidasa	150,000
Denpasar	27,500
Denpasar (Ubung terminal)	37,500
Kuta Beach	15,000
Kuta Beach (over 5km)	20,000
Legian	22,500
Nusa Dua	35,000
Sanur	35,000
Seminyak	22,500
Tanjung Benoa	37,000
Ubud	90,000

You can only share a prepaid airport taxi if all passengers are going to the same place; they won't allow passengers to be dropped off along the way.

If you walk across the airport car park, northeast to Jl Raya Tuban, taxis may stop and take you to your destination for the metered rate, which might be cheaper than a prepaid airport taxi.

Using a metered taxi *to* the airport should cost less than the prepaid taxi rates.

OJEK

Around some major towns, and along roads where bemos rarely or never venture, transport may be provided by an *ojek* (a motorcycle that takes a paying pillion passenger). However, with increased vehicle ownership in Bali, *ojek* are becoming increasingly less common. *Ojek* riders hang around certain spots in towns, and are often identified by yellow helmets; in rural areas you'll see bunches of them at road junctions. *Ojek* are usually limited to one adult passenger. They're OK on quiet country roads, but a high-risk option in the big towns. The fare is negotiable, but about 4000Rp for 5km is fairly standard.

DOKAR

The small *dokar* (pony cart) still provides local transport in some remote areas, and even in areas of Denpasar, but they're extremely slow and are not particularly cheap. Prices start at 1000Rp per person for a short trip, but are very negotiable, depending on demand, number of passengers, nearby competition, and your bargaining skills. The tourist price can be high if the driver thinks the tourist will pay big-time for the novelty value.

BICYCLE

A famous temple carving shows the Dutch artist WOJ Nieuwenkamp pedalling through Bali in 1904. Bali's roads have improved greatly since then, but surprisingly few people tour the island on a *sepeda* (bicycle). But many visitors are using bikes around the towns and for day trips; good quality rental bikes are available, and several companies organise full-day cycle trips in the back country. Mountain bikes are widely available, and their low gear ratios and softer tyres are much better suited to Bali than a 10-speed touring bike.

Some people are put off cycle touring by Bali's tropical heat, heavy traffic, frequent showers and high mountains. But when you're riding on the level or downhill, the breeze really moderates the heat, and once you're out of the congested southern region, and especially on the back roads, traffic is lighter. Frequent roadside food stalls are great for a drink, a snack, or as shelter from a downpour. Multigear mountain bikes make it possible to get up the higher mountains, but with a bit of negotiating and patience, you can get a bemo or minibus to take you and your bike up the steepest sections.

The main advantage of seeing Bali by bicycle is the quality of the experience. By bicycle you can be totally immersed in the environment – you can hear the wind rustling in the rice paddies, the sound of a gamelan orchestra practicing, and catch the scent of the flowers. Even at the height of the tourist season, cycle tourers on the back roads experience the friendliness that seems all but lost on the usual tourist circuit.

You can usually bring your bicycle with you by air, but may have to pay a fee or pay for excess baggage. You may have to box the bike, take the pedals off and/or turn the handlebars sideways. Some airlines will provide a bike box for a small charge – contact the airline in advance to make arrangements.

Rental & Purchase

There are plenty of bicycles for rent in Kuta, Legian, Sanur and Ubud, but many of them are in poor condition (check to see if all the nuts are securely tightened, especially those attached to the seat, the wheel nuts, the brake linkage cables and the brake rims, which tend to loosen with vibration). The best place to rent a good quality mountain bike is in Ubud. If you want to buy a new bike, start by looking along Jl Kartini in Denpasar, and also in the big department stores.

Touring

See Roads in the Car & Motorcycle section earlier for more information, and make sure your bike is equipped for these conditions.

Even the smallest village has some semblance of a bike shop – a flat tyre should cost about 4000Rp to fix. Denpasar has a number of shops selling spare parts and complete bicycles – look along Jl Kartini.

HITCHING

You can hitchhike on Bali, but it's not a very useful option for getting around, as public transport is so cheap and frequent. If you are standing by the side of the road, waving down vehicles, about the only thing that will stop is a public bus or bemo, for which you will have to pay, or a private vehicle, which will in all likelihood also expect payment.

Bear in mind, also, that hitching is never entirely safe in any country and we don't recommend it. Travellers who decide to hitch should understand that they are taking a small but potentially serious risk. People who do choose to hitch will be safer if they travel in pairs and let someone know where they plan to go.

WALKING

Bali is ideal for some leisurely walking between villages, up mountains and across rice fields. Trekking in the Activities section in the Facts for the Visitor chapter has more information.

BOAT

Small boats go to a number of islands around Bali, notably those in the Nusa Penida group. Usually they'll pull up to a beach, and you have to wade to the boat with your luggage and clamber aboard over the stern. It's difficult with a heavy pack, and you might consider wrapping items like cameras in plastic bags. You, and your luggage, may also be drenched by spray if the water is rough. Life jackets are not usually provided and safety standards may not satisfy everyone.

Lombok

Ferry Public ferries travel nonstop between Padangbai (Bali) and Lembar 24 hours a day

(10,000Rp, 3½ hours, every 1½ hours). Motorcycles cost 25,000Rp and cars cost 173,000Rp. Food and drink is sold on board.

Warning There have been some unpleasant scenes with luggage porters at Lembar – if you allow someone to carry your bags for you, agree on the price beforehand.

Fast Boat The **Padangbai Express** (☎ 0361-755260; e pbxpress@indosat.net.id) departs for Lembar (75,000Rp, 90 minutes) twice daily at 9.30am and 2pm.

Catamaran Modern passenger catamarans provide a faster, more comfortable and more expensive service than the regular ferries.

Mabua Express (☎ 0361-721212, fax 723615, on Lombok ☎ 0370-681195, fax 681224; e mabuaexp@indosat.net.id) travels daily between Benoa harbour (Bali) and Lembar harbour (Lombok). The fare is US$30/25 for upper/lower deck class. The boat departs Benoa at 8.30am and arrives in Lembar at 11am, then departs Lembar at 2.30pm and arrives in Benoa at 5pm. You can book at travel agencies on Lombok or Bali. The fare does not include transfers to/from the harbour, but some agents can arrange this. In Lembar, a taxi and shuttle service (minimum of 4 people) transports passengers to Bangsal, Mataram, Senggigi and Kuta.

Bounty Cruises (☎ 0361-726666, on Lombok ☎/fax 0370-642321; w www.balibounty group.com) operates a round trip on Tuesday, Thursday, Saturday and Sunday between Benoa, Nusa Lembongan and Gili Meno on Lombok. From Gili Meno it continues on to Teluk Nare (near Bangsal) in Lombok, where passengers can be bussed to central Senggigi. The Benoa–Lembongan economy fare is US$23/41 one way/return (45 minutes); the Lembongan–Gili Meno economy fare is US$23/41 one way/return (90 minutes). Currently it departs Benoa at 8am daily and returns at 4pm; tickets can be bought from travel agents. Local boats can be chartered from Gili Meno to the other Gili islands.

Tourist Shuttle Bus/Boat The Bali-based company **Perama** (☎ 0361-751551, fax 751170; Jl Legian 39, Kuta) runs shuttle buses to/from Padangbai and Lembar harbours connecting (more or less) with the regular public ferries there. This provides a convenient service between the main tourist centres on Bali (Kuta-Legian, Sanur, Ubud, Candidasa etc) and Lombok (Mataram, Senggigi, Bangsal, Tetebatu and Kuta). Several other companies offer similar services at similar prices, and may be more convenient from some locations.

Shuttle buses are more expensive than public buses and bemos, but they save considerable hassle changing bemos and arranging ferry tickets.

ORGANISED TOURS

Many travellers end up taking one or two organised tours because it can be such a quick and convenient way to visit a few places, especially where public transport is limited (eg, Pura Besakih) or nonexistent (eg, Ulu Watu after sunset). All sorts of tours are available from the tourist centres – the posh hotels can arrange expensive day tours for their guests, while tour companies along the main streets in the tourist centres advertise cheaper trips for those on a budget.

There is an extraordinarily wide range of prices for basically the same sort of tour. The cheaper ones may have less comfortable vehicles, less qualified guides and be less organised, but the savings can be considerable. Higher priced tours may include a buffet lunch, an English-speaking guide and air-conditioning, but generally a higher price is no guarantee of higher quality. Some tours make long stops at craft shops, so you can buy things and the tour company can earn commissions for the tour operator. Tours are typically in an eight- to 12-seat minibus, which picks you up and drops you off at your hotel.

Tours can be booked at the desk of any large hotel, but these will be much more expensive than a similar tour booked at a travel agency with the price in rupiah. If you can get together a group of four or more, most tour agencies will arrange a tour to suit you; or you can easily create your own tour by chartering a vehicle.

Day Tours

You can take a huge range of organised tours from Kuta-Legian, Sanur or Ubud for about the same price. For most tours, prices will be higher from Nusa Dua or Candidasa. Smaller operators or charter drivers will generally do tours for far less than an organised tour you might book through a mid-range or top-end hotel.

Denpasar Tour Takes in the arts centre, markets, museum and perhaps a temple or two

Sunset Tour Includes Mengwi, Marga, Alas Kedaton and the sunset at Tanah Lot

Singaraja–Lovina Tour Goes to Mengwi, Bedugul, Gitgit, Singaraja, Lovina, Banjar and Pupuan

Kintamani–Gunung Batur Tour Takes in the craft shops at Celuk, Mas and Batuan, a dance at Batubulan, Tampaksiring and views of Gunung Batur. Alternatively, the tour may go to Goa Gajah, Pejeng, Tampaksiring and Kintamani

Besakih Tour Includes craft shops at Celuk, Mas and Batuan, Gianyar, Semarapura (Klungkung), Pura Besakih, and return via Bukit Jambal

East Bali Tour Includes the usual craft shops, Semarapura (Klungkung), Kusamba, Goa Lawah, Candidasa and Tenganan

Bedugul Tour Includes Sangeh or Alas Kedaton, Mengwi, Jatiluwih, Candikuning and sunset at Tanah Lot

Other Tours

Some tour agencies also offer one night/two day organised tours, skipping through most of Bali. Short tours to Taman Burung Bali Bird Park, for example, or scheduled dance performances offer little more than transport and entry to the attraction. Possible special interest tours for diving, surfing and other activities are discussed in the Facts for the Visitor chapter. The best plan is to visit a few travel agencies, pick up a handful of brochures and spend some time choosing what will suit you best.

Also, some agencies, including **Suta Tours** (☎ 0361-465249, fax 466783; ⓦ www .sutatour.com), arrange trips to see cremation ceremonies and special temple festivals, for around US$15. It may seem in poor taste to advertise for paying visits to a cremation, but good tour companies are sensitive about these occasions, and will ensure that their participants dress and behave appropriately.

Lombok

Some companies organise day tours around Lombok from Bali, crossing on the *Mabua Express* or by plane, then tearing through Senggigi and a few villages by minibus. A longer tour, with more time for sightseeing and relaxing, will be more expensive but more satisfying.

Denpasar

☎ 0361

Bali's capital has been the focus of a lot of the island's growth and wealth over the last four decades, and now has much of the bustle and congestion of many fast-growing cities in Asia, without any of the first-world infrastructure. There are still tree-lined streets and some pleasant gardens, but the traffic, noise and pollution can make it difficult to enjoy. A limited range of accommodation is available, so naturally most visitors find it convenient to stay in Kuta-Legian, Sanur or Ubud, and visit Denpasar as a day trip. Denpasar might not be a tropical paradise, but it's as much a part of 'the real Bali' as the rice paddies and cliff-top temples, and it's not touristy – you can still catch a *dokar* (pony cart) to get around in some parts of Denpasar.

HISTORY

Denpasar, which means 'Next to the Market', was an important trading centre, and the seat of local rajahs before the colonial period. The Dutch gained control of northern Bali in the mid-19th century, but their takeover of the south didn't start until 1906. The Dutch attacked at Sanur, and the Balinese retreated to Denpasar. There, under the threat of Dutch artillery, three princes of the kingdom of Badung destroyed their own palaces and made a suicidal last stand – a ritual *puputan* – in which the old kingdoms of the south were wiped out.

The northern town of Singaraja remained the Dutch administrative capital, but a new airport was built in the south. This made Denpasar a strategic asset in WWII, and when the Japanese invaded, they used it as a springboard to attack Java. After the war, the Dutch moved their headquarters to Denpasar and in 1958, some years after Indonesian independence, the city became the official capital of the province of Bali. Formerly a part of the Badung district, Denpasar is now a self-governing municipality that includes Sanur and Benoa harbour (see the South Bali chapter).

Many of Denpasar's residents are descended from immigrant groups, such as Bugis mercenaries (from Sulawesi) and Chinese, Arab and Indian traders. More recent immigrants, including civil servants, artisans, business people and labourers, have come

Highlights

- Checking out the art, architecture, carvings and costumes from all corners of Bali at Museum Negeri Propinsi Bali
- Visiting Bali's state temple, Pura Jagatnatha, which has some of the biggest festivals in all of Bali
- Shopping for spices, sarongs and CDs at the markets

ⓞ DENPASAR pp126-7

from Java and all over Indonesia, attracted by the opportunities in the growing Balinese capital. Non-Balinese tend to live in detached houses or small apartments, but the Balinese communities still maintain their traditions and family compounds, even as their villages are engulfed by an expanding conurbation.

ORIENTATION

The main road, Jl Gunung Agung, starts at the western side of town. It changes to Jl Gajah Mada in the middle of town, then Jl Surapati and finally Jl Hayam Wuruk. This name changing is common in Denpasar, and confusing.

Another problem is one-way traffic restrictions, sometimes for only part of a street's length, which often change and are rarely marked on any maps. The traffic jams can be intense and parking can be difficult, so avoid driving in Denpasar – take taxis, *bemos* (small pick-up trucks), or walk.

In contrast to the rest of Denpasar, the Renon area, southeast of the town centre, is laid-out on a grand scale, with wide streets, large car parks and huge landscaped blocks of land. This is where you'll find the government offices, many of which are impressive structures, built with lavish budgets in modern Balinese style.

Maps
The map in this guidebook will be enough for most visitors. If you're driving, the Denpasar inset on the Periplus *Bali* map is the best reference available to navigate the many one-way streets.

INFORMATION
Tourist Offices
The **Denpasar Tourist Office** (☎ 234569, fax 223602; *Jl Surapati 7; open 7.30am-3.30pm Mon-Thur, 8am-1pm Fri*) deals with tourism in the Denpasar municipality (including Sanur), but it has some information about the rest of Bali. It's not terribly helpful apart from handing out brochures, including the useful *Calendar of Events* booklet, *Discover Denpasar* and the *Hello Bali* tourist magazine. There's a far more helpful **tourist office**, however, at the Ubung Bus and Bemo Terminal.

Bali's regional **Departemen Parawisata, Seni dan Budaya** (☎ 222387; *open 7am-2pm Mon-Thur, 7am-11am Fri, 7am-12.30pm Sat*), in Renon, is mainly a bureaucratic facility. If you go to the back of the main building, staff happily hand out yet more brochures and maps, but it's not worth the trek or taxi ride.

Consulates
The Australian, Japanese and US consulates are in Renon. For details of these and other consulates on Bali, and embassies in Jakarta, see the Facts for the Visitor chapter.

Money
All major Indonesian banks have offices in Denpasar, and most have ATMs. Several are on Jl Gajah Mada, near the corner of Jl Arjuna, and there are some around Robinson's and Matahari department stores. **Bank Exim** (*cnr Jl Hasanudin & Jl Udayana*) is reliable for changing money and arranging overseas transfers. The rates offered by the moneychangers along the northern end of Jl Diponegoro are better than the banks, but not as good as the moneychangers at Kuta or Sanur.

Post
The **main post office** (☎ 223565; *open 8am-8pm daily*), with poste restante service, is inconveniently located in Renon. Post offices in Kuta, Sanur or Ubud are more convenient for poste restante mail.

Telephone
The **Telkom office** is also inconveniently located in Renon, but there are *wartels* (public telephone offices) all over town. For telephone calls and faxes, the smaller Telkom offices just north of the Denpasar Tourist Office, and along Jl Teuku Umar (further south) are handy.

Email & Internet Access
The **warnet** (*warung Internet; open 8am-9pm Mon-Sat, 9am-6pm Sun*) on the eastern side of the post office has Internet access. There are also several warnets in the Pasar Burung area.

Bookshops
One of the best bookshops on Bali is the **Gramedia Book Shop** (☎ 237364; *Jl Teuku Umar*) in the basement of the Matahari department store. It has a large range of souvenir books about Bali in English, French, German and Japanese. It also has some language guides and reference material, a fair selection of English paperbacks, and the usual range of Bali maps.

Medical Services
The city's general hospital, **Rumah Sakit Umum Propinsi Sanglah** (*RSUP Sanglah;* ☎ 227911; *Sanglah; open 24hr*) has English-speaking staff, and a casualty room. It's the best hospital on the island. For an ambulance call ☎ 227911, or ☎ 118.

Private medical practices that deal with foreigners include **Gatotkaca Klinik** (☎ 223 555; *Jl Gatotkaca*) and **BIMC** (☎ 761263; *Jl Ngurah Rai 100X, Kuta*) which is a modern Australian-run clinic not too far away.

There are plenty of pharmacies in town.

Emergency
The **police station** (☎ 424346; *Jl Pattimura*) is the place for any general problems. The general police emergency number is ☎ 110. The **main police station** (☎ 424346; *Jl Sangian*) is about 4km west of Puputan Square, but there's no reason for tourists to go there.

In case of fire call ☎ 225113, or ☎ 113.

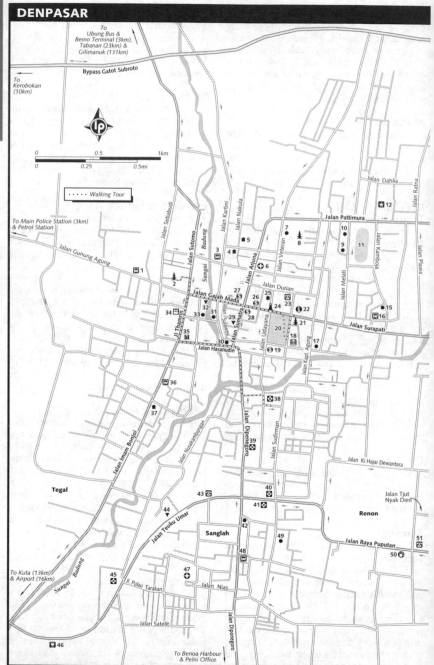

DENPASAR

To
Ubung Bus &
Bemo Terminal (3km),
Tabanan (23km) &
Gilimanuk (131km)

Bypass Gatot Subroto

To
Kerobokan
(10km)

Walking Tour

To Main Police Station (3km)
& Petrol Station

Jalan Gunung Agung

Jalan Dahlia

Jalan Pattimura

Jalan Ratna

Jalan Kartini

Jalan Nakula

Jalan Setiabudi

Jalan Sutomo

Jalan Badung

Jalan Kamboja

Jalan Pluwa

Jalan Melati

Jalan Veteran

Jalan Arjuna

Jalan Gajah Mada

Jalan Sungai

Jalan Durian

Jalan Surapati

J J Thamrin

Jalan Somaratna

Jalan Udayana

Jalan Kapt. Agung

Jalan Hasanudin

Jalan Imam Bonjol

Jalan Nusakambangan

Jalan Diponegoro

Jalan Sudirman

Jalan Ki Hajar Dewantara

Tegal

Jalan Tjut
Nyak Dien

Renon

Jalan Teuku Umar

Sanglah

Jalan Raya Puputan

To Kuta (13km)
& Airport (16km)

Sungai Badung

Jl. Pulau Tarakan

Jalan Nias

Jalan Satelit

To Benoa Harbour
& Pelni Office

DENPASAR

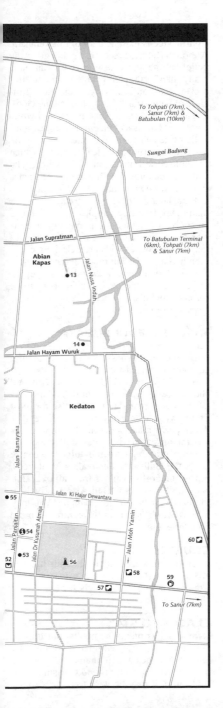

DENPASAR

PLACES TO STAY
4 Nakula Familar Inn
5 Adi Yasa
25 Natour Bali Hotel; Bouraq Airlines
37 Hotel Taman Suci

PLACES TO EAT
29 Mie 88; Restoran Betty
32 Restaurant Hong Kong
44 Ayam Bakar Taliwang Baru

BEMO/BUS TERMINALS
1 Gunung Agung
3 Wangaya
16 Kereneng
36 Tegal
48 Sanglah

OTHER
2 Pura Maospahit
6 Gatotkaca Klinik
7 Pasar Burung (Bird Market)
8 Pura Sutriya
9 Merpati Office
10 Garuda Office
11 Stadium
12 Police Station (for Driving Licences)
13 STSI (School of Dance)
14 Taman Wedhi Budaya (Arts Centre)
15 Pasar Malam Kereneng (Night Market)
17 Indonesia Australia Language Foundation
18 Museum Negeri Propinsi Bali
19 Bank Exim
20 Puputan Square
21 Pura Jagatnatha
22 Denpasar Tourist Office
23 Telkom Office
24 Catur Muka Statue
26 Bank Bali
27 Bank BNI
28 Bank Rakyat Indonesia
30 Kampung Arab
31 Pasar Badung (Main Produce Market)
33 Pasar Kumbasari (Handcraft & Textiles Market)
34 Wisata Cineplex
35 Puri Pemecutan; Hotel Pemecutan Palace
38 Tiara Dewata Shopping Centre
39 Bali Mall (Mal Bali)
40 Robinson's Department Store; ATMs
41 Matahari Department Store; ATMs
42 Pelni Ticket Agency
43 Telkom Office
45 Libby Plaza (Shopping Centre);
   Hero Supermarket; BNI ATM
46 Kak Man Pub
47 RSUP Sanglah Hospital
49 University Udayana
50 Petrol Station
51 Main Telkom Office
52 Main Post Office; Warnet Office
53 Immigration Office
54 Departemen Parawisata, Seni dan Budaya
55 Foreign Driving Licence Service
56 Monument
57 Japanese Consulate
58 Australian Consulate
59 Petrol Station
60 US Consulate

MUSEUM NEGERI PROPINSI BALI

The museum (☎ 222680; adult/child 750/250Rp; open 7.30am-3.30pm Sat-Thur, 7.30am-1pm Fri) was originally established in 1910 by a Dutch Resident who was concerned by the export of culturally significant artefacts from the island. Destroyed in a 1917 earthquake, it was rebuilt in the 1920s, but used mainly for storage until 1932. At that time, German artist Walter Spies and some Dutch officials revived the idea of collecting and preserving Balinese antiquities and cultural objects, and creating an ethnographic museum. Now it's quite well set up, and most displays are labelled in English. You can climb one of the towers inside the grounds for a better view of the whole complex.

The museum comprises several buildings and pavilions, including examples of the architecture of both the palace (puri) and temple (pura), with features like a split gateway (candi bentar) and a warning drum (kulkul) tower. The **main building**, to the back as you enter, has a collection of prehistoric pieces downstairs, including stone sarcophagi, and stone and bronze implements. Upstairs are examples of traditional artefacts, including types still in everyday use. Look for the fine wood and cane carrying cases for transporting fighting cocks, and tiny carrying cases for fighting crickets.

The **northern pavilion** is in the style of a Tabanan palace and houses dance costumes and masks, including a sinister rangda, a healthy looking barong and a towering barong landung figure. See the Glossary, later in the book, for explanations of mythical figures.

The **central pavilion**, with its wide veranda, is like the palace pavilions of the Karangasem kingdom (based in Amlapura), where rajahs held audiences. The exhibits here are related to Balinese religion, and include ceremonial objects, calendars and priests' clothing.

The **southern pavilion** is in the style of a Buleleng palace (from northern Bali), and has a varied collection of textiles, including endek, double ikat, songket and prada (see the special section 'Balinese Arts & Crafts' for more on Balinese textiles).

PURA JAGATNATHA

Next to the museum, the state temple, Pura Jagatnatha is dedicated to the supreme god, Sanghyang Widi. Built in 1953, part of its significance is its statement of monotheism. Although Balinese recognise many gods, the belief in one supreme god (who can have many manifestations) brings Balinese Hinduism into conformity with the first principle of Pancasila – the 'Belief in One God'.

The shrine (padmasana) is made of white coral, and consists of an empty throne (symbolic of heaven) on top of the cosmic turtle and two naga (mythological serpents), which symbolise the foundation of the world. The walls are decorated with carvings of scenes from the Ramayana and Mahabharata.

Pura Jagatnatha is more frequently used than many Balinese temples – local people come every afternoon to pray and make offerings – so it can often be closed to the public. Two major festivals are held here every month, during the full moon and new moon, and feature wayang kulit (shadow puppet plays). Ask at the Denpasar Tourist Office for exact details, or refer to its Calendar of Events booklet.

TAMAN WEDHI BUDAYA

This arts centre (☎ 222776; admission free; open 8am-5pm Tues-Sun) is a sprawling complex in the eastern part of Denpasar. It was established in 1973 as an academy and showplace for Balinese culture, and has lavish architecture and not much else for most of the year (there are no longer regular dance performances here). The impressive-looking art gallery has a fair collection.

From mid-June to mid-July, the centre hosts the **Bali Arts Festival**, with dances, music and crafts displays from all over Bali (see the boxed text 'Bali Arts Festival' in the Facts for the Visitor chapter). You may need to book tickets at the centre for more popular events.

COURSES

Courses in Bahasa Indonesia and Balinese arts are available in Denpasar – see the Courses section in the Facts for the Visitor chapter for details.

PLACES TO STAY

Denpasar has plenty of hotels, but they're not very good value compared with nearby Kuta. At times when many Indonesians travel (July, August, around Christmas and Idul Fitri), it may be wise to book a room.

Waiting for a fare in colourful dokar at the Denpasar market

Fishing boat at sunrise, Sanur

The entrance to Museum Negeri Propinsi Bali

Bustling tourism on Kuta Beach, southern Bali

RICHARD I'ANSON

Sailing boats for hire on Sanur Beach

RICHARD I'ANSON

PAUL KENNEDY

Kids from Nusa Dua – not so camera shy!

JOHN BORTHWICK

Cliff-top Pura Ulu Watu

Sunset sprint along Seminyak Beach

Walking Tour

This walk includes most of the attractions in the middle of town and is shown as a dotted line on the Denpasar map. It will take around two or three hours – more if you stop at the museum or for shopping.

Starting at the Denpasar Tourist Office, head south to the state temple, **Pura Jagatnatha**, and the adjacent **museum**. Opposite the museum is **Puputan Square**, a park that commemorates the heroic but suicidal stand of the rajahs of Badung against the invading Dutch in 1906. A monument depicts a Balinese man, woman and two children in heroic pose, brandishing the weapons that were so ineffective against the Dutch guns. The woman also has jewels in her left hand, as the women of the Badung court reputedly flung their jewellery at the Dutch soldiers to taunt them. The park is popular with locals at lunch time and in the early evening.

Back on Jl Surapati is the towering **Catur Muka statue** (cnr Jl Surapati & Jl Veteran), which represents Batara Guru, Lord of the Four Directions. The four-faced, eight-armed figure keeps a close eye (or is it eight eyes?) on the traffic swirling around him. West of the statue the street is called Jl Gajah Mada (named after the 14th-century Majapahit prime minister). Follow it west, past banks, shops and restaurants to the bridge over the grubby Sungai Badung (Badung River). Just before the bridge, on the left, is the original site of **Pasar Badung**, the main produce market. At the time of writing the market is being rebuilt after a fire swept through the complex. It has set up temporarily on a smaller scale next to the original site. On the left, just after the bridge, **Pasar Kumbasari** is a handcraft and textiles market.

At the next main intersection, detour north up Jl Sutomo, and turn left along a small *gang* (lane) leading to the **Pura Maospahit** temple. Established in the 14th century, at the time the Majapahit arrived from Java, the temple was damaged in a 1917 earthquake and has been heavily restored since. The oldest structures are at the back of the temple, but the most interesting features are the large statues of Garuda and the giant Batara Bayu.

Turn back, and continue south along Jl Thamrin, to the junction of Jl Hasanudin. On this corner is the **Puri Pemecutan**, a palace destroyed during the 1906 invasion. It's now rebuilt and operating as a hotel, but you can look inside the compound.

Go east on Jl Hasanudin, then north onto Jl Sulawesi, and you'll be in the area of the gold shops, known as **Kampung Arab** for the many people there of Middle Eastern or Indian descent. Continue north past Pasar Badung market to return to Jl Gajah Mada.

Alternatively, go east on Jl Hasanudin and head south and then east to **Tiara Dewata** shopping centre, for a bite to eat at its food court.

PLACES TO STAY – BUDGET

Adi Yasa (☎ 222679; Jl Nakula 23B; singles/doubles 25,000/40,000Rp) is where budget travellers have crashed since the 1970s. It's still centrally located (although its front yard resembles a building site) and friendly, but the rooms are very basic.

Nakula Familar Inn (☎ 226446; Jl Nakula 4; singles/doubles 50,000/75,000Rp) is across the road and a few metres west from the Adi Yasa. Rooms are decent (cold water showers only) and clean, and all have a small balcony area. The traffic noise isn't too bad. Breakfast is not included, but is available for around 10,000Rp. Tegal-Kereneng bemos go along Jl Nakula.

The unusual **Hotel Pemecutan Palace** (☎ 423491; Jl Thamrin 2; singles/doubles with air-con 70,000/80,000Rp) is located in the rebuilt Puri Pemecutan (the palace of a Badung rajah). Rooms are dilapidated, but it could make for an interesting stay.

PLACES TO STAY – MID-RANGE

Most mid-range places cater to Indonesian business travellers. There are no hotels in the top-end category.

Natour Bali Hotel (☎ 225681, fax 235347; Jl Veteran 3; singles/doubles from 275,000/315,000Rp, suites 550,000Rp) is a government-owned hotel. There are no real luxury hotels in Denpasar, but the suites are comfortable here and overlook a garden, and are relatively peaceful and quiet (a rare thing in Denpasar!). It dates from the Dutch days and retains a few nice Art Deco details. Rooms have hot water,

DENPASAR

phone and TV. The hotel is a good base for the **Ogoh Ogoh parades** that take place the day before Nyepi, as they pass right by the front of the hotel.

Hotel Taman Suci *(☎ 484445, fax 484724;* **w** *www.tamansuci.com; Jl Imam Bonjol 45; rooms 225,000-325,000Rp)* is a modern, multifloor building on the western side of town. Rooms are moderately well insulated from the noise and grime outside.

PLACES TO EAT

Most places cater to local people and Indonesian visitors, so they offer a good selection of authentic food at reasonable prices. The cheapest places are **warung** (food stalls) at the bemo/bus terminals and the markets. Around Pasar Kumbasari and Pasar Burung, the bird market, the various warung work till about 10pm (after most restaurants in town have closed), while at **Pasar Malam Kereneng** (Kereneng Night Market) dozens of vendors dish it up till dawn.

A number of places along Jl Teuku Umar cater to the more affluent locals. Several specialise in spicy Lombok-style chicken – try **Ayam Bakar Taliwang Baru** *(mains 15,000-20,000Rp, additional dishes 3500-6000Rp),* which is always full of locals, for an authentic version.

Most of the shopping centre eateries also serve a wide variety of cheap Indonesian and Chinese food in hygienic, air-conditioned comfort, at low prices. The food court at **Tiara Dewata Shopping Centre** is especially recommended. The shopping centres also cater to fast-food junkies.

Restaurant Hong Kong *(Jl Gajah Mada 99; dishes 20,000-100,000Rp)* has a good reputation locally and is air-conditioned and cool inside. It has a huge range of Indonesian and Chinese dishes on offer.

Mie 88 *(Jl Sumatra 44; dishes 6,000-11,000Rp)* is a cheap and not very cheerful Chinese restaurant that is worth trying for a quick bite, or something special such as fried pigeon.

Restoran Betty *(Jl Sumatra 56; dishes 6500-9000Rp)* is calm compared to the madness of the street outside. It has a good range of juices and Indonesian dishes, including the delicious *sayur assam,* a thin soup of vegetables with tamarind and star fruit (4500Rp).

Natour Bali Hotel *(☎ 225681, fax 235347; Jl Veteran 3)* is known for its old-fashioned dining room, which still serves its fine *rijstaffel,* a Dutch-Indonesian-style meal with rice and a selection of tasty treats (23,000Rp per person).

ENTERTAINMENT
Bars & Clubs

No one comes to Denpasar for the nightlife – in fact, locals go to Kuta-Legian or Sanur for a night out, rather than stay in Denpasar.

Kak Man Pub *(☎ 227188; Jl Teuku Umar 135; dishes 10,000-25,000Rp; open 9am-10pm)* is in a relatively serene traditional Balinese setting. There are other nightclub/karaoke places along Jl Teuku Umar, Jl Diponegoro, or around Robinson's and the Matahari department stores.

Cinemas

The younger, more affluent denizens of Denpasar congregate around shopping centres in the evening, and often later around the local cinema, **Wisata Cineplex** *(☎ 424023; Jl Thamrin 21; tickets 10,000Rp),* which has five screens that show B-grade Western flicks, subtitled in Bahasa Indonesia, as well as a few Indonesian films.

SHOPPING

You'll find some craft shops along Jl Gajah Mada, and further west, on the corner with Jl Thamrin, but for most souvenirs you'll do better in the tourist areas.

Markets

The **Pasar Badung** is busy in the morning and evening, and is a great place to browse and bargain. Jl Sulawesi, east of Pasar Badung, has many **shops** with batik, ikat and other fabrics; and in nearby **Kampung Arab** gold jewellery is sold by the ounce, and can be made to order. On the opposite side of the river, **Pasar Kumbasari** has handcrafts, fabrics and costumes decorated with gold.

Further north on Jl Veteran, **Pasar Burung** is a bird market with hundreds of caged birds and small animals, such as guinea pigs, rabbits and monkeys for sale. It's an interesting sight. On sale are wonderfully gaudy and colourful birdcages, as well as traditional wooden cages. You wonder how many endangered species are traded behind the scenes.

An impromptu dog market also operates directly opposite the market. (While you're here, have a look at the elaborate Pura Sutriya, just east of the market.)

Just north of Kereneng bus terminal, the busy **Pasar Malam Kereneng**, on Jl Kamboja, sells mainly food and goods for the local community.

Shopping Centres
Western-style shopping centres are very fashionable. The main stores are **Matahari**, **Robinson's**, and **Bali Mall** (Mal Bali). They sell a wide range of clothes, cosmetics, leather goods, sportswear, toys and baby things, all at marked prices that are quite inexpensive by international standards. The brand-name goods are genuine – if you want cheap fakes, go to Kuta or the markets.

Most shopping centres have a food court with stalls serving Asian food, as well as international fast-food franchises. Some have amusement centres for the kids, and **Tiara Dewata** also has a good-sized swimming pool.

Hero Supermarket (Teuku Umar), in Libi Plaza, is the place to stock up on those Indonesian spices and sauces.

GETTING THERE & AWAY
Denpasar is the hub of road transport on Bali – you'll find buses and minibuses bound for all corners of the island. The Getting There & Away chapter has details of transport between Bali and Lombok and other Indonesian islands.

Air
It is not necessary to come to Denpasar to arrange bookings, tickets or reconfirmation of flights – travel agencies in Kuta, Sanur, Ubud and other tourist centres can do this. Some airline offices are in Denpasar, but most are at the airport, as well as in Sanur – see the Getting There & Away chapter for details.

Bemo
Denpasar is *the* hub for bemo transport around Bali. The city has several terminals, so if you're travelling independently from one part of Bali to another, you'll often have to go via Denpasar, and transfer from one terminal to another. The terminals for transport around Bali are Ubung, Batubulan and Tegal, while the Gunung Agung, Kereneng, Sanglah and Wangaya terminals serve destinations in and around Denpasar. Each terminal has

regular bemo connections to the other terminals in Denpasar for 3000Rp.

Bemos and minibuses cover shorter routes between towns, while full-size buses are often used on longer, more heavily travelled routes. Buses may be slightly cheaper than smaller vehicles on a long route, and probably quicker and more comfortable, but they're less frequent.

Ubung Well north of the town, on the road to Gilimanuk, Ubung is the terminal for northern and western Bali. There is a very helpful tourist office in the complex, which can provide help with fares and schedules.

destination	fare (Rp)
Gilimanuk (for the ferry to Java)	17,500
Kediri (for Tanah Lot)	2500
Mengwi	2500
Negara	7000
Pancasari (for Danau Bratan)	5000
Singaraja (via Pupuan or Bedugul)	9000
Tabanan	4000

Batubulan This terminal, a very inconvenient 6km northeast of Denpasar, is for destinations in eastern and central Bali. It can be hard for foreigners to get bemos at the local rate from Batubulan terminal. One ploy is to get tourists into a vehicle with no other passengers and start driving – the tourists then discover they have chartered the whole bemo to their destination at an enormous price. Try to arrive early at the terminal, when there are lots of locals coming and going, and get on a bemo with a group of them.

destination	fare (Rp)
Amlapura	5500
Bangli	2500
Gianyar	3000
Kintamani (via Tampaksiring)	4500
Nusa Dua (via Sanur)	3000
Padangbai (for the Lombok ferry)	4000
Selat (via Semarapura & Amlapura)	10,000
Semarapura	4000
Singaraja (via Kintamani)	8500
Singaraja (via Semarapura & Amlapura)	12,500
Tampaksiring (via Ubud)	3,500
Ubud	2500

To Besakih, go first to Semarapura (Klungkung); for Tirta Gangga and Tulamben, go first to Amlapura; for Candidasa, go first to Semarapura or Padangbai.

Tegal On the western side of town on Jl Iman Bonjol, Tegal is the terminal for Kuta and the Bukit peninsula.

destination	fare (Rp)
Airport	2500
Jimbaran	3000
Kuta	2500
Legian	2500
Nusa Dua/Bualu	4000

For Ulu Watu, go first to Kuta.

Gunung Agung This new terminal, at the northwestern corner of town (look for orange bemos), is on Jl Gunung Agung, and has bemos to Kerobokan and Canggu (3000Rp).

Kereneng East of the town centre, Kereneng has bemos to Sanur (1000Rp) and to every other terminal in Denpasar.

Sanglah On Jl Diponegoro, near the main hospital in the south of the city, bemos go to Suwung and Benoa harbour (3000Rp), and also to Kereneng terminal.

Wangaya From this tiny terminal near the river, bemos go up the middle of Bali – to Pelaga (4500Rp), via Sangeh; and to Ubung and Kereneng terminals (3000Rp).

Bus
The usual route to Java is a bus from Denpasar to Surabaya, which includes the short ferry trip across the Bali Strait. Other buses go as far as Yogyakarta and Jakarta, usually travelling overnight. There are also regular buses from Denpasar, via Padangbai and the ferry, to Mataram, Lombok. Buses also go further east to Sumbawa, but it's generally better to do this trip in shorter stages.

Book directly at offices in the Ubung terminal, 3km north of the city centre. To Surabaya or even Jakarta, you may get on a bus within an hour of arriving at Ubung, but at busy times you should buy your ticket at least one day ahead.

None of the tourist shuttle bus companies travel to/from Denpasar.

Boat
Tickets for Pelni (the government shipping line) boats are sold by the **Pelni ticket agency** (☎ 234680; Jl Diponegoro 165), as well as at the **Pelni offices** in Tuban and Benoa harbour (see the Getting There & Away chapter for more on Pelni).

GETTING AROUND
To/From the Airport
Bali's Ngurah Rai airport is just south of Kuta (although it is referred to internationally as Denpasar). A taxi from the airport to Denpasar is 27,500Rp.

Bemo
The main form of public transport is the bemo – these small minibuses take various circuitous routes from and between the bus/bemo terminals. They line up for various destinations at each terminal, or you can hail them from anywhere along the main roads – look for the destination sign above the driver's window. The Tegal–Nusa Dua bemo (dark blue) is handy for Robinson's and Matahari department stores, and Renon; and the Kereneng–Ubung bemo (turquoise) travels along Jl Gajah Mada, past the museum and Denpasar Tourist Office, and turns north up Jl Veteran.

Dokar
Despite the traffic, *dokar* (pony carts) are still used in quieter parts of Denpasar. They should cost the same as a bemo, but tourists are always charged more. They are slow, and definitely not recommended on busy streets.

Taxi
Many taxis prowl the streets of Denpasar looking for fares – they often beep at pedestrians. Try to get a metered taxi and if the driver says the meter isn't working, get another taxi. If you can't find one on the street, call **Bali Taxi** (☎ 701111).

Chartering a Vehicle
If you want to travel a lot in and around the city, ask at your hotel about chartering a car and driver for the day.

South Bali

In Balinese terms, the mountains are always much more auspicious than the sea, but economically, the southern coastline is the most important and dynamic part of the island and the site of its major industry – tourism. If you're looking for a window on traditional Balinese village life, go elsewhere, but for a one-week sun, surf and sand holiday the area offers some of the best beaches, nightlife and shopping, and some outstanding restaurants amongst the tourist fodder.

History
Following the bloody defeat of the three princes of the kingdom of Badung in 1906, the Dutch administration was relatively benign, and southern Bali was little affected until the first Western tourists and artists started to arrive. Although Denpasar became the capital of Bali after independence, the phenomenal growth in southern Bali is almost entirely a result of the booming tourism industry.

Sanur had the first big hotel on Bali in 1965, but it was such an eyesore that the local *banjar* (community council) placed subsequent controls on tourist developments.

The growth of mass tourism dates from August 1969, when Ngurah Rai international airport opened. The first planned tourist resort was conceived in the early 1970s, by 'experts' working for the United Nations (UN) and the World Bank. As luxury hotels were built at Nusa Dua, unplanned development raced ahead from Kuta to Legian. People made the most of their opportunities, and small-scale, low-budget businesses were set up with limited local resources.

At first, development was confined to designated resort areas, such as Kuta, Sanur and Nusa Dua, but the boom of the 1990s saw tourism developments spreading north and south of Kuta, extending as far as Jimbaran Bay, and north of Nusa Dua to Tanjung Benoa, while real estate speculators grabbed prime coastal spots around the Bukit peninsula.

Many developments were backed by companies linked to the Soeharto family. With Soeharto's demise and the general economic crisis, several big projects stalled. Street protests and riots across Indonesia

Highlights

- Sunbathing and shopping at Kuta Beach
- Enjoying the beachfront hotels, fine food and family-friendliness of Sanur
- Soaking up the superb sunsets, beautiful bay and fresh fish at Jimbaran
- Discovering Bukit peninsula's cliff-top temples, killer surf, secluded beaches, water sports and luxury resorts

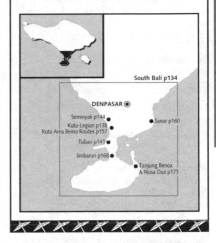

South Bali p134

DENPASAR ◉

Seminyak p144
Kuta-Legian p138
Kuta Area Bemo Routes p157
Tuban p141
Jimbaran p168

Sanur p160

Tanjung Benoa & Nusa Dua p173

SOUTH BALI

had a ripple effect on the Balinese economy, keeping tourists away, as did the events of 11 September, 2001 in New York and the airline and travel bankruptcies in Australia. The bombings of October 2002 (see the boxed text 'The Bali Bombings – Paradise Lost?' later) dealt an even bigger blow, but even with tourist numbers at a low, development is expected to continue.

Kuta

☎ 0361

The Kuta region is overwhelmingly Bali's largest tourist resort. Most visitors come here sooner or later because it's close to the airport, and has the best range of hotels, restaurants and tourist facilities. Some find the area overdeveloped and seedy, but if you have a taste for a busy beach scene,

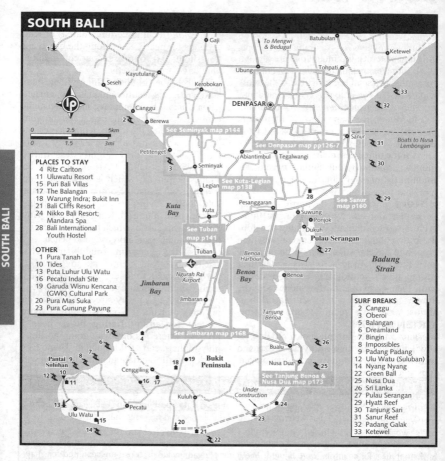

SOUTH BALI

PLACES TO STAY
4 Ritz Carlton
11 Uluwatu Resort
15 Puri Bali Villas
17 The Balangan
18 Warung Indra; Bukit Inn
21 Bali Cliffs Resort
24 Nikko Bali Resort;
    Mandara Spa
28 Bali International
    Youth Hostel

OTHER
1 Pura Tanah Lot
10 Tides
13 Puta Luhur Ulu Watu
16 Pecatu Indah Site
19 Garuda Wisnu Kencana
    (GWK) Cultural Park
20 Pura Mas Suka
23 Pura Gunung Payung

SURF BREAKS
2 Canggu
3 Oberoi
5 Balangan
6 Dreamland
7 Bingin
8 Impossibles
9 Padang Padang
12 Ulu Watu (Suluban)
14 Nyang Nyang
22 Green Ball
25 Nusa Dua
26 Sri Lanka
27 Pulau Serangan
29 Hyatt Reef
30 Tanjung Sari
31 Sanur Reef
32 Padang Galak
33 Ketewel

shopping and nightlife, you will probably have a great time.

It's easy to disparage Kuta for its rampant development, low-brow nightlife and crass commercialism, but the cosmopolitan mixture of beach-party hedonism and entrepreneurial energy can be exciting. It's not pretty, but it's not dull either, and the amazing growth is evidence that a lot of people find something to like in Kuta.

HISTORY
Mads Lange, a Danish copra trader and 19th-century adventurer, set up a successful trading enterprise near modern Kuta in 1839, and successfully mediated between local rajahs and the Dutch, who were encroaching from the north. His business soured in the 1850s,

and he died suddenly, just as he was about to return to Denmark. His death may have been the result of poisoning.

The original Kuta Beach Hotel was started by a Californian couple, Louise and Bob Koke, in the 1930s. The guests, mostly from Europe and the US, were housed in thatched bungalows built in Balinese style (the Dutch Resident called them 'filthy native huts'). The hotel closed in 1942, when the Japanese occupied Bali, but a modern version opened on the same site in 1959, was rebuilt in 1991 and is now run by the government's hotel chain as Natour Kuta Beach. Louise Koke wrote *Our Hotel in Bali*, a memoir about their experiences (see the boxed text 'Western Visitors in the 1930s' in the Facts for the Visitor chapter).

Kuta really began to change in the late 1960s, when it became known as a stop on the hippy trail between Australia and Europe. At first, most visitors stayed in Denpasar and made day trips to Kuta, but more accommodation opened and, by the early 1970s, Kuta had relaxed *losmen* (basic accommodation) in pretty gardens, friendly places to eat and a delightfully laid-back atmosphere. Surfers also arrived, enjoying the waves at Kuta and using it as a base to explore the rest of Bali's coastline. Enterprising Indonesians seized opportunities to profit from the tourist trade, often in partnership with foreigners seeking a pretext for staying longer.

Legian, the village to the north, sprang up as an alternative to Kuta in the mid-1970s. At first it was a totally separate development, but these days you can't tell where one ends and the other begins. Legian now merges with upmarket Seminyak, the next village north, and Kuta merges seamlessly with Tuban in the south and sprawls all the way to the airport.

ORIENTATION

Kuta is a disorienting place – it's flat, with few landmarks or signs, and the streets and alleys are crooked and often walled on one or both sides so it feels like a maze. The *kelurahan* (local government area) of Kuta extends for nearly 8km along the beach and foreshore, and comprises four communities that have grown together.

Kuta is the original fishing-village-cum-budget beach resort, and has the greatest choice of hotels, restaurants, shops and nightclubs, the best part of the beach and the worst traffic. North of Jl Melasti, Kuta merges into Legian, which has almost as many tourist businesses, and only slightly less traffic. Somewhere around Jl Arjuna, Legian becomes Seminyak, which is less densely developed, but has some of the best restaurants and coolest nightspots, and great shopping. Somewhere along Jl Kartika Plaza, Kuta merges with Tuban, which has quite a few upmarket hotels, and a pretty good beach.

Busy Jl Legian runs roughly parallel to the beach from Seminyak in the north through Legian to Kuta (the northern end is also called Jl Seminyak or Jl Raya Seminyak). It's a two-way street in Legian, but in most of Kuta it's one-way going south, except for an infuriating block near Jl Melasti where it's one-way going north. At the southern end of Jl Legian is 'Bemo Corner', a small roundabout at the junction with

The Bali Bombings – Paradise Lost?

On Saturday 12 October, 2002, two bombs exploded on Kuta's bustling Jalan (Jl) Legian. The popular Sari Club and Paddy's Bar were obliterated, and the blast and fire balls that followed destroyed or damaged neighbouring clubs, pubs, shops and houses.

Close to midnight on the busiest night of the week, the area was packed. More than 300 people from at least 23 countries were injured. The number dead, including those unaccounted for, may reach 200. Most of these are Australians and Indonesians.

Who was responsible? Initial suspicion fell on radical sectarian Islamic groups targeting Western culture and politics. The effectiveness of the attacks has temporarily discouraged tourism and destabilised the local – and possibly national – economy.

So is Bali a paradise lost? No. Changed, certainly. But behind the destruction – and renewal – of Jl Legian, behind the tourist strips of Kuta and around the island and the colourful, good-natured interchange between tourists and locals, traditional life goes on. The household temples, sacred places and fields of old Bali remain intact; the conscious practice of rituals, culture and social behaviour that distinguish Bali and its charming people continues.

And tourism helps these traditions continue. Considerable amounts of income derived from the sale of traditional crafts and performances are channelled back to strengthen these. In the aftermath of the Kuta bombing, of course we should check our governments' travel advisories and consider personal safety, as we should for any destination. And hopefully we'll continue to enjoy holidays in Bali that both support the Balinese and reaffirm that the world belongs to all people to travel together without fear.

Virginia Jealous, with thanks to Professor Ken Taylor of Canberra University

SOUTH BALI

Jl Pantai Kuta (Kuta Beach Rd). This one-way street runs west from Bemo Corner then north along the beach to Jl Melasti, and has now been extended right up to the Double Six Club, at the end of Jl Double Six (also known as Jl Arjuna).

Between Jl Legian and the beach is a tangle of narrow streets, tracks and alleys, with a hodgepodge of tiny hotels, souvenir stalls, *warung* (food stall), bars, building construction sites and even a few coconut palms.

Most of the bigger shops, restaurants and low-rent nightspots are along Jl Legian and a few of the main streets that head towards the beach. There are also dozens and dozens of travel agents, souvenir shops, banks, moneychangers, motorcycle- and car-rental outlets, postal agencies, *wartels* (public telephone offices) and Internet cafés – everything a holiday-maker could possibly want.

Maps

It's hard to find a detailed, accurate map that covers the whole Kuta strip, but the maps in this book will be sufficient for most visitors. Periplus maps of Bali have excellent inset maps of the Kuta region.

INFORMATION
Tourist Offices

The **Bali Tourist Office** (☎ 754090, fax 758521; Jl Benesari 7; open 8am-9pm daily), in the Century Plaza building, is responsible for the whole of the island. The friendly staff can answer specific local queries and have limited information about hotels and activities, and a few brochures and maps to hand out.

The **Badung Tourist Office** (☎/fax 756176; Jl Raya Kuta 2; open 7am-2pm Mon-Thur,

7am-11am Fri, 7am-12.30pm Sat) is responsible for the Kuta region, Nusa Dua and the Bukit peninsula, but is *not* worth venturing into. You'll be given an obligatory brochure, a sleepy smile and be sent on your way.

Other places that advertise themselves as 'tourist information centres' are usually commercial travel agents, and some can be helpful, especially for booking organised tours, activities and transport.

The gay-friendly tour operator and guide **Hanafi** (☎ 756454, fax 752561; e hanafi@ consultant.com; Poppies Gang I 77) operates from a small souvenir craft shop. He's a valuable source of information on the gay scene and can also organise accommodation.

Money

There are several banks and ATMs along Jl Legian, at Kuta Square and Jl Pantai Kuta. The numerous 'authorised' moneychangers are faster, efficient, open longer hours and offer better exchange rates. Rates can vary considerably, but be sceptical about those that are markedly better than average – they may not have mentioned that they charge a commission or, judging by the number of readers' letters we've received, they may well make their profit by adeptly short-changing their customers.

Here's how the scam works. The moneychanger counts out the money in front of you. Everything seems OK. Then, they can't quite find the last bit of change for you and a mate comes over to find it from his pocket... The moment your attention is diverted about a quarter of your cash is swept off the table into an open drawer or elsewhere behind the counter. They pile the money for you – shake your hand (the worst insult in retrospect!), say thanks and shoo you out the door. We went back to complain but of course the shop was closed for the day... So please take care and make sure you are the last to count the money and then hold on to it. Better still go to a bank or change it at your accommodation. It'll be cheaper.
Debra & Howard Robinson, Australia

Numerous ATMs take Visa, MasterCard, Cirrus and/or Plus cards. (The ubiquitous Circle K minimarts also have ATMs attached to each shop.) Most give a maximum withdrawal of 600,000Rp. Many banks provide Visa or MasterCard cash advances, and charge around 20,000Rp per 1,000,000Rp advance.

Gangland

A small lane or alley is known as a *gang*, and most of them lack signs or even names. Some are referred to by the name of a connecting street, eg, Jl Padma Utara is the *gang* going north of Jl Padma. Many are too small for cars, although this doesn't stop some drivers trying. The best-known in Kuta are Poppies Gang I, a tiny path between Jl Legian and the beach, and Poppies Gang II, a crooked lane a little further north. They're both named (unofficially) for one of Kuta's first businesses.

Street Names

Most streets in the Kuta area are unofficially named after a well-known temple and/or business establishment, or according to the direction they head. Several small back streets don't have names at all. Recently there has been an attempt to impose official names on all the streets, but the old, unofficial names are by far the most common usage – the only place you're likely to encounter the new names is on some new, small street signs, and on brochures for upmarket hotels. For example, in Legian there's a crooked street that is commonly called Jl Pura Bagus Taruna (after a temple that is now in the grounds of the Hotel Jayakarta), or sometimes referred to as Rum Jungle Rd (after the Rum Jungle Restaurant), but now has an inconspicuous sign identifying it as Jl Werkudara.

In this guide, both old and new names are shown on the maps, but in the text, the old, commonly used names have been retained. For reference, here are the old and new names, from north to south.

old/unofficial	new/official
Jl Oberoi	Jl Lasmana
Jl Dhyana Pura/Jl Gado Gado	Jl Abimanyu
Jl Double Six	Jl Arjuna
Jl Pura Bagus Taruna/Rum Jungle Rd	Jl Werkudara
Jl Padma	Jl Yudistra
Poppies Gang II	Jl Batu Bolong
Poppies Gang I	Poppies Gang I
Jl Pantai Kuta	Jl Pantai Banjar Pande Mas
Jl Kartika Plaza	Jl Dewi Sartika
Jl Segara	Jl Jenggala
Jl Satria	Jl Kediri

A number of hotels have safety deposit boxes, where you can leave airline tickets or other valuables without worrying about them during your stay on Bali.

Post

The **main post office** *(kantor pos; open 7am-2pm Mon-Thur, 7am-11am Fri, 7am-12.30pm Sat)* is on a small road east of Jl Raya Kuta. It's small, efficient and has an easy, sort-it-yourself poste restante service. This post office is well practised in shipping large packages. Other postal agencies, that can send but not receive mail, are dotted around the place (and indicated on the relevant maps). The postal agency on the ground floor of the **Matahari department store** *(Kuta Square; open 8am-9.30pm daily)* has a fax and poste restante service.

There are several cargo agencies in the Kuta area. Try **Nominasi Cargo** *(Jl Melasti, Legian)* or **Putri Dewi Sri International Cargo** *(☎/fax 756880; Jl Padma Utara 8X)*.

Telephone

Wartels are concentrated in the main tourist areas, particularly along Jl Legian, the main roads between Jl Legian and the beach, and along Jl Dhyana Pura in Seminyak. Hours are generally 7am to 9pm, but some are open later. In most places, you can make international calls and send faxes (shop around for international calls, as prices do vary), and arrange collect calls for a small fee. You can find Home Country Direct (HCD) telephones on the ground floor of the Matahari department store at Kuta Square, and near the left-luggage counter at the international terminal at the airport.

Email & Internet Access

There are numerous Internet centres in Kuta and Legian, and the standard rate is 500Rp per minute. One of the cheapest places is **Bol @ Bali** *(Jl Benesari)*, which charges 250Rp per minute.

Travel Agents

Many travel agents will arrange transport or car and motorcycle rental. They also sell tickets for tourist shuttle buses, Balinese dance performances, adventure activities and a variety of organised tours. Most will also change money. Many travel agents can also book airline tickets, or will change an existing flight booking for a fee. It may,

SOUTH BALI

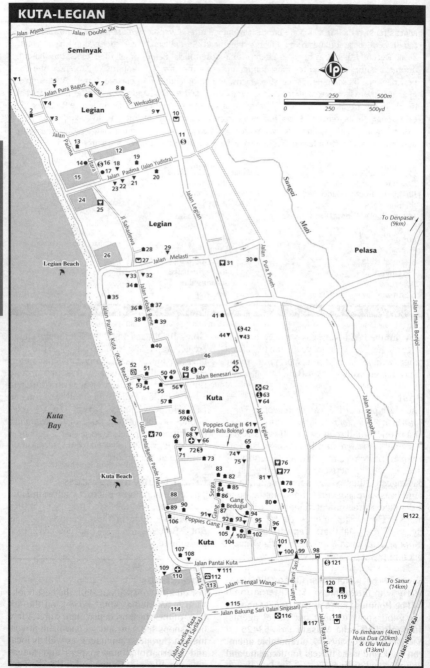

KUTA-LEGIAN

KUTA–LEGIAN

PLACES TO STAY
2 Puri Tantra Beach Bungalows
6 Court Yard Hotel & Apartments; Hot Mango Bar
8 Su's Cottages
12 Three Brothers Inn
13 Sinar Indah; Sudani Bookshop
15 Hotel Padma Bali; Mandara Spa
19 Casa Padma
20 Legian Beach Bungalow
24 Bali Mandira Hotel, Café & Spa; Spa Me; Parasol Mediterranean Restaurant
26 Legian Beach Hotel
28 Darsana Beach Inn
34 Apolina Gallery; Senen Beach Inn
35 Alam Kul Kul; Jamu Spa; Papa's Café
36 Adus Beach Inn
37 Bali Matahari Hotel; Rosani Hotel
38 Hotel Camplung Mas
39 Hotel Puri Tanah Lot
40 Hotel Sayang Maha Mertha (Hotel Sayang Beach Lodging)
41 Kuta Legian Village Hotel; The Bounty
51 Hotel Lusa
54 Komala Indah I
55 Un's Hotel
57 Maharani II Hotel
58 Taman Ayu II
60 Simpang Inn
69 Hotel Bounty
73 Bali Sandy Cottages
78 Aquarius Star Hotel; Este de Massa
82 Kedin's II
83 Hotel Sorga Kuta
84 Mimpi Bungalows
85 Suji Bungalow
86 Berlian Inn
87 Rita's House
88 Kuta Seaview Cottages
90 Kuta Puri Bungalows
92 Ayu Beach Inn
94 Lima Satu Cottages; Puri Agung; Taman Ayu I
95 Komala Indah I
102 Poppies Cottages I
104 Fat Yogis
105 Masa Inn
106 Sari Yasa Samudra Bungalows
107 Hard Rock Hotel; Hard Rock Cafe
117 Jesen's Inn II

PLACES TO EAT
1 Kafe Warna
3 Poco Loco
4 Warung Banyu Mas
5 Swiss & Austrian Consular Agent; Swiss Restaurant; Rhum
7 Rum Jungle Road Bar & Restaurant
9 Restoran Enak Glory
18 Joni Bar Restaurant
21 Wayan & Friends
22 Kin Khao
23 Take
29 Gosha Bar & Restaurant
32 Copa Café & Internet
33 Legian Garden Restaurant; Restaurant Puri Bali Indah
43 Nero Bar & Restaurant
44 Aroma's Cafe
50 The Balcony
53 Komala Indah II Café
56 Brasil Bali Cantinho
61 Kopi Pot
64 Ketupat; Jonathon's Gallery
66 Bali Corner
67 Warung 96; Warung Wulon
71 Rainbow Café
74 Rumah Makan ACC Baru; Tubes Surf Bar & Restaurant
75 Fajar; Warung Indonesia
81 Mini Restaurant
91 Treehouse Cafe
93 Bamboo Corner
96 Poppies Restaurant
97 Kunti Japanese
100 Made's Warung
101 Un's Restaurant
108 Hard Rock Deli
109 Mentari

BARS & NIGHTCLUBS
25 Hulu Café
31 Peanuts
48 Latino's
76 Miller Time Cafe; Apache
77 Bounty II

OTHER
10 Postal Agency
11 ATM
14 Putri Dewi Sri International Cargo
16 Bank Bali
17 Sumanindo Graha Wisata
27 Nominasi Cargo; Postal Agent
30 Bali Bungy
42 Bank Bali (ATM)
45 Legian Medical Clinic; Pharmacy
46 Legian Arcade; Guardian Pharmacy; BCA (ATM)
47 Bali Tourist Office
49 Redz; Circle K Minimart
52 Bol @ Bali
59 Bank Bali (ATM)
62 Matahari Department Store; Timezone; McDonalds
63 Bali Lombok Tourist Info
65 Circle K Minimart
68 Legian Clinic
70 Tourist Police
72 Bank Bali (ATM)
79 Pharmacy
80 Perama Office
89 Circle K Minimart; ATM
98 Bemos to Tegal, Jimbaran, Uluwatu & Nusa Dua
99 Bemo Corner
103 Hanafi
110 SOS Natour Clinic; Wartel
111 Suci Bar & Restaurant
112 Kambodja Wartel
113 Matahari Department Store; Postal Agency; M-Media; HCD Telephones
114 Kuta Art Market; Artists Cafe
115 Pharmacy
116 Agung Supermarket
118 Main Post Office
119 Chinese Temple
120 Police Station; Badung Tourist Office
121 Bank BCA
122 Bemos to Nusa Dua; Petrol Station

SOUTH BALI

however, be better to do this yourself directly with the airline.

The Poppies Gangs and Jl Benesari areas are good spots to hunt out travel agents. **Sumanindo Graha Wisata** (☎ 753425; Jl Padma Utara 2G, Legian), a reputable agent, can book and issue tickets for domestic and international airlines.

Bookshops
For quality books about Bali, the best bookshop is **M-Media** (Kuta Square), on the 4th floor of the Matahari department store. A few bookshops sell new and second-hand novels in most European languages, as well as local and international newspapers and magazines; the Poppies Gangs and Jl Benesari are

the obvious places to look. **Sudani Bookshop** (*Jl Padma Utara, Legian*) a book exchange near Sinar Indah losmen, has a varied range of English-, European- and Scandinavian-language titles, as well as travel guides.

Laundry
Most hotels, even top-end ones, do laundry for a comparatively low price. Back-street laundries are only marginally cheaper – about 1500Rp for jeans; 1000Rp for a shirt or shorts; 500Rp for underwear and you have less recourse if something goes awry. We don't recommend Komalah Indah II White Water Laundry on Jl Benesari; we've had reports of clothes being returned damaged and dirtier than when they were dropped off.

Medical Services
BIMC (*☎ 761263; Jl Ngurah Rai 100X*) is a modern, professional Australian-run clinic on the bypass road just east of Kuta – and is easily reached by taxi. It can do blood tests, hotel visits, midwife checks, transfers to hospitals and medical evacuation. At US$60 for a minimum consultation it's relatively expensive compared to other clinics catering to foreigners, but your travel insurance will cover it.

The **Legian Medical Clinic** (*☎ 758503; Jl Benesari; on call 24 hrs daily*) has an ambulance and dental service. It's 150,000Rp for a consultation with an English-speaking Balinese doctor, or 200,000Rp for an emergency visit to your hotel room. It has a well-stocked pharmacy attached to the clinic. It also has another clinic on Poppies Gang II (*☎ 768117*). Also accessible is the small **SOS Natour Clinic** (*☎ 751361; Jl Pantai Kuta*), opposite the Hard Rock Beach Club, which charges 150,000Rp per consultation.

Guardian Pharmacy in Legian Arcade, Kuta, will meet most medical or cosmetic needs, while in Seminyak there is a 24-hour **pharmacy** right next door to the Bintang Supermarket.

Emergency
The **local police station** (*☎ 751598; Jl Raya Kuta*) is next to the Badung Tourist Office. There are one or two temporary tourist police posts along Jl Legian, and a **tourist police post** on Jl Pantai Kuta. If you have any major problem, go to the **main police station** (*☎ 234928; Jl Pattimura, Denpasar*).

Dangers & Annoyances
See Dangers & Annoyances in the Facts for the Visitor chapter for general information.

Theft This is not a big problem, but visitors do lose things from unlocked hotel rooms or from the beach. Going into the water and leaving valuables on the beach is simply asking for trouble (in any country). Snatch thefts are rare. Valuable items can be left at your hotel reception.

Surf The surf can be very dangerous, with a strong current on some tides, especially up north in Legian. Lifeguards patrol swimming areas of the beaches at Kuta and Legian, indicated by red-and-yellow flags. If they say the water is too rough or unsafe to swim in, they mean it.

Water Pollution The sea water around Kuta is quite commonly contaminated by runoff from both built-up areas and surrounding farmland, especially after heavy rain. The water usually looks and smells just fine, but many people suffer from ear infections after swimming.

Hawkers Hawkers have been hassling tourists here for years, and the problem became worse as the economic crisis induced people from other parts of the country to try their luck on Bali. In early 2000, the Kuta *banjar* finally acted against street vendors – after a couple of warnings, all the hawkers were rounded up, some were beaten, and many vendors' carts were burned.

Today it's rare to find any food carts in the Kuta tourist area, but street selling is making a comeback, especially on hassle street, Jl Legian. To get more of that that old-style hassle, stroll along the upper part of the beach, where souvenir sellers and licensed massage ladies are allowed to tout for business. Closer to the water, you can lie on the sand in peace – you'll soon find where the invisible line is.

ACTIVITIES
From Kuta, you can easily go surfing, sailing, diving, fishing or rafting anywhere in the southern part of Bali, and be back for the start of happy hour in the evening. See the Activities section in the Facts for the Visitor chapter for information on individual activities.

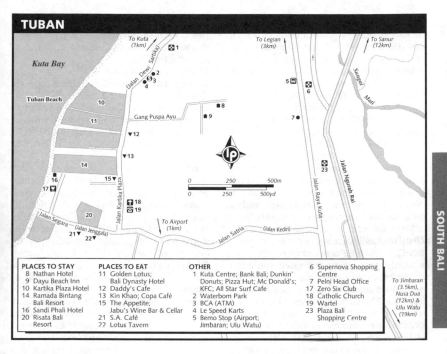

TUBAN

To Kuta (1km)
To Legian (3km)
To Sanur (12km)

Kuta Bay

Tuban Beach

Jalan Dewi Sartika

Gang Puspa Ayu

Jalan Kartika Plaza

Jalan Segara

(Jalan Jenggala)

To Airport (1km)

Jalan Satria   (Jalan Kediri)

Sungai Mati

Jalan Ngurah Rai

Jalan Raya Kuta

0   250   500m
0   250   500yd

To Jimbaran (3.5km), Nusa Dua (12km) & Ulu Watu (19km)

PLACES TO STAY	PLACES TO EAT	OTHER	6 Supernova Shopping
8 Nathan Hotel	11 Golden Lotus;	1 Kuta Centre; Bank Bali; Dunkin'	Centre
9 Dayu Beach Inn	Bali Dynasty Hotel	Donuts; Pizza Hut; Mc Donald's;	7 Pelni Head Office
10 Kartika Plaza Hotel	12 Daddy's Cafe	KFC; All Star Surf Cafe	17 Zero Six Club
14 Ramada Bintang	13 Kin Khao; Copa Café	2 Waterbom Park	18 Catholic Church
Bali Resort	15 The Appetite;	3 BCA (ATM)	19 Wartel
16 Sandi Phali Hotel	Jabu's Wine Bar & Cellar	4 Le Speed Karts	23 Plaza Bali
20 Risata Bali	21 S.A. Café	5 Bemo Stop (Airport;	Shopping Centre
Resort	22 Lotus Tavern	Jimbaran; Ulu Watu)	

Surfing

The beach break called Halfway Kuta, off-shore near the Hotel Istana Rama, is the best place to learn surfing. More challenging breaks are on the shifting sandbars off Legian, around the end of Jl Padma; and also at Kuta Reef, 1km out to sea off Tuban Beach (see Surfing in the Activities section in the Facts for the Visitor chapter). Several shops on Jl Legian sell big-brand surf gear and surfboards. Smaller shops on the side streets hire out surfboards (for a negotiable 35,000Rp per day) and boogie boards, repair dings, sell new and used boards, and some can arrange transport to nearby surfing spots. **Redz** (☎ 763980; e redzsurf@iol.it; Jl Bene-sari) is a reputable operator for board rental.

Tubes Surf Bar is *the* surfers' hangout. It shows surfing videos, and publishes a tide chart, which is widely circulated. Also keep an eye out for free surfing magazines.

For information on surf schools in Kuta, see Courses in the Facts for the Visitor chapter, and for information on surfing tours to Nusa Lembongan, Java and further afield see the Surfing section in the Facts for the Visitor chapter.

Massage & Spas

Professional masseurs, with licence numbers on their conical hats, offer massages on the beach. A realistic price is about 20,000Rp for a half-hour massage, or 40,000Rp for one hour, but you might have to bargain hard to get near this price. Professional massages in your room or in a small massage establishment cost a negotiable 65,000Rp per hour. Most spas also offer facials and waxing.

Alamanda Spa & Salon (☎ 732163; Jl Legian 494, Seminyak) offers a full range of massages and beauty treatments in luxurious surroundings.

Este de Massa (☎ 757451; Jl Legian; open 9am-10pm daily), in calm surroundings, behind the Aquarius Star Hotel, is good value compared to other spas nearby. A 60-minute massage in Balinese, Shiatsu or Thai style is US$18, while a 30-minute *lulur* (body mask) of turmeric and sandalwood or Balinese Boreh (body scrub of cloves, ginger, nutmeg, galangal and rice powder) is US$10.

Jamu Spa (☎ 752520; w www.jamutraditio nalspa.com; Alam Kul Kul hotel) is in a typically calm setting. Indoor massage rooms open onto a pretty garden courtyard, and the

SOUTH BALI

spa offers exotic body treatments such as the 'New Age' body wrap treatment of papaya, kemiri and mint (US$45). A 60-minute massage is US$30.

Sicilia Spa (☎ 0818 355 602; Jl Arjuna, Seminyak) has a pleasant set-up of open-air massage and treatment rooms. A 60-minute massage starts at 60,000Rp.

Spa Me (☎ 765809; e spame@dps.centrin .net.id; Bali Mandira Hotel & Spa) is a deliciously relaxed and ambient spa, redolent with Balinese style. The stone walled massage rooms are light-filled. Reflexology massage, body scrubs, Javanese *lulur*, manicures and pedicures are available. A 50-minute massage is 240,000Rp and a romantic massage for two is 880,000Rp.

Mandara Spa (W www.mandaraspa-asia .com) has facilities in several top-end hotels including **Hotel Padma Bali** (☎ 752111), where the divine spa is decorated with water features and impressive stone sculptural reliefs. **Waterbom Park** also has a Mandara Spa villa. Massages start from US$30.

Waterbom Park
The popular Waterbom Park (Tuban map; ☎ 755676; W www.waterbom.com; Jl Kartika Plaza; adult/child/family US$16.50/8.80/44; open 8.30am-6pm daily), south of Kuta, is set on 3.5 hectares and has assorted water slides, swimming pools, play areas, a supervised childrens park for children under five years old, and a 'lazy river' ride. Other indulgences include eateries, a bar and the Mandara Spa (see Massage & Spas under Activities earlier). There are Australian-trained lifeguards and it's well supervised, but children under 12 years of age must be accompanied by an adult.

Swimming Pools
Most hotels will allow nonguests to use their pool for a fee. The most impressive (and expensive) is at the **Hard Rock Hotel** (☎ 761869; Jl Pantai Kuta; adult/child/family 100,000/50,000/250,000Rp; open from 11am), where you could easily hang out for the entire day. The snaking pool features water slides and small sandy beach areas, and is patrolled by lifeguards.

For the Kids
Timezone video arcades, in the two Matahari department stores, have lots of hi-tech games. Just south of Waterbom Park is **Le Speed Karts** (Tuban map; ☎ 757850), which charges 40,000Rp for five minutes' zipping around a tiny track.

Bungy Jumping
This not-so-cheap thrill is entirely in keeping with the Kuta ethos, and it's no surprise that Kuta has three bungy jump operators. Prices are competitive – US$45 or US$50 will get you two jumps and a T-shirt that brags about it.

AJ Hackett Bungy Co (Seminyak map; ☎ 731144, 730666; Jl Double Six), beside the beach in Legian, has a great view of the coast.

Bali Bungy (☎ 752658; Jl Pura Puseh) offers the extra thrill of 'sky surfing' – you're put in a hang-glider harness, hauled backwards up to 50m, then released to swoop over the pool at 120km/h in a super swing. Call for a free pick-up.

Horse Riding
Umalas Stables (☎ 731402; W www.99bali .com/adventure/umalas), north of Seminyak in Kerobokan, have a stable of 30 horses and ponies, and offer one-hour rice field tours for US$30, and two-/three-hour beach rides for US$50/70. Lessons in equestrian events such as dressage and showjumping can also be arranged.

ORGANISED TOURS
A vast range of tours all around Bali, from half-day to three-day tours can be booked through travel agents or hotels in the Kuta region. These tours are a quick and easy way to see a few sights if your time is limited, and you don't want to rent or charter a vehicle. See Organised Tours in the Getting Around chapter for popular itinerary options.

PLACES TO STAY
Kuta, Legian, Tuban and Seminyak have hundreds of places for you to stay. The top-end hotels are along the beachfront, mid-range places are mostly on the bigger roads between Jl Legian and the beach, and the cheapest losmen are generally along the smaller lanes in between. Tuban, Seminyak and the northern parts of Legian have mostly mid-range and top-end hotels – the best places to find budget accommodation are Kuta and southern Legian.

The cheapest places cost about 30,000/40,000Rp for singles/doubles, usually with a fan, a private bathroom with a cold shower, and a Western-style toilet. It is often worth paying more to stay in the cheapest rooms at a mid-range hotel, which will usually have a nice garden and a swimming pool. The better mid-range hotels have air-con rooms, and often hot water (as do more expensive rooms in the budget category). The top-end hotels or resorts have all the trimmings, including telephone, TV, hot water, minibar and room service.

With hotel names, be sceptical about words such as 'beach', 'seaview', 'cottage', and 'bungalows'. Places with 'beach' in their name may not be anywhere near the beach and a featureless, three-storey hotel block may rejoice in the name 'cottages'. Note that hotels on Jl Pantai Kuta are separated from the beach by a busy main road, even if the hotel is described as being 'on the beachfront'. This road has extended north of Jl Melasti, so now very few hotels have absolute beach frontage.

In all categories in this section, the hotels are grouped by location, from Tuban to Seminyak, and then listed alphabetically within the group. Prices quoted in this section are the peak season published rates – prices for budget accommodation include tax and service and prices for mid-range and top-end accommodation exclude tax and service charges unless otherwise stated.

PLACES TO STAY – BUDGET

The best budget accommodation is in a losmen with rooms facing a central garden. Look for a place that is far enough off the main roads to be quiet, but close enough so that getting to the beach, shops and restaurants is no problem. Many losmen still offer a simple breakfast.

Kuta

There are a couple of budget places near each other, just south of Jl Bakung Sari.

The friendly **Jesen's Inn II** (☎ 752647; singles/doubles 80,000/100,000Rp, rooms with air-con 120,000Rp) is a clean and modern place to stay.

Many of the cheap places are along the tiny alleys and lanes between Jl Legian and the beach in central Kuta. This is a good place to base yourself: it's quiet, but only a short walk from the beach, shops, bars and restaurants. A few places on the eastern side of Jl Legian are close to the bars and restaurants, but can be noisy and a fair hike from the beach. Jl Benesari is a great place to stay, close to the beach and quieter than the Poppies Gangs. There are a few reasonable cheapies on Gang Bedugul, off Poppies Gang I, such as **Lima Satu Cottages** (☎/fax 754944; singles/doubles 100,000/150,000Rp), which has rooms with hot water, air-con and a pool; **Puri Agung** (☎ 750054; singles/doubles 30,000/40,000Rp); and also **Taman Ayu I** (☎ 751855; singles/doubles 35,000/50,000Rp).

Ayu Beach Inn (☎ 752091, fax 752948; Poppies Gang I; room with/without hot water 120,000/100,000Rp) has simple rooms around a small round pool (so small in fact it's more like a plunge pool).

Adus Beach Inn (☎ 755326; Jl Lebak Bene; rooms 75,000-120,000Rp, with air-con 160,000-260,000Rp), set in a family compound, has clean but cramped rooms, all with cold water (except the most expensive).

Berlian Inn (☎ 751501; off Poppies Gang I; singles/doubles 50,000/60,000Rp, with hot water 90,000/100,000Rp), a quiet, friendly place has pleasant rooms with ikat bedspreads, and unusual open-air bathroom design.

Fat Yogis (☎ 751665; e fatyogi@telkom.net; Poppies Gang I; singles/doubles 60,000/80,000Rp, with air-con & hot water 140,000/160,000Rp) is in a central position and has decent rooms and a pool, although the bathrooms look a little grubby.

In leafy grounds, **Hotel Lusa** (☎ 753714; Jl Benesari; singles 75,000-165,000Rp, doubles 90,000-220,000Rp) has spartan rooms and the cheapest have cold water only. The drawcard is the pool.

Kedin's II (☎ 763554; Gang Sorga; singles/doubles 60,000/70,000Rp) is far cleaner than many other options and actually has white (as opposed to old and yellowed) sheets! Set in a leafy garden, rooms are in a two-storey building.

Komala Indah I (☎ 751422; Poppies Gang I; singles/doubles 25,000/35,000Rp), an old place, is clean and great value for the prime location. Rooms are simple with squat toilet and *mandi* (Indonesian bath), and it's always full, so book ahead.

Komala Indah I (☎ 753185; Jl Benesari; singles 30,000-95,000Rp, doubles 40,000-

135,000Rp), not to be confused with the losmen of the same name on Poppies Gang I, has a range of rooms with fan or air-con, set around a pleasant garden. The cheaper rooms have squat toilets and twin beds only. Breakfast isn't included.

Masa Inn (☎ 758507, fax 752606; W www .masainn.com; Poppies Gang I, 27; singles/ doubles 115,000/135,000Rp, with air-con 150,000/180,000Rp), a friendly and central place, offers decent value, since all rooms have hot water. The pool is an attraction.

Mimpi Bungalows (☎/fax 751848; off Gang Sorga; singles/doubles 80,000/120,000Rp, with hot water 200,000/300,00Rp) boasts plenty of shade and privacy, as well as nice rooms with a slightly Mexican feel, and friendly staff.

Rita's House (☎ 751760; singles/doubles 40,000/50,000Rp), just north of Poppies Gang I, isn't fancy but it's cheap, and hence a long-standing favourite of budget travellers.

Taman Ayu II (☎ 754376, fax 754640; off Poppies Gang II; singles 35,000-45,000Rp, doubles 50,000-65,000Rp, with air-con 70,000/ 100,000Rp) has a range of clean rooms with bamboo walls and most come with open-air bathrooms.

Legian

A few places are crowded along the two busy main roads in Legian – Jl Padma and Jl Melasti, or in areas between. Jl Pura Bagus Taruna is a quieter stretch of road.

Darsana Beach Inn (off Jl Sahadewa; singles/doubles 40,000/45,000Rp), a rundown

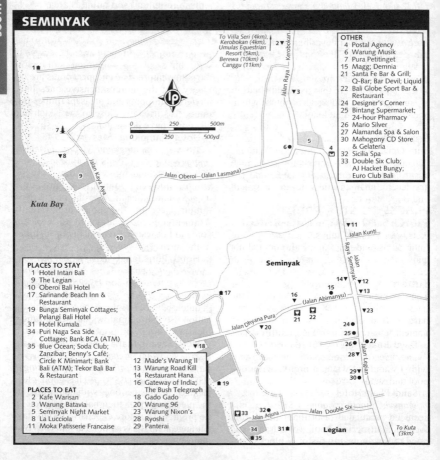

SEMINYAK

To Villa Seri (4km),
Kerobokan (4km),
Umulas Equestrian
Resort (5km),
Berewa (10km) &
Canggu (11km)

Jalan Raya Kerobokan

Jalan Raya Kerobokan

Jalan Kaya Aya

Kuta Bay

Jalan Oberoi – (Jalan Lasmana)

Jalan Kaya Aya

Seminyak

Jalan Kunti

Jalan Raya Seminyak

(Jalan Abimanyu)

Jalan Dhyana Pura

Jalan Legian

Jalan Arjuna

Jalan Double Six

Legian

To Kuta
(3km)

OTHER
4 Postal Agency
6 Warung Musik
7 Pura Petitinget
15 Magg; Demnia
21 Santa Fe Bar & Grill;
   Q-Bar; Bar Devil; Liquid
22 Bali Globe Sport Bar &
   Restaurant
24 Designer's Corner
25 Bintang Supermarket;
   24-hour Pharmacy
26 Mario Silver
27 Alamanda Spa & Salon
30 Mahogony CD Store
   & Gelateria
32 Sicilia Spa
33 Double Six Club;
   AJ Hacket Bungy;
   Euro Club Bali

PLACES TO STAY
1 Hotel Intan Bali
9 The Legian
10 Oberoi Bali Hotel
17 Sarinande Beach Inn &
   Restaurant
19 Bunga Seminyak Cottages;
   Pelangi Bali Hotel
31 Hotel Kumala
34 Puri Naga Sea Side
   Cottages; Bank BCA (ATM)
35 Blue Ocean; Soda Club;
   Zanzibar; Benny's Café;
   Circle K Minimart; Bank
   Bali (ATM); Tekor Bali Bar
   & Restaurant

PLACES TO EAT
2 Kafe Warisan
3 Warung Batavia
5 Seminyak Night Market
8 La Lucciola
11 Moka Patisserie Francaise

12 Made's Warung II
13 Warung Road Kill
14 Restaurant Hana
16 Gateway of India;
   The Bush Telegraph
18 Gado Gado
20 Warung 96
23 Warung Nixon's
28 Ryoshi
29 Panterai

0   250   500m
0   250   500yd

but rustic place, is set in a family compound with chooks running around.

Legian Beach Bungalow (☎ 751087; Jl Padma; singles/doubles 50,000/70,000Rp), friendly, unassuming, and centrally located, has a small pool and smallish rooms that are great value but can be noisy at night.

Senen Beach Inn (☎ 755470; Gang Camplung Mas 25; singles/doubles 30,000/35,000Rp), off Jl Melasti, is a low-key place run by friendly young guys. Rooms have outdoor bathrooms of sorts (cold water mandi) and are set around a small garden. It's an atmospheric, quiet place to stay because there's a small furniture-making workshop in the same compound where you can watch stuff being made. Breakfast isn't included.

Sinar Indah (☎ 755905; e wayansuda@ hotmail.com; Jl Padma Utara; singles/doubles 80,000/100,000Rp, with air-con 125,000/150,000Rp), a standard, fairly basic losmen handy to the beach, but without a pool, offers plain, clean rooms. All rooms have hot water.

Su's Cottages (☎ 752127, fax 750372; Jl Pura Bagus Taruna; rooms 130,000Rp, with air-con 160,000Rp) has stylish rattan beds in its simple, clean and bright rooms, which open onto a deep-blue pool.

Seminyak

Blue Ocean (☎ 730289, fax 730590; rooms 100,000-120,000Rp) is right on the beach beside Benny's Cafe in Seminyak. Rooms are decent, all with hot water and pleasant outdoor bathrooms.

PLACES TO STAY – MID-RANGE

All hotels listed in this section offer swimming pools, and many have air-con and hot water.

Tuban

There is some decent accommodation in the back streets east of Jl Kartika Plaza but it's hard to find, and it's also not very convenient for the beach or the nightlife areas.

Dayu Beach Inn (☎ 752263; off Jl Puspa Ayu; singles/doubles US$20/30) has rooms with TV and hot water, a pretty swimming pool and shady gardens.

Sandi Phala Hotel (☎ 753780, fax 236021; Jl Jenggala; singles/doubles US$20/25) is a secluded place with a brilliant beachfront location, attractive pool, restaurant, and good rooms in neat two-storey blocks.

Kuta

Central Kuta Many of these places are handy to the beach.

Aquarius Star Hotel (☎ 756573, fax 751762; e aquariushotel@yahoo.com; Jl Legian 116; singles 110,000-230,000Rp, doubles 125,000-250,000Rp) has clean, comfortable bungalows. The more expensive rooms are on the 2nd floor and are somewhat closeted and small but have TV and fridge.

Bali Matahari Hotel (☎ 763707, fax 763704; w www.balimatahari.com; Jl Lebak Bene; doubles US$20-40, family rooms US$80), off Jl Melasti, has impressive contemporary architecture. Many rooms, although small, are just by the pool, and the split-level family rooms are excellent. All rooms have air-con and TV, and there's also a plush restaurant and billiards area.

Bali Sandy Cottages (☎ 753344, fax 750791; off Poppies Gang II; singles 125,000-190,000Rp, doubles 150,000-225,000Rp) has been revamped and there are no cottages in sight, but a curving swimming pool is now the main feature. The cheaper rooms are ordinary, but the more expensive ones have modern bathrooms and pleasant timber furniture. It's friendly, close to the beach and all rooms have hot water.

Hotel Camplung Mas (☎ 751461, fax 751869; e camplung@indo.net.id; Jl Melasti; singles & doubles US$45) has Balinese stone architecture, and most bungalows are set within walled compounds – so if privacy is what you are after then this hotel is a good option. Even so, the rooms aren't really worth raving about, although all have air-con and hot water. Breakfast isn't included in the rates.

Hotel Puri Tanah Lot (☎ 752281, fax 755626; Jl Lebak Bene; singles/doubles US$17/20, with air-con US$25/30, poolside with air-con US$30/35), south of Jl Melasti, is quiet, but accessible to the beach and the action. Stylish bungalows are set around a pleasant garden and pool.

Hotel Sayang Maha Mertha (Hotel Sayang Beach Lodging; ☎/fax 751249; w www.sayanghotel.com; off Jl Lebak Bene; singles US$8-40, doubles US$10-45) has good, clean rooms. The cheaper ones with cold water are the nicest, although their balconies lack a little privacy. The more expensive rooms have a lounge area. It has a pool, bar and convivial atmosphere.

SOUTH BALI

The popular, three-storey **Hotel Sorga Kuta** (☎ 751897, fax 752417; e sorga@idola.net.id; singles 100,000-140,000Rp, doubles 132,000-184,000Rp) is located on a small site with a pool squeezed onto it. More expensive rooms have air-con and TV, and all of the rooms have hot water.

Kuta Puri Bungalows (☎ 751903, fax 752585; Poppies Gang I; singles/doubles US$17/20, with hot water US$24/28, with air-con & hot water US$30-40/35-45), with a convenient location, a pool and spacious gardens, is run down but OK value.

Kuta Seaview Cottages (Hotel Kuta Segara Ceria; ☎ 751961, fax 751962; w www.kuta seaviewhotel.com; Jl Pantai Kuta; singles US$45-80, doubles US$60-90, family room US$210) has stylishly decorated cottages, complete with fresh flowers on the beds, and is set among lovely gardens. It's popular with a younger crowd and its pool is perfectly placed facing the ocean.

Maharani II Hotel (☎/fax 756288; Gang Wina; singles/doubles US$50/60) is on a gang off Jl Pantai Kuta. The two-storey hotel has clean, modern rooms, all with air-con and a minibar, set around a landscaped pool area.

Rosani Hotel (☎ 761042, fax 761044; w www.rosani.com; Jl Lebak Bene; rooms 200,000Rp), next door to Bali Matahari Hotel, has clean, cold-water rooms.

Sari Yasa Samudra Bungalows (☎ 751562, fax 752948; Jl Pantai Kuta; singles/doubles US$20/23, with air-con US$35-40) has an excellent location directly opposite the beach. It has stylish bungalows that are pleasant, apart from some of the awful bed coverings. A few of the rooms are in a garden and poolside setting (although the swimming pool has seen better days). Breakfast isn't included.

Simpang Inn (☎ 761306; e simpanginn@ denpasar.wasantara.net.id; Jl Legian 133; singles US$22-46, doubles US$27-60) is a perfectly clean, functional place set around a pool. If you want to be close to the bars and nightlife it's ideal, and there's minimal traffic noise.

Suji Bungalow (☎ 765804, fax 752483; w www.sujibglow.co.id; off Poppies Gang I; singles US$19-26, doubles US$22-29) is a fine, friendly place with a choice of bungalows set in a spacious, quiet garden around a pool. It's not flash but it's better than

many similarly priced options. There's also a shady poolside café.

Un's Hotel (☎ 757409, fax 758414; e uns hotel@denpasar.wasantara.net.id; Jl Benesari; singles/doubles US$20/23, with air-con US$28/31, family rooms US$32-43), tucked away, but close to restaurants and the beach, is a relaxed two-storey place with bougainvillea spilling over the balconies, which face a pool. The spacious rooms have solar hot water, phones and open-air bathrooms. Breakfast isn't included.

Legian

Court Yard Hotel & Apartments (☎ 750242; w www.courtyard-bali.com; Jl Pura Bagus Taruna; rooms US$50-75, one-/two-bedroom apartments US$100/150) is a sleek, contemporary two-storey hotel cleverly designed so that all rooms face the pool. The rooms, decorated with abstract art, have a summery, airy ambience, and top-end facilities. **Hot Mango Bar** is a cool little whitewashed bar at the front of the hotel.

Puri Tantra Beach Bungalows (☎/fax 753195; Jl Padma Utara 50X; singles/ doubles/family US$35/40/55) has six charming, traditional, fan-only cottages, all with outdoor bathrooms and hot water, right by the beach.

Three Brothers Inn (☎ 751566, fax 756082; Jl Padma Utara; rooms from US$20, with air-con from US$30) has bungalows on huge shady grounds, nestled among twisting banyan trees. The fan rooms are the best option, but all rooms are spacious, some have lovely outdoor bathrooms, and most have solar hot water. Some rooms are suitable for families and there's a pleasant poolside café.

Seminyak

Bunga Seminyak Cottages (☎ 730239, fax 730905; Jl Camplung Tanduk; rooms US$65-80), off Jl Dhyana Pura, has lovely rooms with polished floorboards, huge bathrooms, and individual design touches. A small timber gate in the leafy gardens provides beach access.

Hotel Kumala (☎ 732186, fax 730407; w www.kumalahotel.com; Jl Pura Bagus Taruna; rooms 260,000-360,000Rp) has large rooms furnished with teak furniture, modern bathrooms, and two pools in a garden filled bamboo stands, frangipani and bougainvillea.

Puri Naga Sea Side Cottages (☎ 730761, fax 730524; Jl Arjuna; rooms US$65-90), right at the beach end of Jl Double Six, has a small pool and pleasant rooms, with lovely balcony views.

A delightful little hideaway, **Sarinande Beach Inn** (☎ 733604, fax 733605; e sarinand @dps.centrin.net.id; singles/doubles with air-con 60,000/180,000Rp) is one of the best places in Seminyak. It's secluded, but offers free transfers to Kuta and the airport. Rooms are excellent value and include TV and fridge.

A great little romantic hideaway, **Villa Seri** (☎ 730262, fax 730784; w www.villaseri.com; Br Umalas Kauh; rooms US$55-65) is located in Kerobokan. The rooms have four-poster beds and lots of Indonesian touches, as well as spacious balcony areas, that come complete with TVs.

PLACES TO STAY – TOP END

Hotels in Tuban and Seminyak might have genuine beach frontage, but those in Kuta and Legian are separated from the beach by a busy main road.

Tuban

Most of the top-end places are along Jl Kartika Plaza, the main road through Tuban, or on the side street Jl Segara.

Kartika Plaza Hotel (☎ 751067, fax 754585; w www.kartika-plaza.com; Jl Kartika Plaza; rooms US$180-200, family rooms US$200-300) is a large hotel with beach frontage, expansive gardens and a gigantic swimming pool.

Nathan Hotel (☎ 752825, fax 753222; e nathanhotel@eksadata.com; Gang Puspa Ayu; rooms US$80-95) is a stylish new place with rooms surrounding a pool.

Ramada Bintang Bali Resort (☎ 753292, fax 753288; w www.bali-paradise.com/ bintang-bali; Jl Kartika Plaza; singles US$145-285, doubles US$155-285), a big hotel fronting Tuban beach, has a wonderful pool, tennis courts, health club, nightclub and karaoke.

Risata Bali Resort (☎ 753340, fax 753354; w www.risatabali.com, Jl Segara; rooms US$100-210) has pleasant, spacious rooms. The resort is set around a pool in a lovely colouful garden. It's a short walk to the beach, but a fair way from most of Kuta's shops and nightlife.

Kuta

Alam Kul Kul (☎ 752520, fax 752519; w www .alamresorts.com; Jl Pantai Kuta; rooms/villas US$125/250) is in a gorgeous setting among majestic, gnarled banyan trees. Rooms and villas have contemporary styling with lots of attention to detail, and there's a kids' daycare centre. The **Jamu Spa** is on-site (see the Massage & Spas entry under Activities earlier in this chapter).

Hard Rock Hotel (☎ 761869, fax 762162; w www.hardrockhotelbali.com; Jl Pantai Kuta; rooms US$180-750, family suite US$360) has themed rooms, which all feature appropriate memorabilia (as well as Hard Rock logos here, there and everywhere). It's totally formulaic and feels like a theme park, but…it's different. All rooms have TV, a music system and spa bath, and the hotel has a kids' club, spa (one-hour massage US$45) and there's a gym.

Hotel Bounty (☎ 753030, fax 752121; w www.balibountygroup.com; Poppies Gang II; doubles US$93-103, duplex US$175) has two pools in leafy grounds – one is quiet and low key, while the other has a busy bar, loud dance music and plenty of under-30s lounging in the sun. All rooms have air-con, phone and TV, and the duplex rooms are ideal for groups.

Kuta Legian Village Hotel (☎ 750888, fax 750815; w www.kutalegianvillage.com; off Jl Legian; rooms US$98, with pool view US$118, villas US$158) is at the end of a long bamboo-lined path off Jl Legian – so it's relatively quiet. The thatch-roofed hotel is in a new, blindingly white building set off by colourful hibiscus blooms. Rooms are lovely, although the standard ones face a wall. Those with pool views are a step away from the pool. There's also an in-house spa.

Poppies Cottages I (☎ 751059, fax 752364; w www.poppies.net; Poppies Gang I; singles/doubles US$80/85) is a Kuta institution and has a lush garden setting for its thatch-roofed cottages. A big attraction is that the cottages have outdoor sunken baths. The peaceful pool is surrounded by stone sculptures and water fountains.

Legian

Most of the top-end places in Legian are directly opposite the beach. However, in all cases a road separates their lush gardens from the sand.

Bali Mandira Hotel & Spa (☎ 751381, fax 752377; W www.balimandira.com; Jl Pantai Kuta; rooms US$130-250) has gardens filled with bird of paradise flowers. Cottages have modern interiors, and the bathrooms are partly open-air. The drawcard here is the stunning pool at the peak of a stone ziggurat, offering uninterrupted ocean views. It also has a pleasant open-air beachfront café. For information on the hotel's spa, Spa Me, see Massage & Spas under Activities earlier in this chapter.

Casa Padma (☎ 753073, fax 755925; e casapadma@indo.com; Jl Padma; rooms US$70-120) is a small, stylish place designed around neutral beach-washed tones. All of the rooms have air-conditioning and the best rooms are by the pool. Breakfast isn't included.

Hotel Padma Bali (☎ 752111, fax 752140; W www.hotelpadma.com; Jl Padma; rooms US$160-190, family room US$220), a sprawling upmarket hotel by the beach, has lush gardens landscaped with lotus ponds. Balinese artwork graces the tasteful decorated rooms. It has several restaurants, including Italian and Japanese (dishes around 50,000Rp). For information on the spa, see Massage & Spas under Activities earlier in this chapter.

Legian Beach Hotel (☎ 751711, fax 752651; W www.legianbeachbali.com; Jl Melasti; rooms US$130, bungalows US$150-170, family room US$160-170) has thatched bungalows set amongst lovely gardens of tall coconut palms. Rooms are comfortable, if a bit formulaic. The scenic pool area has a great view of the ocean and the horizon from the swim-up bar, and there's also a shallow pool for kids.

Seminyak

There are a few top-end hotels along the coast in Seminyak. All of them offer almost total seclusion, and a full range of services because there are very few shops and restaurants nearby. Most of these hotels provide a free shuttle bus service to Kuta and Legian.

Hotel Intan Bali (☎ 730777, fax 730778; e intan@denpasar.wasantara.net.id; singles US$130-190, doubles US$140-190) is a wonderfully isolated four-star hotel with beautiful gardens, a spa, full sporting facilities and spacious rooms.

Oberoi Bali Hotel (☎ 730361, fax 730791; cottages & villas US$255-850), an elegant place with beach frontage and relaxing gardens, has tasteful and understated Balinese cottage-style architecture.

Pelangi Bali Hotel (☎ 730346, fax 730947; W www.pelangibali.com; Jl Dhyana Pura; rooms US$80-130, suite US$360) is a new hotel with absolute beachfront access. A contemporary double-storey place on a small site, it has very smart rooms. There are sculptures throughout the grounds and a cascading pool overlooking the beachfront. It also has a spa.

The Legian (☎ 730622, fax 730623; e reservation@thelegianbali.com; rooms US$236-366) features compelling ocean outlooks from the restaurant, pool area and every room. Rooms and suites are decorated with fine Indonesian arts and crafts.

Umalas Equestrian Resort (☎ 731402, fax 731403; Jl Lestari 9X, Br Umalas, Kerobokan; rooms US$150-225, walk in rates US$83-93), north of Seminyak, is a magical place to stay – especially if you are a horse lover. The comfortable rooms, complete with horse motifs, pristine modern bathrooms and rice paddy views, are above the stables, so it is all very atmospheric. A café overlooks the pool.

Long-term Accommodation

Many villas are available for longer stays. Typically they have a kitchen (with fridge and basic cooking facilities), living room and private garden, and often two or more bedrooms, so they are suitable for a family or a group of friends. For rentals, check out either **House of Bali** (☎ 739541, fax 412804; e kerobokan@houseofbali.com; W www.houseofbali.com) or **The Agencies Bali Villas** (☎ 730068, fax 733851; e info@agencies-bali-villas.com; W www.agencies-bali-villas.com).

PLACES TO EAT

There are countless places to eat around the Kuta region, from small warung to gourmet hotel restaurants. The cuisine is international and multicultural, so dining on Japanese or Thai food or Balinese fusion are standard options.

You'll find some of the best and cheapest food available in Kuta at Seminyak night market, and there are also travellers cafés everywhere in the area.

Tuban

The restaurants in the top-end hotels along Jl Kartika Plaza are worth considering, particularly the **Golden Lotus** (☎ 752403; dishes 40,000-100,000Rp) in the Bali Dynasty Hotel, which focuses on Chinese cuisine. One of the more obvious non-hotel choices is the **Lotus Tavern** (☎ 753797; Jl Segara; dishes 22,000-50,000Rp), part of a Bali-wide chain that serves good quality Western and Asian cuisine in a pleasant setting.

S.A. Café (Jl Segara; dishes 15,000-30,000Rp) is a cheap option if you're staying at one of the resort hotels, and serves all the usual suspects.

The Appetite (Jl Kartika Plaza; dishes 26,000-55,000Rp) is a swanky place featuring a grand piano and water fountains. Dishes are internationally inspired, as well as Indonesian and Chinese. Wines are available by the glass or bottle from Jabu's Wine Bar & Cellar, next door.

Daddy's Cafe (dishes 25,000-45,000Rp) does kebabs, moussaka, meze and other Greek and Mediterranean fare in low-key surroundings.

Kin Khao (☎ 757808; Jl Kartika Plaza; dishes 16,000 35,000Rp), part of a chain, serves authentic, inexpensive Thai food in a pleasant setting.

Copa Café (☎ 762028; Jl Kartika Plaza 172; dishes 15,000-60,000Rp) has tourist fodder of pizzas and pasta as well as a small selection of Balinese food, and there's a kids' menu. The upstairs area has Internet terminals and is much more pleasant than downstairs.

Further north, in and around the Kuta Centre shopping centre, those in need of a fast-food fix will find the usual Western options. Also here is the **All Star Surf Cafe** (☎ 757933; 2nd Flr, Kuta Centre; dishes 20,000-56,000Rp), which serves up crowd pleasers of burgers, enchiladas and pizzas.

Kuta

South Kuta East of the hotel, **Hard Rock Deli** (☎ 761869; dishes 12,000-43,000Rp) is a tiny café, and is perfect to stock up on comfort food such as pastries, coffee, savoury pies and ice cream.

Matahari Food Court, on the top floor of the Matahari department store, has an excellent selection of economical Asian food stalls popular with locals.

Made's Warung (Jl Pantai Kuta; dishes 18,000-90,000Rp) may be one of the few restaurants where you'll dine amongst locals, but staff are surly and you'll be forced to sit at 'sociable shared tables', where diners awkwardly make a point of ignoring one another, while entry is barred to the peaceful and empty upstairs section. On offer are sandwiches, salads, and overpriced Indonesian and Western dishes.

At the southern end of the beachfront, there are limited options. **Mentari** (dishes 15,000-50,000Rp), part of the Natour Kuta Beach Hotel, serves up international dishes such as risotto and paella. If you sit at the front tables, you'll get hassled by hawkers.

Central Kuta A welcome retreat after the noise and hassle of Jl Legian, **Poppies Restaurant** (☎ 751059; dishes 20,000-40,000Rp) was one of the first restaurants in Kuta (hence Poppies Gang I is named after it), and is popular for its garden setting and romantic atmosphere. The menu is international and the food is perfectly presented, though not outstanding. You may need to make a dinner reservation.

Un's Restaurant (☎ 752607; dishes 26,000-70,000Rp), a stylish place, is down a narrow lane south of Poppies Gang I. It has several very European offerings, as well as Indonesian dishes.

Bamboo Corner (Poppies Gang I; dishes 7000-15,000Rp) is dark and stuffy but it's always crowded with travellers – due to the bargain prices and decent food – juices are only 3000Rp and a large Bintang is 8500Rp. Sandwiches, seafood and Chinese and Indonesian dishes are on offer.

Fat Yogis (☎ 751665; Poppies Gang I; dishes 10,000-37,000Rp) serves yet more traveller ghetto fare of pasta and wood-fired pizzas.

Treehouse Café (dishes 6000-50,000Rp) is a low-key, relaxed place serving cheap juices and beers, and standard travellers fare from its international menu, such as *tempeh* burgers, complete with gherkin and fries (9500Rp).

Along Jl Legian The possibilities along Jl Legian are endless, but avoid tables close to the busy street.

Just north of Bemo Corner, **Kunti Japanese** (dishes 25,000-30,000Rp) has all the

Japanese standards of udon, soba, tempura, sushi and sashimi, and all the right Japanese flavours, but it's not worth going out of your way to eat here.

Further north, **Mini Restaurant** (☎ 751651; No 77; dishes 20,000-70,000Rp) was being restored at the time of writing, following damage from the bombings. It is a huge place, despite the name, and had a busy, bustling ambience. It did a good line in barbecued seafood and Chinese food.

Tucked down a small laneway at the rear of Voodoo Dolls shop, the tiny and friendly **Bali's Best Bistro – Legian's Little Purple Palace** (☎ 750649; No 62; dishes 5000-10,000Rp, large Bintang 11,000Rp) is a locals' favourite. Tuck into simple, but generous dishes such as *bakso* (meat balls) and *nasi campur*.

Ketupat (☎ 754209; dishes 25,000-120,000Rp), hidden behind the Jonathan Gallery, is a calm, serene oasis ideal for either lunch or dinner. The dining pavilions all centre on a strikingly blue bathing pool. Dishes originate from across Indonesia, including Javanese curries, such as *nasi hijau harum* (fried rice with greens, shrimps and herbs).

Kopi Pot (☎ 752614; cakes 14,000-17,000Rp; dishes 22,000-40,000Rp; open until midnight) is popular for its choice of coffees, fresh salads and yum cakes, as well as seafood, European and Indonesian main courses. The upstairs dining area is more relaxed than the twee outdoor area which is at street level.

Nero Bar & Restaurant (☎ 750756; **w** www.nerobali.com; dishes 26,000-60,000Rp; open 10am-midnight) has a slick, architectural interior. Bar prices are reasonable (small/large Bintang 11,000/18,000Rp) and the international menu has a Mediterranean bent, while the seafood choices include mouth-watering options, like tuna brochette in lime olive oil.

Aroma's Cafe (☎ 751003; dishes 25,000-38,000Rp) may be in a gentle garden setting encircled by water fountains, but expect similar prices to what you would pay at home for just better than average juices, breakfast and coffee (then again it does have very flash toilets – make sure you go at least once to get your money's worth!). International mains meals are also available, at more reasonable prices.

On & Near Poppies Gang II Poppies Gang II has the biggest concentration of cheap travellers eateries – most with indistinguishable menus, such as **Bali Corner** (dishes 8000-15,000Rp), which serves up the usual range of Indonesian, Western and Chinese food, and of course crowd pleaser pizza. Many of the eateries along here also show video movies at night.

Rumah Makan ACC Baru (dishes 5,000-10,000Rp; open 24hr), next door to Tubes Surf Bar, serves up generous Sumatran Padang dishes, with big dollops of hot sambal. A little further down, opposite Hotel Bounty, the **Rainbow Cafe** (☎ 765730; Poppies Gang II 23; dishes 7000-17,500Rp), a nice little travellers café, has large comfy sofas and is a good place to watch life on the gang.

On the lane to the south, a group of small, totally unpretentious cheapies, such as **Warung Indonesia** and **Fajar** (dishes 5000-16,000Rp) serve up typical travellers fare. Many also show videos during the day and evening.

On another unnamed lane going north, **Warung 96** (dishes 6000-25,000Rp) is a good, fail-safe option if you're really hungry. It serves up a big range of sandwiches, Western, Indonesian and Chinese food, and yes, pizza. Opposite is a great little **warung Padang**, while next door **Warung Wulon** (dishes 6000-17,000Rp) is dark and cool inside and serves up similar food to Warung 96. They also do great banana smoothies (6000Rp) – cold, icy and very banana. The beers are also cheap.

Further up this lane at the Jl Benesari corner, the Brazilian founders of **Brasil Bali Cantinho** (☎ 752692; dishes 15,000-30,000Rp) have long since moved on, although the Brazilian paraphernalia remains (if a little grimy these days), as does the menu of favourites like *feijoada* (a soup of rice and beans). The restaurant is always surprisingly busy and has a good vibe.

The Balcony (☎ 757409; Jl Benesari 16; breakfast 17,000-25,000Rp, dishes 34,000-90,000Rp) has a breezy tropical design. It is located on the first floor which separates it from the hub-bub below. The generous dishes are mostly Mediterranean – on offer is gazpacho, seafood brochettes, tapas and paella. If you're thirsty, happy hour is between 5pm and 8pm.

Komala Indah II Cafe (☎ 754258; dishes 5000-17,000Rp) shows films nightly and has a little more atmosphere than some of the other travellers cafés around.

On the Beach Only the hum of motorbikes interrupt the seaside ambience at **Bali Mandira Hotel Café** (☎ 751381; Jl Pantai Kuta; dishes 25,000-43,000Rp), a fine place to start the evening off with cocktails (38,000Rp to 51,000Rp) or beers (small/large Bintang 17,000/24,000Rp). On offer are tasty dishes such as red snapper fillet on a sesame seed bun with tartar sauce and fries.

Papa's Café (☎ 755055; e papasbali@hot mail.com; Jl Pantai Kuta; dishes 28,000-90,000Rp), part of the Alam Kul Kul hotel, is a breezy Italian café. Partake of some chilled *limoncello* liqueur or gelato while taking in the ocean views, or dine on simple meals of foccacia, antipasto and pizza, or more elaborate pasta and seafood dishes.

In a great spot, **Parasol Mediterranean Restaurant** (☎ 751381; dishes 40,000-90,000Rp) is part of the Bali Mandira Hotel & Spa and overlooks the beach. Be sure to call to reserve an outdoor table for dinner.

Legian

On Jl Melasti, several places cater mainly to package tourists from the nearby hotels.

Gosha Bar & Restaurant (☎ 759880; Jl Melasti; dishes 20,000-80,000Rp) has an airy bamboo interior where the focus is more on food than décor. It specialises in charcoal grilled crayfish.

Legian Garden Restaurant has cheap all-you-can eat buffet breakfasts (12,500Rp) and an excellent happy hour (but not much else going for it). For Chinese, head to **Restaurant Puri Bali Indah** (☎ 751644; dishes 12,000-60,000Rp), which has a typically epic menu of 174 items, with plenty of seafood options, including abalone.

Copa Café & Internet (☎ 767312; Jl Melasti; dishes 13,500-28,000Rp) is doing a suck job for the Australian package tourists, with 'Aussie' paraphernalia decorating its open-air tropical interior. It's not too nauseating, however, and is actually a decent, friendly place to eat. Plenty of interesting local dishes are on offer, including *pepes ikan* (grilled fish in banana leaf), and there's a comfortable Internet area upstairs (300Rp per minute).

Around the corner, Jl Padma is well supplied with eateries and bars. **Take** (☎ 763376; dishes 24,000-80,000Rp, set menus 59,000-70,000Rp) is pricey by Balinese standards but it serves among the best Japanese food in Kuta. You will be greeted by a spirited *irrashaimase* (welcome) from Balinese staff in kimono and *yukata* dress.

Jl Padma also has another of the **Kin Khao** (dishes 16,000-35,000Rp) restaurants, serving tasty Thai dishes.

Joni Bar Restaurant (Jl Padma; dishes 17,000-46,000Rp), across the road, has a party atmosphere around the swimming pool. Tex-Mex meals and an evening happy hour (6pm to 8.30pm) are on offer. Balinese dance performances are also held on Monday and Friday at 7.30pm.

Wayan & Friends (☎ 761024; Jl Padma; dishes 9000-40,000Rp) is a relaxed place with batik tablecloths and low lighting. It has some delicious offerings, such as vegetable juices, and gourmet sandwiches made from freshly baked baguettes, filled with Australian cheeses and meats. A kids' menu is also available.

Further north, things get more expensive, but the standards are higher – this is the fashionable end of town. There are, however, plenty of smaller warung. Try **Warung Banyu Mas** (☎ 755956; Jl Padma Utara; dishes 6000-13,000Rp), a refreshingly low-key place serving inexpensive Indonesian dishes, such as a spicy *nasi campur* with roasted peanuts, fish, green beans and corn fritters.

Kafe Warna (Jl Pantai Arjuna; dishes 11,000-40,000Rp) is a shady, easygoing spot opposite the beach at the cusp of Legian and Seminyak. On offer are Tex-Mex dishes as well as the usual Indonesian suspects. A good selection of pastries (13,000Rp to 30,000Rp) is also available.

Restoran Enak Glory (☎ 751091; Jl Legian 445; Balinese buffet adult/child 40,000/20,000Rp) is a long-standing place, worth heading to on a Saturday night to try a Balinese buffet.

Poco Loco (☎ 756079; Jl Padma Utara; dishes 25,000-50,000Rp; open 6pm-late daily), on the lane south of Jl Pura Bagus Taruna, is a popular, brightly decorated Mexican restaurant and bar, serving tasty food – Tex-Mex chicken is a good choice.

Jl Pura Bagus Taruna has a big selection. **Swiss Restaurant** (☎ 761511; Jl Pura Bagus

Taruna; dishes 15,000-56,000Rp), adjacent to the Swiss and Austrian consular agents, has been serving up Swiss favourites since 1977 (long enough in any case for the décor to morph into a jarring collage of Swiss and Balinese design). Indonesian dishes are also on offer, and a Legong dance performance is held every Saturday at 8pm.

Rhum (☎ 762297; Jl Pura Bagus Taruna; dishes 10,000-25,000Rp), next door, is a contemporary, funkster bar/café with plenty of atmosphere and nil attitude. Chilled music, newspapers and comfy lounges make this a place to sit and while away the holiday hours. The food's not bad either, with delicious breakfast and main options, including basics like *soto ayam*, satay and Thai fish cakes. Movies are also played nightly (except Friday and Sunday) at 7pm and 9pm.

Rum Jungle Road Bar & Restaurant (dishes 20,000-40,000Rp) is a reliable eatery that's been on the tourist scene for some time.

Seminyak

Seminyak Night Market gets going around 6pm and plenty of warung sell delicious *bakso* and *soto ayam*. Loud music plays and there's a real convivial atmosphere. Not many travellers seem to make it here, which makes the trip for dinner well worth it. In Seminyak itself, you'll still see *bakso* sellers and small warung, which gives it a less Western atmosphere than elsewhere in Kuta. At the western end of Jl Double Six, several bar/eateries line-up along the beach, all with cool breezes and a sunset drinks scene, and all much hipper than equivalent places in Kuta.

Benny's Cafe (☎ 731305; dishes 14,000-48,000Rp), with gorgeous ocean views and a comfortable, beach holiday atmosphere, is one of the few restaurants in Kuta (or Bali for that matter) that has *bakso* on the menu. Also on offer are salads, pasta, pizza and a big range of Indonesian dishes. Bintang is reasonably priced and the banana milkshakes are thick and creamy.

Zanzibar (☎ 733529; dishes 21,000-44,000Rp) comes into its own at sunset, but during the day you'll bake a little in the shade-free café. The menu features vegetarian and pasta dishes, including calzone.

Soda Club (☎ 732777; dishes 22,000-86,000Rp) is another stylish place on this little strip, with tables on ascending terraces,

which take advantage of the sea views. The menu is interesting, featuring lots of fresh seafood.

Tekor Bali Bar & Restaurant (☎ 735268; dishes 17,000-42,000Rp) is a shady place offering good breakfast choices, and Thai, Indian, Italian and Western dishes, as well as a big range of authentic Balinese dishes. Try *tumbabi* (minced pork in banana leaf) or *jaja dadar guling* (Balinese pancakes).

Gado Gado (☎ 736966; lunch 45,000-75,000Rp, dinner 85,000-110,000Rp) offers light, seasonal dishes reflecting Asian, Japanese and Mediterranean influences, such as lobster tempura with seaweed. It's very much a smart, international restaurant, without a hint of anything Balinese about it. There's also a chic lounge area, ideal for sipping on cocktails.

The main road offers a few options, including **Ryoshi** (☎ 731152; Jl Legian; dishes 28,000-60,000Rp), a reliable Japanese restaurant, and **Panterai** (☎ 732567; Jl Legian; dishes 25,000-50,000Rp), which is known for its fine Greek-Mediterranean seafood. Or, for a fraction of the price, head to **Warung Nixon**, a friendly locals' place offering good Indonesian food.

At the Jl Dhyana Pura junction, Jl Legian changes name to Jl Raya Seminyak, and you'll find **Warung Road Kill** (☎ 736222), which serves sanitized versions of traditional warung dishes (point and select from the display) at smart little tables. The name is appropriate given the crazy traffic flow on this corner!

JP's Warung Club (☎ 731622; Jl Dhyana Pura; dishes 15,000-38,000Rp) is a relaxed place, which has comfy lounges and very long tables. On offer are health juices, delish sandwiches, such as tuna ciabatta with capers and mayonnaise, as well as interesting Indonesian and Italian dishes. There's live music here on Tuesday to Friday nights.

Gateway of India (☎ 732940; Jl Dhyana Pura 10; dishes 25,000-45,000Rp) is a popular spot for curries and tandoori dishes.

Made's Warung II (☎ 732130; Jl Raya Seminyak; dishes 18,000-90,000Rp) is in a private courtyard area, set back from the road (although traffic noise is still ever present). The menu is the same as Made's Warung in Kuta, although the setting is more spacious, and features well-prepared Indonesian- and Asian-style dishes, cakes and coffee.

Across the road, the Japanese **Restaurant Hana** (☎ 732778; *Jl Raya Seminyak; dishes 20,000-50,000Rp*) offers great sushi from 8000Rp to 20,000Rp per piece, served with style at dark wood tables with cushions on the floor.

Moka Patisserie Francaise (☎ 731424; *Jl Raya Seminyak; dishes 15,000-45,000Rp*) is a good French-style bakery, which is popular for breakfast. French cuisine is also served for lunch and dinner.

Follow the road north towards Kerobokan, and you'll pass **Warung Batavia** (*dishes 15,000-30,000Rp*), which has a big choice of excellent, authentic Indonesian dishes, and **Kafe Warisan** (☎ 731175; *Jl Raya Kerobokan; dishes 27,000-60,000Rp*), which serves fine French-Mediterranean cuisine in a romantic atmosphere.

Follow Jl Oberoi to the end and check out the delightful seaside setting of **La Lucciola** (☎ 730838; *dishes 30,000-60,000Rp*), where an Italian and seafood menu awaits.

ENTERTAINMENT

Around 6pm, the sunset at the beach is the big attraction, perhaps while enjoying a drink at a café with a sea view. After a good dinner, many visitors are happy with a video movie, another drink (or two) and a stroll in the cool evening air. But a lot of people are on holiday and here to party, and in Kuta that means lots of drinking, loud music and late nights. The more sophisticated nightspots are mainly in Seminyak, where the ambience is decidedly hipper, and where the clubs don't get going until after 11pm.

A few prostitutes cruise the central part of Jl Legian after 11pm, but mostly they are now confined to a couple of bars. 'Kuta Cowboys' practice their pick-ups in many of the busier tourist bars and clubs. There are also cruising transvestites (*orang bencong* or *waria*) late at night. Gays are welcome almost everywhere, but only a couple of places have a noticeable gay scene.

It's generally safe to walk the main streets late at night, but avoid isolated parts of the beach and take care outside nightclubs.

Bars & Clubs

Most bars are free to enter, and often have special drink promotions and 'happy hours' between about 6pm and 9pm. During the low season, when tourist numbers are down, you might have to visit quite a few venues to find one with any life.

Tuban Starting right down south, **Zero Six Club** (☎ 753196) is by the beach, and has a happy hour at sunset, live music on some nights and a DJ after midnight.

All Star Surf Club (☎ 757933) offers raucous entertainment, such as live sumo wrestling on some nights of the week, as well as karaoke and DJs. Movies are also played.

Jabu's Wine Bar & Cellar (☎ 763861; *Kartika Plaza 99X; open 10am-1am*) is a stylish bar where fairly ordinary French and Australian wines can be ordered by the glass. More promising options are available by the bottle. You can also order wine here but dine at The Appetite, next door.

Kuta & Legian The landmark, **Hard Rock Cafe** (☎ 755661; *Jl Pantai Kuta*) is a merchandising outlet disguised as a nightclub, and a magnet for Asian yuppies. It gets going after 11pm, when a (usually) slick band plays classic rock covers. It's also a venue for occasional overseas artists.

Further south on Jl Legian, **Miller Time Cafe** (*small/large Bintang 8500/12,500Rp*) has a big outdoor seating area and stage, where bad cover bands play even worse Beatles covers, while hammered foreigners 'sing' along. Go down a side lane near here to **Apache**, where a local reggae band starts at 11pm every night (it's deserted before then). It gets a lively crowd of locals, Japanese and Westerners. The pedestrian court south of here has various venues, including the **Bounty II**.

Just south of Poppies Gang II, **Tubes Surf Bar & Restaurant** (*small/large Bintang 7500/14,000Rp*) is a cavernous place that's deserted during the day, but attracts an interesting mixed crowd in the evening. The music is commercial and a long way from the bad cover bands found elsewhere. A kiosk opens in the evening with info on surf lessons and trips. Surfing videos and pool tables offer an alternative to straight up drinking.

The Bounty (*Jl Legian*) is a ludicrous building shaped like a sailing ship, where wait staff are dressed like Captain Stubing and Gopher from the *Love Boat*. Awful live

SOUTH BALI

'music' plays nightly at 9pm. The happy hour goes from 9pm until 11pm – where the infamous 'jam jar' drinks provide maximum alcohol for minimum rupiah, multiplied by quantum hangover. A 'discotheque' kicks on until 6am.

Near the Jl Legian and Jl Melasti intersection, the all-class Kuta institution, **Peanuts** (☎ 754226) is yet another place to go if you're hankering for a killer hangover. It organises the Peanuts Pub Crawl on Tuesday and Saturday nights (15,000Rp), which provides special buses and entry to a selection of local watering holes (does it get any better than this?). *Arak* and 'Jungle Juice' feature big time. It has a big outer bar with pool tables and loud live rock or reggae, and a large dance floor inside. It attracts plenty of local gigolos and, all in all, is a sad and sorry place.

Suci Bar & Restaurant (☎ 751330; Jl Pantai Kuta; dishes 7000-25,000Rp) is a good people-watching spot that has been around forever. It has an impressive bar list, with cocktails from 23,000Rp to 28,000Rp.

Seminyak Some of the hippest bars are in Seminyak – and thankfully there's not a 'jam jar' in sight!

Santa Fe Bar & Grill (☎ 731147; Jl Dhyana Pura 11A; dishes 15,000-40,000Rp) will do a tequila sunrise or meal 24 hours a day. It's actually a relaxed, low-key bar with candle-lit tables, which has a good reputation as a live music venue from Tuesday to Thursday and Saturday.

Q-Bar (☎ 762361; Jl Dhyana Pura; open until 2am) is a swish, dimly lit gay bar that has regular DJs playing alternative music. The upstairs area has clubbing clothes for both genders on sale, as well as Internet access. A simple menu of Q-snacks is available.

Bar Devil (☎ 730931; Jl Dhyana Pura; dishes 25,000-35,000Rp) has a Japanese owner who doubles as the DJ on Friday and Saturday nights and spins some mean vinyl in the dark, narrow interior of this very cool, Tokyo-esque bar.

Liquid (☎ 730894; Jl Dhyana Pura) and its blue illuminated bar and kaleidoscopic lights trailing the walls is very lush and very sexy. The bar gets going at around 1am and a guest DJ plays every Wednesday, Friday and Saturday night.

Alternatively, the chic and streamlined **Gado Gado** (☎ 736966; open till 4am or later),

by the beach, has DJs on Friday and Saturday nights and a comfortable lounge area to sip cocktails; it's also a very smart restaurant (see Places to Eat earlier in this chapter).

Later on, but never before 1am, the action shifts to the beachside **Double Six Club** (☎ 731266; open midnight-7am), a huge, thatch-roofed pavilion overlooking a pool and the 'classy' AJ Hackett bungy jump.

Euro Club Bali (☎ 733441; call for pick up) is another big open-air place across from the beach beside Double Six Club. It features live music, including a Salsa night every Thursday.

Gay & Lesbian Venues

In the Kuta-Legian-Seminyak area, the most openly gay venues are **Cafe Luna** in Legian and **Hulu Café** (Jl Sahadewa) in Kuta, which has drag shows several nights a week.

In Seminyak, **Double Six** is popular with gays (as well as everyone else), as is **Q-Bar** (☎ 762361; Jl Dhyana Pura). The beach, especially at the end of Jl Dhyana Pura, is a cruising area, but activity is sometimes restricted when the *banjar* decides to crackdown on beach crimes.

Video Movies & Sports Telecasts

Video movies are featured at numerous bar/restaurants, particularly along or near Poppies Gang II. They are pretty loud and easy to find, and they start as early as 3pm, with a new movie every couple of hours. Other places show live sports telecasts.

The Bush Telegraph Pub (☎ 732963; Jl Dhyana Pura 10XX, Seminyak; dishes 23,500-49,500Rp) is a cavernous place where staff dress in awful blue-and-yellow branded Fosters-beer uniforms. There's a big screen and the focus here is on sports coverage, including live crossovers to Australian Football League (AFL) games on weekends. You can also tuck into Australian steaks, hamburgers and general pub fare.

Bali Globe Sport Bar & Restaurant (☎ 730323; Jl Dhyana Pura 9, Seminyak; dishes 17,000-55,000Rp) is a breezy, relaxed place to hang out. It has pool tables as well as Starsport and other cable sports channels. The menu is typically international.

Latino's (☎ 756529; Jl Benesari; dishes 19,000-50,000Rp) is a spacious open-air pavilion that offers billiard tables, a big screen and an international menu.

Balinese Dance
Large hotels and restaurants present the best-known Balinese dances, and these are well publicised. A Balinese buffet is usually included.

Travel agents and hotels can also arrange evening trips to see traditional dances at Batubulan and Denpasar. If you can, it's cheaper to arrange it yourself. If you're heading to Ubud, it's a much better place to see Balinese dancing. For more information see the 'Balinese Dance' special section.

SHOPPING
Parts of the Kuta region are door-to-door shops and over the years these have steadily become more sophisticated. But there are still many simple stalls, where T-shirts, souvenirs and beachwear are the main lines, and where the price depends on your bargaining ability. Many of these stalls are crowded together in 'art markets' like the one near the beach end of Jl Bakung Sari or the one on Jl Melasti. The bigger, Western-style shops generally have higher quality goods at higher fixed prices. Don't be pressured into buying things during the first few days of your stay – shop around for quality and price first.

Supermarkets & Department Stores
For everyday purchases like groceries, toiletries and stationery, there are shops and minimarkets, such as Circle K, along busy streets. The two **Matahari department stores** *(open 9.30am-10pm)* have fairly uninspiring clothing, a floor full of souvenirs, jewellery, cheap eateries and plenty of other ways to spend your money. These continue around to Jl Pantai Kuta, where there is a **Lotte Japanese** department store.

Clothing
The local fashion industry has diversified from beach gear to sportswear to fashion clothing. Most of the fashion shops are on or near Jl Legian. Inexpensive everyday clothing is sold in the Matahari department stores. **Kuta Square** has the most sophisticated group of shops, including brand-name clothing shops such as Mooks and Stussy, and locally based fashion outlets such as **Animale** *(☎ 485450; e animale@indosat.net.id)* and **Ulu Watu Lace** *(☎ 755342; Jl Pantai Kuta)*.

Body & Soul *(☎ 767169; Jl Legian 162)* is also worth checking out for women's fashion.

From the intersection of Jl Pura Bagus Taruna and Jl Legian, north to Seminyak, you'll find some of the more interesting women's (and men's) clothing shops (far removed from the teen-girl hype of Surfer Girl), as well as interesting homewares shops (often the two are combined). Jl Pura Bagus Taruna also has decent shopping.

In Seminyak, fashion shops are much more funkier. Interesting shops along Jl Dhyana Pura include **Magg**, filled with princessy cushions of bright velours trimmed with gold brocade, as well as cool sandals; and **Demnia**, next door, which has funky shoes.

Designer's Corner *(Jl Legian, Seminyak)* has a collection of clothes from Jakarta designers. The most interesting collection is the menswear by Denny Kho; the other garments have their design base firmly rooted in Indonesian traditions and are less creative.

Beachwear & Surf Shops
A huge range of surf shops sell big-name surf gear – including brands such as Mambo, Rip Curl, Quicksilver and Billabong – although the quality may not be as good as you'll find overseas, and is only marginally cheaper. Local names include Surfer Girl and Dreamland. If you just want shorts, T-shirts or dresses, check the stalls in the art markets.

Film & Processing
A wide variety of slide and print film is available in the shopping centres at reasonable prices, though it may have been stored in suboptimal conditions. Check the expiry dates on film.

Lots of places process print film within an hour or so, quite cheaply. Slide film is generally not processed locally – it's best to take it home with you.

Arts & Crafts
Kuta shops sell arts and crafts from almost every part of the island, from Mas woodcarvings to Kamasan paintings to Gianyar textiles, and just about everything else in between. There are also many interesting pieces from other parts of Indonesia, some of questionable authenticity and value. There's a good selection of quality **craft shops** on Jl Legian, between Poppies Gang II and Jl Padma.

For souvenirs, sarongs and more mass-produced handicrafts, shop around **Jl Melasti** or the **Kuta Art Market**. In the Kuta Art Market, the Artists Café exhibits the works of local artists.

An offbeat place worth heading to is **Apolina Gallery** (☎ 751334; Gang Camplung Mas, Legian), near Senen Beach Inn, off Jl Melasti, which is run by local musos and an alternative crowd. The paintings of artist Wahyoe Wijaya are on display, as well as some unique jewellery pieces. Staff are happy for you to stop by for a coffee and chat, and artists and musos are particularly welcome.

Music
Many music shops offer a huge range of cassette tapes and CDs of Western, Indonesian and Balinese music – all at fixed prices.

Silverwork & Jewellery
Many shops sell silver and jewellery, although none of it is particularly breathtaking. Before you buy anything from street vendors or smaller shops, look at the style, quality and fixed prices on offer at well-established shops, such as **Jonathan Gallery** (☎ 754209; e legian100@hotmail.com; Jl Legian 109; open 8am-11.30pm), **Yusef Silver** and **Suarti** (both with outlets on Jl Legian and elsewhere) and **Mario Silver** (☎ 730977, fax 730926; w www.mariosilver.com; Jl Raya Seminyak 19), which also has shops on Jl Melasti and Jl Legian.

Watches
Fake fashion watches are sold in many small shops, and you'll still have the challenge of bargaining with the vendors. From a ridiculously high first price they should come down to around 40,000Rp. Most of these 'copy watches' are pretty convincing, but some have token design deviations, like TG instead of TAG, on the watch's face.

GETTING THERE & AWAY
Air
If you want to buy or change an airline ticket, start by contacting the office of the appropriate airline – most are at the airport or in Sanur (see the Getting There & Away chapter for details). You may have to visit the office to pay for or collect the ticket, but call first. The myriad travel agents within the Kuta region will reconfirm your flight for a small fee. Big hotels should reconfirm for their guests free of charge.

Bemo
Public *bemos* (small pick-up trucks) regularly travel between Kuta and the Tegal terminal in Denpasar – the fare should be 2500Rp but tourists are often charged more. Most 'S' bemos go only to the terminal area in Kuta (on Jl Raya Kuta just east of Bemo Corner).

If you can't get a public bemo in the tourist area (some drivers don't stop for tourists), go to the terminal area on the street east of Bemo Corner. Southbound bemos go through Tuban, detour past the airport entrance, then continue south to Jimbaran and east to Nusa Dua. Northbound bemos go to Tegal terminal in Denpasar, where you can get another bemo to the appropriate Denpasar terminal for any other destination on Bali.

Bus
Travel agents in Kuta sell bus tickets to Java and Lombok that depart from Ubung terminal in Denpasar; you'll have to get yourself to Ubung. The tickets will be slightly more expensive than if you buy them at Ubung, but it's worth it to avoid a trip into Ubung and to be sure of a seat when you want to go. For public buses to anywhere else on Bali you will have to go first to the appropriate terminal in Denpasar, and pay your money there (see the Denpasar chapter for details).

Tourist Shuttle Bus
Shuttle bus tickets are sold at most travel agents – buy them a day ahead, or call the company and pay when you check in.

Perama (☎ 751551; Jl Legian 39) is the best-known shuttle bus operation, and will pick you up from your hotel for free (although don't always count on this). Perama has frequent buses to Sanur (10,000Rp) and Ubud (20,000Rp), and one daily to Kintamani (30,000Rp), Lovina (50,000Rp) and Bedugul (30,000Rp). Buses to Padangbai (30,000Rp, three daily), Candidasa (30,000Rp, three daily), Tirta Gangga (45,000Rp, one daily) and Tulamben (50,000Rp, one daily) may go via Ubud and take quite a while.

There's bus-ferry-bus services to destinations in Lombok, including Mataram

(105,000Rp, two daily), Senggigi Beach (65,000Rp, two daily), Bangsal for boats to the Gili islands (90,000Rp, one daily), as well as Kuta (Lombok) and Tetebatu.

Car & Motorcycle

There are many car- and motorcycle-rental places, so prices are very competitive (see the Getting Around chapter for details on prices and conditions). Avoid taking a car or taxi on Poppies Gang I or II in central Kuta, or on the narrow lanes in between.

GETTING AROUND
To/From the Airport

A taxi from the airport costs 15,000Rp to Bemo Corner, 22,500Rp to Legian and 22,500Rp to Seminyak. Between 6am and 4pm, you could walk 700m across the car park to the main road and wait for a blue bemo to Bemo Corner (2000Rp), but it's probably not worth the trouble.

From Kuta *to* the airport, get a metered taxi for around 12,000Rp. Tourist shuttle buses cost 10,000Rp, but may not travel at suitable times. A public bemo from Jl Raya Kuta is cheaper, but very inconvenient.

Bemo

Dark-blue bemos do a loop from Bemo Corner along and up Jl Pantai Kuta, along Jl Melasti, then up Jl Legian for a short while before returning down Jl Legian to Bemo Corner (about 2000Rp around the loop). Drivers can be reluctant to stop for tourists and, in any case, bemos are infrequent in the afternoon and nonexistent in the evening.

Charter Transport

It's easy to find a vehicle to charter – just walk down Jl Legian and you will be assailed with offers of 'transport', and in case you don't understand, the driver will effusively gesticulate the motions of driving a car. You may well think he's pretending to run and shouting 'sport' at you!

Negotiate the fare before you get on board. You should be able to get from the middle of Kuta to the middle of Legian for around 6000Rp, but bargain hard.

A full-day, eight-hour charter should run to between 150,000 and 200,000Rp, but more if it's nonstop driving over a long distance. You can estimate a price for shorter trips on a proportional basis, but you'll have

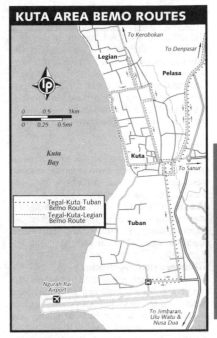

KUTA AREA BEMO ROUTES

to bargain. The 'first price' for transport can be truly outrageous. Chartered vehicles should cost about the same as an equivalent trip in taxi.

Taxi

Plenty of taxis work the Kuta region. Most use their meters and are quite cheap – 3000Rp flagfall plus about 1000Rp per kilometre. Taxis are indispensable for getting around town at night, and they can be hired for longer trips anywhere in southern Bali, and even as far as Ubud (you'll pay a 30% surcharge with Blue Taxis if you travel outside the Kuta/Seminyak/Denpasar region (for example, to Tanah Lot or Ubud).

Bicycle

Cycling is a good way to get around as Kuta is pretty flat – you can go up the narrowest gang, park anywhere and even push your bike the wrong way up a one-way street (though technically this is illegal). To find a bicycle, ask at your hotel. A bike shouldn't cost more than 15,000Rp per day. Check the bike carefully, and make sure you get a lock and key.

Around Kuta

☎ 0361

Any place on the Bukit peninsula, and anywhere as far away as Bedugul, Padangbai, Ubud and Tanah Lot, can be easily visited on a day trip from Kuta by private transport, or even by bemo if you start early. A couple of beaches north of Kuta are worth exploring.

BEREWA

This greyish beach, secluded among stunning paddy fields, is a few kilometres up the coast from Kuta. There is no public transport, but the two hotels in the area provide shuttle services to/from Kuta. The turn-off is along the road heading west from Kerobokan. You can eat in the hotel restaurants, or in one of the several decent **cafés** and **warung** in the village, about 200m from the two hotels.

Bolare Beach Bungalows (☎ 730258, fax 731663; e bolare@indosat.net.id; singles US$65-80, doubles US$65-85) has a great beachfront location, lush gardens and renovated rooms, with open-air bathrooms.

CANGGU

A popular surf spot with right- and left-hand breaks, Canggu is surprisingly undeveloped. Surfers congregate at the unnamed **warung** a few metres from the beach.

Hotel Tugu Bali (☎ 731701, fax 731704; w www.tuguhotels.com; Jl Pantai Batu Bolong, Desa Canggu; rooms US$270-475), a unique hotel set amongst rice paddies, crosses the boundaries into a museum and gallery, especially the Walter Spies and Le Mayuer Pavilions, where memorabilia from the artists' lives decorates the rooms. A range of dining options is also available.

To get to Canggu, go west at Kerobokan and south at Kayutulang. Bemos leave from Gunung Agung terminal in Denpasar (3000Rp).

Sanur

☎ 0361

Sanur is a slightly upmarket sea, sun and sand Bali holiday alternative to Kuta. The white-sand beach is sheltered by a reef, but is suffering from erosion – the best stretch of beach is in front of the high-rise abomination Grand Bali Beach Hotel. At low tide the beach is wide, but the water is shallow and you have to pick your way out over rocks and coral through knee-deep water. At high tide the swimming is fine, but the beach is narrow and almost nonexistent in places. There's also a classic, but fickle, surf break on the reef, and a range of water sports. Sanur still hasn't been totally engulfed by the excesses of tourism as Kuta has – as a walk along the beachside pathway will reveal. You'll see gnarled fishermen in woven bamboo hats standing in the shallows rod-fishing for a living and, at the northern end of the beach, elderly men convivially gather at sunrise and beyond for *meditasi* – swimming and baking in the black volcanic sand found only at that end of the beach.

HISTORY

Inscriptions on a stone pillar found near modern Sanur tell of King Sri Kesari Varma, who came to Bali to teach Buddhism in AD 913. The pillar, behind Pura Belangjong, is Bali's oldest dated artefact and has ancient inscriptions recounting military victories of more than 1000 years ago. These inscriptions are in Sanskrit and are evidence of Hindu influence 300 years before the arrival of the Majapahit era.

The area was home to priests and scholars from the early days of Hinduism on Bali, and chronicles refer to Sanur priests from the 13th to the 16th century. Mads Lange, the Danish trader based in Kuta, documented close alliances between Sanur and the kings of Denpasar in the mid-19th century.

Sanur was one of the places favoured by Westerners during their pre-war discovery of Bali. Artists Miguel Covarrubias, Adrien Jean Le Mayeur and Walter Spies, anthropologist Jane Belo and choreographer Katharane Mershon all spent time here. The first simple tourist bungalows appeared in Sanur in the 1940s and 1950s, and more artists, including Australian Donald Friend and Ian Fairweather, made their homes in Sanur. This early popularity made Sanur a likely locale for Bali's first big tourist hotel, the (then) Bali Beach Hotel, built in the Soekarno era with war reparation funds from Japan.

Over this period, Sanur was ruled by insightful priests and scholars, who recognised both the opportunities and the threats presented by the expanding tourism. Horrified at the high-rise Bali Beach Hotel, they imposed the famous rule that no building could be higher than a coconut palm. They also established village co-operatives that own land and run tourist businesses, ensuring that a good share of the economic benefits remains in the community.

The priestly influence remains strong, and Sanur is one of the few communities still ruled by members of the Brahmana caste. It is known as a home of sorcerers and healers, and a centre for both black and white magic. The black-and-white chequered cloth known as *kain poleng,* which symbolises the balance of good and evil, is emblematic of Sanur.

ORIENTATION

Sanur stretches for about 5km along an east-facing coastline, with the landscaped grounds of expensive hotels fronting right onto the beach. The conspicuous, 1960s-style highrise Grand Bali Beach Hotel is at the northern end of the strip, and fronts the best stretch of beach. West of the beachfront hotels is the noisy main drag, Jl Danau Tamblingan, with hotel entrances, wall-to-wall tourist shops and restaurants. Most streets are named after Indonesian lakes, such as Jl Danau Tamblingan and Jl Danau Buyan. A scenic paved walkway runs the length of the beach, past markets, restaurants and the grounds of top-end hotels.

Jl Bypass Ngurah Rai, commonly called Bypass Rd or Jl Bypass, skirts the western side of the resort area, and is the main link to Kuta and the airport.

INFORMATION

There's no tourist office. Notice boards at Hotel Santai and the expat hang-out Cafe Batu Jimbar have some local information. Hotel Santai is also home to **Pusat Pendidikan Lingkungan Hidup** *(PPLH; ☎ 287314; ⓦ www.pplhbali.or.id),* an environmental education centre working on sustainability issues, which has a small library. Money from the hotel and the adjacent Cafe Tali Jiwa funds the centre (so eat up!).

Money

Moneychangers in Sanur offer marginally lower exchange rates than in Kuta and, it seems, have the same reputation for dishonesty. There are several ATMs along the main street (including one inside Circle K minimart) and several banks – change your money there unless you have a recommendation for a reliable moneychanger.

Post & Communications

Sanur's **post office** *(☎ 754012; Jl Danau Buyan)* is west of Jl Bypass Ngurah Rai, but there are more convenient postal agencies on Jl Danau Tamblingan, as well as a few wartels. Cyber cafés on Jl Danau Tamblingan can provide Internet access from about 400Rp to 500Rp per minute. Recommended is **Sunshine Holiday** *(☎ 287376; 400Rp per minute),* which also rents bicycles (25,000Rp per day), and also **Hotel Santai** (300Rp per minute). There is also a cluster of cyber cafés that are directly opposite the bemo stop on Jl Mertasari.

Emergency

There is a **medical clinic** *(☎ 288511, ext 1102)* in the grounds of the Grand Bali Beach Hotel, which charges US$35 per consultation, while **Sanur Clinic** *(☎ 282678; Jl Danau Tamblingan 27)* is on call 24 hours and charges 100,000Rp per consultation. The **police station** *(☎ 288597)* is on Bypass Rd.

MUSEUM LE MAYEUR

The Belgian artist Adrien Jean Le Mayeur de Merpes (1880–1958) lived in this house from 1935 until his death, when Sanur was still a quiet fishing village. The house must have been a delightful place then – a peaceful and elegant home right by the beach. It's an interesting example of Balinese-style

The Artist from Belgium

Adrien Jean Le Mayeur de Merpes arrived on Bali in 1932 and stayed at first near Denpasar, where he met Ni Polok, renowned as a beautiful Legong dancer, who began to model for him. He soon fell in love with the island and with her, and they married – he was 55, she was 15. They rented land in Sanur and built a house, which Le Mayeur decorated with antique stone and wood carvings collected from across Bali. On his death, he willed the house to the Indonesian government to become a museum. His widow, Ni Polok, maintained the house until her death in 1985.

architecture – notice the beautifully carved window shutters that recount the story of Rama and Sita from the *Ramayana*.

Some Le Mayeur paintings are displayed inside the museum (☎ 286201; adult/child 750/250Rp; open 7.30am-3.30pm Sun-Thur, 7.30am-1pm Fri, closed Sat), with information in Indonesian and English, but many of them are yellowed, dirty and poorly lit. Some of the early works are interesting, Impressionist-style paintings from his travels in Africa, India, Italy, France and the South Pacific. Paintings from his early period on Bali are romantic depictions of Balinese daily life and beautiful Balinese women. Those that look like they're done on Hessian bags are actually on palm fibre, which Le Mayeur used during WWII when he couldn't obtain canvas. The more recent works, from the 1950s, are in much better condition and show less signs of wear and tear, with the vibrant colours that later became popular with young Balinese artists. Of particular interest are the black-and-white photos of Le Mayeur's Balinese wife, the dancer, Ni Polok.

ACTIVITIES

Rafting, cycling and other activities are available on day trips from Sanur (see Activities in the Facts for the Visitor chapter for details). It's not far to Kuta for bungy jumping, surfing lessons and Waterbom Park. Sanur itself is a good base for water sports.

Diving

The diving near Sanur is not great, but the reef has a good variety of fish and offers quite good snorkelling. Sanur is the best departure point for dive trips to Nusa Lembongan. A recommended local operator is **Global Aquatic Adventure Tours** (☎/fax 289077; W www.globalaquatic.com; Jl Tambak Sari, Gang 5, No. 1, off Bypass Rd).

Water Sports

Various water sports are offered at **kiosks** along the beach: close to Museum Le Mayeur; near Sanur Beach Market; and at **Surya Water Sports** (☎ 287956; I Duyung; W www.suryadive.gb.net). Prices at all three places are similar, and are based on a minimum of two people. You can go parasailing (US$10 per go), jet-skiing (US$20, 15 minutes), water-skiing (US$20, 15 minutes),

SANUR

snorkelling by boat (US$25, two hours), windsurfing (US$25, one hour), or be towed on an inflatable banana (US$10, 15 minutes).

Blue Oasis Beach Club (☎ 288011; e blue oasisbc@geocities.com), at **Sanur Beach Hotel**, also offers water sports activities, including windsurfing and kite-surfing clinics for all levels ($80 per four hours for beginners) and surf safaris around Sanur ($10 by boat, not including equipment). It hires out sea kayaks for US$4 per hour and surfboards for US$10 per day.

Three good surf breaks on the Sanur reef need a big swell to work well, and they are only good in the wet season (October to March), when winds are offshore. Boats to Nusa Lembongan, another great surf spot, leave from the northern end of the beach.

Fishing
Atlantis Big Game Fishing (☎/fax 283676; e atlantiskb@hotmail.com; Jl Mertasari), next door to Trophy Pub, offers coral fishing trips for four/six hours for US$75/90.

Massage & Spas
Natural Spa (☎ 283677; e naturalspa@hot mail.com; Jl Danau Tamblingan 23) is a huge operation, which offers standard massages ($40 for two hours), reflexology ($25 for 1½ hours) and body treatments ($50 for two hours), including an after-sun treatment. The young female staff are, however, nauseatingly obsequious (no doubt by management decree). Nearby is the friendly **Tapak Sole** (☎ 282209; Jl Danau Tamblingan 27E), a small Chinese reflexology and massage studio. There are also several reflexology places on Jl Pantai Sindhu.

SOUTH BALI

SANUR

	PLACES TO STAY				
4	Watering Hole (Agung & Sue) & Restaurant; Miramar Mini-Restaurant; Mini Market	74	Puri Santrian Hotel	16	Telkom Wartel
		81	Watering Hole II	19	Sanur Beach Market; Water Sports Kiosk
		82	Sanur Beach Hotel; Blue Oasis Beach Club	20	Bali International Sports Bar
7	Diwangkara Beach Hotel			22	Pasar Sindhu 'Night Market' & Art Market
10	Grand Bali Beach Hotel; Northwest Airlines; Quantas; Thai Airways		**PLACES TO EAT**	25	Bank Bali (ATM)
		1	Kafe Wayang & Bakery	26	Natural Spa; Tapak Sole
17	Desa Segara	14	Splash Bakery	27	Sanur Clinic; Circle K & ATM Bank Bali; Meidy
29	La Taverna Bali Hotel	18	Warungs		
30	Tandjung Sari Hotel	21	Arri's	31	Telkom Wartel
32	Tamu Kami Hotel Restaurant & Bar; Alise's Restaurant; The Village	23	Randy's Café Bar & Restaurant; Rare Angon	35	French Consular Agent
		24	Benno's Corner Cafe; Mango Bar	37	Speakezy's
33	Yulia Home-stay; Coco Homestay			40	Mama Leon
		28	Warung Lobi-Lobi	42	German Consulate
36	Gazebo Cottages Beach Hotel; Piazza Gazebo Bakery & Restaurant	34	Lotus Pond Restaurant	45	Swastika II
		44	Retro Café & Gallery	46	Bank Danamon
		51	Cafe Batu Jimbar; Sari Bumi; Ryoshi	47	Bank Bali (ATM)
38	Keke Homestay			48	Supermarket; BNI (ATM)
39	Flashbacks; Nogo Bali Ikat Centre	56	Telaga Naga	49	Petrol Station
		59	Elang Laut	52	BCA (ATM)
41	Griya Santrian	77	Sari Laut; Cybercafes	55	Sunshine Holiday
43	Yulia 2 Homestay; Billy's Kafe	78	Sari Bundo II	57	Koki Pub
50	Hotel Santai; Cafe Tali Jiwa; Pusat Pendidikan Lingkungan Hidup	80	Warung Blanjong	58	Putih Pino
				60	Bali Hyatt; Medical Clinic
			OTHER	61	Toko Bagus
53	Hotel Paneeda View	2	Jazz Bar & Grille	62	Wartel & Internet
54	Jati Homestay	3	Warung Pojok; Perama Office	63	Surya Water Sports
65	Hotel Segara Agung	5	Boats to Nusa Lembongan	64	Banjar Club
67	Hotel Palm Gardens	6	Museum Le Mayeur; Water Sports Kiosk	66	Double U Shopping Centre
68	Abian Boga			72	Jaya Kesuma Art Market
69	Stana Puri Gopa Hotel	8	Wartel	75	Trophy Pub; Atlantis Big Game Fishing; Postal Agency
70	Hotel Kusumasari	9	Bemo Stop		
71	Sativa Sanur Cottages	11	Police Station	76	Bemo Stop
73	Natah Bale Villas; Essence Restaurant & Bar	12	Supermarket	79	Pura Belangjong
		13	Main Post Office		
		15	Postal Agent		

Other Activities

The **ten-pin bowling centre** (open 6pm-midnight daily) in the Grand Bali Beach Hotel charges US$2.50 per person per game. The hotel also has a nine-hole **golf course**, which charges US$53 per round (including caddie), plus US$15 for a full set of clubs.

ORGANISED TOURS

All the big hotels arrange tours for their guests, but it may be cheaper to buy tour tickets from a travel agent on the main street (see Organised Tours in the Getting Around chapter for details of the standard tours).

PLACES TO STAY

There's a scarcity of decent budget and mid-range accommodation in Sanur. Facades look promising, but room interiors and facilities can often be disappointing.

PLACES TO STAY – BUDGET

Abian Boga (☎ 287174; e abian@indo.net.id; Jl Kesumasari 5; doubles 135,000-150,000Rp) has only two rooms behind its restaurant but they're good value and close to the beach. Each is decorated with ornate Chinese furniture and has a modern bathroom with hot water.

Coco Homestay (☎ 287391; singles/doubles 40,000/50,000Rp) is worth recommending only because it's cheap, clean and central, but lacking in any appeal.

Keke Homestay (☎ 287282; Jl Danau Tamblingan 96; singles/doubles 60,000/75,000Rp), set back a little from the noisy main road, welcomes travellers with quiet, clean rooms.

Watering Hole (Agung & Sue; ☎ 288289; e agungsuewateringhole@yahoo.com; Jl Hang Tuah 37; singles/doubles 60,000/80,000Rp, with air-con 100,000/125,000Rp, family-sized rooms 150,000Rp), in the northern part of Sanur, is a busy, friendly place, with pleasant, clean rooms over a few storeys. Breakfast is not included.

Watering Hole II (☎ 270545; singles/doubles 80,000/100,000Rp, with air-con 120,000/150,000Rp, family-sized rooms 200,000Rp) is at the southern end of Sanur and has a pool.

Yulia Home-stay (☎ 288089; Jl Danau Tamblingan 38; singles/doubles from 60,000/70,000Rp, new rooms 100,000Rp) is one of the best places to stay and, in an ironic twist, one of the cheapest. In lovely grounds, the bungalows are in a traditional Balinese family compound filled with hanging birdcages and birdsong. Rooms are clean and pleasant, and the newer bungalows are good value and have modern bathrooms (cold water only).

Yulia 2 Homestay (☎ 287495; e kf_billy@indo.net.id; Jl Danau Tamblingan; singles/doubles 60,000/70,000Rp), further south of Yulia 1 and on the beach side, has clean, pleasant rooms in a fairly cramped compound.

Around Sanur

Bali International Youth Hostel (☎ 720812; Jl Mertesari 19M Sidakarya; singles/doubles 20,000/40,000Rp, with air-con 30,000/40,000Rp) is the only point of interest in this village a few kilometres west of Sanur (see the South Bali map). It's clean and friendly enough, and has a restaurant and pool; it's not popular with travellers, mostly because the location is out of the way, but it does provide daily free transfer to/from Kuta and Sanur.

PLACES TO STAY – MID-RANGE

Diwangkara Beach Hotel (☎ 288577, fax 288894; singles/doubles US$47/56), facing the beach near the end of Jl Hang Tuah, is a tad old-fashioned, but the smaller bungalows are right by the beach, as is the pool.

Flashbacks (☎ 281682; w www.flashbacks-chb.com/location.html; Jl Danau Tamblingan 106; rooms 125,000Rp, with air-con US$30) is a gorgeous little place. Rooms and bungalows are extremely inviting and well set-up, as is the lush and intimate pool area.

Gazebo Cottages Beach Hotel (☎ 286927, fax 288300; w www.baligazebo.com; singles US$65-72, doubles US$70-80) has slightly cramped, but well-furnished two-storey bungalows, all with hot water and air-con, set amongst pleasant landscaped gardens and a pool.

Hotel Kusumasari (☎ 287492, fax 288876; Jl Mertasari; singles US$20-35, doubles US$25-40) has decent rooms with spacious balconies overlooking a pool.

Hotel Palm Gardens (☎ 287041, fax 289571; e plmgrd@indosat.net.id; Jl Kesumasari 3; rooms US$60, family suite US$120) has pleasant rooms, including some apartment-style family rooms, close to the beach.

Hotel Paneeda View (☎ 288425, fax 286224; w www.paneedaview.com; Jl Danau

Tamblingan 89; bungalows US$55-70), with three pools and beach frontage, is great value. Much attention to detail is devoted to the modern interiors. Breakfast is not included.

Hotel Santai *(☎/fax 287314;* e *santai@ indosat.net.id; Jl Danau Tamblingan 148; singles/doubles 140,000/170,000Rp)* has clean, somewhat dreary rooms facing a pool.

Hotel Segara Agung *(☎ 288446, fax 286113;* w *www.segaraagung.com; Jl Duyung 43; rooms US$20-30, with hot water US$35)*, down a quiet unpaved residential street, is only a few minutes walk to the beach. Rooms are clean and pleasant, staff are friendly and there's a big swimming pool. Suites and family rooms are also available.

Jati Homestay *(☎ 281730, fax 289157; rooms 175,000-200,000Rp)*, situated in pretty grounds, has pleasant and clean rooms, with small but well-organised kitchen ensuites and hot water.

Stana Puri Gopa Hotel *(☎ 289948;* w *www.purigopabali.com; Jl Kesumasari 4; singles US$30-40, doubles US$35-45)* has traditional Balinese architecture, modern bathrooms, and a pool. It's a short walk to the beach and all rooms have air-con.

PLACES TO STAY – TOP END

An attractive hotel, **Desa Segara** *(☎ 288407, fax 287242;* e *segara1@denpasar.wasantara .net.id; singles US$65-110, doubles US$75-135)* has typically lovely gardens and swimming pools.

La Taverna Bali Hotel *(☎ 288497, fax 287126;* w *www.latavernahotel.com; Jl Danau Tamblingan 29; rooms US$110-240)*, right on the beach, has comfortable rooms set in a beautifully landscaped garden.

Griya Santrian *(☎ 288181, fax 288185;* w *www.santrian.com; Jl Danau Tamblingan 47; rooms with garden view US$105-110, beach view US$110-115, pool view US$120)* features great beach frontage, two swimming pools and very stylish pool-view rooms.

Natah Bale Villas *(☎ 287429, fax 287429;* e *natah_bale_villa@yahoo.com; Jl Mertasari; one-bed/two-bed villas US$110/210)* are absolutely stunning and excellent value. On a large stretch of land dotted with coconut palms, expect a modern, stylish fully furnished villa, including a versatile open-air kitchen.

Puri Santrian Hotel *(☎ 288009, fax 287101;* w *www.santrian.com; Jl Mertasari; rooms*

US$125-200), a fine-looking place, has a lush garden, three pools, tennis court, beach frontage as well as comfortable, well-equipped rooms.

Sativa Sanur Cottages *(☎/fax 287881; Jl Mertasari; singles US$60-78, doubles US$70-88, suite US$96)*, close to the beach, has appealing two-storey thatched bungalows, with TV and fridge, set around a snaking pool fringed by frangipani trees.

Tamu Kami Hotel Restaurant & Bar *(☎ 282510, fax 282520;* w *www.tamukami .com; Jl Danau Tamblingan 64X; rooms US$95-120, family room US$155)* has large, modern rooms and bungalows, finished with Indonesian touches, overlooking a swimming pool.

Tandjung Sari Hotel *(☎ 288441, fax 287930;* w *www.tandjungsari.com; Jl Danau Tamblingan 29; bungalows US$170-210)*, at the end of a shaded driveway, was one of the first Balinese bungalow hotels – it started as an extension to a family home in 1962. Gorgeous traditional-style bungalows are superbly decorated with crafts and antiques.

PLACES TO EAT

There's great eating in Sanur at every budget level. Cheap **warung** and **street food carts** can be found around the Pasar Sindhu night market, at the beach end of Jl Segara Ayu, and along Jl Danau Poso, at the southern end of Sanur, beyond the resort area.

Bypass Road

West of the main Sanur strip, Bypass Rd is ignored by most tourists, but several places are patronised by those in the know. At the northern end, **Kafe Wayang & Bakery** *(☎ 287591; dishes 25,000-70,000Rp)* is popular with expats and wealthy locals. Traffic noise is blocked out in the cool, air-con interior, and menu offerings include sandwiches, pasta and contemporary Asian fare. A kids' menu is available. Live music gigs are held regularly (see Entertainment later in this section).

Splash Bakery *(☎ 288186)*, further south, makes a good selection of bread, cakes, pastries and pies. It has a small eat-in area.

Northern Sanur & the Beach

Watering Hole (Agung & Sue) Restaurant *(dishes 10,000-40,000Rp)* is popular for Chinese, Indonesian and Western meals at decent prices. Recommended is the black rice pudding for breakfast (order the day before). On Thursday night at 8pm, a Balinese buffet with Legong dance and live music costs 50,000Rp.

Mirama Mini-Restaurant *(dishes 8500-19,000Rp)*, next door, is a pleasant, clean place serving Chinese and Indonesian food and inexpensive juices.

The esplanade has restaurants, warung and bars where you can catch a meal, a drink or a sea breeze. There are several near the end of Jl Hang Tuah, and at Jl Segara Ayu. **Benno's Corner Cafe** *(dishes 20,000-30,000Rp)* looks over the water and is good for snacks and drinks. A few places near here have sunset drinks specials (though the beach faces east).

Arri's *(☎ 289880; Jl Pantai Sindhu 7; dishes 13,000-50,000Rp)* is a neat, compact place that serves Balinese, Javanese and, surprisingly enough, West Yorkshire specialities. The chef trained in the UK, so expect cottage pie, Lancashire soup and traditional English breakfasts. Free pick-up in Sanur is available.

Jl Danau Tamblingan

Apart from the constant traffic noise, **Randy's Café Bar & Restaurant** *(☎ 288962; Jl Danau Tamblingan 17; dishes 12,000-30,000Rp, small/large Bintang 8000/12,500Rp)* is a nice little Canadian-themed place. On offer are great sandwiches, veggie burgers and for a treat, they also have chocolate brownies with ice cream.

Lotus Pond Restaurant *(☎ 289398; W www.lotus-restaurants.com; dishes 35,000-105,000Rp)* is ideal for couples. The high-thatched building surrounded by lotus ponds (of course) serves pastas, wood-oven pizzas, seafood and a few Indonesian dishes. Legong is performed on Sunday, Tuesday and Wednesday at 8pm.

Warung Lobi-Lobi *(☎ 289138; dishes 15,000-35,000Rp)* is a small, unprepossessing Chinese restaurant serving tasty dishes such as *sup ayam tahu* (minced chicken with beancurd in vegetable soup).

Alise's Restaurant *(☎ 282510; dishes 20,000-60,000Rp, set menus 50,000-65,000Rp)*, part of the Tamu Kami Hotel, has a romantic, lantern-lit outdoor dining area by the pool and serves excellent European, Indonesian and Japanese dishes and delicious pasta. If you enjoy music, quality musicians perform at the restaurant on Sunday, Tuesday, Thursday and Friday from 7.30pm to 10pm.

The Village *(☎ 285025; Jl Danau Tamblingan 66; dishes 26,000-40,000Rp)* is an airy and romantic Italian restaurant. Wood-fired oven pizzas, such as the tonno pizza, a mélange of tomato, tuna, capers and olive oil, are on offer as well as delicious pastas.

Piazza Gazebo Bakery & Restaurant *(☎ 288212; Jl Danau Tamblingan 37)* is worth stopping by for pastries, sandwiches, cakes and excellent coffee. It has a rather swish bar/restaurant behind it.

Billy's Kafe *(☎ 287495; dishes 8000-17,000Rp)*, at Yulia 2 Homestay, is a nice place to hang out or head to for a cheap breakfast. It has a few Western favourites (banana muffins even!), but offerings are mostly simple Indonesian tastes, such as *soto ayam*.

Retro Café & Gallery *(☎ 282472; Jl Danau Tamblingan; dishes 28,000-45,000Rp)* has a relaxed back section, well away from the traffic noise, where the walls are filled with paintings.

Cafe Tali Jiwa *(☎ 287314; dishes 10,000-31,000Rp)*, in front of Hotel Santai, has an appetizing choice of dishes, from icy smoothies to filling chickpea veggie burgers. It doesn't have the expat ambience of Batu Jimbar, but it's better food and better value.

Cafe Batu Jimbar *(☎ 287374; Jl Danau Tamblingan 152; dishes 25,000-35,000Rp; open 8am-11pm Mon-Sat & 8am-4pm Sun)*, a local expat meeting place, is sheltered by shady palm trees from the constant motorbike cacophony of the main drag. It serves fresh vegetable and fruit juices, soups, home-made pastas, curries and cakes and biscuits. The coffee is also worth seeking out if you need a fix.

Ryoshi *(dishes 30,000-60,000Rp)*, next door to Cafe Batu Jimbar, executes all the usual Japanese standards well enough.

Telaga Naga *(☎ 281234; dishes 25,000-100,000Rp; open dinner only)*, opposite the Bali Hyatt, serves Cantonese and Sichuan cuisine. Torches light the pathway to the restaurant and bright red lanterns glow over the tables. Offerings are gourmand, such as *abalone masak jamur hitan* (abalone with black mushrooms).

Elang Laut *(Sea Eagle; ☎ 282552; Jl Danau Tamblingan 188; dishes 20,000-45,000Rp)* features a long list of Dutch specialities, including Javanese *rijstaffel* (100,00Rp). The interior has a beautifully arranged triptych of the Dutch royal family (with Megawati presiding above).

South Sanur

Abian Boga *(☎ 287174; Jl Kesumasari 5; dishes 15,000-35,000Rp, small/large Bintang 9000/13,500Rp)*, a cavernous place with dowdy furniture, is redeemed by its nightly Legong performances at 8.30pm. The menu is predominantly Chinese, with a few Western and Indonesian dishes thrown in. It has a wide range of set menus.

Essence Restaurant & Bar *(☎ 2822208; Jl Danau Tamblingan 58; dishes 19,000-55,000Rp, small/large Bintang 8500/10,500Rp)* is a new place worth going to for its creative, modern cuisine and good service. There's a bar menu if you feel like a snack over a beer or wine (and a kids' menu).

A cluster of *warung* by the bemo stop offer cheap dining. Among them is **Sari Laut** *(☎ 289151; dishes 12,500-25,000Rp)*, which is always full of locals. For Padang food, **Sari Bundo II** *(Jl Danau Poso)* is very good and cheap. Opposite, **Warung Blanjong** *(☎ 285613; dishes 15,000-30,000Rp)* is more tourist-oriented, but has authentic Indonesian and Balinese dishes – try the *tipat*, a Balinese *gado gado* with sticky rice, vegetables and peanut sauce.

ENTERTAINMENT
Bars & Clubs

Bali International Sports Bar *(Jl Pantai Sindhu; open 8am-midnight)* shows international sporting events, especially football and rugby, on two big screens.

Jazz Bar & Grille *(☎ 285892; Komplek Sanur; Jl Bypass Ngurah Rai; dishes 35,000-75,000Rp; open 11am-2pm)* has live jazz from around 9.30pm nightly and an international menu, including Australian steaks and Mexican fare.

Kafe Wayang & Bakery *(☎ 287591; Komplek Sanur; Jl Bypass Ngurah Rai)* has Latin on Wednesday night from 8pm, and Latin fusion on Friday and Saturday from 9pm. Bar snacks are available.

Koki Pub *(☎ 287503; Jl Bypass Ngurah Rai; dishes 28,000-50,000Rp; open 4pm-2am)* is like walking into a European pub – which can come as a bit of a shock! It's totally sheltered from the noise, sun and heat. Expect to find pool tables, televised sporting events, beefy types at the bar, and a menu focusing on German cuisine and Australian wines.

Mango Bar *(small/large Bintang 10,500/12,500Rp)*, which looks like it's run by the local reggae Mafioso, and **Banjar Club**, both on the beachfront, are worth trying for live reggae.

Trophy Pub *(☎ 285010; Jl Mertasari)* is an open-air, nondescript bar that attracts an older crowd.

Speakezy's *(☎ 288825; Jl Danau Tamblingan 94; small/large Bintang 8000/15,000Rp)* is a cheesy-theme bar, but has live music nightly.

Balinese Dance & Music

Restaurants with regular Balinese dance performances include **Watering Hole (Agung & Sue) Restaurant**, **Lotus Pond Restaurant** and **Abian Boga**. **Swastika II** has Legong performances every Thursday and Sunday evening at 8.30pm, while **Alise's Restaurant** has live music.

At the top-end hotels, dinner with a dance performance will cost around US$25 per person, plus drinks. **Grand Bali Beach Hotel** *(☎ 288511)*, **Bali Hyatt** *(☎ 281234)* and **Hotel Sanur Beach** *(☎ 288011)* have some of the most lavish productions.

For something more authentic, see the Barong performance at Batubulan. Local travel agents can arrange this, or you can arrange it independently for much less.

SHOPPING

Good shopping is to be had in Sanur. For serious shopping, look at the shops on Jl Bypass Ngurah Rai and up past Batubulan on the way to Ubud. Villages on this route are centres for stone-carving, woodcarving, jewellery, weaving and basketware (see the Denpasar to Ubud section in the Ubud & Around chapter).

Locally, there are several painting studio shops, with a wide selection of paintings on offer, on the main street and also around Jl Pantai Sindhu. Batik cloth is also easy to find and Sanur has a plenty of tailors on the main strip if you want something special made up. Try **Batik Winotosastro** *(☎ 462069; Jl Bypass Ngurah Rai 96, Tohpati)*, a huge place that stocks hand-wax processed batik fabrics and clothes, sourced from Gianyar; or **Nogo Bali Ikat Centre** (☎ 288765; e nogo@indo.net.id; Jl Danau Tamblingan 100), which has a range of fabrics made in the Gianyar area from threads imported from overseas. It has a clothes range that is pretty awful (it seems to specialise in kaftans for the morbidly obese), but the centre can tailor-make anything from an outfit to quilt covers.

For fashion, head to **Meidy** (☎ 282572), near Sanur Clinic, a great little shop stocked to the brim with very feminine funky gear; or else go upmarket at **Mama Leon** (☎ 288044; w www.mamaleon.com; Jl Danau Tamblingan 99A), a women's fashion shop specialising in cool, classic cuts and colours, where many of the designs feature embroidery.

For homewares try **Putih Pino** (☎ 287889), which sells a range of natural textiles and homewares, as well as a few Chinese-style tops, and shoes. **Sari Bumi** (☎ 284101), in the same courtyard as Cafe Batu Jimbar, has a range of ceramic homewares from Jengalla Keramics in Jimbaran. **Piazza Gazebo** has an upmarket selection of shops selling homewares, clothes and books set around the Piazza Gazebo Bakery and Restaurant.

For souvenirs, try the numerous shops on the main street, or one of the various 'art markets'. **Sanur Beach Market**, off Jl Segara Ayu, is fun to browse around and has a wide selection of souvenirs. **Jaya Kesuma Art Market**, **Pasar Sindhu Art Market** and **Double U** shopping centre all have numerous stalls selling T-shirts, sarongs, woodcarvings and other items.

For groceries and personal items, there are supermarkets on Jl Bypass Ngurah Rai, and Jl Danau Tamblingan. The biggest, which also sells a wide range of alcohol, is around the middle of Jl Danau Tamblingan. **Toko Bagus**, at the southern end of Jl Danau Tamblingan doubles as a pharmacy and minimart. There's also a minimart next door to the Watering Hole in northern Sanur. The **Pasar Sindhu night market** (open during the day also) sells fresh vegetables, dried fish, pungent spices and various household goods.

GETTING THERE & AWAY
Bemo
The public bemo stops are at the southern end of Sanur on Jl Mertasari, and just outside the entrance to the Grand Bali Beach Hotel.

You can hail a bemo anywhere along Jl Danau Tamblingan and Jl Danau Poso.

Green bemos go along Jl Hang Tuah and up Jl Hayam Wuruk to the Kereneng terminal in Denpasar (1000Rp).

Tourist Shuttle Bus
The **Perama office** (☎ 287594) is at **Warung Pojok** (Jl Hang Tuah 31), at the northern end of town. It runs buses to these destinations.

destination	services (daily)	fare (Rp)
Bedugul	1	30,000
Candidasa	3	30,000
Kintamani	1	30,000
Kuta	7	10,000
Lovina	2	50,000
Padangbai	3	30,000
Tirta Gangga	1	45,000
Tulamben	1	55,000
Ubud	7	15,000

Boat
Public boats to Nusa Lembongan leave from the northern end of Sanur beach at 8am (30,000Rp, 1½ hours); the public 'shuttle boat' leaves at 10.30am (40,000Rp).

From Nusa Lembongan to Sanur, public boats leave Jungutbatu beach at 7am, and shuttle boats at 8am. The Perama boat to Sanur leaves at 8.30am and connects with a through service to Kuta (60,000Rp) and Ubud (65,000Rp).

GETTING AROUND
To/From the Airport
A prepaid taxi from the airport to Sanur costs 35,000Rp. Going to the airport from Sanur, a metered taxi will cost less. Shuttle buses from Sanur to the airport cost 10,000Rp. Bemos to/from the airport are cheap, inconvenient and nonexistent after 4pm.

Bemo
Bemos go up and down Jl Danau Tamblingan and Jl Danau Poso for 1000Rp.

Car, Motorcycle & Bicycle
Agencies along the main road in Sanur rent cars, motorcycles and bicycles. If you want a vehicle for more than a couple of days, head to Kuta, where rates are slightly lower.

Taxi
Metered taxis can be flagged down in the street, or call **Bali Taxi** (☎ 701111).

Around Sanur

PULAU SERANGAN

Only about 250m offshore, south of Sanur, Pulau Serangan (Turtle Island) is connected to the mainland by a causeway and bridge. This link, and a large area of landfill on the eastern and southern sides of the island, were part of a massive, abortive development project associated with Soeharto's infamous son Tommy. The earthworks obliterated the island's sandy beaches, destroyed the coral reefs and created wide stretches of barren land, where hotels and a theme park were supposed to be. The project is also believed to have caused the increased erosion of Sanur's once wide and sandy beach. The island was named for the turtles that used to lay eggs here, but the turtles have disappeared, along with their nesting sites and the beaches themselves.

The island has two villages, Ponjok and Dukuh (see the South Bali map), and an important temple, **Pura Sakenan**, just east of the causeway. Architecturally, the temple is insignificant, but it's one of the holiest on Bali, and major festivals attract huge crowds of devotees, especially during the Kuningan festival.

The only other reason to come here is for the irregular **surf break** at the southern end of the landfill area, where a row of **warung** has appeared to provide food, drinks and souvenirs. The wide, unsealed road to the island branches off Jl Bypass Ngurah Rai just east of the Benoa harbour turnoff – a booth at the end of the causeway collects a 1000Rp fee.

BENOA HARBOUR

Bali's main port is at the entrance of Teluk Benoa, the wide but shallow bay east of the airport runway. Benoa harbour is on the northern side of the bay – a square of docks and port buildings on reclaimed land, linked to mainland Bali by a 2km causeway. It's referred to as Benoa port, or Benoa harbour to distinguish it from Benoa village, on the southern side of the bay (see the Bukit Peninsula section later).

Benoa harbour is the port for the fast *Mabua Express* and *Bounty* boats to Lombok (see Getting There & Away in the Lombok chapter), and for Pelni ships to other parts of Indonesia (see the Getting There & Away chapter). It is also the main departure point for many of the luxury cruises, and fishing, diving and surfing trips (see the Activities section in the Facts for the Visitor chapter for details).

Getting There & Away

Visitors must pay a toll to go on the causeway (1000Rp per vehicle). Public bemos (1000Rp) leave from Sanglah terminal in Denpasar (the driver pays the toll). A chartered bemo or taxi from Kuta or Sanur should cost around 8000Rp one way, plus the toll.

Bukit Peninsula

The southern peninsula is known as Bukit (*bukit* means 'hill' in Indonesian), but was known to the Dutch as Taffelhoek (Table Point). Once a reserve for royal hunting parties, and a place of banishment for undesirables, the Bukit peninsula was sparsely inhabited. Its only significant site was Pura Luhur Ulu Watu, the spectacular 'sea temple' at the southwestern tip of the peninsula.

Over the last few decades, a university campus and a cement industry have been established, as well as hotel developments at Jimbaran and the luxury tourist enclave at Nusa Dua. The western and southern coasts are magnificent, and have some lovely, isolated beaches and great surf (for details about Bukit peninsula surf breaks, see the Surfing section in Activities in the Facts for the Visitor chapter; routes around the Bukit peninsula are shown on the South Bali map).

JIMBARAN
☎ 0361

South of Kuta and the airport, Teluk Jimbaran (Jimbaran Bay) is a superb crescent of white sand and blue sea, fronted by a long string of seafood warung, and ending at the southern end in a bushy headland, home to the Four Seasons Resort. The sunset towering over the horizon is what brings travellers to Jimbaran to feast on seafood grilled over coconut husks, fresh from the local fishing fleet. The fish market is well worth an early morning exploration, as it is one of the best in Bali. Jimbaran is home to some of Bali's luxury resorts and a host of small boutique hotels, but budget and midrange accommodation is limited.

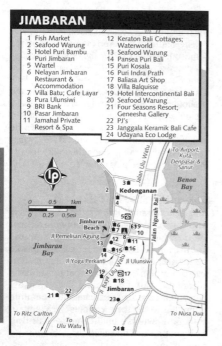

JIMBARAN

1 Fish Market	12 Keraton Bali Cottages;
2 Seafood Warung	Waterworld
3 Hotel Puri Bambu	13 Seafood Warung
4 Puri Jimbaran	14 Pansea Puri Bali
5 Wartel	15 Puri Kosala
6 Nelayan Jimbaran	16 Puri Indra Prath
Restaurant &	17 Baliasa Art Shop
Accommodation	18 Villa Balquisse
7 Villa Batu; Cafe Layar	19 Hotel Intercontinental Bali
8 Pura Ulunsiwi	20 Seafood Warung
9 BRI Bank	21 Four Seasons Resort;
10 Pasar Jimbaran	Geneesha Gallery
11 Jamahal Private	22 PJ's
Resort & Spa	23 Janggala Keramik Bali Cafe
	24 Udayana Eco Lodge

Facilities are limited. Jl Raya Uluwatu has moneychangers and a BRI bank. **Baliasa Art Shop** (☎ 701058; e baliasa@indosat.net.id; Jl Uluwatu 47) has slow Internet access for 400Rp per minute. The owner also has a good reputation as a guide.

Water sports and diving trips are available at **Waterworld** (☎ 701961; e wtrworld@ indosat.net.id; Keraton Bali Cottages). And if you plan to surf the **Airport Rights** surf break is accessible by boat from the beach.

The **Ganeesha Gallery** at the Four Seasons Resort has exhibitions by international artists and is worth seeking out.

Places to Stay

Places to Stay – Budget A ramshackle place, **Puri Indra Prath** (☎/fax 701552; Jl Uluwatu 28; rooms with/without air-con 200,000/100,000Rp) has a less-than clean pool, but its fan rooms offer one of the few budget options in Jimbaran.

In a central location, **Nelayan Jimbaran Restaurant & Accommodation** (☎/fax 702253; rooms 125,000Rp, with air-con 200,000-400,000Rp) has a maze of different category rooms (all with cold water only),

including family rooms, all crowded onto a small site by the beach.

Places to Stay – Mid-Range On a side road 200m from the beach, **Hotel Puri Bambu** (☎ 701377; w www.puribambu.com; singles US$55-75, doubles US$65-90), has air-con rooms in three-storey blocks around a pool; it also has character and friendly staff.

Villa Balquisse (☎/fax 701695; w www .balquisse.com; Jl Uluwatu 18X; rooms US$90) is a charming and intimate little hideaway. Each light-filled room has a four-poster bed, high bamboo ceilings, an open-air bathroom and a small outdoor lounging area. A relaxed open-air living room sits at one end of the pool.

Villa Batu (☎/fax 703186; Jl Pemelisan Agung 21A; rooms with/without air-con 280,000/160,000Rp), behind Cafe Layar, has small rooms with open-air bathrooms (cold water only), but it's in a good spot.

Places to Stay – Top End Catering to the honeymoon market, **Four Seasons Resort** (☎ 701010, fax 701020; w www.fourseasons .com; villas with/without ocean views US$650/ 570) is absolutely divine. On a hillside, each villa is designed in a traditional Balinese manner complete with a carved entrance-way, which opens onto an open-air dining pavilion overlooking a plunge pool. The spa is open to guests only.

The massive **Hotel Intercontinental Bali** (☎ 701888, fax 701777; e ali@interconti.com; rooms US$240-260, suites US$325-650) is a fortress-like place, but it's beautifully decorated with fine Balinese arts and handicrafts.

Jamahal Private Resort & Spa (☎ 704394, fax 704597; w www.jamahal.net; Gang Batu Putih 1; suites US$195-225) has contemporary suites, some with private plunge pools. Traffic noise from nearby Jl Uluwatu manages to slip through, but the water fountains in the grounds cleverly mask the buzz. It also has a dreamy spa and pool.

Pansea Puri Bali (☎ 701605, fax 701320; w www.pansea.com; Jl Yoga Perkanti; cottages US$199-235) is set in gorgeous grounds complete with a figure-eight pool that looks on to open ocean. Cottages have private gardens and stylish room design.

Around Jimbaran In the hills near Udayana University, **Udayana Eco Lodge**

(☎ 261204, fax 701098; e lodge@denpasar. wasantara.net.id; singles/doubles with air-con US$45/50; students & Indonesians 220,000Rp) is a peaceful and ecofriendly place set in 70 hectares of bushland, with a swimming pool surrounded by lush vegetation. All profits are reinvested in environmental protection, and it's a great place to meet visiting academics, researchers and expats. Udayana also has an ecolodge in Labuan Bajo in Flores, which operates under the same environmental protection principles.

Ritz Carlton (☎ 702222, fax 701555; e ritz bc@indosat.net.id; rooms US$280-400, suites & villas US$310-730) is about 5km southeast of Jimbaran. Its over-the-top opulence is hidden in vast private grounds overlooking the sea. Rooms are large and lavishly decorated.

Places to Eat & Drink

Three groups of **seafood warung** do fresh barbecued seafood every evening (and many are also open for lunch). The simple open-sided shacks are right by the beach and perfect for enjoying sea breezes and sunsets. Tables and chairs are set up on the sand almost to the water's edge. The usual deal is to select your seafood fresh from an ice bucket and pay according to weight. Per 100g, expect to pay around 22,500Rp for live lobster, 20,000Rp for fresh lobster, 13,000Rp to 18,000Rp for prawns, and 5000Rp for fish, squid and clams. Prices are open to negotiation and rumours abound that scales are weighted in the restaurants' favour.

The longest row of restaurants is at the northern end of the beach. In the middle of the beach, a smaller strip of **warung** is substantially cheaper and offers a similar deal. At the southern end of the beach, a third, smaller cluster of warung is less accessible and a little less crowded.

By day, options include **Nelayan Jimbaran** (dishes 20,000-37,000Rp), which serves typical traveller fare of banana pancakes, T-Bone steak and nasi campur. The balcony restaurant is airy, if somewhat sterile, and has good views to the busy street below. **Cafe Layar** is another inexpensive option (but its toilet could do with a bit of elbow grease, a lock and a light).

Jenggala Keramik Bali Cafe (☎ 703310; Jl Raya Uluwatu; dishes 16,000-34,000Rp; open 9am-6pm) is an art gallery café with slick Nordic design and international café offerings, including cheesecake and espresso.

The resorts all have restaurants, but the stand-out is **PJ's** (☎ 701010; dishes 100,000-180,000Rp; open 11am-10pm), part of the Four Seasons. In an enviable position, PJ's smart open-air dining pavilion overlooks the beach, and is known for its Mediterranean-fusion dishes.

Pansea Puri Bali has cocktail specials (40,000Rp) in its waterfront café between 6pm and 7pm, and is a fine place to kick off the night before heading to one of the seafood warung.

Shopping

Jenggala Keramik Bali (☎ 703310; w www .jenggala-bali-com; Jl Uluwatu II; open 9am-6pm daily) is a modern warehouse showcasing slick homeware ceramics and a smattering of hand painted pieces by local artists, but don't expect any bargains here – all prices are in US dollars. There's also a viewing area where you can watch ceramic production. **Ceramic courses** (US$15/30, two/six sessions) and **ceramic painting workshops** are held regularly.

Getting There & Away

Public bemos from Tegal terminal in Denpasar go via Kuta to Jimbaran (3000Rp), and continue to Nusa Dua. They don't run after about 4pm, but plenty of taxis wait around the beachfront warung in the evening to take replete diners back to Kuta, Sanur or wherever.

Cafe Layar can organise transport to the Airport, Kuta or Ulu Watu (25,000Rp), Tanah Lot, Ubud, Kintamani and Bedugul (36,000Rp).

WEST BUKIT
☎ 0361

Jl Ulu Watu goes south of Jimbaran, climbing 200m up the hill for which the peninsula is named, affording fine views back over the airport and southern Bali. For years the only tourist facilities on the west coast of the Bukit were a few warung at the surf breaks, but in the late 1990s speculation ran rampant. A huge real estate development, Bali Pecatu Indah, went bankrupt, leaving an imposing road network in empty fields, and making part of the coast almost inaccessible. But one of the most grandiose tourist attractions ever conceived for Bali is still going ahead.

Garuda Wisnu Kencana (GWK) Cultural Park

The centrepiece of GWK (☎ 703603; W www .gwk-bali.com; admission 15,000Rp) is the yet to be completed 66m-high statue of Garuda, to be erected on top of a shopping and gallery complex, at a total height of 140m. Touted as the biggest and highest statue in the world, it is to be surrounded by performance spaces, art galleries, a food court and an adventure playground. The approaches to the statue will feature 250m lotus ponds in artificial canyons cut into the hillside, and huge murals of the *Ramayana* carved into limestone cliffs.

Over time GWK has been criticised vehemently for commercialising the Hindu religion and reducing Balinese culture to theme-park status. Many feel that the enormous investment (US$200 million) would be better used for more practical purposes, but this is a privately funded project.

As it stands, the deserted site is not worth going out of your way for. If you do, however, your admission fee includes a guided tour (in indecipherable English) of a statue of Vishnu (a mere 22m high). There's also an interesting art gallery, Kecak dances on Tuesday and Friday, some impressive excavations, and two empty restaurants, serving Chinese and Indonesian food, albeit with great views over southern Bali. Call GWK for the latest information.

Surfing

To reach the surf break at **Balangan** you'll need your own transport – go all the way through the deserted development of Pecatu Indah, and at the locked gate on the far side, go right and follow the rough dirt track. Going left through Pecatu Indah should get you to **Dreamland**, another good surf break. Neither beach is good for swimming.

A newly paved road goes northwest from Pecatu village to **Padang Padang**, with a small side road branching off to **Bingin** – both have savage surf and sandy beaches, but only Padang Padang is a good place to swim. The road crosses a new bridge at Padang Padang, and winds on to **Suluban** and **Ulu Watu**.

Places to Stay & Eat

Warung Indra (☎ 702846; Jl Uluwatu 32; rooms 50,000-60,000Rp) gets some road noise, but is reasonably clean. Breakfast is not included.

Near Warung Indra, **Bukit Inn** (Villa Koyo; ☎ 702927, fax 703362; Jl Uluwatu; W www .bukitinn.com; rooms 200,000-400,000Rp; bungalows 600,000Rp), is a modern mid-range hotel with air-con, hot water, and a pool. Ask for a room away from the road.

The Balangan (☎ 708080, fax 708022; Banjar Cenggiling 88; W www.thebalangan.com; villas from US$350-450), off the road to the west in Cenggiling, is an isolated boutique hotel with luxury villas, each with a private plunge pool and stunning views. There's also a gorgeous spa and a restaurant.

There's a whole string of cheap and very basic surfing dives on the road to Padang Padang, many with shared bathrooms, including **Tete Bali Inn** (rooms 60,000Rp) and **Emma Accommodation** (rooms 50,000Rp).

Better options include **Rocky Bungalows** (☎ 0817 346 201; Jl Pantai Suluban 33, off Jl Uluwatu; singles/doubles 150,000/200,000Rp), a low-key, well-maintained place, which has great water views from its balconies.

Padang Padang Inn (☎ 0812 3913 617; Jl Melasti 432; singles/doubles 50,000/80,000Rp) has clean rooms with private bathrooms and a nice little café.

Ayu Guna Inn (☎ 0823 611 517; Jl Melasti 39X; bungalows 75,000Rp) has pleasant rice-barn style bungalows dotted among gardens and there's plenty of room for parking.

Most of the hotels and losmen have restaurants, but the best place to go is **Yeye's Warung** (Jl Labuan Sait; dishes 18,000-25,000Rp), which has an easy going ambience, cheapish beers and tasty food, such as sliced chicken breast fried with basil. It was unsigned at the time of writing – look out for the peach-coloured facade.

ULU WATU
Pura Luhur Ulu Watu

The temple of Ulu Watu (admission 3000Rp, including sarong & sash rental; parking 500Rp; open daily) is one of several important temples to the spirits of the sea along the south coast of Bali. In the 11th century, the Javanese priest Empu Kuturan first established a temple here. The temple was added to by Nirartha, another Javanese priest who is known for the seafront temples at Tanah Lot, Rambut Siwi and Pura Sakenan. Nirartha retreated to Ulu Watu for his final days, when he attained *moksa* (freedom from earthly desires).

The temple is perched precipitously on the southwestern tip of the peninsula, atop sheer cliffs that drop straight into the pounding surf. You enter through an unusual arched gateway flanked by statues of Ganesha. Inside, the walls of coral bricks are covered with intricate carvings of Bali's mythological menagerie. The small inner temple is only open to Hindu worshippers.

The real attraction is the location – for a good angle, especially at sunset, walk around the cliff-top to the left (south) of the temple. Watch out for the monkeys, who like to snatch sunglasses and handbags, as well as hats and anything else within reach.

Balinese Dance An enchanting **Kecak dance** *(tickets 35,000Rp)* is held in the temple grounds at sunset from 6pm to 7pm on Wednesday, Friday and Saturday evenings. Although obviously set up for tourists, the gorgeous setting makes it one of the best performances on the island.

Surfing

Ulu Watu, or Ulu's, is a legendary surf spot – the stuff of dreams and nightmares. Just before you reach the temple area, a sealed side road goes north for about 3km to Pantai Suluban. At the end of the road, park (500Rp) and walk down the concrete steps, over the small bridge then up to the row of warung, where you get an overview of Ulu's five main surf breaks (see Surfing in the Activities section in the Facts for the Visitor chapter for descriptions). There's no real beach as such, but a rickety ladder goes down to a sandy cave floor, and you walk through the cave to reach the water. The warung sell and rent surfboards, and provide food, drink, ding repairs or a massage – whatever you need most.

Places to Stay & Eat

The temple car park has quite a few basic **restaurants** selling drinks, souvenirs and simple meals. The surfers' **warung** sell basic rice and noodles, toasted sandwiches, burgers and beer.

Uluwatu Resort *(☎ 0823 611 008, fax 774266; w www.uluwaturesort.com; Jl Pantai Suluban, off Jl Uluwatu; rooms US$65)*, above the clifftop, is a new, stylish place where bungalows have impressive ocean views.

Tides *(☎ 416070; Jl Labuan Sait; dishes 28,000-55,000Rp)*, in a spectacular setting

overlooking the ocean, is a young clubbers bar, where you can hang out eating and drinking by the pool or restaurant, and then head down to the Ulu Watu break for a surf.

Getting There & Away

Public bemos to Ulu Watu are infrequent, and stop running by mid-afternoon. Some of the dark blue bemos from Tegal terminal in Denpasar to Kuta will continue to Tuban, Jimbaran and Ulu Watu – it's best to catch one in Kuta (on Jl Raya Kuta, outside the Supernova shopping centre) or Jimbaran (on Jl Ulu Watu).

To see the sunset or the Kecak dance, you'll need an organised tour or your own wheels. Many travel agents in Kuta and Sanur arrange sunset trips to the temple, sometimes with a side trip to a beach or to Jimbaran. Chartering a taxi or bemo is often cheaper than a tour, and **Perama** *(☎ 751551; Jl Legian 39)* also offers return transport for 75,000Rp (departs at 4pm).

SOUTH COAST
☎ 0361
The south coast has high cliffs and big swells.

Bali Cliffs Resort *(☎ 771992, fax 771993; e bcr@indosat.net.id; rooms US$175-250)*, at the very southern end of the Bukit peninsula, is a huge luxury hotel built by Soeharto's cronies. Two transparent elevators go down the cliff to a restaurant, bar and the beach. Just east of the resort is a separate car park where a steep track goes down to the beach and the **Green Ball** surf break.

Puri Bali Villas *(☎ 701362, fax 701363; Jl Uluwatu; w www.puribalivillas.com; villas US$135)*, on a side road, is a more understated luxury option. The sumptuous villas have magnificent views of the ocean. The **restaurant** is an open-sided pavilion at the cliff-top, serving Asian and European dishes. The track down to the **Nyang Nyang** surf break is beside the restaurant.

NUSA DUA
☎ 0361
Nusa Dua translates literally as 'Two Islands' – the islands are actually small raised headlands, each with a little temple. Nusa Dua is better known as Bali's top-end beach resort enclave – a gilded ghetto of five-star hotels. There are no independent developments, no hawkers, no warung, no traffic,

no pollution and no noise. The drawbacks are the high cost of everything at the resort hotels, and the isolation from any sense of Balinese community life.

But reality is on the march just outside the enclave gates. The village of Bualu is a burgeoning Balinese town, home to many of the hotel staff and visitors confined to Nusa hotels who are escaping here, to shops with Asian prices, and to tourist restaurants that would not be out of place in Kuta. You'll see lots of **warung Muslim** (halal food) and **makan Padang** (Padang food) eateries too.

Orientation & Information

As a planned resort, Nusa Dua is easy to make sense of when looking at a map, but it's very spread out. You enter the enclave through one of the big gateways, and inside there are expansive lawns, manicured gardens and sweeping driveways leading to the lobbies of grand hotels. In the middle of the resort, the **Galeria Nusa Dua** shopping centre has banks, moneychangers, ATMs, a postal agent, wartel and plenty of pricey restaurants. Big hotels have the lowest exchange rates.

Some hotels may provide Internet access for their guests. Otherwise, there are Internet cafés just north of the resort on Jl Pratama and just west on Jl Pantai Mengiat in Bualu.

The modern, well-equipped medical **Klinik Gawat Darurat** (☎ 772118) is on call 24 hours.

Surfing & Beaches

The beach at Nusa Dua is shallow at low tide, and not especially attractive. The surf breaks at Nusa Dua are way out on reefs to the north and south of the two 'islands'. They work best with a big swell during the wet season. **Sri Lanka** is a right-hander in front of Club Med. The so-called **Nusa Dua** breaks are peaks, reached by boat from the beach south of the Hilton – go past the golf course and turn left on a dirt road. Nonsurfers from all over southern Bali also flock to this pretty beach, which now has a dozen warung.

Diving & Water Sports

Most diving and water sports are based in Tanjung Benoa.

Golf

The **Bali Golf & Country Club** (☎ 771791) is a superb 18-hole course. Greens fees are US$142, including buggy and caddie, or US$85 for just the front nine holes. Club rental is US$25.

Places to Stay

The Nusa Dua hotels all have beach frontage, large swimming pools, gorgeous gardens, several restaurants, bars, entertainment and five-star facilities. Extras such as meals, drinks, tours and activities are all expensive at these resorts and can add hugely to the cost of a stay. The following hotels are all in the Nusa Dua enclave itself, listed from north to south.

Nusa Dua Beach Hotel & Spa (☎ 771210, fax 771229; e reservations@nusaduahotel .com; rooms from US$150-380) has rooms and suites featuring attractive Balinese decor. Tennis, squash and a gym are available, but the emphasis is on spa treatments (US$30 for a 50-minute massage).

Tourism – Nusa Dua Style

Nusa Dua is a planned tourist resort, designed with advice from World Bank 'experts'. The site was chosen not just for its fine weather and white beaches, but also because the area was dry, relatively barren and sparsely populated. The objective was an isolated luxury resort, which would bring in the tourist dollars while having minimal impact on the rest of Bali. The underlying philosophy represented a new development in tourism strategy.

The idea of 'cultural tourism' had emerged in Ubud as a reaction to the hedonism and 'cultural pollution' of Kuta. The aim was to protect Bali's culture by selectively promoting and presenting aspects of it to tourists. But as mass tourism boomed, the sheer number of visitors was seen as a problem. The solution was a new strategy of 'elite tourism', which would derive more revenue from fewer visitors.

The authorities were probably not so naive as to think that rich tourists would all be culturally sensitive – but at least their impact could be largely confined to resort enclaves, where the cultural tourist attractions could be recreated with visiting dance troupes and Balinese decor.

TANJUNG BENOA & NUSA DUA

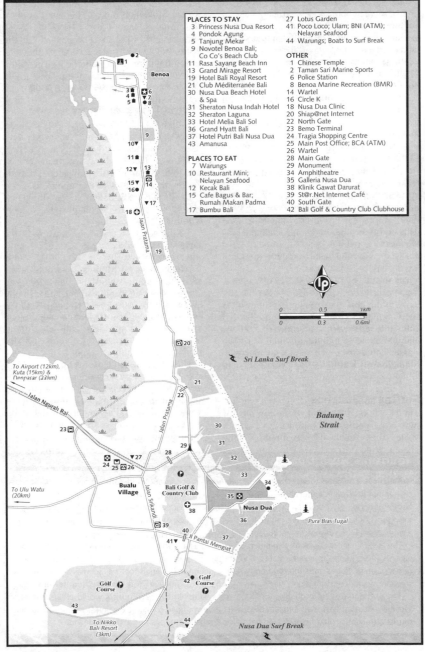

PLACES TO STAY
3 Princess Nusa Dua Resort
4 Pondok Agung
5 Tanjung Mekar
9 Novotel Benoa Bali;
   Co Co's Beach Club
11 Rasa Sayang Beach Inn
13 Grand Mirage Resort
19 Hotel Bali Royal Resort
21 Club Méditerranée Bali
30 Nusa Dua Beach Hotel
   & Spa
31 Sheraton Nusa Indah Hotel
32 Sheraton Laguna
33 Hotel Melia Bali Sol
36 Grand Hyatt Bali
37 Hotel Putri Bali Nusa Dua
43 Amanusa

PLACES TO EAT
7 Warungs
10 Restaurant Mini;
   Nelayan Seafood
12 Kecak Bali
15 Cafe Bagus & Bar;
   Rumah Makan Padma
17 Bumbu Bali

27 Lotus Garden
41 Poco Loco; Ulam; BNI (ATM);
   Nelayan Seafood
44 Warungs; Boats to Surf Break

OTHER
1 Chinese Temple
2 Taman Sari Marine Sports
6 Police Station
8 Benoa Marine Recreation (BMR)
14 Wartel
16 Circle K
18 Nusa Dua Clinic
20 Shiap@net Internet
22 North Gate
23 Bemo Terminal
24 Tragia Shopping Centre
25 Main Post Office; BCA (ATM)
26 Wartel
28 Main Gate
29 Monument
34 Amphitheatre
35 Galleria Nusa Dua
38 Klinik Gawat Darurat
39 St@r.Net Internet Café
40 South Gate
42 Bali Golf & Country Club Clubhouse

Benoa

To Airport (12km),
Kuta (15km) &
Denpasar (23km)

Jalan Ngurah Rai

Jalan Pratama

Jalan Pratama

Sri Lanka Surf Break

Badung
Strait

To Ulu Watu
(20km)

Bualu
Village

Bali Golf &
Country Club

Jalan Srikandi

Nusa Dua

Pura Bias Tugal

Jl Pantai Mengiat

Golf
Course

Golf
Course

To Nikko
Bali Resort
(3km)

Nusa Dua Surf Break

0   0.5   1km
0   0.3   0.6mi

SOUTH BALI

Sheraton Laguna (☎ 771327, fax 772163; singles/doubles US$225/235, min 3 nights) is unashamedly luxurious, featuring a vast swimming pool (it's called a swimmable lagoon) with sandy beaches, landscaped islands and cascading waterfalls.

Hotel Melia Bali Sol (☎ 771510, fax 771360; w www.meliabali.com; singles/ doubles from US$215/235) offers some Mediterranean touches with its food and good entertainment.

Grand Hyatt Bali (☎ 771234, fax 772038; e baligh.reservation@hyattintl.com; rooms from US$220-335, suites US$440-1110) is a vast place with extensive gardens and a river-like swimming pool, a health centre and children's activity centre.

Hotel Putri Bali Nusa Dua (☎ 771020, fax 771139; e putribali@indo.com; rooms US$193 -242), not as expensive as some Nusa Dua palaces, offers a big range of recreational facilities (all at extra cost).

Just outside the resort enclave there's a larger variety of hotels.

Amanusa (☎ 772333, fax 772335; w www .amanresorts.com; villas US$600-1200), overlooking the golf course, is one of the finest hotels on Bali, with elegant, understated architecture, superb decorations, brilliant views and just 35 individual villas. Cooking classes and a range of tours are available.

Nikko Bali Resort & Spa (☎ 773377, fax 773388; www.nikkobali.com; rooms US$180-280), about 3km south of the enclave, dramatically built up a cliff facing the sea, has about 16 floors in total, a whole complex of swimming pools and a private cove with a white sandy beach. The treatments at the Mandara Spa start at US$42 for a massage.

Places to Eat

The Galeria Nusa Dua shopping centre has a variety of themed tourist fare, such as pizza and pasta at **Uno** (dishes 48,000-70,000Rp), burgers and hot stone cooking at **On the Rocks** (☎ 773653; dishes 30,000Rp), Indonesian at **Rayunan** (dishes 30,000-100,000Rp), delicious Spanish and Mediterranean at **Olé Olé** (☎ 774208; dishes 95,000-260,000Rp) and both German and Swiss dishes at **Sendok** (☎ 772850; dishes 48,000-100,000Rp).

Matsuri (☎ 772267; set meals 80,000-165,000Rp; open 11.30am-11pm) serves very tasteful Japanese and is set in beautiful grounds of raked sand and water features. Expect to pay more than similar eateries outside the centre (and anywhere else in Bali).

La Risya Café & Bakery in the Tragia Galeria is the best place for an inexpensive meal within Galeria Nusa Dua.

To the south, the various **warung** at the surfers' beach serve some very good stuff, and are almost cheap.

Along Jl Pantai Mengiat, just outside the gate, there are a string of eateries offering an unpretentious alternative to Nusa Dua dining (phone for free transport). **Nelayan Seafood** (☎ 773534; Jl Pantai Mengiat; dishes 18,000-31,000Rp) is part of a local chain, while **Ulam** (☎ 771902; Jl Pantai Mengiat; dishes 27,000-56,000Rp) is good for quality Balinese, such as grilled whole chicken, and fresh seafood.

Poco Loco (☎ 773923; Jl Pantai Mengiat; dishes 27,000-72,000Rp; open 4pm-late) is a colourful, open-air place on the 2nd floor, where Margaritas, Mexican and 'cowboy' steaks are on offer.

Other inexpensive restaurants are on the main road in Bualu, including **Lotus Garden**

Eating Bali

In addition to some pretty good tourist restaurants, Benoa has **Bumbu Bali** (☎ 774502; dishes 33,000-46,000Rp), which serves authentic Balinese cuisine from a traditional kitchen with all local ingredients. For an appetiser, try the shredded chicken with shallots and lemongrass; follow with grilled duck, chicken or squid in a banana leaf with coconut, lime and basil; and finish with a selection of desserts like black-rice pudding, coconut pancake and palm sugar, or sticky rice cake. Especially recommended is the *rijstaffel* (135,000Rp per person), which lets you sample a wide selection, and is typical of the way Balinese would enjoy a ceremonial feast.

Bumbu Bali is run by Heinz von Holzen, one-time executive chef of the Grand Hyatt Hotel and author of *The Food of Bali*. He also runs a one-day cooking course that starts at 6am in the fish and vegetable markets, stops for coffee in a typical warung, covers 21 recipes and three complete meals, and finishes with a full *rijstaffel* dinner at Bumbu Bali.

(☎ 773378; dishes 24,000-64,000Rp), which serves Chinese options such as prawns in chilli sauce.

Entertainment
The **Galeria Nusa Dua** *(☎ 771662; e galleria@ indo.net.id; open 9am-10pm)* shopping centre offers free entertainment, including Kecak and Legong dances from Sunday to Monday at 7.30pm, and live music on Saturday at 6pm. The **resort hotels** have Balinese dance performances in their restaurants, which include a buffet dinner and show). The **restaurant-bars** on Jl Pantai Mengiat and in Tanjung Benoa can be lively at night.

Shopping
The **Galeria Nusa Dua** *(☎ 771662; e galleria@ indo.net.id; open 9am-10pm)* shopping centre has 70-plus shops selling souvenirs, sporting goods, leather goods and clothing – mostly of the brands and high quality favoured by Japanese tourists. **Galleri Keris** *(☎ 771303)* department store has lots of crafts, expensive brand clothing and a Periplus bookshop. Visit the information booth in Galleri Keris for a map of the complex – you'll need one.

Just outside the resort, Bualu village has some reasonably priced tourist shops, as well as the low-rent **Tragia Shopping Centre** *(☎ 772170; Jl By Pass Nusa Dua; open 9am-10pm)*, a department store and supermarket which has an entire floor devoted to souvenirs, and several fast-food outlets and ATMs. There's actually a bit of Kuta bustle out here, and it's a refreshing change from the orderly, uncrowded enclave. Jl Pantai Mengiat also has some **souvenir shops** with sensible prices.

Getting There & Away
The fixed taxi fare from the airport is 35,000Rp; a metered taxi *to* the airport will be cheaper. Public bemos travel between Denpasar's Tegal terminal and the terminal at Bualu (the bemo also goes through Bualu village) for 4000Rp. From Bualu, it's at least a kilometre to the hotels. Bemos also run from Denpasar's Batubulan terminal (3000Rp).

Getting Around
Find out what shuttle bus services your hotel provides before you start calling taxis. A free **shuttle bus** *(☎ 771662; runs 9am-10pm)* connects all Nusa Dua and Tanjung

Benoa resort hotels with the Galleria shopping centre about very hour.

TANJUNG BENOA
☎ 0361
The peninsula of Tanjung Benoa extends about 4km north from Nusa Dua to Benoa village. Benoa village is one of Bali's multi-denominational corners, with an interesting **Chinese temple**, a **mosque** and a **Hindu temple** within 100m.

Orientation & Information
Restaurants and hotels are spread out along Jl Pratama, which runs the length of the peninsula. The police station and wartel are easy to find. **Nusa Dua Clinic** *(☎ 778098l; Jl Pratama 81)* charges 150,000Rp per consultation. **Shiap@net Internet** *(Jl Pratama 77)* has a minimum charge of 6000Rp for 30 minutes, and only two computers.

Activities
Quite a few water sports centres along Jl Pratama offer diving, cruises, windsurfing, parasailing, water-skiing etc. Check equipment and credentials before you sign up. Most have a bar and restaurant attached to their premises. For diving, cruises and fishing trips, you can book with many of the travel agents in southern Bali.

Established water sports operators include **Taman Sari Marine Sports** *(☎ 772583; w www.balibagus.com/tamansaridiving)* and **Benoa Marine Recreation** *(BMR; ☎ 771757, fax 775252)*. All operators will have similar prices for **diving** (about US$75/85 for 1/2 dives around Tanjung Benoa, including equipment rental; US$100 for two dives in Tulamben; US$350 for a three-day PADI open-water course). A minimum of two people is required for most dive trips and courses. See Activities in the Facts for the Visitor chapter for more information on dive sites and operators. **Snorkelling** trips include equipment and a boat ride to a reef (minimum two people) for US$20 per hour per person.

Other water sports include the very popular **parasailing** (US$15 per round) – so many people try it that it looks like an airborne invasion – and **jet-skiing** (US$20 for 15 minutes). You'll need at least two people for **water-skiing** (US$20 for 15 minutes) or **banana-boat** rides (US$15 for 15 minutes), or **glass-bottom boat trips** (US$20 per hour per person), and a maximum of five in a **speedboat** (US$200 per hour).

For a three-hour **fishing** trip, it is US$35 to US$80 per person, when there's two or more people, depending on boat size, and for sunset fishing it's US$35, including dinner.

Places to Stay – Budget

A few adjacent places near the top of Jl Pratama offer no frills accommodation across the road from the beach.

Pondok Agung *(☎/fax771143; rooms 90,000-120,000Rp, with air-con 120,000-175,000Rp)* is an attractive place; air-con rooms have TV.

Tanjung Mekar *(☎ 772063; rooms 90,000Rp)* is a small guesthouse, with just four pleasant rooms.

Rasa Sayang Beach Inn *(☎ 771643, fax 777268; rooms 75,000Rp, with air-con 125,000-175,000Rp)* is friendly, very clean and great value – it's the best option out of the three.

Places to Stay – Top End

In Benoa village, **Princess Nusa Dua Resort** *(☎ 771604, fax 771394; rooms US$75-100, family rooms US$150)*, is an attractive place with a pool and gardens.

Novotel Benoa Bali *(☎ 772239, fax 772237; e info@novotelbali.com; rooms US$206-352)*, straddles both sides of the road, and rooms and facilities are extremely tasteful. It has a health centre and spa, where massages start at US$22 for one hour.

Grand Mirage Resort *(☎ 771888, fax 772148; w www.grandmirage.com; rooms US$225-305)* is a huge complex with a four-storey interior waterfall and a Thalasso spa (w www.thalassobali.com), which offers massage, facials, aquamedics and aromatherapy. Individual treatments start from US$25 and packages start from US$95

Hotel Bali Royal Resort *(☎ 771039, fax 771885; suites US$169-218)* is the small place you will reach heading further south from the Grand Mirage. The 14 air-con suites all have living rooms, and are set in a pretty garden.

Places to Eat

Each hotel has several restaurants, and nonguests are welcome. One worth keeping in mind is **Co Co's Beach Club** *(☎ 772239)* at the Novotel Benoa Bali, where buffets focusing on different cuisines are held nightly.

On the 'border' with Nusa Dua, some cheap **warung** cater to hotel staff and offer the best value for money, while several busy **local warung** are clustered around the police station to the north.

There's several tourist restaurants in or near Benoa. **Restaurant Mini** *(☎ 973303; dishes 14,000-55,000Rp)* has a pleasant alfresco setting and offers Chinese and Indonesian dishes; Balinese dance shows are held on Monday and Friday night at 7.30pm. Next door **Nelayan Seafood** *(☎ 776868; Jl Pratama 101; dishes 18,000-31,000Rp)* offers less traffic noise and free hotel transfers.

Kecak Bali *(☎ 775533; w www.kecakbali .com; Jl Pratama; dishes 30,000-40,000Rp)*, under an *alang alang* canopy, has Balinese specialities as well as *rijstaffel* (105,000Rp for one), and offers free transport in the Nusa Dua area. It also organises cooking classes.

Cafe Bagus & Bar *(☎ 772716; dishes 20,000-45,000Rp)* is away from the beach, but is a reasonable spot for a pizza and a happy-hour beer between 7pm and 8pm (small/large Bintang 5500/10,500Rp).

Rumah Makan Padma *(☎ 773958; Jl Pratama 90; dishes 19,000-35,000Rp)* is a low-key place where the back wall is covered in graffiti. It offers fresh seafood, such as tuna, barracuda and lobster, which is best ordered the day before. *Rijstaffel* for two is 85,000Rp.

Getting There & Away

You can reach Bualu by public bemo from Kuta, then take one of the green bemos that shuttle up and down Jl Pratama (2000Rp) – after about 3pm bemos become scarce on both routes. A metered taxi or chartered bemo would be easier and quicker.

Getting Around

Bemos are infrequent on Jl Pratama, so taxis or walking are the main options.

Ubud & Around

Perched on the gentle slopes leading towards the central mountains, Ubud now matches Kuta for pace and tack. Ubud, though, continues to maintain its identity as the centre of 'cultural tourism' on Bali, and is a must-see destination for anyone interested in Balinese art, craft, music and dance. Around Ubud are temples, ancient sites and whole villages producing various handicrafts (albeit for tourists). Although the growth of Ubud has engulfed several neighbouring villages, leading to an urban sprawl, much of the surrounding countryside remains unspoiled and offers scenery of lush rice paddies, almost iridescent in the fierce sunlight, towering coconut trees, and small friendly villages. This all translates into delightful possibilities for walking and cycling.

Denpasar to Ubud

The road between Denpasar and Ubud is lined with places making and selling handicrafts. Try not to be put off by the rampant development and commercialism – the craft villages are much more interesting when you stop and look. Many tourists shop along the route, sometimes by the busload, but much of the craftwork is actually done in small workshops and family compounds on quiet back roads. You may enjoy these places more after visiting Ubud, where you'll see some of the best Balinese arts and develop some appreciation of the styles and themes.

From Batubulan terminal (see Getting There & Away in the Denpasar chapter) *bemos* (small pick-up trucks) to Ubud stop at the craft villages along the main road. For serious shopping, it's worth renting or chartering your own transport from Ubud, so you can explore the back roads and carry your purchases, without any hassles. If you decide to charter a vehicle, the driver may receive a commission from any place you spend your money – this can add 10% or more to the cost of purchases. Also, a driver is likely to steer you to workshops or artisans that he favours, rather than those of most interest to you.

Highlights

- Sampling the world-class multicultural cuisine of Bali's culinary capital
- Browsing through art shops, workshops and galleries, for arts, crafts and antiques
- Experiencing Bali's unique and elaborate cultural life through the vibrant performing arts of Ubud, Peliatan, Batubulan and Batuan
- Visiting Ubud's Neka and ARMA musums, showcasing the history of Balinese art
- Enhancing your health and beauty by indulging and soaking in some heavenly spas
- Exploring Gunung Kawi, the home of ancient, strange stone statues cut into the cliffs of the picturesque Pakerisan valley
- White water rafting through gorgeous gorges

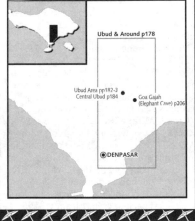

BATUBULAN

The start of the road from Denpasar is lined with outlets for stone sculptures – stone carving is the main craft of Batubulan (which means 'Moonstone'), and workshops are found all along the road to Tegaltamu, where the main road to Ubud does a sharp right turn. Batubulan is the source of the temple-gate guardians seen all over Bali. The stone used is a porous grey volcanic

UBUD & AROUND

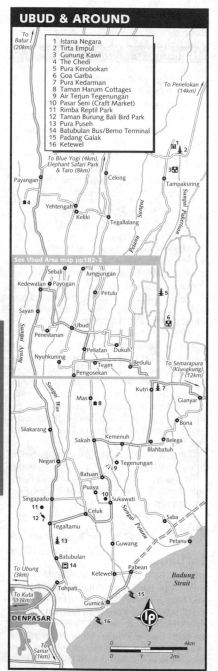

UBUD & AROUND

1 Istana Negara
2 Tirta Empul
3 Gunung Kawi
4 The Chedi
5 Pura Kerobokan
6 Goa Garba
7 Pura Kedarman
8 Taman Harum Cottages
9 Air Terjun Tegenungan
10 Pasar Seni (Craft Market)
11 Rimba Reptil Park
12 Taman Burung Bali Bird Park
13 Pura Puseh
14 Batubulan Bus/Bemo Terminal
15 Padang Galak
16 Ketewel

UBUD & AROUND

rock called *paras,* which resembles pumice; it's soft and surprisingly light.

The temples around Batubulan are, naturally, noted for their fine stonework. Just 200m to the east of the busy main road, **Pura Puseh** is worth a visit for its unusual decorations. The statues draw on ancient Hindu and Buddhist iconography and Balinese mythology, however, they are not old – many are based on illustrations from books on Javanese archaeology.

Batubulan is also a centre for making 'antiques', textiles and woodwork, and has numerous craft and antique shops. Several venues offer regular performances of traditional **Barong and Rangda dances**, often during the day, and commonly included in organised tours from southern Bali.

TAMAN BURUNG BALI BIRD PARK & RIMBA REPTIL PARK
☎ 0361

The bird park (☎ 299352; adult/child 70,000/35,000Rp; open 8am-6pm daily) boasts more than 1000 birds from over 250 species, including rare birds of paradise (cendrawasih) from Irian Jaya and highly endangered Bali starlings – many of which are housed in special walk-through aviaries. The two hectares of landscaped gardens feature a fine collection of tropical plants, and a couple of Komodo dragons. With some foreign assistance, the park is also actively involved in captive-breeding programmes.

Next door, Rimba Reptil Park (☎ 299344; adult/child 66,000/33,000Rp; open 8am-6pm daily) has about 20 species of creatures from Indonesia and Africa, as well as more Komodo dragons, turtles, crocodiles, and a python.

You can buy a combination ticket to both parks for 125,000/90,000Rp per adult/child. Allow at least two hours for the bird park alone, which also has an excellent **restaurant. Warung Lesehan 2M**, nearby on the road towards Ubud, is also a good, inexpensive place to eat.

Many organised tours stop at the parks, or you can take a Batubulan–Ubud bemo, get off at the junction at Tegaltamu, and follow the signs north for about 600m.

SINGAPADU
Singapadu is largely uncommercial and preserves a traditional appearance, with walled

family compounds and shady trees. The area has a strong history of music and dance, specifically the *gong gede* gamelan, the older *gong saron* gamelan and the Barong dance. Local artisans specialise in producing masks for Topeng and Barong dances.

Singapadu's dancers now perform mostly at large venues in the tourist areas – there are no regular public performances. There are not many obvious places in the town to buy locally produced crafts, as most of the better products are sold directly to dance troupes or quality art shops. Ask around to find some of the workshops, but even at the source the best quality masks will still be quite expensive. If you are relying on public transport wait for a bemo at the junction at Tegaltamu.

CELUK

Celuk is the silver and goldsmithing centre of Bali. The bigger showrooms are on the main road, and have marked prices that are quite high, although negotiation is possible. The variety and quality of the designs on display is not as good as those in the shops of Kuta and Ubud, and the prices are no cheaper, except for commercial buyers.

Hundreds of silversmiths and goldsmiths work in their homes on the back streets north of the main road. Most of these artisans are from *pande* families, members of a subcaste of blacksmiths whose knowledge of fire and metal has traditionally put them outside the usual caste hierarchy. Their small workshops are interesting to visit, and have the lowest prices, but they don't keep a large stock of finished work. They will make something to order if you bring a sample or sketch.

SUKAWATI

Once a royal capital, Sukawati is now known for a number of specialised crafts and for the daily **Pasar Seni**, a two-storey craft market where every type of quality craftwork and touristy trinket is on sale. One group of artisans, the *tukang prada,* make temple umbrellas, beautifully decorated with stencilled gold paint, which can be seen at roadside shops. The *tukang wadah* make cremation towers, which you're less likely to see. Other craft products include intricate patterned *lontar* (palm) baskets and wind chimes.

The craft market is on the western side of the main road – public bemos stop right outside. Across the road is the colourful morning **produce market**, which also sells sarongs and temple ceremony paraphernalia.

Sukawati is also renowned for its **traditional dances** and *wayang kulit* (shadow puppet) performances.

Puaya, about a kilometre northwest of Sukawati, specialises in high-quality leather shadow puppets and Topeng masks.

BATUAN

Batuan's recorded history goes back 1000 years, and in the 17th century its royal family controlled most of southern Bali. The decline of its power is attributed to a priest's curse, which scattered the royal family to different parts of the island.

In the 1930s two local artists began experimenting with a new style of painting using black ink on white paper. Their dynamic drawings featured all sorts of scenes from daily life – markets, paddy fields, animals and people crowded onto each painting – while the black-and-white technique evoked the Balinese view of the super natural.

Today, this distinct Batuan style of painting is noted for its inclusion of modern elements. Sea scenes often include a windsurfer, while tourists with video cameras or riding motorcycles pop up in the otherwise traditional Balinese scenery. There are good examples in galleries along, or just off, the main road in Batuan, and also in Ubud's Museum Puri Lukisan.

Batuan is also noted for its traditional dance, and is a centre for carved wooden relief panels and screens. The ancient **Gambuh dance** is performed in Batuan's **Pura Puseh** every full moon.

MAS
☎ 0361

Mas means 'Gold' in Bahasa Indonesia, but woodcarving is the principal craft in this village. The great Majapahit priest Nirartha once lived here, and **Pura Taman Pule** is said to be built on the site of his home. During the three-day **Kuningan festival** (see the Public Holidays & Special Events section in the Facts for the Visitor chapter), a performance of *wayang wong* (an older version of the *Ramayana* ballet) is held in the temple's courtyard.

Carved timber lion figures are produced in Mas' many workshops

Carving was a traditional art of the priestly Brahmana caste, and the skills are said to have been a gift of the gods. Historically, carving was limited to temple decorations, dance masks and musical instruments, but in the 1930s carvers began to depict people and animals in a naturalistic way, and the growth of tourism provided a market for woodcarving, which has become a major cottage industry. More abstract styles appeared in the 1960s and 1970s, with elongated figures and demonic forms emerging from the natural shapes of tree branches and roots. Now Mas is the centre of Bali's burgeoning furniture industry, producing chairs, tables and reproduction antiques, mainly from teak imported from other Indonesian islands.

North of Mas, woodcarving shops make way for art galleries, cafés and hotels, and you soon know that you're approaching Ubud.

Places to Stay
Taman Harum Cottages (☎ 975567, fax 975149; ⓦ www.tamanharumcottages.com; rooms from US$35, family villas US$45), along the main road in Mas, has elegant, individual bungalows, some with balconies overlooking the paddy fields, plus a swimming pool. It's behind a gallery, which is also a venue for a range of art and cultural courses (see the Courses section in the Facts for the Visitor chapter).

ALTERNATIVE ROUTES
Via the Coast
An alternative route between Denpasar and Ubud goes through the coastal village of **Gumicik**, which has a broad, black beach. This bypasses the congested roads of Batubulan and Celuk, and is the first completed section of a new, east coast road going via Lebih to Kusamba. The coast around here has some good wet-season **surfing** – Padang Galak, a right-hand beach break at low- to mid-tide; and Ketewel, a barrelling right-hander at high tide.

The beach at **Pabean** is a site for irregular religious purification ceremonies, and cremated ashes are ritually scattered here, near the mouth of the Sungai Wos (Wos River). Just north of Ketewel town, **Guwang** is another small woodcarving centre.

Via Blahbatuh
From Sakah, along the road between Batuan and Ubud, you can continue east for a few kilometres to the turn-off to Blahbatuh and continue to Ubud via Kutri and Bedulu.

In Blahbatuh, **Pura Gaduh** has a 1m-high stone head, said to be a portrait of Kebo Iwa, the legendary strongman and minister to the last king of the Bedulu kingdom. Gajah Mada – the Majapahit strongman – realised that he could not conquer Bedulu (Bali's strongest kingdom) while Kebo Iwa was there. So Gajah Mada lured him away to Java (with promises of women and song) and had him killed. The stone head possibly predates the Javanese influence on Bali, but the temple is a reconstruction of an earlier one destroyed in the great earthquake of 1917.

About 2km southwest of Blahbatuh, along Sungai Petanu, is **Air Terjun Tegenungan** (Tegenungan Waterfall; also known as Srog Srogan). Follow the signs from Kemenuh village for the best view of the falls, from the western side of the river.

Kutri North of Blahbatuh, Kutri has the interesting **Pura Kedarman** (also known as Pura Bukit Dharma). If you climb Bukit Dharma behind the temple, there's a panoramic **view** and a **hilltop shrine**, with a stone statue of the eight-armed goddess Durga killing a demon-possessed water buffalo.

Bona On the back road between Blahbatuh and Gianyar, Bona is credited as the modern home of the Kecak dance, however, Kecak and other dances are no longer held here for tourists. Bona is also a **basket-weaving** centre and has many articles made from lontar leaves. Nearby, **Belega** is a centre for **bamboo furniture** production.

Ubud

☎ 0361

In addition to the cultural attractions outlined at the start of this chapter, Ubud also has charming accommodation for all budgets and some of the best food on Bali. It's just high enough to be cooler than the coast during the evening and early morning and also during the wet season, but the days are just as fierce as the lowlands, but it's also noticeably wetter. There's an amazing amount to see in and around Ubud. You need at least a few days to appreciate it properly, and Ubud is one of those places where days can become weeks and weeks become months, as the noticeable expatatriate community demonstrates.

HISTORY

In the late 19th century, Cokorda Gede Sukawati established his branch of the Sukawati royal family in Ubud and began a series of alliances and confrontations with neighbouring kingdoms. In 1900, along with the kingdom of Gianyar, Ubud became (at its own request) a Dutch protectorate and, no longer troubled by local conflicts, was able to concentrate on its religious and cultural life.

The Cokorda's descendants encouraged Western artists and intellectuals to visit the area in the 1930s, most notably Walter Spies, Colin McPhee and Rudolf Bonnet (see the boxed text 'Western Visitors in the 1930s' in the Facts for the Visitor chapter). They provided an enormous stimulus to local art, introduced new ideas and techniques, and began a process of displaying and promoting Balinese culture worldwide. As mass tourism arrived on Bali, Ubud became an attraction not for beaches or bars, but for the arts.

ORIENTATION

The once small village of Ubud has expanded to encompass its neighbours – Campuan, Penestanan, Padangtegal, Peliatan and Pengosekan are all part of what we see as Ubud today. The centre of town is the junction of Monkey Forest Rd and Jl Raya Ubud, where the bustling market and crowded bemo stops are found, as well as Ubud palace and the main temple, Pura Desa Ubud. Monkey Forest Rd (officially Jl Wanara Wana, but always known by its unofficial name) runs south to Monkey Forest Sanctuary – the northern part of the road is one-way, heading north.

Jl Raya Ubud ('Ubud Main Rd' – usually Jl Raya for short) is the main east–west road. West of Ubud, the road drops steeply down to the ravine at Campuan, where an old suspension bridge, next to the new one, hangs over the Sungai Wos. West of Campuan, the pretty village of Penestanan is famous for its painters and bead-work. East and south of Ubud proper, the 'villages' of Peliatan, Pengosekan and Nyuhkuning are known variously for painting, traditional dance and woodcarving. The area north of Ubud is less densely settled, with picturesque paddy fields interspersed with small villages, many of which specialise in a local craft.

Maps

The maps in this guidebook will be sufficient for most visitors, but if you want to explore the surrounding villages on foot or by bicycle, the best map to buy is the pocket-sized *Ubud* map published by Periplus Handimaps. *Bali Pathfinder* is also worth picking up. Both are readily available from bookshops in town.

The Statue of Kutri

This statue on the hilltop shrine at Kutri is thought to date from the 11th century and shows strong Indian influences.

One theory is that the image is of Airlangga's mother, Mahendradatta, who married King Udayana, Bali's 10th-century ruler. When her son succeeded to the throne she hatched a plot against him and unleashed *leyak* (evil spirits) upon his kingdom. She was defeated, but this led to the legend of Rangda, the widow-witch and ruler of evil spirits. The temple at the base of the hill has images of Durga, and the body of a *barong*, the mythical lion-dog creature, can be seen in one of the pavilions (the sacred head of the barong is kept elsewhere).

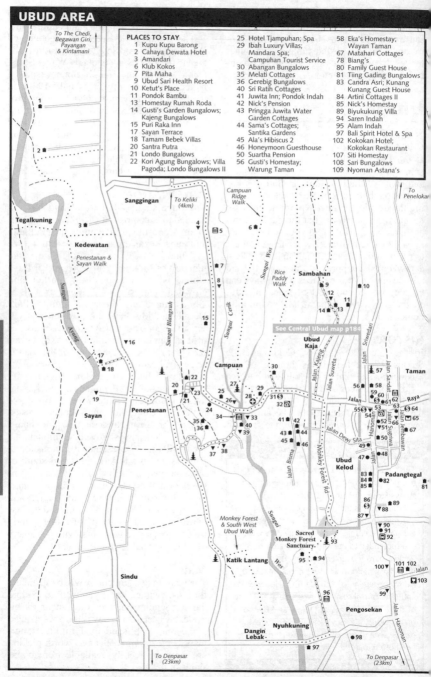

UBUD AREA

PLACES TO STAY
1 Kupu Kupu Barong
2 Cahaya Dewata Hotel
3 Amandari
6 Klub Kokos
7 Pita Maha
9 Ubud Sari Health Resort
10 Ketut's Place
11 Pondok Bambu
13 Homestay Rumah Roda
14 Gusti's Garden Bungalows; Kajeng Bungalows
15 Puri Raka Inn
17 Sayan Terrace
18 Tamam Bebek Villas
20 Santra Putra
21 Londo Bungalows
22 Kori Agung Bungalows; Villa Pagoda; Londo Bungalows II

25 Hotel Tjampuhan; Spa
29 Ibah Luxury Villas; Mandara Spa; Campuhan Tourist Service
30 Abangan Bungalows
35 Melati Cottages
36 Gerebig Bungalows
40 Sri Ratih Cottages
41 Juwita Inn; Pondok Indah
42 Nick's Pension
43 Pringga Juwita Water Garden Cottages
44 Sama's Cottages; Santika Gardens
45 Ala's Hibiscus 2
46 Honeymoon Guesthouse
50 Suartha Pension
56 Gusti's Homestay; Warung Taman

58 Eka's Homestay; Wayan Taman
67 Matahari Cottages
78 Biang's
80 Family Guest House
81 Tiing Gading Bungalows
83 Candra Asri; Kunang Kunang Guest House
84 Artini Cottages II
85 Nick's Homestay
89 Biyukukung Villa
94 Saren Indah
95 Alam Indah
97 Bali Spirit Hotel & Spa
102 Kokokan Hotel; Kokokan Restaurant
107 Siti Homestay
108 Sari Bungalows
109 Nyoman Astana's

UBUD AREA

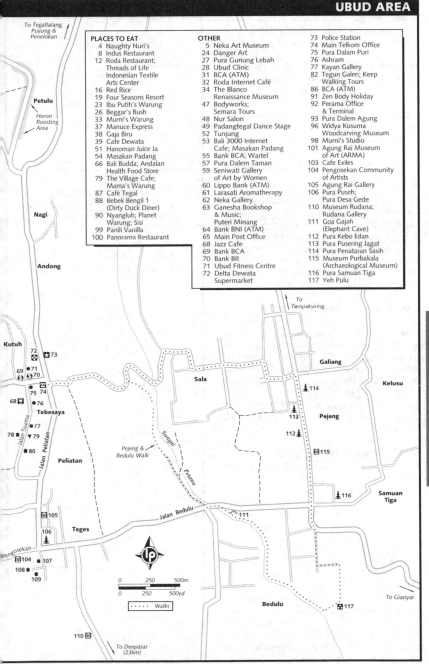

PLACES TO EAT
- 4 Naughty Nuri's
- 8 Indus Restaurant
- 12 Roda Restaurant;
    Threads of Life
    Indonesian Textile
    Arts Center
- 16 Red Rice
- 19 Four Seasons Resort
- 23 Ibu Putih's Warung
- 26 Beggar's Bush
- 33 Murni's Warung
- 37 Manuce Express
- 38 Gaja Biru
- 39 Cafe Dewata
- 51 Hanoman Juice Ja
- 54 Masakan Padang
- 66 Bali Budda; Andalan
    Health Food Store
- 79 The Village Cafe;
    Mama's Warung
- 87 Café Tegal
- 88 Bebek Bengil 1
    (Dirty Duck Diner)
- 90 Nyangluh; Planet
    Warung; Sisi
- 99 Panili Vanilla
- 100 Panorama Restaurant

OTHER
- 5 Neka Art Museum
- 24 Danger Art
- 27 Pura Gunung Lebah
- 28 Ubud Clinic
- 31 BCA (ATM)
- 32 Roda Internet Café
- 34 The Blanco
    Renaissance Museum
- 47 Bodyworks;
    Semara Tours
- 48 Nur Salon
- 49 Padangtegal Dance Stage
- 52 Tunjung
- 53 Bali 3000 Internet
    Cafe; Masakan Padang
- 55 Bank BCA; Wartel
- 57 Pura Dalem Taman
- 59 Seniwati Gallery
    of Art by Women
- 60 Lippo Bank (ATM)
- 61 Larasati Aromatherapy
- 62 Neka Gallery
- 63 Ganesha Bookshop
    & Music;
    Puteri Minang
- 64 Bank BNI (ATM)
- 65 Main Post Office
- 68 Jazz Cafe
- 69 Bank BCA
- 70 Bank BII
- 71 Ubud Fitness Centre
- 72 Delta Dewata
    Supermarket

- 73 Police Station
- 74 Main Telkom Office
- 75 Pura Dalam Puri
- 76 Ashram
- 77 Kayan Gallery
- 82 Tegun Galeri; Keep
    Walking Tours
- 86 BCA (ATM)
- 91 Zen Body Holiday
- 92 Perama Office
    & Terminal
- 93 Pura Dalem Agung
- 96 Widya Kusuma
    Woodcarving Museum
- 98 Murni's Studio
- 101 Agung Rai Museum
    of Art (ARMA)
- 103 Cafe Exiles
- 104 Pengosekan Community
    of Artists
- 105 Agung Rai Gallery
- 106 Pura Puseh;
    Pura Desa Gede
- 110 Museum Rudana;
    Rudana Gallery
- 111 Goa Gajah
    (Elephant Cave)
- 112 Pura Kebo Edan
- 113 Pura Pusering Jagat
- 114 Pura Penataran Sasih
- 115 Museum Purbakala
    (Archaeological Museum)
- 116 Pura Samuan Tiga
- 117 Yeh Pulu

UBUD & AROUND

INFORMATION
Along the main roads, you'll find banks, ATMs, moneychangers, travel agents and several *wartels* (public telephone offices).

Tourist Offices
Ubud Tourist Information *(Yaysan Bina Wisata;* ☎ *973285; Jl Raya; open 8am-9pm daily)* has a good range of pamphlets and a notice board advertising current happenings and activities. The staff can answer most regional questions and have up-to-date information on ceremonies and traditional dances held in the region; dance tickets are sold here.

Post
The **main post office** *(Jl Jembawan; open 8am-4pm Mon-Thur, 8am-11am Fri, 8am-12.30pm Sat)* is east of the centre, south off Jl Raya (see the Ubud Area map). It has a sort-it-yourself poste restante system – address poste restante mail to Kantor Pos, Ubud 80571, Bali, Indonesia. There are also several postal agencies on the main roads.

Email & Internet Access
Internet centres are easy to find on Monkey Forest Rd, Jl Hanoman, Jl Kajeng and Jl Bisma – basically wherever there are concentrations of places to stay. One of the better places is the airy **Bali 3000 Internet Cafe** *(☎ 978538; Jl Raya; dishes 8000-20,000Rp)*, which has a big range of espresso coffee, cakes, croissants and sandwiches that you can tuck into while you're emailing. Charges are 250Rp per minute.

Bookshops & Music Shops
The middle of Jl Raya has two good places for new books, including maps, travel guides and specialist titles on Bali and Indonesia – try **Ary's Bookshop** and **Ubud Bookshop** *(☎ 975362)*. **Ganesha Bookshop & Music** *(☎ 970320;* W *www.ganeshabooksbali.com)*, at the eastern end of Jl Raya, has a good selection of titles on Indonesian studies, travel, women's issues, arts and music, including a few titles in French. The **Neka Art Museum** (not to be confused with the Neka Gallery) has a particularly good range of art books.

For second-hand books in most major European languages, try **Igna Bookshop** *(Monkey Forest Rd)*, which also has a small range of new titles, or go to **Pondok Pecak Library & Learning Centre**.

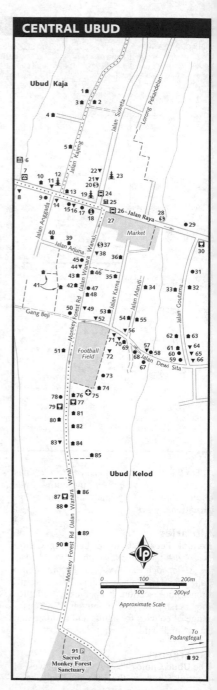

CENTRAL UBUD

PLACES TO STAY
1 Padma Accommodation & Painting Collection
2 Arjana Accommodation
3 Artja Inn
4 Siti Bungalows
5 Roja's Bungalows
10 Puri Saraswati Bungalows
13 Pradha Guesthouse & Restaurant
32 Shana Homestay
33 Darta Homestay
34 Sayong House
35 Gandra House
36 Yuni's House; Hibiscus Bungalows
39 Puji Bungalows
40 Anom Bungalows; Jungut Inn
41 Oka Wati Hotel
42 Puri Muwa Bungalows; Pharmacy
43 Alit House
46 Pandawa Homestay
48 Gayatri Bungalows
51 Nyuh Gading Accommodation
53 Surawan House
54 Budi Bungalows; Anugrah House; Sen Sen Warung
55 Esty's House
61 Agung Cottages
62 Nirwana Pension & Gallery; Toko Tako
63 Donald Homestay; Sundana Homestay
69 Masih Bungalow
74 Loka House
76 Cendana Resort & Spa; Le Chat; Postal Agent
80 Ubud Village Hotel
81 Frog Pond Inn; Postal Agency; Wartel
82 Komaneka Resort & Spa; Komaneka Art Gallery
84 Lumbung Sari; Three Brothers
85 Rice Paddy Bungalows
86 Ubud Bungalows
89 Kubu Saren
90 Ubud Terrace Bungalows
92 Kubuku

PLACES TO EAT
8 Sababa; Casa Luna
11 Cafe Lotus
14 Ryoshi
16 Ary's Warung
21 Warung Babi Guling; Bumbu Restaurant
22 Terazo; Ang Ka Sa
38 Canderi's Warung
44 Ayu's Kitchen
49 Ibu Rai Bar & Restaurant
52 Bamboo Restaurant
56 Tutmak Cafe
57 Kafe Batan Waru
64 Dewa Warung
65 Warung Mini
66 Fairway Cafe & Internet
70 Kanpai
71 Do Drop In; Kertas Gingsir
72 Aries Warung
83 Cafe Wayan & Bakery

OTHER
6 Museum Puri Lukisan; Art & Cultural Workshops
7 Wartel
9 Tino Supermarket; Ubud Bookshop
12 Pura Taman Saraswati
15 Treasures – a Gallery of Gold Creations
17 Ary's Bookshop
18 Ubud Tourist Information (Yaysan Bina Wisata)
19 Pura Desa Ubud
20 BNI (ATM)
23 Pura Merajan Agung
24 Bemo Stop
25 Ubud Palace; Puri Saren Agung
26 Bemo Stop
27 Pasar Seni (Art Market)
28 Bank Danamon
29 Lempad's House
30 Nomad's
31 Studio Perak
37 Bank BNI (ATM)
45 Era 21
47 Zarong
50 Igna Bookshop
58 Olala; Bulan Madu
59 Alamkara
60 Acupuncture & Chinese Herbal Clinic
67 Dewangga Bunglows & Gallery
68 Galeri Déjà vu
73 Pondok Pecak Library & Learning Centre; Beranda Café & Restaurant
75 MF Medical Service; Milano Salon; Bebek Bengil 2
77 Sai Sai Bar
78 Alamkara
79 Putra Bar
87 Bulan Baru
88 Meditation Shop
91 Parking (for Monkey Forest Sanctuary)

Era 21 (☎ 970820; Monkey Forest Rd) has a good music selection, including traditional Balinese CDs and contemporary international discs.

Libraries

Pondok Pecak Library & Learning Centre (☎ 976194; e pondok@indo.net.id; Monkey Forest Rd; open 9am-9pm Mon-Sat, noon-5pm Sun) is a relaxed place, which also has a children's book section. It charges a 30,000Rp membership fee per month. It also runs a range of courses for adults and children and has a small café.

Emergency

The **Ubud Clinic** (☎ 974911; Jl Raya), west of Central Ubud, is the best medical centre around. It's open 24 hours and charges 150,000Rp for a clinical consultation, or 250,000Rp to 300,000Rp for a hotel visit (payment by credit card is available). **MF Medical Service** (☎ 971426; Monkey Forest Rd), near Milano Salon, is on call 24 hours. The **Acupuncture & Chinese Herbal Clinic** (☎ 971969; Jl Goutama 16) is staffed by an Australian-trained herbalist. There's also a **pharmacy** next door to Puri Muwa Bungalows on Monkey Forest Rd.

The **police station** (☎ 975316) is out on the eastern side of town at Andong.

MUSEUMS

As well as numerous galleries where paintings are exhibited for sale, Ubud has several art museums.

Museum Puri Lukisan

Museum Puri Lukisan *(Museum of Fine Arts; fax 975136;* W *www.mpl-ubud.com; admission 10,000Rp; open 8am-4pm daily)* was opened in 1956, and displays fine examples of all schools of Balinese art. It was in Ubud that the modern Balinese art movement started; where artists first began to abandon purely religious themes and court subjects for scenes of everyday life. Rudolf Bonnet was part of the Pita Maha artists' cooperative, and together with Cokorda Gede Agung Sukawati (a prince of Ubud's royal family) they helped to establish a permanent collection.

The pavilion straight ahead as you enter has a collection of early works from Ubud and the surrounding villages. These include examples of classical Wayang-style paintings, fine ink drawings by I Gusti Nyoman Lempad and paintings by Pita Maha artists. The pavilion on the left as you enter has some colourful examples of the 'Young Artist' style of painting and a good selection of 'modern traditional' works. The pavilion on the right as you enter the grounds is used for temporary exhibitions, which change every month or so. Paintings are well displayed and labelled in English, and artwork for sale is also on display.

Art & Cultural Workshops (☎ *971159, fax 975136;* W *www.dwibhumi.com),* based at the rear of the building to the right, run creative courses, including the art of making offerings, Kecak (traditional Balinese dance, based on the *Ramayana*) singing,

kite making and woodcarving, mask painting and Balinese dance. Costs range, for example, from 65,000Rp for a 90-minute gamelan class, to 235,000Rp for a full-day woodcarving class. Visit the workshop to see what's on offer (alternatively, the ticket office should have an activities folder).

Neka Art Museum

The Neka Art Museum (☎ *975074; admission 10,000Rp; open 9am-5pm daily),* which is quite distinct from Neka Gallery, was opened in 1976, and is the creation of Suteja Neka, a private collector and dealer in Balinese art. It has an excellent and diverse collection and is the best place to learn about the development of painting on Bali.

The **Balinese Painting Hall** provides an overview of local painting, many influenced by *wayang kulit* puppetry. The **Arie Smit Pavilion** features Smit's works on the upper level, and examples of the Young Artist school, which he inspired, on the lower level. The **Lempad Pavilion** houses Bali's largest collection of works by I Gusti Nyoman Lempad.

The **Contemporary Indonesian Art Hall** has paintings by artists from other parts of Indonesia, many of whom have worked on Bali. The upper floor of the **East–West Art Annexe** is devoted to the work of foreign artists, such as Louise Koke, Miguel Covarrubias, Rudolf Bonnet, Han Snel, Donald Friend and Antonio Blanco.

The **temporary exhibition hall** has changing displays, while the **Photography Archive**

The Real Bali

A mythical place called 'the real Bali' is supposed to exist somewhere near Ubud, and many who scorn Kuta will pretend that Ubud is untainted by tourism. In fact, Ubud is not a traditional Balinese rural village, nor is it typical of modern Bali. It has undergone tremendous development in the past few years, seen some unfortunate buildings go up on the main street and now has traffic congestion in its centre and urban sprawl on its edges. Its two main streets are completely lined with restaurants, travel agents, fashion shops and Internet cafés, while the fast disappearing paddy fields are a bankable backdrop for some of the most expensive hotels on Bali.

Ubud and its surrounding villages, however, are still *desa adat* – communities adhering to traditional custom – with a priestly caste and a local royal family. Although the arts, crafts, music and dances are important parts of the cultural tourism industry, they also serve to support the religious rituals and ceremonies that are integral to community life. The making of offerings and the preparations for ceremonies are almost continuous, and if you stay at a 'homestay' in a traditional family compound, you'll notice that the family temple is as elaborately carved, painted and decorated as anything sold to tourists in a gallery or art market.

Centre features black and white photography of Bali in the early 1930s and 1940s.

Any Ubud–Kintamani bemo will stop outside the museum.

Museum Rudana

This large, imposing museum (☎ 976479; admission 10,000Rp; open 8am-5pm daily), to the southeast of Ubud in Peliatan, was opened in December 1995. The three floors contain interesting traditional paintings, including a calendar dated to the 1840s, some Lempad drawings, and more modern pieces. The museum is beside the **Rudana Gallery**, which has a large selection of paintings for sale.

Agung Rai Museum of Art (ARMA)

Founded by Agung Rai as a museum, gallery and cultural centre, the impressive ARMA (☎ 976659; w www.chica.com/arma; Jl Pengosekan; admission 10,000Rp; open 9am-6pm daily) is on the southeastern side of Ubud. It's the only place on Bali to see works by the influential German artist Walter Spies. It also has work by 19th-century Javanese artist Raden Saleh. It exhibits classical Kamasan paintings, Batuan-style work from the 1930s and 1940s, and works by Lempad, Affandi, Sadali, Hofker, Bonnet and Le Mayeur (see the special section 'Balinese Arts & Crafts' for more details). The collection is well labelled in English and Japanese.

It's interesting to visit ARMA between 3pm and 5pm from Monday to Friday and 10am to noon on Saturday, when local children practice Balinese dancing, while gamelan practice takes place on Tuesday, Thursday and Sunday at 5pm. Regular **Kecak performances** (50,000Rp) are held here every full moon and new moon at 7pm; book at Ubud Tourist Information.

You can enter the museum grounds from the southern end of Jl Hanoman (there's parking near Kafe ARMA), but the main entrance is around the corner on Jl Pengosekan. The Ubud–Gianyar bemo will drop you here.

Threads of Life Indonesian Textile Arts Center

This small, professional textile gallery and educational studio (☎ 972187, fax 976582; w www.threadsoflife.com; Jl Kajeng 24) sponsors the production of naturally-dyed,

The Plastic Bottle Pile-up

A number of businesses are attempting to confront the huge waste problem created by the disposal of plastic water bottles (think about how much water you drink per day and think about the fact that there are no recycling plants in Bali). Inexpensive filtered water refills are available at **Roda Internet Cafe** (☎ 973325; e rodanet@denpasar.wasantara.net.id; Jl Bisma), **Roda Restaurant** (Jl Kajeng 24), **Pondok Pecak Library & Learning Centre** (Jl Hanoman) and **Aries Warung** (across Football Field, Monkey Forest Rd).

handmade ritual textiles, helping to recover skills in danger of being lost to modern dyeing and weaving methods. Commissioned pieces are displayed in the gallery. It also runs regular textile appreciation courses (see Courses in the Facts for the Visitor chapter).

Widya Kusuma Woodcarving Museum

This tiny museum (admission by donation; open 10am-5pm daily) is a short walk south of Monkey Forest Sanctuary – follow the signs past Pura Dalem Agung in the sanctuary. The walk there is probably more of a highlight, as the museum only has a few pieces, but it does show a variety of styles and subjects. In spite of the official opening hours, you might have to ask around for someone to open it.

GALLERIES

Ubud is dotted with galleries – every street and lane seems to have a place exhibiting artwork for sale. They vary enormously in the choice and quality of items on display. Several major galleries display a huge variety of work, generally of a very high quality, but at prices that are often similarly elevated. A few others in the surrounding villages, such as the **Pengosekan Community of Artists**, are also worth visiting. All of the following galleries appear on the Ubud Area map.

Agung Rai Gallery

In Peliatan, the gallery's collection covers the full range of Balinese styles. It works as a cooperative, with the work priced by the artist and the gallery adding a percentage.

Neka Gallery

Operated by Suteja Neka, the commercial Neka Gallery (☎ 975034) is quite distinct from Neka Art Museum, and is on the other side of town in Taman. It has an extensive selection from all the schools of Balinese art, as well as works by European residents such as Arie Smit.

Seniwati Gallery of Art by Women

This small commercial gallery (☎/fax 975 485) exhibits works by Balinese, Indonesian and resident foreign women artists. The gallery and workshop aims to publicise Balinese women artists and to encourage the next generation. The art shop on the main street nearby is also well worth browsing.

Danger Art

Founded by the contemporary American artist Symon, the gallery/studio (☎ 974721; W www.symonbali.com; Jl Raya) is a rambling place full of huge, colourful, exotic portraits. A sign at the entrance reads: 'Warning: Full frontal nude noveltys (sic) exhibited upstairs' – just so you know what to expect!

ARTISTS' HOMES
Lempad's House

The home of the great I Gusti Nyoman Lempad is open to the public, but it's mainly used as a gallery for a group of artists, which includes Lempad's grand-children. There are only a few of Lempad's own works here. The family compound itself is a good example of traditional Balinese architecture and layout – Lempad was an architect and sculptor before he started painting and drawing. The Puri Lukisan and Neka museums have more extensive collections of Lempad's drawings.

The Blanco Renaissance Museum

Beside the Campuan suspension bridge, a driveway leads to the superbly theatrical house of Antonio Blanco (☎ 975502; Jl Raya; admission 20,000Rp; open 8am-5pm daily), who came to Bali from Spain via the Philippines. Blanco specialised in erotic art, illustrated poetry and playing the role of an eccentric, self-adulatory artist. He died on Bali in December 1999, and his home is now a museum.

Other Artists' Homes

The home of Walter Spies is now part of the Hotel Tjampuhan. Aficionados can stay in the 'Spies house' if they book well in advance. Dutch-born artist Han Snel lived in Ubud from the 1950s until his death in early 1999, and his family runs Siti Bungalows on Jl Kajeng, where his work is exhibited in a separate gallery.

Arie Smit (1916–) is the best-known and the longest surviving Western artist in Ubud. He worked in the Dutch colonial administration in the 1930s, was imprisoned during WWII, and came to Bali in 1956. In the 1960s, his influence sparked the Young Artists school of painting in Penestanan, earning him an enduring place in the history of Balinese art. His home is not open to the public.

Murni (Gusti Kadek Murniasih) is one of Bali's most innovative contemporary artists. If you're down in Pengosekan, it's well worth dropping into her studio (☎ 976453) to see what's on display.

SACRED MONKEY FOREST SANCTUARY

This cool and dense swathe of jungle, officially called Mandala Wisata Wanara Wana (adult/child 3000/1500Rp; open 8.30am-6pm daily), at the southern end of Monkey Forest Rd, houses three holy temples. The sanctuary is inhabited by a band of grey-haired and greedy long-tailed Balinese macaques, who are ever vigilant for passing tourists who just might have peanuts and ripe bananas available for a quick handout. They can put on ferocious displays of temperament if you fail to come through with the goods. The macaques have been known to bite if provoked, and you should definitely not hand food directly to the less than endearing creatures.

The interesting Pura Dalem Agung (Temple of the Dead) is in the forest, for this is the inauspicious kelod side of town. Look for the Rangda figures devouring children at the entrance to the inner temple. (See the Glossary at the back of the book for explanations of various terms.)

You can enter through one of the three gates: at the southern end of Monkey Forest Rd; 100m further east, near the car park; or from the southern side, on the lane from Nyuhkuning.

ELEPHANT SAFARI PARK

North of Ubud, in Taro in the cool, wet highlands, **Bali Adventure Tours** (☎ 721480; W www.baliadventuretours.com) runs the enjoyable **Elephant Safari Park** (admission adult/child US$7.50/3.75; tour package including elephant ride & transport adult/child US$68/47).

PETULU

Every evening at around 6pm, thousands of big, white, water birds fly in to Petulu, squabbling over the prime perching places before settling into the trees beside the road, and becoming a minor tourist attraction. The herons, mainly Java pond heron, started their visits to Petulu in 1965 for no apparent reason. Villagers believe they bring good luck (as well as tourists), despite the smell and the mess. A few *warung* (food stalls) have been set up in the paddy fields, where you can have a drink while enjoying the spectacle. Walk quickly under the trees if the herons are already roosting – the copious droppings on the road will indicate if it's unwise to hang around.

A bemo from Ubud to Puyung will drop you off at the turn-off just south of Petulu (the trip should take about 10 to 15 minutes), but it's more convenient with your own transport. It would make a pleasant walk or bicycle ride on any of several routes north of Ubud, but if you stay for the herons you'll be heading back in the dark.

WALKS AROUND UBUD

The growth of Ubud has engulfed a number of nearby villages, although they have still managed to retain distinct identities. There are lots of interesting walks in the area, to surrounding villages or through the paddy fields. You'll frequently see artists at work in open rooms and on verandas, and the timeless tasks of rice cultivation continue alongside luxury villas.

In most places there are plenty of warung or small shops selling snack foods and drinks, but bring your own water anyway. Also bring a good hat, decent shoes and wet-weather gear for the afternoon showers; long pants are better for walking through thick vegetation.

It's good to start walks at daybreak, before it gets too hot. Don't leave your return too late if you're planning to get a bemo back to town, as they become infrequent after 5pm, after which you may have to charter transport, or walk back in the dark.

Keep Walking Tours (☎/fax 970581; e keepwalk@hotmail.com; Jl Hanoman), based next door to Tegun Galeri, offers one-to seven-hour guided and themed walking tours around Ubud, including walks to rural villages and the herons at Petulu from 45,000Rp to 150,000Rp. It also organises treks of Gunung Batur for US$55. If the office is closed, you should seek information from Tegun Galeri.

Monkey Forest & Southwest Ubud

This walk can be attempted from either Monkey Forest Rd or Campuan; our route begins from the Monkey Forest Sanctuary.

Take your time strolling through the forest, then take the sealed road at the southwestern corner of the forest near the temple. Continue south on the lane to the woodcarvers' village of **Nyuhkuning**. At the southern end of the village at Bale Banjar Nyuhkuning (Nyuhkuning Community Hall), turn right and follow the paved road across the bridge over Sungai Wos to Dangin Lebak (this busy road is the most unpleasant part of the trip but should only take around 15 minutes). Take the track to the right just after the large Bale Banjar Dangin Lebak (Dangin Lebak Community Hall). From here follow paths due north through the paddy fields, and either veer left, westwards through the rice paddies or head down a short goat track to a paved road to reach **Katik Lantang**, where you join a paved road that continues north to **Penestanan**. Many artists live here, and you can stop at their homes/studios/galleries and see paintings for sale. Follow the paved road through the village, veering east, and go down through a deep cutting and back to Campuan and Ubud.

This whole circuit is well under 8km, but could take a whole day, with pleasant stops for eating, drinking and enjoying the sights.

Campuan Ridge

This walk passes over the lush river valley of the Sungai Wos, offering views of Gunung Agung and glimpses of small village communities. Two round trip routes are possible (via Payogan, or via Sebali and

Keliki). Both routes take around two hours return, and water is available en route.

At the confluence of the Sungai Wos and Sungai Cerik is **Campuan**, which means 'Where Two Rivers Meet'. The walk starts here at the Ibah Luxury Villas. Enter the hotel driveway and take the path to the left, where a walkway crosses the river to Pura Gunung Lebah. From there follow the concrete path north, climbing up onto the ridge between the two rivers. Fields of elephant grass, traditionally used for thatched roofs, slope away on either side.

Continuing north along the Campuan ridge past Klub Kokos (a convenient drink stop), the road improves as it passes through paddy fields and the small village of **Bangkiang Sidem**. From here either head west to the small village of **Payogan** and Ubud (see directions following), or continue due north to the neighbouring villages of **Sebali** and **Keliki**. Beyond **Sebali** and **Keliki**, you could keep going for another 20km and reach the great volcanic crater around Gunung Batur.

On the outskirts of Bangkiang Sidem, an unsigned road heads west, which winds down to Sungai Cerik (the west branch of Sungai Wos), then climbs steeply up to **Payogan**. From here you can walk south to the main road, and walk (40 minutes) or catch a ride back to Campuan and Ubud.

Rice Paddy Walk

This one hour walk will take you through peaceful and gently terraced emerald paddy fields fringed with coconut palms. You will see the Sungai Wos valley, flocks of ducks and domestic chickens, and you may even be offered a freshly picked coconut.

Walk west along Jl Raya from central Ubud and head up the driveway of Abangan Bungalows, keeping them on your left. Turn left at the first driveway to head west along the southern edge of a paddy field. If you stick to the higher footpath as it curves northwards between high walls you will come to the western edge of the paddy field. The paved path heading north will give way to a dirt track as the view across the valley to the Campuan ridge opens up to your left.

After around 20 minutes of walking north you will pass a small group of thatched huts directly to your left. Moving on you will find yourself on a high ridge looking steeply down a valley.

Soon after you become aware of a river on your right, the path forks. Take the path leading to the right and down to a channel that you can jump over (approximately 1m wide), then turn left and north to a concrete bridge. Cross the channel and turn right and along this bank southwards towards Ubud. This path involves some narrow channel banks so you will need to do some balancing acts along the way, and in the wet season, this may be very slippery.

The path forks at the sharp end of a triangular walled compound. Take the wider left-hand fork, keeping the wall to your right. Crossing a small bridge, the road bends right, beside an embankment wall until you reach Jl Kajeng, which will take you back to Jl Raya Ubud.

Penestanan & Sayan

Just west of the Campuan bridge, past the Blanco Renaissance Museum, a steep uphill road bends away to the left and winds across the forested gully of the Sungai Blangsuh to the Young Artists village of Penestanan. West of Penestanan is Sayan, site of Colin McPhee's home in the 1930s, amusingly described in his book, *A House in Bali*. The homes of a number of modern-day McPhees are perched overlooking the deep valley of the magnificent Sungai Ayung. The best place to get down to the riverside is just north of the bungalows at **Sayan Terrace** – some would-be guides hang around here, and you might find them very helpful to negotiate the network of tracks in the valley.

Following the trails north, along the eastern side of the Ayung, you traverse steep slopes, cross paddy fields and pass some irrigation canals and tunnels. After about 1.5km you'll reach the finishing point for many of the white water rafting trips – a good trail goes from there up to the main road at **Kedewatan**, where you can get a bemo (or walk) back to Ubud. Alternatively, cross the river on the nearby bridge and climb up to the very untouristy village of **Tegalkuning** on the other side. Another option is to continue upstream on the eastern side of the river, through the maze of paddy fields beneath the upmarket Amandari hotel. After about a kilometre, a trail to the right leads back up to the main road near Cahaya Dewata Hotel.

Pejeng & Bedulu

The temples of Pejeng and the archaeological sites of Bedulu (see the Around Ubud section later in this chapter) can be visited in a day's walk. As most of the attractions are on sealed roads, you can also go by bicycle.

If you have the time and energy, do the entire loop by going to the far eastern end of Jl Raya, and taking the small road that continues east from there. It passes the garbage dump and descends steeply to cross the Sungai Petanu, then climbs to the village of Sala. Some back roads will take you east through Pejeng to the main road, where you turn south to pass several important temples and archaeological sites.

You can keep walking south down through Bedulu to the carved cliffs of **Yeh Pulu**. From there it's possible to follow Sungai Petanu upstream to **Goa Gajah** (Elephant Cave), but you may have trouble finding the right trail through the paddy fields. If you've had enough, grab one of the many Ubud–Gianyar bemos that go past Goa Gajah. Alternatively, follow the trail by Sungai Petanu back to the small road by the garbage dump – most of it is pretty, despite this landmark.

Bird-Watching

The legendary Victor Mason's **Bali Bird Walks** (☎ 975009) start at 9am at the Beggar's Bush pub in Campuan on Tuesday, Friday and Saturday. Most walks are actually guided by one of Victor's staff. The cost is US$33 per person, for the three-hour walk and includes drinking water and lunch at the pub. Confirm that you'll receive your own set of binoculars, given the price of the tour.

CYCLING

Many shops, agencies and hotels in central Ubud, especially on Monkey Forest Rd, rent mountain bikes. A good place is **Campuhan Tourist Service** (☎ 975298; Jl Raya), next door to Ibah Villas. It rents bikes for 25,000Rp per day or 20,000Rp per day over three days. In general, the land is dissected by rivers running south, so any east–west route will involve a lot of ups and downs as you cross the river valleys. North–south routes run between the rivers, and are much easier going, but can have heavy traffic. Some of the walking routes described are also suitable for cycling, especially southwest to Nyuhkuning and Penestanan, and southeast to Pejeng and Bedulu.

RAFTING

The nearby Sungai Ayung is the most popular river on Bali for white water rafting, so Ubud is a convenient base for rafting trips – see Rafting in the Activities section in the Facts for the Visitor chapter.

MASSAGE & SPAS

Ubud has several salons and spas where you can seriously pamper yourself, as well as a gym – **Ubud Fitness Centre** (☎ 974804; Jl Jero Gading), which charges a registration fee of 50,000Rp and 25,000Rp per visit.

Bodyworks (☎ 975720; W www.ubudbody workscentre.com; Jl Hanoman) is set in a traditional Balinese compound and treatment rooms are light-filled, although there is some traffic noise. A 60-minute massage is 85,000Rp, a facial is 75,000Rp, while a spice, salt, milk or seaweed bath costs from 125,000Rp to 150,000Rp.

Cendana Resort & Spa (☎ 971927; Monkey Forest Rd) has a nice set up, including an open-air jacuzzi and open-air rooms upstairs. The couples' massage room is particularly pleasant. One-day use of the hotel's pool, sauna and steam room is available for US$5. Massage (US$12, 1 hour), massage and mud bath (US$18, 1 hour) and milk bath with massage (US$18, 1 hour) are all options. The spa also does colonic irrigation, which it euphemistically calls 'Total Tissue Cleansing'.

Komaneka Resort & Spa (☎ 976090, fax 977140; W www.komaneka.com; Monkey Forest Rd) offers open-air treatments for singles and couples in lush surrounds. A one-hour massage featuring stretching, acupressure and Swedish massage techniques is US$30. It's US$40 for a 90-minute aromatherapy massage.

With open views of the thatched roof tops of the hotel, **Mandara Spa** (Ibah Luxury Villas; ☎ 974466, fax 974467; W www.ibahbali.com), as to be expected, has a very calm wooden interior and a jacuzzi. A 50-minute Balinese massage is US$42.

Milano Salon (☎ 973448; Monkey Forest Rd) offers facials and massage.

Nur Salon (☎ 975352; Jl Hanoman 28; open 9am-8pm daily) offers 60-minute massage for 65,000Rp, 90-minute massage, scrub and bath treatments from 95,000Rp and 60-minute facials for 65,000Rp.

Hotel Tjampuhan Spa (☎ 975368, fax 975137; e tjampuan@indo.net.id) which is in a unique grotto setting, overlooking the river, and features organic carved stone reliefs. A 60-minute massage is US$25, use of the sauna and steam room is US$15 and a *mandi lulur* (body mask) is from US$33 to US$120.

Ubud Sari Health Resort (☎ 974393, fax 976305; ☒ www.ubudsari.com; Jl Kajeng) seems to have more staff than clients, so it may not be totally relaxing! It offers 60-minute massages for US$15, as well as a host of other services.

Zen Body Holiday (☎ 970976; ☒ zen_body holiday@yahoo.com; Jl Hanoman), near the Perama office, has a good reputation. It offers one-hour Balinese massage for 60,000Rp, body scrubs, 90-minute *mandi lulur* and massage treatments (90,000Rp).

COURSES

Ubud is a very pleasant place to spend a few weeks developing your artistic or language skills, or learning about Balinese music, dance and cuisine. To find what courses are on offer see the Courses section in the Facts for the Visitor chapter, or check at the tourist office, Pondok Pecak Library & Learning Centre, the Art & Cultural Workshops section in Museum Puri Lukisan, and Studio Perak for jewellery making courses.

Meditation & Yoga

Ubud Sari Health Resort offers daily morning yoga classes for US$5, and private guided meditation classes, while the **Meditation Shop** (☎ 976206; Monkey Forest Rd; open 5pm), part of the Brahma Kumaris Society, offers silent meditation practice between 6pm and 7pm daily, and 5-day meditation courses.

Yoga classes are available at **Tegun Galeri** (☎ 973361; Jl Hanoman 40), as well as at **Indus Restaurant**.

ORGANISED TOURS

Taking an organised tour or two is a good idea as many of the attractions around Ubud are quite difficult to reach by public transport, and finding your way around this part of Bali isn't easy, even with your own vehicle.

All travel agencies in Ubud can arrange organised tours, but it's worth shopping around, as prices vary (eg, check if entrance fees are included in the price). **Ubud Tourist Information** runs interesting half-day trips to a huge range of places including Mengwi, Alas Kedaton and Tanah Lot, or Goa Gajah,

Pejeng, Gunung Kawi, Tampaksiring and Kintamani.

Semara Tours (☎/fax 975576; ☒ semara@ indo.net.id; Jl Hanoman 27A), next door to Bodyworks massage salon, runs treks to Gunung Batur ($30 per person; make sure they provide you with a torch), as well as overnight Borobodur tours for US$230, including Yogyakarta airfare.

See the Organised Tours section in the Getting Around chapter for general information, and the Activities section in Facts for the Visitor.

PLACES TO STAY

Ubud has hundreds of places to stay. Generally, accommodation in Ubud offers good value for money. A simple, clean room within a family home compound is the least expensive option available. The mid-range hotels generally offer swimming pools and hot water, while the really expensive, top-end hotels are perched on the edges of the deep river valleys, with superb views.

Addresses in Ubud can be imprecise – but signage at the end of a road will often list the names of all the hotels and *losmen* (basic accommodation). Away from the main roads, especially out in Penestanan, there are no streetlights and it can be very difficult to find your way after dark.

PLACES TO STAY – BUDGET

Many inexpensive family lodgings are very small, often with just two, three or four rooms.

Central Ubud

On & Around Monkey Forest Rd Near the top of Monkey Forest Rd, some simple rooms in small, secluded family compounds are very central but surprisingly tranquil, and include **Pandawa Homestay** (☎ 975698; singles/doubles 40,000/50,000Rp) and **Gayatri Bungalows** (☎ 973391; singles/doubles 40,000/50,000Rp).

Near the top of the street, **Puri Muwa Bungalows** (☎ 976441; Monkey Forest Rd; singles/doubles 50,000/75,000Rp) is a basic family-run place, which is reasonably quiet considering its location. Some rooms are cold water only.

Alit House (☎ 973284; Monkey Forest Rd 64; singles/doubles 40,000/50,000Rp) has basic rooms in a small, treeless compound

Shrines carved into the rock face at Gunung Kawi, near Ubud

Carrying elaborate cremation towers through Ubud

Example of the Young Artists painting style at Neka Museum, Ubud

Girls dressed in traditional costume for a full-moon festival

The bathing pools at Goa Gajah, near Ubud

Residents of the Ubud Monkey Forest

Women with temple offerings, Pura Dalem Agung

that doubles as a colourful open-air art gallery – hence you'll have to deal with people browsing at all hours – which could make for an interesting or tiresome stay.

A small side street, Jl Arjuna, has several more, basic, low-budget possibilities, including **Anom Bungalows**, **Puji Bungalows** and **Jungut Inn**, which all cost around 40,000/50,000Rp for singles/doubles.

Nyuh Gading Accommodation *(Bendi's; ☎ 973410; singles/doubles 40,000/70,000Rp)*, in a quiet garden enclosure opposite the football field, has clean, simple rooms, some with hot water.

Loka House *(☎ 973326; singles/doubles 90,000/100,000Rp)*, across the football field, is a very peaceful place, where the two-storey main building overlooks a small carp pond in the garden. Rooms have hot water and fans.

Further down Monkey Forest Rd, other budget options include: the quiet, ultra-basic but friendly **Frog Pond Inn** *(singles 20,000-30,000Rp, doubles 30,000-40,000Rp)*, which has open-air bathrooms and cold water; **Rice Paddy Bungalows** *(singles/doubles 70,000/80,000Rp)*, where better rooms have paddy-field views; and **Kubu Saren** *(☎ 975704, fax 974683; singles/doubles 70,000/90,000Rp)*, which is good value for hot-water rooms. With lovely paddy-field views, **Kubuku** *(☎ 974742; rooms 150,000-200,000Rp)* has a small-bar café with lounging *bales*.

East of Monkey Forest Rd Small streets east of Monkey Forest Rd, including Jl Karna, have numerous, family-style homestays, which are secluded but still handy to the centre.

In a shady garden, **Hibiscus Bungalows** *(☎ 970475; singles/doubles 30,000/40,000Rp)* offers traditional-style lodgings. The other appealing places on Jl Karna include the nice and friendly **Yuni's House** *(☎ 975701; singles/doubles from 40,000/50,000Rp, with hot water 60,000/80,000Rp)*; **Gandra House** *(☎ 976529; Jl Karna; singles/doubles 35,000/50,000Rp)*, which has modern bathrooms and spacious gardens; and also **Surawan House** *(☎ 975307; singles/doubles 40,000/50,000, with hot water 50,000/60,000Rp)*.

Budi Bungalows *(☎ 973307; Jl Maruti; singles/doubles 40,000/50,000Rp)*, a block further east of Jl Karna, has traditional *alang alang* (grass thatched) roofs and is clean, quiet and comfortable. Right next door to

Budi, **Anugrah House** *(singles/doubles 30,000/40,000Rp, new rooms 100,000Rp)* has new rooms with modern bathrooms, which have cold water only. The cheaper rooms are good value. Directly opposite, **Esty's House** *(☎ 977679; singles/doubles 30,000/35,000Rp)* is also clean and quiet, as is **Masih Bungalow** *(☎ 975062; Jl Dewi Sita; singles/doubles 80,000/90,000Rp)*.

Sayong House *(☎ 973305; Jl Maruti; singles/doubles from 80,000/100,000Rp)*, at the northern end of this deliciously quiet lane, has simple hot-water rooms, but there's a gorgeous pool in a private location set well away from the family compound.

Jl Goutama This street has several more cheap, quiet and accessible places to stay.

Shana Homestay *(☎ 970481; Jl Goutama 7; rooms 40,000-60,000Rp)* has basic rooms, some with private patios.

Donald Homestay *(☎ 977156; Jl Goutama; singles/doubles 40,000/50,000Rp, with hot water 50,000/75,000Rp)* is better than it looks from the outside. The setting is pretty and the small rooms are good value. **Sudana Homestay** *(☎ 976435; Jl Goutama 11; singles/doubles 40,000/50,000Rp)* and **Darta Homestay** *(☎ 970559; Jl Goutama 6; singles/doubles 30,000/45,000Rp)* are also good options.

Jl Sriwedari In a central location, **Gusti's Homestay** *(☎ 971731; Jl Sriwedari 2; rooms 40,000Rp, with hot water 60,000Rp)* has clean, pleasant rooms with bamboo furniture.

Eka's Homestay *(Jl Sriwedari 8; singles/doubles 40,000/50,000Rp)* is a nice little place and is the home of Wayan Pasek Sucipta, a teacher of Balinese music (see Courses in the Facts for the Visitor chapter).

Jl Bisma Unpaved Jl Bisma goes south of Jl Raya, just west of central Ubud, and is handy to town.

Ala's Hibiscus 2 *(☎/fax 970476; Jl Bisma; singles/doubles 100,000/150,000Rp)* is smack bang in the middle of rice paddies, about 100m down a path off Jl Bisma. Rooms have exceptional views and hot water, and are decorated with local handicrafts.

Juwita Inn *(☎ 976056, fax 975734; Jl Bisma; singles/doubles 110,000/140,000Rp)* is looking a little tired. Rooms, in a lush garden, are fairly basic with only wall fans, but the breakfast area and pool vista make up for this.

Pondok Indah (☎ 966323; off Jl Bisma; singles/doubles 80,000/100,000Rp) is a quiet, peaceful place where the top-floor balconies look over paddy fields. All rooms have hot water. To find it, follow the path beyond Juwita Inn.

Padangtegal
East of central Ubud, but still conveniently located, this area has a few budget lodgings along Jl Hanoman (see the Ubud Area map).

Suartha Pension (☎ 974244; Jl Hanoman 17; singles/doubles 40,000/60,000Rp, with hot water 60,000/100,000Rp) has a charming, traditional family setting. Ikat and decorative features are a very welcoming setting.

Candra Asri (☎ 970517; Jl Hanoman 43; singles/doubles 50,000/60,000Rp, with hot water 90,000/120,000Rp) has comfortable rooms, perfect for lounging around and taking in the paddy field views, as is **Kunang Kunang Guest House** (☎ 976052; singles/doubles 80,000/90,000, upstairs 90,000/120,000Rp), next door, where all rooms have hot water.

Nick's Homestay (☎ 975525; e nicksp@ indosat.net.id; Jl Hanoman; singles/doubles 50,000/70,000Rp) is a really nice place, with spacious grounds, carp ponds, caged birds and amazingly enough, well-fed dogs roaming the compound!

Tebesaya
A little further east, this quiet village comprises little more than its main street, Jl Sukma, which runs between two streams.

Biangs (☎ 976520; Jl Sukma 28; singles/doubles 60,000/80,000Rp) has well-maintained rooms, with hot water, and offers lush views.

Family Guest House (☎ 974054; Jl Sukma; singles 88,000-165,000Rp, doubles 165,000-220,000Rp), a popular place set in a pleasant garden, is another gem, with friendly staff, hot water and modern bathrooms.

Teges
At the southeastern fringe of the Ubud area, the small community of Teges has a cluster of quiet, decent places. Including **Siti Homestay** (☎ 975599; singles/doubles 35,000/45,000Rp); plus **Sari Bungalows** (☎ 975541; rooms 30,000Rp, with hot water 35,000Rp), which is in a pleasant compound right next door to the paddy fields; and also **Nyoman Astana's**

(☎ 975661; singles/doubles 55,000/60,000Rp), which has a nice garden.

North of Jl Raya
Both Jl Kajeng and Jl Suweta, leading north from Jl Raya, offer an excellent choice of budget lodgings, some quite close to the centre of town, others almost a kilometre to the north. Most of these are on the Central Ubud map while the more distant ones are on the Ubud Area map.

Roja's Bungalows (☎ 975107; Jl Kajeng 1; singles 50,000-60,000Rp, doubles 70,000-90,000Rp), one of the first places on Jl Kajeng, maintains a friendly atmosphere. Rooms are clean and well kept.

Artja Inn (☎ 974425; singles/doubles 50,000/60,000Rp), a small, friendly place, offers basic rooms with cold water mandi (Indonesian bath) and no fans. The rooms are separate from the family compound down a small slope, in a lush jungle-like setting filled with butterflies.

Arjana Accommodation (☎ 975583; Jl Kajeng 6; singles/doubles 30,000/50,000Rp), across the road from the Artja Inn, is good value. Bathrooms are outdoors in a mini-jungle, and rooms are clean.

Homestay Rumah Roda (Ubud Area map; ☎ 975487, fax 975682; e rumahroda@indo .net.id; Jl Kajeng 24; bungalows 50,000Rp), next door to Threads of Life gallery, is an ever friendly and understandably popular homestay. Bungalows have hot water.

Kajeng Bungalows (Ubud Area map; ☎ 975018; Jl Kajeng; singles/doubles from 60,000/85,000Rp, with hot water 75,000/100,000Rp), opposite the Rumah Roda, has a swimming pool and a stunning setting overlooking a lush valley. The hot-water rooms have the best views.

Padma Accommodation & Painting Collection (☎ 977247, fax 975115; e aswatama@ hotmail.com; Jl Kajeng 13; rooms 100,000Rp) is a new, very friendly place with only two adjoining, very private bungalows in a tropical garden. Rooms are decorated with local crafts and the modern outdoor bathroom has hot water. Nyoman Sudiarsa, a painter and family member, has a studio on the grounds.

Gusti's Garden Bungalows (Ubud Area map; ☎ 973311; Jl Kajeng; rooms 100,000Rp, with hot water 150,000Rp) opens onto a stunning garden, where rooms, some with hot water, are perched overlooking a swimming pool. The downside is that the bathrooms looked somewhat grubby. There is also a restaurant by the pool.

Campuan & Penestanan

West of Ubud (see the Ubud Area map), but still within walking distance, Campuan has mainly mid-range accommodation, but many places in the paddy fields of Penestanan are pitched at those seeking low-priced, longer-term lodgings. Most will offer discounted weekly rates, and some bigger bungalows are quite economical if you can share with four or more people.

Londo Bungalows II (☎ 976764; bungalows 50,000Rp), next door to Kori Agung Bungalows, is ridiculously cheap – perhaps expect a price hike when you call or visit. Bungalows have gorgeous paddy views and morning views of Gunung Batukau.

Londo Bungalows (☎/fax 976548; e londobungalows@hotmail.com; rooms with hot water 75,000-100,000Rp) has two-storey bungalows, with a carp pond fronting each bungalow.

Santra Putra (☎ 977810, fax 977321; e karjabali@yahoo.com; Penestan; rooms US$12-15), run by internationally exhibited abstract artist I Wayan Karja whose studio/gallery is also on-site, has big, open airy rooms with paddy field views from all vantage points. Intensive painting and drawing classes are offered by the artist.

South of Londo Bungalows, **Gerebig Bungalows** (☎/fax 974582; singles/doubles 125,000/150,000Rp) has wonderful views and good-value two-storey bungalows.

PLACES TO STAY – MID-RANGE
Central Ubud

Jl Raya Part of the Ubud royal family's old palace, **Puri Saren Agung** (☎ 975057; rooms US$50-65) is behind the courtyard where the regular dance performances are held. Accommodation is in traditional Balinese pavilions, with big verandas, four-poster beds, antique furnishings and hot water.

Puri Saraswati Bungalows (☎/fax 975164; e purisaraswati@yahoo.com; singles US$19-50, doubles US$21-60) is very central, pleasant and reasonably well kept (although bathrooms seem a little grotty), with a pool, lovely gardens and a friendly atmosphere. Rooms are well back from Jl Raya, so it's surprisingly quiet.

Monkey Forest Rd The cheaper standard rooms at **Cendana Resort & Spa** (☎ 973242, fax 971930; Monkey Forest Rd; singles US$40-80, doubles US$45-90) face a lone paddy field and are decidedly ordinary and not good value. The two more expensive rooms, however, have modern bathrooms and both face pools. The landscaping is superb, with the pools appearing to cascade over the rice paddies.

The new and stylish **Lumbung Sari** (☎ 976396; e palupi@indo.net.id; rooms with/without air-con US$60/30) is in a central location. Lots of artwork decorates the walls of the rooms and the bathrooms are very modern.

Oka Wati Hotel (☎ 973386; w www.okawatihotel.com; singles US$25-40, doubles US$40-55), a quiet place off Gang Beji, off the western side of Monkey Forest Rd, is an old Ubud standard. It now has two sites on opposite sides of a rare and endangered Ubud paddy field, along with a swimming pool, and heavily decorated rooms and suites.

Most other mid-range places on this road are a fair way further south, but all appear on the Central Ubud map.

Ubud Bungalows (☎ 975537, fax 971298; Monkey Forest Rd; singles 100,000-200,000Rp, doubles 150,000-250,000Rp, with air-con US$35/50), south of the Puri Garden, is pleasant enough, with a pool, gardens and spacious rooms with hot water.

Ubud Terrace Bungalows (☎ 975690; Monkey Forest Rd; singles 80,000-250,000Rp, doubles 100,000-300,000Rp) is good value for a place with a pool and hot water.

Jl Bisma Overlooking the river, **Sama's Cottages** (☎ 973481; Jl Bisma; singles/doubles 150,000/200,000Rp) is a lovely little hideaway terraced down a hill. It also has a well-maintained pool in a private spot on the grounds.

Honeymoon Guesthouse (☎ 970708, fax 973282; w www.casalunabali.com; Jl Bisma; singles 150,000-400,000Rp, doubles 180,000-400,000, family room 700,000Rp), run by the Casa Luna clan and set in a family compound, has a high rate of return visitors and is a good value option, so book ahead.

Jl Goutama A really comfortable option is **Nirwana Pension & Gallery** (☎/fax 975415; Jl Goutama 10; rooms 150,000Rp) where you'll find *alang alang* roofs, decorative paintings, ornate doorways and modern bathrooms with hot water. Batik courses also take place here (see Courses in the Facts for the Visitor chapter).

Agung Cottages (☎ 975414; Jl Goutama; singles/doubles 200,000/250,000Rp, villa 300,000Rp) is a gem of a place and has huge, spotless rooms with hot water, lovely gardens and friendly staff – local art hangs on the walls.

East of Ubud
Artini Cottages II (Ubud Area map; ☎ 975689, fax 975348; Jl Hanoman; rooms US$40), in Padangtegal, has a nice setting with paddy fields on two sides. Comfortable rooms are in three-storey blocks round a pretty pool. It's a sociable, well-run place, but you're ultimately paying for the pool.

Matahari Cottages (☎ 975459; w www .matahariubud.com; Jl Jembawan; singles US$25-40, doubles US$35-60) has flamboyant, fantasy-themed rooms, including the 'Batavia Princess' and the 'Indian Pasha'. It also offers high tea between 2pm and 5pm for 55,000Rp.

Overlooking a rainforest valley, **Tiing Gading Bungalows** (☎ 973228; e tiing@ indosat.net.id; Jl Sukma; singles/doubles US$40/45), has attractive views from its pool and restaurant, and the rooms are tastefully presented.

South of Ubud
Biyukukung Villa (☎ 978976; Jl Sugriwa; rooms US$35-65), off Jl Hanoman, is a new place with a pool, that has stylish two-storey rooms, which all face magnificent paddy fields.

North of Ubud
In a good spot, **Pradha Guesthouse & Restaurant** (☎ 975122, fax 974291; Jl Kajeng 1; rooms US$75), overlooking a deep lush pool and café, has pleasant rooms , but expect some traffic noise from Jl Raya Ubud.

Siti Bungalows (☎ 975699, fax 975643; Jl Kajeng 3; cottages from US$50) is owned by the family of the late Han Snel, a well-known Ubud painter for many years. Some rooms are perched right on the edge of the river gorge.

Ubud Sari Health Resort (Ubud Area map; ☎ 974393, fax 976305; w www.ubudsari.com; Jl Kajeng; singles US$25-35, doubles US$35-44) offers charming bungalows. It also has a small **café** (dishes 15,000-20,000Rp). Prices include use of the steam room, whirlpool and sauna.

Known for its Balinese feasts, **Ketut's Place** (Ubud Area map; ☎ 975304, fax 973424; e mmnet@dps.centrin.net.id; Jl Suweta 40; singles/doubles 150,000/200,000Rp) has a fine atmosphere and comfortable rooms – as well as a stunning pool overlooking the river valley.

Klub Kokos (☎/fax 978270; w www.klub kokos.com; singles/doubles US$42/46), a half an hour walk north in the small village of Bangkiang Sidem on the Campuan ridge, is a secluded place with a big pool and spotless rooms. Two-bedroom and family bungalows are also available.

West of Ubud
Several good places are on or near Jl Bisma (see the Ubud Area map).

Nick's Pension (☎ 975636; e nicksp@indo sat.net.id; Jl Bisma; singles US$20-25, doubles US$25-35) is a popular choice in a tranquil setting with a pool, and hot-water rooms terraced down a deep ravine. While the road access is from Jl Bisma, you can also reach Nick's by walking west of Monkey Forest Rd on Gang Beji, so it's very handy to the centre of town.

Abangan Bungalows (☎ 975977, fax 975 082; Jl Raya; singles/doubles US$20/30, with air-con US$30/40), up a steep driveway, has a lovely setting, a pool and views of treetops by the river.

Campuan & Penestanan On the western side of the road in a paddy field, **Puri Raka Inn** (☎ 975213; singles/doubles 300,000/ 400,000Rp) has a wonderfully sited swimming pool and five very attractive rooms.

Just west of the Campuan bridge, a steep side-road branches off to the left, and climbs up and around to Penestanan.

Sri Ratih Cottages (☎ 975638, fax 976550; rooms US$25), on this steep side-road, has a pool with a view of the lotus flower inspired roof of Antonio Blanco's house, spacious grounds and clean, neat rooms.

Walking tracks north of this road give access to the various bungalows tucked away in the paddy fields. One of these is **Melati Cottages** (☎ 974650, fax 975088; single/

double/family US$25/35/45) which has traditional-style rooms with indoor bathrooms and a café by the pool.

Kori Agung Bungalows (☎ 975166; rooms US$15-20) also has a lovely setting and nice double-storey bungalows with hot water. The easiest way to reach it is by tracks through the paddy fields or by the steps up from the main road.

Villa Pagoda (☎ 979265; rooms US$65), next door to Kori Agung Bungalows, is very luxurious and rooms have a kitchen and their own plunge pool.

Sayan With a million-dollar view of the Sungai Ayung Valley below, **Sayan Terrace** (☎ 974384, fax 975384; rooms US$40-80, villas US$110) is good value.

PLACES TO STAY – TOP END

Top-end places generally have all mod-cons, including air-con, IDD phone, minibar and TV.

Central Ubud

Monkey Forest Rd A stylish place, **Ubud Village Hotel** (☎ 975571, fax 975069; e ubudvlg@indo.net.id; singles US$65-80, doubles US$70-90, deluxe villa US$150) features a big pool, lush garden and tasteful, fully equipped rooms. Breakfast is not included. The hotel also has an impressive tree-house restaurant and an open air spa.

Komaneka Resort & Spa (☎ 976090, fax 977140; w www.komaneka.com; deluxe rooms US$155-210, garden villa US$230, pool villa US$250) exudes contemporary elegance. Room are beautifully decorated in rough-hewn furniture, while the pool and gardens are lovely. The **Komaneka Art Gallery** is at the front of the hotel.

Jl Bisma On a quiet street, **Pringga Juwita Water Garden Cottages** (Ubud Area map; ☎ 975734, fax 975734; w www.thefibra .com/pringga; singles US$57-125, doubles US$65-150) has ponds and a swimming pool in one of the prettiest gardens in Ubud.

Santika Gardens (☎ 975443; fax 970850; e santik@indosat.net.id; Jl Bisma; doubles/ suite/villa US$95/125/325) is a modern, very stylish boutique hotel. Rooms have traditional alang alang ceilings and the balconies are draped in white bougainvillea. The mosaic-tiled pool is spectacular.

South of Ubud

Kokokan Hotel (☎ 976659, fax 975332; e kokokan@dps.mega.net.id; singles US$90-220, doubles US$100-250) is in Pengosekan, next to the ARMA art museum. It features fine views, imaginative architecture and attractive decor.

Alam Indah (☎/fax 974629; w www.alam -indah.com; rooms US$50-96), just south of the Monkey Forest in Nyuhkuning, has a prime riverside location and rooms that are beautifully finished in natural materials, some with river valley views.

Bali Spirit Hotel & Spa (☎ 974013; w www .balispirit.com; rooms US$69-99), further south from the Alam Indah and also overlooking the Wos valley, has stylish rooms and great views from its restaurant.

Saren Indah (☎ 971471, fax 974683; w www.saren.balisite.com; rooms US$80-100), in a rural setting in Nyuhkuning village, has good facilities, an inviting pool, paddy views and comfortable rooms.

West of Ubud

Campuan Overlooking the lush Wos valley, **Ibah Luxury Villas** (☎ 974466, fax 974467; w www.ibahbali.com; Jl Raya; suites US$200-500) offers an elegant environment, Mandara Spa facilities, and spacious, stylish individual suites. The delightful garden is decorated with stone carvings, hand-crafted pots and antique doors, and the swimming pool is set into the hillside beneath an ancient-looking stone wall.

Hotel Tjampuhan (☎ 975368, fax 975137; e tjampuan@indo.net.id; rooms US$70, with air-con US$115, Walter Spies' House US$175) is a venerable place, overlooking the confluence of Sungai Wos and Campuan. The influential German artist Walter Spies lived here in the 1930s, and his former home, which sleeps four people, is now part of the hotel. There are individual bungalows in the wonderful garden. The hillside swimming pool is especially delightful, and was originally designed by Spies. The hotel also has a spa overlooking the rivers.

Sanggingan With a dramatic location, **Pita Maha** (☎ 974330, fax 974329; w www .slh.com/pitamaha; villas US$300-480) has no shortage of style in its spectacular balcony restaurant or its scenic swimming pool. Each of the elegant individual villas is in its own small private compound, but not all of them enjoy the best views.

Ayung Valley Two kilometres west of Ubud, the fast flowing Sungai Ayung has carved out a deep valley, its sides sculpted into terraced paddy fields or draped in thick rainforest. Overlooking this verdant valley are some of the most stylish, luxurious and expensive hotels on Bali.

Taman Bebek Villas (☎ 975385, fax 976 532; e tbvbali@dps.mega.net.id; villas US$65-200), overlooking the valley, is a much more affordable place which is pleasantly old-fashioned, with Balinese furnishings and a beautifully located pool.

Amandari (☎ 975333, fax 975335; w www .amanresorts.com; suites US$600-1200), in Kedewatan village, is unquestionably classy with superb views over the paddies and down to the river – the main swimming pool seems to drop right over the edge. Private pavilions are spacious and exquisitely decorated. The most expensive rooms have their own private swimming pool.

Kupu Kupu Barong (☎ 975478, fax 975079; w www.kupu-barong.com; bungalows US$335 -699), further north, clings precariously to the steep sides of the valley – the views from the rooms, pool and the restaurant are just truly unbelievable.

The Chedi (Ubud & Around map; ☎ 975963, fax 975968; w www.chedi-ubud .com; deluxe rooms US$305, suites US$465), near Payangan, offers great views and modern luxury amid rural tranquillity.

Begawan Giri (☎ 978888, fax 978889; w www.begawan.com; suites US$495-2950), well secluded in a remote location, is arguably the most opulent hotel in Bali. Set amid acres of riverside forest and paddy field, the 22 unique suites are grouped into five 'residences', each with its own swimming pool, library, kitchen and butler. You;ll find the architecture emphasises the natural surroundings.

PLACES TO STAY – RENTALS

For information about houses to rent or share, check the notice boards at Pondok Pecak Library, Ubud Tourist Information and Casa Luna restaurant. Penestanan (west of Ubud) has the most places for rent, and it's worth asking around. Also look in the *Bali Advertiser* broadsheet.

PLACES TO EAT

Ubud's restaurants offer the most diverse and delicious food on the island. It's a good place to try authentic Balinese dishes, as well as a range of other Asian cuisine. The quintessential Ubud restaurant has fresh ingredients, a delightful ambience and an eclectic menu, with European-, US- and Asian-inspired dishes. Unusual dining experiences on offer include high tea at Matahari Cottages and 'painter's salads' using the colour palette of French artists at Panili Vanilla! There are also many inexpensive warung serving Sumatran, Indonesian and Chinese dishes, and for a Balinese speciality, head to Warung Babi Guling opposite the rear of Ubud Palace.

If you're self-catering **Andalan Health Food Store** (☎ 976324; e adalan@indo.net.id) sells fresh organic fruit and vegetables, lots of Australian produce such as muesli and olive oils, and home baked bagels and cookies; supermarkets are listed under Shopping.

Central Ubud

Jl Raya Well worth a visit for its Balinese 'fusion' fare, **Ary's Warung** (☎ 978359; Jl Raya; mains 30,000-50,000Rp) is something of a misnomer as crisp table linen, architectural food presentation, well-trained waiters and high prices won't be found in any other warung!

Near Ary's Warung, **Ryoshi** (☎ 972192; dishes 28,000-60,000Rp) is one of the local chain of Japanese restaurants, and serves reliable Japanese fare.

Cafe Lotus (☎ 975357; Jl Raya; dishes 26,000-55,000Rp) was for a long time *the* place to eat. It's been well and truly surpassed in the cuisine stakes, but a leisurely meal overlooking the lotus pond is still a relaxing enough option. The menu features wood-fired pizza and home-made pasta.

Sababa (☎ 972294; Jl Raya; dishes 15,000-25,000Rp), near Casa Luna, is an authentic Middle Eastern café that serves delicious falafel rolls, chicken and lamb kebabs as well as salads. It's oppressively hot in the small, narrow interior, so it's best to eat at the few café tables outside or order take-away.

Casa Luna (☎ 977409; w www.casaluna bali.com; Jl Raya; breakfast 9000-18,000Rp, dishes 15,000-32,000Rp) has a creative international menu, health tonics, and a delicious range of bread, pastries, cakes and biscuits from its own bakery. Crisp salads, homemade pasta and simple main courses are not to be missed. The owner runs regular Balinese cooking courses (see Courses and the boxed text 'Do-It-Yourself Gado Gado' in the Facts for the Visitor chapter).

Masakan Padang (Ubud Area map; Jl Raya; dishes 6000-12,000Rp), further east from Nomad's, is a Padang-style eatery, where you choose from the plates on display – these are some of the cheapest, tastiest eats in town. **Puteri Minang** next door to Ganesha Bookshop & Music, is another Masakan Padang place that comes recommended.

Warung Taman (Jl Sriwedari; dishes 10,000-20,000Rp), near Gusti's Homestay, is an inviting little warung, which serves consistently good Indonesian and Chinese food. Rough-hewn tables and friendly staff give it a relaxed atmosphere.

Bali Buddha (☎ 976324; Jl Jembawan 1; dishes 12,000-35,000Rp), on the corner of Jl Raya and upstairs from Andalan Health Food Store, offers a full range of jamu (health tonics), salads, bagels, tofu curries, savoury crepes and pizza, as well as gelato. It has a comfy lounging area and is candlelit in the evening. The café also doubles as an exhibition space for local artists.

Matahari Cottages (☎ 975459; Jl Jembawan) offers grand high tea in an open-air pavilion between 2pm and 5pm for 55,000Rp.

Jl Suweta For probably the best meal you'll have in Ubud, head to **Warung Babi Guling** (dishes 10,000Rp), opposite Ubud Palace, which is a locals' favourite for Balinese-style roast piglet.

Bumbu Restaurant (☎ 974217; Jl Suweta 1; dishes 18,000-50,000Rp) has an Indian, Balinese and vegetarian focus, and many of its candlelit tables face Ubud Palace. It also offers a cooking course (see Courses in the Facts for the Visitor chapter).

Terazo (☎ 978941; Jl Suweta; dishes 38,000-40,000Rp), further up from the Bumbu Restaurant, is a stylish place serving brilliantly presented, eclectic cuisine.

Ketut's Place (Ubud Area map; ☎ 975304; Jl Suweta; 'feast' for two 150,000Rp), almost a kilometre up the street, does its famous Balinese feast on Friday nights. The meal is also an excellent introduction to Balinese life and customs. There's usually an interesting group, so it's very sociable.

Jl Kajeng Above Threads of Life Indonesian Textile Art Center, **Roda Restaurant** (Jl Kajeng 24; dishes 6000-10,000Rp) is a pleasant little restaurant. It has all Indonesian dishes, including hard-to-find Balinese desserts, such as the Moorish jaja Bali (sticky rice, coconut, palm sugar and fruit steamed in banana leaves). Filtered water refills are also possible (750/1500Rp small/large). The restaurant also holds traditional meals (30,000Rp per person; minimum 5 people), but you'll need to book in advance.

Along Monkey Forest Rd There are plenty of inexpensive eateries that are good for a quick bite along Monkey Forest Rd, including **Canderi's Warung** (dishes 8000-28,000Rp), a popular but unappealing place serving Western staples such as potato wedges, **Ayu's Kitchen** (dishes 13,000-20,000Rp) and **Ibu Rai Bar & Restaurant** (dishes 20,000-50,000Rp).

Bebek Bengil 2 (☎ 978954; Monkey Forest Rd; dishes 18,000-50,000Rp), near Milano

UBUD & AROUND

A Balinese Feast

A complete Balinese feast is something local people would have only a couple of times a year, at a major religious or family occasion. A typical feast would include smoked duck, roast pork or Balinese satay (minced and spiced meat wrapped around a wide stick – quite different from the usual Indonesian satay). Vegetable dishes include items that Westerners think of as fruits – like papaya, jackfruit (nangka) and starfruit (blimbing). Paku is a form of fern and ketela potton is tapioca leaves, both prepared as tasty vegetables. Red onions (anyang) and cucumber (ketimun) will also feature. Then there might be Balinese-style gado gado and mie goreng, and a dish of duck livers cooked in banana leaves and coconut.

Standard accompaniments include rice (white, red or both), prawn crackers (krupuk) and Balinese rice wine (brem). To finish there are desserts like sumping, a leaf-wrapped sticky rice concoction with coconut, palm sugar and banana or jackfruit, as well as Balinese coffee.

Salon, is another branch of the long-established 'Dirty Duck Diner' and offers the same range of duck specialties.

Cafe Wayan & Bakery (☎ 975447; mains 20,000-50,000Rp, Balinese buffet 95,000Rp per person) is another old Ubud favourite, popular for its relaxed and pleasant garden-setting ambience and for its food, such as its Sunday Balinese buffets and desserts.

Jl Dewi Sita & Jl Goutama Reasonable Indonesian dishes, a large range of beers, wines and cocktails, and a breezy upstairs setting, as well as Internet access are on offer at **Bamboo Restaurant** (☎ 975307; dishes 12,000-30,000Rp). Nearby, the **Do Drop In** (☎ 975309; dishes 12,000-28,000Rp) has tables so close to the football field you can rule on the local kids' offside disputes! It's a friendly place with decent food.

Serving excellent food, **Kanpai** (☎ 972259; dishes 28,000-50,000Rp) is an ultra-slick, contemporary Japanese restaurant. Happy hour is from 4pm to 7pm.

For a really good cup of coffee, head to **Tutmak Cafe** (☎ 975754; Jl Dewi Sita; dishes 30,000-50,000Rp), a stylish, low-key place that serves serious cakes and Western dishes.

Kafe Batan Waru (☎ 977528; Jl Dewi Sita; dishes 20,000-35,000Rp) claims to use organic meats and vegetables when possible. It's a popular place, with a quiet rear section lined with bamboo. Smoked duck and suckling pig can be ordered in advance. Off Jl Dewi Sita on Jl Maruti, **Sen Sen Warung** (dishes 5000-8000Rp) is a nice little hole-in-the-wall place with a simple menu. It's next door to Budi Bungalows.

Perched above Jl Goutama, **Fairway Cafe & Internet** (☎ 970810; cnr Jl Dewi Sita & Jl Goutama; dishes 8000-11,000Rp) has a casual, easy-going atmosphere. Dishes are simple and include some Japanese favourites. Water refill is available and there's also a small Internet café annexe.

Warung Mini (Jl Goutama; dishes 5000-13,000Rp) is a relaxed place that serves up a range of home-style Japanese, Chinese, and seafood dishes, including seafood laksa.

Dewa Warung (Jl Goutama; dishes 4000-7000Rp), in a shady position and elevated above the street, has inexpensive offerings, such as tempeh curry with rice and is busy in the evenings with young Japanese and Balinese. Beers are also cheap.

Toko Tako (Jl Goutama) is a tiny outdoor Japanese teashop and café opposite Donald Homestay. It's very sweet.

East of Ubud

Jl Hanoman Framed by vines at its entrance, **Hanoman Juice Ja** (☎ 971056; dishes 6000-13,000Rp) is a simple café serving health juices, including wheatgerm grass and ginseng shots, and bagels, salads, sandwiches and soups.

Bebek Bengil 1 (Dirty Duck Diner; ☎ 975489; dishes 18,000-50,000Rp) is an original place that does a special line in crispy deep-fried duck dishes and has a delightful dining area.

Nyangluh (☎ 975894; dishes 17,000-40,000Rp) is a newish restaurant-bar that focuses on Balinese cuisine, such as shredded pork and coconut satay and sweet treats such as sumping waluh (ground rice, pumpkin and coconut milk steamed in banana leaf). It has a great open-air space upstairs, which is perfect to watch the sunset. DJs or bands play on Saturday nights.

Cafe Tegal (☎ 971555; dishes 13,000-30,000Rp) has a big range of seafood and Chinese dishes.

Down past the Perama office, Jl Hanoman is busy, but a couple of nice places are set well back and enjoy restful views overlooking the paddy fields. **Panorama Restaurant** (☎ 973335; Jl Raya Pengosekan; dishes 15,000-30,000Rp) has a small menu focusing on Balinese dishes and a dining area, which is completely open to a picture-perfect paddy outlook.

South of Ubud

Panili Vanilla (☎ 971224; Pengosekan; dishes 15,000-40,000Rp), a French café, has a rustic, relaxed alfresco setting (apart from the traffic noise of course). On offer are veggie juices, French specialities, such as crepes, and very creative salads. Friday evening is 'world food night'.

Kokokan Restaurant (☎ 973495; Jl Pengosekan; mains 35,000-50,000Rp), past the ARMA art museum, serves superb Thai and seafood dishes. The beautiful, open-sided, upstairs dining area has marble floors, potted palms, linen tablecloths and a general air of understated elegance. Phone for transport.

Jl Sukma Part of Rona Accommodation, **The Village Cafe** *(dishes 7500-20,000Rp)* has friendly staff and serves up the usual suspects as well as tasty juice concoctions, such as watermelon, carrot and apple juice. **Mama's Warung** *(dishes 5000-11,000Rp)*, nearby, is also worth checking out if you're staying in the area.

West of Ubud

Campuan Next to the Campuan bridge, **Murni's Warung** *(☎ 975233; Jl Raya; dishes 16,000-47,000Rp)* is an old Ubud favourite. It has a beautiful setting and a four-level dining room overlooking the forest canopy by the river. Indonesian dishes, curries and Western options are available. There's a cosy bar on the second level down, which is great for an early afternoon drink.

Overlooking the river, **Beggar's Bush** *(☎/fax 975009; dishes 20,000-35,000Rp, small/large Bintang 10,000/15,000Rp)* is an expansive open-air place without a whole lot of character, which still manages to pull in the punters. Pub fare such as Australian steaks, pastas and sandwiches are on offer.

Indus Restaurant *(☎ 977684; dishes 15,000-42,000Rp)*, perched on a ridge above the Sungai Cerik valley, is yet another top-class Ubud eatery with a creative modern menu. To make the most of the panoramic views, come for lunch or an early dinner.

Naughty Nuri's *(dishes 14,000-20,000Rp)*, opposite the Neka Museum, has big slab tables and a Japanese-style bar and is a lively place in the evenings. It is especially popular for its fresh grilled tuna.

Penestanan Choices are limited if you're staying in Penestanan. The road that curves round the southern side of Penestanan, Jl Raya Penestanan, has a few restaurants.

Cafe Dewata *(dishes 10,000-20,000Rp)* serves standard tourist fare and is popular for its breezy setting.

Gajah Biru *(☎ 979085; dishes 42,000-55,000Rp; open 6pm-midnight)* offers a range of Indian curries. It has also opened a restaurant in central Ubud, but the food there is decidedly ordinary.

Manuce Express *(dishes 8000-12,000Rp)* is a no-frills place that seems far removed from the rest of the tourist trap eateries nearby.

Ibu Putih's Warung *(☎ 976146; dishes 6000-10,000Rp)* is a shady place at the top of the stairs leading to Penestanan from Jl Raya. It has a friendly, family ambience, and the food is simple and excellent. There are also rooms available here from 40,000Rp to US$50!

Sayan If you want to get a taste of Bali's best hotels, try lunch or dinner at the **Amandari** *(☎ 975333)* or **Four Seasons Resort** *(☎ 977577)* – they both offer excellent food in a sophisticated atmosphere. Call for reservations.

Red Rice *(☎ 974433; Jl Sayan; dishes 30,000-60,000Rp)*, an alternative to Four Seasons Resort or Amandari, is a 'warung with wine' where the decor is minimalist and the menu is innovative and based on Balinese 'fusion'.

ENTERTAINMENT

No-one comes to Ubud for wild nightlife – the entertainment is mainly cultural. A few bars do get quite lively around sunset and later into the night, but the venues certainly don't aspire to the extremes of beer-swilling debauchery and first-world hip clubs found at some of the southern beach resorts – Ubud is all middle-ground!

Balinese Music & Dance

If you're in the right place at the right time you may see dances performed in temple ceremonies for an essentially local audience. These dances are often quite long and not as entertaining to the uninitiated. Dances performed for tourists are usually adapted and abbreviated to some extent to make them more enjoyable, but most are done with a high degree of skill and commitment, and usually have appreciative locals in the audience (or peering over the fence!). It's also common to combine the features of more than one traditional dance in a single performance.

In a week in Ubud, you can see Kecak, Legong and Barong dances, *Mahabharata* and *Ramayana* ballets, *wayang kulit* puppets and gamelan orchestras. The main venues are the **Ubud Palace**, **Padangtegal dance stage**, the **ARMA open stage**, and **Pura Dalem Puri** in Peliatan. Other performances are in nearby towns like Batuan, Mawang and Kutuh. The central Ubud Palace is the most attractive and accessible venue, but arrive early for a seat near the front.

UBUD & AROUND

Ubud Tourist Information has performance information, and sells tickets (25,000Rp to 50,000Rp). For performances outside Ubud, transport is usually included in the price. Tickets are also sold at many travel agencies and hotels, and by street-sellers who hang around outside Ubud Palace – all charge the same price as the tourist office.

For free entertainment, it's interesting to see children's dance and gamelan rehearsals at Ubud Palace or ARMA (see Agung Rai Museum of Art entry under Museums earlier in this chapter for details). For more information on *wayang kulit* puppets and gamelan, see the Performing Arts section in the Facts about Bali chapter, and for details of dances see the special section 'Balinese Dance'.

Bars
Bars close early in Ubud – around 1am – by local ordinance. The two old standbys are the dimly lit bar-restaurant at **Nomad's** (☎ 975721; Jl Raya; dishes 15,000-35,000Rp) and the upstairs bar at **Beggars Bush** – they're both good for a quiet drink until midnight, and Nomad's often has a gamelan player. More lively though is the **Jazz Cafe** (☎ 976594; e jazzcafe@indo.net.id; Jl Sukma; dishes 35,000-60,000Rp, small/large beer 15,000/28,000Rp; closes at 12.30am), which has a relaxed atmosphere in a garden of coconut palms and ferns, good food and live music from Tuesday to Saturday from 8pm. Free pick up and drop off around Ubud is also on offer.

Sai Sai Bar (Sai 2 Bar; ☎ 976698; Monkey Forest Rd) is bright and spacious, has occasional video movies, and attracts a relaxed crowd in the evening. Further down Monkey Forest Rd, **Putra Bar** (draught beer 12,000Rp; open 9am-1am) is darker and noisier, and features live music on Sunday, Tuesday, Wednesday and Friday nights from 9pm, and video movies or sports telecasts on others. **Bulan Baru**, nearby, is also worth seeking out.

On Jl Suweta, next door to Terazo restaurant, **Ang Ka Sa** (☎/fax 977395; small/large Bintang 9000/14,000Rp) is a small, stylish bar-café, which is great for an early evening drink.

Planet Warung (☎ 973343; Jl Hanoman; small/large Bintang 9000/14,000Rp) promises to be lively. Live reggae and acoustic music is performed several nights a week from around 9pm and there are also pool tables.

Nyangluh (☎ 975894; Jl Hanoman), a restaurant-bar, has either DJs or bands on Saturday nights.

In Padangtegal, not far from ARMA art museum, **Cafe Exiles** (☎ 974812; Jl Pengosekan Kaja; dishes 19,000-28,000Rp; open 9am-1am) is an open-air café-bar with a grassy outlook, which pulls in a crowd on Saturday nights, when there's live music. The menu is international and includes tapas.

Video Movies & Sports Telecasts
Casa Luna shows movies nightly in a separate video room. **Sai Sai Bar** often shows films, while **Putra Bar** shows films or live telecasts of international sports events. **Beranda Cafe & Restaurant** (☎ 972360), next door to Pondok Pecak Library and Learning Centre, shows movies nightly on a big screen, and offers reasonably priced meals.

SHOPPING
Ubud has a variety of art shops and galleries, and you can use Ubud as a base to explore craft and antique shops all the way down to Batubulan (see the Denpasar to Ubud section earlier in this chapter). For concentrated souvenir shopping go to Pasar Seni or Jl Hanoman, both are stocked to the brim with basketware, textiles, paintings, mirrors, mosaics, bags, kites, drums – even didgeridoos! In Ubud, for unusual handicrafts and jewellery, head to **Tegun Galeri** (☎ 973361; w www.balitrade.net; Jl Hanoman 40).

Paintings
You'll find paintings for sale everywhere. The main galleries like **Agung Rai** (Jl Peliatan), and **Neka** (Jl Raya), have excellent selections, and they're very interesting to look through, but most paintings are well over the US$100 mark. Prices will be far lower if you buy directly from the artist's workshop. The small landscape paintings with intricate wooden frames make great souvenirs – prices start from around 100,000Rp.

Interesting places to browse include **Galeri Déjà Vu** (☎ 978225; Jl Dewi Sita), which holds changing exhibitions of young local painters and photographers, including expat artists; and **Dewangga Gallery** (☎ 973302; Jl Dewi Sita) at Dewangga Bungalows, which features the limited edition wood-cut prints of female artist **Mega Sari**, who has developed a following among Japanese collectors.

Woodcarvings

Small shops at the market and by Monkey Forest Rd often have good woodcarvings, particularly masks. There are other good woodcarving places along Jl Bedulu east of Teges, and along the road between Nyuhkuning and the southern entrance to Monkey Forest Sanctuary.

Surrounding villages also specialise in different styles or subjects. Along the road from Teges to Mas, look for masks and some of the most original carved pieces with natural wood finishes. North of Ubud, look for carved Garudas in Junjungan, and painted flowers and fruit in Tegallalang.

Clothes

For fashion and fabrics, the most interesting shops are found on Monkey Forest Rd, Jl Dewi Siti and Jl Hanoman. Many will make or alter to order.

Zarong (☎ 977601; *Monkey Forest Rd*) is a slightly offbeat, hippy, chic fashion store. Be warned that some of it is slightly NQR (not quite right), although the leather slip-on sandals are definitely worth checking out!

Le Chat (*Monkey Forest Rd*) has some stylish designer pieces, especially men's shirts, as well as unusual homewares.

Olala (☎ 977925; *Jl Dewi Sita*) features the work of a Japanese designer, including gorgeous Japanese kimono-cut shirts, made from heavy ikat fabric. Next door **Bulan Madu** (☎ 977465; *Jl Dewi Sita*) has smart, simple tie-dyed women's clothes. Further east **Putu Di Noto** (☎ 971628; *Jl Dewi Sita*) has interesting lightweight men's and women's clothing.

For kids clothing, head to **Tunjung** (☎/fax 974078; *Jl Hanoman 10*). You'll find very sweet batik print outfits for newborns to 10-year-olds. Plus dolls clothes to fit Barbie and Ken in traditional Indonesian outfits!

Sisi (e sisibali@hotmail.com; *Jl Hanoman*), near Nyangluh, has a shop full of groovy fabric handbags by a Japanese designer. There's also another store on Jl Sukma.

Jewellery

Jl Dewi Siti is a jewellery hub, and several shops on Monkey Forest Rd also have original silver jewellery.

Alamkara (☎ 972213, 971004) has two locations, one on Monkey Forest Rd and the other on Jl Dewi Sita, and is one of the best jewellery galleries in Ubud, if not Bali, where the craftsmanship is of a high standard. On display are unusual, but very wearable designs in gold and silver, featuring black pearls and gems. The work of foreign and local jewellers is on display.

Treasures – a Gallery of Gold Creations (☎ 976697; w *www.dekco.com; Jl Raya*), next door to Ary's Warung, has expensive, gem encrusted gold jewellery by international artists. Much of it looks more Mediterranean than Balinese, but the pieces are exquisite either way.

Ashram (☎ 43354; *www.baliashram.com; Jl Sukma*) is a colourful, funky gallery of works by Jeli Lala, a foreign jeweller whose work is marked by a playful, naïve style. It's a fun place to browse, although you might not buy anything!

Kayan Gallery (☎ 980424; e *kayan@denpasar.wasantara.net.id; Jl Sukma 17*) shows the distinctive work of Dutch jeweller Jan Van, which features black pearls, leather and silver chokers, and interestingly shaped rings.

Other Items

The two-storey art market, **Pasar Seni**, sells a wide range of clothing, sarongs, footwear and souvenirs. Some other good buys include leather goods, batik, baskets and silverware. 'Antiques' in Ubud tend to be overpriced – bargain hard or go back to Batubulan, Denpasar or even Kuta. Ubud's colourful **produce market**, adjacent to Pasar Seni starts early in the morning, but winds up by lunch time.

Tino Supermarket (*Jl Raya*) sells most things, including newspapers and maps. On the eastern side of town, **Delta Dewata Supermarket** has a good range of groceries, stationery and CDs and is the cheaper of the two supermarkets.

Larasati Aromatherapy (☎ 971225; e *para dise_on_sea@yahoo.com; Jl Raya Ubud 4*) sells blended essential oils and also pre-packaged body treatments. It runs courses in aroma crafts.

Kertas Gingsir (☎ 973030; *Jl Dewi Sita*), next door to the Do Drop In, specialises in interesting paper handmade from banana, pineapple and taro plants. There are a few other homewares shops on Jl Dewi Sita.

In central Ubud, several photography shops sell slide and print film, and also develop film.

UBUD & AROUND

GETTING THERE & AWAY
Bemo
Ubud is served by two main bemo routes, but does not have a bemo terminal as such – bemos stop at one of two convenient points, north of the market in the centre of town, and nearby, at the southern end of Jl Suweta.

Small bemos travel between Ubud and Gianyar (2000Rp), which has bus and bemo connections to most of eastern Bali.

Brown bemos go to/from Batubulan terminal (4000Rp), with connections to Kereneng terminal in Denpasar itself (another 3000Rp).

To Bedugul, western Bali and Java, go via Batubulan and Kereneng to Ubung terminal, and get a bus or bemo from there. To Kuta, the airport and the Bukit peninsula, go via Batubulan and Kereneng to Tegal terminal, and get a bemo from there. An alternative public transport connection to southern Bali is a bemo to Batubulan in Denpasar (2500Rp).

Going north to Kintamani, get a brown bemo (4000Rp). To Singaraja, Lovina, and northern Bali, go to Kintamani and make a connection there.

Tourist Shuttle Bus
Plenty of companies offer shuttle buses – check the billboards outside shops and travel agencies for current prices and times. **Perama** *(☎ 973316; Jl Hanoman)* is the major operator, but its terminal is inconveniently located in Padangtegal. Seven services run to Kuta, the airport (15,000Rp) and Sanur (20,000Rp). There's one service daily to Bedugul and Kintamani (30,000Rp), three to Padangbai and Candidasa (20,000Rp), one daily to Tirta Gangga (45,000Rp) and Tulamben (50,000Rp) and two daily to Lovina (50,000Rp). Perama shuttle buses, with a public ferry connection, go to Mataram and Senggigi on Lombok and to the Gili islands.

Taxi
There are very few taxis in Ubud – just a few that have brought in passengers from southern Bali and are hoping for a fare back.

GETTING AROUND
To/From the Airport
Regular tourist shuttle buses go to the airport from Ubud, while prepaid taxis from the airport to Ubud cost 90,000Rp. If you really need a taxi, ask your hotel or a travel agent to charter transport one day ahead, or bargain with one of the ubiquitous transport touts. By bemo, go to Batubulan terminal in Denpasar, catch another bemo to Tegal terminal, and then another to the airport – it may be cheap, but it is slow and extremely inconvenient.

Bemo
Bemos don't directly link Ubud with nearby villages; you'll have to catch a bemo going to Denpasar, Gianyar, Pujung or Kintamani and get off where you need to. Small bemos to Gianyar travel along eastern Jl Raya, down Jl Peliatan and east to Bedulu. To Pujung, bemos head east along Jl Raya and then north through Andong and past the turn-off to Petulu.

To Payangan, they travel west along Jl Raya, past Campuan and turn north at the junction after Sanggingan. Larger brown bemos to Batubulan terminal go east along Jl Raya and down Jl Hanoman.

Ojek
If you are staying in the 'suburbs' of Ubud and want to get into town (or vice-versa), ask around for an *ojek* – a motorcycle that will take you as a paying pillion passenger. Prices are negotiable – anywhere in Ubud should cost 5000Rp to 10,000Rp.

Car & Motorcycle
A rented car or motorcycle is very convenient for getting around the outskirts of Ubud, visiting nearby attractions, and travelling further afield. Prices are quite competitive in Ubud, and you might avoid the horrors of driving around Kuta, Denpasar and other congested areas of southern Bali. The ubiquitous Suzuki Jimny jeep costs about 80,000Rp per day with minimal insurance cover – a little bit less for a longer period. A bigger Toyota Kijang costs about 100,000Rp, and a motorcycle costs around 30,000Rp.

Numerous agencies on Monkey Forest Rd, Jl Hanoman and Jl Raya will happily arrange car rental. One of the few places with new cars is **Three Brothers** *(☎ 973240; Jl Hanoman)*, with new Daihatsus from 100,000Rp to 200,000Rp. It's just beside Lumbung Sari hotel.

Around Ubud

The region east and north of Ubud has many of the most ancient monuments and relics on Bali. Many of them predate the Majapahit era and raise as-yet-unanswered questions about Bali's history. Some sites are more recent, and in other instances, newer structures have been built on and around the ancient remains. They're interesting to history and archaeology buffs, but not that spectacular to look at – with the exception of Gunung Kawi. Perhaps the best approach is to plan a whole day walking or cycling around the area, stopping at the places that interest you, but not treating any one as a destination in itself.

If you're travelling by public transport, start early and take a bemo to the Bedulu intersection southeast of Ubud, and another due north to Tirta Empul, about 15km from Ubud (see the Ubud & Around map at the start of this chapter). From the temple of Tirta Empul, follow the path beside the river down to Gunung Kawi, then return to the main road and walk south for about 8km to Pejeng (see the Ubud Area map), or flag down a bemo going towards Gianyar.

BEDULU

Bedulu was once the capital of a great kingdom. The legendary Dalem Bedaulu ruled the Pejeng dynasty from here, and was the last Balinese king to withstand the onslaught of the powerful Majapahit from Java. He was defeated by Gajah Mada in 1343. The capital shifted several times after this, to Gelgel and then later to Semarapura (Klungkung).

The Legend of Dalem Bedaulu

A legend relates how Dalem Bedaulu possessed magical powers that allowed him to have his head chopped off and then replaced. Performing this unique party trick one day, the servant entrusted with lopping off his head and then replacing it unfortunately dropped it in a river and, to his horror, watched it float away. Looking around in panic for a replacement he grabbed a pig, cut off its head and popped it upon the king's shoulders. Thereafter the king was forced to sit on a high throne and forbade his subjects to look up at him; Bedaulu means 'He Who Changed Heads'.

The ornately carved entrance to Goa Gajah – the Elephant Cave

Goa Gajah

Two kilometres southeast of Ubud on the road to Bedulu, a large car park and a slew of souvenir shops indicate that you've reached a big tourist attraction – Goa Gajah *(Elephant Cave; adult/child 3100/1600Rp, car parking 400Rp, motorbike parking 300Rp; open 8am-6pm daily)*. There were never any elephants on Bali; the cave probably takes its name from the nearby Sungai Petanu, which at one time was known as Elephant River, or perhaps because the face over the cave entrance might resemble an elephant.

The origins of the cave are uncertain – one tale relates that it was created by the fingernail of the legendary giant Kebo Iwa. It probably dates to the 11th century, and was certainly in existence during the Majapahit takeover of Bali. The cave was rediscovered by Dutch archaeologists in 1923, but the fountains and pool were not found until 1954.

The cave is carved into a rock face and you enter through the cavernous mouth of a demon. The gigantic fingertips pressed beside the face of the demon push back a riotous jungle of surrounding stone carvings.

Inside the T-shaped cave you can see fragmentary remains of the *lingam*, the phallic symbol of the Hindu god Shiva, and its female counterpart the *yoni*, plus a statue of

UBUD & AROUND

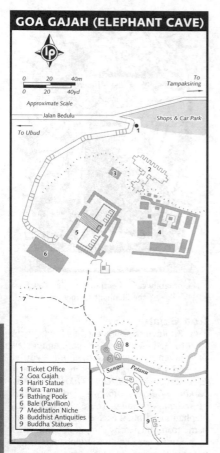

GOA GAJAH (ELEPHANT CAVE)

To Tampaksiring

Approximate Scale

Jalan Bedulu

Shops & Car Park

To Ubud

1 Ticket Office
2 Goa Gajah
3 Hariti Statue
4 Pura Taman
5 Bathing Pools
6 Bale (Pavilion)
7 Meditation Niche
8 Buddhist Antiquities
9 Buddha Statues

Sungai Petanu

Yeh Pulu

This 25m-long carved cliff face (adult/child 3100/1600Rp) is believed to be a hermitage dating from the late 14th century. Apart from the figure of elephant-headed Ganesha, the son of Shiva, there are no obvious religious scenes here. The energetic frieze includes various scenes of everyday life, although the position and movement of the figures suggests that it could be read from left to right as a story. One theory is that they are events from the life of Krishna, the Hindu god.

One of the first recognisable images is of a man carrying a shoulder pole with two jugs, possibly full of *tuak* (palm wine). He is following a woman whose jewellery suggests wealth and power. There's a whimsical figure peering round a doorway, who seems to have armour on his front and a weapon on his back. The thoughtful seated figure wears a turban, which suggests he is a priest.

The hunting scene starts with a horseman and a man throwing a spear. Another man seems to be thrusting a weapon into the mouth of a large beast, while a frog imitates him by disposing of a snake in the same manner. Above the frog, two figures kneel over a smoking pot, while to the right, two men carry off a slain animal on a pole. Then there's the depiction of the woman holding the horse's tail – is she begging the rider to stay or being dragged off as his captive?

The Ganesha figures of Yeh Pulu and Goa Gajah are quite similar, indicating a close relationship between them. You can walk between the sites, following small paths through the paddy fields, but you might need to pay a local kid to guide you. By car or bicycle, look for the signs to 'Relief Yeh Pulu' or 'Villa Yeh Pulu', east of Goa Gajah.

From the entrance, it's a pleasant 300m walk to Yeh Pulu.

Pura Samuan Tiga

The majestic Pura Samuan Tiga (Temple of the Meeting of the Three) is about 200m east of the Bedulu junction. The name is possibly a reference to the Hindu trinity, or it may refer to meetings held here in the early 11th century. Despite these early associations, all the temple buildings have been rebuilt since the 1917 earthquake. The imposing main gate was designed and built by I Gusti Nyoman Lempad, one of Bali's renowned artists and a native of Bedulu.

Shiva's son, the elephant-headed god Ganesha. In the courtyard in front of the cave are two square bathing pools with water trickling into them from waterspouts held by six female figures. To the left of the cave entrance, in a small pavilion, is a statue of Hariti, surrounded by children. In Buddhist lore, Hariti was an evil woman who devoured children, but under the influence of Buddhism she reformed completely to become a protector of children and a symbol of fertility.

From Goa Gajah you can clamber down through the rice paddies to Sungai Petanu, where there are crumbling **rock carvings** of *stupas* (domes for housing Buddhist relics) on a cliff face, and a small **cave**.

Try to see it before 10am, when the big tourist buses start to arrive.

Museum Purbakala

This archaeological museum (☎ 942534; admission by donation; open 8am-3pm Mon-Thur, 8am-12.30 Fri, closed Sat & Sun) has a reasonable collection of artefacts from all over Bali, and most displays are in English. The exhibits include some of Bali's first pottery from near Gilimanuk, and sarcophagi dating from as early as 300 BC – some originating from Bangli are carved in the shape of a turtle, which has important cosmic associations in Balinese mythology. The museum is about 500m north of the Bedulu junction, and easy to reach by bemo or by bicycle.

Getting There & Away

About 3km east of Teges, the road from Ubud reaches a junction where you can turn south to Gianyar or north to Pejeng, Tampaksiring and Penelokan. Ubud–Gianyar bemos will drop you off at this junction, from where you can walk to the attractions. The road from Ubud is reasonably flat, so coming by bicycle is a good option.

PEJENG

Continuing up the road towards Tampaksiring you soon come to Pejeng and its famous temples. Like Bedulu, this was once an important seat of power, as it was the capital of the Pejeng kingdom, which fell to the Majapahit invaders in 1343.

Penis Envy

The fearsome Giant of Pejeng may represent Bima, a hero of the *Mahabharata,* dancing on a dead body, as in a myth related to the Hindu Shiva cult. Another theory is that the statue is trampling on a copulating couple, rather than a dead body, but it takes some imagination to see this. There is some conjecture about the giant's genitalia – it has either six small penises or one large one, and if that large thing is a penis, what are those interesting lumps and that big hole in the side?

The associated legend tells how Bima lusted after a woman, but his penis was too big for her, so she found a less well-endowed lover. When Bima caught them at it, he was really pissed off, and stomped them both to death. There's probably a moral in this somewhere.

Pura Kebo Edan

Also called the Crazy Buffalo Temple, this is not an imposing structure, but it is famous for its 3m-high statue, known as the **Giant of Pejeng**, thought to be approximately 700 years old.

Pura Pusering Jagat

The large Pura Pusering Jagat (Navel of the World Temple) is said to be the centre of the old Pejeng kingdom. Dating from 1329, this temple is visited by young couples who pray at the stone *lingam* and *yoni*. Further back is a large stone urn, with elaborate but worn carvings of gods and demons searching for the elixir of life in a depiction of the *Mahabharata* tale 'Churning the Sea of Milk'. The temple is on a small track running west of the main road.

Pura Penataran Sasih

This was once the state temple of the Pejeng kingdom. In the inner courtyard, high up in a pavilion and difficult to see, is the huge bronze drum known as the **Moon of Pejeng**. The hourglass-shaped drum is more than 2m long, the largest single-piece cast drum in the world. Estimates of its age vary from 1000 to 2000 years, and it is not certain whether it was made locally or imported – the intricate geometric decorations are said to resemble patterns from as far apart as Irian Jaya and Vietnam. Even in its inaccessible position, you can make out these patterns and the distinctive heart-shaped face designs.

Balinese legend relates that the drum came to earth as a fallen moon, landing in a tree and shining so brightly that it prevented a band of thieves from going about their unlawful purpose. One of the thieves decided to put the light out by urinating on it, but the moon exploded and fell to earth as a drum, with a crack across its base as a result of the fall.

TAMPAKSIRING

Tampaksiring is a small town with a large and important temple and the most impressive ancient monument on Bali (see the Ubud & Around map).

Gunung Kawi

On the southern outskirts of town, a sign points east off the main road to Gunung Kawi (adult/child 3100/1600Rp; open 7am-5pm daily). From the end of the access road, a steep, stone stairway leads down to the river, at one point making a cutting through an embankment of solid rock. There, in the bottom of this lush green valley, is one of Bali's oldest and largest ancient monuments.

Gunung Kawi consists of 10 rock-cut *candi* (shrines) – memorials cut out of the rock face in imitation of actual statues. They stand in 7m-high sheltered niches cut into the sheer cliff face. A solitary candi stands about a kilometre further down the valley to the south; this is reached by a trek through the rice paddies on the western side of the river.

Each *candi* is believed to be a memorial to a member of the 11th-century Balinese royalty, but little is known for certain. Legends relate that the whole group of memorials was carved out of the rock face in one hard-working night by the mighty fingernails of Kebo Iwa.

The five monuments on the eastern bank are probably dedicated to King Udayana, Queen Mahendradatta, their son Airlangga and his brothers Anak Wungsu and Marakata. While Airlangga ruled eastern Java, Anak Wungsu ruled Bali. The four monuments on the western side are, by this theory, to Anak Wungsu's chief concubines. Another theory is that the whole complex is dedicated to Anak Wungsu, his wives, concubines and, in the case of the remote 10th *candi*, to a royal minister.

Tirta Empul

A well-signposted fork in the road north of Tampaksiring leads to the holy springs at Tirta Empul (*adult/child 3100/1600Rp; open 8am-6pm daily*), discovered in AD 962 and believed to have magical powers. The springs bubble up into a large, crystal-clear tank within the temple and gush out through waterspouts into a bathing pool – they're the main source of Sungai Pakerisan, the river that rushes by Gunung Kawi only 1km or so away. Next to the springs, Pura Tirta Empul is one of Bali's most important temples.

You'll need a sarong or long pants, and maybe a scarf. Come in the early morning or late afternoon to avoid the tourist buses. You can also use the clean, segregated and free **public baths** in the grounds.

Overlooking Tirta Empul is Soekarno's palace, **Istana Negara**, an unspectacular, single-storey structure, designed by Soekarno himself and built in 1954 on the site of a Dutch rest house. Soekarno, whose mother was Balinese, was a frequent visitor to the island. It's said that he had a telescope here to spy on girls bathing in the pools below.

Other Sites

There are other groups of *candi* and monks' cells in the area encompassed by the ancient Pejeng kingdom, notably **Pura Krobokan** and **Goa Garba**, but none so grand as Gunung Kawi. Between Gunung Kawi and Tirta Empul, **Pura Mengening** temple has a free-standing *candi*, similar in design to those at Gunung Kawi.

NORTH OF UBUD
☎ 0361

The usual road from Ubud to Batur is through Tampaksiring, but there are other lesser roads up the gentle mountain slope. One of the most attractive goes north from Peliatan, past Petulu, and through Tegallalang and Pujung, to bring you out on the crater rim between Penelokan and Batur. It's a sealed road all the way. Tegallalang, Jati and Pujung are all noted woodcarving centres. The Elephant Safari Park is in the area at Taro (see the Ubud section earlier).

Blue Yogi Cafe (☎ 901368; *dishes 15,000-40,000Rp*), about 12km from Ubud, is a good lunch stop with picturesque paddy-field views, although the service can be slow.

A smaller road goes north through **Keliki**, where you'll find **Alam Sari** (☎ 240308; ⓦ *www.alamsari.com; rooms US$66-77*), a fine, small hotel in a wonderfully isolated location, with a pool and a great view.

Balinese Dance

Balinese Dance

RICHARD I'ANSON

GREGORY ADAMS

RICHARD I'ANSON

GREGORY ADAMS

PAUL BEINSSEN

Previous page: A rather ferociously masked performer in a Legong dance (photograph by John Banagan)

Top: A performance of the Barong Landung dance in Batubulan

Middle Top: Elaborately costumed Condong dancer in the classical Legong dance

Middle Bottom Left: A performance of the epic Ramayana Ballet at Ubud Palace

Middle Bottom Right: A masked Topeng dancer performing

Bottom : In the Sanghyang Jaran dance, a boy in a trance state rides his 'horse' around coconut-husk fire

Balinese dance is definitely not some sterile art form requiring a fine arts degree to appreciate – with just the slightest effort it can be exciting and enjoyable for almost anyone.

Balinese dances are not hard to find as there are performances virtually every night at all the tourist centres – admission is generally 25,000Rp to 50,000Rp for visitors. Dances are put on regularly at the tourist centres to raise money, but they are also an integral part of almost every temple festival, and Bali has no shortage of these. Many of the performances held for tourists offer a smorgasbord of Balinese dances – a little Topeng, a taste of Legong and some Baris to round it all off. A nice introduction perhaps, but some dances should be experienced in their entirety. It will be a shame if the 'instant Asia' mentality takes too strong a grip on Balinese dance.

Dances take various forms, but with a few notable exceptions (in particular, Kecak and the Sanghyang trance dance), they are all accompanied by music from the *gamelan* (traditional Balinese percussion orchestra). Some dances are almost purely for the sake of dancing, like the technically precise Legong, its male equivalent, the Baris, or various solo dances like the Kebyar. Mask dances like the Topeng or the Jauk also place a high premium on dancing ability.

In the Barong & Rangda dance, powerful forces are at work and elaborate preparations must be made to ensure that a balance is maintained between good and evil. All masked dances require great care as, in donning a mask, you take on another personality and it is wise to ensure that the mask's personality does not take over. Masks used in the Barong & Rangda dance are treated with particular caution. A Rangda mask must be kept covered until the instant before the performance starts (a Rangda is a widow-witch and ruler of evil spirits). These masks can have powerful *satki* (spirits), and the unwary must be careful of their magical, often dangerous, spiritual vibrations.

The Mexican artist Miguel Covarrubias pointed out in the 1930s that the Balinese like a blend of seriousness and slapstick, and this still shows in their dances. Some have a decidedly comic element, with clowns who convey the story and also act as a counterpoint to the staid, noble characters. The noble characters may use the high Balinese language or classical Kawi, while the clowns, usually servants of the noble characters, converse in everyday Balinese. There are always two clowns – the leader, or *punta*, and his follower, the *kartala*, who never quite manages to carry off his mimicry.

Most dancers on Bali are not professionals, just ordinary people who dance in the evening or in their spare time. Dance is learned by performing, and long hours may be spent in practice, usually by carefully following the movements of an expert. There's little of the soaring leaps of Western ballet or the smooth flowing movements often found in Western dance. Balinese dance tends to be precise, jerky, shifting and jumpy, and is remarkably like Balinese music, with its abrupt changes of tempo and dramatic contrasts between silence and crashing noise.

To the expert, every movement of wrist, hand and fingers is important; even facial expressions are carefully choreographed to convey the character of the dance. To local children, it's as entertaining as a pantomime – watch how they cheer the good characters and cringe back from the stage when the demons appear.

KECAK

Probably the best known of the many Balinese dances, the Kecak is unusual in that it does not have a gamelan accompaniment. Instead the background is provided by a chanting 'choir' of men who provide the 'chak-a-chak-a-chak' noise. Originally, this chanting group was known as the Kecak and was part of a Sanghyang trance dance. Then, in the 1930s, the modern Kecak developed in Bona, near Gianyar in eastern Bali, where the dance is still held regularly.

The Kecak tells a tale from the *Ramayana*, one of the great Hindu holy books, about Prince Rama and his Princess Sita. With Rama's brother, Laksamana, they have been exiled from the kingdom of Ayodya and are wandering in the forest. The evil Rawana, King of Lanka, lures Rama away with a golden deer (which is really Lanka's equally evil prime minister, who has magically changed himself into a deer). When Rama fails to return, Sita persuades Laksamana to search for him. When the princess is alone, Rawana pounces and carries her off to his hideaway.

Hanuman, the white monkey-god, appears before Sita and tells her that Rama is trying to rescue her. He brings her Rama's ring to show that he is indeed the prince's envoy and Sita gives him a hairpin to take back to Rama. When Rama finally arrives in Lanka he is met by the evil king's evil son, Megananda, who shoots an arrow at him, but the arrow

GREGORY ADAMS

magically turns into a snake, which ties Rama up. Fortunately, Rama is able to call upon a Garuda, a mythical creature, part man and part bird, for assistance and thus escapes. Finally, Sugriwa, the king of the monkeys, comes to Rama's assistance with his monkey army and, after a great battle, good wins out over evil and Rama and Sita return home.

Throughout the dance the surrounding circle of men, all bare-chested and wearing checked cloth around their waists, provide a nonstop accompaniment that rises to a crescendo as they play the monkey army and fight it out with Rawana and his cronies. The chanting is superbly synchronised; members of the monkey army sway back and forth, raise their hands in unison, flutter their fingers and lean left and right, all with an eerily exciting coordination.

Left: A dancer portrays a golden deer from the *Ramayana*. The deer is actually a decoy sent by the evil Rawana to lure Rama away from the beautiful Sita.

BARONG & RANGDA

The Barong & Rangda dance rivals the Kecak as Bali's most popular dance for tourists. Again it's a straightforward battle between good (the Barong) and bad (the Rangda). The Barong is a strange creature – half shaggy dog, half lion – propelled by two men like a pantomime horse. It's definitely on the side of good, but is a mischievous and fun-loving creature. By contrast, the widow-witch Rangda is bad through and through, and certainly not someone you'd like to meet on a midnight stroll through the rice paddies.

Barong can take various forms, but in the Barong & Rangda dance it will be as the Barong Keket, the most holy of the Barong. The Barong flounces in, snaps its jaws at the gamelan, dances around a bit and enjoys the acclaim of its supporters – a group of men with kris (ceremonial daggers). Then Rangda makes her appearance, her long tongue lolling, terrible fangs protruding from her mouth, human entrails draped around her neck, and pendulous parody breasts.

The Barong and Rangda duel, using their magical powers, but when things look bad for the Barong, its supporters draw their kris and rush in to attack the Rangda. Using her magical powers the Rangda throws them into a trance and the men try to stab themselves with their kris. But the Barong also has great magical powers and casts a spell that stops the kris from harming the men. This is the most dramatic part of the dance. As the gamelan rings crazily the men rush back and forth, waving their kris around, all but foaming at the mouth, sometimes even rolling on the ground in a desperate attempt to stab themselves. There often seems to be a conspiracy to terrify tourists in the front row!

Finally, the Rangda retires, defeated, and good has triumphed again. However, this still leaves a large group of entranced Barong supporters who need to return to the real world. This is usually done by sprinkling them with holy water, sanctified by dipping the Barong's beard in it. Performing the Barong & Rangda dance is a touchy operation – playing around with all that powerful magic, good and bad, is not to be taken lightly. Extensive ceremonies have to be performed, a *pesmangku* (temple guardian and priest for temple rituals) must be on hand to end the dancers' trance and, at the end, a chicken must be sacrificed to propitiate the evil spirits.

LEGONG

The Legong is the most graceful of Balinese dances, and to connoisseurs it's the one of most interest and discussion. A *legong* (as a Legong dancer is known) is a girl – often as young as eight or nine years, and rarely older than her early teens. Such importance is attached to the dance that in old age a classic dancer will be remembered as a 'great *legong*', even though her brief period of fame may have been 50 years previously.

There are various forms of this dance, but the Legong Keraton (Legong of the Palace) is the one most often performed. Peliatan's famous dance troupe, which visitors to Ubud often get a chance to see, is particularly noted for its Legong. The story behind the Legong is very stylised and symbolic – if you didn't know the story it would be impossible to tell what was going on.

The Legong involves three dancers – the two *legong* and their 'attendant', the *congong*. The *legong* are dressed in gold brocade, so tightly bound that it's surprising they can move so rapidly. Their faces are elaborately made up, their eyebrows plucked and repainted, and their hair decorated with frangipani. The dance relates how a king takes a maiden, Rangkesari, captive. When Rangkesari's brother comes to release her, Rangkesari begs the king to free her rather than go to war. The king refuses and on his way to the battle meets a bird bringing ill omens. He ignores the bird and continues on, meets Rangkesari's brother and is killed.

That's the story, but the dance tells only of the king's preparations for battle and ends with the bird's appearance – when the king leaves the stage it's to join the battle where he will meet his death. The dance starts with the *congong* dancing and then departing as the two *legong* come on. The *legong* dance in close formation and in mirror image, as when they dance a nose-to-nose 'love scene'. The dance tells of the king's sad departure from his queen, Rangkesari's bitter request that he release her and then the king's departure for the battle. The *congong* reappears with tiny golden wings as the bird of ill fortune and the dance ends.

BARIS

The warrior dance, known as the Baris, is traditionally a male equivalent of the Legong – femininity and grace give way to energetic and warlike martial spirit. The Baris dancer must convey the thoughts and emotions of a warrior preparing for action, and then meeting an enemy in battle. The dancer has to show his changing moods through facial expression as well as movement – chivalry, pride, anger, prowess and, finally, a little regret. Though it's a solo dance, the Baris requires great energy and skill, and is said to be one of the most complex of all Balinese dances.

KEBYAR

The Kebyar is a male solo dance like the Baris, but with greater emphasis on the performer's individual abilities. Development of the modern Kebyar is credited in large part to the famous prewar dancer Mario. There are various forms of Kebyar, including the Kebyar Duduk, where the 'dance' is done from the seated position and facial expressions, as well as movements of the hands, arms and torso, are all-important. In the Kebyar Trompong, the dancer joins the gamelan and plays the *trompong* drum while dancing.

RAMAYANA BALLET

The *Ramayana* is a familiar tale on Bali, but the dance is a relatively recent addition to the Balinese repertoire. Basically, it tells the same story of Rama and Sita as told in the Kecak, but without the monkey ensemble and with a usual gamelan gong accompaniment.

The *Ramayana* provides plenty of opportunity for improvisation and comic additions. Rawana may be played as a classic bad guy, Hanuman can be a comic clown, and camera-clicking tourists among the spectators may come in for a little imitative ribbing.

BARONG LANDUNG

The giant puppet dances known as Barong Landung are not an every-day occurrence – they take place annually on the island of Pulau Serangan and a few other places in southern Bali. The legend of their creation relates how the demon Jero Gede Macaling popped over from Nusa Penida, disguised as a standing Barong, to cause havoc on Bali. To scare him away, the people had to make a big Barong just like him.

The Barong Landung dance, a reminder of that ancient legend, features two gigantic puppet figures – a horrific male image of black Jero Gede and his female sidekick, white Jero Luh. Barong Landung performances are often highly comical.

JANGER

The Janger is a relatively new dance that appeared in the 1920s and 1930s. Both Miguel Covarrubias and Hickman Powell commented on this strange, almost un-Balinese, courtship dance. Today, it is an accepted part of the standard repertoire. In the Janger, formations of 12 young women and 12 young men do a sitting dance, and the gentle swaying and chanting of the women contrasts with the violently choreographed movements and loud shouts of the men. It has similarities to several other dances, including the Sanghyang, where the relaxed chanting of the women is contrasted with the violent 'chak-a-chak-a-chak' of the men.

TOPENG

This is a mask dance where the dancers have to imitate the character represented by the mask. (Topeng means 'Pressed Against the Face', as with a mask.) The Topeng Tua is a classic solo dance where the mask is that of an old man and the dancer has to dance like a creaky old gentleman. In other dances there may be a small troupe who perform various characters and types. A full collection of Topeng masks may number 30 or 40.

RICHARD I'ANSON

Right: Topeng dancer

JAUK

The Jauk is a mask dance, and strictly a solo performance – the dancer plays an evil demon, his mask an eerie face with bulging eyes and fixed smile, while long wavering fingernails complete the demonic look. Mask dances are considered to require great expertise because the dancer is not able to convey the character's thoughts and meanings through his facial expressions – the dance has to tell all. Demons are very unpleasant, frenetic and fast-moving creatures, so a Jauk dancer has to imitate all of these things.

SANGHYANG

These dances originally developed to drive out evil spirits from a village – Sanghyang is a divine spirit who temporarily inhabits an entranced dancer. The Sanghyang Dedari dance is performed by two young girls who dance a dream-like version of the Legong, but with their eyes closed. They perform the intricate pattern of the Legong in perfect harmony, with their eyes firmly shut. Male and female choirs, the male choir being a Kecak, provide a background chant, but when the chant stops the dancers slump to the ground in a faint. Two women bring them around, and at the finish a *pemangku* blesses them with holy water and brings them out of the trance. The modern Kecak dance developed from the Sanghyang.

In the Sanghyang Jaran, a boy in a trance dances around and through a fire of coconut husks, riding a coconut palm 'hobby horse'. It's labelled the 'fire dance' for the benefit of tourists. Like other trance dances (such as the Barong & Rangda dance) great care must be taken to control the magical forces at play. Experts must always be on hand to take care of the entranced dancers and to bring them out of the trance at the close, but in tourist centres the 'trance' is often staged.

OTHER DANCES

Old dances fade out and new dances emerge. New developments of old dances still appear – dance on Bali is not a static art form. The Oleg Tambulilingan was developed in the 1950s, originally as a solo female dance. Later, a male part was added and the dance now mimics the flirtations of two *tambulilingan* (bumblebees).

Pendet, an everyday dance of the temples, is a small procedure performed before making temple offerings. You may often see the Pendet being danced by women bringing offerings to a temple for a festival, but it is also sometimes danced as an introduction and a closing for other dance performances.

One of the most popular comic dances is the Cupak, which tells a tale of a greedy coward (Cupak) and his brave but hard-done-by younger brother Grantang, and their adventures while rescuing a beautiful princess.

The Arja is a sort of Balinese soap opera, long and full of high drama. Since it requires much translation of the noble's actions by the clowns, it's hard for Westerners to understand and appreciate. Drama Gong is in some ways a more modern version of the same romantic themes.

WHERE ARE THE DANCES?

You might catch a quality dance performance anywhere if there's a special festival or celebration happening. The annual Bali Arts Festival, in Denpasar during June and July, is a feast for dance fans. You'll encounter all sorts of dances at hotels and restaurants in the main tourist areas, with varying degrees of professionalism. But to see good Balinese dance on a regular basis, you should stay in or near Ubud, where the tourist office has information and tickets for a full programme of performances.

Balinese Dance Styles & Locations

Barong & Kris Dance Padangtegal: Monday; Batubulan: most days
Barong & Rangda Dance Ubud Palace: Friday; Batubulan: most days
Kecak Dance Peliatan: Thursday; Agung Rai Museum of Art (ARMA) Open Stage: every full moon and new moon
Kecak Fire Dance Junjungan: Monday
Kecak Fire & Trance Dance Padangtegal: Sunday, Tuesday, Wednesday and Saturday; Pura Dalem Ubud: Friday
Legong Dance Ubud Palace: Monday and Saturday; ARMA Open Stage: Sunday; Peliatan: Tuesday and Friday
Ramayana Ballet Ubud Palace: Tuesday

East Bali

The eastern end of Bali is dominated by the mighty Gunung Agung, known as the 'navel of the world' and Bali's 'Mother Mountain'. This towering 3142m-high volcano last erupted in 1963, causing a major disaster. Today, Gunung Agung is quiet, but the 'Mother Temple' of Pura Besakih, perched high on its slopes, attracts a steady stream of devotees and tourists.

The main route east from Denpasar and Ubud goes through Gianyar and Semarapura (also known as Klungkung), and then close to the coast past Kusamba, the bat-infested temple of Pura Goa Lawah and the turn-off to the port of Padangbai. A new coast road is currently under construction, which will relieve the heavy traffic through the main towns. It currently extends from Sanur in south Bali to the Saba area.

From Padangbai and Candidasa, there are plenty of places to stay and lots of coast to explore. An alternative route goes round the southern flank of Gunung Agung, with fine scenery and small villages. From Amlapura, another old kingdom capital, you can continue north past the rice fields of Tirta Gangga to reach the far east coast, a region with great diving and a relaxed seaside scene.

Organised Tours
Sobek (☎ 0361 287059, fax 289448; W www.sobekbali.com) runs a one-day 4WD tour of eastern Bali, starting in Bangli (see Activities in the Facts for the Visitor chapter).

GIANYAR
☎ 0361
Gianyar is the administrative capital and main market town of the Gianyar district, which also includes Ubud. It's on Bali's main eastern road, which carries heavy traffic between Denpasar and Padangbai port. The town has a number of factories producing batik and ikat fabrics, and the palace of the surviving royal family, but it's of minimal interest to most visitors. People sometimes come to sample market food, like *babi guling* (roast piglet), for which the town is noted.

Information
A huge, white statue of Arjuna in his chariot marks the western end of Jl Ngurah Rai, the

Highlights

- Exploring Bali's 'Mother Mountain', Gunung Agung – a classic conical volcano and the toughest trekkers' climb
- Learning about Bali's most lurid legends at Semarapura's Kertha Gosa (Hall of Justice)
- Experiencing the elaborate festivals of Pura Besakih, the 'Mother Temple'
- Wandering around Padangbai, a bustling little port with walks to idyllic beaches
- Diving and snorkelling around the islets off Candidasa, coral reefs off Amed and a WWII wreck off Tulamben
- Soaking up stunning scenery of sculpted rice terraces, rugged seascapes and superb sunrises

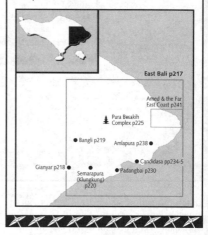

East Bali p217

Amed & the Far East Coast p241

Pura Besakih Complex p225

● Bangli p219   Amlapura p238 ●

Gianyar p218 ●

Semarapura (Klungkung) p220

● Candidasa pp234-5

● Padangbai p230

main street. The **police station** (☎ 93110; Jl Ngurah Rai) doubles as the tourist information office (but very little English is spoken). On the main street, **Gianyar Paradiso Internet** (☎ 943478; Jl Ngurah Rai) has Internet access and is also a **wartel** (public telephone office), and there are several **banks** (with ATMs).

Puri Gianyar
The palace dates from 1771, but was destroyed in a conflict with the neighbouring kingdom of Klungkung in the mid-1880s and rebuilt. Under threat from its aggressive neighbours, the Gianyar kingdom requested

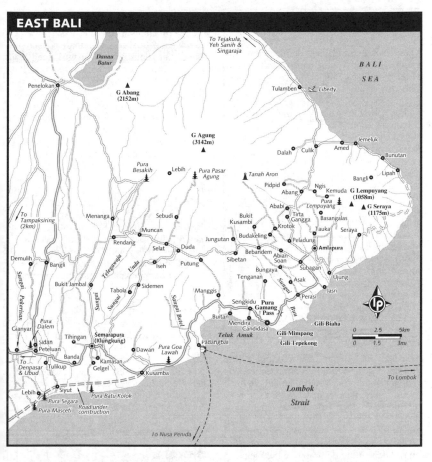

EAST BALI

Dutch protection, and a 1900 agreement allowed Gianyar's ruling family to retain its status and its palace, though it lost all political power. The palace *(puri)* was damaged in the 1917 earthquake, but was restored soon after and appears little changed from the time the Dutch arrived. It's a fine example of traditional palace architecture, but tourists are not usually allowed inside. If you report to the guard inside the complex, you may be allowed a quick look around. Otherwise, you can see some of it through the gates.

Places to Stay & Eat
Pondok Wisata Gianyar (☎ 942165; *Jl Anom Sandat 10X; doubles 45,000Rp*), with small, clean rooms, is the best and most central place to stay in Gianyar.

For the local speciality, *babi guling* (6000Rp), head straight to the stalls inside the open-air **food market** from about 11am to 2pm, or try one of the small **restaurants** nearby in the main street, or the **food stalls** in the main market from about 6pm to 9pm. **Gianyar Paradiso Internet** (*dishes 6000-10,000Rp*) is a nice little café to stop by for coffee or *nasi goreng* (fried rice). **Dunkin' Donuts** is a conspicuous alternative in the main street.

Shopping
There are a few textile factories at the western end of town, including **Tenun Ikat Setia Cili** (☎/fax 943409; e yunpande@yahoo .com; open 9am-5pm), **Cap Bakti** and **Cap Togog** (☎ 943046; *Jl Astina Utara 11; open*

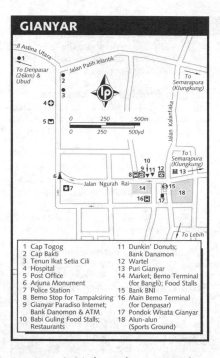

GIANYAR

1 Cap Togog
2 Cap Bakti
3 Tenun Ikat Setia Cili
4 Hospital
5 Post Office
6 Arjuna Monument
7 Police Station
8 Bemo Stop for Tampaksiring
9 Gianyar Paradiso Internet;
   Bank Danomon & ATM
10 Babi Guling Food Stalls;
   Restaurants
11 Dunkin' Donuts;
   Bank Danamon
12 Wartel
13 Puri Gianyar
14 Market; Bemo Terminal
   (for Bangli); Food Stalls
15 Bank BNI
16 Main Bemo Terminal
   (for Denpasar)
17 Pondok Wisata Gianyar
18 Alun-alun
   (Sports Ground)

8am-5pm daily), have showrooms where you can buy material by the metre, or you can have it tailored. You can go out the back to see a lone weaver at work and see how the thread is dyed before weaving to produce the vibrantly patterned weft ikat, which is called *endek* on Bali. Prices cost 40,000Rp to 55,000Rp per metre for cotton fabric, depending on how fine the weaving is – costs will rise if it contains silk. Handmade batik is also for sale here. Tenun Ikat Setia Cili also will run textile courses on demand, and these range from two-hour to six-month courses.

Getting There & Away
There are regular *bemos* (small pick-up trucks) that cost 5000Rp and travel between Batubulan terminal near Denpasar and Gianyar's main terminal, which is behind the market, before heading to Semarapura and Amlapura (9000Rp). Bemos to Sidan and Bangli (2500Rp) use the same area. Bemos to/from Tampaksiring (2500Rp) use the bemo stop across the road from the market. (If you are heading to Ubud, you have to change at Tampaksiring.)

LEBIH & THE COAST
South of Gianyar, the coast is fringed by black-sand beaches and small coastal villages like Lebih, but you will need your own transport to get around. Sungai Pakerisan (Pakerisan River), which starts near Tampaksiring, reaches the sea near Lebih. Here, and at other coastal villages south of Gianyar, cremation formalities reach their conclusion when the ashes are consigned to the sea. Ritual purification ceremonies for temple artefacts are also held on these beaches. The impressive **Pura Segara** temple looks across the strait to Nusa Penida, home of Jero Gede Macaling – the temple helps protect Bali from his evil influence.

Further west is **Pura Masceti**, one of Bali's nine directional temples. On the beach, the local villagers have erected a huge and somewhat horrific swan in an attempt to create a tourist attraction. One of the best **beaches** along this stretch of coast is just south of Siyut.

SIDAN
Continuing east from Gianyar you come to the turn-off to Bangli about 2km out of Peteluan. Follow this road for about 1km until you reach a sharp bend, where you'll find Sidan's **Pura Dalem**, a good example of a temple of the dead, with very fine carvings. Note the sculptures of Durga with children by the gate and the separate enclosure in one corner of the temple – this is dedicated to Merajapati, the guardian spirit of the dead.

BANGLI
☎ 0366
Halfway up the slope to Penelokan, Bangli, once the capital of a kingdom, is said to have the best climate on Bali. It has an interesting temple, and the town makes a pleasant base for exploring the area, but accommodation is limited.

History
Bangli dates from the early 13th century. In the Majapahit era it broke away from Gelgel to become a separate kingdom, even though it was landlocked, poor and involved in long-running conflicts with neighbouring states.

In 1849 Bangli made a treaty with the Dutch, giving it control over the defeated north-coast kingdom of Buleleng, but Buleleng rebelled and the Dutch imposed direct

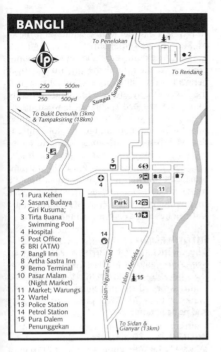

BANGLI

To Penelokan

To Rendang

0   250   500m
0   250   500yd

Sungai Sangsang

To Bukit Demulih (3km)
& Tampaksiring (18km)

Park

1 Pura Kehen
2 Sasana Budaya
   Giri Kusuma;
3 Tirta Buana
   Swimming Pool
4 Hospital
5 Post Office
6 BRI (ATM)
7 Bangli Inn
8 Artha Sastra Inn
9 Bemo Terminal
10 Pasar Malam
   (Night Market)
11 Market; Warungs
12 Wartel
13 Police Station
14 Petrol Station
15 Pura Dalem
   Penunggekan

Jalan Ngurah Road
Jalan Merdeka

To Sidan &
Gianyar (13km)

rule there. In 1909 the rajah of Bangli chose to become a Dutch protectorate rather than face complete conquest by neighbouring kingdoms or the colonial power.

Orientation & Information
Bangli is a neat and well-planned town, although its facilities are limited. There is a **police station** (☎ 91072) and **public hospital** (☎ 91020), and **Bank Rakyat Indonesia** (BRI) has an ATM.

Pura Kehen
Pura Kehen (*admission by donation; open 8am-5pm daily*), the state temple of the Bangli kingdom, is one of the finest temples in eastern Bali – it's a miniature version of Pura Besakih. It is terraced up the hillside, with a flight of steps leading to the beautifully decorated entrance. The first courtyard has a huge banyan tree with a *kulkul* (warning drum) entwined in its branches. The Chinese porcelain plates were set into the walls as decoration, but most of the originals have been damaged or lost. The inner courtyard has an 11-roofed *meru* (shrine), and there are other shrines with thrones for the

Hindu trinity – Brahma, Shiva and Vishnu. The carvings are particularly intricate.

There's a counter opposite the temple entrance where you make your donation. You'll pay extra for sarong or sash rental.

Sasana Budaya Giri Kusuma
Supposedly a showplace for Balinese dance, drama, gamelan and the visual arts, this large arts centre rarely seems to have anything on.

Bukit Demulih
Three kilometres west of Bangli is the village of Demulih, and a hill called Bukit Demulih. If you can't find the sign pointing to it, ask local children to direct you. After a short climb to the top, you'll see a small **temple** and good **views** over south Bali.

On the way, a steep side road leads down to Tirta Buana, a **public swimming pool** in a lovely location deep in the valley.

Pura Dalem Penunggekan
Just south of Bangli, the wall of this fascinating 'temple of the dead' features vivid relief carvings of wrong-doers getting their just desserts in the afterlife. It's definitely adults-only viewing.

Places to Stay & Eat
A former palace residence, **Artha Sastra Inn** (☎ 91179; Jl Merdeka; singles/doubles 30,000/45,000Rp) is still run by descendants of the last royal family. It's not fancy, but cheap, pleasant and friendly.

Bangli Inn (☎/fax 91419; Jl Rambutan 1; singles/doubles 70,000/150,000Rp) is a little more modern, but just as friendly, with clean, simple rooms.

A *pasar malam* (night market), on the street beside the bemo terminal, has some excellent **warung** (food stalls), and you'll also find some in the market area during the day.

Getting There & Away
Bangli is easy to reach by bemo: it's on the main road between Denpasar's Batubulan terminal (2500Rp) and Kintamani (4500Rp), via Penelokan. Bemos also regularly leave Gianyar and go up the pretty, shaded road to Bangli, although it's often quicker to get a connection at the junction near Peteluan.

Tourist shuttle buses travelling between Ubud and Gunung Batur usually go via Tampaksiring and bypass Bangli.

EAST BALI

SEMARAPURA (KLUNGKUNG)
☎ 0366

Semarapura was once the centre of Bali's most important kingdom, and a great artistic and cultural focal point. Today, the capital of Klungkung district, with its distinctly Chinese character, is a major public transport junction and has a chaotic market **Pasar Senggol**. The town has been officially renamed Semarapura, but is still more commonly called Klungkung. The new name now appears on some signs and maps, and on the front of bemos and buses. The Kertha Gosa complex is worth visiting, and there are some fascinating attractions in the surrounding area, but accommodation is very limited.

History
Successors to the Majapahit conquerors of Bali established themselves at Gelgel (just south of modern Semarapura) in around 1400, and the Gelgel dynasty strengthened with the growing Majapahit presence on Bali. During the 17th century, the successors of the Gelgel line established separate kingdoms and the dominance of the Gelgel court was lost. The court moved to Klungkung (as it was called then) in 1710, but never regained a pre-eminent position.

In 1849 the rulers of Klungkung and Gianyar defeated a Dutch invasion force at Kusamba. Before the Dutch could launch a counter attack, a force from Tabanan had arrived and the trader Mads Lange was able to broker a peace settlement.

For the next 50 years, the south Bali kingdoms squabbled, until the rajah of Gianyar persuaded the Dutch to support him. When the Dutch finally invaded the south, the king of Klungkung had a choice between a suicidal *puputan* (fight to the death), like the rajah of Denpasar, or an ignominious surrender, as Tabanan's rajah had done. He chose the former. In April 1908, as the Dutch surrounded his palace, the Dewa Agung and hundreds of his relatives and followers marched out to certain death from Dutch gunfire, or the blades of their own kris. It was the last Balinese kingdom to succumb.

Information
The **district tourist office** (☎ 21448; open 8am-2pm daily) is in the Museum Semarajaya building of Taman Kertha Gosa. The main street, Jl Diponegoro, has several **banks** with ATMs. The **post office**, **wartel** and **police station** (☎ 21115) are further west.

Taman Kertha Gosa
When the Dewa Agung dynasty moved here in 1710, a new palace, the Semara Pura, was established. It was laid out as a large square, believed to be in the form of a mandala, with courtyards, gardens, pavilions and

SEMARAPURA (KLUNGKUNG)

To Burkit Jambal, Rendang, Pura Besakih (23km) & Selat (29km)

To Kusamba, Padangbai (19km), & Amlapura (40km)

Sungai Unda

Jalan Gajah Mada

Jalan Gunung Batukaru

Jalan Besakih

Gunung Rinjani

Jalan Surapati

Jalan Diponegoro

Jalan Nakula

Jalan Sahadewa

Jalan Puputan

To Tihingan, Museum Seni Lukis Klasik (6km), Gianyar (16km) & Denpasar (39km)

Taman Kertha Gosa

To Terminal Kelod

To Gelgel & Kamasan

PLACES TO STAY		OTHER	
19 Loji Ramayana Hotel		1 Police Station	10 Tragia Supermarket
		2 Post Office	11 Pura Taman Sari
PLACES TO EAT		3 Museum Semarajaya; Tourist Office	12 Pasar Senggol
16 Bali Indah		4 Bale Kambang	13 Bank Pembangunan; Bank Danamon
17 Sumber Rasa		5 Puputan Monument	14 Bank BCA
		6 Kertha Gosa	15 Market
		7 Parking	18 Mosque
		8 Wartel	19
		9 Bemo Terminal (for Besakih & Rendang)	

EAST BALI

moats – the complex is sometimes referred to as Taman Gili (Island Garden). Most of the original palace and grounds were destroyed by Dutch attacks in 1908 – the **Pemedal Agung**, the gateway on the south side of the square, is all that remains of the palace itself (it's worth a close look to see the carvings). Two important buildings are preserved in a restored section of the grounds, and with a museum they comprise the Taman Kertha Gosa complex *(adult/child 5000/2000Rp; open 8am-6pm daily)*.

Kertha Gosa In the northeastern corner of the complex, the 'Hall of Justice' was effectively the supreme court of the Klungkung kingdom, where disputes and cases that could not be settled at the village level were eventually brought. This open-sided pavilion is a superb example of Klungkung architecture, and its ceiling is completely covered with fine paintings in the Klungkung style. The paintings, done on asbestos sheeting, were installed in the 1940s, replacing cloth paintings, which had deteriorated.

The rows of ceiling panels depict several different themes. The lowest level illustrates five tales from Bali's answer to the *Arabian Nights,* where a girl called Tantri spins a different yarn every night. The next two rows are scenes from Bima's travels in the afterlife, where he witnesses the torment of evildoers. The gruesome tortures are shown clearly, but there are different interpretations of what punishment goes with what crime. (There's a pretty authoritative explanation in *The Epic of Life – A Balinese Journey of the Soul,* available for reference in the pavilion.) The fourth row of panels depicts the story of Garuda's search for the elixir of life, while the fifth row shows events on the Balinese astrological calendar. The next three rows return to the story of Bima, this time travelling in heaven, with doves and a lotus flower at the apex of the ceiling.

Bale Kambang The ceiling of the beautiful 'Floating Pavilion' is painted in Klungkung style. Again, the different rows of paintings deal with various subjects. The first row is based on the astrological calendar; the second on the folk tale of Pan and Men Brayut and their 18 children; and the upper rows on the adventures of the hero Sutasona.

Museum Semarajaya There are a few archaeological pieces and some quite interesting contemporary accounts of the 1908 *puputan* on display in this tumbledown museum, although you'll find that most displays are in Indonesian.

Pura Taman Sari
The quiet lawns and ponds around this temple make it a relaxing stop. The towering 11-roofed *meru* (multiroofed shrine) indicates that this was a temple built for royalty.

Places to Stay & Eat
Loji Ramayana Hotel *(☎ 21044; rooms 70,000Rp)* has several adequate rooms, all with cold water, set around a spacious family compound.

Two Chinese-style restaurants on Jl Nakula, **Bali Indah** *(dishes 10,000-17,000Rp)* and **Sumber Rasa** *(dishes 8000-15,000Rp)*, are clean, cheap and have quite OK food, but neither appears to be frequented by locals. **Pasar Senggol** *(open 4pm-midnight)*, a night market, is by far the best spot to eat – Bollywood tuncs blast out from CD stalls amid satay stalls and Chinese woks.

Shopping
One or two shops along Jl Diponegoro sell Kamasan-style paintings, temple umbrellas and textiles from the nearby villages. The **Tragia supermarket** *(Jl Gunung Batukaru)* has anything else you are likely to need. The chaotic **markets** are definitely worth a look around.

Getting There & Away
Frequent bemos and minibuses from Denpasar (Batubulan terminal) pass through Semarapura (minibus 4000Rp) on the way to Padangbai, Amlapura, Selat and Singaraja. They can be hailed from the main road in Semarapura.

Bemos heading north to Besakih (6000Rp) leave from the centre of Semarapura, a block northeast of Kertha Gosa. Most other bemos leave from the inconvenient Terminal Kelod, about 2km south of the city centre.

Tourist shuttle buses between southern Bali or Ubud and Padangbai, or Candidasa, will stop in Semarapura on request. Kertha Gosa is a regular stop-off for bus tours of eastern Bali.

EAST BALI

AROUND SEMARAPURA (KLUNGKUNG)

Gelgel

About 3km south of Semarapura, Gelgel was once the seat of Bali's most powerful dynasty. Its decline started in 1710, when the court moved to present-day Semarapura, and finished when the Dutch bombarded the place in 1908.

Today the wide streets and the surviving temples are only faintly evocative of past grandeur. The **Pura Dasar** is not particularly attractive, but its vast courtyards are a real clue to its former importance, and festivals here attract large numbers of people from all over Bali.

A little to the east, the **Masjid Gelgel** is Bali's oldest mosque. It was established in the late 16th century for the benefit of Muslim missionaries from Java, who were unwilling to return home after failing to make any converts.

Kamasan

This quiet, traditional village is the place where the classical Kamasan painting style originated, and several artists still practise this art – you can see their workshops and small showrooms along the main street. The work is often a family affair, with one person inking the outlines, while another mixes the paints and yet another applies the colours. The paintings depict traditional stories or Balinese calendars, and although they are sold in souvenir shops all over Bali, the quality is better here. Look for smooth and distinct line-work, evenly applied colours and balance in the overall composition (see the Arts & Crafts special section for more information). The village is also home to families of *bokor* artisans, who produce the silver bowls used in traditional ceremonies.

To reach Kamasan, go about 2km south of Semarapura and look for the turn-off to the left (east).

Bukit Jambal

The road north of Semarapura climbs steeply into the hills, via Bukit Jambal, which is understandably popular for its magnificent views. There are several **restaurants** here that provide buffet lunches for tour groups. This road continues to Rendang and Pura Besakih.

Sungai Unda & Sungai Telagawaja

East of Semarapura, the main road crosses the dammed up Sungai Unda. Further upstream, both the Unda and its tributary the Telagawaja are used for white-water rafting trips (see the Activities section in the Facts for the Visitor chapter).

Tihingan

Tihingan has several workshops producing gamelan instruments. Small foundries make the resonating bronze bars and bowl-shaped gongs, which are then carefully filed and polished until they produce the correct tone. Some pieces are on sale, but most of the instruments are produced for musical groups all over Bali. It's not really set up for visitors, but the workshops with signs out the front will receive visitors (albeit sometimes grudgingly) – the work is usually done very early in the morning. From Semarapura, head west along Jl Diponegoro and look for the signs.

Museum Seni Lukis Klasik

Nyoman Gunarsa, one of the most respected and successful modern artists in Indonesia, established this museum and arts centre (*admission adult/child 10,000Rp/free; open 9am-5pm daily*) near his home village. The huge three-storey building exhibits an impressive variety of older pieces, including stone- and woodcarvings, architectural antiques, masks, ceramics and textiles. Many of the classical paintings are on bark paper and are some of the oldest surviving examples of this style. The top floor is devoted to Gunarsa's own work of colourful, semi-abstract depictions of traditional dancers and musicians.

There's a large performance space downstairs, and some fine examples of traditional architecture just outside.

The museum is about 6km from Semarapura, near a bend on the road to Denpasar – look for the mannequin policemen at the base of a large statue nearby.

Goa Jepang

About 1km west of the museum, just past a big bridge, some small U-shaped tunnels dug into the roadside were the work of Japanese soldiers who occupied Bali in WWII. A signpost marks them as Goa Jepang (Japanese Cave), but they're hardly worth a stop.

The Coast

The coast south of Semarapura is striking, with seaside temples, black-sand beaches and pounding waves, but the sea is not suitable for swimming. Roads don't run quite next to the coast; you need to take side tracks to the sea at places like **Siyut** and **Pura Batu Kolok**. It's difficult without your own transport.

East of Semarapura, the main road crosses Sungai Unda, then swings south towards the sea. Lava from the 1963 eruption of Gunung Agung destroyed villages and cut the road, but the lava flows are now overgrown.

Kusamba A side road goes south to the fishing and salt-making village of Kusamba, where you will see lines of colourful fishing *prahu* (outriggers) lined up all along the beach. The fish market in Kusamba is really excellent. The fishing is usually done at night and the 'eyes' on the front of the boats help navigation through the darkness. Local boats travel to the islands of Nusa Penida and Nusa Lembongan, which are clearly visible from Kusamba (but you can get faster and safer boats from Padangbai port). Both east and west of Kusamba, there are small salt-making huts lined up in rows along the beach – see the boxed text 'Making Salt While the Sun Shines' later in this chapter for more information.

A Short History of Kusamba

In 1849 Kusamba was the site of a key battle that delayed Dutch control of southern Bali for more than 50 years. The Dutch had landed an invasion force here, which outraged the Balinese by desecrating a temple. While the Dutch were weakened by an outbreak of dysentery, Dewa Agung Isteri, known as the 'virgin queen' of Klungkung, led an attack in which the Dutch suffered numerous casualties and their leader was fatally wounded.

Historically, Kusamba was also one of the original Muslim settlements on Bali, and a centre for metal-workers who produced weapons, including the sacred kris. Kusamba still has mosques and kris-makers, although neither wants to attract visitors.

Pura Goa Lawah (Bat Cave Temple) is one of nine diectional temples on Bali and is devoted to the diety Naga Basuki

Pura Goa Lawah Three kilometres east of Kusamba is the Pura Goa Lawah *(Bat Cave Temple; admission 3000Rp, car park 1000Rp, sash rental 1000Rp; open daily)*, which is one of nine directional temples on Bali. The cave in the cliff face is packed, crammed and jammed full of bats, and the complex is equally way overcrowded with tour groups. There is a distinctly batty stench exuding from the cave, and the roofs of the temple shrines, which are in front of the cave, are liberally coated with bat droppings. Superficially, the temple is small and unimpressive, but it is very old and of great significance to the Balinese.

It is said that the cave leads all the way to Besakih, but it's unlikely that you'd want to try this route. The bats provide sustenance for the legendary giant snake, the diety Naga Basuki, which is also believed to live in the cave.

EAST BALI

SIDEMEN ROAD

☎ 0366

A less travelled route to Pura Besakih goes northeast from Semarapura, via Sidemen and Iseh, to the Rendang–Amlapura road. The area offers marvellous paddy-field scenery, a delightful rural character and exciting views of Gunung Agung (when the clouds permit). The road is sealed, though decidedly rough in places, and regular bemos shuttle up and down from Semarapura.

Sidemen was a base for Swiss ethnologist Urs Ramseyer, and is also a centre for culture and arts, particularly *endek* cloth and *songket*, which is woven with threads of silver and gold. German artist Walter Spies lived in Iseh for some time from 1932. Later, the Swiss painter Theo Meier, nearly as famous as Spies for his influence on Balinese art, lived in the same house.

Places to Stay & Eat

Pondok Wisata Sidemen (☎ 23009; singles/doubles 200,000/400,000Rp), at the south end of Sideman, has clean, simple rooms with four-poster beds and great views. Accommodation includes an excellent breakfast and dinner of traditional Balinese foods.

Near the centre of Sidemen, a track heads west, signposted with the names of several places to stay, including the following.

Lihat Sawah (☎/fax 24183; singles/doubles with hot water 150,000/175,000Rp), a very friendly place, is also the most affordable. All rooms have views of the valley and mountain, and there's also a **restaurant** (dishes 12,500-25,000Rp).

Sacred Mountain Sanctuary (☎ 24330; ⓦ www.sacredmountainbali.com; villas US$80-130), closer to the river, is a rusticated resort, with a new-age image, a brilliant spring-fed swimming pool and luxurious bamboo villas, which all have open-air bathrooms. The resort has a **restaurant** that specialises in Thai food (dishes 21,000-32,000Rp) and can arrange treks of Gunung Agung (one/two people US$55/40), as well as a range of courses. Massage (US$15 for an hour) is also available.

Another fork in the road takes you to Nirarta (Centre for Living Awareness; ☎ 24122, fax 21444; ⓦ www.awareness-bali.com; Br Tabola, Sideman; singles US$25-50, doubles US$30-55), which conducts programmes for personal and spiritual development, including meditation intensives, but usually welcomes casual visitors in its comfortable bungalows; some are well suited to families and groups.

Patal Kikian (☎/fax 23005; villas per person US$70), several kilometres north of Nirarta, on the eastern side of the Sidemen road, has a steep driveway. They have three spacious, stylishly furnished villas with vast verandas overlooking terraced hillsides to the towering peak of Gunung Agung. The price includes all meals, which are served as private banquets on your own veranda (half-board and breakfast-only rates are also available).

PURA BESAKIH

Perched nearly 1000m up the side of Gunung Agung is Bali's most important temple, Pura Besakih. In fact, it is an extensive complex of 23 separate-but-related temples, with the largest and most important being Pura Penataran Agung. It's most enjoyable during one of the frequent festivals, when hundreds, perhaps thousands, of gorgeously dressed devotees turn up with beautifully arranged offerings. The panoramic view and mountain backdrop are impressive too, but try to arrive early before the mist rolls in, along with the tour buses. A major disappointment for some is that tourists are barred from entering the temples.

The Tourism Fee office can answer basic questions. Well-informed official temple guides will greet you nearby (30,000Rp), and it's worth going with them to add extra insight to the complex.

History

The precise origins of Pura Besakih are not totally clear, but it almost certainly dates from prehistoric times. The stone bases of Pura Penataran Agung and several other temples resemble megalithic stepped pyramids, which date back at least 2000 years. There are legendary accounts of Sri Dangkyang Markendaya conducting meditation and ceremonies here in the 8th century AD, while stone inscriptions record a Hindu ritual on the site in AD 1007. There are some indications of Buddhist activity, but it was certainly used as a Hindu place of worship from 1284, when the first Javanese conquerors settled on Bali, and this is confirmed by accounts from the time of the Majapahit conquest in 1343. By the 15th century, Besakih had become a state temple of the Gelgel dynasty.

PURA BESAKIH COMPLEX

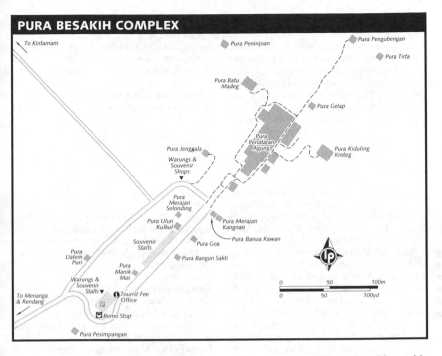

To Kintamani

Pura Peninjoan

Pura Pengubengan

Pura Tirta

Pura Batu Madeg

Pura Gelap

Pura Penataran Agung

Pura Jenggala

Warungs & Souvenir Shops

Pura Kiduling Kreteg

Pura Merajan Selonding

Pura Ulun Kulkul

Pura Merajan Kangnan

Pura Banua Kawan

Souvenir Stalls

Pura Goa

Pura Dalem Puri

Pura Manik Mas

Pura Bangun Sakti

Warungs & Souvenir Stalls

To Menanga & Rendang

Tourist Fee Office

Bemo Stop

Pura Pesimpangan

The central temple was added to over the years, and additional temples were built for specific family, occupational and regional groups. The complex was neglected during the colonial period, perhaps because of lack of royal patronage, and was virtually destroyed in the 1917 earthquake. The Dutch assisted with its reconstruction, and the dependent rajahs were encouraged to support the maintenance of the temples.

Entrance

Entry to Besakih is 3100Rp *(camera 1000Rp, car park 500Rp)*. If you don't have a sarong, you'll have to rent one, though long pants or a long skirt are considered modest enough, as temple entry is forbidden to tourists. The best time to come is at about 8am, before the souvenir stalls open and the tourist buses start to unload their passengers.

Pura Penataran Agung

This is the central temple of the complex – in significance, if not exactly in position. It is built on six levels, terraced up the slope, with the entrance approached from below, up a flight of steps. This entrance is an imposing

split gateway *(candi bentar)*, and beyond it, the even more impressive *kori agung* is the gateway to the second courtyard.

Tourists are not permitted inside, so for the best view, climb the steps to the left of the main entrance and follow the path around the western side. From here, you can just see over the wall into the second courtyard (don't climb up on the wall), where the *padmasana* is. In most modern temples this is a single throne for the supreme god, but Besakih stresses the Hindu trinity, and it has a triple throne called *padmasana tiga,* or *padmasana trisakti,* with separate seats for Brahma, Vishnu and Shiva. This point is the spiritual centre of the temple, and indeed, of the whole Besakih complex.

Continuing on the footpath around the temple, you can see quite a few imposing *meru*, the multiroofed towers through which gods can descend to earth, but otherwise the temple is unspectacular. The upper courtyards are usually empty, even during festivals. One of the best views is from the path at the northeastern end, where you can look down past the many towers and over the temple to the sea.

EAST BALI

Other Temples

None of the other temples is striking, except when decorated for festivals, but each one has a particular significance, sometimes in conjunction with other temples. The Hindu trinity *(trimurti)* is represented by the combination of Pura Penataran Agung as Shiva, Pura Kiduling Kreteg as Brahma and Pura Batu Madeg as Vishnu. Just as each village on Bali has a *pura puseh* (temple of origin), *pura desa* (village temple) and *pura dalem* (temple of the dead), Pura Besakih has three temples that fulfil these roles for Bali as a whole – Pura Basukian, Pura Penataran Agung and Pura Dalem Puri, respectively.

The Balinese concept of *panca dewata*, which embodies a centre and four cardinal points, is represented by Pura Penataran Agung (the centre), Pura Kiduling Kreteg (south), Pura Batu Madeg (north), Pura Gelap (east) and Pura Ulun Kulkul (west). Each district of Bali is associated with a specific temple at Besakih, and the main temples of Bali are also represented by specific shrines here. Some temples are associated with families descended from the original Gelgel dynasty, and there are shrines and memorials going back many generations. Various craft guilds also have their own temples, notably the metal-workers, whose Pura Ratu Pande is built onto the side of the main temple.

Festivals

Besakih is at its best when a festival is on, and with so many temples and gods represented here, there seems to be one every week or so. Ask at a tourist office anywhere on Bali, and try to identify which part of the Besakih complex will be the focus of attention. The founding of Besakih itself is celebrated at **Bhatara Turun Kabeh**, around the full moon of the 10th lunar month (usually in March and April), when all the gods descend at once. The annual rites at Pura Dalem Puri, usually in January, attract thousands who make offerings for the dead. In addition, each individual temple has its own *odalan,* held annually according to the 210-day *wuku* calendar.

Even more important are the great purification ceremonies of **Panca Wali Krama**, theoretically held every 10 years, and the **Eka Dasa Rudra** held every 100 years. In fact, the exact dates of these festivals are determined after long considerations by priests, and they have not been exactly regular. An Eka Dasa Rudra was held in 1963, but was disrupted by the disastrous eruption of Gunung Agung, and restaged successfully in 1979. The last Panca Wali Krama was in 1999.

Places to Stay & Eat

Lembah Arca *(☎ 23076; singles/doubles 70,000/80,000Rp, with hot water 100,000/125,000Rp)*, about 5km below Besakih, is prettily situated in a valley by a bend in the road. Rooms are clean with valley views from the balconies, but the bathrooms are run-down. The **restaurant** *(dishes 10,000-20,000Rp)* serves Chinese and Indonesian dishes.

There are several inexpensive **warung** around the car park and the approaches to the temple, as well as some pricey places on the approach roads, which do buffet lunches by the tour-busload.

Getting There & Away

The usual route to Besakih is by minibus or bemo from Denpasar (Batubulan) via Semarapura (6000Rp). Ask the driver to take you to the temple entrance, not to the village of Besakih about 1km south of the temple complex. You may want to charter a vehicle (best from southern tourist areas), as public transport is infrequent; make sure you leave the temple by 3pm if you want to return to either Semarapura or Denpasar by bemo. Besakih is a *major* feature on any organised tour of eastern and northern Bali.

GUNUNG AGUNG

Bali's highest and most revered mountain, Gunung Agung is an imposing peak from most of south and east Bali, although it's often obscured by cloud and mist. Most books and maps give its height as 3142m, but some say it lost its top in the 1963 eruption and with subsequent erosion and is now only 3014m. The summit is an oval crater, about 700m across, with its highest point on the western edge above Besakih.

Climbing Agung

It's possible to climb Agung from various directions. The two shortest and most popular routes are from Pura Besakih, on the southwest side of the mountain, or from Pura Pasar Agung, on the southern slopes. The latter route goes to the lower edge of the crater rim (2900m), but you can't make your way from there around to the very highest point. You'll have great views south and east, but you won't be able to see central Bali. If you want to say you've been to the very top, climb from Besakih.

To have the best chance of seeing the view before the clouds form, get to the top before 8am, or preferably before sunrise at about 6am. You'll have to start at night, so plan your climb when there will be some moonlight (for religious reasons, many local guides don't want to do it on the night of the full moon, but a day before or after is OK). Take a strong torch (flashlight), extra batteries, plenty of water (2L per person), snack food, waterproof clothing and a warm jumper. The descent is especially hard on the feet, so you'll appreciate strong shoes or boots (and cut your toenails before you start).

You should take a guide for either route. Before you start, or early in the climb, the guide will stop at a shrine to make an offering and say some prayers. This is a holy mountain and you should show respect. Besides, you will want to have everything going for you.

It's best to climb during the dry season (April to September); July to September are the most reliable months. At other times, the paths can be slippery and dangerous, and you probably won't see anything of the view. Climbing Gunung Agung is not allowed when major religious events are being held at Pura Besakih, which generally includes most of April. No guide will take you up at these times, from either Besakih or Pura Pasar Agung, and there are horror stories about those who defied the ban and came to a sticky end on Gunung Agung.

From Pura Besakih This climb is much tougher than from the south and is only for the very physically fit. For the best chance of a clear view before the clouds close in, you should start at midnight. Allow at least six hours for the climb, and four to five hours for the descent. The starting point is Pura Pengsubengan, northeast of the main temple complex, but it's easy to get lost on the lower trails, so definitely hire a guide. The tourist information office near the car park at Pura Besakih can arrange a guide – the asking rate is about 400,000Rp to 500,000Rp for a group of up to four people. It might, however, be

better to arrange a guide in Muncan or Selat, or with one of the companies in Ubud or south Bali. Near Selat market, **Gung Bawa Trekking** (☎/fax 0366-24379), next door to the police station, charges 500,000Rp per guided group.

From Pura Pasar Agung This route involves the least walking, because Pura Pasar Agung (Agung Market Temple) is high on the southern slopes of the mountain (around 1500m) and can be reached by a sealed road north from Selat. From the temple you can climb to the top in three or four hours, but it's a pretty demanding trek. With or without a guide, you must report to the police station at Selat before you start; if you don't have a guide the police will strongly encourage you to take one.

In Muncan, **Ketut Uriada** (☎ 0812 364 6426) is an experienced guide, who can also arrange accommodation and meals. It's easiest if you have your own car, but he can arrange transport for an extra fee (look for his small sign on the road east of the village). **Gung Bawa Trekking** (☎/fax 0366-24379) in Selat is a reliable operation that charges 400,000Rp per guided group, including food, water and homestay accommodation (alternatively accommodation can be arranged at Pondok Wisata Puri Agung near Selat). **Nengan Kari** (☎ 24336; Jl Gunung Agung 5), based in Selat, has also been recommended by readers, and can arrange pick up and drop off, for an all-inclusive fee of 300,000Rp.

If none of these three is available, ask at the police station in Selat or at nearby **Pondok Wisata Puri Agung** (☎ 0366-23037). Most of the places to stay in the area, including those around Sidemen and Tirta Gangga, will recommend guides for Gunung Agung climbs, but it's more convenient to start from a base nearer the mountain, and the local guides are more experienced. A last resort is to head to Pura Pasar Agung the day before and ask around at the temple – some of the people there know the route, but they won't be able to arrange food or equipment, and they probably won't speak much English. If they let you doss in one of the huts there, a donation to the temple would be appropriate.

It is much better to stay the night near Muncan or Selat (see the following Rendang to Amlapura section), and drive up early in the morning to Pura Pasar Agung. This temple has been greatly enlarged and improved, in part as a monument to the 1963 eruption that devastated this area.

Start climbing from the temple at around 3am. There are numerous trails through the pine forest but after an hour or so you'll climb above the tree line. Then you're climbing on solidified lava, which can be loose and broken in places, but a good guide will keep you on solid ground. At the top, you can gawk into the crater, watch the sun rise over Lombok and see the shadow of Agung in the morning haze over southern Bali.

Allow at least two hours to get back down to the temple. If you don't have a car waiting for you, walk down to Sebudi, from where there are public bemos down to Selat.

RENDANG TO AMLAPURA

A scenic road goes around the southern slopes of Gunung Agung from Rendang to near Amlapura. It runs through some superb countryside, descending more or less gradually as it goes further east. If you have your own wheels, you'll find it very scenic, with some interesting places to stop. It's possible by public bemo, but awkward. Starting from Semarapura, the bemo heads to Menanga, Rendang and Selat (2000Rp). From Selat, either take a bemo to Duda and pick up a bemo for Amlapura from there, or

The 1963 Eruption

The most disastrous volcanic eruption on Bali this century took place in 1963, when Gunung Agung blew its top in no uncertain manner at a time of considerable prophetic and political importance.

Eka Desa Rudra, the greatest of all Balinese sacrifices and an event that only takes place every 100 years on the Balinese calendar, was to culminate on 8 March 1963. It had been well over 100 Balinese years since the last Eka Desa Rudra, but there was dispute among the priests as to the correct and most propitious date.

Naturally, Pura Besakih was a focal point for the festival, but Gunung Agung was acting strangely as final preparations were made in late February. The date of the ceremony was looking decidedly unpropitious, but President Soekarno had already scheduled an international conference of travel agents to witness the great occasion as a highlight of their visit to the country, and he would not allow it to be postponed. By the time the sacrifices began, the mountain was glowing, belching smoke and ash, and rumbling ominously, but Gunung Agung contained itself until the travel agents had flown home.

On 17 March Gunung Agung exploded. The catastrophic eruption killed more than 1000 people (some estimate 2000) and destroyed entire villages – 100,000 people lost their homes. Streams of lava and hot volcanic mud poured right down to the sea at several places, completely covering roads and isolating the eastern end of Bali for some time. The entire island was covered in ash and crops were wiped out everywhere.

Torrential rainfall followed the eruptions, and compounded the damage as boiling hot ash and boulders were swept down the mountainside, wreaking havoc on many villages, including Subagan, just outside Amlapura, and Selat, further along the road towards Rendang. The whole of Bali suffered a drastic food shortage, and many Balinese were resettled in western Bali and Sulawesi.

Although Pura Besakih is high on the slopes of Gunung Agung, only about 6km from the crater, the temple suffered little damage from the eruption. Volcanic dust and gravel flattened timber and bamboo buildings around the temple complex, but the stone structures came through unscathed. The inhabitants of the village of Lebih, also high up on Gunung Agung's slopes, were all but wiped out. Most of the people killed at the time of the eruption were burnt and suffocated by searing clouds of hot gas that rushed down the volcano's slopes. Agung erupted again on 16 May, with serious loss of life, although not on the same scale as the March eruption.

The Balinese take signs and portents seriously – that such a terrible event should happen as they were making a most important sacrifice to the gods was not taken lightly. Soekarno's political demise two years later, following the failed Communist coup, could be seen as a consequence of his defiance of the volcanic deity's power. The interrupted series of sacrifices finally recommenced 16 years later in 1979.

pick up one that goes straight through from Selat. You can do it in either direction, but by bicycle it's better going eastward.

Starting from the west, **Rendang** is an attractive town, easily reached by bemo from Semarapura or via the very pretty, minor road from Bangli. Approximately 4km along a winding road, the old-fashioned village of **Muncan** has quaint shingle roofs. East of Muncan, the road passes through some of the prettiest rice country on Bali before reaching **Selat**, where you turn north for Pura Pasar Agung, the starting point for the easiest route up Gunung Agung. **Pondok Wisata Puri Agung** (*☎ 0366-23037; singles/ doubles 100,000/150,000Rp*) is on the road between Selat and Duda. It has clean and comfortable rooms, although the service can be erratic and staff may even be absent when you arrive.

Further on is **Duda**, where another scenic route branches southwest via Sidemen to Semarapura (see the Sidemen Road section earlier). Further east, a side road (about 800m) leads to **Putung**, where **Bukit Putung Resort** (*☎ 0366-23039*) has wonderful views down the southern slopes to the coast. It's a good stop for a snack or drink. This area is superb for **hiking**: there's an easy-to-follow track from Putung to **Manggis**, about 8km down the hill.

Continuing east, **Sibetan** is famous for growing *salak,* the delicious fruit with a curious 'snakeskin' covering – you can buy *salak* from roadside stalls. Nearby, a poorly signposted road leads north to Jungutan with its **Tirta Telaga Tista** – a decorative pool and garden complex built for the water-loving old Rajah of Karangasem.

The scenic road finishes at Bebandem, where there's a **cattle market** every three days, and plenty of other stuff for sale as well. Bebandem and several nearby villages are home to members of the traditional metal-workers caste, which includes silversmiths as well as blacksmiths.

Homestay Lila (*singles/doubles 30,000/ 50,000Rp*), in **Abian Soan** further east, is family-run with a friendly atmosphere and basic rooms. It's a good place to base yourself for walks around the area, and you can arrange a guide here (see Around Tirta Gangga, later in this chapter, for information about this area). The homestay also organises trips to Bebandem cattle market.

PADANGBAI
☎ 0363

On a perfect bay lined with colourful *prahu* and picturesque views of Nusa Penida, Padangbai is the port for Bali–Lombok ferries and passenger boats to Nusa Penida. A popular travellers' stop, offering excellent diving and snorkelling, and walks to nearby beaches, it has a relaxed ambience, added to by the main street's unpaved road and the exuberance of local children swimming at the eastern end of the beach. The quiet is punctuated only by the blare of horns and the ripple of activity as ferries arrive and depart.

Information

A number of unofficial tourist information booths operate in the harbour area and there's a **wartel** on the main street. Made's Homestay has an **Internet café** (*350Rp per minute*) and can also organise transport. **Ozone Cafe** also has the **Internet. Moneychangers** at hotels and along the main street offer rates slightly lower than in the south Bali tourist resorts – check the rates at **Bank BRI** first. **Ryan Shop** (*Jl Segara 38*), a book exchange, has a fair selection of second-hand paperbacks, as well as a few new books and maps.

Geko Dive is active in the local community in plastic recycling projects, as well as raising the standard and accessibility of health care and education to locals. Donations to this cause are welcome. (See the following Things to See & Do section for details)

Female travellers will notice a change in attitude towards women here (more commonly on Lombok), especially around the ferry terminal area. Expect snide remarks and unwanted stares.

Things to See & Do

If you walk southwest from the ferry terminal and follow the trail up the hill, you'll soon come to idyllic **Bias Tugal**, also called Pantai Kecil (Little Beach), on the exposed coast outside the bay. Be very careful in the water, which is subject to strong currents. There are a couple of daytime **warung** here.

On a headland at the northeastern corner of the bay, a path uphill leads to three **temples**, including Pura Silayukti where Empu Kuturan – who introduced the caste system to Bali in the 11th century – is said to have lived. On the other side of this headland is another small, sandy beach.

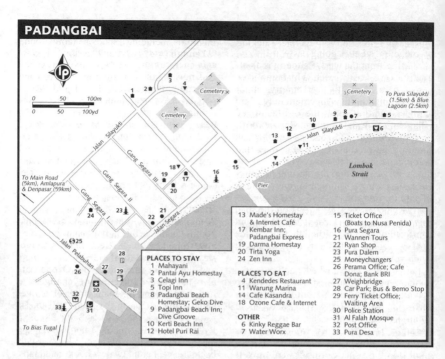

PADANGBAI

To Pura Silayukti (1.5km) & Blue Lagoon (2.5km)

Lombok Strait

To Main Road (5km), Amlapura & Denpasar (59km)

To Bias Tugal

PLACES TO STAY
1 Mahayani
2 Pantai Ayu Homestay
3 Celagi Inn
5 Topi Inn
8 Padangbai Beach Homestay; Geko Dive
9 Padangbai Beach Inn; Dive Groove
10 Kerti Beach Inn
12 Hotel Puri Rai
13 Made's Homestay & Internet Café
17 Kembar Inn; Padangbai Express
19 Darma Homestay
20 Tirta Yoga
24 Zen Inn

PLACES TO EAT
4 Kendedes Restaurant
11 Warung Marina
14 Cafe Kasandra
18 Ozone Cafe & Internet

OTHER
6 Kinky Reggae Bar
7 Water Worx
15 Ticket Office (Boats to Nusa Penida)
16 Pura Segara
21 Wannen Tours
22 Ryan Shop
23 Pura Dalem
25 Moneychangers
26 Perama Office; Cafe Dona; Bank BRI
27 Weighbridge
28 Car Park; Bus & Bemo Stop
29 Ferry Ticket Office; Waiting Area
30 Police Station
31 Al Falah Mosque
32 Post Office
33 Pura Desa

Diving There's some pretty good diving on the coral reefs around Padangbai, but the water can be a little cold and visibility is not always ideal. The most popular local dives are **Blue Lagoon** and **Teluk Jepun** (Jepun Bay), both in Teluk Amuk, the bay just east of Padangbai. There's a good variety of soft and hard corals and varied marine life, including sharks, turtles and wrasse, and a 40m wall at the Blue Lagoon.

Several good local outfits offer diving trips in the area, including Gili Tepekong and Biaha, and on to Tulamben and Nusa Penida. All dive prices are competitive, costing US$40 to US$70 for two boat dives, depending on the site, and courses ranging from PADI open-water course (around US$280) to dive master. Dive instructors at all three schools are German- and English-speakers.

The longest established operator is **Geko Dive** (☎ 41516, fax 41790; ⓦ www.geko dive.com; Padangbai Beach Homestay).

Water Worx (☎ 41220, fax 41462; ⓦ www .waterworxbali.com; Jl Silayukti) is the newest dive operator on the scene.

Dive Groove (☎ 8123 989 746; ⓦ www .divinggroove.com; Padangbai Beach Inn; Jl Silayukti) offers a fish briefing before heading into the water.

Snorkelling One of the best and most accessible walk-in snorkel sites is **Blue Lagoon**, which can be reached by walking east on Jl Silayukti and following the signs (note that it is subject to strong currents when the tide is out). Other sites such as Teluk Jepun can be reached by local boat (or check with the dive operators to see if they have any room on their dive boats). Snorkel sets cost about 20,000Rp per day.

Boating & Fishing Local *jukung* (boats) offer snorkelling (bring your own snorkelling gear) and fishing trips around Padangbai (120,000Rp), and as far away as Nusa Lembongan (200,000Rp) for two passengers. These are advertised on boards around the village, or ask your hotel what's on offer. Alternatively, a small fibreglass glass-bottom boat can be hired for snorkelling or fishing (with professional fishing equipment); book at **Geko Dive** (☎ 41516, fax 41790; ⓦ www.gekodive.com; Padangbai Beach Homestay).

EAST BALI

Places to Stay

Most accommodation is desperately lacking in personality in Padangbai (apart from Zen Inn), not to mention water views, but cleanliness is at least a common denominator. Most are also in the budget category. Hotel Puri Rai is the only place with a pool.

In the village, there are several tiny places in the alleys, some with a choice of small, cheap downstairs rooms or bigger, brighter upstairs rooms. Including **Darma Homestay** (☎ 41394; **e** putungeres@hotmail.com; Gang Segara III; rooms 40,000-60,000Rp), **Kembar Inn** (☎/fax 41364; singles/doubles with fan 70,000/85,000Rp, with air-con and hot water 150,000Rp), which both have basic rooms, while the friendly **Tirta Yoga** (Gang Segara III; rooms 30,000Rp) has very simple rooms. **Made's Homestay** (☎ 41441; Jl Silayukti; rooms 70,000-80,000Rp) has clean rooms that are in need of a paint job. Among the best is **Mahayani** (Gang Luhur 6; singles/doubles 25,000/30,000Rp), a friendly little place where three rooms are set around a stone temple shrine.

Celagi Inn (☎ 41505; rooms 60,000-75,000Rp), away from the beach and on three levels, has pleasant rooms with private balconies. The top floor is a communal area with ocean views.

Hotel Puri Rai (☎ 41385, fax 41386; Jl Silayukti 3; rooms 150,000Rp, with air-con 250,000Rp) is the most upmarket option in town. Shady fan rooms in a double-storey stone building, pleasantly facing the pool, are the best option, while the air-con rooms have a charming view of the grubby driveway.

Kerti Beach Inn (☎ 41391; Jl Silayukti; singles 30,000/50,000Rp, doubles 80,000/100,000Rp) and **Padangbai Beach Inn** (☎ 41517; rooms 60,000-100,000Rp) both have rice-barn style two-storey cottages, with a bathroom downstairs and an oppressively hot, boxy bedroom upstairs.

Pantai Ayu Homestay (☎ 41396; rooms 40,000-60,000Rp), away from the beach, has small rooms and a pleasant restaurant with water views.

Padangbai Beach Homestay (☎ 41516, 0812 360 7946, fax 41790; Jl Silayukti; singles/doubles 95,000/125,000Rp) has gorgeous new bungalows, with open-air bathrooms, in a classic Balinese garden setting.

Topi Inn (☎ 41424; Jl Silayukti; rooms 35,000Rp, family room 150,000Rp), at the end of the bay, is in a serene location with pleasant rooms, including a spacious family room.

Zen Inn (☎ 41418; Gang Segara 1; singles/doubles 50,000/70,000Rp), closest to the ferry terminal, is a new place where each room is eclectically designed and decorated, with a heavy emphasis on kitsch.

Places to Eat & Drink

Don't expect anything gourmand in Padangbai. Eating out is to stave off hunger, and not much else! Most of the places to stay have a restaurant, and a few have occasional entertainment as well – mainly video nights or sports telecasts. The beachfront restaurants on Jl Segara and Jl Silayukti have similar menus and prices, harbour views during the day and cool breezes in the evening.

Warung Marina (mains 10,000-25,000Rp; Jl Silayukti), right on the water's edge, has breezy views and serves tasty basic dishes and cheap beers. Another reasonable place is **Cafe Kasandra** (dishes 8000-25,000Rp), a deliciously low-key place overlooking the water, which is ideal to kick back in the afternoon with a drink and soak up the sea breezes. Bubur ayam (rice porridge with vegetables and chicken) is worth trying.

Ozone Cafe (☎ 41501; dishes 19,000-23,000Rp) is a popular travellers gathering spot at night, with walls covered in mildly amusing Indolish graffiti. Its menu of pizza, pasta and Indonesian dishes is pricey compared to elsewhere in Padangbai, but beers are cheapish. Back from the beach, **Kendedes Restaurant** (dishes 8000-10,000Rp) is also worth a try.

Kinky Reggae Bar, run by typically long-haired, guitar-toting local lads, sets up on the eastern end of the beach in the late afternoon and is a fine spot for a sunset tipple.

The walls of Zen Inn's **bar/restaurant** (☎ 41418; Gang Segara 1; dishes 15,000-25,000Rp) are covered in painted cinema posters. Beers are cheap (small/large Bintang 6000/11,000Rp) and wood-fired pizza is an option.

Getting There & Away

Bemo Padangbai is 2km south of the main Semarapura–Amlapura road. Bemos leave from the car park in front of the port – orange bemos go east through Candidasa to Amlapura (3000Rp); blue or white bemos go to Semarapura (5000Rp).

Bus Several buses travel daily between Denpasar (Batubulan terminal) and Padangbai (4000Rp). These are theoretically timed to connect with ferries to Lombok, but don't depend on it. Buses also pass through Padangbai on the way to Surabaya (100,000Rp) and Yogyakarta (135,000Rp) on Java. You can buy tickets at **Wannen Tours** (☎ 41287, Jl Segara).

Tourist Shuttle Bus Situated in a complex with Cafe Dona and Bank BRI, **Perama** (☎ 41419; Café Dona, Jl Pelabuhan) stops here on trips around the east coast. Services include three buses daily each to Kuta or Sanur (30,000Rp), Ubud (20,000Rp) and Candidasa (10,000Rp); two daily to Lovina (60,000Rp), and one to Tirta Gangga (30,000Rp) and Tulamben (40,000Rp). Perama, and a few other agencies along the esplanade, also organise services to Lombok, including Senggigi (75,000Rp), from where you can get a connection to the Gili islands (40,000Rp). Alternatively, buy your own ferry ticket and organise Lombok connections when you arrive on Lombok.

Boat
Lombok Daily public ferries travel nonstop between Padangbai and Lembar (10,000Rp, 3½ hours, every 1½ hours). Motorcycles cost 25,000Rp and cars cost 173,000Rp – go through the weighbridge at the west corner of the car park. Food and drink is sold on board.

Anyone who carries your luggage on or off the ferry will expect to be paid, so agree on the price first or carry your own stuff – the luggage porters here have a reputation (perhaps undeserved) as being aggressive. Expect more hassle at Lembar.

The **Padangbai Express** (☎ 0361-755260; e pbxpress@indosat.net.id) departs for Lembar twice daily (75,000Rp, 90 minutes, 9.30am and 2pm). A travel agent next to the Kembar Inn sells tickets.

Nusa Penida On the beach just east of the car park you'll find the twin-engine fibreglass boats that run across the strait to Nusa Penida (25,000Rp, one hour, 7am and noon). The inconspicuous ticket office is nearby.

PADANGBAI TO CANDIDASA
It's 11km along the main road from the Padangbai turn-off to the beach resort of Candidasa, and there are bemos or buses every few minutes. Between the two is an attractive stretch of coast, which has some tourist development and a large oil storage depot in Teluk Amuk.

After about 4km, beyond the turn-off to the pretty village of **Manggis**, a discreetly marked side road leads to the exclusive **Amankila** (☎ 41333, fax 41555; w www.amankila.com; suites US$600-1400). It features an isolated seaside location and understated architecture – classically simple rectangular structures with thatched roofs and lots of natural wood and stone. The three main swimming pools step down into the sea, in matching shades of blue. Nonguests can visit the **Terrace** (lunch around US$40) or **The Restaurant** (dinner around US$60), but call first. The 'Beachclub' pool (150,000Rp) is also open to nonguests.

Buitan (Balina Beach)
☎ 0363
Balina Beach is the name bestowed on the small tourist development at the village of Buitan. It's an attractive area on a quiet coastal stretch, though the beach is being lost to erosion and what's left is black sand and stones. To find the turn-off, look for the small yellow sign 'Balina' from the main road.

A couple of diving operations here are handy to dive sites off southeastern Bali – try **Spicedive** (☎ 41725, fax 41001; w www.damai.com/spicedive) at Balina Beach Resort.

Places to Stay & Eat Near Balina Beach Resort, **Lumbung Damuh** (☎/fax 41553; e tania@ionker.com; Jl Pantai; cottages 150,000-350,000Rp) is a deliciously low-key place right beside the water. There are only a few lumbungs (traditional rice-barn dwellings) on the small site, and all are very comfortable with outdoor bathrooms, inviting interiors and views.

Balina Beach Resort (☎ 41002, fax 41001; e balina@denpasar.wasantara.net.id; singles/doubles US$35/45) has pretty gardens and a pool facing the black-sand beach. Rooms are pleasant, and all have hot water.

The Serai (☎ 41011, fax 41015; w www.ghmhotels.com; rooms US$180-310), east of Balina Beach Resort, has elegant, white thatch-roofed buildings in spacious lawn gardens facing a beautiful stretch of secluded beach. Rooms are very comfortable, with smart modern interiors. The restaurant features excellent nouvelle Bali cuisine, and offers a well-regarded, if pricey, cooking course (see Courses in the Facts for the Visitor chapter). The Serai also has a **Mandara Spa** on the grounds by the beach.

There are several small cafés near Lumbung Damuh, including **Nyoman Café** and **Warung Made**. Car rental is also possible from the cafés.

Mendira & Sengkidu

Coming from the west, there are hotels and *losmen* (basic accommodation) off the main road at Mendira and Sengkidu, several kilometres before you reach Candidasa. For most of these places, get a bemo that will stop at Sengkidu – look for the turn-off with signs to the hotels. The beach has suffered badly from erosion, and somewhat unsightly sea walls have been constructed.

Homestay Dewi Utama (☎ 41053; rooms with bath 70,000Rp), a friendly little place, offers seclusion and basic accommodation.

Pondok Pisang (☎ 41065; singles 80,000-250,000Rp, doubles 100,000-350,000Rp), just west of the Homestay Dewi Utama, is a wonderful alternative, with five, spacious bungalows, set apart, facing the sea. Each bungalow has a unique interior, including mosaic-tiled

---

The Legend of Tenganan

There's a delightful legend about how the villagers of Tenganan came to acquire their land. The story pops up in various places in Indonesia, but in slightly different forms.

The Tenganan version relates how Dalem Bedaulu lost a valuable horse. When the villagers of Tenganan found the carcass, the king offered them a reward. They asked that they be given the land where the horse was found – that is, the entire area where the dead horse could be smelled.

The king sent a man with a keen nose who set off with the village chief and walked an enormous distance without ever managing to get away from the foul odour. Eventually accepting that enough was enough, the official headed back to Bedaulu, scratching his head. Once out of sight, the village chief pulled a large hunk of dead horse out from under his clothes.

---

bathrooms. Yoga intensives are held here in August in a *bale* facing the ocean.

Near the Candi Beach Cottages, **Amarta Beach Inn Bungalows** (☎ 41230; singles/ doubles 65,000/70,000Rp) has a gorgeous location and friendly atmosphere, and is good value, although it's looking a bit tumbledown these days.

Nirwana Cottages (☎ 41136, fax 41543; singles US$30-40, doubles US$40-60), about 1km west of the start of Candidasa, down a long driveway, is delightful with only 12 rooms in a quiet location. The less expensive rooms are without air-con, the mid-range rooms have leafy outdoor bathrooms, while the deluxe rooms are split level and more spacious.

There are a couple of cheap **warung** in the main street, including **Bintang Restoran**, part of Homestay Dewi Utama, but you'll probably end up eating at your hotel or another one nearby.

Tenganan

Tenganan is a village of Bali Aga people, the descendants of the original Balinese who inhabited Bali before the Majapahit arrival. The village is surrounded by a wall, and consists basically of two rows of identical houses stretching up the gentle slope of the hill. The Bali Aga are reputed to be exceptionally conservative and resistant to change, but even here the modern age has not been totally held at bay – a small forest of TV aerials sprouts from those oh-so-traditional houses. The most striking feature of Tenganan, however, is its exceptional neatness, with the hills providing a beautiful backdrop. As you enter the village you'll be greeted by a guide who will take you on a tour of the village (and generally lead you back to their family compound to look at textiles and *lontar* palm strips), however, there's no pressure to buy anything.

A peculiar, old-fashioned version of the gamelan known as the gamelan *selunding* is still played here, and girls dance an equally ancient dance known as the Rejang. There are other Bali Aga villages nearby, including **Tenganan Dauh Tenkad**, 1.5km west off the Tenganan road, with a charming old-fashioned ambience and several weaving workshops. At **Asak**, southeast of Tenganan, another ancient instrument, the gamelan *gambang*, is still played.

Festivals Tenganan is full of unusual customs, festivals and practices. At the month-long **Usaba Sambah Festival**, which usually starts in May or June, men fight with sticks wrapped in thorny pandanus leaves – similar events occur on the island of Sumba, far to the east in Nusa Tenggara. At this same festival, small, hand-powered Ferris wheels are brought out and the village girls are ceremonially twirled around.

Shopping A magical cloth known as *kamben gringsing* is woven here – a person wearing it is said to be protected against black magic. Traditionally this is made using the 'double ikat' technique, in which both the warp and weft threads are resist dyed before being woven. It's very time-consuming, and the pieces of double ikat available for sale are quite expensive (from about 600,000Rp). Other interesting textiles are sold here – some are handmade by local craftswomen, but much comes from other parts of Bali and Indonesia. Many locally made baskets are on sale, made from *ata* palm. Another local craft is traditional Balinese calligraphy, with the script inscribed onto *lontar* palm strips, in the same way that ancient *lontar* books were created. Most of these *lontar* books are Balinese calendars or depictions of the *Ramayana* epic. They cost 150,000Rp to 400,000Rp, depending on quality.

Getting There & Away Tenganan is 4km up a side road just west of Candidasa. At the turn-off, a posse of motorcycle riders offer *ojek* rides to the village for about 5000Rp. Otherwise, wait at the turn-off for an infrequent bemo (1000Rp). A nice option is to take an *ojek* up to Tenganan, and enjoy a shady downhill walk back to the main road.

CANDIDASA
☎ 0363

Until the 1970s, Candidasa was a just a quiet little fishing village, then beachside losmen and restaurants sprang up and suddenly it was *the* new beach place on Bali. As the facilities developed, the beach eroded – unthinkingly, offshore barrier-reef corals were harvested to produce lime for cement for the orgy of construction that took place – and by the late 1980s Candidasa was a beach resort with no beach.

Mining stopped in 1991 and concrete sea walls and groins have limited the erosion, and now provide some sandy swimming spots, but it's not your typical, tropical stretch of golden-sand beach. Still, the relaxed seaside ambience, where many of the hotels are built right on the water appeals to a more sedate, often older crowd of travellers – compare Candidasa with hanging out in a *bale* by the ocean in Gili Trawangan, for example, and it just doesn't cut it. Even

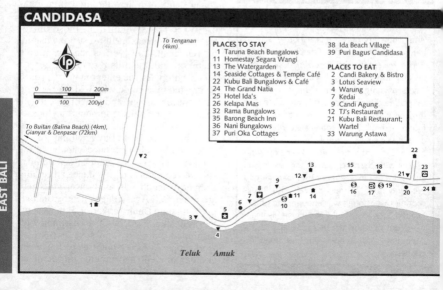

CANDIDASA

To Tenganan (4km)

0   100   200m
0   100   200yd

To Buitan (Balina Beach) (4km),
Gianyar & Denpasar (72km)

PLACES TO STAY
1 Taruna Beach Bungalows
11 Homestay Segara Wangi
13 The Watergarden
14 Seaside Cottages & Temple Café
22 Kubu Bali Bungalows & Café
24 The Grand Natia
25 Hotel Ida's
26 Kelapa Mas
32 Rama Bungalows
35 Barong Beach Inn
36 Nani Bungalows
37 Puri Oka Cottages
38 Ida Beach Village
39 Puri Bagus Candidasa

PLACES TO EAT
2 Candi Bakery & Bistro
3 Lotus Seaview
4 Warung
7 Kedai
9 Candi Agung
12 TJ's Restaurant
21 Kubu Bali Restaurant;
   Wartel
33 Warung Astawa

Teluk   Amuk

EAST BALI

if it is lacking in travellers' street-cred, it's still a good base from which to explore the interior of east Bali and the east coast's famous diving and snorkelling sites. Another downside of Candidasa is its position on a major road.

Information

The Candidasa **tourist office** *(open 8am-2pm Mon-Sat)* has some brochures and maps. Easily found along the main street are **postal agencies**, **wartels** and **moneychangers**. A Bank BNI ATM is opposite Foto Asri on the main drag, while the **Regional Development Bank of Bali** *(open 9am-1pm Mon-Fri)* will change travellers cheques. There are plenty of Internet options around, including **Safari Internet**, next door to Foto Asri, and **Happy Internet**. A small tourist/expat newsletter *Suara Candidasa*, published by Taruna Beach Bungalows, is available from many hotels, and is a useful source of cultural and event information.

Ashram Gandhi Chandi *(☎/fax 41108; e gandhiashram@yahoo.com)*, a community by the lagoon, follows the pacifist teachings of Mahatma Gandhi. Guests are welcome to stay for short or extended periods, but are expected to participate in the life of the community, including waking early for daily yoga practice. Simple guest cottages are by the ocean, and payment is by donation.

Dewi Spa *(Jl Raya Candidasa; open 9am-9pm)* is a pleasant enough massage treatment spa that specialises in papaya scrubs. You should expect to be smeared all over with freshly pureed fruit!

Things to See & Do

Candidasa's temple, **Pura Candidasa** *(entry by donation)*, is on the hillside across from the lagoon at the eastern end of the village strip. The fishing village, just beyond the lagoon, has colourful *prahu* drawn up on what's left of the beach. In the early morning you can watch the boats coasting in after a night's fishing. The owners canvas visitors for **snorkelling trips** to the reef and the nearby islets.

The main road east of Candidasa spirals up to **Pura Gamang Pass** *(gamang* means 'to get dizzy') from where there are fine **views** down to the coast. If you follow the coastline from Candidasa towards Amlapura, a trail climbs up over the headland, with fine views over the rocky islets off the coast. Beyond this headland there's a long sweep of wide, exposed black-sand beach. Further east, turn right at Perasi (about 6km from Candidasa) to reach **Pasir Putih**, a pretty white-sand beach.

Apart from the Bali Aga village of Tenganan, there are several traditional villages inland from Candidasa and attractive countryside for walking.

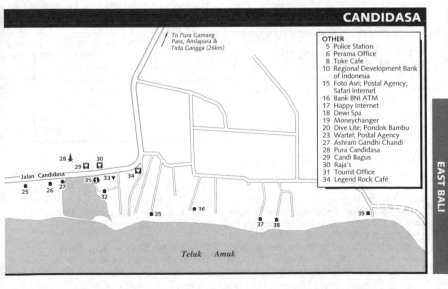

CANDIDASA

To Pura Gamang Pass, Amlapura & Tirta Gangga (26km)

OTHER
5 Police Station
6 Perama Office
8 Toke Cafe
10 Regional Development Bank of Indonesia
15 Foto Asri; Postal Agency; Safari Internet
16 Bank BNI ATM
17 Happy Internet
18 Dewi Spa
19 Moneychanger
20 Dive Lite; Pondok Bambu
23 Wartel; Postal Agency
27 Ashram Gandhi Chandi
28 Pura Candidasa
29 Candi Bagus
30 Raja's
31 Tourist Office
34 Legend Rock Café

Jalan Candidasa

Teluk   Amuk

EAST BALI

Diving & Snorkelling Gili Tepekong, which has a series of coral heads at the top of a sheer drop-off, is perhaps the best dive site. It offers the chance to see lots of fish, including some larger marine life. Other features include an underwater canyon, which can be dived in good conditions, but is always potentially hazardous. The currents here are strong and unpredictable, the water is cold and visibility is variable – it's recommended for experienced divers only.

Other dive sites are beside Gili Mimpang, further east at Gili Bahia, and Nusa Penida. A recommended dive operator is **Dive Lite** (☎ 41660, fax 41661; ⓦ www.divelite.com) opposite Kubu Bali, which dives Tulamben, Amed, Nusa Penida/Lembongan and Menjangan (US$55-75 for two dives). A four-day PADI Open Water Course is US$360. Snorkelling tours are US$25. Several other dive shops operate in Candidasa.

Hotels and shops along the main road rent snorkel sets for about 20,000Rp per day. For the best snorkelling, take a boat to offshore sites or to Gili Mimpang (a one-hour boat trip should cost about 80,000-100,000Rp for up to three people).

Places to Stay

Candidasa's main street is well supplied with seaside accommodation, as well as restaurants and other tourist facilities. More relaxed, but less convenient, are the places east of the lagoon, hidden among the palm trees near the original fishing village.

Places to Stay – Budget

Taruna Beach Bungalows (☎ 41823; ⓔ taruna_bungalows@hotmail.com; rooms 35,000-80,000Rp), west of the town centre, has themed rooms – the gecko room, the fish room, the dolphin room etc. It's all a bit cheesy and lacking in Balinese style, but rooms are clean and OK value. Tax is not included.

Homestay Segara Wangi (☎ 41159; singles/doubles 40,000/60,000Rp) is a small-scale place that's pleasant enough, although its bathrooms have seen better days.

The clean **Seaside Cottages & Temple Café** (☎ 41629; ⓦ www.bali_seafront_bungalows.com; singles 30,000-65,000Rp, doubles 45,000-80,000Rp, sea-view singles with hot-water 130,000-200,00Rp, doubles 145,000-230,000Rp) is a well-run place, with homey

touches. At low tide, a small beach surfaces just in front of the hotel. Breakfast is not included. The **café** (dishes 12,000-28,000Rp) has meals for homesick travellers.

Hotel Ida's (☎/fax 41096; bungalows 80,000-100,000Rp), set in a shady, rambling seaside garden, has thatched bungalows with open-air bathrooms. Rustic balcony furniture, including a daybed, make relaxing that much easier!

Rama Bungalows (☎ 41778; singles/doubles from 35,000/40,000Rp) by the lotus-filled lagoon is a double-storey stone structure of red temple design. Upstairs rooms have views of the lagoon, while downstairs rooms have open-air bathrooms.

Barong Beach Inn (☎ 41137; singles/doubles 35,000/50,000Rp) and **Nani Bungalows** (☎ 41829; singles/doubles 70,000/90,000Rp), right by the beach, are quiet, laid-back and good choices. Nani Bungalows is blessed with a beach at low tide.

Places to Stay – Mid-Range

The Grand Natia (☎ 42007, fax 41889; ⓔ hotelnatia@yahoo.com; Jl Candidasa; rooms US$70, pool view US$80) is a swish, modern hotel resembling a modern water palace – elegant pathways are lined with waterways teeming with carp. Each room has air-con and an open-air bathroom. The small pool drops away to an gorgeous ocean view. The hotel also has a smart **restaurant** (dishes 12,000-75,000Rp).

Kelapa Mas (☎ 41369, fax 41947; ⓦ www.welcome.to/kelapamas; rooms US$10-20, with hot water US$25-30), a relaxing hideaway, deserves its name – the grounds are filled with tall coconut palms. Bamboo rooms with lounging verandas are set in lush gardens, with even a little sand on the seashore.

Puri Oka Cottages (☎ 41092; rooms US$15-40) has small, boxy cheaper rooms, and tastefully decorated rooms with water views. The pool is looking a little tired, but there's a small beach out the front at low tide.

Ida Beach Village (☎ 41118, fax 41041; bungalow US$55-60) has pleasantly decorated, Balinese rice-barn style bungalows, each with a private garden. There's also a seaside swimming pool.

Places to Stay – Top End

The Watergarden (☎ 41540; ⓦ www.watergardenhotel.com; rooms US$70-85, 2-bedroom *suites US$160)* is a delightfully different place, with a swimming pool and fish-filled ponds that wind around the buildings and through the lovely garden. The design has a Japanese influence, and each room has a veranda projecting over the lily ponds.

Kubu Bali Bungalows *(☎ 41532, fax 41531; singles US$50-60, doubles US$55-65)*, behind Kubu restaurant, has beautifully finished individual bungalows. Streams, ponds and a swimming pool are landscaped into the steep hillside, with views over palm trees, the coast and the sea. You'll have to climb a bit to get to your room (so it's only for the fit). Breakfast is not included. There's also a café by the pool with wonderful views.

Puri Bagus Candidasa *(☎ 41131, fax 41 290; e pbcandi@denpasar.wasantara.net.id; rooms US$115-135)*, at the eastern end of the beach, is a handsome beachfront hotel hidden away in the palm trees in very grand grounds. A sandy beach area set up with cabanas is by the pool and restaurant. Rooms are pleasant, all with open-air bathrooms and air-con, although there's no wow factor.

Places to Eat

The food in Candidasa is a vast improvement on Padangbai's meagre offerings, although there's plenty of dross around as well. Many of the hotels have seafront restaurants that are lovely at lunchtime and idyllic in the early evening, although the food in restaurant hotels is generally hit and miss. One such place is **Pondok Bambu** *(☎ 41534; dishes 17,000-30,000Rp)*.

Other restaurants are dotted along Jl Raya Candidasa, and the traffic noise can be particularly unpleasant, although it improves after dark. Among the cheapest and tastiest eateries are the **warung** and **kaki lima** (food carts) that spring up every evening (and to a lesser extent during the day) at the western end of town where the main road almost crashes into the sea. If you're staying at the eastern end of Candidasa, you can easily walk to the main road for meals (although the area is unlit at night) or try any of the warung clustered outside the hotels in the area – there are several.

Candi Bakery & Bistro *(☎ 41883; Jl Tenganan; dishes 10,000-21,000Rp)*, about 50m up from the Tenganan turn-off is a real find. The tiny bakery specialises in delicious authentic German pastries and cakes (worth stocking up on!), coffee and simple hot Indonesian dishes.

Lotus Seaview *(☎ 41257; dishes 22,000-50,000Rp)*, one of the Bali-wide chain of restaurants, has a wonderful ocean outlook.

Kedai *(☎ 42020; mains 28,000-53,000Rp)*, in a gorgeous open-air pavilion under a high conical thatched roof, is no doubt one of Candidasa's best restaurants and even rivals restaurants in Ubud. The service is excellent as are the mouth-watering array of dishes, such as crispy Balinese crab cakes. Worth trying also is the four-course tasting menu (75,000Rp).

Candi Agung *(☎ 41672; dishes 17,500-35,000Rp)* has a pleasant atmosphere even with the unnerving traffic noise. It serves pizza and pasta standards, and has Legong (classic Balinese) dance performances. It also offers free transport from as far away as Sengkidu.

TJ's Restaurant *(☎ 41540; dishes 15,000-40,000Rp)*, part of the Watergarden Hotel, overlooks a carp pond and fan palms, and somehow manages to maintain a peaceful atmosphere amid the traffic noise. The food is excellent, including Asian specialities, such as laksa, tempura and Thai dishes. Its breakfasts are also worth experiencing.

Kubu Bali Restaurant *(☎ 41532; dishes 18,000-50,000Rp)* is a big place with an open kitchen out the front, where Indonesian and Chinese dishes are turned out with great energy and panache.

Warung Astawa *(☎ 41363; set menu 10,000-19,000Rp, dishes 15,000-30,000Rp)* is popular for its set-menu specials and congenial ambience – not to mention the happy hour.

Entertainment

Many restaurants advertise happy hours with cheap beer between 5pm and 8pm – look for the signs out the front. **Candi Agung** presents free Legong dances in the evening at 7.45pm (ask who the dancer is and you'll probably find it's one of the waitresses!); while **Raja's, Candi Bagus** and others show movies – look for the notices nailed to pretty much every tree in Candidasa.

Legend Rock Cafe *(dishes 9000-24,000Rp; large Bintang 14,000Rp)*, a bar that also serves Western and Indonesian meals, has live gigs in the high season from Monday to Thursday and Saturday (bands often come from Jakarta). It also shows movies nightly at 8pm. The upstairs pavilion at **Toke Café** is a nice place for a drink.

Shopping

Sarongs, silver, souvenirs and beachwear are available in shops along the main road. Hand-woven textiles are produced locally, as are fine baskets, but the nearby village of Tenganan has a more interesting selection and lower prices. **Kedai** (☎ 42020; ⓦ www .deckco.com) has a small shop selling textiles, homewares and jewellery. **Foto Asri** has groceries and most other basics.

Getting There & Away

Candidasa is on the main road between Amlapura and Denpasar, but there's no terminal, so hail down bemos (buses probably won't stop).

Perama (☎ 41114) is at the western end of the strip. It runs three tourist shuttle buses per day to Padangbai (10,000Rp) and Sanur and Kuta/Airport (30,000Rp) and Ubud (20,000Rp), two services per day to Lovina (60,000Rp), as well as daily services to Tirta Gangga and Tulamben (20,000Rp).

Getting Around

Suzuki jeeps (about 80,000Rp per day), Kijangs (about 150,000Rp per day) and motorcycles (40,000Rp per day) can be rented from agencies along the main road. For exploring the nearby area, full-day and half-day tours and chartered vehicles are also available.

AMLAPURA

Amlapura is the capital of Karangasem district, and the main town and transport junction in eastern Bali. The smallest of Bali's district capitals, it's a sprawling, multicultural place with Chinese shophouses, several mosques and confusing one-way streets. It's worth a stop to see Puri Agung Karangasem, but Tirta Gangga is a more picturesque, laid-back place to stay.

Information

The many friendly staff at the **tourist office** (☎/fax 21196) will be spellbound if any traveller walks in requesting information. **Bank BRI** and **Bank Danamon** will change money; Bank Danamon has an ATM, which accepts Visa.

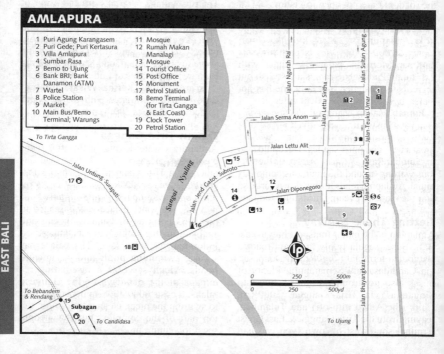

AMLAPURA

1 Puri Agung Karangasem
2 Puri Gede; Puri Kertasura
3 Villa Amlapura
4 Sumbar Rasa
5 Bemo to Ujung
6 Bank BRI; Bank Danamon (ATM)
7 Wartel
8 Police Station
9 Market
10 Main Bus/Bemo Terminal; Warungs
11 Mosque
12 Rumah Makan Manalagi
13 Mosque
14 Tourist Office
15 Post Office
16 Monument
17 Petrol Station
18 Bemo Terminal (for Tirta Gangga & East Coast)
19 Clock Tower
20 Petrol Station

Puri Agung Karangasem

Amlapura's three palaces, on Jl Teuku Umar, are decaying reminders of Karangasem's period as a kingdom, at its most important when supported by Dutch colonial power in the late-19th and early-20th centuries.

Outside Puri Agung Karangasem (admission 3000Rp; open 8am-6pm daily) there is an impressive three-tiered entry gate and beautiful sculpted panels. After you pass through the entry courtyard, a left turn takes you to the main building, known as the Maskerdam (Amsterdam), because it was the Karangasem kingdom's acquiescence to Dutch rule that allowed it to hang on long after the demise of the other Balinese kingdoms. Inside you can see several rooms, including the royal bedroom and a living room with furniture that was a gift from the Dutch royal family. The Maskerdam faces the ornately decorated Bale Pemandesan, which was used for royal tooth-filing ceremonies. Beyond this, surrounded by a pond, is the Bale Kambang, still used for family meetings and dance practice.

Other royal palace buildings, Puri Gede and Puri Kertasura, are on the west side of the road, but are not open to visitors.

Places to Stay & Eat

Villa Amlapura (☎ 23246; Jl Teuku Umar; rooms 60,000-100,000Rp) is part funkster pad, part Moroccan palace! Affiliated with Zen Inn in Padangbai, rooms are stylish but eclectically designed, but only one has hot water. It also has an excellent café.

Rumah Makan Manalagi (Jl Diponegoro) is always busy with locals due to its proximity to a mosque. On offer is satay kambing (goat satay) and other staples. You could also try Sumbar Rasa (Jl Gajah Madah) or the various warung around the main bus/bemo terminal. Amlapura tends to shut down early, so don't leave your evening meal until too late.

Getting There & Away

Amlapura is the major transport hub in east Bali. Buses regularly ply the main road to Batubulan terminal (7000Rp) in Denpasar, via Candidasa and Semarapura. Plenty of buses also go around the north coast to Singaraja (via Tirta Gangga, 3000Rp), Culik (the Amed turn-off) and Tulamben, leaving from the Tirta Gangga & East Coast terminal southwest of town (you can hail

these from outside Villa Amlapura). Bemos climb the road around the southern slopes of Gunung Agung to Rendang and Besakih, but it is much better to do this with your own transport (see the Rendang to Amlapura section earlier).

UJUNG

Five kilometres south of Amlapura, Taman Ujung (admission by donation) is an extensive, picturesque and crumbling ruin of a once-grand water palace complex. The last king of Karangasem completed the palace in 1921, but it has been deteriorating for some time and was extensively damaged by an earthquake in 1979. An old photo in the palace in Amlapura shows how wonderful it was. You can wander around the remnants of the main pool, admire the views from the pavilion higher up the hill above the rice fields, or continue a little further down the road to Ujung, a fishing village on the coast. Regular blue bemos leave from the main terminal in Amlapura.

TIRTA GANGGA
☎ 0363

The tiny village of Tirta Gangga (Water of the Ganges), high on a ridge with sublime rice paddy vistas, is a relaxing place to stop for a day or so. The main attraction is the old water palace and guided treks through the gorgeous landscape (Good Karma or Genta Bali are good places to find a guide). Facilities are limited; Kertha Wisata Internet Café is at the entrance path to the water palace and charges 200Rp per minute.

Taman Tirta Gangga

Amlapura's water-loving rajah, after completing his masterpiece at Ujung, had another go at Tirta Gangga (adult/child 3100/1600Rp, camera 1000Rp; open 24 hr, ticket office open 7am-6pm daily). Originally built in 1948, the water palace was damaged in the 1963 eruption of Gunung Agung and again during the political events that rocked Indonesia two years later. The palace has several swimming pools and ornamental ponds, which serve as a fascinating reminder of the old days of the Balinese rajahs. It costs 6000/4000Rp per adult/child to swim in the nicer, cleaner 'pool A' in the top part of the complex, but few people seem to venture in.

EAST BALI

Places to Stay & Eat

Dhangin Taman (☎ 22059; rooms 35,000-70,000Rp), adjacent to the water palace, has a range of simple rooms – the cheapest ones facing the rice paddies are the best – and a **restaurant** (dishes 5000-8000Rp).

Good Karma (☎ 22445; singles/doubles 40,000/60,000Rp), in the middle of a picturesque rice paddy, has very clean and pleasant bungalows. The **restaurant** (dishes 10,000-16,000Rp) serves excellent food in a comfortable setting; try the green tempeh curry with vegetables.

Pondok Lembah Dukah (singles 25,000-40,000Rp, doubles 40,000-60,000Rp), down the path to the right of Good Karma and past Dua Homestay, has only three bungalows and is a bit of a climb, but worth it. Rooms are clean and simple, and have incredible views.

Puri Sawah Bungalows (☎ 21847, fax 21939; bungalows 80,000-200,000Rp) is just up the road from the palace. It has a few comfortable and spacious rooms with great views, and larger, two-bedroom bungalows, which sleep six (with hot water). The **restaurant** (dishes 16,000-22,000Rp) has rice paddy views.

Puri Prima (☎/fax 21316; singles 50,000-80,000Rp, doubles 70,000-100,000Rp), about 800m from central Tirta Gangga, offers outstanding views and pleasant rooms. It's best to book ahead as it often holds conferences. It has a small **restaurant** (dishes 10,000-16,000Rp). Staff can also organise trekking to Gunung Agung (600,000Rp for two people).

Genta Bali (☎ 22436; dishes 10,000-12,000Rp), across the road from Good Karma, is well recommended, and puts together pasta and Indonesian food. It also has an impressive pudding list, served with coconut milk, brown sugar and coconut.

Tirta Ayu Homestay (☎ 22697, fax 21383; singles 150,000-200,000Rp, doubles 200,000-250,000Rp, villas US$70-90), actually within the palace compound, has pleasant bungalows (cold water only) and spacious villas; free use of the palace swimming pool is included. A **cafe** (dishes 10,000-25,000Rp) overlooks the palace grounds.

A couple of places are at **Desa Ababi**, on the hills above Tirta Gangga – call the hotels first for directions (see following two entries).

Geria Semalung (☎ 22116; singles/doubles 75,000/120,000Rp, with hot water 120,000/180,000Rp) offers complete seclusion and breathtaking views, although rooms are very ordinary.

Pondok Batur Indah (☎ 22342; rooms 70,000Rp) can be reached by walking up the steps from the water palace.

Getting There & Away

Regular bemos and minibuses pass through Tirta Gangga on routes north of Amlapura – they'll stop on request. Two Perama shuttle buses pass through daily, once in either direction (buses stop at Good Karma). Heading south and east the buses go to Candidasa (20,000Rp), Padangbai (30,000Rp), Ubud (45,000Rp), Sanur (45,000Rp) and Kuta/Airport (45,000Rp). Heading north the buses go past Yeh Sanih, Culik (the turn-off for Amed) to Tulamben (20,000Rp) and Lovina (40,000Rp). Several shops in Tirta Gangga sell tickets – look for the noticeboards.

AROUND TIRTA GANGGA

The rice terraces around Tirta Gangga are some of the most beautiful on Bali. They sweep out from Tirta Gangga, almost like a sea surrounding an island. Back roads and walking paths take you to many picturesque traditional villages. Going to smaller, more remote villages, it's sensible and inexpensive to engage a guide – ask at your hotel or else contact **Nyoman Budiasa** at Genta Bali or **Komang Gede Sutama** at Good Karma, both in Tirta Gangga. Another good place to arrange hikes is **Homestay Lila** in Abian Soan (see the Rendang to Amlapura section earlier). Guide prices are negotiable, at around 15,000Rp per person per hour for local treks, plus transport and food.

Pura Lempuyang

This is one of Bali's nine directional temples, perched on a hilltop at 768m. Turn south off the Amlapura–Tulamben road to Ngis (2km), a palm sugar and coffee growing area, and follow the signs another 2km to Kemuda (ask directions if the signs confuse you). From Kemuda, climb 1700 steps to Pura Lempuyang (allow at least two hours, one way). If you want to continue to the peaks of Lempuyang (1058m) or Seraya (1175m), you should take a guide.

Bukit Kusambi

This small hill has a big view – at sunrise Lombok's Gunung Rinjani throws a shadow

Sunset over Gunung Agung, Bali's mighty 'Mother Mountain', which last erupted in 1963

ANDREW LUBRAN

Soft coral forest in waters near Tulamben

EDWARD AM SNIJDERS

Bats at Pura Goa Lawah, near Kusamba

GREG ELMS

The lagoon at Candidasa beach

The floating pavilion at Kertha Gosa, Semarapura

The impressive Pura Besakih temple complex, 1000m up the side of Gunung Agung

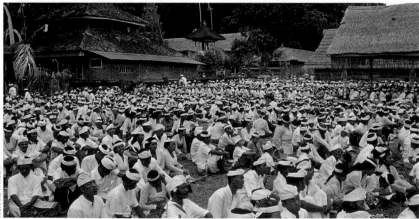

A festival crowd at Tenganan, a village of the traditional 'Bali Aga' people

on Gunung Agung. It is easy to reach from Abian Soan – look for the obvious large hill to the northwest, and follow the tiny canals through the rice fields. On the western side of the hill, a set of steps leads to the top.

Budakeling & Krotok
Budakeling, home to several Buddhist communities, is on the back road to Bebandem, a few kilometres southeast of Tirta Gangga. It's a short drive, or a pleasant three-hour walk through rice fields, via Krotok, home of traditional blacksmiths and silversmiths.

Tanah Aron
This imposing monument is gloriously situated on the southeastern slopes of Gunung Agung. The road is quite good, or you can walk up and back in about six hours from Tirta Gangga.

AMED & THE FAR EAST COAST
This once-remote stretch of coast, from Amed to Bali's far eastern tip, continues to develop as a new resort area. The coastline is superb and still largely unspoilt, with views across to Lombok and behind to Gunung Agung. Hotels, restaurants, dive operators and other facilities continue to expand as an increasing number of visitors come to enjoy the fine scenery, the relaxed atmosphere, and the excellent diving and snorkelling.

Amazingly, this growth has occurred in an area that still lacks regular public transport, and has only very recently seen the addition of a fixed telephone line. Amed itself has no standard tourist centre, so it's the perfect hideaway if you want to simply stay put and never leave your hotel, apart from to swim or snorkel. If you're after a more dynamic holiday destination, head elsewhere.

Traditionally, this area has been quite poor, with thin soils, low rainfall and very limited infrastructure. Salt production is still carried out on the beach at Amed, and you'll see numerous rows of evaporating troughs in the dry season (or big stacks of them for the rest of the year). Villages further east rely on fishing, and colourful *jukung* line up on every available piece of beach. Inland, the steep hillsides are generally too dry for rice – corn, peanuts and vegetables are the main crops.

Orientation
In the rest of Bali, and to identify itself as a destination, this whole strip of coast is commonly called 'Amed' but, strictly speaking, Amed is just the first of several *dusun* (small villages) set in a dramatic landscape of black-sand beaches, spread over 10km. Most of the development is around two bays, Jemeluk and Lipah, but hotels continue to appear on the headlands in between, and right around to Aas in the southeast.

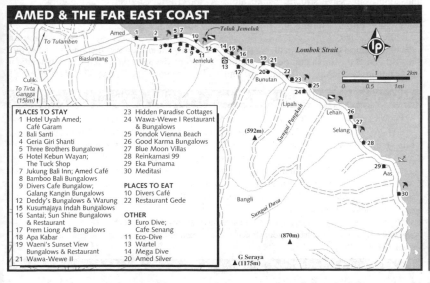

AMED & THE FAR EAST COAST

PLACES TO STAY
1 Hotel Uyah Amed;
   Café Garam
2 Bali Santi
4 Geria Giri Shanti
5 Three Brothers Bungalows
6 Hotel Kebun Wayan;
   The Tuck Shop
7 Jukung Bali Inn; Amed Café
8 Bamboo Bali Bungalows
9 Divers Cafe Bungalow;
   Galang Kangin Bungalows
12 Deddy's Bungalows & Warung
15 Kusumajaya Indah Bungalows
16 Santai; Sun Shine Bungalows
   & Restaurant
17 Prem Liong Art Bungalows
18 Apa Kabar
19 Waeni's Sunset View
   Bungalows & Restaurant
21 Wawa-Wewe II

23 Hidden Paradise Cottages
24 Wawa-Wewe I Restaurant
   & Bungalows
25 Pondok Vienna Beach
26 Good Karma Bungalows
27 Blue Moon Villas
28 Reinkarnasi 99
29 Eka Purnama
30 Meditasi

PLACES TO EAT
10 Divers Café
22 Restaurant Gede

OTHER
3 Euro Dive;
   Cafe Senang
11 Eco-Dive
13 Wartel
14 Mega Dive
20 Amed Silver

Information

There's no tourist office or post office, there is, however, a tourist tax! It's the only one of its kind in Bali and was set up by the local community in January 2002. Expect to pay a one-off fee of 3000Rp per person at a tollbooth on the outskirts of Amed. Part of the tax goes towards local infrastructure and services.

In mid-2002 telephone services were connected as far as Lipah. There's a **wartel** near Kusamajaya Indah Bungalows in Jemeluk. **Hotel Kebun Wayan** changes US dollar travellers cheques and has a small **minimart** next door. There are several other **moneychangers** in Lipah near Hidden Paradise Cottages. **Hidden Paradise** rents bicycles for 25,000Rp per day. Shopping is limited, but **Amed Silver** (☎ 22166) near Waeni's is a small silversmithing studio.

Diving & Snorkelling

Snorkelling is excellent at several places along the coast. Jemeluk is a protected area where you can admire live coral and plentiful fish within 100m of the beach. There's a relatively recent Japanese shipwreck near Aas, offshore from Eka Purnama bungalows, and coral gardens and colourful marine life at Selang. As in much of Indonesia and the Indian Ocean, the reefs here suffered from 'coral bleaching' in the 1998 El Niño event, and some impressive structures like table corals have been lost. Almost every hotel rents snorkelling equipment for about 20,000Rp per day.

Scuba diving is also excellent, with dive sites off Jemeluk, Lipah and Selang featuring coral slopes and drop-offs with soft and hard corals, and abundant fish. Some are accessible from the beach, while others require a short boat ride. The *Liberty* wreck at Tulamben is only a 20-minute drive away.

Euro Dive (fax 0363-22958; W www.euro divebali.com), a PADI Resort, is a well-recommended operation that dives around Amed, Tulamben and Gili Selang. Dives start from US$45, and a PADI Open-Water Course is US$310. Snorkelling equipment is available for rent. Euro Dive also operates **Cafe Senang** (small/large Bintang 8000/12,000Rp), a small, sleek bar/café. Other dive operators in Amed include **Eco-dive** (W www.ecodive bali.com) and **Mega Dive** (W www.mega -dive.com; Amed Beach Cottage).

Trekking

Quite a few trails go inland from the coast, up the slopes of Gunung Seraya (1175m) and to some little-visited villages. The countryside is sparsely vegetated and most trails are well defined, so you won't need a guide for shorter walks – if you get lost, just follow a ridge top back down to the coast road. Allow a good three hours to get to the top of Seraya, starting from the rocky ridge just east of Jemeluk Bay, near Prem Liong Art Bungalows. To reach the top for sunrise, you'll need to start in the dark, so a guide is probably a good idea – ask at your hotel. A fair rate is around 15,000-20,000Rp per hour for an English-speaking guide.

Places to Stay

The Amed area is very spread out, so take this into consideration when choosing accommodation. If you want to venture to restaurants beyond your hotel's own, for example, you'll

Making Salt While the Sun Shines

In the volcanic areas near Kusamba, and around the northeast coast between Amed and Yeh Sanih and Selang, you can see the thatched roofs of salt-making huts along the beach. Sand that has been saturated with seawater is collected from the beach, dried out and then taken inside a hut, where more sea water is strained through it to wash out the salt. This very salty water is then poured into a shallow trough (palungan), made of palm tree trunks split in half. Hundreds of these troughs are lined up in rows along the beaches during the salt-making season, and as the hot sun evaporates the water, the almost-dry salt is scraped out and put in baskets. The salt is used mainly for processing dried fish, not as table salt.

It's a laborious process, yielding a meagre income in the dry season and none at all in the wet season when rain stops production. Tourists who stop, look and take photos should consider leaving a small donation.

have to either walk or pay for transport. No hotel offers free transport.

Places to Stay – Budget

There's a wide range of budget accommodation to choose from.

Amed Village Area Both the **Bali Santi** *(singles/doubles 50,000/100,000Rp)* and also the **Geria Giri Shanti** *(singles/doubles 60,000/ 100,000Rp)* have clean rooms and are inexpensive options.

Three Brothers Bungalows *(singles 100,000-120,000Rp, doubles 120,000-150,000Rp)*, opposite Geria Giri Shanti, has popular beachfront accommodation, and an adjoining **café** *(dishes 10,000-25,000Rp)*.

Hotel Kebun Wayan *(fax 0363-22166; singles/doubles 80,000/100,000Rp, with air-con & hot water US$25/30)*, opposite Amed Café, offers small but charming rooms in pleasant grounds.

Bamboo Bali Bungalows *(singles/doubles from 35,000/40,000Rp, with air-con to 150,000Rp)*, about 300m east of Pondok Kebun Wayan, on a hillside overlooking the water, has a small pool and simple rooms with open-air bathrooms.

Jemeluk Facing the beach and offering clean rooms in stone bungalows terraced up the hill is **Divers Cafe Bungalows** *(singles/ doubles 80,000/ 100,000Rp, with hot water 110,000/150,000Rp)*. The **café** *(dishes 11,000-25,000Rp)* has a few Indonesian dishes worth ordering in advance, such as *pepes ikan bakar* (grilled fish in spicy sauce). **Galang Kangin Bungalows** *(singles/doubles 45,000/ 80,000Rp)* has clean rooms and is a decent, inexpensive option.

Deddy's Bungalows & Warung *(*e* warung _deddys@hotmail.com; singles/doubles 65,000/ 80,000Rp)* is a clean, pleasant place on the hillside.

Waeni's Sunset View Bungalows & Restaurant *(fax 0363-21044;* e *madesani@ hotmail.com; rooms 60,000-100,000Rp; dishes 14,000-30,000Rp)* has unusual rustic stone cottages with gorgeous views of the mountains behind and bay below. The restaurant is the perfect place to stop for a drink and watch the sunset.

Wawa-Wewe II *(fax 0363-22074;* e *wawa wewevillas@hotmail.com; singles/doubles/ quads 125,000/150,000/250,000Rp)* is a nice

and peaceful place offering cold-water, fan-cooled villas. The simple little **restaurant** *(dishes 18,000-23,000Rp)* overlooks the water.

Lipah The road swings down to **Lipah**, which has a mostly sandy beach, a shop, several eateries and more accommodation. Run by local hipsters, **Wawa-Wewe I Restaurant & Bungalows** *(*e* rodanet@depasar.wasan tara.net.id; singles/doubles 50,000/75,000Rp)* has simple rooms with outdoor bathrooms. The café has a limited menu.

Selang In an isolated position, **Good Karma Bungalows** *(singles US$9-17, doubles US$10-24, bigger bungalows US$18-25)* has a fittingly resident longhaired guru-esque owner. A range of rooms in the Sulawesi-style thatch-roofed bungalows, all with open-air bathrooms, is on offer, including bungalows that sleep up to four. The bungalows and peaceful **restaurant** *(dishes 8000-22,000Rp)* overlook a black-sand beach crowded with *jukung*. The same owner has a similarly inviting hideaway, **Reinkarnasi 99** *(singles/doubles 80,000/150,000Rp)*, 1km further along.

Eka Purnama *(fax 0363-21044;* e *geoco wan@yahoo.com; singles/doubles 200,000/ 250,000Rp)* is a gorgeous, cold-water only place set high on a hill. The balconies, complete with hammocks, have pure ocean views. It also has a pleasant **restaurant** *(dishes 17,000-25,000Rp)*.

Aas Two kilometres beyond Reinkarnasi 99, **Meditasi** *(fax 0363-22166; singles/doubles 100,000/135,000Rp)* is a chilled place where the bamboo bungalows have dreamy balconies overlooking the beach. There's also an open-air restaurant by the water and good snorkelling nearby.

Places to Stay – Mid-Range & Top End

There are some good value mid-range and top-end options around.

Amed Village Area Overlooking the salt-works of Amed and, hence, without the most scenic views, **Hotel Uyah Amed** *(☎ 0868 1210 3665; rooms 250,000-320,000Rp)* is a new, swish place featuring four-poster beds, creative interiors and a pool.

Jukung Bali Inn *(singles 130,000-150,000Rp, doubles 150,000-200,000Rp)* is a great new place, which, at the time of writing, only had two bungalows. Balconies, each with a day bed, face the water, and the smartly designed interiors feature four-poster beds, ikat curtains and open-air bathrooms.

Jemeluk A sandstone-paved pool overlooks the beach at **Kusumajaya Indah Bungalows** (☎ 0363-21250; singles 100,000-150,000Rp, doubles 200,000-250,000Rp). The rooms here are pleasant enough.

Santai (☎/fax 0363-23487; w www.santai bali.com; single/double with garden view US$60/70, with ocean view US$80/90), a gorgeous top-end option has a lovely ambience. Rooms have four-poster double beds, timber floors, open-air bathrooms and big comfy balcony sofas. A snaking swimming pool, fringed by purple bougainvillea, adds to the atmosphere. The **restaurant** (dishes 18,000-52,000Rp) faces the beach and serves imported steaks, savoury crepes, pasta and delish desserts.

Sun Shine Bungalows & Restaurant (☎/fax 0361-243 929 or 0811 387 473; rooms 350,000-600,000Rp) is a two-storey building designed around a pool. Modern, spacious, somewhat bland rooms all have air-con and hot water. A small café overlooks the water.

Prem Liong Art Bungalows (☎ 0363-22 859; w www.bali-amed.com; singles/doubles/quads 100,000/250,000/400,000Rp), near Santai, has a kind of hippyish feel to its Javanese-style two-storey bungalows terraced up the hillside. The open-air bathrooms are lush and almost double as a garden, while the balconies have comfy cushions and day beds. Rooms are ideal for families or groups. The **restaurant** (dishes 11,000-27,000Rp) here focuses on Balinese dishes, such as green papaya soup.

Apa Kabar (☎ 0868 1210 3753, fax 0363-21044; w www.apakabarvillas.com; 1-bedroom villa US$35, 2-bedroom villa for 2/4 persons US$100/120), right by the water, has deliciously stylish and spacious villas overlooking a swimming pool.

Lipah Both **Hidden Paradise Cottages** (☎/fax 0363-431273; w www.hiddenpar adise-bali.com; cottages US$40-45, with air-con US$50-55) and **Pondok Vienna Beach** (fax 0363-21883; w www.bali-amed.com; rooms US$22-30, rooms with hot water &

air-con US$40) have reasonable accommodation by the beach, but they're only worth considering in the discounted low season.

Selang Straight out of the pages of a glossy magazine, **Blue Moon Villas** (☎ 0868 1210 3650, fax 0363-21044; w www.bluemoon villa.com; single/doubles US$60/65, penthouse US$200) is an upmarket place, complete with a stylish pool perfect for lounging. The café, **Komang John's** (dishes 20,000-25,000Rp), serves dishes such as pizza and burgers, as well as Indonesian favourites.

Places to Eat
Amed Café (dishes 15,000-25,000Rp) is serene if a bit swank. It has an extensive seafood menu, as well as the usual pizza, pasta and Indonesian dishes.

Restaurant Gede (dishes 16,000-33,000Rp) has a huge menu, focusing on Chinese dishes, with a few Balinese dishes as well. It's a bit hit and miss but worth a try if you're staying in Amed for any length of time.

Café Garam (Amed village area; dishes 14,000-39,000Rp) has a nice ambience, pool tables and features live Genjek music every Wednesday and Saturday at 8pm. The café also has a small exhibition on salt-making, and local salt is on sale.

Getting There & Around
All the places east of Amed can be difficult to reach by public transport. Plenty of minibuses and bemos from Singaraja and Amlapura go through Culik, the turn-off for Amed. Infrequent public bemos go from Culik to Amed (3.5km), and at least some of them continue to Selang (another 8km), mostly in the morning and never after noon. A public bemo should cost around 2500Rp from Culik to Lipah, but if you arrive at Culik after noon, you'll probably have to charter transport for a negotiable 25,000Rp or so. Alternatively, if you're travelling light, you can get an *ojek* from Culik to Jemeluk, Lipah or Selang for about 5000Rp to 10,000Rp (also negotiable). When negotiating the fare, be careful to specify which part of the coast, or which hotel, you wish to go to – if you agree on a price to 'Amed', you may be taken only as far as Amed village, then be asked to pay more to get to a hotel.

Tourist shuttle buses going to/from Tulamben will also drop you at Culik, but probably too late for a public bemo connection to Amed and beyond. Perama buses from Tirta Gangga to Tulamben will pass through Culik at about 2.30pm; in the other direction, they pass Culik at approximately 10.30am.

If you have your own transport, the coast road from Amed to Amlapura via the market town of Seraya and Ujung has recently been paved. The narrow, winding route passes through spectacular scenery.

TULAMBEN
☎ 0363

The big attraction here is the wreck of the US cargo ship *Liberty* – among the best and most popular dive site on Bali. Other great dive sites are nearby, and even snorkellers can easily swim out and enjoy the wreck and the coral. Tulamben's beachfront is quite different from other beach resorts – heavy, black, round boulders and pebbles make it more akin to the shore of Santorini in Greece, or other volcanic islands. Tulamben itself is a quiet place, and is essentially built around the wreck – the hotels, all with restaurants, and many with dive shops, are spread along a 3km stretch either side of the main road. You can change cash at a few signposted places at the eastern end of the main road, while the better hotels take travellers cheques.

Diving & Snorkelling

The wreck of the *Liberty* is about 50m directly offshore from Puri Madya Bungalows (there's also a car park here). Swim straight out and you'll see the stern rearing up from the depths, heavily encrusted with coral, and swarming with dozens of species of colourful fish – and with scuba divers most of the day. The ship is more than 100m long, but the hull is broken into sections and it's easy for divers to get inside. The bow is in quite good shape, the midships region is badly mangled and the stern is almost intact – the best parts are between 15m and 30m deep. You will want at least two dives to really explore the wreck.

Many divers commute to Tulamben from Candidasa, Lovina or even the south Bali resorts, and the wreck can get quite crowded between 11am and 4pm, with up to 50 divers there at a time. It's better, and cheaper, to get yourself to Tulamben, stay the night and do your dives early in the day, or perhaps between noon and 2pm, when visiting divers

take a lunch break. Amed is also a convenient base for Tulamben dives.

Most hotels have their own diving centre, and some will give a discount on accommodation if you dive with their centre, but not all of them can be recommended for inexperienced divers.

Reputable dive operations include **Tauch Terminal** (☎ *0361-730200, fax 730201;* Ⓦ *www.tauch-terminal.com*), a Gold Palm Padi Resort. The Padi Open-Water certificate, held over four days, costs US$380. **Deep Blue Studio** (☎ *22919;* Ⓦ *www.scubaqua.com*) charges US$250 for a non-Padi International Association of Nitrox and Technical Divers (IANTD) certified dive course. Expect to pay about US$35/60 for one/two dives at Tulamben, and a little more for a night dive and for dives around Amed. Most hotels and dive centres rent out snorkelling gear for anything from 20,000Rp to US$5 per day.

Places to Stay & Eat

Puri Madha Bungalows (☎ *22921; singles/ doubles 50,000/60,000Rp*) is the first hotel you approach from the west, and faces the wreck; it has a few small, clean rooms that face the beachfront.

Tauch Terminal Resort (☎ *0361-730200, fax 730201;* Ⓔ *dive@tauch-terminal.com; rooms US$40, with sea view US$80*), east of Puri Madhya Bungalows, is reached by a side road. Expect high quality rooms, with a spacious terrace. It also has an idyllic beachfront pool, beach bar and **restaurant** (*dishes 16,000-38,000Rp*). Pasta, Indonesian and German dishes are on offer. This is definitely the better place to eat!

Deep Blue Studio (☎ *22919;* Ⓦ *www .scubaqua.com*), on the inland side of the road, near Tauch Terminal, has basic, but clean rooms for US$10 with rooftop balcony views and a small pool; car rental is available.

Bali Coral Bungalows (☎/*fax 22909; rooms US$10-30, hot water US$3 extra*), on the same side road as Tauch Terminal, has a cluster of pleasant, clean bungalows with modern bathrooms, some with sea views.

Gandu Mayu Bungalows (☎ *22912; singles/doubles 50,000/70,000Rp*), on the inland side of the main road, has OK rooms, which may get some traffic noise. This is also the Perama office.

Puri Aries (*singles/doubles 45,000/ 50,000 Rp*), next door to Gandu Mayu, has small,

clean bungalows in a really lush, green garden setting.

Further east, on the ocean side of the
road, are three places in a row, including
Paradise Palm Beach Bungalows *(☎ 22910,
fax 22917; rooms 60,000Rp, rooms with hot
water 180,000-280,000Rp)*, which has neat,
clean, quite ordinary rooms with verandas
overlooking a pretty garden. The big plus is
that it has direct beach access. The **restaurant**
(dishes 10,000-20,000Rp) has Indonesian options as well as pizza.

Matahari Tulamben Resort *(☎ 22907;
singles/doubles 40,000/60,000Rp, with air-
con 150,000/250,000Rp)* is a small place,
with pleasant rooms, and a swimming pool
and **restaurant** *(dishes 8000-15,000Rp)* overlooking the water.

Mimpi Resort *(☎/fax 21642; **w** www
.mimpi.com; rooms US$80-150)*, designed by
Australian architects and overlooking a picturesque stretch of beach, has a range of stylish bungalows with outdoor bathrooms, and
a beachfront pool, dive centre and spa. It also
has a **restaurant** *(dishes 22,000-55,000Rp)*.

Getting There & Away

Plenty of minibuses, buses and bemos travel
between Amlapura and Singaraja and will
stop anywhere along the Tulamben road, but
they're infrequent after 2pm. Public buses
and bemos ask high fares for people leaving
Tulamben. Daily Perama shuttle buses,
based at Gandu Mayu Bungalows, will drop
you anywhere along the main road. They
continue from Tulamben around the northeast coast to Yeh Sanih (20,000Rp) and Lovina (40,000Rp), and in the other direction,
past Culik (the Amed turn-off), Tirta Gangga
(20,000Rp), Candidasa (30,000Rp), Padangbai (40,000Rp), Ubud (50,000Rp), Sanur
(55,000Rp) and Kuta/Airport (50,000Rp).

TULAMBEN TO YEH SANIH

North of Tulamben, a good sealed road continues to skirt the slopes of Gunung Agung,
with frequent evidence of lava flows from
the 1963 eruption. Further around, the outer
crater of Gunung Batur slopes steeply down
to the sea. The rainfall is low and you can
generally count on sunny weather. The
scenery is very stark in the dry season, but
glimpses of the ocean and a series of unspoilt villages make it an interesting trip.
The route has regular public transport, but
it's easier to make stops and detours with
your own vehicle.

Alam Anda *(☎/fax 0362-22222;* **w** *www
.alamanda.de; singles/doubles €50/60; villa
for 1 week €1300)* is the only place to stay
near **Sambirenteng**. It's a delightful resort on
the beach, with a fine coral reef just offshore.
It boasts its own diving centre, a pretty pool
and very attractive bungalows in a garden
setting, as well as cheaper rooms. The beachfront restaurant *(dishes €3-8)*, has daily buffets and whole fresh fish is often an option

At Les, a road goes inland to lovely **Air
Terjun Yeh Mampeh** *(Yeh Mampeh Waterfall)*, said to be one of Bali's highest. Bemos
or minibuses may make the 1.5km detour,
or look for an *ojek* at the turn-off, and then
walk the last 2.5km or so on an obvious
path by the stream. A donation is requested.

The next main town is **Tejakula**, famous
for its stream-fed public bathing area, said
to have been built for washing horses, and
often called the **horse bath**. The renovated
bathing areas (separate for men and women)
are behind walls topped by rows of elaborately decorated arches, and are regarded as
a sacred area. The baths are 100m inland on
a narrow road with lots of small shops – it's
a quaint village, with some finely carved
kulkul towers.

At **Pacung**, about 10km before Yeh
Sanih, you can turn inland to **Sembiran**,
which is believed to be a Bali Aga village,
although it doesn't promote itself as such.
The most striking thing about the place is its
hillside location and the brilliant coastal
views it offers.

Nusa Penida

Nusa Penida, an administrative region within the Klungkung district, comprises three islands – Nusa Penida itself, the smaller Nusa Lembongan to the northwest and tiny Nusa Ceningan in between. Nusa Lembongan attracts the most visitors for its surf, seclusion and quiet beaches. The island of Nusa Penida has several villages, but is right off the tourist track and has few facilities for visitors, while Nusa Ceningan is very sparsely populated.

Lembongan is a wonderful place, where surfers and nonsurfers alike can get away from the relative chaos of southern Bali. Low-budget bungalows are ideal for extended stays by the seaside, while boutique hotels offer instant indulgence. For an even shorter visit, take a comfortable cruise boat, stopping to snorkel or bask on a beach, or do a more specialised diving or surf trip. A new service connects Nusa Lembongan with Lombok (see Getting There & Away under Nusa Lembongan, later).

It's been a poor region for many years and there has been some transmigration from here to other parts of Indonesia. Thin soils and a lack of fresh water do not permit the cultivation of rice, but other crops such as maize, cassava and beans are staples grown here. The main cash crop, however, is seaweed.

Diving

There are great diving possibilities around the islands, from shallow and sheltered reefs, mainly on the northern side of Lembongan and Penida, to very demanding drift dives in the channel between Penida and the other two islands. Vigilant locals have protected their waters from dynamite bombing by renegade fishing boats, so the reefs are still intact, although the Quicksilver mooring at Toyapakeh is said by local dive operators to have destroyed sections of coral. The best local dive operation, based at Nusa Lembongan, is **World Diving** (☎ 0812 390 0686; w www.world-diving.com).

If you arrange a dive trip from Sanur, Candidasa or Nusa Dua, stick with the most reputable operators, as conditions here can be tricky and local knowledge is essential. A particular attraction is the large marine animals, including turtles, sharks and manta rays. The

Highlights

- Exploring spectacular rugged coast and remote villages
- Diving for big fish, caves, coral walls and drift dives
- Surfing the classy right-hand reef breaks off Nusa Lembongan
- Luxuriating in the seclusion of idyllic Mushroom Bay, Nusa Lembongan's luxury getaway
- Enjoying the tranquillity on Nusa Lembongan

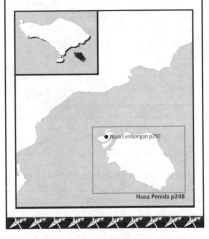

Nusa Lembongan p250

Nusa Penida p248

large and unusual sunfish *(mola mola)* is sometimes seen around the islands between July and September, while manta rays are often seen south of Nusa Penida.

NUSA PENIDA
☎ 0366

The island of Nusa Penida is a limestone plateau with white-sand beaches on its north coast, and views over the water to the volcanoes on Bali – these beaches are not good for swimming as most of the shallows are filled with bamboo frames used for seaweed farming. The south coast has limestone cliffs dropping straight down to the sea and a row of offshore islets – it's rugged and spectacular scenery. The interior is hilly, with sparse-looking crops, and old-fashioned villages.

NUSA PENIDA

DIVE SITES
1. Big Rock
2. Ped SD
3. Quicksilver Pontoon
4. Ceningan Wall
5. Shark Cave
6. Malibu Point
7. Batu Aba
8. Batu Lumbung

The rainfall is low, and there are large tanks known as *cabang*, in which water is stored for the dry season.

The population of around 45,000 people is predominantly Hindu, although there are some Muslims in Toyapakeh. The culture is distinct from that of Bali: the language is an old form of Balinese no longer heard on the mainland, and there is also local dance, architecture and craft, including a unique type of red ikat weaving. Nusa Penida was once used as a place of banishment for criminals and other undesirables from the kingdom of Klungkung, and still has a somewhat sinister reputation.

Cruises

Bali Hai (☎ 0361-720331; W www.balihai cruises.com) does an 'ocean-rafting' trip in a high-speed inflatable boat that takes in the dramatic south coast and the Ceningan channel for US$64.

Quicksilver (☎ 0361-283664; W www.bali -tours.com/quicksilver) runs day cruises from Benoa harbour to its pontoon off Toyapakeh for US$70/35 per adult/child. The fare includes hotel transfers, a buffet lunch,

snorkelling and a village walking tour. Options such as cycling tours are possible. Book at travel agents or on-line.

Sampalan

There's nothing inspiring about Sampalan, the main town on Penida, but it's quiet and pleasant, with a market, schools and shops strung out along the curving coast road. The market area, where the *bemos* (small pick-up trucks) congregate, is in the middle of town.

Made's Homestay (☎ 081 834 5204; singles/doubles 60,000/75,000Rp) is a friendly place with small, clean rooms and a pleasant garden. Breakfast is included. A small side road leads here between the market and the harbour.

Bungalow Pemda (☎ 21448; rooms from 25,000-50,000Rp), opposite the police station a few hundred metres east of the market, is the government resthouse, and has four recently renovated rooms, which are good value. The older rooms are basic.

There are a few simple **warung** (food stalls) along the main road and around the market. **Kios Dewi**, east of the market, serves Padang-style food.

Toyapakeh

If you come by boat from Lembongan, you'll probably be dropped at the beach at Toyapakeh, a pretty town with lots of shady trees. The beach has clean white sand, clear blue water, a neat line of boats, and Gunung Agung as a backdrop. Step up from the beach and you're at the roadhead, where bemos can take you to Ped or Sampalan (1000Rp). Few travellers stay here, but **Losmen Terang** *(singles/doubles 40,000/45,000Rp)* is near the waterfront.

Around the Island

A trip around the island, following the north and east coasts, and crossing the hilly interior, can be completed in a few hours by motorcycle. You could spend much longer, lingering at the temples and the small villages, and walking to less accessible areas, but there's no accommodation outside the two main towns. The following description goes clockwise from Sampalan.

The coastal road from Sampalan curves and dips past bays with rows of fishing boats and offshore seaweed gardens. After about 6km, just before the village of Karangsari, steps go up on the right side of the road to the narrow entrance of **Goa Karangsari** caves. There are usually people who can provide a pressure lantern and guide you through the cave for a small negotiable fee of around 10,000Rp. The limestone cave extends more than 200m through the hill and emerges on the other side to overlook a verdant valley.

Continue south past a naval station and several charming **temples** to Suana. Here the main road swings inland and climbs up into the hills, while a very rough side track goes southeast, past more interesting temples to **Semaya**, a fishing village with a sheltered **beach** and one of Bali's best **dive sites** offshore.

About 9km southwest of Suana, **Tanglad** is a very old-fashioned village and a centre for **traditional weaving**. Rough roads south and east lead to isolated parts of the coast.

A scenic ridge-top road goes northwest from Tanglad. At Batukandik, a rough road leads to a spectacular **waterfall**. Limestone cliffs drop hundreds of feet into the sea, with offshore rock pinnacles surrounded by crashing surf. At the base of these cliffs, underground streams discharge fresh water into the sea – a pipeline has been made to bring the water up to the top. You can follow the pipeline down the cliff-face on an alarmingly exposed metal stairway. From it, you can see the remains of rickety old wooden scaffolding – women used to clamber down this and return with large pots of water on their heads.

Back on the main road, continue to Batumadeg, past **Bukit Mundi** (the highest point on the island at 529m), through Klumpu and **Sakti**, which has traditional stone buildings. Return to the north coast at Toyapakeh.

The important temple of **Pura Dalem Penetaran Ped** is near the beach at Ped, a few kilometres east of Toyapakeh. It houses a shrine for the demon Jero Gede Macaling. The temple structure is crude, which gives it an appropriately sinister ambience. From there, the road is straight and flat back to Sampalan.

Getting There & Away

The strait between Nusa Penida and southern Bali is very deep and subject to heavy swells – if there is a strong tide, boats often have to wait. You may have to wait a while for the public boat to fill up with passengers.

Padangbai Fast public boats operate every day between Nusa Penida and Padangbai (25,000Rp, one hour). Boats leave from the beach at Buyuk, a few hundred metres west of the market.

Kusamba Slower *prahu* (traditional boats) carry goods, and the occasional passenger,

---

Jero Gede Macaling – Demon

Nusa Penida is the legendary home of Jero Gede Macaling, the demon who inspired the Barong Landung dance. Many Balinese believe the island is a place of enchantment and evil power *(angker)* – paradoxically, this is an attraction. Although few foreigners visit, thousands of Balinese come every year for religious observances aimed at placating the evil spirits.

The island has a number of interesting temples dedicated to Jero Gede Macaling, including Pura Dalem Penetaran Ped, near Toyapakeh. It houses a shrine, which is a source of power for practitioners of black magic, and a place of pilgrimage for those seeking protection from sickness and evil.

between Sampalan and Kusamba, the port closest to Semarapura. The boats leave when full and cost 5000Rp one-way for locals and around 25,000Rp for tourists. They are much slower than the boats from Padangbai, and may be heavily loaded with provisions.

Nusa Lembongan There is a public boat connection between Toyapakeh and Jungutbatu (Nusa Lembongan) between 5am and 6am (5000Rp), which takes about 20 minutes. Ask at your hotel or on the beach. Alternatively, charter a whole boat between the two islands for a negotiable 200,000Rp.

Getting Around

Bemos regularly travel along the sealed road between Toyapakeh and Sampalan, and sometimes on to Suana and up to Klumpu, but beyond these areas the roads are rough or nonexistent and transport is limited. You may be able to negotiate an *ojek* (a motorcycle that carries paying pillion passengers) for about 20,000Rp per hour. If you really want to explore, bring a mountain bike and camping equipment from the mainland (but remember, Nusa Penida is hilly). Alternatively, plan to do some serious hiking, but come well prepared.

NUSA LEMBONGAN

The most developed island for tourism is the deliciously laid-back Nusa Lembongan, which is totally free of cars, motorcycle noise and hassles of any form. It has a local population of about 7000 people, mostly

NUSA LEMBONGAN

PLACES TO STAY & EAT
6 Bungalo Jungutbatu
7 Bungalo Tarci; Linda Bungalows; Kainalu (The Surf Café)
9 Sukanusa 2003
11 Nusa Lembongan Bungalows
12 Agung's Lembongan Lodge
13 Main Ski Inn & Restaurant
14 Two Thousand Café & Bungalows; Ketut's Bungalows
17 Nusa Indah Bungalows

19 Pondok Baruna; World Diving
23 Bungalow Number 7
26 Coconut Beach Resort
27 Villa Wayan Cottages
28 Hai Tide Huts; Winda Sari Warung
29 Waka Nusa Resort
30 Nusa Lembongan Resort; The Anchorage

DIVE SITES
1 Jackfish Point
5 Blue Corner
31 Ceningan Point

OTHER
2 Pura Sakenan
3 Snorkelling Area
4 Lighthouse
8 Ronnie Billyard Warung
10 Ketut's Warung
15 Clinic
16 Pura Empuaji
18 Perama Office; Mandara Beach Bungalows
20 Bounty & Bali Hai Pontoons
21 Public Boats
22 Bank Pembangunan Daerah Bali
24 Pura Segara
25 Pura Dalem

Badung Strait

Shipwreck Surf Break

Lacerations Surf Break

Playground Surf Break

To Sanur

Mushroom Bay

Lembongan

Ceningan Reef Surf Break

To Toyapakeh

Pantai Selegimpak

Jungutbatu

Nusa Ceningan

Nusa Penida

0   0.5   1km
0   0.25   0.5mi

living in two small villages, Jungutbatu and Lembongan. Many of the locals are involved in the seaweed industry and tourism is a secondary source of income. Most surfers, divers and budget travellers stay at Jungutbatu beach, while more upmarket accommodation is further south, around Mushroom Bay, where many of the day-trip cruise boats stop.

Information

There's no tourist office, but your hotel or the **Perama office** on Jungutbatu beach at Mandara Beach Bungalows should be able to answer most questions. **Bank Pembangunan Daerah Bali** can exchange travellers cheques and cash, as will the Perama office; although it's advisable to bring sufficient cash with you, as rates are very poor. Ketut's Warung, behind Nusa Lembongan Bungalows, will change cash only.

There's no post office, although the Perama office has a postbox if you bring your own stamps. Main Ski Inn operates a **wartel** (public telephone office) and a **cybercafé**. Note that the telephone numbers given in this section are either mobile phones, or contact numbers of offices on mainland Bali. A small grocery shop is near the bank.

Electricity operates from 4pm to 9am from Monday to Saturday and all day Sunday), but the upmarket places have their own generators.

Any of the hotels can refer you to the local doctor in Jungutbatu village, although the consultation fee is a pricey 250,000Rp. The nurse's clinic in the village, opposite the path to Ketut's Bungalows, is a better option for simple problems.

Ketut's Bungalows rent pushbikes for 25,000Rp per day, surfboards for 30,000Rp to 40,000Rp per day, snorkelling gear for 20,000Rp to 30,000Rp per day, and motorbikes for 30,000Rp per hour.

Surfing

Surfing here is best in the dry season (April to September), when the winds come from the southeast. It's definitely not for beginners, and can be dangerous even for experts. There are three main breaks on the reef, all aptly named. You can paddle out to **Shipwreck**, but for **Lacerations** and **Playground** it's better to hire a boat. Prices are negotiable – from about 10,000Rp for a one-way trip, and around 100,000Rp waiting time. See Surfing under Activities in Facts for the Visitor for information on each break.

The surf can be crowded here even when the island isn't – charter boats from Bali sometimes bring groups of surfers for day trips from the mainland, or as part of a longer surfing trip between Bali and Sumbawa. For day trips boats can be chartered from Sanur Beach for a minimum of 500,000Rp. A tour operator with a good reputation is **Surf Travel Online** (☎ 0361-750550; e office@surftravelonline.com; Gang Sorga, off Poppies Gang II), based in Kuta, which runs all-inclusive overnight surfing trips to Lembongan, staying at Pondok Baruna, for 210,000Rp.

Diving

The excellent **World Diving** (☎ 0812 390 0686; w www.world-diving.com), based at Pondok Baruna on Jungutbatu Beach, has full PADI Resort status. It offers a full range of courses, including five-day PADI Open Water courses for US$295, and dive trips for US$30 per dive to sites around all three islands. There are several other dive operators based at Jungutbatu that operate from the various hotels.

That Seaweed Something

The cultivation of seaweed (rumput laut) is now a well-established industry, for which the shallow waters around Nusa Penida and Lembongan are particularly suitable. Because rainfall is low, the seawater maintains a high level of salinity, which is ideal for seaweed growth. Small pieces of a marine algae (Eucheuma) are attached to strings that are stretched between bamboo poles – these underwater fences can be seen off many of the beaches, and especially in the shallows between Lembongan and Ceningan. Growth is so fast that new shoots can be harvested every 45 days. The seaweed is then spread out on mats to dry in the sun – a sight and smell that you'll notice as you stroll around the seashore at Lembongan. The dried red and green seaweed is shipped to Padangbai, and then exported to Hong Kong, Japan and Europe, where its main use is for carrageen, an emulsifying and gelling agent in processed foods and cosmetics.

Snorkelling

There's good snorkelling just off the Bali Hai and Bounty pontoons off Jungutbatu Beach, as well as in areas off the north coast of the island. You can charter a boat from 30,000Rp to 50,000Rp per hour per boat, depending on demand, distance and the number of passengers; for more information ask at your hotel. Snorkelling gear can be rented for 20,000Rp to 30,000Rp per day. World Diving allows snorkellers to join dive trips and charges 50,000Rp for a four-hour trip.

Cruises

A number of cruise boats offer day trips to Nusa Lembongan from Benoa harbour. Trips include hotel transfer from the southern resorts, snorkelling and a substantial buffet lunch. Most of the companies listed have overnight accommodation at Mushroom Bay, if you are interested in extending your stay.

Bali Hai (☎ 0361-720331; w www.balihai cruises.com) has an ugly offshore pontoon for snorkelling and water play (it seriously looks like something out of the *Waterworld* movie). Reef cruises cost US$85/42.50 per adult/child, and catamaran cruises are US$75/50. Cruises depart Benoa harbour at 9.15am and return at 4.15pm.

Bounty Cruises (☎ 0361-726666; w www .balibountygroup.com) has an offshore pontoon and offers similar cruises to the Bali Hai for US$85/42.50, although the trip also includes a village tour on Lembongan. Cruises depart at 9am and return at 4.30pm. Pondok Baruna sells tickets.

Bali Happy Cruises (☎ 0361-728088; w www.baliseacruises.com/islandexplorer) has two fast boats and a yacht, offering day trips from US$49, and sports fishing cruises for US$115.

Waka Louka (☎ 0361-723629; w www .wakaexperience.com) is a luxury sailing catamaran and runs trips for US$86/43 per adult/child, which depart from Benoa at 9am and return at 6pm.

Other Activities

The Anchorage (☎ 0361-413375; admission US$10), part of Nusa Lembongan Resort, has two pools, a small water slide and a café-bar. It offers a mangrove tour US$10, which departs at 10.45am. Snorkel hire is available ($5).

Jungutbatu

Most visitors to Nusa Lembongan come for the reef surf breaks, and they stay around the quiet beach at Jungutbatu. The beach, a lovely arc of white sand with clear blue water, has superb views across to Gunung Agung on mainland Bali. The village itself is pleasant, with quiet lanes, no cars and a couple of temples, including **Pura Segara** and its enormous banyan tree. There's no jetty – the boats usually beach in the shallows by the village. The Perama boat stops outside Mandara Beach Bungalows, while the public shuttle boat stops further south.

Places to Stay & Eat Most places to stay in Jungutbatu are basic and breakfast isn't included unless otherwise stated. Most *losmen* (basic accommodation) have beachfront restaurants serving typical travellers fare.

A host of fairly nondescript, charmless accommodation is on offer in Jungutbatu, including **Nusa Indah Bungalows** (☎ 0366-24480; singles/doubles 40,000/60,000Rp), which is basically a doss-house for surfers; **Main Ski Inn & Restaurant** (☎ 0361-283065, 0811 394 426; singles 40,000Rp, doubles 60,000-80,000Rp); **Linda Bungalows** (☎ 0812 394 3988; rooms 75,000-190,000Rp); the clean and neat **Bungalo Tarci** (rooms 50,000-60,000Rp, 4-bed bungalow 100,000Rp); **Nusa Lembongan Bungalows** (☎ 0818 344 453; bungalows 50,000-100,000Rp), which has interesting rice-barn style bungalows that are painted in bright colours; and **Two Thousand Café & Bungalows** (☎ 0812 394 1273; rooms 125,000Rp).

A better option is **Bungalow Number 7** (☎ 0366-24497; doubles/triples 50,000/100,000Rp), which is a good, clean and friendly place. It has a **beachfront restaurant** (dishes 7000-20,000Rp) serving simple dishes.

Pondok Baruna (☎ 0812 390 0686; e putu baruna@yahoo.com; w www.world-diving.com; singles/doubles 50,000/80,000Rp) shares the same premises as World Diving and is without a doubt the best place to stay. Staff are deliciously friendly, rooms are pleasant and balconies face the ocean. The **restaurant** (dishes 10,000-18,000Rp) serves good meals, including club sandwiches.

Ketut's Bungalows (☎ 0366-24487; singles/doubles 70,000/140,000Rp, room with hot water 200,000Rp) has enormous beds (!)

and views of the ocean from most balconies. It's a scenic place where the small sandy area out the front fills with lounging travellers by day.

Agung's Lembongan Lodge (☎ 0361-422266; e agungs_lembongan@mailcity.com; singles 40,000-60,000Rp, doubles 50,000-70,000Rp, bungalows 100,000Rp) has colourful rice-barn style bungalows, as well as smaller rooms. The bathrooms are looking very tired, but are clean. The **restaurant** (dishes 6000-15,000Rp) has hanging bird cages, ocean views and a much nicer atmosphere than many others.

In more of a village atmosphere, **Bungalo Jungutbatu** (☎/fax 0361-723846; e sariwi@ dps.centrin.net.id; bungalows 250,000Rp) has bungalows set back from the beach in a pleasant garden. Rooms are cold water only, but have TV and fridge. It has rental bikes for guests.

Coconut Beach Resort (☎ 0361-728088; bungalows US$56, with air-con US$76), south of the village, has unusual, spacious, circular bungalows staggered up the hillside overlooking a lovely pool and the sea.

Sukanusa 2003 (dishes 15,000-30,000Rp) is a pleasant café-bar about 100m inland from Nusa Lembongan Bungalows.

Kainalu (The Surf Café) (dishes 14,000-26,000) has a pool table and serves up pizza, pasta and seafood dishes.

Entertainment Video movies are sometimes shown at **Agung's Lembongan Lodge**. **Ronnie Billyard Warung**, near Sukanusa 2003, is a locals' pool hall that plays loud music and karaoke, and could make for an interesting afternoon or evening.

Lembongan Village

About 4km southwest along the sealed road from Jungutbatu is Lembongan village, the island's other town. Leaving Jungutbatu you climb up a knoll that offers a wonderful view back over the beach. You can go right around the island, following the rough track that eventually comes back to Jungutbatu, but the roads are steep for cyclists and walkers.

Mushroom Bay

This gorgeous little bay, unofficially named for the mushroom corals offshore, has a perfect crescent of white-sand beach. It's the destination of most of the day cruises to

Lembongan, and the focus of Lembongan's upmarket tourist developments. During the day, the tranquillity may be disturbed by banana boat rides or parasailing. In the morning and the evening, it's delightful.

The most pleasant way from Jungutbatu is to walk along the trail that starts from the southern end of the main beach and follows the coastline for a kilometre or so, past a couple of little beaches. Alternatively, get a boat from Jungutbatu (or ask the captain of the boat from Sanur to drop you at Mushroom Bay before he goes on to Jungutbatu).

Places to Stay & Eat At the Bali Hai Beach Club, **Hai Tide Huts** (☎ 0361-720331; hut US$64, ocean view 74) has small but well-finished rice-barn thatched bungalows, albeit without private bathrooms – you'll have to head over to the bathroom block. Still, it's a relaxed place looking onto a clear stretch of beach, and there's a flash swimming pool. Packages are available for US$100/74 per adult/child, which includes the Bali Hai boat transfer.

Waka Nusa Resort (☎ 0361-7233629, fax 772077; W www.wakaexperience.com; bungalows US$143) has thatch-roofed bungalows set in sandy grounds. The beachside restaurant and bar is delightfully located under coconut palms. There is a US$80 transfer fee if you arrive via the Waka Louka cruise.

Villa Wayan Cottages (Chelegimbai; ☎ 0361-287431; W www.lembongan-discov ery.com; rooms US$21-59), just north of Mushroom Bay, near another delightful little bay called Pantai Selegimpak, has a few, varied and unusually decorated rooms, some suitable for families or groups.

Nusa Lembongan Resort (☎ 0361-413375, fax 413376; W www.nusa-lembongan.com; garden villas US$200, ocean villas US$250) has private and stylish villas overlooking a gorgeous sweep of ocean. Breakfast is included. The resort has a smart **restaurant** (lunch 50,000Rp, dinner 55,000-90,000Rp), and it's possible to dine over six-courses at ocean-side private pavilions for 350,000Rp per person.

Winda Sari Warung (dishes 10,000-30,000Rp), near Waka Nusa Resort, has a few dishes worth investigating, such as *ledok Penida* (rice porridge with chicken and eggs) and Balinese cakes served with grated coconut and ginger sauce.

Getting There & Away

Apart from luxury cruises, there are regular boats to/from Sanur, Kusamba and Nusa Penida.

Sanur & South Bali Boats leave from the northern end of Sanur Beach. Public boats leave at about 8am (30,000Rp, 90 minutes); the public 'shuttle' boat leaves at 10.30am and costs 40,000Rp – be there 30 minutes before departure. The strait between Bali and Nusa Penida is very deep and huge swells can develop – you may get wet with spray, so be prepared. A Perama boat leaves daily from Sanur at 10.30am (50,000Rp), with shuttle bus connections from Kuta and Ubud.

Returning to Sanur, the boats leave from Jungutbatu beach at 7am, and public shuttle boats at 8am. The Perama boat leaves at 8.30am and connects with a through service to Kuta (60,000Rp) and Ubud (65,000Rp).

Kusamba Most boats from Kusamba go to Toyapakeh on Nusa Penida, but sometimes they go to Jungutbatu on Lembongan. Boats from Sanur are safer and quicker.

Nusa Penida Boats take locals between Jungutbatu and Toyapakeh between 5.30am to 6am for 5000Rp. Otherwise, charter a boat for 200,000Rp one-way.

Benoa & Lombok Bounty Cruises (☎ 0361-726666; W www.balibountygroup .com) operates on Tuesday, Thursday, Saturday and Sunday between Benoa, Nusa Lembongan and Gili Meno on Lombok. The Benoa–Lembongan economy fare is US$23/41 for a one-way/return ticket (45 minutes), and the Lembongan–Gili Meno economy fare is US$23/41 (90 minutes). Tickets can be bought on Nusa Lembongan at Pondok Baruna/World Diving.

Getting Around

The island is fairly small and you can easily walk around it in a few hours, however, the roads across the middle of the island are quite steep.

NUSA CENINGAN

There is a narrow suspension bridge crossing the lagoon between Nusa Lembongan and Nusa Ceningan, which makes it quite easy to explore the network of tracks on foot or by bicycle – not that there is much to see. The lagoon is filled with frames for seaweed farming and there's also a fishing village and several small agricultural plots. Although the island is quite hilly, if you're up for it, you'll get glimpses of great scenery as you wander or cycle around the rough tracks.

Central Mountains

Most of Bali's mountains are volcanoes – some are dormant, some are definitely active. The mountains divide the gentle sweep of fertile rice land to the south from the narrower strip to the north. In east Bali, there is a small clump of mountains right at the end of the island, beyond Amlapura. Then there's the mighty volcano Gunung Agung (3142m), the island's 'Mother Mountain'. Northwest of Gunung Agung is the stark and spectacular caldera that contains the volcanic cone of Gunung Batur (1717m), Danau Batur (Lake Batur) and numerous smaller craters.

Further west, in the Danau Bratan (Lake Bratan) area, lush vegetation covers another complex of volcanic craters, these ones long dormant and interspersed with several lakes. A string of smaller mountains stretches off to the sparsely inhabited western region. Small, uncrowded roads cross Bali's steep central and western regions, through little-visited villages.

The popular round trip to the north coast crosses the mountains by one route (eg, via Gunung Batur) and returns by another (from Singaraja via Bedugul), thus covering the most interesting parts of the central mountain region. You can do the circuit easily in either direction, and while getting to more remote areas by public transport is a little tricky, it's not impossible.

Trekking to the peak of Gunung Batur to watch the sunrise is popular, but there are many other possibilities around the central mountains and lakes. Be prepared for weather that's considerably cooler and wetter than on the coast.

Gunung Batur Area

This area is like a giant dish, with the bottom half covered with water and a set of volcanic cones growing in the middle. The road around the southwestern rim of the Gunung Batur dish is one of Bali's most important north–south routes and has one of Bali's most spectacular vistas. However, most overnight visitors stay in the villages around the shores of Danau Batur, and plan an early start to climb the volcano.

Highlights

- Exploring the vast double caldera, crater lake, lava flows, hot springs, smoking cones, and let's not forget the mountain mafia of Gunung Batur
- Enjoying the beauty of the surrounding mountains reflected in the mountain lakes – Bratan, Buyan and Tamblingan
- Discovering Pura Ulun Danu Bratan – a truly beautiful, meditative temple
- Trekking through Bali's back country of winding roads and walking tracks through superb scenery and rural villages

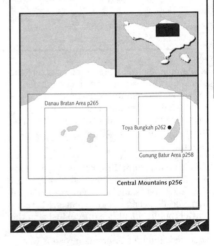

Danau Bratan Area p265

Toya Bungkah p262 ●

Gunung Batur Area p258

Central Mountains p256

Warning

The Gunung Batur area has a well-deserved reputation as a money-grubbing place. Keep an eye on your gear and don't leave any valuables in your car, especially at the start of any trail up the volcano. There's a complaints box at the ticket offices in Penelokan and Kubupenelokan, which is worth using if you encounter problems when trekking Gunung Batur (see 'The Mountain Monopoly' boxed text later).

ORIENTATION

The villages around the crater rim have grown together in a continuous, untidy strip. The main village is Kintamani, though the whole area is often referred to by that name.

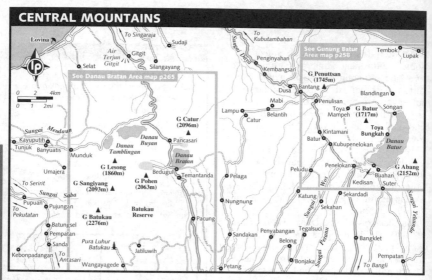

CENTRAL MOUNTAINS

Kintamani itself is a dreary place where the locals never look quite warm enough. Coming from the south, the first village is Penelokan, where tour group busloads stop to gasp at the view, eat a buffet lunch and be hassled by souvenir sellers.

INFORMATION

The **tourist information office** (*Yayasa Bintang Danu; ☎ 0366-23370; open 9am-2pm*), at Penelokan, has some information about local transport fares and trekking routes. There's a **wartel** (public telephone office) just near the turn-off down to the lake, and several postal agencies along the Kintamani road.

Entry Tickets

If you arrive by private vehicle, you'll be stopped at ticket offices at either Penelokan or Kubupenelokan; to save any hassle, you should stop by and buy a ticket. Entry is adult/child 3000/1500Rp, plus 100Rp insurance, plus 1000Rp for a car or 200Rp for a bicycle. This is for the whole Gunung Batur area; you shouldn't be charged any more down at the lakeside. Keep the tickets if you drive back and forth around the crater rim, or you may have to pay again and again. The entry ticket should be included in any organised tour. If you're passing through on a public bus or *bemo* (small pick-up truck) you don't have to pay anything.

Money

You can change money only at **Bank BRI** in Kintamani, and at a number of nearby **stalls** in Penelokan. Lakeside Cottages in Toya Bungkah changes money for guests only.

TREKKING

The climb to see the sunrise from Gunung Batur is still the most popular trek, even with the exorbitant fees charged, not to mention the unsavoury reputation, of the HPPGB (the guides organisation).

Warning

The volcanically active area west of the main peak can be deadly, with explosions of steam and hot lava, unstable ground and sulphurous gases. To find out about current conditions, ask at the trekking agencies in Toya Bungkah, or alternatively look at the website of the **Directorate of Volcanology and Geographical Hazard Mitigation** (**w** *www.vsi.dpe.go.id*). The active areas are sometimes closed to visitors for safety reasons – if this is the case, don't try it alone, and don't pay extra for an extended main crater trek that you won't be able to do.

Think twice about trekking in the wet season, because the trails can be muddy and slippery, and clouds often block the views. Note that monsoonal rains in early 2002 caused landslides in some mountain areas.

Millions of fruit bats fly over the coast at Nusa Penida

Watermelons for sale

Surfers return from the reef at Nusa Lembongan

Spot a spotted moray eel

Pura Ulun Danu Bratan, a Hindu/Buddhist temple built on islands in Danau Bratan

Smoking crater on Gunung Batur

Boats for hire at Danau Batur

Descending the black volcanic ash slopes of Gunung Batur

The Mountain Monopoly

For years, guides around Gunung Batur have competed with each other to overcharge would-be trekkers – and for the past few years they have *joined forces* to overcharge would-be trekkers. The *organisasi* is a cartel called HPPGB, which has an effective monopoly on the mountain – no-one else is permitted to work as a Gunung Batur trekking guide, even people who have done so many times in the past. The HPPGB office in Kedisan (near Pura Jati) has fixed the rates at 300,000Rp for a sunrise climb to the top (which covers from one to four trekkers and should take about six hours total), and 500,000Rp for a longer trek to the summit and around the new volcanic cones (about eight hours), again for a group of up to four people. (These prices are very high by Balinese standards, especially given the short length of the climb.) An anomaly, however, is that the HPPGB office in the village of Toya Bungkah, provides a different set of prices, stating that the full 300,000Rp is for travellers who arrive by car with a driver. Instead it quotes a price of 150,000Rp for a maximum of 4 people who arrive without a driver.

The Kedisan HPPGB makes a number of claims about the fee. It says that the Bangli local government supports the organisation and receives 15% of the fee; that the bulk of the money goes into the individual guides hands (although, other sources say guides receive only 10% of the fee); and that the rest is used for maintenance work on the mountain. Its main office, however, can't even seem to pay for pens to take down trekkers' names...so where is the money going?

While it is definitely recommended to take a guide if you start your climb in the dark, the problem is that trekkers' freedom of choice to make this decision has effectively been hijacked by the HPPGB, who aggressively discourage independent trekkers through intimidatory tactics. Numerous readers' letters have quoted similar stories of HPPGB guides waiting outside their hotel at 4am as they embark on an independent climb, only to be harassed and/or attacked when they refuse to take a guide. One traveller even wrote of hiding in bushes with a mountain mafia vigilante group in search of him, while another wrote of threats to kill her and her friends. Many travellers turned back out of genuine fear for their safety. The HPPGB also has most routes covered, and will try to prevent you from climbing without an official guide.

It seems likely that blatant overcharging, intimidation and aggression will prevail in the future, and while it does a Gunung Batur trek is a relatively expensive and unappealing outing. If this is the sort of environment you wish to climb in (whether independently or not), then so be it, but try to get a full group of four people together to share the cost, or seriously consider an alternative trek. Remember that Gunung Rinjani is just across the water and offers a far more spectacular climb. And Rinjani, unlike Batur, has had its own mountain mafia quashed.

To sum up, one traveller comments on the validity of including Gunung Batur in this guide at all: *This is by far the most piratical place in Bali. It really is questionable whether you should be recommending people to trek here at all. Rip-offs begin from the time a cop stops your bike outside Penelokan to extract a 'toll' and end with you crawling up a precipitous mountain side in the dark without a torch having parted with hundreds of thousands of rupiah, only to have to pay someone to drive you back to your hotel if you should live to make it back down to the base...'*

Michael Day, Australia

Trekking Agencies

Even reputable and highly competent adventure tour operators from elsewhere on Bali cannot take their customers up Gunung Batur without paying the HPPGB and using one of their guides, so these tours are relatively expensive.

Trekking agencies in Toya Bungkah must also use guides from the organisation for Gunung Batur treks, but they *may* be able to help you to get a full group together, and ensure that you get one of the better guides from the HPPGB. Alternatively, they can arrange other treks in the area, to Gunung Abang or the outer rim of the crater, or to other mountains such as Gunung Agung.

Two good local agencies worth checking with, even if you don't trek with them, are **Arlina's** (☎ 0366-51165), at Arlina's Bungalows, which charges US$20/25/38 for a short/medium/long climb of Batur, and **Jero Wijaya Tourist Service** (☎ 0366-51249,

fax 51250; **W** *www.balitrekking.com*), affiliated with Lakeside Cottages. It charges
US$30 per person (minimum of 5 people
needed) for the sunrise climb of Batur. It
also offers treks up Gunung Agung (US$75)
and in Taman Nasional Bali Barat (US$90).

Hotel Segara in Kedisan quotes a trekking
fee of 150,000Rp per person for a group of
four, while **Hotel Miranda** in Kintamani
quotes 150,000Rp per person for a group of
five, or 350,000Rp for solo climbers.

Equipment

If you're climbing before sunrise, take a
torch (flashlight) or be absolutely sure that
your guide provides you with one. You'll
need good strong footwear, a hat, a sweater
and drinking water.

Gunung Batur

Vulcanologists describe Gunung Batur as a
'double caldera', ie, one crater inside another. The outer crater is an oval about 14km
long, with its western rim about 1500m
above sea level. The inner crater is a classic
volcano-shaped peak that reaches 1717m.
Activity over the last decade has spawned
several smaller cones on its western flank,
unimaginatively named Batur I, II, III and
IV. More than 20 minor eruptions were
recorded between 1824 and 1994, and there
were major eruptions in 1917, 1926 and
1963. As recently as November 1997, about
3000 minor tremors were recorded, and
there was more activity in 1999 and 2000.

Ideally, trekkers should get to the top for
sunrise (about 6am), before mist and cloud

GUNUNG BATUR AREA

PLACES TO STAY
3 Hotel Miranda
18 Lakeview Hotel &
   Puncak Sari Restaurant
20 Hotel Astra Dana
21 Hotel Segara & Restoran;
   Hotel Surya
22 Hotel Putra Mulya
23 Hotel Baruna

PLACES TO EAT
10 Gunung Sari Restaurant;
   Perama Stop
13 Kintamani
14 Puri Dewata
15 Gunawan

OTHER
1 Pura Puncak
   Penulisan
2 Bank BRI
4 Pura Ulun Danu
5 Pura Bukit Mentik
6 Car Park
7 Pura Ulun Danu Batur
8 Pura Jati
9 HPPGB Guides Office
11 Post Office
12 Ticket Office
16 Tourist Information
   Office (Yayasa
   Bintang Danu)
17 Wartel
19 Ticket Office
24 Ticket Office

Tembok
To
Singaraja   To Tulamben
                 & Amlapura
                              Lupak

Siakin

G Penulisan
(1745m)
To
Kubutambahan
          1
To   Penulisan
Pelaga

                 Blandingan

Kintamani
3   2

                              Songan 7
      5   Toya Mampeh
                        6
4   G Batur
                       (1717m)

Batur
                                    Kuban (Cemetery)
11   Kubupenelokan   Toya Bungkah
12   10   Trunyan
13   9   8
      15   Penelokan
14   17   20   Danau Batur
To   16   18   21
Payangan   19
                 22   Kedisan   Abang
Peludu   Boat Terminal
                              G Abang
Beyunggede   Buahan   (2152m)
                    23
To Ubud
     To Sekardadi,   To Bangklet   To Suter,
     Tampaksiring &   & Bangli   Pempatar
     Ubud   & Rendang   24

0   1.5   3km
0   0.75   1.5mi

obscure the view. It's a magnificent sight, though hardly a wilderness experience – it's not uncommon to have 100 people on top for sunrise in the tourist season. However, it's not necessary to be at the top for sunrise – a halfway point is fine. If you start at 5am, you'll avoid the crowds.

Guides will usually provide breakfast on the summit, and this often includes the novelty of cooking an egg or banana in the steaming holes at the top of the volcano (although this isn't recommended for hygiene reasons). Unfortunately, the practice has resulted in an accumulation of litter around the summit, although it's not as bad as it once was. Please take your rubbish with you. There are several refreshment stops along the way, and people with buckets full of cold drinks. Agree on a price before they open the bottle – they can ask over 10,000Rp for a small soft drink. Some small **warung** (food stalls) at the top offer tea, coffee and toasted sandwiches for quite high prices – and brilliant views for free (although check where the water comes from for the coffee and tea).

From Toya Bungkah The basic trek is to start climbing from Toya Bungkah at about 3am, reach the summit for sunrise, and possibly walk right around the main cone, then return to Toya Bungkah. The route is pretty straightforward – walk out of the village towards Kedisan and turn right just after the car park. There are a few separate paths at first but they all rejoin sooner or later – just keep going uphill, tending southwest and then west. After about 30 minutes you'll be on a ridge with quite a well-defined track; keep going up. It gets pretty steep towards the top and it can be hard walking over the loose volcanic sand – climbing up three steps and sliding back two. Allow about two hours to reach the top, which is at the northern edge of the inner crater.

You can follow the rim to the western side, with a view of the area of the most recent volcanic activity, continue to the southern edge, and then return to Toya Bungkah by the route you climbed up. Alternatively, descend on a more southerly route through the lava field to Pura Jati, and walk (or get a bemo) along the road back to Toya Bungkah.

Longer trips go around the new volcanic cones southwest of the summit. This has the most exciting volcanic activity, with smoking craters, bright yellow sulphur deposits, and steep slopes of fine black sand. If the activity is *too* exciting, the area may be closed for trekking, though the summit can still be OK. The most satisfying round trip is to climb Gunung Batur from Toya Bungkah, follow the inner crater rim around to the west, then go south through the area of the most recent volcanic activity, descend to the east, and traverse through the lava field to Pura Jati.

Climbing up, spending a reasonable time on the top and then strolling back down takes four or five hours; for the longer treks around the newer cones, allow around eight hours.

From Pura Jati If you stay at Kedisan rather than Toya Bungkah, you might want to start at Pura Jati. The shortest trek is basically across the lava fields, then straight up (allow about two hours to the top). If you want to see the newer cones west of the peak (assuming the area is safe to visit), go to the summit first – don't go walking round the active area before sunrise.

From the Northeast The easiest route is from the northeast, if you can get transport to the trailhead at 4am. From Toya Bungkah take the road northeast towards Songan and take the left fork after about 3.5km. Follow this small road for another 1.7km to a badly signposted track on the left – this climbs another kilometre or so to a parking area – if you don't get lost. From here, the walking track is easy to follow to the top, and should take less than an hour.

Warning The parking area is not secure, so don't leave anything of value in your car, or even a helmet with your motorcycle. There's a high risk of damage to your vehicle if you don't use an official guide, and no guarantee of its safety even if you do. The best way to do this route is probably to engage one of the HPPGB guides, and ask him to arrange transport (for an extra cost) to the trailhead, climb to the top, then walk back by the southeastern trail to Toya Bungkah.

From Kintamani From the western edge of the outer crater, trails go from Batur and Kintamani down into the main crater, then up Gunung Batur from the west side. However, this route passes close to the volcanically active area and may be closed for safety reasons. Check the current status with the guide at Hotel Miranda in Kintamani.

The Outer Crater

An increasingly popular place to see the sunrise is on the outer crater rim northeast of Songan. You'll need transport to Pura Ulun Danu Batur, near the northern end of the lake. From there you can climb to the top of the outer crater rim in under 30 minutes, and see Bali's northeast coast, about 5km away. At sunrise, the silhouette of Lombok looms across the water, and the first rays strike the great volcanoes of Batur and Agung. If you can reconnoitre this route in daylight, you'll be able to do it without a guide.

Trails follow the outer rim to the north and south, and provide delightful trekking, with the sea on one side, the lake and volcanoes on the other. The Toya Bungkah trekking agents know many minor trails that can bring you back to the lakeside.

Another option is an easy downhill stroll to the coast road at Lupak, from where you can take public transport back to Toya Bungkah via Kubutambahan and Penelokan. If you start early, you could complete this round trip in a single day.

Gunung Abang

It's possible to hike up Gunung Abang (2152m), at the southeastern edge of the outer crater. It's the highest point on the crater, though the potentially panoramic view is largely obscured by forest. Go as far southeast around the rim as possible by road and, where the road swings south, look for the walking trail that continues eastwards and upwards. Beyond Abang there are little-used trails around the crater and beside the lake that can get you down to Trunyan or right around to Songan, but you'll need a good guide – talk to the trekking agents in Toya Bungkah.

See the Activities section in the Facts for the Visitor chapter for recommended tours, which include 4WD tours of the crater and mountain bike tours.

VILLAGES AROUND GUNUNG BATUR
☎ 0366

There are several small villages around Gunung Batur, where you can choose to base yourself.

Penelokan

Penelokan means 'Place to Look' – and you will be gobsmacked by the view across to Gunung Batur and down to the lake at the bottom of the crater. Apart from the view, there's not much here – a large hotel under renovation, several ugly monolithic restaurants peering over the crater, and numerous desperate souvenir sellers.

Places to Stay & Eat Right on the edge of the crater with a brilliant view of the lake, **Lakeview Hotel & Puncak Sari Restaurant** (☎/fax 51464; e lakeview@baliparadise.com; rooms from US$30) was under renovation at the time of writing, but should be reopening quite soon.

The road around the rim has several monstrous, overpriced restaurants geared to busloads of tour groups, including **Gunawan, Puri Dewata** and **Kintamani**. They all have fine views, and provide buffet-style lunches from 60,000Rp to 80,000Rp or more. Most will have a relatively expensive a la carte alternative if you ask. Dotted among these restaurants are some decent **warung** with similar views, and meals for about 20,000Rp.

Batur & Kintamani

The original village of Batur was down in the crater but was wiped out by a violent eruption in 1917. It killed thousands of people and destroyed more than 60,000 homes before the lava flow stopped at the entrance to the village's main temple.

Taking this as a good omen, the village was rebuilt, but Gunung Batur erupted again in 1926. This time, the lava flow covered everything but the loftiest temple shrine. Fortunately, the Dutch administration anticipated the eruption and evacuated the village (partly by force), so very few lives were lost. The village was relocated up on the crater rim, and the surviving shrine was also moved up there and placed in the new temple, **Pura Ulun Danu**. Spiritually, Gunung Batur is the second most important mountain on Bali (only Gunung Agung outranks it) so this temple is of considerable importance.

The villages of Batur and Kintamani now virtually run together. Kintamani is famed for its large and colourful **market** held every three days. It starts early and by 11am it's all over.

Places to Stay & Eat The **Hotel Miranda** (☎ 52022; Jl Raya Kintamani; singles/doubles 25,000/50,000Rp) is the only reliable accommodation here; it's very basic but clean and does have good food and a congenial open fire at night. The informative owner can act as a trekking guide (see the Trekking Agencies entry under Trekking earlier).

Penulisan

The road gradually climbs along the crater rim beyond Kintamani, and is often shrouded in clouds, mist or rain. Penulisan is where the road bends sharply and heads down towards the north coast. Near the bend, several steep flights of steps lead to Bali's highest temple, **Pura Puncak Penulisan**, at 1745m. Inside the highest courtyard are rows of old statues and fragments of sculptures in the open *bale* (pavilions). Some of the sculptures date back to the 11th century. The temple views are superb: facing north you can see over the rice terraces clear to the Singaraja coast – weather permitting.

With your own transport you can continue further around the crater rim, with a great view of the northern side of Gunung Batur. After a while, the road leaves the ridge top and descends towards the north coast – you'll get glimpses of brilliant coastal scenery through the tall trees, but the road doesn't go all the way down.

Getting There & Around

The two main routes to Penelokan from the south, via Bangli and Tampaksiring, meet just before Penelokan, and are both good roads. You can also take the rougher road to/from Rendang via Menanga, which turns off a few kilometres east of Penelokan, and goes on to Semarapura. In clear weather, you'll have fine views of Gunung Agung. The other roads are OK, but have little public transport.

You can also get to Penelokan from the north coast – the road climbs steeply from Kubutambahan, near Yeh Sanih, and has regular public transport.

Bemo & Bus From the Batubulan terminal in Denpasar, bemos regularly go to Kintamani, via various routes, including Ubud and Payangan (6000Rp), Bangli, or Tampaksiring (4500Rp). They also run between Denpasar (Batubulan) and Singaraja via Kintamani and Penelokan (8500Rp).

Orange bemos regularly shuttle back and forth around the crater rim, between Penelokan and Kintamani (5000Rp for tourists). To Penulisan, try to flag down a minibus going to Singaraja. Public bemos from Penelokan to the lakeside villages go mostly in the morning (tourist price about 4000Rp to Toya Bungkah). Later in the day, you may have to charter transport (maybe 30,000Rp).

Tourist Shuttle Bus On Perama there's one daily service to/from Kuta (30,000Rp), Sanur (30,000Rp) and Ubud (30,000Rp), which stops at Gunung Sari Restaurant at Kubupenelokan and along the road through Kintamani to Penulisan, on request. A daily south-bound Perama bus comes from Lovina (30,000Rp) via Singaraja, and continues to Ubud and southern Bali. Lakeside Cottages in Toya Bungkah also arranges transport for one to five passengers to Ubud (100,000Rp), Padangbai or Sanur (130,000Rp), Candidasa, Lovina or Kuta/airport (150,000Rp) and Amed (180,000Rp).

Ojek An *ojek* (motorcycle taking a pillion passenger) can be a really easy way to get around if you don't have much luggage. Fares are negotiable, but from Penelokan try to not pay more than 6000Rp to Kedisan, 7000Rp to Buahan or 12,000Rp to Toya Bungkah.

AROUND DANAU BATUR
☎ 0366

A hairpin-bend road winds its way down from Penelokan to the shore of Danau Batur. At the lakeside you can go left along the quaint little switchback road that winds its way through lava fields to Toya Bungkah, the usual base for climbing Gunung Batur.

The road gets rougher as it continues round to Songan, under the northeastern rim of the crater, and an even rougher side road goes around to the north side of Gunung Batur, via Toya Mampeh. This round-the-volcano road is interesting, as it passes through a huge layer of solidified black lava from the 1974 eruption, but it now carries a huge number of large trucks hauling sand and gravel – which make it hazardous and unpleasant. If you want to risk it, go clockwise round the crater, and at least you won't be meeting the trucks head-on.

Alternatively, go east around the lakeside, through Kedisan and Buahan. Another option is a boat trip across the lake, to the ancient village of Trunyan and its alfresco cemetery.

Toya Bungkah

The main tourist centre is Toya Bungkah (also known as Tirta), with its hot springs (*tirta* and *toya* both mean 'water'). Toya Bungkah is a scruffy little village, but many travellers stay here so they can climb Gunung Batur early in the morning – most of them leave quickly afterwards.

Information   The infamous **HPPGB** (☎ 52362; e volcanotrek@hotmail.com), the *organisasi* of Gunung Batur guides that currently exploits a monopoly on the trekking business, has an office in Toya Bungkah (see the Gunung Batur section earlier).

Jero Wijaya Tourist Service changes money for Lakeside Cottage guests only.

Hot Springs   Hot springs bubble out in a couple of spots, and have long been used for bathing pools. Beside the lake, with a wonderful mountain backdrop, **Tirta Sanjiwani Hot Springs Complex** (☎ 51205; adult/child US$5/2.50; open 8am-6pm) is appealing enough, though often deserted. Entry includes use of the cold-water pool and hot spa; some hotels sell discount entry vouchers.

Places to Stay   The main road through town is used by large gravel trucks day and night, so try to get rooms at hotel backs. There are plenty of small, cheap *losmen* (basic accommodation), but not many worth recommending. Most have cold water only.

Hotel Dharma Putra (☎ 52043; singles 40,000-60,000Rp, doubles 50,000-70,000Rp) has (just) adequate rooms.

Arlina's Bungalows (☎ 51165; singles/doubles 30,000/50,000Rp, with hot water 40,000/60,000Rp) is clean, comfortable, friendly and above the average standard.

Under the Volcano I (☎ 51166; singles/doubles/triples 30,000/40,000/50,000Rp) has large rooms around a small garden. The **restaurant** (dishes 12,000-20,000Rp) serves the local speciality *ikan mujair*.

Under the Volcano II (☎ 51666; singles/doubles 50,000/60,000Rp), with a lovely, quiet lakeside location opposite vegetable plots, has clean rooms, with a glimmer of personality.

Lakeside Cottages (☎ 51249, fax 51250; w www.balitrekking.com; singles/doubles US$8/10, with hot water US$20/25, with hot water & satellite TV US$28/35), at the end of the track on the water's edge, is definitely one of the better places.

Hotel Puri Bening Hayato (☎ 51234, fax 51248; bungalow US$20, rooms US$55-80), an incongruous three-storey place, has a few quaint water-view bungalows and oversized wannabe 'deluxe' rooms all with hot water and lake views. The hotel has a **restaurant** (dishes 12,000-24,000Rp), which is cool and quiet inside, but often deserted.

Places to Eat   Small, sweet lake fish known as *ikan mujair* are the delicious local speciality. The dish is barbecued to a crisp with onion, garlic and bamboo sprouts, making the bones crunchy and edible. Most of the hotels have restaurants, and **Arlina's** and **Under the Volcano I** are worth seeking out, as is **Lakeside Cottages** (dishes 9000-14,000Rp). Its restaurant is worth trying for home-style Japanese dishes, such as *oyakodon* (rice topped with egg and chicken).

Volcano Breeze (☎ 51824; dishes 10,000-18,000Rp) is a sociable travellers café, well away from the constant truck noise.

Getting There & Around   Bemos between Toya Bungkah and Penelokan (on the crater

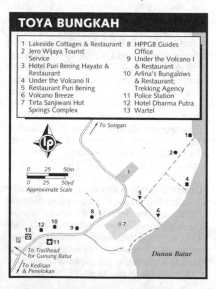

TOYA BUNGKAH

1 Lakeside Cottages & Restaurant	8 HPPGB Guides Office
2 Jero Wijaya Tourist Service	9 Under the Volcano I & Restaurant
3 Hotel Puri Bening Hayato & Restaurant	10 Arlina's Bungalows & Restaurant; Trekking Agency
4 Under the Volcano II	11 Police Station
5 Restaurant Puri Bening	12 Hotel Dharma Putra
6 Volcano Breeze	13 Wartel
7 Tirta Sanjiwani Hot Springs Complex	

To Songan

0   25   50m
0   25   50yd
Approximate Scale

To Trailhead for Gunung Batur
To Kedisan & Penelokan

Danau Batur

rim) go mostly in the morning. Later you may have to charter transport (around 20,000Rp). Jero Wijaya (affiliated with Lakeside Cottages) can organise a shuttle bus for a minimum of five people to the Perama stop in Kintamani, or elsewhere.

Advertised transport to tourist areas like Ubud and Kuta is often by charter vehicle, and may require a minimum of six people to run.

Songan

Two kilometres around the lake from Toya Bungkah, Songan is a large and interesting village with market gardens extending to the lake's edge. At lakeside road end is **Pura Ulun Danu Batur**, under the edge of the crater rim.

Toya Mampeh

A turn-off in Songan takes you on a rough but passable road around the crater floor. Much of the area is very fertile, with bright patches of market garden and quite strange landforms. On the northwestern side of the volcano, Toya Mampeh village (also called Yeh Mampeh) is surrounded by a vast field of chunky black lava – a legacy of the 1974 eruption.

Further on, **Pura Bukit Mentik** was completely surrounded by molten lava from this eruption, but the temple itself, and its really impressive banyan tree, were quite untouched – it's called the 'Lucky Temple'. The enjoyment is constantly shattered, however, by a continuous procession of trucks hauling out volcanic gravel and sand.

Kedisan & Buahan

The villages around the south end of the lake have a few places to stay, in a fairly isolated setting. Buahan is a pleasant 15-minute stroll from Kedisan, with market gardens going right down to the lakeshore.

Places to Stay & Eat Right at the bottom of the road from Penelokan is **Hotel Surya** (☎ 51378; singles/doubles 30,000/40,000Rp, with hot water 60,000/80,000Rp), with a big range of somewhat grimy rooms – the more expensive have views and hot water. Its **restaurant** (dishes 7000-12,000Rp), in a nice elevated position, has a better view than some of the expensive tourist restaurants in Penelokan. Free pick-up is offered from Ubud and Semarapura.

Hotel Segara & Restoran (☎ 51136; fax 51212; rooms 40,000-80,000Rp), next door to Hotel Surya, has bungalows set around a courtyard. The more expensive rooms have hot water. It's clean and comfortable enough for a night. No rooms have lake views.

Hotel Astra Dana (☎ 52091; rooms 40,000-60,000Rp), which is nearby, overlooks the lake. Rooms are decent enough, and the more expensive ones have hot water and views.

Hotel Putra Mulya (☎ 51818; singles/doubles 30,000/50,000Rp), east of Hotel Segara, has OK, somewhat grubby, rooms in a quiet yard away from the road.

Hotel Baruna (rooms 50,000Rp), out past the edge of the village, is a restful, very isolated place, with a lovely outlook. It offers simple, clean rooms.

Trunyan & Kuban

The village of Trunyan is squeezed between the lake and the outer crater rim. It is inhabited by Bali Aga people, descendants of the original Balinese who inhabited Bali before the Majapahit arrival. Trunyan is not a welcoming place, unlike Tenganan, the other well-known Bali Aga village in eastern Bali.

Trunyan is famous for the **Pura Pancering Jagat** temple, with its 4m-high statue of the village's guardian spirit, but tourists are not allowed to go inside. There are also several traditional Bali Aga–style dwellings, and a large banyan tree, said to be over 1100 years old. Touts and guides want large tips for brief and barely comprehensible commentaries, and solicit large 'offerings' at the temple or the graves – 2000Rp is sufficient.

A little beyond Trunyan, and accessible only by boat (there's no path) is the **village cemetery** at Kuban. The people of Trunyan do not cremate or bury their dead – they lie them out in bamboo cages to decompose, although strangely there is no stench. A collection of skulls and bones lies on a stone platform. This is a tourist trap for those with macabre tastes.

Getting There & Away Getting across the lake from Kedisan to Trunyan was once one of Bali's great rip-offs. After negotiating a sky-high price, your boatman would then want to renegotiate halfway across. Meanwhile, your motorcycle was being stripped back at Kedisan. It got so bad that the government took over and set the prices.

Boats leave from a jetty near the middle of Kedisan, where there is a ticket office and a secure car park. Tourists are not allowed to catch the public boat! The price for a round trip Kedisan–Trunyan–Kuban; cemetery–Toya Bungkah–Kedisan (8am to 5pm, two hours) depends on the number of passengers, with a maximum of seven (one/two people 196,500/199,000Rp), and finally seven people for 211,500Rp. Try to go before 10am, when the water is calmer and Gunung Batur is most photogenic.

If you want to do it on the cheap, don't consider hiring a canoe and paddling yourself – the lake is bigger than it looks from the shore and it can get rough. An alternative is to follow the footpath around the lake to Trunyan, an easy one- or two-hour walk (the walk will be the best part of the trip). From Trunyan, you may be able to negotiate a boat to the cemetery, Toya Bungkah or Kedisan, but it won't be cheap.

PELAGA
☎ 0362

A scenic road heads north from Ubud, via Sangeh and Petang, and continues through the pretty village of Pelaga to finish near Penulisan at the northwestern edge of Gunung Batur's outer crater. The road is sealed, little trafficked, and would make a fine cycling trip. Pelaga has great possibilities for hiking in the surrounding countryside.

There are bemos up this road all the way from Wangaya terminal in Denpasar (4500Rp), via Sangeh, but it's best with your own transport. With some directions, you could walk the 8km from Bedugul (near Danau Gratan) to Pelaga.

Danau Bratan Area

Approaching from the south, you gradually leave the rice terraces behind and ascend into the cool, damp mountain country around Danau Bratan. Candikuning is the main village in the area, and has an important and picturesque temple. Bedugul is at the south end of the lake, with the most touristy attractions. About 4km north of the lake, Pancasari has the local market, the main bemo terminal and a famous golf course. Danau Buyan and Danau Tamblingan are pristine lakes northwest of Danau Bratan, beyond

which are some interesting villages. To the south and west there are other beautiful highland areas, little visited by tourists.

While the choice of accommodation near the lake is limited, much of the area is geared towards domestic, not foreign, tourists. On Sunday and public holidays, the lakeside can be crowded with courting couples on motorcycles and Kijangs bursting with day-tripping families.

BEDUGUL
☎ 0368

The name Bedugul is sometimes used to refer to the whole lakeside area, but strictly speaking, Bedugul is just the first place you reach at the top of the hill when coming up from south Bali. At the large billboard, take a right turn to the southern edge of the lake, where a harmless tourist trap awaits.

Taman Rekreasi Bedugul

Lakeside eateries, a souvenir supermarket and a selection of **water sports** – parasailing, water- and jet-skiing plus speedboats – are the features at this tacky recreation park (☎ 21197; admission 3300Rp, parking 1500Rp), which attracts many tour buses.

Trekking

From the water sports area, a trail around the south side of the lake goes to **Goa Jepang** (Japanese Cave), dug during WWII. From there, a difficult path ascends to the top of **Gunung Catur** (2096m), where the old **Pura Puncak Mangu** temple is popular with monkeys. Allow about four hours to go up and back from Taman Rekreasi.

Places to Stay & Eat

Bedugul Hotel & Restaurant (☎/fax 21197; hill view 195,000Rp, lake view 250,000Rp), in the recreation park, has clean, modern but charm-free rooms. The restaurant does buffet lunch (45,000Rp), or you can eat à la carte at tables overlooking the lake (dishes 13,000Rp to 40,000Rp).

Hotel Bukit Permai (☎ 21443; rooms 80,000-250,000Rp), on a hillside away from the lake, overlooking the village below, seems to attract few guests, though the rooms are comfortable and the views are excellent.

Upmarket hotels on the slope south of Bedugul offer outstanding views to the east and west.

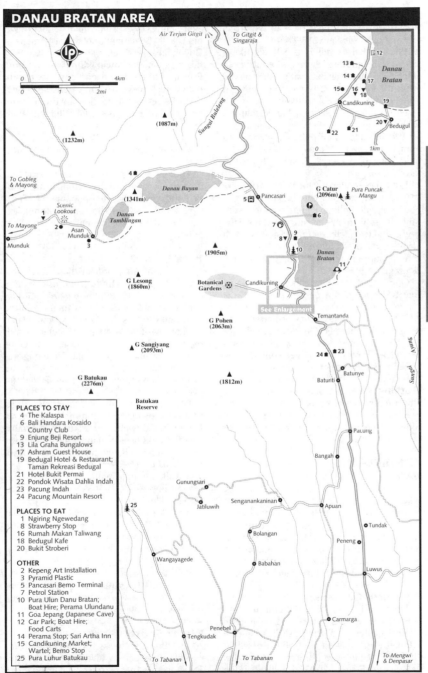

DANAU BRATAN AREA

Inset map (Danau Bratan enlargement)
12
13
14
17
15 16 18
Candikuning 19
20 Bedugul
22 21

0   1km

Main map labels

Air Terjun Gitgit
To Gitgit & Singaraja

(1087m)

Sungai Baleleng

(1232m)

To Gobleg & Mayong

4
Danau Buyan
(1341m)
5 Pancasari

G Catur (2096m)
Pura Puncak Mangu

Scenic Lookout
1
2 Asan Munduk
3
Danau Tamblingan
6

To Mayong

Munduk

7
9
8 10
Danau Bratan
11

(1905m)

G Lesong (1860m)

Botanical Gardens
Candikuning

See Enlargement

Temantanda

G Pohen (2063m)

G Sangiyang (2093m)

24 23

Batunye
Baturiti

G Batukau (2276m)

(1812m)

Batukau Reserve

CENTRAL MOUNTAINS

Pacung

Bangah

Gunungsari
Senganankaninan
Apuan

Jatiluwih
Tundak

25
Bolangan
Peneng

Wangayagede
Babahan
Luwus

Penebel
Carmarga

Tengkudak
To Mengwi & Denpasar

To Tabanan   To Tabanan

Legend

PLACES TO STAY
4 The Kalaspa
6 Bali Handara Kosaido Country Club
9 Enjung Beji Resort
13 Lila Graha Bungalows
17 Ashram Guest House
19 Bedugal Hotel & Restaurant; Taman Rekreasi Bedugal
21 Hotel Bukit Permai
22 Pondok Wisata Dahlia Indah
23 Pacung Indah
24 Pacung Mountain Resort

PLACES TO EAT
1 Ngiring Ngewedang
8 Strawberry Stop
16 Rumah Makan Taliwang
18 Bedugul Kafe
20 Bukit Stroberi

OTHER
2 Kepeng Art Installation
3 Pyramid Plastic
5 Pancasari Bemo Terminal
7 Petrol Station
10 Pura Ulun Danu Bratan; Boat Hire; Perama Ulundanu
11 Goa Jepang (Japanese Cave)
12 Car Park; Boat Hire; Food Carts
14 Perama Stop; Sari Artha Inn
15 Candikuning Market; Wartel; Bemo Stop
25 Pura Luhur Batukau

On a busy main road, **Pacung Mountain Resort** (☎ 21038; fax 21043; W www.bali-pacung.com; singles US$90-185, doubles US$100-200) from the facade looks like a tourist trap, but it's built on a steep terraced slope overlooking an exquisite valley carved with rice fields and early morning views of Gunung Batukau, and is actually a quiet and tasteful option. There is a bar-restaurant, with gorgeous views of course, which serves a buffet lunch (55,000Rp) between noon and 3pm, or à la carte is also available (22,000Rp to 78,000Rp). It's worth dropping by just to have a drink.

Just opposite, **Pacung Indah** (☎ 21020, fax 21964; W www.pacung.com; rooms 190,000-750,000Rp) doesn't have quite the same sublime views, but rooms are still a cut above the average and all include a private courtyard. It also serves a buffet lunch (39,000Rp) or à la carte options (19,000Rp to 45,000Rp), such as pizza.

Opposite the Taman Rekreasi turn-off, **Bukit Stroberi** (Strawberry Hill; ☎ 21265; singles/doubles 40,000/50,000Rp; dishes 11,000-17,000Rp) has a cosy restaurant with polished floorboards. On offer are dishes such as burgers and soto ayam. It has simple, clean rooms, which get some traffic noise. Breakfast is not included.

Getting There & Away

Any minibus or bemo between south Bali and Singaraja will stop at Bedugul on request (see the Candikuning section for details).

CANDIKUNING
☎ 0368

Spread out along the western side of the lake, Candikuning is the horticultural focus of central Bali. Its daily market was once the main supplier of vegetables, fruit and flowers for the southern hotels, but now it mostly supplies herbs, spices and potted plants for tourists. There's a **wartel** beside the market, and several **moneychangers**.

Botanical Gardens

Coming north from Bedugul, at a junction conspicuously marked with a large, phallic corncob sculpture, a small side road goes a kilometre or so west to Bali's **Botanical Gardens** (Kebun Raya Eka Karya Bali; ☎/fax 21273; admission 3000Rp, car parking 1000Rp, motorcycle parking 500Rp; open 8am-6pm daily). Established in 1959 as a branch of the national botanical gardens at Bogor, near Jakarta, they cover over 120 hectares on the lower slopes of Gunung Pohen. Although the gardens are poorly maintained, they boast an extensive collection of trees and a small collection of wild orchids. Some plants are labelled with their botanical names, and the booklet Six Self Guided Walks in the Bali Botanical Gardens, sold at the ticket office for 20,000Rp, is helpful.

The gardens are cool, shady, scenic and usually uncrowded, but on Sunday and public holidays they're very popular with Balinese families. Cars (but not motorcycles) can be taken into the park for an extra 5000Rp.

Pura Ulun Danu Bratan

A few kilometres north of the market, this very important Hindu-Buddhist temple (adult/child 3300/1800Rp, parking 2000Rp; open 8.30am-6pm daily) was founded in the 17th century. It is dedicated to Dewi Danu, the goddess of the waters, and is actually built on small islands, which means it is completely surrounded by the lake. Both pilgrimages and ceremonies are held here to ensure that there is a supply of water for farmers all over Bali.

It is truly beautiful, with classical Hindu thatch-roofed meru (multiroofed shrines) reflected in the water and silhouetted against the often cloudy mountain backdrop – one of the commonest photographic images of Bali. A large banyan tree shades the entrance, and you walk through manicured gardens and past an impressive Buddhist stupa to reach the lakeside.

An unfortunate aspect is the small animal zoo, left of the main entrance, where tourists are encouraged to be photographed alongside snakes, bats and a caged bear cat, all of which appear to be kept in less than humane conditions.

Perama Ulundanu (☎ 21191; dishes 15,000-30,000Rp; open 9am-5pm) in the grounds has a pleasant outdoor terrace.

Water Sports

At the temple gardens, you can hire a four-passenger speedboat with a driver (50,000Rp, 15 minutes), a five-person boat with boatman

(60,000Rp, 30 minutes), or a two-person pedal boat (30,000Rp, 30 minutes). Canoes rented from the lakeside near the Ashram Guest House should cost a negotiable 90,000Rp for half a day.

For an almost surreal experience, take a quiet paddle across the lake and see Pura Ulun Danu Bratan at sunrise – arrange it with a boatman the night before.

Places to Stay

Pondok Wisata Dahlia Indah (☎ 21233; rooms 40,000Rp) in the village, along a lane near the road to the Botanical Gardens, is a decent budget option with comfortable, clean, hot-water rooms.

Ashram Guest House (☎ 21450, fax 21101; rooms 40,000 & 100,000Rp), southeast of Sari Artha Inn, has somewhat scruffy, utilitarian rooms and decidedly unfriendly staff. The only upside is its setting overlooking the lake. It has a range of rooms starting with shared bathroom and no hot water, more for a private bathroom, more still for hot water, and top price for everything, plus a view of the lake.

On the uphill side of the road, **Lila Graha Bungalows** (☎ 21446; singles 60,000-200,000Rp, doubles 80,000-250,000Rp) is a shambolic place, where only the cheapest rooms (including the best views) are worth considering.

Enjung Beji Resort (☎ 21490, fax 21022; cottages US$30-67, family cottage US$100), just north of the temple and overlooking the lake, is a peaceful, pleasant option. The superior cottages are excellent quality and have outdoor showers, sunken baths, a day bed and TV.

Places to Eat

Food stalls at Candikuning market offer cheap eats, and there are **food carts** further north at the car park overlooking the lake. At the entrance to Pura Ulun Danu Bratan are several **Padang warung**, and a restaurant in the grounds.

Several roadside restaurants cater to Indonesian day-trippers, and offer really good Indonesian food at very reasonable prices. Try **Rumah Makan Taliwang** (dishes 10,000-30,000Rp), which does spicy Lombok-style chicken, or **Bedugul Kafe** (dishes 15,000-30,000Rp), with barbecued fish and a nice cold beer.

For something different, try the **Strawberry Stop** (☎ 21060; dishes 6000-15,000Rp), north of Bedugul, which makes good use of locally grown strawberries in shakes, juices and pancakes. Jaffles and other simple dishes are also available.

Getting There & Away

Danau Bratan is beside a main north–south road, so it's easy to reach from Denpasar or Singaraja.

Bemo & Bus The main bemo terminal is a few kilometres further north at Pancasari, but most minibuses and bemos will stop along the main road in Bedugul and Candikuning. There are frequent connections from Denpasar's Ubung terminal (5000Rp) and Singaraja's Sukasada terminal (5000Rp). To get to Ubud, change bemos in Denpasar. For Gunung Batur, get a connection in Singaraja.

The big, fast through buses may not stop anywhere in the Danau Bratan area – and if they do the fare is the same as for a cross-Bali trip.

Tourist Shuttle Bus Daily Perama shuttle buses are by far the easiest way to get to the area from Kuta (30,000Rp), Sanur (30,000Rp), Ubud (30,000Rp) or Lovina (30,000Rp). The Perama stop is at Sari Artha Inn (☎ 21011) in Candikuning, but the driver should drop you off anywhere between Bedugul and Pancasari.

PANCASARI

The broad, green valley north and west of Danau Bratan is actually the crater of an extinct volcano. In the middle of the valley, on the main road, Pancasari is a non-tourist town with a bustling market and the main terminal for public bemos.

Just south of Pancasari, you will see an impressive split gate. This is not a temple, but is in fact the entrance to the **Bali Handara Kosaido Country Club** (☎ 22646, fax 23048; rooms US$100-150), a superbly situated, world-class golf course with luxurious accommodation. The green fees for 18 holes are US$100 (including caddy), and club hire is US$20. The sterile restaurant (dishes 32,000-100,000Rp) has typically gorgeous views and serves both Japanese and international cuisine.

DANAU BUYAN & DANAU TAMBLINGAN

Northwest of Danau Bratan are two more lakes, Buyan and Tamblingan – neither is developed for tourism. There are several tiny villages and abandoned **temples** along the shores of both lakes, but the frequently swampy ground makes it unpleasant in parts to explore.

A **hiking** trail goes around the southern side of Danau Buyan, then over the saddle to Tamblingan, and on to Asan Munduk, but you spend too much time in the forest and not enough admiring the lakes. **Sobek** (☎ 0361-287059, fax 289448; W www.sobek bali.com) organises treks offering views of this region for adult/child US$49/30, including transport from south Bali and lunch.

MUNDUK
☎ 0362

Heading north from Pancasari, the main road climbs steeply up the rim of the old volcanic crater. It's worth stopping to enjoy the **views** back over the valley and lakes – watch out for monkeys on the road. Turning right at the top will take you on a scenic descent to the coastal town of Singaraja, via the Gitgit waterfalls (see the North Bali chapter). Taking a sharp left turn, you follow a ridge-top road with Danau Buyan on one side and a slope to the sea on the other – coffee is a big crop in the area.

This road reaches a T-junction where you'll see a strange, stepped pyramid about 4m high. This is the **Pyramid Plastic**, one of several art installations in the area. It's made of melted down plastic waste, partly as a statement about the environmental problems plastic has caused on Bali.

If you turn left at this junction, a trail leads to near Danau Tamblingan, among forest and market gardens. Turning right takes you along beautiful winding roads to the main village of Munduk. On the way is another **art installation** – oversize versions of the old Chinese coins called *kepeng,* standing on edge in front of a superb panorama.

There's archaeological evidence of a developed community in the Munduk region between the 10th and 14th centuries, and accounts of the first Majapahit emissaries visiting the area. When the Dutch took control of north Bali in the 1890s, they experimented with commercial crops, establishing plantations for coffee, vanilla, cloves and cocoa. Quite a few Dutch buildings are still intact along the road in Munduk and further west, and the mountain scenery is sublime.

Trekking

Numerous trails are suitable for two- or three-hour hikes to coffee plantations, waterfalls, villages, and around Tamblingan and Buyan lakes. Arrange a guide through your lodgings, or join one of the treks from Puri Lumbung Cottages (US$5 per hour per guide).

Places to Stay & Eat

The Kalaspa (☎ 0826 361 034; W www.bali -kalaspa.com; 3-day/2-night complete package US$760), on the road to Munduk and with mountain views to the sea, has luxurious two-room cottages, featuring private courtyards and bathrooms with garden views. It also has its own spa, yoga room and restaurant.

Puri Lumbung Cottages (☎ 92810; W www.travelideas.net/bali.hotels/lumbung .html; bungalow singles/doubles US$47/52, family cottages US$76) is on the right-hand side of the road as you enter Munduk from Bedugul. The hotel offers 15 trekking options, and a range of courses, including dance and cooking. It's a delightful place to stay, and has well-finished thatched bungalows overlooking red-rice fields. **Warung Kopi Bali** (dishes 15,000-24,000Rp), in the hotel, has a great outlook and serves great food, including the local dish *timbungan be-siap* (clear chicken soup with sliced cassava and fried shallots).

Simpler, cheaper accommodation is available at three homestays just down the road, including **Guru Ratna** (☎ 92182; singles/ doubles 150,000/175,000Rp), the least expensive place, with comfortable rooms in an old Dutch house and newer, very comfortable rooms. The **restaurant** here does good meals for around 12,500Rp. **Meme Surung** and **Mekel Ragi** (☎/fax 92811) are atmospheric old Dutch houses, with rooms for US$20/30, including all meals.

Ngiring Ngewedang (☎ 41126; dishes 15,000-40,000Rp; open 10am-4pm) is a coffee shop on the road to Munduk, which has views of the ocean when it's not clouded over. The café sells its own brand of coffee and staff will also take you through the coffee production process.

Getting There & Away

Bemos leave Ubung terminal in Denpasar for Munduk frequently (15,000Rp); alternatively head to Singaraja and take a bemo from there. Bemos from Candikuning also stop in Munduk (10,000Rp). If you're driving to/from the north coast, a decent road west of Munduk goes through a number of picturesque villages to Mayong, then down to the sea at Seririt.

GUNUNG BATUKAU

West of the Mengwi–Bedugul–Singaraja road rises Gunung Batukau (2276m), the 'Coconut-shell Mountain'. This is the third of Bali's three major mountains and the holy peak of the island's western end.

If you want to climb it, you'll need a guide, as there are many false trails. You'll also need to be very fit – it's an arduous climb. From the temple, a guide will cost a negotiable 500,000Rp. It takes about five or six hours to the top, and four hours to get down, through quite thick forest. If you want to get to the top before the mist rolls in, you'll need to spend a night near the summit, so bring a tent.

Pura Luhur Batukau

On the slopes of Batukau, this was the state temple when Tabanan was an independent kingdom. It has a seven-roofed *meru* to Maha Dewa, the mountain's guardian spirit, as well as shrines for Bratan, Buyan and Tamblingan lakes. It's surrounded by forest, and often damp and misty. Sarongs can be rented and a donation to the temple is requested. Temple guardians will not allow pregnant or menstruating women into the grounds (unlike most other temples, which waive these rules).

There are several routes to the temple. The easiest way is to follow the road north from Tabanan to Wangayagede, the last village before the temple.

Wangayagede

Warung Kaja (☎ 0812 397 0173; e pkater@ dps.centrin.net.id; single/doubles 90,000/ 125,000Rp) has lovely, clean, simple wooden bungalows with modern bathrooms and views of surrounding coffee plantations. Treks in the local area, including bird watching, can be organised from here. To reach it, turn right on the Pura Luhur Batukau road at the white Sekolah Desar and continue for another 500m.

Prana Dewi Mountain Resort (☎/fax 732032; w www.balipranaresort.com; bungalows US$40-50), past the village and signposted to the left off the main Pura Luhur Batukau road, is set amongst rice paddies and a snaking carp-filled stream. The rustic, beautifully furnished bungalows have thick slab timber floors and floor to ceiling views. The **restaurant** (dishes 19,000-37,000Rp), surrounded by low, terraced red-rice fields, has a closed, lush vista. Most of the vegetables, *tempeh* and rice is produced organically at the resort.

Jatiluwih

For an alternative route to Pura Luhur Batukau, turn off the Mengwi–Singaraja road south of Pacung, and follow the rough road to Senganankaninan. From there, an even rougher road goes in a westerly direction to Wangayagede, via Jatiluwih. The name Jatiluwih means 'Truly Marvellous', and the view truly is – it takes in a huge chunk of south Bali.

Sobek (☎ 0361-287059; w www.sobek bali.com) runs an interior trek in the Batukau valley around Jatiluwih for adult/child US$55/30, including a massage or spa at Yeh Panes Resort (see the West Bali chapter). It also runs a cycle trip (the Batukau Trail) in the area, which combines road and off-road riding for adult/child US$55/45.

North Bali

North Bali, the district of Buleleng, makes an interesting contrast with the south of the island. The Lovina beaches are popular with budget travellers, offering good-value places to stay and eat, but nothing like the chaos of the Kuta region. Many travellers coming from Java go straight from Gilimanuk to the north coast, rather than taking the south coast road, which would leave them in Denpasar or, horror of horrors, Kuta.

Buleleng has a strong artistic and cultural tradition. Its dance troupes are highly regarded and a number of dance styles have originated here, including Janger. Gold- and silverwork, weaving, pottery, instrument-making and temple design all show distinctive local styles. The Sapi Gerumbungan, a distinctive Buleleng tradition, is a bull race where style is as important as speed.

History
The north coast has been subject to European influence for a long time. Having first encountered Balinese troops on Java in the 18th century, the Dutch became the main purchasers of Balinese slaves – many of whom served in the Dutch East India Company armies.

Various Balinese kings provided the Dutch with soldiers, but in the 1840s, disputes over shipwreck salvage, together with fears that other European powers might establish themselves on Bali, prompted the Dutch to make treaties with a number of the Balinese rajahs. However, the treaties proved ineffective, the plundering continued apace, and disputes arose with Buleleng's rajah.

During 1845 the rajahs of Buleleng and Karangasem formed an alliance, possibly to conquer other Balinese states or, equally possibly, to resist the Dutch. In any case, the Dutch became worried and attacked Buleleng and Karangasem in 1846, 1848 and 1849, seizing control of north Bali on the third attempt.

YEH SANIH
☎ 0362

About 15km east of Singaraja, Yeh Sanih (also called Air Sanih) is a deliciously hassle-free seaside spot with a string of guesthouses on the black-sand beachfront (albeit with a

Highlights

- Relaxing in the quiet, hassle-free beach-front village of Yeh Sanih

- Partying at Lovina – the north's very own Kuta, and popular with budget backpackers

- Discovering the temples with their 'Bali baroque' carvings featuring bicycles and biplanes

- Diving and snorkelling at the great sites around the north

- Soaking in Air Panas Banjar – a natural spa of hot springs in a lush rainforest setting

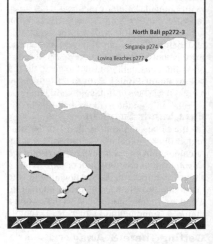

North Bali pp272-3

Singaraja p274

Lovina Beaches p277

retaining wall). It's named for its freshwater springs **Air Sanih** *(adult/child 2000/1000Rp; open 8am-6pm daily)*, which are channelled into swimming pools before flowing into the sea. The pools are particularly picturesque at sunset, when throngs of locals bathe under heavily blooming frangipani trees.

A welcome surprise in the area is **Art Zoo** (w *www.symonbali.com*), west of Yeh Sanih on the Singaraja road. The American artist Symon, formerly of Danger Art in Ubud, has a gallery, bursting with vibrant, exotic and often homoerotic paintings and sculpture.

Places to Stay & Eat
At Sembiran, outside Yeh Sanih on the Singaraja road, **Pondok Sembiran** (☎ *0868 1210*

3677) is 20m from the beach and has pleasant bungalows, which have kitchens and hot water.

In the Air Sanih springs gardens, **Puri Sanih Bungalows** *(☎ 26563; singles/doubles 70,000/80,000Rp)*, facing the sea, is looking a bit worse for wear, but is still OK value and clean. There's also a restaurant here.

Approximately 300m east of Puri Sanih Bungalows, **Cilik's Beach Garden** *(☎/fax 26561; w www.ciliksbeachgarden.com; lumbung singles/doubles €30/50, villas singles €50-85, doubles €65-115, triples €80-130)* is excellent value. All accommodation is in beautifully furnished *lumbung* (rice barn-style bungalows), very private and set in a delightful, quiet garden facing the ocean. A host of other services are available, including tours and delicious meals.

Hotel Tara *(☎ 26575; rooms 60,000Rp, with air-con 100,000Rp)*, a kilometre or so east of Cilik's Beach Garden, is wonderfully isolated and right on the beach. It has basic but acceptable rooms.

Puri Bagus Ponjok Batu *(☎ 21430; dishes 15,000 27,000Rp)* is a lovely spot 7km west of Yeh Sanih on the road to Singaraja by the temple Ponjok Batu, overlooking the water. It offers a big range of grilled fish, prawns and seafood, and Balinese dishes.

Opposite Air Sanih springs, **Archipelago Restaurant** *(dishes 9000-18,000Rp)* is up a flight of stairs under an imposing *bale* (an open-sided pavilion), and has an interesting menu of Indonesian and Western options, including eggplant and lentil curry.

Getting There & Away
Yeh Sanih is on the main road along the north coast. Frequent *bemos* (small pick-up trucks) and buses from Singaraja stop outside the springs (3000Rp). Perama buses will stop here on request, en route to Lovina.

SINGARAJA
☎ 0362
With a population of over 100,000 people, Singaraja (which means 'Lion King') is Bali's second-largest city, but is far more low-key than Denpasar. With its tree-lined streets, Dutch colonial buildings and charmingly decrepit waterfront area, north of Jl Erlangga, it's worth wandering around for a few hours, but most people prefer to stay in nearby Yeh Sanih or Lovina.

Singaraja was the centre of Dutch power on Bali and remained the administrative centre for the Lesser Sunda Islands (Bali through to Timor) until 1953. It is one of the few places on Bali where there are visible reminders of the Dutch period, but there are also Chinese and Muslim influences. The port of Singaraja was for years the usual arrival point for visitors to Bali – it's where all the pre-war travel books started. Some writers complained it was too commercial and preferred south Bali because it was less developed. Today Singaraja is a major educational and cultural centre, and its two university campuses provide the city with a substantial, and sometimes vocal, student population.

The 'suburb' of Beratan, to the south of Singaraja, is the silverwork centre of northern Bali. You'll find a few traditional pieces, such as *cucuk* (gold headpieces) on display, but it mostly has uninspiring tourist jewellery. A few workshops in and around Singaraja produce hand-woven sarongs – especially *songket*, woven with silver or gold threads.

Orientation & Information
The main commercial areas are in the northeastern part of town, south of the harbour. Most hotels, restaurants and bus company offices are along Jl Jen Achmed Yani. Traffic does a few complicated one-way loops around town, but it's easy enough to get around on foot or by bemo.

Diparda *(☎ 25141 ext 22; cnr Jl Veteran & Jl Gajah Mada; open 7.30am-4pm Mon-Fri)*, the tourist office, is not particularly helpful. The main banks will change money, and some of them have ATMs. There are several **wartels** (public telephone offices) along the main streets and there is **Internet access** at the rear of the post office (6000Rp per hour). Singaraja's **RSUP hospital** *(☎ 22046)* is the largest in northern Bali, and there is also a major **police station** *(☎ 41510)* located here.

Old Harbour & Waterfront
The conspicuous **Yudha Mandala Tama** monument commemorates a freedom fighter killed by gunfire from a Dutch warship early in the struggle for independence. Close by, there's the colourful Chinese temple **Ling Gwan Kiong**.

NORTH BALI

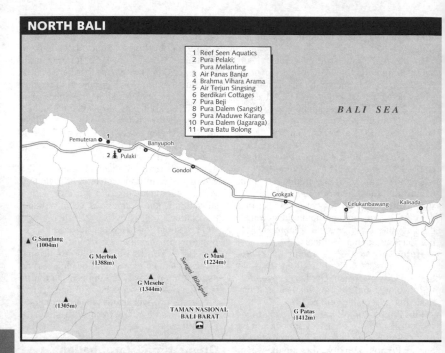

1 Reef Seen Aquatics
2 Pura Pelaki;
  Pura Melanting
3 Air Panas Banjar
4 Brahma Vihara Arama
5 Air Terjun Singsing
6 Berdikari Cottages
7 Pura Beji
8 Pura Dalem (Sangsit)
9 Pura Maduwe Karang
10 Pura Dalem (Jagaraga)
11 Pura Batu Bolong

BALI SEA

Pemuteran 1
Banyupoh
2 Pulaki
Gondoi
Grokgak
Celukanbawang   Kalisada

▲ G Sanglang
   (1004m)

▲ G Merbuk
   (1388m)

▲ G Musi
   (1224m)

Sungai Bilukpoh

▲ G Mesehe
   (1344m)

▲ (1305m)

**TAMAN NASIONAL
BALI BARAT**

▲ G Patas
   (1412m)

Lontar Books

The Gedong Kirtya Library has the world's largest collection of works that are inscribed on *lontar*. You will find some 4000 historic Balinese manuscripts covering everything from the literary to mythological and historical to religious themes. They are written in fine Sanskrit calligraphy, and some are elaborately decorated.

Lontar is made from the fan-shaped leaves of the *rontal* palm. The process involves the following steps. Initially, the leaf is dried, soaked in water, cleaned, steamed, dried again, then flattened, dyed and eventually cut into strips. Then the strips are inscribed with words and pictures using a very sharp blade or point, then coated with a black stain which is wiped off. This process ensures that the black colour remains in the inscribed surface. A hole in the middle of each lontar strip is threaded onto a string, with a carved bamboo 'cover' at each end to protect the 'pages', and the string is secured with a couple of pierced Chinese coins, or *kepeng*.

Gedong Kirtya Library

This small historical library (☎ 22645; admission by donation; open 7am-2pm Mon-Thur), next to the tourist office, was established in 1928 by Dutch colonialists and named after the Sanskrit word 'to try'. It has a collection of *lontar* books (written on palm leaves), as well as some even older written works, in the form of inscribed copper plates called *prasasti*. Dutch publications, dating back to 1901, may interest students of the colonial period.

Pura Jagat Natha

Singaraja's main temple, the largest in northern Bali, is not usually open to foreigners. You can appreciate its size and admire the carved stone decorations from the outside.

Places to Stay & Eat

There are slim accommodation pickings in Singaraja, and there's no real reason to stay here. Most hotels cater for Indonesian travellers.

Hotel Gelar Sari (☎ 21495; Jl Achmed Jen Yani; singles/doubles from 20,000/40,000Rp) has basic, clean rooms, with what look like

NORTH BALI

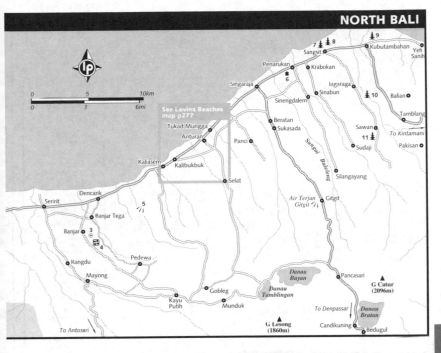

NORTH BALI

ex-hospital beds, in a colonial-era Dutch-style house.

Hotel Wijaya (☎ 21915, fax 25817; Jl Pudak; singles/doubles with fan from 20,000/25,000Rp, with air-con 90,000/95,000Rp) is the most comfortable place in town, although economy fan rooms have an outside bathroom. It also has a restaurant.

Cafe Lima Lima (dishes 3500-7500Rp) and **Kantin Koka** (dishes 3000-7500Rp) are clean, inexpensive places side by side on Jl Achmed Jen Yani, and attract a few students. **Depot Merdeka** (☎ 29917; Jl Pramuka; dishes 4000-5000Rp) is another cheapie popular with students. In the evening, there are **food stalls** in the night market on Jl Durian, and various **warung** (food stalls) around the bemo/bus terminals.

Getting There & Away
Bemo & Bus Singaraja is the transport hub for the northern coast, with three main bemo/bus terminals. From the main **Sukasada terminal**, about 3km south of town, minibuses go to Denpasar (Ubung terminal, 9000Rp) via Bedugul/Pancasari (5000Rp) about every 30 minutes from 6am

to 4pm. There is also a tiny bemo stop, next to the *puskesmas* (community health centre) in Sukasada, with services to Gitgit.

The **Banyuasri terminal**, on the western side of town, has buses heading for Seririt (3000Rp), Gilimanuk (9000Rp) and Java (see below), and plenty of blue bemos to Lovina (3000Rp).

The **Penarukan terminal**, a couple of kilometres east of town, has bemos to Yeh Sanih (3000Rp) and Amlapura (6000Rp) via the coastal road; and also minibuses to Denpasar (Batubulan terminal; 8500Rp) via Kintamani.

Java From Singaraja, several bus companies have overnight services to Surabaya on Java, via Gilimanuk and the public ferry – book at Banyuasri terminal one day before. Many travel agencies along the western end of Jl Jen Achmed Yani also sell bus tickets.

Tourist Shuttle Bus All of the shuttle buses going to Lovina from south Bali, whether via the east coast, Bedugul or Kintamani, can drop you off in Singaraja.

SINGARAJA

BALI SEA

PLACES TO STAY
13 Hotel Gelar Sari
15 Hotel Wijaya
   & Restaurant

PLACES TO EAT
11 Cafe Lima Lima;
   Kantin Koka
19 Depot Merdeka

OTHER
1 Yudha Mandala
  Tama Monument
2 Ling Gwan Kiong
  Chinese Temple
3 Old Harbour &
  Warehouse Area
4 Mosque
5 Mosque
6 Night Market
7 Post Office;
  Internet Access
8 Telkom Office
9 Bank BCA; ATM
10 Bank Danamon
  (ATM)
12 University
14 Banyuasri
  Bemo/Bus Terminal
  (for Lovina
  & Gilimanuk)
16 Police Station
17 Pura Jagat Natha
18 Bank BRI
20 Bank BRI
21 RSUP (Hospital)
22 Gedong Kirtya
  Library
23 Diparda
  (Tourist Office)
24 Market

Getting Around

Plenty of bemos link the three main bemo/bus terminals, and hurtle along all main roads in between. The bemos are all well signed and colour-coded, and cost about 1000Rp for a ride anywhere around town. The green Banyuasri–Sukasada bemo goes along Jl Gajah Mada to the tourist office; and this bemo, as well as the brown one between Penarukan and Banyuasri terminals, also goes along Jl Jen Achmed Yani.

AROUND SINGARAJA

Interesting sites around Singaraja include some of Bali's best-known temples. The north-coast sandstone is very soft and easily carved, allowing local sculptors to give free rein to their imaginations, and you'll find some delightfully whimsical scenes carved into a number of the temples.

Although temple architecture is similar in both northern and southern Bali, there are some important differences. The inner courtyards of southern temples usually house a number of multiroofed shrines *(meru)*, together with other structures, whereas in the north, everything is grouped on a single pedestal. On the pedestal you'll find 'houses' for the deities to use on their earthly visits; they're also used to store religious relics.

Sangsit

A few kilometres northeast of Singaraja, you can see an excellent example of the colourful architectural style of north Bali. Sangsit's **Pura Beji** is a *subak* temple, dedicated to the goddess Dewi Sri, who looks after irrigated rice fields. The sculptured panels along the front wall set the tone with their Disneyland-like demons and amazing *naga* (mythological serpents). The inside also has a variety of sculptures covering every available space. It's about 500m off the main road towards the coast.

The **Pura Dalem** shows scenes of punishment in the afterlife, and other humorous and sometimes erotic pictures. It's in the rice fields, about 500m northeast of Pura Beji.

An accommodation option nearby is **Berdikari Cottages** (☎ 25195; rooms 70,000, with air-con 150,000Rp), which has a range of decent rooms.

Buses and bemos going east from Singaraja's Penarukan terminal will stop at Sangsit, and at the hotel.

Jagaraga
It was the capture of the local rajah's stronghold at Jagaraga that marked the arrival of Dutch power on Bali in 1849. The village, which is a few kilometres south of the main road, has the interesting **Pura Dalem**. The small temple has delightful sculptured panels along its front wall, both inside and out. On the outer wall look for a vintage car driving sedately past, a steamer at sea and even an aerial dogfight between early aircraft. Jagaraga is also famous for its Legong troupe, said to be the best in north Bali, but performances are irregular. Bemos from the Penarukan terminal in Singaraja stop at Jagaraga on the way to Sawan.

Sawan
Several kilometres inland from Jagaraga, Sawan is a centre for the manufacture of gamelan gongs and gamelan instruments. You can see the gongs being cast and the intricately carved gamelan frames being made. The strange-looking **Pura Batu Bolong** is also worth a look. Around Sawan, there are **cold water springs** that are believed to cure all sorts of illnesses. Regular bemos to Sawan leave from Penarukan terminal in Singaraja.

Kubutambahan
About a kilometre east of the turn-off to Kintamani is **Pura Maduwe Karang** (Temple of the Land Owner). Like Pura Beji at Sangsit, the temple is dedicated to agricultural spirits, but this one looks after non-irrigated land.

This is one of the finest temples in north Bali and is particularly noted for its sculptured panels, including the famous bicycle relief that depicts a gentleman riding a bicycle with flowers for wheels. It's on the base of the main plinth in the inner enclosure. The cyclist may be WOJ Nieuwenkamp, a Dutch artist who, in 1904, brought probably the first bicycle to Bali.

The temple is easy to find in the village. Kubutambahan is on the road between Singaraja and Amlapura, and there are regular bemos and buses.

Gitgit
About 11km south of Singaraja, a well-signposted path goes 800m west from the main road to the touristy waterfall of **Air Terjun Gitgit** (adult/child 3100/1600Rp). The path is lined with souvenir stalls, and persistent guides offer their services. The 40m waterfalls are quite pretty, and a great place for a picnic, but far from pristine. You buy a ticket about halfway down the path, and you also pay to park (1000Rp). There are **warung** along the path to the falls.

About 2km further up the hill, **Gitgit Multi-tier Waterfall** (donation requested) is about 600m off the western side of the main road, by a small side track then a good walking path, with only a few clusters of souvenir stalls. The path crosses a narrow bridge and follows the river up past several sets of waterfalls, through verdant jungle and with several places to swim – if you're careful.

Getting There & Away Regular bemos and minibuses between Denpasar (Ubung terminal) and Singaraja (Sukasada terminal) stop at Gitgit. More regular bemos to Gitgit (2500Rp) leave from outside the health centre (puskesmas) near Sukasada terminal – let the driver know where you want to get off. Gitgit is also a major stop on organised tours of north and central Bali.

LOVINA
☎ 0362

Almost merging into Singaraja to the west, a string of coastal villages – Pemaron, Tukad Mungga, Anturan, Kalibukbuk, Kaliasem and Temukus – collectively known as Lovina, are a popular budget beach resort, living off the back of the schools of dolphins offshore. It's still a low-rise development, but hotels and restaurants are fast eating up the surrounding rice fields, and the quiet pace expected of the north of Bali isn't evident – the main street, Jl Raya Lovina is incredibly busy as trucks and vehicles edge toward Gilimanuk, and locals are even more aggressive than in Kuta in their fervour to sell dolphin trips, snorkelling tours and transport. Still you can get away from the hassle, and Lovina is a convenient base for trips around the north coast or the central mountains.

The beaches are of washed-out grey and black volcanic sand, and they are mostly clean near the hotel areas, but generally unspectacular. Reefs protect the shore, so the water is mostly calm and clear. Every afternoon, at fishing villages like Anturan, you can see *prahu*, the outrigger canoes, being prepared for the night's fishing, and as sunset reddens the sky, the lights of the fishing boats appear as bright dots across the horizon.

Orientation

The Lovina tourist area stretches over 8km, but the main focus is Kalibukbuk, 10.5km west of Singaraja. It's hard to know where one village ends and the next one begins, but signposts along Jl Raya Lovina indicate the location of various hotels and restaurants and make convenient landmarks.

Information

The **tourist office** (☎ 41910) shares the same premises as the **police station**. It offers brochures of Lovina, and staff who do their best to answer any questions (although they may not be the most objective answers). There are plenty of moneychangers around Lovina. There's also **Bank BPD Bali**, which changes travellers cheques, an **ATM** on Jl Bina Ria, and another on the Jl Raya Lovina intersection.

The **main post office** is a kilometre west of central Kalibukbuk, but **postal agencies** and **wartels** are dotted along Jl Raya Lovina, the main road.

Several **Internet cafés** on Jl Bina Ria and elsewhere in Kalibukbuk provide Internet access from 400Rp to 500Rp per minute; there are also one or two in Anturan.

The **Lovina Clinic** (☎ 41106, Jl Raya Lovina, Kalibukbuk) has English-speaking doctors, on call 24 hours a day, who can deal with minor ailments. A consultation costs 150,000Rp.

The grassed beach area in front of Nirwana Seaside Cottages is popular for sunbathing.

Bull Races

The **Yayasan Budaya Den Bukit Lovina** (Lovina Culture Foundation; ☎ 41293) organises

---

The Dawn Charging Patrol

At sunrise, the dawn patrol mobilises for the daily money-making ritual ahead. Tourists sit in wooden *prahu*, with monikers such as 'James Bond' or bows painted with gun motifs, and motor along to the open sea. Tourists from top-end resorts glow in orange life-jackets – ironic because with so many other boats on the water – at least 30 – there is no chance of flailing in the water unnoticed.

Boats motor out a few kilometres offshore and the tragicomedy begins – the drivers putter around, not knowing which way to turn, going in ever-widening circles, while tourists sit desperately clutching cameras, scanning the waters and breathing in petrol fumes from the crowd of boats. When a dolphin school is finally spotted, all 30 or so boats go full throttle and charge to surround it, and the sorry chase begins. The dolphins stay up long enough to breathe and arc out of the water, and then disappear, and the James Bond flotilla recommences its aimless motoring through the water. This replays several times through the sunrise hour.

Dolphin 'watching' Lovina-style is on a par with hunting without a spear – dolphins are chased mercilessly through the water, and there is no sense of playfulness or interactivity on their part, just a doggedness to outrun the flotilla. As your boat returns to the shore, you'll be greeted surreally by young boys selling carved dolphins neatly laid on a platter, and offers of massage and snorkelling.

If you really want to see dolphins in the wild, as opposed to dolphins intimidated for the purpose of making tourists happy, make contact with local tuna fisherman at the southern end of the beach. They leave at 4.30am and use the dolphins to help track the tuna catch. Or to create minimum interference in the local ways, whenever you next get a chance, visit an aquarium…

Kate Daly

LOVINA BEACHES

Kalibukbuk

BALI SEA

To Singaraja

Tukad Mungga

JL Kubu Gembong

Anturan

To Singaraja (Back Rd)

Jalan Raya Lovina

JL Pantai Banyualit

Jalanket epang

JL Bina Ria

To Gilimanuk (79km)

See Enlargement

Kaliasem

To Kaya Putih

PLACES TO STAY
1 Billibo Beach Cottages
3 Parma Hotel
4 Aditya Bungalows; Wartel
8 Hotel Mutiara Beach
9 Mangalla Homestay; John's House
10 Hotel Purnama
11 Lovina Beach Hotel
15 Nirwana Seaside Cottages
19 Rini Hotel
20 Bayu Kartika
21 Puri Bali Hotel
23 Rambutan Beach Cottages
25 Taman Lily's
26 Harri's Homestay
27 Pondok Elsa
28 Susila 2 Backpackers Hostel
30 Pulestis Hotel
44 Padang Lovina Hotel & Restaurant
55 Hotel Aneka Lovina
56 Suma; Sartaya
58 Hotel Banyualit
59 Melka Hotel
60 Sunset Ayu
61 Lila Cita
63 Hotel Perama; Perama Office
64 Bayu Mantra; Puspa Rama

66 Gede Home Stay Bungalows
67 Mandhara Cottages
69 Mandhara Chico
70 Hotel Yudha
71 Sri Homestay
72 Bali Taman Beach Resort
73 Kubu Lalang
74 Happy Beach Inn
75 Hotel Puri Bedahulu
76 Baruna Beach Cottages

PLACES TO EAT
6 Octopus Garden
7 Cafe Spice; Watersports; Indiana Massage
13 Sea Breeze Cafe
16 Warung Warubali
22 Barcelona Bar & Restaurant
29 Kakatua Bar & Restaurant
31 Warung Kopi Bali
39 Le Nasi Goreng
42 Bali Apik
45 Malibu Bar & Restaurant
49 Barakuda
50 Khi Khi Restaurant
57 Warung Bias
65 Warung Rasta
68 Warung Bamboo

OTHER
2 Main Post Office
5 Spice Dive (Head Office)
12 Wartel
14 Dolphin Monument; Car Park
17 Spice Dive
18 Temple
24 Perama Agent
32 Spice Cyber; CyberLink
33 Mojo
34 Poco Evolution Bar & Restaurant
35 Lovina Grand Bar de Tommes; Planet Lovina; Lovina Transport
36 Baruna Dive Centre
37 BCA ATM
38 ATM
40 Yayasan Budaya Den Bukit Lovina
41 Postal Agency; Tip Top Shop
43 Tourist Office; Police Station
46 Benny Tantra's Air Brush T-shirts
47 Bank BPD Bali
48 Postal Agent
51 Agung's Massage & Salon
52 Lovina Wellness Spa
53 Lovina Clinic
54 Lia's
62 Wartel

NORTH BALI

traditional Sapi Gerumbungan bull races on Friday at 4pm for 40,000Rp, just west of Kalibukbuk. It's worth checking at the foundation for any other cultural activities.

Dolphin Watching

Sunrise boat trips to see dolphins are Lovina's special tourist attraction – so much so that a large concrete crowned statue has been erected in honour of the over-touted cetaceans, which is fittingly known by local expats as the 'fish on a stick'. Some days, no dolphins are sighted, but about 80% of the time at least a few surface.

Expect hassle from your hotel and touts selling dolphin trips – if you want to go, it's best to buy a ticket the day before. The price is fixed at 30,000Rp per person by the boat owners' cartel. Don't request a refund if you don't see any dolphins – just respect nature.

Snorkelling

Generally, the water is clear and some parts of the reef are quite good for snorkelling, though the coral has been damaged by 'bleaching' and, in places, by dynamite fishing. The best place is to the west, a few hundred metres offshore from Billibo Beach Cottages. A boat trip will cost about 30,000Rp per person for two people for two hours, including equipment. Snorkelling gear costs about 20,000Rp per day.

Diving

Scuba diving on the local reef is better at lower depths and night diving is particularly recommended. Some of the best dive sites on Bali are accessible from Lovina – particularly Pulau Menjangan (Deer Island) in Taman Nasional Bali Barat (West Bali National Park).

For a two-dive trip, including transport and all equipment, expect to pay about US$35/30 for a Lovina reef/night dive; and from US$40 to US$50 to Amed, Tulamben or Pulau Menjangan. **Spice Dive** (☎ 41305, fax 41171; ⓦ www.damai.com/spicedive) has the best reputation and is the only five-star PADI centre in Lovina. It runs PADI open-water certificate courses for US$250. It has a number of outlets in Lovina, including **Spice Cyber**, which is also an Internet café (400Rp per minute) and **Cafe Spice**, but the head office is on Jl Raya Lovina, beyond Kalibukbuk, heading west. The **Baruna Dive Centre** (☎ 41084) is also a long-running operator.

Water Sports
Spice Dive (☎ 41969) offers a range of water sports on the beach in front of Cafe Spice, including parasailing (90,000Rp for 10 minutes), water-skiing (150,000Rp for 20 minutes) and banana boat rides. Book at any Spice Dive office.

Massage & Spas
Agung's Massage & Salon (☎ 42018; Jl Damai), south off Jl Raya Lovina, is a relatively peaceful spot with bamboo walls and a pedicure area facing a garden. A 60-/90-minute massage costs 50,000/54,000Rp. Body treatments use ground coconut or rice bran, and facials are also available.

Lovina Wellness Spa (☎ 0812 377 2046; Jl Ketapang; open 10am-7pm) has some traffic noise, but overall it's a pleasant place, where massage rooms feature pebbled baths. Massage techniques on offer include Balinese (60 minutes for 65,000Rp), Ayerveda (90 minutes for 135,000Rp), and foot massage (40 minutes for 45,000Rp), as well as 're-birthing' (90 minutes for 250,000Rp).

Indiana Massage (☎ 41570; open 11am-sunset) is a tiny open-air pavilion facing the beach nearby Café Spice. It offers a range of massage, from shiatsu or reflexology to acupressure and Thai for 75,000Rp for 75 minutes.

Organised Tours
Most local transport touts and some travel agencies offer tours of local attractions, such as Beratan, Gitgit, the central mountains area, Banjar hot springs and eastern destinations. They can be a good option if your time is limited. A full day tour with a chartered vehicle and driver will cost between 150,000Rp and 200,000Rp, depending on the season, your choice of destinations and your bargaining skills.

Places to Stay
Hotels are spread out along Jl Raya Lovina, and on the side roads going off to the beach. There are many budget places that would fit into the mid-range category elsewhere in Bali – but room rates are very competitive here. During high season, accommodation may be tight, so it's wise to arrive early.

Places to Stay – Budget
Singaraja to Anturan Happy Beach (or Pantai Bahagia), at the end of a side road around Tukad Mungga village, is very quiet.

Happy Beach Inn (☎ 41017; rooms 50,000Rp), right by the beach, is a bit run-down, especially the open-air bathrooms, but rooms are simple and clean.

Sri Homestay (☎ 41135; singles/doubles 45,000/50,000Rp), tucked in behind Bali Taman Beach Resort, facing the sea, is friendly and has a great location and basic, smallish rooms. It's just a short walk along the beach to the eateries of Anturan.

Anturan Continuing west, a few tiny side tracks and one proper sealed road, Jl Kubu Gembong, lead to this lively little fishing village, busy with swimming locals and moored fishing boats. It's a real travellers' hang-out, courtesy of the proximity of the Perama stop in front of Hotel Perama. It's a long way from Lovina nightlife though – expect to pay around 20,000Rp for transport back to Anturan from Kalibukbuk after 6pm when the bemos stop operating.

At the back of the Perama office on the main road, **Hotel Perama** (☎ 41161; singles/ doubles 40,000/50,000Rp, with air-con 90,000/135,000Rp) is a perfectly clean and decent place if you can't be bothered to find a room elsewhere. It claims to run a shuttle bus into central Lovina from 9am to 8pm.

On Jl Kubu Gembong, there are some good-value places, including **Puspa Rama** (☎ 42070; singles/doubles 60,000/70,000Rp) and **Bayu Mantra** (☎ 41930; singles/doubles

50,000/80,000Rp, with hot water 60,000/ 100,000Rp), both of which are clean and have modern bathrooms.

Gede Home Stay Bungalows (☎ 41526; singles/doubles 35,000/40,000Rp, with air-con & hot water 65,000/70,000Rp) is a friendly and popular place, while **Mandhara Cottages** (☎ 41476; singles/doubles 50,000/60,000Rp) has clean rooms set in pleasant grounds, as does **Mandhara Chico** (rooms 50,000-80,000Rp). **Hotel Yudha** (☎ 41183, fax 41160; rooms 60,000-70,000Rp, with hot water 100,000-120,000Rp) is a longstanding place with a variety of very clean rooms, as well as a good pool and a great beachfront position.

Anturan to Kalibukbuk Situated right on the beachfront, **Lila Cita** (rooms 40,000-70,000Rp, with hot water 100,000Rp) is scruffy and run-down, but it's the place to go if you want to get away from it all.

The next road west is Jl Pantai Banyualit, with a good selection of hotels, although the beachfront area is not very inspiring.

Suma (☎ 41566; singles/doubles 35,000/ 50,000Rp), in a very pretty stone building, has views of the sea from its upstairs rooms. Rooms are basic but fine. There's also a pleasant **café** (dishes 10,000-20,000Rp).

Built in traditional Balinese style, **Sartaya** (☎ 422240; singles/doubles 40,000/50,000Rp, with air-con 100,000Rp) has clean, decent rooms with 'warm' water.

Sunset Ayu (☎/fax 41054; singles 40,000-80,000Rp, doubles 50,000-100,000Rp) is a small place with a nice atmosphere.

Kalibukbuk A little over 10km from Singaraja, the 'centre' of Lovina is the village of Kalibukbuk, with the biggest concentration of hotels, restaurants and services.

Taman Lily's (☎ 41307; singles/doubles 80,000/100,000Rp, Jl Ketapang), across the road from Rambutan cottages, has a friendly atmosphere and good-value rooms.

Puri Bali Hotel (☎ 41485; rooms 60,000-80,000Rp, with hot water 100,000Rp, with air-con 150,000Rp) has a pool and the air-con rooms are very comfortable.

The next turn-off, Jl Bina Ria, has a handful of bars and restaurants before it ends at the beach.

Pulestis Hotel (☎ 41035; e pulestis@ hotmail.com; Jl Bina Ria; singles/doubles 70,000/100,000Rp) has bungalows with a funky exterior, clean rooms, pebbled open-air bathrooms and a café overlooking a modern pool. The downside is some traffic noise and no hot water.

Susila 2 Backpackers Hostel (☎ 41080; e angsoka@singaraja.wasantara.net.id; singles/ doubles 40,000/50,000Rp), on a side street, has clean, adequate rooms. Guests can use the Angsoka Hotel pool nearby.

Another small side track leads to several other cheap but pleasant places, such as the family-run **Harri's Homestay** (☎ 41152; singles/doubles 40,000/50,000Rp), **Padang Lovina Hotel** (rooms from 70,000Rp), which has good, large rooms, and **Pondok Elsa** (☎ 41186; singles/doubles 60,000/80,000Rp, with air-con 80,000/120,000Rp), a two-storey heavily ornate building, with pleasant rooms.

West of Kalibukbuk Near the Bali Lovina Beach Cottages, **Lovina Beach Hotel** (☎ 41005, fax 41473; w www.lovinabeach hotel.com; rooms 70,000Rp, with hot water from 150,000-175,000Rp) has a great beachfront location, although the cheaper rooms are closer to Jl Raya Lovina. Bland but clean rooms in heavily detailed Balinese bungalows are set in pleasant grounds.

A string of cheapies along Jl Raya Lovina here includes: **Hotel Purnama** (☎ 41043; singles/doubles 25,000/40,000Rp) and the pleasant **Mangalla Homestay** (☎ 41371; singles/doubles 40,000/60,000Rp), both of which have clean fan rooms, set around a small courtyard, but expect some traffic noise; the popular **John's House** (☎ 42189; rooms 70,000Rp), with only two small, basic beachfront rooms (accessed via Mangalla Homestay or via the beach); and **Hotel Mutiara Beach** (☎ 41132; singles/doubles 30,000/40,000Rp), which is clean but noisy and doesn't have much atmosphere.

Parma Hotel (☎ 41555; singles/doubles 40,000/50,000Rp) is a bit tumble-down, but its rooms are clean and reasonably well-protected from traffic noise. Rooms that face the sea are good value.

Places to Stay – Mid-Range
Tukad Mungga to Anturan The **Hotel Puri Bedahulu** (☎ 41731; rooms with fan 150,000Rp, with air-con 200,000Rp) overlooks the beach and has heavily decorated Balinese-style rooms, which are clean and well maintained.

Kubu Lalang (☎ 42207; e kubu-lalang@ cu-media.com; singles/doubles 120,000/ 150,000Rp), which means 'small house of long grass', has bungalows designed in traditional rice-barn style. Edged in between rice paddies, each bungalow is different, exotically decorated and has a modern open-air bathroom. This is a great place for couples to chill in peace. It also has an excellent restaurant (see Places to Eat).

Only stay at **Baruna Beach Cottages** (☎ 41745; e balibara@singaraja.wasantara .net.id; rooms US$17-24, with hot water US$32-52) if you can get a sizeable discount, as rooms are a bit run-down. However, it does have some nice touches, such as crafted wooden furniture and a shady, quiet beachside location.

Anturan to Kalibukbuk Coming complete with its own animal menagerie and a beer garden, the idiosyncratic **Melka Hotel** (☎ 41552, fax 41543; e melka@singaraja .wasantara.net.id; singles US$12-36, doubles US$15-42; Jl Pantai Banyualit) has a range of excellent rooms to suit all budgets.

Hotel Banyualit (☎ 41789; e banyualit@ singaraja.wasantara.net.id; Jl Pantai Banyualit; singles/doubles 70,000/105,000Rp, singles with air-con & hot water 150,000-600,000Rp, doubles 200,000-700,000Rp), back from the beach, has a pool and a lush garden of snaking vines. There's a big choice of rooms, though some are dark and dreary.

Kalibukbuk Close to the beach, **Rini Hotel** (☎/fax 41386; e rinihotel@telkom.net; Jl Ketapang; rooms 100,000-250,000Rp) is a super-clean and well-run place, which features a saltwater pool, a range of rooms with fan and much bigger, better air-con rooms.

Nirwana Seaside Cottages (☎ 41288, fax 41090; e nirwana@singaraja.wasantara.net.id; off Jl Bina Ria; bungalows from 100,000-200,000Rp, with seaview 225,000Rp) is on large and lovely beachfront grounds. All bungalows have some character and hot water, and fan rooms have open-air bathrooms. There's also a pool. Don't confuse this Nirwana with Nirwana Water Gardens, nearby on Jl Bina Ria.

Bayu Kartika (☎ 41055; w www.nusa -bali.com/bayu-kartika; rooms 155,000Rp, with hot water 315,000Rp, with air-con and hot water 355,000Rp) has a range of pleasant

rooms set on sprawling grounds with a small creek running through it. There's also a pool.

In a central Kalibukbuk location **Rambutan Beach Cottages** (☎ 41388; Jl Ketepang; w www.rambutan.org; singles/doubles US$12/ 15, singles with hot water US$27-55, doubles with hot water US$30-55, villas US$95-150), is so family-friendly it has a creative children's play area, but it also caters to honeymooners and couples. The hotel, on a large area of land, features two swimming pools and charming gardens. Rooms, and more especially the villas, are tasteful with lashings of Balinese style.

West of Kalibukbuk Almost Chinese in style, **Aditya Bungalows** (☎ 41059; e aditya @singaraja.wasantara.net.id; rooms US$30-60) is a big place with beach frontage, a pool, shops and a range of rooms with good facilities.

Billibo Beach Cottages (☎/fax 41358; rooms with fan 150,000Rp, with air-con & hot water 200,000-250,000Rp) faces a fine stretch of beach. Rooms are in good condition and all face the water. The café (dishes 15,000-40,000Rp) has a relaxed atmosphere, with big comfy lounges.

Places to Stay – Top End
Facing Jl Raya Lovina, but extending down to the beach, **Bali Taman Beach Resort** (☎ 41126, fax 41840; e balitaman@singaraja .wasantara.net.id; singles US$35-75, doubles US$40-85) is a small but attractive upmarket place, with a pool facing the ocean, and leafy gardens. Rooms have air-con, TV, mini-bar and hot water.

Extending all the way to the beach, **Hotel Aneka Lovina** (☎ 41121, fax 41827; e ank -lovina@singaraja.wasantara.net.id; singles/ doubles from US$71/77, villa/cottage US$89/ 101) is a pleasant place. Rooms have air-con, mini-bar and modern, but bland bathrooms.

Places to Eat
Just about every hotel has a restaurant. In addition there are **food carts**, **warung**, **cafés** and some excellent **restaurants**, including a few in Kayu Putih in the hills above Lovina. Lunch tours to **Sanda Bukit Villas & Restaurant** (☎/fax 0828 369 137; w www.sandavillas .com; Pupuan) can also be arranged (see Routes to the North Coast in the West Bali chapter).

Anturan In a lovely setting surrounded by a carp pond **Warung Bias** (☎ 411692; Jl Pantai Banyualit; dishes 10,000-38,000Rp) is worth going out of your way for. On offer are homemade Bavarian bread, French bread, muffins and cookies, as well as Indian curries, European dishes such as wiener schnitzel, pastas and pizzas.

Warung Rasta (☎ 41275; Jl Kubu Gembong; dishes 15,000-35,000Rp) amusingly serves 'vegetarian Rasta food', such as spaghetti with cheese – go figure! Apart from the Rasta obsession, it has a great chill-out ambience by the waterfront. Views are framed by fishing boats, and fresh fish is grilled at the front of the restaurant.

At the end of Jl Kubu Gembong, walk east along the beach to **Warung Bamboo** (dishes 9000-30,000Rp), a small, open-fronted place, which fronts a lively section of beachfront. It serves typical travellers' fare, cheapish beer and has a relaxed feel.

The restaurant at **Kubu Lalang** (☎ 42207; dishes 18,000-30,000Rp) is a foodie's paradise. On offer is homemade ice cream (including sirsak fruit flavour), Austrian pastries and homemade pasta, including one made from fresh squid ink served with fresh squid, lime and chilli. There's a lovely view from the restaurant of rice paddies and the ocean.

Kalibukbuk On Jl Ketepang, **Barakuda** (dishes 12,500-20,000Rp) has uninspiring décor but a big seafood selection and a good range of Balinese dishes, including sup libi manis (sweet potato soup) and fried banana with palm sugar. Balinese specialities can be ordered the day before.

Barcelona Bar & Restaurant (dishes 10,000-30,000Rp) has a lovely, open-air, shady area out the back where you can finally get away from the endless motorcycle noise. The food is excellent, and includes sate pelecing (fish satay with Balinese spices) and pepesan babi guling (suckling pig slices wrapped in banana leaf).

Warung Warubali (☎ 41533; mains 8500-26,500Rp), at the beach end of the road, has a lively atmosphere and is one of the best places to watch the sunset, which coincides with happy hour (small/large Bintang 5000/10,000Rp; 6.30pm to 8.30pm).

Warung Kopi Bali (☎ 41361; dishes 10,000-20,000Rp) is popular for reasonable meals at reasonable prices.

Kakatua Bar & Restaurant (☎ 41344; dishes 7000-30,000Rp), noticeable by the caged and shrieking sulphur-crested cockatoo at the front of the restaurant (best to avoid this place if you have a hangover), has an overly ambitious menu of Mexican, Thai, Indian and Balinese (and let's not forget pizza) – all of which it does adequately. Don't expect any taste sensations, however.

Le Nasi Goreng (dishes 10,000-30,000Rp) is a nice little place on Jl Bina Ria, shaded by tall lemongrass.

At the end of Jl Bina Ria, turn left to find the **Sea Breeze Cafe** (dishes 13,000-38,000Rp). Right by the beach with an uninterrupted outlook, it has a big choice of pastries and cakes, and a range of Indonesian and Western dishes, including vegetarian lasagne, grilled tuna and tasty pizzas.

Malibu Bar & Restaurant (☎ 41225; dishes 10,000-30,000Rp), on Jl Raya Lovina, is known for its pizzas, filled baguettes, croissants and brownies. It has pool tables, movies nightly at 7.30pm and reggae music in the high season (which hopefully drowns out the traffic noise).

Also on this stretch of road, **Khi Khi Restaurant** (☎ 41548; dishes 12,500-135,000Rp), a big barn of a place filled with fishy aromas, specialises in Chinese food and grilled seafood. It's down-at-heel, and you'll even find yourself eating among locals.

Off Jl Bina Ria, **Bali Apik** (☎ 41050; dishes 7000-25,000Rp) is a low-key bar-restaurant with years of beer-fuelled graffiti splattered on the walls. Food is good value, but novel – soto ayam served with hot chips?! It probably has the cheapest happy hour in Lovina (8000Rp for a large Bintang) and is refreshingly free of cheesy staff and cheesy lovesong atmospherics.

West of Kalibukbuk An ambitious global culinary array is available at **Octopus Garden** (☎ 42031; Jl Raya Lovina; dishes 14,000-35,000Rp), including simple home-style Japanese dishes, such as gyudon (rice topped with beef). The wait staff, though, are uncomfortably obsequious – loosen up guys!

Cafe Spice (dishes 24,000-42,000Rp, off Jl Raya Lovina), an open space whose walls are covered in artwork, has a delicious range of options, such as onion pie with salad, as well as some claypot Indonesian dishes. It's mercifully quiet and faces a long stretch of beach.

Entertainment

Balinese Dance A number of the hotel restaurants offer Balinese dancing with a Balinese buffet meal, or Dutch-style *rijs-taffel* ('rice table' banquet). **Rambutan Beach Cottages** holds performances every Wednesday and Sunday (25,000Rp).

Bars & Clubs Usually between 6pm and 9pm, many restaurants have 'happy hours' – at such times there's an outbreak of happy hour war (much to the delight of thirsty travellers) when a large Bintang is only around 10,000Rp.

Lovina's social scene centres on Jl Bina Ria, which is happy hour HQ, and has several bar-restaurants, none of them with much class, including the always busy **Poco Evolution Bar**. The night begins with acoustic guitar, followed by a cover band. On Sundays there's occasional live entertainment, including drag queens. It has a comfortable lounge area at the back of the bar, and also has a **restaurant** *(dishes 5000-35,000Rp)*, which serves generous crowd pleasers such as burgers, imported Australian steaks and you can guess the rest...

Next door, **Mojo** *(small/large Bintang 5000/10,000Rp)*, a small place on two levels, has slightly more street cred. Walls are covered in artwork, and acoustic guitar (ho hum) plays most nights from 8pm to midnight.

Malibu Bar & Restaurant on Jl Raya Lovina is a good place to head to for a game of pool and a pizza and has live reggae music in the high season after 9pm.

Options on Jl Raya Lovina, near the Jl Bina Ria intersection, have a touch more style. **Lovina Grand Bar de Tommes** *(☎ 42265; dishes 10,000-40,000Rp)* has live music on Tuesday, Thursday and Saturday and club nights on Saturday. It serves up a range of good Dutch food in fairly stylish surroundings. Nearby, **Planet Lovina** has disco meets Bob Marley decor and is a comfortable, interesting place, with live music most nights and occasional DJs.

Videos Several of the eateries along Jl Bina Ria show videos, as does **Malibu**. Keep an eye out for posters advertising videos.

Shopping

Tip Top Shop, on the main street, stocks all of your basic necessities, including some second-hand books. Shops on Jl Ketepang have an assortment of clothing, crafts and souvenirs, but nothing like you'd find in Kuta or Sanur. For something different, check the amusing range of T-shirts and postcards at **Benny Tantra's Air Brush T-Shirts**, which portray to an uncanny degree the daily life of a tourist in Lovina.

Getting There & Away

Bus & Bemo To reach Lovina from south Bali by public transport, you'll need to change in Singaraja (see the earlier Singaraja section for details). Regular blue bemos go from Singaraja's Banyuasri terminal to Kalibukbuk (about 2000Rp) – you can flag them down anywhere on the coast road.

Java Public buses between Surabaya (Java) and Singaraja will drop you anywhere along the main Lovina road, so you won't have to backtrack from Singaraja. **Lovina Transport** *(☎ 41384)*, next door to Planet Lovina, at the corner of Jl Bina Ria and Jl Raya Lovina, sells tickets to Java. Destinations include the following: Mt Bromo (85,000Rp), Yogyakarta (95,000Rp), Surabaya (90,000Rp) and Jakarta (200,000Rp).

Tourist Shuttle Bus Perama links Lovina with Kuta, Sanur and Ubud (50,000Rp), twice daily, via Bedugul (30,000Rp, daily) or Kintamani (30,000Rp, daily). **Perama** buses stop at their office, in front of Hotel Perama, in Anturan *(☎ 41161)*, and then ferry passengers to other points on the Lovina strip for a fee. There's also a **Perama ticket agent** *(☎ 41104; Jl Ketapang)* in Kalibukbuk.

Getting Around

The Lovina strip is *very* spread out, but you can easily travel back and forth on bemos (1000Rp).

Car & Motorcycle Lovina is an excellent base from which to explore north and central Bali, and rental prices are reasonable, but check rental vehicles very carefully – absolutely go on a test run first, and if you're heading anywhere near the central mountains, thoroughly check gear and brake quality. Approximate rates per day are 35,000Rp for a motorcycle and 90,000Rp for a Suzuki Jimny jeep. A chartered vehicle and driver will cost about 170,000Rp per day.

Rentals and charters can be organised through your hotel, or at a shop-cum-travel agency, but look around, because prices do vary between operators. Most transport rental companies are clustered around Jl Raya Lovina near Jl Bina Ria.

Bicycle Rent bicycles at **Lia's** (*Jl Damai*) for 20,000Rp per day. Jl Raya Lovina is flat, but busy. The back road between Kalibukbuk and Singaraja, which runs a kilometre or so inland, is recommended for cyclists.

SOUTH OF LOVINA
☎ 0362

In the hills around Lovina there are a couple of interesting places. At the main junction in Kalibukbuk, go south on Jl Damai and follow the road for about 4km.

Damai Lovina Villas (☎ 41008, fax 41009; W *www.damai.com; rooms US$190*), facing a fabulous view of the ocean in the distance, has just eight luxury bungalows, all interestingly furnished with beautiful wood and fabrics and antiques. A divine pool seemingly spills onto a landscape of coconut palms. The restaurant (*lunch US$4-10, 5-course dinner US$38*), on a raised pavilion fringed by cerise bougainvillea and distant sea views, focuses on beautifully presented gourmet Asian-European nouvelle cuisine using home-grown produce – call for a dinner reservation and free transport.

Pojok Indah (☎ 41571; *dishes 25,000-60,000Rp*), a couple of kilometres on from Damai Lovina Villas on a narrow stretch of road without many parking opportunities, has breathtaking views and a small menu that specialises in Australian steaks. It's associated with the nearby **Bali Fruit Drink Winery**, which produces a range of white wines from tropical fruits, such as banana, pineapple and even *sirsak*. Try a glass (27,500Rp) while you watch the sun sink into the Bali Sea.

WEST OF LOVINA

A good road goes west of Lovina, passing several interesting attractions and following an unspoiled coast, where a few resorts and diving centres take advantage of the secluded beaches and coral reefs. The road continues to the Taman Nasional Bali Barat and the port of Gilimanuk (see the West Bali chapter).

Air Terjun Singsing

About 5km west of Kalibukbuk, a sign points to Air Terjun Singsing (Daybreak Waterfall). About 1km from the main road, there is a warung on the left and a car park on the right. Walk past the warung and along the path for about 200m to the lower falls. The waterfall is not huge, but the pool underneath is ideal for swimming. The water isn't crystal clear, but it's cooler than the sea and very refreshing.

Clamber further up the hill to another waterfall, **Singsing Dua**, which is slightly bigger and has a mud bath, which is supposedly good for the skin. This one also cascades into a deep swimming pool.

The area is pretty and makes a nice day trip from Lovina. The falls are more spectacular in the wet season, and may be just a trickle in the dry season.

Banjar

Brahma Vihara Arama Bali's single Buddhist monastery, only vaguely Buddhist in appearance, with colourful decorations, a bright orange roof and statues of Buddha, has very Balinese decorative carvings and door guardians. It's quite a handsome structure in a commanding location, with **views** down the valley and across the rice fields to the sea. You should wear long pants or a sarong (which can be hired for a small donation). The monastery doesn't advertise any regular courses or programs, but visitors are welcome to meditate in special rooms.

The temple is about 3.3km off the main road – take the obvious turn-off in Dencarik. If you don't have your own transport, arrange an *ojek* at the turn-off (tourist price 5000Rp). The road continues past the monastery, winding further up into the hills to Pedewa, a **Bali Aga village**.

Air Panas Banjar Not far from Brahma Vihara Arama, these hot springs (*adult/child 3000/1500Rp, parking 500Rp; open 8am-6pm daily*) are beautifully landscaped with lush tropical plants. You can relax here for a few hours and have lunch at the restaurant, or even stay the night.

Eight fierce-faced carved stone *naga* pour water from a natural hot spring into the first bath, which then overflows (via the mouths of five more *naga*), into a second, larger pool. In a third pool, water pours from 3m-high spouts to give you a pummelling massage. The water is slightly sulphurous and pleasantly hot, so you might enjoy it more in the morning or the evening than in the heat of the day. You must wear a swimsuit and you shouldn't use soap in the pools, but you can do so under an adjacent outdoor shower.

The change rooms and lockers are under the restaurant, on the right-hand side.

Pondok Wisata Grya Sari (☎ 0362-92903, fax 92966; singles/doubles 80,000/100,000Rp, suites 150,000Rp) is in a wonderful setting on a hillside very close to the baths; however, the rooms are slightly grotty, though they do have outdoor bathrooms. Treks into the surrounding countryside can be organised from here.

Restoran Komala Tirta (dishes 8000-16,000Rp), which overlooks the baths, does good, inexpensive Indonesian food.

It's only about 3km from the monastery to the hot springs if you take the short cut – go down to Banjar Tega, turn left in the centre of the village and follow the small road west and then north to Banjar village. From there it's a short distance uphill before you see the 'air panas 1km' sign on the left (it's on the corner by the police station). From the main road to the hot springs you can take an *ojek*; going back is a 2.4km downhill stroll.

Seririt
☎ 0362

Seririt is a junction for roads that run south over the mountains to Pulukan or Antosari, on the way to Denpasar. The road running west along the coast towards Gilimanuk is quite good, with pretty coastal scenery and few tourists. There's a BCA **ATM** at the Lovina end of Seririt. There are many **warung** and *rumah makan* (restaurants) in the market area, just north of the bemo stop.

Celukanbawang
☎ 0362

Celukanbawang is the main cargo port for north Bali, and has a large wharf. Bugis schooners – the magnificent sailing ships that take their name from the seafaring Bugis people of Sulawesi – can sometimes be seen anchoring here.

Pulaki
☎ 0362

Pulaki is famous for its many grape vines and for **Pura Pulaki**, a coastal temple that was completely rebuilt in the early 1980s, and is home to a large troop of monkeys.

A few hundred metres east of the temple, a well-signposted 3km paved road leads to **Pura Melanting**. This temple is set dramatically in the foothills, and is gloriously devoid of tourists and hawkers. A donation is expected to enter the complex, although you're not permitted in the main worship area.

Pemuteran
☎ 0362

This wonderfully isolated area, with limited facilities, has extensive, untouched coral reefs about 3km offshore, good snorkelling, and is handy for dive sites on Pulau Menjangan to the west. The area is home to the Reef Seen Turtle Project, run by the Australian-owned **Reef Seen Aquatics** (☎/fax 92339; e reefseen@denpasar.wasantara.net.id). Turtle eggs and small turtles purchased from locals are looked after until they're ready for ocean release. More than 4000 turtles have been released since 1994. You can visit the small hatchery and make a donation of US$5 to sponsor and release a tiny turtle.

Reef Seen also offers diving, boat cruises and horse riding. A PADI open-water certificate is US$310, and dives at Pemuteran/Pulau Menjangan are US$55/70 for two dives. Sunset and sunrise cruises cost US$10 per person and glass-bottom boat trips cost US$15 per person for two hours. Horse riding treks pass through the local villages and beaches and cost US$30 for a 90-minute horse ride or US$20 for a 30-minute pony ride. It's possible to take the horses into the ocean for a swim after the trek. Simple accommodation is available to dive guests and horse riders.

Easy Divers (☎ 753673, fax 753683) comes well recommended and offers a worthwhile five-day PADI open-water course for US$350. Dive trips to Tulamben and Menjangan cost US$65.

Three charming small hotels here, all set amid spacious lawns running down to the sea, have their own dive operations, as does Matahari Beach Resort, which rivals the best hotels in Bali. There are several small warung along the main drag. **Balinese dancing**, sponsored by Reef Seen is held every Saturday evening at the Reef Seen café (admission by donation), and dance training takes place on Wednesday and Saturday from 3pm to 5pm.

Taman Selini Beach Bungalows *(☎/fax 93449;* W *www.tamanselini.com; singles/ doubles US$75/85)* is the first place you'll see coming from the east. The thatch-roofed bungalows have four-poster beds and big outdoor bathrooms, which open onto a small garden area. Balconies also have day beds, and there's an inviting pool. **Caffe Selini** *(dishes 18,000-33,000Rp)* is a picturesque, relaxed spot featuring Indonesian and Greek cuisine – tuck into options like *pastitsi*, prawn *saganaki* or *kefte!*

Pondok Sari *(☎/fax 92337; singles/doubles 253,000/301,000Rp, with air-con & hot water 326,000/362,000Rp)* has pleasant bungalows with traditional rooms and lovely flower-filled open-air bathrooms. Snorkelling is possible to the left and right of the beach. **Yos Diving** is based here. The **restaurant** *(dishes 14,000-30,000Rp)* features pasta and cheeseburgers, and *rijstaffel* can be ordered two hours beforehand.

Taman Sari Bali Cottages *(☎/fax 288096;* W *www.balitamansari.com; bungalows US$35-65)*, has gorgeous bungalows and an eco-bent and the **Archipelago Dive Centre** is also situated there.

Matahari Beach Resort & Spa *(☎ 92312, fax 92313;* W *www.matahari-beach-resort .com; singles US$169-424, doubles US$186-466)* is an absolutely elegant place in an isolated location on the eastern outskirts of Pemuteran. Beautifully furnished bungalows are set in attractive gardens, and the pool overlooks the black-sand beach. It offers diving, tennis, windsurfing, mountain bikes, gym and library facilities. The most amazing part of the resort however is the spa, which is like a grand water palace. The central entrance area features a huge lily pond, surrounded by fountain statues, while relief sculptures line the massage room walls. **Dave's Dive Centre** is based at the Matahari.

West Bali

Most of the places regularly visited in west Bali, like Sangeh or Tanah Lot, are easy day trips from Denpasar, Ubud or the Kuta region. Further west, there's lots of through traffic going to/from Java, but the area is well off the main tourist trails. There are a few secluded places to stay, long stretches of deserted black-sand beaches, a few surf spots and countless side tracks to villages that rarely see a tourist.

In the latter half of the 19th century, this was an area of warring kingdoms. However, with the Dutch takeover in the early 20th century, the princes' lands were redistributed among the general population. With this bounty of rich agricultural land, the region around Tabanan was cultivated with beautiful rice fields and became one of the wealthiest parts of Bali.

KAPAL

About 10km north of Denpasar, Kapal is the garden gnome and temple curlicue centre of Bali. If you need a new temple guardian, technicolour deer, roof ornament, planter pot or any of the other countless standard architectural decorations, you've come to shop at the right place.

The most important temple in the area is **Pura Sadat**. It was possibly built in the 12th century, then damaged in an earthquake early in the 20th century and subsequently restored after WWII.

TANAH LOT
☎ 0361

The brilliantly located Tanah Lot *(adult/child 3300/1800Rp, car park 1500Rp)* is possibly the best-known and most photographed temple on Bali. It's an obligatory stop on many tours from southern Bali, very commercialised, and especially crowded at sunset. At the time of writing, the quaint temple, perched on a little rocky islet, was surrounded by conservation construction works financed by the Japanese government, which are due to be completed in 2004. The project aims to construct an artificial rock platform around the temple to halt the erosion that currently threatens it.

For the Balinese, Tanah Lot is one of the most important and venerated sea temples.

Highlights

- Soaking up superb sunset silhouettes of the serene sea temple of Rambut Siwi
- Viewing the *sawah* scenery, especially the picturesque rice fields of the district of Tabanan
- Trekking in Taman Nasional Bali Barat and maybe spotting an endangered Bali starling
- Diving at the popular Pulau Menjangan
- Visiting small villages, walking to waterfalls and traversing the island on Bali's back roads

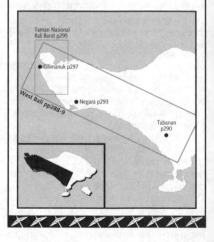

Like Pura Luhur Ulu Watu, at the tip of the southern Bukit peninsula, and Pura Rambut Siwi to the west, it is closely associated with the Majapahit priest Nirartha. It's said that each of the 'sea temples' was intended to be within sight of the next, so they form a chain along Bali's southwestern coast – from Tanah Lot you can certainly see the clifftop site of Ulu Watu, and the long sweep of sea shore around to Perancak, near Negara.

Tanah Lot, however, is a well-organised tourist trap. To reach the temple, a walkway runs through a sort of sideshow alley with dozens of souvenir shops and out of place brand-name American clothes stores down to the sea. You can walk over to the temple itself at low tide (but non-Balinese are not allowed to enter), or walk up the slope to the left and sit at one of the many tables along the cliff top. Order an expensive drink, or a more expensive dinner, get your camera ready – and wait for 'The Sunset'.

Places to Stay & Eat

To really appreciate the area (and avoid the heavy traffic after sunset), you can stay overnight. There are cheap **warung** (food stalls) around the car park, and more expensive **restaurants** inside the grounds and on the clifftops facing the temple.

Pondok Wisata Astiti Graha (☎ 812955; rooms 60,000Rp), about 800m before the car park, is clean and friendly and has rooms facing farmland views.

Dewi Sinta Restaurant & Villa (☎ 812933, fax 813956; e dewisinta@denpasar.wasantara .net.id; singles US$12-50, doubles US$16-55) is on souvenir shop alley, not far from the ticket office. There's a range of rooms, and some look across the pool and beyond to rural views. It's a good base to explore the west of Bali. Its **restaurant** (dishes 18,000-60,000Rp, buffet lunches 50,000Rp) offers buffet lunches between noon and 3pm, and evening Balinese dance performances from Thursday to Saturday.

Le Meridien Nirwana Golf Spa & Resort (☎ 815900, fax 815901; w www.lemeridien -bali.com; rooms US$190-490), close to Mutiara Tanah Lot, was one of the most controversial hotel developments on Bali in the 1990s. The resort's position at a higher level than the temple was a prime issue, but it also raised concerns about the additional demand for water, the displacement of traditional landholders and the lack of local participation in the decision-making process. It's a huge development, with over 270 rooms and an 18-hole golf course. The grounds are especially attractive and have a wonderful view of Tanah Lot, albeit from a disrespectful viewpoint.

Getting There & Away

Coming from south Bali with your own transport, take the new coastal road west from Kerobokan, which is north of the Kuta area, and follow the signs or the traffic. From other parts of Bali, turn off the Denpasar to Gilimanuk road near Kediri and follow the signs. To avoid the traffic jams on your journey back, leave very promptly

after sunset to beat the rush, or stay for a leisurely dinner and return after dark.

By *bemo* (small pick-up truck), go from Denpasar's Ubung terminal to Tanah Lot via Kediri (3000Rp). Bemos usually stop running by nightfall, so if you want to see the sunset, you may need to stay overnight at Tanah Lot or charter a vehicle back. Alternatively, take an organised tour from Ubud or South Bali, which may include other sites such Bedugul, Mengwi and Sangeh.

MENGWI

The huge state temple of **Pura Taman Ayun** (adult/child 3300/1800Rp; open 8am-6pm daily), surrounded by a wide, elegant moat, was the main temple of the Mengwi kingdom, which survived until 1891, when it was conquered by the neighbouring kingdoms of Tabanan and Badung. The large, spacious temple was built in 1634 and extensively renovated in 1937. It's a lovely place to wander around, especially before the tour buses arrive. The first courtyard is a large, open, grassy expanse and the inner courtyard has a multitude of *meru* (multitiered shrines).

Any bemo running between Denpasar (Ubung terminal) and Bedugul or Singaraja can drop you off at the roundabout in Mengwi, where signs indicate the road (250m) to the temple. Pura Taman Ayun is a stop-off on many organised tours from Ubud or southern Bali.

BELAYU

In the small village of Belayu (or Blayu), 3km north of Mengwi, traditional *songket* sarongs are woven with intricate gold threads. These are for ceremonial use only and not for everyday wear. Take any bemo or bus between Denpasar (Ubung terminal) and Bedugul or Singaraja, get off at the turnoff to Belayu and walk about 1km west; alternatively bemos go directly from Ubung terminal in Denpasar to Belayu (2500Rp).

MARGA

Between the walls of traditional family compounds, there are some beautifully shaded roads in Marga – but this town wasn't always so peaceful. On 20 November 1946, a much larger and better-armed Dutch force, fighting to regain Bali as a colony after the departure of the Japanese, surrounded a force of 96 independence fighters. The outcome was

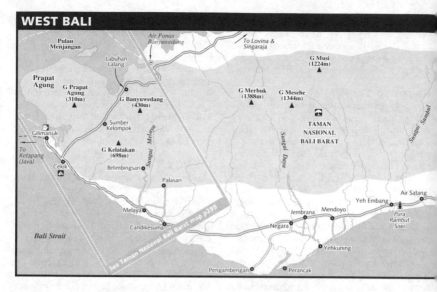

WEST BALI

(map showing:) Pulau Menjangan, Air Panas Banyuwedang, To Lovina & Singaraja, G Musi (1224m), Labuhan Lalang, Prapat Agung, G Prapat Agung (310m), G Banyuwedang (430m), G Merbuk (1388m), G Mesehe (1344m), Sumber Kelompok, TAMAN NASIONAL BALI BARAT, Sungai Melaya, Sungai Daya, Sungai Sumbul, Gilimanuk, G Kelatakan (698m), To Ketapang (Java), Cekik, Belimbingsari, Palasari, Yeh Embang, Air Satang, Melaya, Jembrana, Mendoyo, Pura Rambut Siwi, Candikesuma, Negara, Bali Strait, See Taman Nasional Bali Barat map p295, Yehkuning, Pengambengan, Perancak

similar to the *puputan* (fight to the death) of 40 years earlier – Ngurah Rai and every one of his men were killed. There was, however, one important difference – this time the Dutch suffered heavy casualties as well, and this may have helped weaken their resolve to hang onto the rebellious colony.

The independence struggle is commemorated at the **Margarana** *(admission 3000Rp; open 9am-5pm daily)*, northwest of Marga village. Tourists seldom visit, but every Balinese schoolchild comes here at least once, and a ceremony is held annually on 20 November. In a large compound stands a 17m-high pillar, and nearby there's a **museum**,

with a few photos, home-made weapons and other artefacts from the conflict. Behind is a smaller compound with 1372 small stone memorials to those who gave their lives for the cause of independence – they're like gravestones in a military cemetery, though bodies are not actually buried here. Each memorial has a symbol indicating the hero's religion, mostly the Hindu swastika, but also Islamic crescent moons and even a few Christian crosses. Look for the memorials to 11 Japanese who stayed on after WWII and fought with the Balinese against the Dutch.

To get to the complex take any bemo between Denpasar and Bedugul, and get off at Marga, about 6km north of Mengwi. Walk westward about 2km through Marga. Even with your own transport it's easy to get lost, so ask directions.

SANGEH

About 20km north of Denpasar, near the village of Sangeh, stands the **monkey forest** of Bukit Sari. There's a rare grove of nutmeg trees in the monkey forest and a temple, **Pura Bukit Sari**, with an interesting old Garuda statue. Take care: the monkeys will jump all over you if you have a pocketful of peanuts and don't dispense them fast enough. The Sangeh monkeys have also been known to steal hats, sunglasses, and even sandals, from fleeing tourists. This

---

Famous Last Words

When the Balinese independence fighters at Marga were completely surrounded, outnumbered and outgunned, the Dutch commander called on them to surrender. The Balinese leader, I Gusti Ngurah Rai, replied in a now-famous letter that if the Dutch wanted to negotiate, they should talk with the new Indonesian government on Java, and that he and his men would not surrender. The final words of the letter are engraved in stone panels on the sides of the Margarana memorial – 'Merdeka atau mati!' ('Freedom or death!').

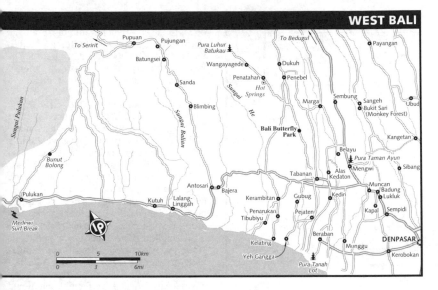

WEST BALI

place is touristy, but the forest is cool, green and shady. The souvenir sellers are restricted to certain areas and are easy to avoid.

You can reach Sangeh on any microbus heading to Plaga from Wangaya terminal in Denpasar (3000Rp). There is also road access from Mengwi and Ubud, but no public transport. Most people visit on an organised tour.

TABANAN
☎ 0361

Tabanan is the capital of the district of the same name. It's a large, well-organised place, with **wartels** (public telephone office) and **Internet access**, **shops**, a **hospital**,

---

> ### The Legend of Sangeh
>
> The monkey forest at Sangeh is featured, or so the Balinese say, in the *Ramayana* epic. Hanuman, the leader of the monkey army, sought to kill the evil Rawana, king of Lanka, by crushing him between the two halves of Mahmeru, the holy mountain. Rawana, who could not be destroyed on the earth or in the air, would thus be trapped in between the two elements. On his way to perform this task, Hanuman dropped a piece of the mountain near Sangeh, complete with a band of monkeys.

---

a **police station** (☎ 91210) and a **market**, but no tourist office and no decent accommodation. There are plenty of basic eateries in the town centre. For something better, try **Taman Senggulan** or **Taliwang Bersandara**, east of town near the side road to the Subak Museum.

Tabanan is also a renowned centre for dancing and gamelan playing. Mario, the renowned dancer of the prewar period, hailed from Tabanan. His greatest achievement was to perfect the Kebyar dance (see the 'Balinese Dance' special section) and he is also featured in Miguel Covarrubias' classic *Island of Bali*.

Mandala Mathika Subak
A *subak* is the village association that deals with water, water rights and irrigation. This quite large complex (☎ 810315; *Jl Raya Kediri; open 8am-7pm*) is devoted to Tabanan's subak organisations and incorporates the **Subak Museum**, which has displays about the irrigation and cultivation of rice, and the intricate social systems that govern it. The exhibits are poorly labelled, but there are sometimes attendants who can show you around and answer questions. It's up a steep road on the left just before you come into town from the east – look out for the sign. Opening hours and visitor service are very casual – a donation may be requested.

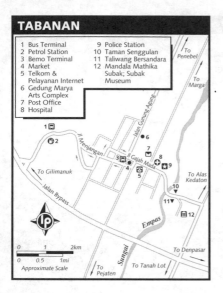

TABANAN

1 Bus Terminal
2 Petrol Station
3 Bemo Terminal
4 Market
5 Telkom &
   Pelayanan Internet
6 Gedung Marya
   Arts Complex
7 Post Office
8 Hospital
9 Police Station
10 Taman Senggulan
11 Taliwang Bersandara
12 Mandala Mathika
   Subak; Subak
   Museum

Getting There & Away

All bemos and buses between Denpasar (Ubung terminal) and Gilimanuk stop at the terminal at the western end of Tabanan. The bemo terminal in the town centre only has transport to nearby villages. If you're driving, note that most main streets are one way, with traffic moving in a clockwise direction around the central blocks. A new road bypasses the south side of town altogether.

SOUTH OF TABANAN

There's not a lot of tourist attractions in the southern part of Tabanan district, but it's easy to access with your own transport. You can reach the main villages by local bemo from Tabanan, especially in the mornings. **Kediri** has Pasar Hewan, one of Bali's busiest **cattle markets**, and is the terminal for bemos to Tanah Lot. About 10km south of Tabanan is **Pejaten**, a centre for the production of traditional pottery, including elaborate ornamental roof tiles. Porcelain clay objects, which are made purely for decorative use, can be seen in a few workshops in the village.

A little west of Tabanan, a road goes south via Gubug to the secluded coast at **Yeh Gangga**, where **Bali Wisata Bungalows** (☎ 0361-261354, fax 812744; ⓦ www.bali wisatabungalows.com; bungalows 150,000-320,000Rp) has stylish accommodation in a superb setting, with a pool and restaurant.

The next road west from Tabanan turns down to the coast via **Kerambitan**, a village noted for its beautiful old buildings (including two 17th-century palaces); a tradition of *wayang*-style painting; and its own styles of music and dance, especially Tektekan, a ceremonial procession. One of the palaces, **Puri Anyar Kerambitan** (☎ 0361-812668, fax 810885; rooms US$30-50), accepts guest bookings in spacious, traditional accommodation in the lively and very welcoming palace compound. Balinese feasts can also be arranged for big groups.

South of Kerambitan, you pass through **Penarukan**, known for its stone-and wood-carvers, and also its dancers. Continue down to the coast, where the beach at **Kelating** is wide, black and usually deserted.

About 4km from southern Kerambitan is **Tibubiyu**, where you'll find **Bibi's Bungalows** (fax 0361-812744; bungalows 80,000-100,000Rp, with hot water 120,000Rp). It's wonderfully isolated, perfectly tranquil and has simple, appealing rice-barn style thatched bungalows decorated with paintings by the owner. The two-storey bungalows have amazing rice-paddy views. The beach is close by (but has strong currents). There's a small, breezy **restaurant** (dishes 14,000-20,000Rp) for guests only. To find Bibi's, head straight from Puri Anyar and then turn left at the T-intersection. At the huge banyan tree, turn right and follow the road through to Tibubiyu. Bibi's is signposted on the left.

NORTH OF TABANAN

The area north of Tabanan is good to travel around with your own transport, but the only regular bemo route is along the road to Penebel.

Another monkey forest, **Alas Kedaton** (adult/child 3300/1800Rp; open 7.30am-6.30pm daily) is a stop-off on many organised tours from Ubud and south Bali. Your ticket includes a guide, who may do little more than fend off avaricious monkeys and lead you to a cousin's sarong shop nearby.

In the village of Wanasari, the **Bali Butterfly Park** (Taman Kupu Kupu Bali; ☎ 0361-814282; adult/child 40,000/20,000Rp; open 8am-5pm daily) has hundreds of mostly Indonesian butterflies in a large, somewhat shabby, enclosed area. The butterflies are most active in the morning, especially on warm, dry days.

Pejaten village is noted for its traditional pottery. The terracotta tiles above feature typical astrological and Hindu motifs.

About 9km north of Tabanan the road reaches a fork. The left road goes to Pura Luhur Batukau (see the Central Mountains chapter), via the **hot springs** at Penatahan. **Yeh Panes Resort** (☎ 0361-262356; e espa_yehpanes@telkom.net; rooms US$80), by the Sungai Yeh Ho (Yeh Ho River), has a small pool, which you can soak in for US$3, where water from the hot springs is piped (although the river looks like a far more inviting option). Rooms are set around the hillside, overlooking the river, and are well maintained. A pleasant open-air **restaurant** (dishes 35,000-38,000Rp) overlooks the picturesque Yeh Ho.

The road to the right continues to Penebel, and then to Dukuh, where you'll find **Taman Sari Bungalow & Coffee House** (☎ 0361-812898; singles/doubles 150,000/200,000Rp). It's a friendly, out-of-the-way place, with some hot-water rooms. It's an ideal base for exploring the area, if you have your own vehicle, but otherwise isn't worth going out of your way for.

LALANG-LINGGAH
☎ 0361

Gajah Mina (☎ 0812 381 1630, fax 731174; w www.gajahminaresort.com; 1-bedroom/2-bedroom suites US$80/120) has only eight exquisitely private, exquisitely furnished bungalows. All have an outdoor and indoor bathroom, and inviting day lounges on the balcony. There are views of the ocean in the near distance from the pool. The **restaurant** (dishes 25,000-50,000Rp) features an international Asian menu. The turn-off is near the village market and the hotel is well away from the noisy main highway.

A little further to the west, the **Taman Rekreasi Indah Soka** is a group of **warung**, with a road leading to the **surf breaks** near the mouth of the river. The break is sometimes called Soka.

ROUTES TO THE NORTH COAST

You can cross between Bali's south and north coasts via Pupuan, well west of the two main cross-island routes (via Kintamani and via Bedugul). From the Denpasar–Gilimanuk road, one road goes north from Pulukan and another road goes north from Antosari – the two roads meet at Pupuan then drop down to Seririt, west of Lovina. Both routes are served by public bemo.

The road from Antosari starts through rice paddies, climbs into the spice-growing country and then descends through the coffee plantations to Pupuan. If you continue 12km or so towards the north coast you reach Mayong, where you can turn east to Munduk and on to Tamblingan and Buyan lakes.

In the foothills of Gunung Batukau, 8km south of Pupuan at Sanda, **Sanda Bukit Villas & Restaurant** (☎/fax 0828 369 137; w www.sandavillas.com; bungalows US$70-95) is a picturesque boutique hotel with a salt-water pool and a relaxed ambience. The **restaurant** (dishes US$3-6) features international and local cuisine.

The Pulukan-Pupuan road climbs steeply up from the coast providing fine views back down to the sea. The route runs through spice-growing country – you'll see (and smell) spices laid out on mats by the road to dry. At one point, the narrow and winding road actually runs right through **Bunut Bolong** – an enormous tree that forms a complete tunnel (the *bunut* tree is a type of ficus; *bolong* means 'hole').

Further on, the road spirals down to Pupuan through some of Bali's most beautiful rice terraces. It is worth stopping off for a walk to the magnificent **waterfall** near Pujungan, a few kilometres south of Pupuan.

Pulukan

Only a few kilometres away from the surf break at Medewi, **Homestay CSB** *(rooms 50,000Rp)*, signposted from the highway on the ocean side, has only two gorgeous bungalows with rice-paddy views and sea views in the near distance. Nearby **Gede Bungalow** *(☎ 0812 397 6668; rooms 50,000Rp)*, only 100m from the beach, has rice-barn style cottages set amidst rice paddies. To reach Gede Bungalows, go past Homestay CSB and take the first right. It's the first building on the left.

JEMBRANA COAST

About 34km west of Tabanan you cross into Bali's most sparsely populated district, Jembrana. The main road follows the south coast most of the way to Negara, the district capital. There's some beautiful scenery, but little tourist development along the way.

Medewi
☎ 0365

Along the main road, a large sign points down the paved road (200m) to the surfing mecca of **Pantai Medewi**. The beach is an impressive stretch of huge, smooth grey rocks interspersed among round black pebbles. It's an idyllic place where cattle graze by the beach. Medewi is noted not for its beach but for its *long* left-hand wave. It works best at mid- to high tide on a 2m swell – get there early before the wind picks up. Non-guests can use the pool at Medewi Beach Cottages for 10,000Rp.

The largest hotel here is **Medewi Beach Cottages** *(☎ 40029, fax 41555; standard doubles/triples 80,000/105,000Rp, garden-view single/doubles US$46/52, ocean-view singles/doubles US$63/69)*. It has an ordinary two-storey building on the western side of the road with second-rate standard cold-water rooms aimed at surfers, and a more stylish

wing on the other side by the pool, with well-furnished rooms featuring air-con, hot water and TV. It's a pleasant-enough and relaxing place, with a plain but big pool and land-scaped gardens. Breakfast is not included. The **restaurant** *(breakfast 15,000-20,000Rp; dishes 15,000Rp-35,000Rp)* serves pasta, steak and seafood and is quite pricey by Balinese standards, with juices for 10,000Rp. It's not a terribly inviting place – toilet paper is humiliatingly rationed out to you if you need to go! A traditional dance performance is held in the restaurant on Sunday evening.

Homestay Gede *(☎ 0812 397 6668; singles/doubles 20,000/30,000Rp)*, an unsignposted place about 20m west of the road behind Medewi Beach Cottages, is a great little low-key homestay with a beach-side **warung** *(dishes 3500-8500Rp)* and *bale* (open-sided pavilion) for lounging. Rooms are basic but suit the 'surfari' hideaway atmosphere. Breakfast isn't included. If you're staying at Medewi Beach Cottages it's worth coming here for breakfast.

Tinjaya Bungalows *(rooms 40,000-45,000Rp)*, a few hundred metres west of the Medewi turn-off, has simple but pleasant rooms in rice-barn style cottages. Its **warung** *(dishes 5000-10,000Rp)* serves cheap and tasty travellers fare.

Near the highway on the Medewi side road, **Kafe Mai Malu** *(dishes 10,000-42,000Rp)* is popular with surfers, serving crowd-pleasing pizza, burgers, steaks and Indonesian meals in its modern, breezy up-stairs eating area.

Pura Rambut Siwi

Picturesquely situated on a clifftop overlooking a long, wide stretch of black-sand beach, this superb temple shaded by flowering frangipani trees is one of the important sea temples of south Bali. Like Tanah Lot and Ulu Watu, it was established in the 16th century by the priest Nirartha, who had such a good eye for ocean scenery. Legend has it that when Nirartha first came here, he donated some of his hair to the local villagers. The hair is now kept in a box buried in this temple, the name of which means 'Worship of the Hair'. Unlike Tanah Lot, it remains a peaceful place and isn't overrun by hordes of local and international tourists.

The caretaker rents sarongs (2000Rp) and is happy to show you around the temple and

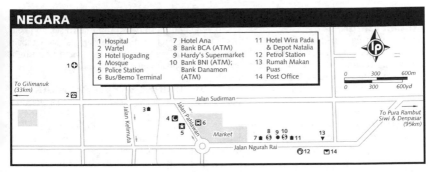

NEGARA

1 Hospital	7 Hotel Ana	11 Hotel Wira Pada
2 Wartel	8 Bank BCA (ATM)	& Depot Natalia
3 Hotel Ijogading	9 Hardy's Supermarket	12 Petrol Station
4 Mosque	10 Bank BNI (ATM);	13 Rumah Makan
5 Police Station	Bank Danamon	Puas
6 Bus/Bemo Terminal	(ATM)	14 Post Office

down to the beach. He then opens the guest book and requests a donation – from 5000Rp to 10,000Rp is a suitable amount, regardless of the much higher amounts attributed to previous visitors.

The temple is between Air Satang and Yeh Embang, at the end of a 300m side road. You'll find it's well-signposted, but look for the turn-off near a cluster of warung on the main road. Any of the regular bemos and buses between Denpasar (Ubung terminal) and Gilimanuk will stop at the turn-off.

Bull Races

This part of Bali is famous for the 'bull races', known as *mekepung*, which culminates in the Bupati Cup in Negara in early August. The racing animals are actually the normally docile water buffalo, which charge down a 2km-long stretch of road or beach pulling tiny chariots. Riders stand or kneel on top of the chariots forcing the bullocks on, sometimes by twisting their tails to make them follow the curve of the makeshift racetrack. The winner, however, is not necessarily first past the post. Style also plays a part and points are awarded for the most elegant runner. Gambling is not legal in Bali but...

Important races are held during the dry season from July to October. Occasional races are set up for tourist groups at a park in Perancak on the coast, and minor races are held at several Perancak sites and several other sites early on Sunday mornings, including Delod Berawan and Yeh Embang, often finishing by noon. Check details with your hotel or the nearest tourist office.

NEGARA
☎ 0365

Negara is a prosperous little town, and not a bad place for a break, though there's not much to see. The town springs to life when the famous bull races are held nearby, in August, September and/or October. Most **banks** change money, and several have ATMs. **Hardy's Supermarket** is on Jl Ngurah Rai.

Places to Stay & Eat
The friendly **Hotel Ana** (☎ 41063; Jl Ngurah Rai 75; singles/doubles with share bathroom 20,000/25,000Rp, singles/doubles with bathroom 25,000/30,000Rp) is clean and good value. Breakfast is not included.

Hotel Wira Pada (☎ 41161; Jl Ngurah Rai 107; singles US$5-10, doubles US$7-15) is probably only worth heading to if you have your own transport, as there's plenty of parking. The cheapest rooms are dark and dreary, while the more expensive ones have air-con. The setting is reasonably pleasant, however.

The Denpasar to Gilimanuk road (Jl Sudirman), which bypasses the town centre, has several cheap lodgings, but the road is very noisy. The quietest and friendliest place along here is **Hotel Ijogading** (☎ 41023; rooms 65,000Rp), with decent rooms.

Depot Natalia (dishes 5000-23,000Rp) at Hotel Wira Pada serves standard Indonesian food in clean surroundings. Other eating options on the main street include **Rumah Makan Puas**, a nice shady spot with good Padang-style food, as well as the assorted **warung** in the market area.

Getting There & Away
Most bemos and minibuses from Denpasar (Ubung terminal) to Gilimanuk drop you in Negara (7000Rp).

AROUND NEGARA
Loloan Timur
At the southern fringe of Negara, this largely Bugis community (originally from Sulawesi) retains 300-year-old traditions. Look for their distinctive houses on stilts, some decorated with wooden fretwork.

Delod Berawan
Turn off the main Gilimanuk–Denpasar road at Mendoyo and go south to the coast, which has a black-sand beach and irregular surf.

Perancak
This is the site of Nirartha's arrival on Bali in 1546, commemorated by a small temple, **Pura Gede Perancak**. Bull races are run at **Taman Wisata Perancak** (☎ 0365-42173), and Balinese buffets are sometimes put on for organised tours from south Bali. If you're travelling independently, give the park a ring before you go out there. In Perancak, ignore the depressing little zoo and go for a walk along the picturesque fishing harbour.

Jembrana
Once capital of the region, Jembrana is the centre of the gamelan *jegog,* a gamelan using huge bamboo instruments that produce a very low-pitched, resonant sound. Performances often feature a number of gamelan groups engaging in musical contest. To see and hear them in action, time your arrival with a local festival, or ask in Negara where you might find a group practising.

BELIMBINGSARI & PALASARI
Christian evangelism on Bali was discouraged by the Dutch, but sporadic missionary activity resulted in a number of converts, many of whom were rejected by their own communities. In 1939 they were encouraged to resettle in Christian communities in the wilds of west Bali.

Belimbingsari was established as a Protestant community, and now has the largest **Protestant church** on Bali. It's an amazing structure, with features of church architecture rendered in a distinctly Balinese style – in place of a church bell there's a *kulkul* (warning drum) like one in a Hindu temple. The entrance is through an *aling-aling*-style gate, and the attractive carved angels look very Balinese. Go on Sunday to see inside.

Palasari is home to a Catholic community, and their **cathedral** is also large and impressive (there could be a little competition here). It also shows Balinese touches in the spires, which resemble the multiroofed *meru* in a Hindu temple, and a facade with

The Bali Starling

Also known as the Bali myna, Rothschild's mynah, or locally as *jalak putih,* the Bali starling (*Leucopsar rothschildi*) is Bali's only endemic bird. It is striking white in colour, with black tips to the wings and tail, and a distinctive bright blue mask. It breeds readily in captivity, and is greatly valued as a caged bird, but in its natural environment it is bordering on extinction. The wild population has been estimated to be as low as 13 – well below the number needed for sustainable reproduction, although experts believe that perhaps several hundred are successfully breeding in captivity around the world.

The internationally supported Bali Starling Project is attempting to rebuild the population by reintroducing captive birds to the wild. At the Bali Starling Pre-Release Centre, formerly caged birds are introduced to the food sources of the natural environment and encouraged to nest in native trees, before being released around Taman Nasional Bali Barat. It's a difficult process, and many attempts have been sadly unsuccessful: birds are often killed by predatory falcons, and on a couple of occasions birds have been stolen from the Pre-Release Centre by armed thieves. Additional assistance is being sought from US conservation group Conservation International (CI).

It is possible to visit the Pre-Release Centre for much of the year, but during the breeding season the parts of Prapat Agung peninsula where the birds congregate are not normally open to visitors. The chances of spotting a Bali starling in the wild are extremely low – to see what you're missing, visit the Taman Burung Bali Bird Park (see the Ubud & Around chapter).

JENNY BOWMAN

the same shape as a temple gate. A few kilometres north of Palasari, a **dam** has created a fine-looking lake among the hills.

These villages are north of the main road, and the best way to see them is with your own transport by doing a loop starting from Melaya, 12km southeast of Cekik. The network of back roads and tracks is very confusing and poorly mapped and signposted, so be prepared to get lost and ask for directions. A bemo or bus will drop you near either turn-off, where you can take an *ojek* (motor-cycle that takes paying pillion passengers).

CEKIK

Cekik is the junction where the road either continues to Gilimanuk or heads east towards Lovina. All buses and bemos to/from Gilimanuk pass through Cekik. Archaeological excavations here during the 1960s yielded the oldest evidence of human life on Bali. Finds include burial mounds with funerary offerings, bronze jewellery, axes, adzes and earthenware vessels from around 1000 BC, give or take a few centuries.

On the southern side of the junction, the pagoda-like structure with a spiral stairway around the outside is a **War Memorial**. It commemorates the landing of Independence forces on Bali to oppose the Dutch, who were trying to reassert control of Indonesia after WWII.

There is a camping ground here; see Places to Stay under Taman Nasional Bali Barat following.

TAMAN NASIONAL BALI BARAT
☎ 0365

The Taman Nasional Bali Barat (West Bali National Park) covers 19,003 hectares of the western tip of Bali. An additional 50,000 hectares are protected in the national park extension, as well as almost 7000 hectares of coral reef and coastal waters. On an island as small and densely populated as Bali, this represents a major commitment to nature conservation.

The **park headquarters** (☎ 61060; open 7am-5pm daily) at Cekik displays a topographic model of the park area, and has a little information about plants and wildlife. You can arrange trekking guides and permits here. There is also the small **Labuhan Lalang visitors' centre** (open 8am-3pm) on the northern coast, where boats leave for Pulau Menjangan.

The main roads to Gilimanuk go through the national park, but you don't have to pay an entrance fee just to drive through. If you want to stop and visit any of the sites within the park, you must buy a ticket (2500Rp).

Flora & Fauna

Most of the natural vegetation in the park is not tropical rainforest, which requires rain year-round, but coastal savanna, with deciduous trees that become bare in the dry season. The southern slopes receive more regular rainfall, and hence have more tropical vegetation, while the coastal lowlands have extensive mangroves.

There are more than 200 species of plants inhabiting the park. Local fauna includes

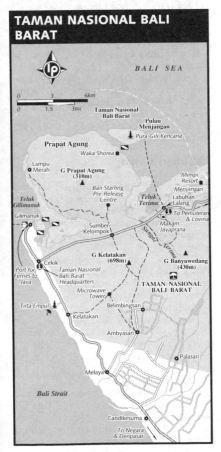

TAMAN NASIONAL BALI BARAT

BALI SEA

Taman Nasional Bali Barat
Pulau Menjangan
Pura Gili Kencana
Prapat Agung
Waka Shorea
Lampu Merah
G Prapat Agung (310m)
Mimpi Resort
Bali Starling Pre-Release Centre
Teluk Terima
Menjangan
Labuhan Lalang
Teluk Gilimanuk
To Pemuteran & Lovina
Gilimanuk
Sumber Kelompok
Makam Jayaprana
G Kelatakan (698m)
G Banyuwedang (430m)
Port for Ferries to Java
Cekik
Taman Nasional Bali Barat Headquarters
TAMAN NASIONAL BALI BARAT
Microwave Tower
Tirta Empul
Belimbingsari
Kelatakan
Ambyasari
Palasari
Melaya
Bali Strait
Candikesuma
To Negara & Denpasar

black monkeys, leaf monkeys and macaques (seen in the afternoon along the main road near Sumber Kelompok); rusa, barking, sambar, Java and mouse deer *(muncak);* and some wild pigs, squirrels, buffalo, iguanas, pythons and green snakes. There were once tigers, but the last confirmed sighting was in 1937 – and that one was shot. The bird life is prolific, with many of Bali's 300 species found here, including the very rare Bali starling (see the boxed text earlier).

Trekking
All trekkers must be accompanied by an authorised guide. It's best to arrive the day before you want to trek, and make inquiries at the park headquarters at Cekik, the visitors' centre at Labuhan Lalang or any hotel in Gilimanuk. Guides may miraculously appear at your hotel within minutes of your arrival, but first make sure they are authorised.

The set rates for guides in the park depend on the size of the group and the length of the trek – with one or two people it's 65,000Rp for one or two hours, 95,000Rp for three or four hours, 207,000Rp for five to seven hours; with three to five people it's 104,000Rp, 152,000Rp or 310,000Rp. Transport and food are extra. Early morning is the best time to start – it's cooler and you're more likely to see some wildlife. The following are some of the more popular treks.

- From a trail west of Labuhan Lalang, hike around the mangroves in Teluk Terima. Then partially follow the Sungai Terima into the hills and walk back down to the road along the steps at Makam Jayaprana. You might see grey macaques, deer and black monkeys (allow two to three hours).
- Starting at Kelatakan village, climb to the microwave tower on Gunung Kelatakan (698m), go down to Ambyasari and get transport back to Cekik (four hours).
- From Sumber Kelompok, go up Gunung Kelatakan, then down to the main road near Kelatakan village (six to seven hours). You may be able to get permission from park headquarters to stay overnight in the forest – if you don't have a tent, your guide can make a shelter.
- From Sumber Kelompok, you can trek around some of Prapat Agung, via the Bali Starling Pre-Release Centre and Batu Lucin – but only from about June to September, when the sensitive Bali starlings move further inland (allow at least five hours). It's easier and quicker to access the peninsula by chartered boat from Gilimanuk.

Boat Trips
The best way to explore the mangroves of Teluk Gilimanuk or the west side of Prapat Agung is by chartering a boat (maximum of three people) for about 100,000Rp per boat per hour from in front of Penginapan Nusantara II homestay in Gilimanuk (see the Gilimanuk map). A guide will cost another 100,000Rp. This is the ideal way to see bird life, including the kingfisher, the Javanese heron and, very rarely, the Bali starling.

Diving
Teluk Gilimanuk is a shallow bay with marine life quite different from other parts of Bali – it's especially interesting for divers with a strong interest in marine biology. The closest and most convenient dive operators are at Pemuteran and Lovina.

Pulau Menjangan is one of Bali's best-known dive areas, with a dozen distinct dive sites. Unfortunately, the coral has suffered somewhat from coral bleaching (caused by warm water during the 1998 El Niño event) and the spread of crown-of-thorns starfish. Nevertheless, the diving is excellent – there's lots of tropical fish (including clown fish, parrot fish, sharks and barracuda), soft corals, great visibility (usually), caves and a spectacular drop-off.

Labuhan Lalang
The jetty at this small harbour is the place to catch a boat to Pulau Menjangan. There's a visitors' centre *(open 8am-3pm)* here, where you can pay the park entrance fee (2500Rp), several **warung** and a pleasant **beach** 200m to the east. Some of the warung rent **snorkelling** gear (50,000Rp per four hours) and can point out where the best sites are. **Waka Dive** (W *www.wakatobi.com)* has a dive shop based here. Parking is 2000Rp for a car and 1000Rp for a motorbike.

Local boat owners have a strict cartel and fixed prices: it costs 200,000Rp for a four-hour trip to Menjangan, and 20,000Rp for every subsequent hour, in a boat holding 10 people (or five scuba divers with equipment).

Pulau Menjangan
This uninhabited island boasts what is thought to be Bali's oldest temple, **Pura Gili Kencana**, dating from the Majapahit period on Java. You can walk around the island in about an hour, but the attractions are mainly

underwater. Snorkellers can find some decent spots not far from the jetty – ask the boatman where to go. **Dive sites** are dotted all around the island, so it's worth discussing the possibilities with the divemaster when you arrange the trip.

Makam Jayaprana

A 20-minute walk up some stone stairs from the southern side of the road, a little west of Labuhan Lalang, will bring you to Jayaprana's grave. There are fine views to the north at the top. Jayaprana, the foster son of a 17th-century king, planned to marry Leyonsari, a beautiful girl of humble origins. The king, however, also fell in love with Leyonsari and had Jayaprana killed. Leyonsari learned the truth of Jayaprana's death in a dream, and killed herself rather than marry the king. This Romeo and Juliet story is a common theme in Balinese folklore, and the grave is regarded as sacred, even though the ill-fated couple were not deities.

Air Panas Banyuwedang

According to a local brochure, water from these hot-water springs (see the West Bali map) will 'strengthen the endurance of your body against the attack of skin disease'. You can soak in the unappealing little bath house (adult/child 3300/1800Rp); the hot springs at Banjar, near Lovina, are far, far better.

Places to Stay

There is a **camp ground** at the park headquarters at Cekik, and several budget hotels in nearby Gilimanuk. There are also several resort hotels.

The **Mimpi Resort Menjangan** (☎ 0361-701070, fax 701074; ⓦ www.mimpi.com; patio rooms US$95, villas US$195-325), at

isolated Banyuwedang, has a large site extending down to a small, mangrove fringed, white-sand beach. The grounds have a sterile atmosphere, while the rooms have stark, simple design, all with open-air bathrooms, while every villa has a hot-spring tub and its own private courtyard. The hotel also has a dive school and spa, where a 60-minute massage is US$25.

Getting There & Away

The national park is too far away for a comfortable day trip from Ubud or southern Bali, though many dive operators do it. It is much more accessible from Lovina or Pemuteran – just get any Gilimanuk-bound bus or bemo to drop you at either the Labuhan Lalang entrance or the park headquarters at Cekik. Alternatively, take an organised tour or even rent a vehicle.

GILIMANUK
☎ 0365

Gilimanuk is the terminus for ferries that shuttle back and forth across the narrow strait to Java. There is a **bank**, **post office**, **wartels** and an uninformative **tourist office** underneath the huge stone quadruped that straddles the road as you enter town (this bizarre edifice comprises four dragons on pedestals, their tails tied together over the middle of the road)

Most travellers to/from Java can get an onward ferry or bus straight away, and won't need to stop in Gilimanuk. There are no attractions as such, but it's a lively place with nonstop port traffic and the profiles of Gunung Merapi and Gunung Raung looming from the other side of the Bali Strait. It's also the closest accommodation to the national park if you want to start an early trek. In the

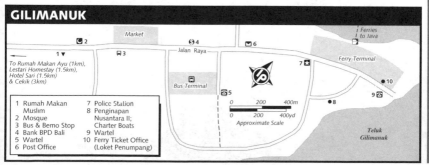

GILIMANUK

To Rumah Makan Ayu (1km),
Lestari Homestay (1.5km),
Hotel Sari (1.5km)
& Cekik (3km)

Jalan Raya

Market

Bus Terminal

Ferry Terminal

i Ferries
to Java

Teluk
Gilimanuk

0   200   400m
0   200   400yd
Approximate Scale

1 Rumah Makan
   Muslim
2 Mosque
3 Bus & Bemo Stop
4 Bank BPD Bali
5 Wartel
6 Post Office
7 Police Station
8 Penginapan
   Nusantara II;
   Charter Boats
9 Wartel
10 Ferry Ticket Office
   (Loket Penumpang)

WEST BALI

windy months of June through August, wind-surfing can be arranged at Hotel Sari.

Places to Stay & Eat

If you have a tent, you can try **camping** at the grounds of the park headquarters at Cekik free of charge. The grounds are not pristine, but the bathroom is clean enough.

There are plenty of cheap lodgings in Gilimanuk close to the ferry terminal, but all are abysmal and not worth recommending. You'll have to head 3km east for decent lodgings.

Lestari Homestay *(☎ 61504; Jl Raya; rooms 35,000-70,000Rp, with air-con 90,000Rp)* is a good, clean, friendly option even though rooms are a touch grotty and there is quite a lot of traffic noise.

Hotel Sari *(☎ 61264; rooms 50,000Rp, with hot water 90,000Rp, suite with private garage 110,000Rp)*, off the ocean side of Jl Raya near Lestari Homestay, is well away from the noisy road. Standard rooms are good value, and hot-water rooms have a phone and TV. It's certainly the most comfortable option for solo female travellers among a relatively unwelcoming hotel scene. The upstairs **restaurant** *(dishes 8000-10,000Rp; open 7pm-10pm)* has Japanese-style cushion seating and delicious, simple dishes.

Assorted cheap-eats options cluster around the market and ferry terminal. **Rumah Makan Muslim** *(Jl Raya; dishes 6000Rp)* is spotlessly clean and inexpensive.

Getting There & Away

Bus & Bemo Frequent buses hurtle along the main road between Gilimanuk and Denpasar (Ubung terminal; 12,000-17,500Rp), or along the north coast to Singaraja (10,000Rp). It's cheaper to catch a bus, rather than a minibus or bemo from outside the market as drivers will probably bump up the fare for tourists, and vehicles are crowded and stop at every place along the way.

Ferry See the Bali Getting There & Away chapter for details about the ferry between Gilimanuk and Ketapang on Java. The pedestrian entranceway for the ticket office is opposite the wartel, while the vehicle entrance is 10m further west.

Getting Around

At the ferry, bemo and bus terminals, you will be thronged by *ojek* riders, who charge 5000Rp for the short ride to the recommended hotels. More leisurely and comfortable, particularly if you have luggage, are the numerous *dokar* (pony carts).

Lombok

Facts about Lombok

HISTORY

The earliest recorded society on Lombok was the relatively small kingdom of the Sasak. The Sasak people were agriculturalists and animists who practised ancestor and spirit worship. The original Sasak are believed to have come overland from northwestern India or Myanmar (Burma) in waves of migration that predated most Indonesian ethnic groups. Only a few archaeological relics remain from the old animist kingdoms, and animism has left its mark on the culture, although the majority of Sasak people today are Muslim. Not much is known about Lombok before the 17th century, at which time it was split into numerous, frequently squabbling states, each presided over by a Sasak 'prince' – a disunity exploited by the neighbouring Balinese.

Balinese princes ruled Lombok from the mid-18th century until the 1890s, when the Dutch sided with the Sasaks and defeated the Balinese in bloody battles (see the boxed text 'The Battle for Lombok' later). Under Dutch rule, the eastern islands of Indonesia were grouped together as the Lesser Sunda Islands, administered from Singaraja, Bali. Taxes resulted in the impoverishment of the majority of peasants and the creation of a new stratum of Chinese middlemen.

Post-Colonial Lombok

When Soekarno proclaimed Indonesian independence on 17 August 1945, the Lesser Sunda Islands were formed into the single province of Nusa Tenggara, which means 'Islands of the Southeast'. This proved far too unwieldy to govern and in 1958 the province was divided into three separate regions – Bali, Nusa Tenggara Barat (West Nusa Tenggara) and Nusa Tenggara Timur (East Nusa Tenggara).

In the wake of the attempted coup and Soekarno's downfall in 1965, Lombok experienced mass killings of communists, sympathisers and ethnic Chinese, as did Bali and other parts of Indonesia. Under President Soeharto's 'New Order', Lombok enjoyed stability and some growth, until crop

Highlights

- Watching magnificent sunsets behind Gunung Agung from the beach at Senggigi
- Visiting the temples and palaces of past rajahs and multiple faiths in and around Mataram
- Shopping for something special while watching village craft workers: sarongs in Sukarara, baskets in Beleka or pottery in Penujak
- Enjoying the rural charm of Lombok: small villages, shady roads, emerald rice fields and rainforest walks
- Exploring the scarcely developed south coast, with perfect bays, hidden beaches, 'secret' surf spots and superb sea views
- Socialising under the coconut palms on the Gili islands while enjoying the simple pleasures of the sun, sea and sand

failures led to famine in 1966 and to severe food shortages in 1973. Many moved away from Lombok under the *transmigrasi* (transmigration) programme.

Tourist development started around 1980, when Lombok attracted attention as an 'unspoilt' alternative to Bali. While low-budget bungalows proliferated at places like the Gili islands and Lombok's south coast, big businesses from outside Lombok became interested and speculation on beachfront land became epidemic. Lombok's tourism planning was dominated by the national government in Jakarta, and many traditional landholders were displaced as outside business interests moved in.

Economic Crisis & Beyond

The political turmoil, economic crisis and civil unrest that beset Indonesia in the late 1990s did not spare Lombok. Students in Mataram and Praya staged protests over the general economic situation as early as 1997, and the local economy was hit hard by the general downturn in Indonesian tourism.

The riots of 17 January 2000 were a surprise and a shock to most local people. A

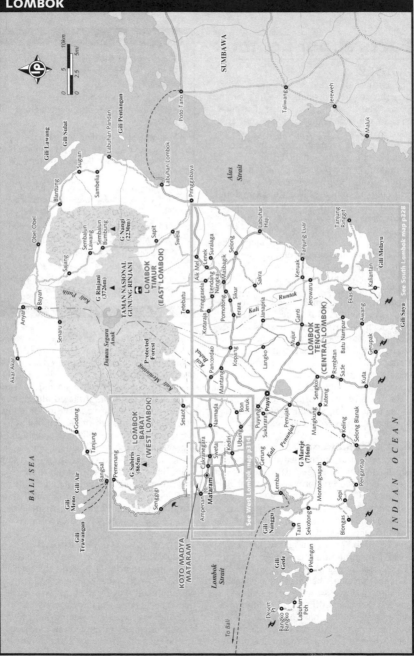

LOMBOK

SUMBAWA

Taiwang

Jereweh

Maluk

Poto Tano

Gili Lawang

Gili Sulat

Sugian

Blantung

Sambelia

Labuhan-Pandan

Gili Petangan

Obel Obel

Sajang

Bayan

Anyar

Sembalun
Lawang

Sembalun
Bumbung

G. Nangi
(2330m)

Sapit

Sweta

Labuhan
Lombok

Pringgabaya

*Alas
Strait*

Akar Akar

Senaru

Kokoq Putih

G Rinjani
(3726m)

TAMAN NASIONAL
GUNUNG RINJANI

LOMBOK
TIMUR
(EAST LOMBOK)

Tetebatu

Aik Mel

Pringgasela

Suralaga

Selong

Labuhan
Haji

Tanjung Luar

Tanjung
Ringgit

Gili Melayu

Godang

*Danau Segara
Anak*

P-rotected
Forest

Kokoq Manuang

Kotaraja

Lendang
Nangka

Masbagik

Sikur

Terara

Kali

Kalantan

Gili Saya

Tanjung

Sesaot

Kokoq Babak

Pancordao

Mantang

Pomotong

Kopang

Langko

Kali

Janapria

Runtak

Mujur

Ganti

Jerowaru

Ekas

Awang

See South Lombok map p328

BALI SEA

Pemenang

Bangsal

LOMBOK
BARAT
(WEST LOMBOK)

G Sahiris
(865m)

Narmada

Sweta

Kedin

Bon
Jeruk

Ubung

Getung

Puyung

Sukarara

Praya

Penujak

Sengkol

Penujak

Mangkung

Kateng

Sade

Batu Nampar

Rembitan

Kuta

LOMBOK
TENGAH
(CENTRAL LOMBOK)

Gerupak

Kali

Gili
Meno

Gili Air

Gili
Trawangan

Cakranegara

Mataram

Ampenan

Lembar

Montongsapah

G Mareje
(716m)

Keling

Selong Blanak

Pengantap

Senggigi

KOTO MADYA
MATARAM

See West Lombok map p314

*Lombok
Strait*

Gili
Nanggu

Taun

Sekotong

Sepi

Blongas

INDIAN OCEAN

Gili
Gede

Pelangan

To Bali

Desert
Pt

Bangko
Bangko

Labuhan
Poh

The Battle for Lombok

In 1894 the Dutch sent an army to back the Sasak people of eastern Lombok in a rebellion against the Balinese rajah, who controlled Lombok with the support of the western Sasak. The rajah quickly capitulated, but the Balinese crown prince decided to fight on.

The Dutch camp at the Mayura Water Palace was attacked late at night by a combined force of Balinese and western Sasak, forcing the Dutch to take shelter in a temple compound. The Balinese also attacked another Dutch camp further east at Mataram, and soon the entire Dutch army on Lombok was routed and forced back to Ampenan where, according to one eyewitness, the soldiers 'were so nervous that they fired madly if so much as a leaf fell off a tree'. These battles resulted in enormous losses of men and arms for the Dutch.

Although the Balinese had won the first battles, they had begun to lose the war. They faced a continuing threat from the eastern Sasak, while the Dutch were soon supported with reinforcements from Java.

The Dutch attacked Mataram a month later, fighting street-to-street against Balinese and western Sasak soldiers and civilians. The Balinese crown prince was killed, and the Balinese retreated to Cakranegara, where they had well-armed defensive positions. Cakra was attacked by a large combined force of Dutch and eastern Sasak. Rather than surrender, Balinese men, women and children opted for the suicidal *puputan* (a fight to the death) and were cut down by rifle and artillery fire.

The Balinese rajah and a small group of commanders fled to Sasari near Lingsar, and though the rajah surrendered, most of the Balinese held out. In late November, the Dutch attacked Sasari and, again, a large number of Balinese chose the *puputan*. With the downfall of the dynasty, the local population abandoned its struggle against the Dutch. The conquest of Lombok, considered for decades, had taken the Dutch barely three months. The old rajah died in exile in Batavia (now Jakarta) in 1895.

public community meeting in Mataram was roused to burn churches and ransack Christians' houses and businesses. Evidence suggests that this apparently spontaneous incident was actually well planned by groups from outside Lombok. Anti-Christian propaganda had been circulated before the meeting, there were planted provocateurs in the crowd and the rioters were directed to a well-identified series of targets.

A high proportion of Lombok's Christians are ethnic Chinese, and though the violence was consistently described as anti-Christian, there may well have been an anti-Chinese element involved. The effect on the tourist industry was immediate, with virtually no visitors for a month, and only a trickle returning some three months later.

The incident caused grave damage to Lombok's reputation and economy, and the government and local tourism industry have been attempting to promote the island since as a safe destination.

CLIMATE

West Lombok, where the main town and tourist areas are based has a climate similar to south Bali, but drier. The wet season, from late October to early May, is less extreme, with December, January and February the wettest months. In the dry season, from June to September, temperatures range from hot to scorching. At higher elevations it can get quite cold at night, so bring some extra layers of clothing and a light jacket. Clouds and mist usually envelop the slopes of Gunung Rinjani from early morning onwards, but the south coast is less humid and has clear skies almost every day.

ECOLOGY & ENVIRONMENT

As in Bali, Lombok's traditional economy was based on intensive wet rice cultivation, supplemented by a few other crops and sea fish. The wooded slopes of Gunung Rinjani have provided timber for building and boats, while coconut palms provided timber, fibre and food. The land use has been environmentally sustainable for many years, and the island retains a natural beauty largely unspoiled by industry, overcrowding or overdevelopment. Some lessons have been learned from the more problematic tourist developments on Bali, and the slowdown in tourism has generally restrained the excesses of resort developers.

Regulations mandate effective sewage treatment and appropriate rubbish disposal, and this is somewhat effective. The main environmental concerns are with unsanctioned activities, such as illegal logging in the forests (forests are now better patrolled than in the past) and destructive fishing practices using explosives and poisons (the coastal area is also better patrolled now). Increases in sea temperature associated with global warming and the 1998 El Niño event have caused some die-off in coral reefs, but they are expected to recover over time.

ECONOMY
Small scale agriculture is still the main economic activity, with the pottery and textiles business now forming a substantial craft industry sector. Infrastructure is improving, with quite good roads around most of the island, reasonably reliable electricity supplies and phones now available in most areas. Various foreign-aid projects have helped to improve water supply, agricultural output and health.

The Tourism Industry
Under the Soeharto regime, tourism policy was determined by the national government, which tried to attract 'quality' tourists and promoted the construction of expensive resort hotels. Large tracts of beachfront land around Senggigi, Kuta and the Gili islands were acquired for codevelopments with Javanese and foreign interests.

Instability in Indonesia has had a disastrous effect on Lombok's tourist industry, with international visitor numbers falling from a peak in 1997 of 245,000 to under 110,000 in 1999 and 2000. Many large tourist developments have failed to materialise at all, and expectations for the industry have become more modest, and perhaps more realistic.

POPULATION & PEOPLE
Lombok has a population of 2.6 million (1997 census), with the majority living in and around the principal centres of Mataram, Praya and Selong. Almost 90% of the people are Sasak, about 10% are Balinese, and there are minority populations of Chinese, Javanese and Arabs.

The Sasak
The Sasak are assumed to have originally come from northwestern India or Myanmar (Burma), and the clothing they wear even today (particularly the women) is very similar to that worn in those areas. Sasak women traditionally dress in long black sarongs called *lambung* and short-sleeved blouses with a V-neck. The sarong is held in place by a 4m-long scarf called a *sabuk*, trimmed with brightly coloured stripes. They wear very little jewellery and never any gold ornaments. Officially, most Sasak people are Muslims, but unofficially many of the traditional beliefs have become interwoven with Muslim ideology.

The Wallace Line

The 19th-century naturalist Sir Alfred Wallace (1822–1913) observed great differences in fauna between Bali and Lombok – as great as the differences between Africa and South America. In particular, there were no large mammals (elephants, rhinos, tigers etc) east of Bali, and very few carnivores. He postulated that during the ice ages, when sea levels were lower, animals could have moved by land from what is now mainland Asia all the way to Bali, but the deep Lombok Strait would always have been a barrier. Thus he drew a line between Bali and Lombok, which he believed marked the biological division between Asia and Australia.

Plant life does not display such a sharp division, but there is a gradual transition from predominantly Asian rainforest species to mostly Australian plants like eucalypts and acacias, which are better suited to long dry periods. This is associated with the lower rainfall as one moves east of Java. Environmental differences, including those in the natural vegetation, are now thought to provide a better explanation of the distribution of animal species than Wallace's theory about limits to their original migrations.

Modern biogeographers do recognise a distinction between Asian and Australian fauna, but the boundary between the regions is regarded as much fuzzier than Wallace's line. Nevertheless, this transitional zone between Asia and Australia is still called 'Walacea'.

The Balinese

The Balinese originally settled in the west of the island, and the majority of Lombok's Balinese still live there and retain their Hindu customs and traditions. Historically, as feudal overlords of Lombok, they earned the ill will of the Sasak. Even today, the Sasak regard the Dutch as liberating them from an oppressive power, but by and large the Balinese and Sasak coexist amicably. The Balinese contributed to the emergence of Lombok's Wektu Telu religion, and Balinese temples, ceremonies and processions are a colourful part of western Lombok's cultural life.

Other Groups

The Chinese first came to Lombok with the Dutch as cheap labour and worked as coolies in the rice paddies. Later they were given some privileges and allowed to set up and develop their own businesses – primarily restaurants and shops. Chinese businesspeople, many of them Christians, owned quite a few shops and restaurants in Ampenan and Cakranegara. These businesses were singled out in the riots of January 2000 – some were ransacked or torched, and many have not reopened.

Ampenan has a small Arab quarter known as Kampung Arab. The Arabs living here are devout Muslims, well educated and relatively affluent.

In the late 19th century, Buginese from south Sulawesi started to settle in coastal areas such as Labuhan Lombok, Labuhan Haji and Tanjung Luar. Their descendants still operate much of the fishing industry.

ARTS

Lombok is home to some unique traditions in both the performing arts and handicrafts.

Dance & Music

Lombok has dances found nowhere else in Indonesia, but they are not widely marketed as tourist attractions. Performances are staged in some luxury hotels and in the village of Lenek, known for its dance traditions. The better-known dances are as follows.

Cupak Gerantang This dance is based on one of the Panji stories, an extensive cycle of written and oral stories originating on Java in the 15th century. It's often performed at traditional celebrations.

Kayak Sando This is another version of a Panji story, but here the dancers wear masks. It is only found in central and eastern Lombok.

Gandrung The Gandrung follows a theme of love and courtship. It is a social dance, usually performed outdoors by young men and women, and most commonly performed in Narmada, Lenek and Praya.

Oncer This war dance, also called *gendang beleq*, is performed by men and boys. It is a highly skilled and dramatic performance, with dancers playing a variety of unusual musical instruments in time to their movements. It is performed at traditional *adat* festivals, in central and eastern Lombok.

Rudat The Rudat is performed by pairs of men dressed in black caps and jackets and black-and-white check sarongs, backed by singers, tambourines and cylindrical drums called *jidur*. The music, lyrics and costumes reveals both a mixture of Muslim and Sasak cultures.

Tandak Gerok This combines dance with music played on bamboo flutes and the bowed lute called a *rebab*, as well as singers imitating the sound of gamelan instruments. It is usually performed after harvesting or other hard labour.

Genggong Using a simple set of instruments, which includes a bamboo flute, a *rebab* and knockers, seven musicians accompany their music with dance movements and stylised hand gestures.

Weaving

Lombok is renowned for its traditional weaving, the techniques being handed down from mother to daughter. Each piece of cloth is woven on a backstrap loom in established patterns and colours. Some fabrics are interwoven with gold thread and many take at least a month to complete. Abstract flower and animal motifs are sometimes used to decorate this exquisite cloth, but you may have to look carefully to recognise forms like buffaloes, dragons, lizards, crocodiles and snakes. Several villages specialise in weaving cloth, while others concentrate on fine baskets and mats woven from rattan or grass.

Other Crafts

Carving is often done to decorate functional items, such as containers for tobacco and spices, and the handles of betel-nut crushers and knives. Materials include wood, horn and bone. A recent fashion is for 'primitive'-style elongated masks, often decorated with inlaid shell pieces. Cakranegara, Sindu, Labuapi and Senanti are centres for carving.

Lombok is noted for its spiral woven rattan basketware, bags made of *lontar* (dried palm leaf) or split bamboo, small boxes made of woven grass and plaited rattan mats. Decorative boxes of palm leaves made in the shape of rice barns and decorated with small shells are another Lombok exclusive. Beleka, Suradadi, Kotaraja and Loyok are noted for fine basketware, while Rungkang, about 1km east of Loyok, combines pottery and basketware. Sayang is known for palm leaf boxes.

Earthenware pots made of local clay *(gerabah)* have been produced on Lombok for centuries. They are shaped entirely by hand (without a potter's wheel), coated with a slurry of clay or ash to enhance the finish, and fired in a simple kiln filled with burning rice stalks. Pots are often finished with a covering of woven cane for decoration and extra strength. Many newer designs feature bright colours and elaborate decorations to meet market demands. Penujak, Banyumulek and Masbagik are some of the main pottery villages. You can also see a good range at the Lombok Pottery Centre in Cakranegara.

Architecture

Lombok's architecture is governed by traditional laws and practices. Construction must begin on a propitious day, always with an odd-numbered date, and the building's frame must be completed on that day. It would be bad luck to leave any of the important structural work to the following day.

In a traditional Sasak village there are three types of buildings – the communal meeting hall *(beruga)*, family houses *(bale tani)* and rice barns *(lumbung)*. The *beruga* and the *bale tani* are both rectangular, with low walls and a steeply pitched thatched roof, although, of course, the *beruga* is much larger. The arrangement of rooms in a *bale tani* is also very standardised. There is an open veranda *(serambi)* at the front and two rooms on two different levels inside – one for cooking and entertaining guests, the other for sleeping and storage.

SOCIETY

Traditional law is still fundamental to the way of life on Lombok today, particularly customs relating to courting and marriage rituals, and circumcision ceremonies. In western Lombok, the Balinese community performs dances, temple ceremonies, and colourful processions with decorative offerings of flowers, fruit and food – just as elaborate as on Bali. Sasak ceremonies are often less visible, but you may see some colourful processions and gatherings, often associated with weddings and circumcisions. If you stay near traditional villages and ask around, you may find some festivals and celebrations, especially around July and August.

Avoiding Offence

Most of Lombok is conservative, and immodest dress and public displays of affection between couples can cause offence. Brief shorts, sleeveless tops and swimwear should not be worn away from the beaches and tourist areas. Elsewhere, long pants or skirts and T-shirts or shirts are the norm (shorts are OK if they cover most of the thighs). Nude bathing or women going topless are also *very* offensive anywhere on Lombok.

Betel Juice

Chewing betel nut *(siri pinang)* is still a custom on Lombok and other outer islands of the Indonesian archipelago. The chewing mix is actually a combination of the betel nut, the green stem of the betel plant, and lime. The lime is a catalyst, which releases a mild intoxicant from the betel, stimulates the production of saliva and gives the whole mess a bright red colour – hence the splotches of red spittle on the ground. Chewing betel can be pretty gross, but it has great cultural significance and it's very bad manners to refuse if you're offered some (put it in your pocket to 'enjoy' later). It's mainly used by older men and women in the more isolated villages, and is becoming less common. Betel chewing helps to relieve the pain of toothache and gum disease, and improved dental health is one reason for its declining use.

Duck man at Singaraja, northern Bali

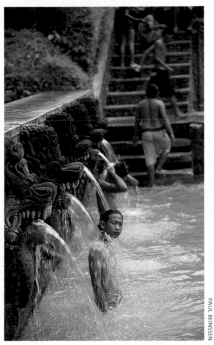

Natural hot springs (Air Panas) at Banjar

Coloured Hindu stone carving, Lovina

Tanah Lot sea temple perches on a rocky outcrop on the west coast

The sacred lotus flower

Iguanas inhabit Taman Nasional Bali Barat

Many people on Lombok fast during the month of Ramadan. During this time it is insensitive and offensive for foreign visitors to eat, drink or smoke in public during the day. Islamic law forbids Muslims from drinking alcohol, and although alcohol is widely available on Lombok, public drunkenness is frowned upon and is particularly offensive near a mosque.

RELIGION

About 90% of Lombok's population are Muslims. Islam reached Indonesia in the 13th century, with peaceful Gujarati merchants arriving on the eastern coast of Lombok via the Celebes (now Sulawesi), and on the western coast via Java.

Islam's traditions and rituals affect all aspects of daily life. Friday afternoon is the official time for worship, and all government offices and many businesses close. Muslim women in Indonesia do not have to wear veils, nor are they segregated or considered second-class citizens.

Wektu Telu

This unique religion originated in the village of Bayan, in north Lombok. Officially only a very small proportion of the population belongs to this faith, which is not one of Indonesia's 'official' religions.

Wektu means 'result' in the Sasak language, while *telu* means 'three' and signifies the three religions that comprise Wektu Telu: Balinese Hinduism, Islam and animism. Members of the Wektu Telu religion regard themselves as Muslims, but are not officially accepted as such by mainstream Muslims.

The fundamental tenet of Wektu Telu is that all important aspects of life are underpinned by a trinity. One example of this principle is the trinity of Allah, Mohammed and Adam. Allah symbolises the one true God, Mohammed is the link between God and human beings, and Adam represents a being in search of a soul.

The Wektu Telu believe they have three main duties – to believe in Allah; avoid the temptations of the devil; and co-operate with, help and love other people. They must pray to Allah every Friday, meditate and undertake to carry out good deeds.

The Wektu Telu do not observe Ramadan; their concession to it is a mere three days of fasting and prayer. They also do not follow

the Muslim practice of praying five times a day in a holy place. While prayer and meditation are important daily rituals, the Wektu Telu believe in praying from the heart when and where they feel the need. All public buildings are designed with a prayer corner or a small room that faces Mecca. As for not eating pork, the Wektu Telu believe that everything that comes from Allah is good, therefore pork is good.

Facts for the Visitor

SUGGESTED ITINERARIES

There's a variety of things to see and do on Lombok – take your pick from the following possibilities and put them together to build your own itinerary.

Mataram Area

In Lombok's main urban area, wander around Ampenan, the faded Dutch colonial port, and visit the markets, handicraft stores, weaving factories or the Pottery Centre. Go a few kilometres east of town to Taman Narmada (a water palace where you can swim) and Pura Lingsar (a multifaith temple).

Beaches

Lombok has some lovely beaches where you can relax for a few days – or weeks. Senggigi is the most developed, with a full range of hotels and tourist services. The Gili islands are simple, inexpensive and popular with young travellers. Kuta has a magnificent beach, and is a good base for exploring Lombok's superb and secluded south coast. To really get away from it all, try the little-developed east coast, or the southeast or southwest peninsulas.

Gunung Rinjani

If the Gunung Rinjani area becomes safe in future (see Dangers & Annoyances later in this section), stay a night in the mountain village of Senaru, walk to the waterfalls and check out the scenery. Perhaps continue to Sembalun, in a cool, fertile valley on the eastern slopes. Trekkers should allow at least a day to reach the crater rim from Senaru, two days to reach the crater lake, three days to climb to the top of Rinjani and four days to traverse the mountain from one village to the other.

Villages & Handicrafts

Several villages around Tetebatu, in central Lombok, have simple lodgings where you can see traditional life, visit waterfalls or watch the timeless cycle of rice cultivation. Other villages specialise in crafts such as pottery, basketwork and weaving – visit them on day trips or on the way to the south coast.

PLANNING
When to Go

The dry season (mid-May to late September) can be hot, but is the best time for trekking and travel to remote areas. The wet season is more humid with frequent tropical rainstorms, and the landscape is greener and more attractive, though some backroads can be washed away. Travel is slightly less convenient during Ramadan, the Muslim fasting month, especially in the traditional rural areas, but in the tourist areas there will be little difference in services.

Maps

The maps in this guidebook will be sufficient for most visitors, but if you're planning on exploring in more detail or trekking, you may need something more detailed. The Periplus *Lombok & Sumbawa* is the best map around, and includes a good street map of Mataram. Also worthwhile is the Nelles *Bali & Lombok* map, which has detailed maps of Mataram and the Gili islands. Both maps are widely available on Bali and in a few shops on Lombok.

HEALTH

Most of the health considerations are the same as for Bali, except that malaria is a greater risk on Lombok. See Health in the Bali Facts for the Visitor chapter for further information.

Malaria

Significant progress has been made in reducing the number of mosquitoes on Lombok, and therefore the risk of malaria and other insect-borne diseases. The risk is greatest in the wet months and in remote areas. The very serious *P. falciparum* strain causes cerebral malaria and may be resistant to many drugs.

Medical Services

The best hospital is in Mataram, and there are more basic ones in Praya and Selong. For anything serious, go to the Bali International Medical Clinic in Kuta, Bali. There are pharmacies in the main towns and tourist centres, but the choice of medicines is limited.

WOMEN TRAVELLERS

Traditionally, women on Lombok are treated with respect, but in the touristy areas, harassment of single foreign women may occur. Would-be guides/boyfriends/gigolos are often persistent in their approaches, and aggressive when ignored or rejected. Western films and TV, as well as the behaviour of many visitors, such as topless bathing and kissing in public, have created fanciful ideas about Western sexual mores. This can be taken to extremes, as a reader's letter reported an attempted rape on Gili Trawangan in 2001. Clothes that aren't too revealing are a good idea – beachwear should be reserved for the beach, and the less skin you expose the better. Two or more women together are less likely to experience problems, and women accompanied by a man are unlikely to be harassed. If walking at night, it's best to walk in a pair.

TRAVEL WITH CHILDREN

Lombok is generally quieter than Bali and the traffic is much less dangerous. People are fond of kids, but less demonstrative about it than the Balinese. The main reservation about bringing kids to Lombok is the risk of malaria. Discuss malaria prevention with your doctor before you go (see the Health section in the Facts for the Visitor chapter).

DANGERS & ANNOYANCES

The traffic is much lighter here than on Bali, but there is still a danger of traffic accidents. Most beaches are protected by coral reefs and are quite safe, but there are strong currents at places around Kuta and the Gili islands (swimming in between the islands is absolutely not recommended – travellers have drowned attempting this), and there are no lifeguards anywhere.

There have been disturbing readers' letters of bandits attacking and robbing surfers in Ekas, east of Kuta, and of robberies from tourists in some villages. At the time of writing, the Australian Department of Foreign Affairs and Trade (w *www.dfat.gov.au/travel*) has warned that travellers to Gunung Rinjani have been the target of criminal activity.

Trekkers should get advice from the local authorities and only use a registered guide (see the Trekking entry under Activities later in this section). In previous years there have been some deaths from falls on Gunung Rinjani or drowning in the crater lake.

Thefts from hotels and *losmen* (basic accommodation) are not unknown, so don't leave valuables lying around your room. Hawker hassles can be overwhelming, especially at Senggigi and Kuta.

EMERGENCIES
In case of emergency call the following numbers.

Police	☎ 110
Fire	☎ 113
Ambulance	☎ 118

Outside the Mataram/Senggigi area, emergency services may be nonexistent, or a long time coming. Don't expect an ambulance to collect injured surfers from the southwest coast. The Gili islands don't have any formal police force.

PUBLIC HOLIDAYS & SPECIAL EVENTS
The Facts for the Visitor chapter has a list of Indonesia's national public holidays. Lombok also has many of its own festivals and holidays. Some are on fixed dates each year, including:

Anniversary of West Lombok April 17 – a government holiday
Ramadan 27 October 2003, 15 October 2004, early October 2005
Idul Fitri (end of Ramadan) 25 November 2003, 14 November 2004, early November 2005
Founding of West Nusa Tenggara December 17 – public holiday

Many festivals take place at the start of the rainy season (around October to December) or at harvest time (around April to May). Most of them do not fall on specific days in the Western calendar, including Ramadan, so planning for them is not really possible.

Ramadan, the month of fasting, is the ninth month of the Muslim calendar. During this period, many restaurants are closed, and foreigners eating, drinking (especially alcohol) and smoking in public may attract a very negative reaction.

Other occasions observed on Lombok include the following.

Harvest Ceremony March or April – Bali Hindu ceremony held at Gunung Pengsong, near Mataram, where a buffalo is sacrificed as a thanksgiving for a good harvest.
Desa Bersih First Thursday in April – a harvest festival held in honour of Dewi Sri, the rice goddess.
Pura Meru A special Bali Hindu ceremony held every June at full moon in the Balinese Pura Meru temple at Cakranegara (in Mataram).
Hari Raya Ketupat Also called Lebaran Topat, seven days after the end of Ramadan, a Wektu Telu celebration held at Batulayar, near Senggigi.
Perang Ketupat Also called Perang Topat, an annual rain festival held at Lingsar, near Mataram, between October and December. Adherents of the Wektu Telu religion and Balinese Hindus give offerings and pray at the temple, then come out and pelt each other with *ketupat* (sticky rice wrapped in banana leaves).
Idul Fitri November or December – also called Hari Raya; celebrates the end of Ramadan. This climax to a month of austerity features wild beating of drums all night, fireworks and no sleep. At 7am everyone turns out for an open-air service. Mass prayers are followed by two days of feasting. Many Indonesians return to their home villages at this time.
Pujawali A Bali Hindu celebration held yearly at Pura Kalasa temple at Narmada, near Mataram, in honour of the god Batara, who dwells on Gunung Rinjani. At the same time, the faithful who have made the trek up the mountain and down to Danau Segara Anak hold a ceremony called *pekelan*, where they throw gold trinkets and objects into the lake.

ACTIVITIES
Lombok has a lot to offer, but often travellers will need to go off the beaten track – particularly surfers.

Surfing
The south and east coasts of Lombok get the same swells that generate the big breaks on Bali's Bukit peninsula – the main problem is getting to them. Lombok's Kuta Beach is the main base for surfers, with accommodation, restaurants and a small surf shop. Boat owners there will take you out to the reefs where the surf breaks. Other south-coast places accessible by road include Selong Blanak, Mawun, Gerupak and Ekas – these are all reef breaks, some accessible by paddling, others that you'll need a boat to reach.

Desert Point, near Bangko Bangko on the southwestern peninsula, is Lombok's most famous break. It's a classic, fast, tubular left, but it's inconsistent and it needs a good size swell to work. A very rough road goes to Bangko Bangko, but there is no regular transport and no visitor facilities.

The easiest way to reach the best of Lombok's breaks is on one of the surf tours from Bali. See the Surfing entry under Activities in the Facts for the Visitor chapter for more information.

Diving & Snorkelling

There is some very good scuba diving and snorkelling off the Gili islands, though much of the coral has been damaged by dynamite fishing. There are also some good reefs near Senggigi. Quite a few dive operators are based on the Gilis and in Senggigi, but some are better than others – check carefully the credentials of the instructor or dive-master who will be responsible for your dive, and remember that any shop selling PADI books can have a PADI logo out the front. With the dearth of tourists on Lombok, diving can be considerably cheaper than on Bali, but don't compromise on safety to save a few bucks.

Trekking

The Gunung Rinjani area is superb for trekking. It's possible to get up to the crater rim and back in a single day, but it's much more rewarding to do a longer trip, which will involve camping out overnight. Note that you'll need good camping equipment and warm, windproof clothing. You can sign up for an all-inclusive trek with an agency, or arrange your own transport to Senaru or Sembulan Lawang (the usual starting points for Rinjani treks), where equipment (including radio communications), guides and porters can be organised through the **Rinjani Trek Centre** (☎ 0868 1210 4132).

See the Organised Tours entry under Getting Around, in this chapter, for details on tour operators.

Warning In recent years, there have been many robberies and some attacks on trekkers in the Gunung Rinjani region, so we can't recommend it at this time – see Dangers & Annoyances earlier in this section for details and advice. At the very least, check the security situation locally before you set out.

SHOPPING

The best buys on Lombok are handicrafts, such as boxes, basketware, pottery and handwoven textiles. Shops in the tourist centres stock items from all over Lombok and from other parts of Indonesia – you'll find a good selection of weavings from Sumbawa, Sumba and Flores.

Nearly every village has basic shops, and a market at least once a week with stalls selling food, clothes, handicrafts and other items. The largest daily market is at Bertais, by the Mandalika bus terminal, east of the Mataram urban area – it's definitely worth seeking out. Mataram Mall has the best range of Western-style goods.

Getting There & Away

Lombok is very accessible by air and sea from the neighbouring islands. The vast majority of travellers arrive from Bali, less than 50km away, while those island-hopping from the east will reach Lombok from Sumbawa.

AIR

Lombok's Selaparang airport is just north of Mataram. It has a hotel reservations desk, café and restaurant, moneychanger and *wartel* (public telephone offices) and Internet access. The only direct international flights are to Singapore and Kuala Lumpur – for any other international destinations, go via Denpasar or Jakarta. Daily domestic flights go to several Indonesian cities.

Airlines

Airlines currently flying to/from Lombok are:

Air Mark (☎ 0370-646847) Selaparang airport
Garuda Indonesia (☎ 0370-637950, fax 637951; W www.ga-citilink.com; open 8.30am-4.45pm Mon-Sat, 9am-1pm Sun) Hotel Lombok Raya, Jl Panca Usaha 11, Mataram
Merpati Nusantara Airlines (☎ 0370-621111, fax 633691; e amidmmz@telkom.net; W www .merpati.co.id) Jl Pejanggik 69, Cakranegara
Silk Air (☎ 0370-628254, fax 628292; W www .silkair.com; open 9am-5pm Mon-Fri, 9am-1pm Sat) Hotel Lombok Raya, Jl Panca Usaha 11, Mataram. There is also an office at Selaparang airport (☎ 0370-636924, fax 636916)

A number of travel agents in Mataram and Senggigi sell tickets and reconfirm flights, and you can also buy tickets at the airport. It's important to reconfirm, because all flights are on small planes and it's very easy to get bumped. Flights are often cancelled at short notice.

Departure Tax
The departure tax is 8000Rp for domestic flights and 75,000Rp for international flights. If you buy tickets on Bali for flights leaving Lombok, make sure the domestic tax is included.

Bali
See the Getting Around chapter for information on travel between Bali and Lombok.

Singapore
The Singapore Airlines subsidiary, Silk Air, has direct flights from Singapore (US$255/ 372 one way/return, four weekly).

Malaysia
Merpati flies several times a week between Mataram and Kuala Lumpur.

Other Indonesian Islands
Departing from Mataram, Merpati flies to Jakarta (830,000Rp, twice daily), Surabaya (445,000Rp, daily), Yogyakarta (550,000Rp, three weekly) and Bima on Sumbawa (240,000Rp, twice weekly). Garuda has daily flights to other Indonesian cities, predominantly via Denpasar, although it flies direct to Surabaya (440,000Rp, daily). Air Mark flies only to Denpasar.

LAND & SEA
See the Getting Around chapter for information on travel between Bali and Lombok.

Sumbawa
Bus Many long-distance public buses travel daily between the Mandalika terminal, east of Mataram, and the major towns on Sumbawa. The bus, complete with passengers and luggage, goes on the public ferry between Labuhan Lombok and Poto Tano. You can buy a ticket at the terminal. It's a good idea to book your ticket a day or two ahead, especially around the time of public holidays. Otherwise, arrive early (before 8am) at the terminal. You may also get a spare seat

on a long-distance bus when it stops at the port, but you can't count on it.

Sometimes you have the choice between a cheaper (economy) bus and a more expensive (luxury) one with air-con and reclining seats, but often there is no option. The official fares are displayed inside the office at Mandalika terminal on an information board, but prices do vary a little from one company to another. All fares include ferry charges.

Buses travel to Sumbawa Besar (31,000/ 45,000Rp economy/luxury, six hours), Dompu (42,000/55,000Rp, 12 hours), Bima (48,000/61,000Rp, 13 hours) and Sape (51,000/64,000Rp, 14 hours).

Ferry Public ferries travel daily between Labuhan Lombok (Lombok) and Poto Tano (Sumbawa), departing every hour. If you are coming from Sumbawa, start early so you can reach Labuhan Lombok by 4pm, because public transport is limited after this time.

Other Indonesian Islands
Bus Long-distance public buses go daily from Mandalika terminal to major cities on Java. The price includes the ferry to Bali, bus across Bali, another ferry to Java and bus to your destination city. Most buses are comfortable, with air-con and reclining seats. Destinations include Denpasar (75,000Rp), Surabaya (110,000Rp, 20 hours), Semarang (155,000Rp, 28 hours), Yogyakarta (165,000Rp, 30 hours) and Jakarta (238,000Rp, 48 hours).

Comfortable long-distance buses also go from Mandalika terminal to the port of Sape (64,000Rp) on Sumbawa, from where you can travel onward to Komodo and Flores.

Pelni Currently three Pelni boats, *Kelimutu, Awu* and *Tilongkabila,* stop at Lembar about once a fortnight. Destinations from Lembar are Bima, Labuanbajo, Ujung Padan, Bau Bau, Surabaya, Larantuka, Kupan, Saumlak, Dobo, Timika and Merauke, but depending on the direction of travel, it may take a long time to get from Lembar to these places. The islands of Bali, Sumbawa and Flores are a journey of four hours, 16 hours and 24 hours respectively from Lembar. You can book tickets at the **Pelni office** (☎ 0370-637212, fax 631604; Jl Majapahit 2, Mataram; open 9am-3pm Mon-Fri, 9am-noon Sat). Pelni also has a small office in **Lembar** (☎ 0370-681204).

Getting Around

Lombok has an extensive network of roads, although many outlying villages are hard to get to by transport. A good road crosses the middle of the island between Mataram and Labuhan Lombok, and quite good roads go to the south of this route. The road around the north coast is paved and in good repair. The road north of Sembalun valley is paved, but narrow, winding and steep; the road south of Sembalun even steeper, but often closed by landslides in the wet season. Roads to the extreme southwest and southeast are mostly unpaved, rough or nonexistent.

Public buses and *bemos* (small pick-up trucks) are generally restricted to the main roads. Away from these, you will have to hire a *cimodo* (pony cart), get a lift on an *ojek* (motorcycle) or walk. Public transport becomes scarce in the afternoon and ceases after dark (or earlier in more remote areas).

During the wet season many unsealed roads are flooded or washed away, while others are impassable because of fallen rocks and rubble, making it impossible to reach out-of-the-way places. The damage may not be repaired until the dry season.

BUS

Buses are the cheapest and most common way of getting around. On rough roads in remote areas, trucks may be used as public transport. Mandalika is the main bus terminal for all of Lombok – it's at Bertais, 900m east of Sweta on the eastern edge of the Mataram urban area. The terminal was formerly at Sweta, and some buses still have 'Sweta' written on them, but to add to confusion the terminal is also referred to as Mandalika or Bertais. There are also regional terminals at Praya and Pancor (near Selong). You may have to go via one or more of these transport hubs to get from one part of Lombok to another.

Boat Trips to Komodo

Boat trips east from Lombok are really only for adventure travellers – most are basic set-ups, offering minimal comforts and few safety provisions. The main destination is Pulau Komodo, an island near Flores, famous for the giant monitor lizards called Komodo dragons. The usual boat trips include stops at other islands for snorkelling, trekking, sightseeing and beach parties. Most trips finish in Labuanbajo on Flores, and passengers then continue eastwards or find their own way back to Lombok. Flying back to Bali may be a good idea, as one reader pointed out:

We took a boat trip from Lombok to the Komodo islands. We got it at a very reasonable price of 300,000Rp per person, including three daily meals. It was a fantastic tour, with lots of good snorkelling...The Komodo islands were a sublime experience, with dragons and snakes and a lot of other animals.

The way back from Flores to Bali was horrible. Thirty-four hours in a bus and ferry with only bread and water/cola. The buses of Sumbawa were a really bad experience. The front windshield was off and replaced by some halfway transparent plastic, where the driver had cut a little rectangular hole to look out through. Thank god it didn't rain. Some of the tourists had to sit on the roof, and that was really dangerous because of the driving in the mountains. Some tourists had bought tickets to the night bus Bima-Mataram, but the buses were overbooked, so they had to stand up for nine hours or sit on their luggage. We had bought a ticket for 125,000Rp per person from Flores to Denpasar, but we were dumped in Padangbai.

Lars No, Denmark

Try to get a recent personal endorsement for a particular trip, and find out *exactly* what the cost includes. Prices can be negotiable, depending particularly on the number of passengers and the itinerary, but they are generally inexpensive – from around 450,000Rp per person for a four-day trip. It's worth paying a little more for a less crowded boat and better conditions.

There are several operators with ticket outlets on Gili Trawangan, Bangsal and in Mataram. They depart several times a week from any of these starting places. From Mataram, the bus travels to a boat waiting in Labuan Lombok.

Road Distances (km)

	Bangsal	Bayan	Kuta	Labuhan Lombok	Labuhan Haji	Lembar	Mataram	Pemenang	Praya	Pringgabaya	Sapit	Senaru	Senggigi	Tetebatu
Bangsal	---													
Bayan	57	---												
Kuta	86	143	---											
Labuhan Lombok	101	66	75	---										
Labuhan Haji	157	100	57	39	---									
Lembar	54	121	64	109	77	---								
Mataram	32	96	54	69	64	27	---							
Pemenang	1	56	79	109	105	53	26	---						
Praya	54	121	26	66	39	39	27	53	---					
Pringgabaya	102	74	83	8	26	102	75	101	62	---				
Sapit	106	47	101	25	43	120	92	119	80	18	---			
Senaru	54	102	140	68	106	116	86	63	117	81	54	---		
Senggigi	18	81	64	79	74	40	10	25	40	88	106	72	---	
Tetebatu	76	120	50	45	32	98	44	75	29	46	63	130	54	---

Public transport fares are fixed by the provincial government, and displayed on a noticeboard outside the terminal office of Mandalika terminal. You may have to pay more if you have a large bag or surfboard.

Tourist Shuttle Bus

Shuttle buses serve the main tourist centres on Lombok – Mataram, Senggigi, Bangsal (the port for the Gili islands), Kuta and Tetebatu. Some routes will require a change of bus in Mataram, but you can normally connect on the same day. Shuttle buses are more convenient, comfortable and reliable than public transport, but more expensive and not as frequent. (If you're travelling in a group of three or more, it may be better to charter a vehicle for a trip – see later entry.)

Perama is the most established operator and has the widest network. Note that Perama has buses to Bangsal, where you get boats to the Gili islands, but it does not offer tickets to the Gili islands themselves. Perama does have representatives on the Gilis, and can sell tickets from there to other destinations on Lombok or Bali. Perama also has a boat service from Senggigi to the Gilis.

CAR & MOTORCYCLE

To explore the backblocks of Lombok, it really helps to have your own vehicle. The roads are improving and traffic is much lighter than on Bali. Check the Getting Around chapter for more details on the joys and perils of driving.

Rental

Car The most professional car-rental firm is **Trac Astra Rent-a-Car** (☎ 626363, fax 627071; W www.trac.astra.co.id; Jl Adi Sucipto 5, Rembiga), which has a range of comfortable vehicles. Prices are much higher than at the tourist agencies, but the quality of vehicles is far superior. It also has agents at the airport, at the **Sheraton Senggigi Beach Resort** (☎ 693333) in Senggigi and the **Novotel Coralia** (☎ 653333) in Kuta.

For more informal hire, it's worth asking at your hotel first, which may have a good contact. Senggigi is the best place to try, with the most competitive prices. A Suzuki Jimny jeep will cost about 85,000Rp to 100,000Rp per day, plus insurance. Larger Toyota Kijang jeeps cost about 175,000Rp per day.

Motorcycle Motorcycles are ideal for Lombok's tiny, rough roads, which may be difficult or impassable by car. Once you get out of the main centres there's not much traffic, apart from people, dogs and water buffalo – watch out for the numerous potholes.

The best place to find rental motorcycles is through your accommodation. Expect to pay about 30,000Rp to 35,000Rp per day for a Honda or Yamaha motor scooter. Some sort of insurance is supposedly included in the price. You should have an International Driving Permit, but owners generally don't mind if it's not endorsed for motorcycles, and the police don't seem to mind either. Ask the rental agency about the current requirements. Always check the condition of the motorcycle, as some are not well maintained and you can quickly find yourself in areas where there's no spare parts or mechanical help.

Petrol is available at stations in and around the larger towns for 1750Rp per litre; out in the villages, petrol is sold from bottles at roadside shops.

Bringing a Car or Motorcycle from Bali Very few agencies on Bali will allow you to take their rental cars or motorcycles to Lombok – the regular vehicle insurance is not valid outside Bali.

CHARTERING A VEHICLE

Chartering a bemo or private car from one place to another, or even for one or more days, is convenient and affordable, especially if you can share costs. With three or more people, a charter vehicle will probably be cheaper than a shuttle bus. Drivers may be reluctant to venture off sealed roads, however.

Prices are strictly negotiable – about 150,000Rp per day (from 8am to 5pm) plus petrol is not unreasonable for a small vehicle. The driver will want more for long waits, rough roads and any other reason he can come up with. You can often arrange a charter vehicle through your hotel or a travel agency, or negotiate directly with a driver at a terminal or on the street.

Check that the vehicle is roadworthy. A trip can quickly turn into a nightmare if you find yourself out after dark, in the rain, without windscreen wipers or headlights.

BICYCLE

Lombok is ideal for touring by bicycle, and excellent for mountain bikes. Bicycles aren't readily available, however. If you are keen, bring a bike from home or Bali.

In the populated areas, the roads are flat and the traffic is less dangerous than on Bali. East of Mataram are several attractions that would make a good day trip from Mataram, or you could go south to Banyumulek via Gunung Pengsong and return (see Around Mataram in the West Lombok section).

Some of the coastal roads have hills and curves like a roller coaster – try going north from Mataram, via Senggigi, to Pemenang, and then (if you feel energetic) return via the steep climb over the Pusuk Pass.

BOAT

There's a regular public boat service between Bangsal and the Gili islands, and tourist shuttle boats from Senggigi to the Gilis. Elsewhere around the coast, it's often possible to charter a local outrigger fishing boat *(prahu)* to reach the more remote islands, snorkelling spots and surf breaks. Rental prices are negotiable and variable, but around 150,000Rp per day including petrol and labour is about the minimum.

LOCAL TRANSPORT

There are plenty of bemos and taxis around Mataram and Senggigi. Most taxis can be chartered for a negotiable price to anywhere in the immediate area – generally it's better to use the meter.

Ojek

An *ojek* is a motorcycle on which you ride as a paying pillion passenger. The cost is highly negotiable, but about 4000Rp to 5000Rp for a short trip (a few kilometres) is not unreasonable. They are very convenient where bemos are infrequent, but only if you don't have much luggage.

Cidomo

The pony cart used on Lombok is known as a *cidomo* – a contraction of *cika* (a traditional handcart), *dokar* (Balinese word for a pony cart) and *mobil* (because car wheels and tyres are used). They are often brightly coloured and the horses decorated with coloured tassels and jingling bells. A typical *cidomo* has a narrow bench seat on either side. The ponies appear to some visitors to be heavily laden and harshly treated, but they are usually looked after reasonably well, if only because the owners depend on them for their livelihood. *Cidomos* are a very popular form of transport in many parts of Lombok, and often go to places that bemos don't, won't or can't.

Fares are not set by the government. The price will always depend on demand, the number of passengers, the destination and your negotiating skills – maybe 2000Rp to 4000Rp per passenger for a short trip.

ORGANISED TOURS

Agencies in Senggigi and Mataram arrange tours, typically half-day trips around Mataram, or day trips to the south coast via several craft villages. Try the options in this entry, or ask at the NTB tourist office about tours and operators. The staff there can also recommend guides, or will work as guides themselves (see Tourist Offices in the following West Lombok section for contact details).

Bidy Tour (☎ 0370-632127, fax 631821; e bidytour@indo.net.id; Jl Ragi Genep 17, Ampenan) organises tours around Lombok and Sumbawa.

Ideal Tours (☎ 0370-633629, fax 636982; Jl Pejanggik 54B, Mataram) organises tours in Lombok, including Gunung Rinjani treks, as well as tours to Komodo.

Rangga Wisata Tours & Travel Services (☎ 0370-640058, fax 646881; Jl Airlangga 17, Mataram) offers tours of Lombok and the Gilis, trekking tours of Gunung Rinjani, Lombok and Sumbawa surfing tours, and Komodo dragon tours.

Dream Divers (☎ 0370-693738; w www.dreamdivers.com), based in Senggigi and the Gili islands, runs overnight trips for advanced divers to Blongas in south Lombok, a dive site which features hammerhead sharks. The trip costs US$165, including accommodation.

West Lombok

☎ 0370

Most travellers who visit Lombok spend some time in West Lombok, if only because the airport and the port for ferries to/from Bali is here. It's the most populous part of Lombok, with the largest urban area centring on Mataram, and the biggest tourist resort area, the Senggigi beach strip. There are a number of attractive villages around Mataram, as well as some hard-to-reach coastal areas on the southwest peninsula.

MATARAM

Lombok's biggest urban area is loosely referred to as Mataram, but it's actually a conglomeration of four main towns – Ampenan, Mataram, Cakranegara and Sweta – as well as some other places on the outskirts, like Rembiga in the north and Bertais in the east.

Some travellers use Mataram as a base, but most head straight to Senggigi or the Gili islands, and don't stay here at all. There are banks, travel agencies, airline offices, and some interesting shops and markets, but they can be visited easily on a day trip from Senggigi.

You may spot a few burnt-out buildings in Ampenan and Mataram. Several churches and Christian-run businesses were torched in the January 2000 riots and the area has never completely recovered.

Orientation

To find your way around, and to locate addresses, it's important to distinguish between Ampenan, Mataram, Cakranegara, Sweta and outer areas like Rembiga and Bertais.

The main street starts in Ampenan as Jl Pabean, quickly becomes Jl Yos Sudarso, changes in Mataram to Jl Langko then Jl Pejanggik, then changes again in Cakranegara to Jl Selaparang. It's a one-way street, running west to east. Another series of one-way roads – Jl Tumpang Sari/Panca Usaha/Pancawarga/Pendidikan – takes traffic back towards the coast. Jl Sriwijaya/Majapahit skirts the south side of town as a sort of bypass road, while Jl Adi Sucipto/Jendral Sudirman forms a northern bypass.

Ampenan Once the main port of Lombok, Ampenan now has just a few fishing boats on its broad beach. The town is run-down and dirty, parts of it resemble a dusty ghost town, but it still has character and a few colonial-era buildings. Apart from the Sasak and Balinese, Ampenan has a few Chinese, plus a small Arab quarter known as Kampung Arab.

Mataram Mataram is the administrative capital of the province of Nusa Tenggara Barat (NTB; West Nusa Tenggara). Some of the buildings, especially the governor's office and the banks, are particularly large and extravagant.

Cakranegara Now the main commercial centre of Lombok, bustling Cakranegara is usually referred to as Cakra (pronounced chakra). Formerly the capital of Lombok under the Balinese rajahs, it has shops, restaurants and a market, with many businesses run by the Chinese community. A number of inexpensive lodgings are run by ethnic Balinese.

LOMBOK

WEST LOMBOK

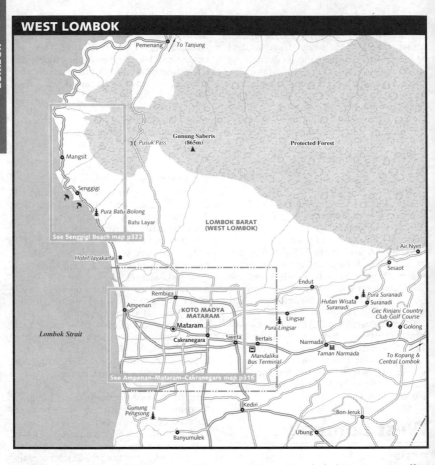

Pemenang | To Tanjung

Pusuk Pass

Gunung Saberis
(865m)

Protected Forest

Mangsit

Senggigi

Pura Batu Bolong

Batu Layar

LOMBOK BARAT
(WEST LOMBOK)

See Senggigi Beach map p322

Air Nyet

Hotel Jayakarta

Sesaot

Endut

Rembiga

Hutan Wisata
Suranadi

Pura Suranadi

Suranadi

Ampenan

KOTO MADYA
MATARAM

Lingsar

Gec Rinjani Country
Club Golf Course

Golong

Mataram

Pura Lingsar

Cakranegara

Sweta

Bertais

Narmada

Lombok Strait

Mandalika
Bus Terminal

Taman Narmada

To Kopang &
Central Lombok

See Ampenan–Mataram–Cakranegara map p316

Gunung
Pengsong

Kediri

Bon Jeruk

Banyumulek

Ubung

Sweta & Bertais Mandalika terminal is the main place to catch buses and bemos to other parts of Lombok, and to Bali, Sumbawa and other islands. See the Getting Around section for more information about the terminal.

On the south side of the terminal is a vast covered market where you'll see stalls spilling over with coffee beans, fruit, eggs, fabric, rice, fish, handicrafts and hardware.

Information
Tourist Offices Mataram has two tourist offices. The most useful one is the **NTB tourist office** (☎ 637233; Jl Singosari 2; open 7am-2pm Mon-Thur, 7am-11am Fri, 7am-12.30pm Sat), the office responsible for the province of Nusa Tenggara Barat.

The **West Lombok district tourist office** (☎ 621658; Jl Suprato) is inconspicuously located a couple of blocks north of the museum in Ampenan. It is officially just for western Lombok, but it does have information about the rest of the island. The opening hours are similar to that of the NTB tourist office.

Immigration Offices Lombok's **kantor imigrasi** (☎ 622520; Jl Udayana) is on the road out to the airport.

Money Most of the banks along Jl Selaparang, in Cakra, will change foreign cash and travellers cheques, although it may take some time. You can also change money at the airport.

Post The **main post office** *(Jl Sriwijaya; open 8am-8pm Mon-Thur & Sat, 8am-11am Fri)*, with a poste restante service, is inconveniently located in the south of Mataram, although you can access the Internet here. The **post office** on Jl Langko is more convenient.

Telephone & Fax The **Telkom office** *(open 24 hrs)* in Ampenan provides telegram and fax services. The international telephone service from this office is efficient, and you can usually get an overseas call connected within a minute or so. There's also a few wartel around town.

Note that Lombok now uses six-digit phone numbers – if you have an old five-digit number (often found on business cards), add a 6 in front of it.

Emergency The best hospital on Lombok is **Rumah Sakit Umum Mataram** *(☎ 622254)*, which has some English-speaking doctors.

The **main police station** *(☎ 631225)* is on Jl Langko. In an emergency, call ☎ 110.

Pura Segara
This Balinese Hindu sea temple is on the beach about 1km north of Ampenan. Nearby are the remnants of a **Muslim cemetery** and an old **Chinese cemetery** – both are worth a wander through if you're visiting the temple.

Museum Negeri Nusa Tenggara Barat
This modern museum *(☎ 632519; Jl Panji Tilar Negara 6; admission adult/child 2500/750Rp; open 8am-1pm & 2pm-4pm daily)* has exhibits on the geology, history and culture of Lombok and Sumbawa, and is worth a look if you have a free hour or so. If you intend buying any antiques or handicrafts, have a look at the *kris* daggers, *songket* (silver or gold-threaded cloth), basketware and masks to give you a starting point for comparison.

Mayura Water Palace
On Jl Selaparang, the main road through Cakra, the Mayura Water Palace was built in 1744 as part of the Balinese kingdom's royal court on Lombok, but most of it was destroyed in the battle of 1894 (see the boxed text 'Battle for Lombok' in this chapter). The main feature remaining is a large artificial lake with an open-sided pavilion in the centre, connected to the shoreline by a raised footpath. This *bale kambang* (floating pavilion) was used as both a court of justice and a meeting place for the Hindu lords. There's not much to see now, but the old palace grounds are a pleasant retreat from the city. Hindus come here to make offerings to their gods, and occasionally exercise their fighting cocks.

The entrance to the walled enclosure of the palace is on a side street on the western side. You may find someone trying to collect entrance fees, but whether they are official is dubious. You should be able to get past them for nothing, or offer 1000Rp if they are insistent.

Pura Meru
Directly opposite the water palace is Pura Meru *(admission by donation; open daily)*, the largest Balinese Hindu temple on Lombok. It was built in 1720 under the patronage of the Balinese prince, Anak Agung Made Karang of the Singosari kingdom, as an attempt to unite all the small kingdoms on Lombok, and as a symbol of the universe, dedicated to the Hindu trinity of Brahma, Vishnu and Shiva.

The outer courtyard has a hall housing the wooden drums that are beaten to call believers to festivals and special ceremonies. In the middle courtyard are two buildings with large raised platforms for offerings.

The inner court has one large and 33 small shrines, as well as three *meru* (multiroofed shrines) that are in a line: the central one, with 11 tiers, is Shiva's house; the one to the north, with nine tiers, is Vishnu's; and the seven-tiered one to the south is Brahma's. The *meru* are also said to represent the three great mountains, Rinjani, Agung and Bromo.

The caretaker will lend you a sash and a sarong if you need one. A major festival is held here every October.

Places to Stay – Budget
Hotel Wisata *(☎ 626971; Jl Koperasi 19, Ampenan; rooms with fan 40,000Rp, singles/doubles with air-con 50,000/75,000Rp)* is a clean and simple option.

A quaint, family-run place, **Oka Homestay** *(☎ 622406; Jl Repatmaja 5, Cakranegara; singles/doubles 25,000/30,000Rp)* has a quiet, shady garden and clean rooms. It has the best atmosphere of all the budget hotels.

LOMBOK

AMPENAN–MATARAM–CAKRANEGARA

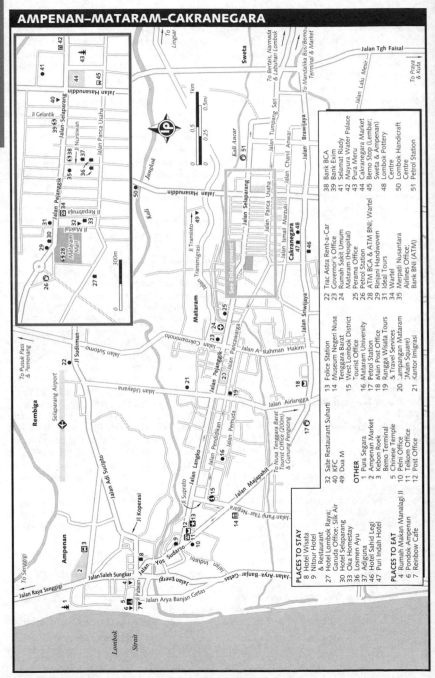

PLACES TO STAY
8   Hotel Wisata
9   Nitour Hotel
    & Restaurant
27 Hotel Lombok Raya;
    Garuda Office; Silk Air
30 Hotel Selaparang
33 Oka Homestay
36 Losmen Ayu
37 Adiguna
46 Hotel Sahid Legi
47 Puri Indah Hotel

PLACES TO EAT
4   Rumah Makan Manalagi II
6   Pondok Ampenan
7   Reinbow Cafe

32 Sate Restaurant Suharti
40 KFC
49 Dua M

OTHER
1   Pura Segara
2   Ampenan Market
3   Kebon Roek
    Bemo Terminal
5   Chinese Temple
10 Pelni Office
11 Telkom Office
12 Post Office

13 Police Station
14 Museum Negeri Nusa
    Tenggara Barat
15 West Lombok District
    Tourist Office
16 Mataram University
17 Petrol Station
18 Main Post Office
19 Rangga Wisata Tours
    & Travel Services
20 Cakrampangan Mataram
    (Main Square)
21 Kantor Imigrasi

22 Trac Astra Rent-a-Car
23 Governor's Office
24 Rumah Sakit Umum
    Mataram (Hospital)
25 Perama Office
26 Petrol Station
28 ATM BCA & ATM BNI; Wartel
29 Rinjani Handwoven
31 Ideal Tours
34 Wartel
35 Merpati Nusantara
    Airlines Office;
    Bank BNI (ATM)

38 Bank BCA
39 Bank Exim
41 Selamat Riady
42 Mayura Water Palace
43 Pura Meru
44 Cakranegara Market
45 Bemo Stop (Lembar;
    Sweta & Ampenan)
48 Lombok Pottery
    Centre
50 Lombok Handicraft
    Centre
51 Petrol Station

Losmen Ayu (☎ 621761; Jl Nursiwan 20, Cakranegara; rooms 25,000-75,000Rp), a Balinese-run hotel, is popular and friendly and well set up for budget travellers. It offers clean comfortable rooms, and the more expensive have air-con. It also has a newer section, with a lovely Balinese-style garden, across the road.

Adiguna (☎ 625946; Jl Nursiwan 9, Cakranegara; rooms 25,000Rp) has clean, basic rooms set around a small garden.

Puri Indah Hotel (☎ 637633; Jl Sriwijaya 132, Cakranegara; rooms 30,000-50,000Rp) is clean, well run and has a restaurant, pool and some air-con rooms, although it's not in a very convenient location.

Places to Stay – Mid-Range

In a central location in Ampenan, **Nitour Hotel** (☎ 623780, fax 625328; Jl Yos Sudarso 4; singles 150,000-300,000Rp, doubles 200,000-350,000Rp) is a quiet and comfortable business travellers' hotel. It has seen better days, although it's still a reasonable option, with rooms with air-con and phone. It also has a **restaurant** (dishes 7000-20,000Rp).

Hotel Selaparang (☎ 632670; Jl Pejanggik 40-42, Cakranegara; singles/doubles with fan 48,000/60,000Rp, with air-con 85,000/108,000Rp) has a good range of rooms; air-con rooms have hot water and TV.

Hotel Lombok Raya (☎ 632305, fax 636478; Jl Panca Usaha 11; singles US$45 55, doubles US$50-60), in Mataram, is a three-star place with attractively furnished, fully equipped rooms, conference facilities and a big swimming pool. The Garuda and Silk Air offices are based here.

Hotel Sahid Legi (☎ 636282, 632681; Jl Sriwijaya 81; rooms US$45), although further from the centre of town than the Lombok Raya, is also good, with a big pool and expansive lawns. Comfortable, modern rooms have TV, telephone and air-con.

Places to Eat

There are several decent restaurants in Ampenan, including the popular no-frills Chinese restaurant **Rumah Makan Manalagi II** (Jl Pabean 28), which is busy all the time with a loyal crowd. No, there are no prices on the menu, but overall it's dirt cheap. Nearby, the **Reinbow Cafe** (Jl Pabean; dishes 6,000-15,000Rp) is a cluttered, colourful little bar featuring a simple menu.

Pondok Ampenan (☎ 645027; Jl Pabean; dishes 9,000-40,000Rp), at the end of Jl Pabean, is a bright, airy place overlooking the bedraggled beach. On offer are seafood, hamburgers, even lamb chops!

Dua M (☎ 622914; Jl Transisto 99; dishes 10,000-20,000Rp), off Jl Transmigrasi, is a locals' favourite for spicy Sasak-style food, such as ayam goreng Taliwang (a spicy grilled chicken) – watch out for the killer sambal. The outdoor area is the most pleasant spot to sit.

Sate Restaurant Suharti (☎ 637958; Jl Maktal 9; satay dishes 6000-9000Rp, seafood 25,000-30,000Rp), in Cakra, is worth visiting for its selection of satays – try anything from liver satay to marrow satay.

Around the western perimeter of Mataram Mall, there are a number of **warung** (food stall) and Internet cafés. Affluent locals are into the conspicuous **KFC** and **McDonald's**, the only Western fast-food outlets on the island, located in Mataram Mall. There's also another **KFC** on Jl Separang.

Shopping

If you don't have time to visit the villages where traditional handicrafts are made, visit the **Lombok Handicraft Centre**, at Sayang Sayang north of Cakra, where a collection of shops have a selection of crafts from Lombok and elsewhere. **Art, craft and 'antique' shops** on Jl Raya Senggigi, the road running north from Ampenan, sell furniture, masks and carvings from Lombok and other parts of Indonesia. Items that are used or dirty are often described as antiques, but very few pieces are more than a few years old.

Lombok Pottery Centre (☎ 640351, fax 640350; Jl Sriwijaya 111A), on the southern edge of Cakra, sells some of the best products available from the various pottery-making villages. It's a little more expensive than buying directly from the villagers, and you don't get to see the pots being made.

Rinjani Handwoven (☎/fax 633169; Jl Pejanggik 44-46), a grubby place, appears to be a throwback to 18th-century working conditions and is where you should still be able to see dyeing and weaving. Interesting ikat or songket fabrics are available by the metre.

Selamat Riady (☎ 631624; Jl Tanun), just east of Jl Hasanuddin, is open on most mornings, and has a shop with textiles and a few other crafts.

Ampenan Market is a colourful produce market worth a look, while the largest (and definitely most lively) daily market is at **Bertais**, by the Mandalika bus terminal. Worth seeking out here is **Toko Anwar** (☎ *671221; Block A, No 5)*, which sells a huge range of textiles (although you'll have to bargain hard).

Getting There & Away
Mandalika terminal is the main bus and bemo terminal for the entire island. It's also the terminal for long-distance buses to Sumbawa, Bali and Java (see the introductory Getting There & Away section in this chapter), and is the eastern terminus for local bemos, which shuttle back and forth to Ampenan.

Long-distance buses leave from behind the main terminal building; bemos and smaller buses for Lombok leave from one of two car parks on either side. Any vehicle without a destination sign on top can usually be chartered for very negotiable prices.

The distances and current fares for buses and bemos from Bertais to major towns and terminal junctions on Lombok are:

destination	distance (km)	price (Rp)
Labuhan Lombok	69	7500
Lembar	22	5000
Praya	27	2000
Kuta	54	4000

The Kebon Roek terminal at Ampenan is for bemos to Senggigi and Mandalika. A trip up the coast to Senggigi costs 2500Rp from Ampenan. Some bemos also travel between Mandalika and Senggigi, but you'll usually have to change in Ampenan.

Getting Around
To/From the Airport Selaparang airport is north of Mataram. Prepaid taxis to anywhere in Mataram cost 9500Rp; it's 15,000Rp to Senggigi, 32,000Rp to Bangsal and Lembar, 62,000Rp to Kuta and 81,000Rp to Senaru. Or, you can walk out of the airport car park to the main road and take one of the frequent No 7 bemos, which go to the Ampenan terminal, or if you have a light load and lots of time, look for a *cidomo* to Mataram from the corner of Jl Sutomo and Jl Sudirman.

Bemo Ampenan-Mataram-Cakra is very spread out, so don't plan to walk from place to place. Yellow bemos shuttle back and forth between the Kebon Roek terminal in Ampenan and the Mandalika terminal. Some make slight detours, but they generally travel along the two main thoroughfares. The fare is a standard 1000Rp, regardless of distance. Outside the market in Cakra, a handy bemo stop has services to Ampenan, Bertais and Lembar. Mandalika and Kebon Roek terminals are good places to charter a bemo.

Car & Motorcycle Most hotels can arrange the rental of motorcycles and cars (if any are available).

Trac Astra Rent-a-Car (☎ *626363, fax 627071;* w *www.trac.astra.co.id; Jl Adi Sucipto 5, Rembiga)*, near the airport, has a range of new vehicles.

Motorcycle owners hang around on Jl Gelantik, off Jl Selaparang near the junction with Jl Hasanuddin, at the Cakra end of Mataram. They rent motorcycles privately for around 35,000Rp for one day, or maybe 30,000Rp per day for a week. There's no insurance, and they may want a passport or licence for security. Check any motorcycle carefully before taking it.

Taxi For an inexpensive metered taxi, call **Lombok Taksi** (☎ *627000)*.

AROUND MATARAM
East of Mataram are small villages and rice field landscapes, and some old temples and palaces. You can easily visit all the following places in half a day if you have your own transport.

Taman Narmada
Laid out as a miniature replica of the summit of Gunung Rinjani and its crater lake, Taman Narmada (*Narmada Park; adult/child 1000/500Rp; open 7am-6pm daily)* takes its name from a sacred Indian river. Its temple, **Pura Kalasa**, is still used and the Balinese Pujawali celebration is held here every year in honour of the god Batara, who dwells on Gunung Rinjani.

Taman Narmada was constructed by the king of Mataram in 1805, when he was no longer able to climb Rinjani to make offerings to the gods. Having set his conscience at rest by placing offerings in the temple, he spent at least some of his time in his pavilion on the hill, lusting after the young girls bathing in the artificial lake. Along one side of the pool are the remains of an aqueduct built by the Dutch and still in use.

This is a beautiful place to spend a few hours, but it tends to be crowded on weekends. Apart from the lake, you can go for a swim at the two **swimming pools** *(adult/child 1000/500Rp)* in the grounds.

Places to Eat Right at the Narmada bemo stop is the local **market**, which sells mainly food and clothing, but is well worth a look. A number of **warung** scattered around sell *soto ayam* (chicken soup) and other dishes.

Getting There & Away Narmada is on a hill about 10km east of Cakra, on the main east–west road crossing Lombok. Frequent bemos from Mandalika take you to the Narmada market, directly opposite the entrance to the gardens.

Pura Lingsar

This large temple complex, built in 1714, is the holiest place on Lombok. The temple combines the Balinese Hindu and Wektu Telu religions in one complex. Designed in two separate sections and on different levels, the Hindu temple in the northern section is higher than the Wektu Telu temple in the southern section.

The Hindu temple has four shrines. On one side is Hyang Tunggal, which looks towards Gunung Agung, the seat of the gods on Bali. The shrine faces northwest rather than northeast, as it would on Bali. On the other side is a shrine devoted to Gunung Rinjani, the seat of the gods on Lombok. Between these two shrines is a double shrine symbolising the union between the two islands. One side is named in honour of the might of Lombok, and the other side is dedicated to a king's daughter, Ayu Nyoman Winton. According to legend, she gave birth to a god.

The Wektu Telu temple is noted for its small, enclosed pond devoted to Lord Vishnu. It has a number of holy eels that look like huge swimming slugs – they can be enticed from their hiding places with hard-boiled eggs, which can be bought from stalls outside and inside the temple complex. You will be expected to hire a sash and/or sarong (or bring your own) to enter the temple, but this is not necessary just to enter the outside buildings.

During the annual rain festival at the start of the wet season (between October and December) the Hindus and Wektu Telu make offerings and pray in their own temples, then come out into the communal compound and pelt each other with *ketupat* (rice wrapped in banana leaves). The ceremony is to bring the rain, or to give thanks for the rain.

Getting There & Away Lingsar is north of Narmada. First, take a bemo from Mandalika terminal to Narmada, then catch another to Lingsar. Ask to be dropped off near the entrance to the temple complex, which is 300m down a well-marked path off the road.

Suranadi

Suranadi is a pleasant little village surrounded by gorgeous countryside. It has a temple, a small pocket of forest, a swimming pool and assorted eateries, making it a popular spot for locals on weekends.

Pura Suranadi This is one of the holiest Hindu temples on Lombok, built around a spring that bubbles icy cold water into pools and a bathing area. Eels and other fish in the pools are also sacred, and well fed with hard-boiled eggs and other offerings. The usual rules for Balinese temple visits apply – you should wear a sash and/or sarong, and you may be asked for a donation.

Hutan Wisata Suranadi Just opposite the village market, an entrance leads to a small **forest sanctuary** *(adult/child 3000/1500Rp; open daylight hours)*. It is a bit neglected, but it's a shady and quiet area for some short **hikes**, and is good for **bird-watching**.

Places to Stay & Eat An interesting old Dutch building, **Suranadi Hotel** *(☎ 633686, fax 623984; rooms 175,000Rp)* has two swimming pools, tennis courts, a restaurant and a bar. It's a lovely place to stay for a while. Casual visitors can enjoy the refreshing, spring-fed **pool** *(adult/child 2500/1500Rp)*.

Pondok Surya *(rooms 30,000Rp)*, near the Suranadi, is casual and friendly, with a nice outlook and good food. Rooms are basic and a bit dark. Look for the sign at the market.

Several **restaurants** along the main road cater for the occasional tour group. Assorted **warung** around the car park provide the usual inexpensive Indonesian standards.

Getting There & Away Occasional public bemos come to Suranadi from Narmada; failing that, charter one for a negotiable 30,000Rp each way.

Golong

About halfway between Suranadi and the main road, on a quiet back road, **Gec Rinjani Country Club** (☎ 633488; e in@lombok golf.com; villas US$60) is where a round of golf will cost US$56 on weekdays and US$79 on weekends, including a caddie. Club rental is US$10. The fine **swimming pool** (adult/child 10,000/5000Rp) can be used by casual visitors. There's no public transport to Golong.

Sesaot

About 5km northeast from Suranadi is Sesaot, a charming, quiet market town on the edge of a forest where wood-felling is the main industry. There are some gorgeous spots for a **picnic**, and you can **swim** in the river. The water is very cool and is considered holy as it comes straight from Gunung Rinjani. Regular bemos come from Narmada, and you can eat at various **warung** along the main street.

Air Nyet

Further east, Air Nyet is another pretty village with more places for **swimming** and **picnics**. Ask directions for the unsigned turn-off in the middle of Sesaot. The bridge and road to Air Nyet are rough, but it's a lovely walk (about 3km) along the forest path. You have to buy tickets (1000Rp) on Sunday and holidays, when the place can be very busy, but otherwise the forest is gloriously empty and serene. You may have to charter a vehicle from Sesaot or Narmada.

GUNUNG PENGSONG

This Balinese temple is built – as the name suggests – on top of a hill. It's 9km south of Mataram and has great views of rice fields, volcanoes and the sea. The area was used by retreating Japanese soldiers to hide during WWII, and remnants of **cannons** can be found, as well as lots of pesky monkeys.

Try to get there early in the morning, before the clouds envelop Gunung Rinjani. Once a year, generally in March or April, a buffalo is taken up the steep 100m slope and sacrificed to give thanks for a good

harvest. The **Desa Bersih festival** also occurs here at harvest time – houses and gardens are cleaned, fences whitewashed, and roads and paths repaired. Once part of a ritual to rid the village of evil spirits, it is now held in honour of the rice goddess Dewi Sri.

There's no set admission charge, but you will have to tip the caretaker. There's no regular public transport from Mataram, so you'll have to rent or charter a vehicle.

BANYUMULEK

This is one of the main pottery centres of Lombok, specialising in decorated pots and pots with a woven fibre covering, as well as more traditional urns and water flasks. It is close to the city, 2km west of the Sweta-Lembar road, which carries frequent bemos. It's easy to combine Banyumulek with a visit to Gunung Pensong if you have your own transport, and it would be a good day trip by bicycle.

LEMBAR

Lembar is the main port on Lombok. The ferries to/from Bali dock here, as do the *Mabua Express*, *Padangbai Express* and Pelni boats. The public ferry terminal is small, with some telephones, a few **warung** and a parking area; the *Padangbai Express* departs from here. The terminal for the *Mabua Express* and Pelni has a separate entrance, 200m to the west.

If you need to stay the night for some reason, the best option is **Tidar** (Jl Raya Pelabuhan; singles/doubles 35,000/40,000Rp), about 750m north of the terminal on the main road. It's a friendly, very clean place, where bathrooms feature an indoor pond! Tasty Indonesian food is also available.

Getting There & Away

Public ferries leave about every two hours, and unless it's a very busy holiday time, you can get tickets at the harbour just before departure. *Mabua Express* tickets are usually available at the terminal too, but it's better to book ahead. See the Lombok entry under the Boat section in the Getting Around chapter for more information.

For a public bemo into town, walk out of the ferry terminal, up the main road and catch one heading to Bertais (3000Rp). If you get a bemo in the ferry car park, it will be at charter rates. Going to Lembar, there

The volcanic cone of Gunung Baru rises from the lake in the crater of Gunung Rinjani

A temple statue at Pura Batu Bolong, Lombok

Children crowd the school bus in Lombok

ANDREW LUBRAN

An idyllic beach on Gili Trawangan

RICHARD I'ANSON

Masks for sale at an art market in Senggigi

MICHAEL AW

A pink flatworm in Lombok waters

are frequent bemos from the Mandalika terminal or the stop next to the market in Cakra.

A taxi and shuttle service (minimum of four people) transports passengers to Bangsal, Mataram, Senggigi and Kuta.

SOUTHWESTERN PENINSULA

Approaching Lembar by ferry you'll see a hilly and little-developed peninsula on your right. A road from Lembar goes round the eastern side of the harbour some distance inland, and after almost 20km reaches a T-junction at Sekotong. From there, the road left goes to the south coast, while the other road follows the coast, more or less, across Lombok's southwest peninsula. The further you go on this road, the rougher it gets. Another option is to charter a small fishing boat – it will take about two hours to reach the end of the peninsula.

The road goes past **Taun**, which has a stunning, empty white sandy beach.

Near Taun, **Sekotong Indah Beach Cottages** (☎ 693040; rooms 30,000-40,000Rp) provides comfortable accommodation and a restaurant near the beach. This place may close in the low season, and plans for other bungalows here are on hold. Boats to Gili Nanggu can be arranged from here.

Continuing east, the road hugs the coast, which has some fine beaches, coral and clear waters, especially near **Pelangan**. It's usually passable by car as far as **Labuhan Poh**, but further east the track gets very rough, and in the wet season you won't even make it with a 4WD. In the dry season, you should be able to make it through **Bangko Bangko**, and from there it's about 2km to **Desert Point**, the famous left-hand surf break. There is no accommodation, but die-hard surfers have been known to camp here for weeks waiting for the fickle break to work. Japanese forces occupied this peninsula in WWII, and you may find a few old caves and guns.

Islands

Two groups of picturesque islands off the northern coast of this peninsula are clearly visible from the ferries going to Lembar. You can reach these islands by chartered *prahu* (outrigger fishing boat) from Lembar or Tuan.

Only a few of these islands are inhabited, and most have beautiful, unspoilt white beaches with plenty of palm trees, and

wonderful snorkelling opportunities (bring your own gear). You can stay on **Gili Nanggu** at the **Gili Nanggu Bungalows** (☎ 62377/623783; singles 80,000-200,000Rp; doubles 100,000-250,000Rp); rates include all meals and bookings are essential.

Further west, **Gili Gede** is in the second group of islands and is the largest of all of them. It has a number of traditional villages (where some Bugis settlers make a living from boat building), more glorious beaches and clear water for snorkelling. It's accessible by boat from Pelangan. There are some quite basic **bungalows** (☎ 623783; rooms 20,000Rp-50,000Rp), as well as an attached restaurant.

SENGGIGI

On a series of sweeping bays north of Ampenan, Senggigi is the most developed tourist area on Lombok, with a full range of facilities and accommodation. The Senggigi coastal strip experienced a rash of ambitious development in the 1980s and 1990s, but with the dearth of tourists after the events of 2000 (and no doubt as a result of the Bali bombing of October 2002), supply continues to exceed demand and Senggigi now has a somewhat deserted atmosphere, with street hawkers sometimes outnumbering tourists.

It is, however, a great place for a quiet holiday at a discount price. Senggigi has some superb beaches and a few good coral reefs just offshore. The sun sets over the mountains of Bali, just across the Lombok Strait, and you can enjoy the panorama from the beach or from one of the beachfront restaurants. As it gets dark, the fishing fleet lines up offshore, each boat with its bright lanterns, like a small city across the water.

Orientation

The Senggigi area has hotels spread out along 10km of coastal road, Jl Raya Senggigi. Most of the restaurants, shops and other tourist facilities are concentrated on this road about 6km north of Ampenan. The road continues north, following the coast past Malimbu Beach, to a junction about 1km from Bangsal (the port for the Gili islands).

Information

You'll find **travel agents**, **photo processors**, handicraft shops and a small **Pacific supermarket** in the central Senggigi strip.

LOMBOK

SENGGIGI BEACH

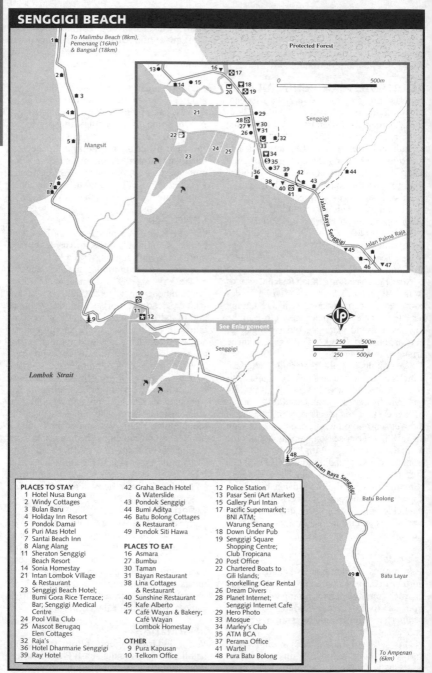

PLACES TO STAY
1 Hotel Nusa Bunga
2 Windy Cottages
3 Bulan Baru
4 Holiday Inn Resort
5 Pondok Damai
6 Puri Mas Hotel
7 Santai Beach Inn
8 Alang Alang
11 Sheraton Senggigi
   Beach Resort
14 Sonia Homestay
21 Intan Lombok Village
   & Restaurant
23 Senggigi Beach Hotel;
   Bumi Gora Rice Terrace;
   Bar; Senggigi Medical
   Centre
24 Pool Villa Club
25 Mascot Berugaq
   Elen Cottages
32 Raja's
36 Hotel Dharmarie Senggigi
39 Ray Hotel

42 Graha Beach Hotel
   & Waterslide
43 Pondok Senggigi
44 Bumi Aditya
46 Batu Bolong Cottages
   & Restaurant
49 Pondok Siti Hawa

PLACES TO EAT
16 Asmara
27 Bumbu
30 Taman
31 Bayan Restaurant
38 Lina Cottages
   & Restaurant
40 Sunshine Restaurant
45 Kafe Alberto
47 Café Wayan & Bakery;
   Café Wayan
   Lombok Homestay

OTHER
9 Pura Kapusan
10 Telkom Office

12 Police Station
13 Pasar Seni (Art Market)
15 Gallery Puri Intan
17 Pacific Supermarket;
   BNI ATM;
   Warung Senang
18 Down Under Pub
19 Senggigi Square
   Shopping Centre;
   Club Tropicana
20 Post Office
22 Chartered Boats to
   Gili Islands;
   Snorkelling Gear Rental
26 Dream Divers
28 Planet Internet;
   Senggigi Internet Cafe
29 Hero Photo
33 Mosque
34 Marley's Club
35 ATM BCA
37 Perama Office
41 Wartel
48 Pura Batu Bolong

Money Several **moneychangers** in central Senggigi exchange foreign currency and travellers cheques, for rates just a little lower than in tourist centres on Bali. Most of the big hotels will also change money, for rates a little lower than the moneychangers. There's a **BCA ATM** by Marley's Club.

Post The **post office** is on the main road, near the shopping centre. Poste restante should be addressed to Senggigi, Lombok, 83355. There are also several **wartel** along the main road. Cybercafés, such as **Planet Internet** and **Senggigi Internet Cafe**, on the central strip, charge around 300Rp per minute – they also double as wartel.

Emergencies The Senggigi **Medical Clinic** (☎ 693856) is based within the Senggigi Beach Hotel. The nearest **hospital** is in Mataram, but any good hotel will have access to an English-speaking doctor. The **police station** is just north of central Senggigi. Call ☎ 110 in the event of an emergency.

Pura Batu Bolong
This temple sits on a rocky point that juts into the sea around 1km south of central Senggigi. The rock underneath the temple has a natural hole that gives the temple its name – *batu bolong* (literally, 'rock with hole'). A Balinese temple, it's oriented towards Gunung Agung, Bali's holiest mountain, across the Lombok Strait. Legend has it that beautiful virgins were once thrown into the sea from the top of the rock. Locals like to claim that this is why there are so many sharks in the water here.

There's a fine view of Senggigi from the point, and it's a nice place to watch the sunset. You will need to wear a sash to enter the temple, and you may be asked to make a donation – 5000Rp to 10,000Rp is appropriate.

Activities
Most activities on offer here involve getting wet. There is a **waterslide** *(adult/child per day 25,000/18,500Rp)* at the Graha Beach Hotel.

Diving Most dive trips from Senggigi go to sites around the Gili islands, so it may be better to base yourself there, unless you prefer to stay in the swankier hotels in Senggigi.

There are several diving centres along the main street in Senggigi. **Dream Divers**

(☎ 693738; W *www.dreamdivers.com)*, also based on the Gili islands, offers PADI open-water courses for US$275 and trips to the Gilis for US$30/50 for one/two dives. It also runs overnight trips for advanced divers.

Snorkelling There's some reasonable snorkelling off the point in central Senggigi, and in the sheltered bay around the headland to the north. Further north in Mangsit, there are some excellent spots on reefs a short distance offshore – just go out from the beach near Alang Alang resort or Windy Cottages, but be careful, as there can be a treacherous current. As a general rule, if the wind is blowing, the current is working, so always check with the Senggigi dive operators about the day's conditions before you snorkel at Mangsit. The reefs have plenty of fish, lobsters, eels and (if you're lucky) turtles. The best time for snorkelling is the dry season (June to September).

Several places rent mask/snorkel/fin sets for about 20,000Rp per day – try at the beach near the Pasar Seni art market or the Senggigi Beach Hotel.

Massage & Spas Several hotels have spas, including the Sheraton, the Holiday Inn and a Mandara Spa at the Senggigi Beach Hotel. The Holiday Inn also has a sauna and gym, which are available to nonguests for 25,000Rp each.

Tennis The Holiday Inn has tennis-court hire for 25,000Rp. Equipment rental is extra.

Organised Tours
It is easy enough to organise day tours from any of the travel agencies along the main road. These tours include most of the usual attractions in west Lombok and some of the craft villages in central Lombok.

Places to Stay
Be aware that continuing tough times have forced some places to scrimp on maintenance, so always check the room first.

Places to Stay – Budget
Make sure your room has a fan that works!

South of Senggigi Well south of the action, in an area called Batu Layar, a few quiet places front a wide beach.

Pondok Siti Hawa *(☎ 693414; cottage singles/doubles 25,500/30,000Rp)* is a ramshackle little hideaway, with small and very basic bamboo cottages that soak up the sea breezes. Home-cooked meals can be arranged.

Senggigi The cheapest places in Senggigi are on the inland side of the main road, away from the beach.

Sonia Homestay *(singles/doubles 20,000/25,000Rp)* is simple, clean and also very cheap.

Bumi Aditya *(☎ 693782; rooms 65,000-100,000Rp, with air-con 150,000Rp)*, a couple of hundred metres up a village path, has a small pool and a range of well-maintained bungalows, each complete with lots of small comforts and detail, such as tie-dyed sheets, lamps, paintings and mosquito nets. The quiet rural setting has a gorgeous mountain backdrop.

Raja's Bungalows *(☎ 693569; e rajas22@yahoo.com; rooms 45,000Rp)*, in a leafy setting, is a great place to hang out and lie low. It has only four very comfortable bungalows, decorated with local pottery.

Ray Hotel *(☎ 0812 375 3500; rooms 40,000Rp, with air-con 60,000Rp)* is a decent place, on an elevated block on the main road. Air-con rooms have a view of the ocean.

With the pool at the front of the complex, **Pondok Senggigi** *(☎ 693273; singles 60,000-100,000Rp, doubles 50,000-150,000Rp)* faces a long stretch of land used to graze horses. Cheaper rooms lack a private balcony, whereas the more expensive rooms are in slightly better condition and deluxe rooms have air-con.

North of Senggigi In Mangsit village, **Pondok Damai** *(☎ 693019; rooms 100,000-125,000Rp, with hot water 175,000Rp)* is a quiet, seaside retreat with comfortable, nicely decorated bamboo cottages. The restaurant is right on the beach.

Santai Beach Inn *(☎/fax 693038; singles 45,000-70,000Rp, doubles 60,000-90,000Rp, with hot water 125,000-140,000Rp)* has sweet *lumbung*-style cottages set among a lush garden. It has a good library and book exchange, and offers Lombok-style **vegetarian meals** *(dishes 12,000-20,000Rp)* in a pleasant pavilion. Call beforehand if you plan to eat here.

Windy Cottages *(☎ 693191, fax 693193; rooms 100,000-125,000Rp, with hot water 140,000Rp)*, 4km north of central Senggigi, is spacious and charming – a perfect place to get away from it all. The beach here is wonderful (great for snorkelling), and the restaurant is good too. The only downside is that only hot-water bungalows have double beds.

Bulan Baru *(New Moon Hotel; ☎/fax 693786; e bulanbaru@hotmail.com; rooms 150,000Rp)*, a friendly, well-run place, has comfortable rooms with open-air bathrooms. The pool and **restaurant** *(dishes 12,000-48,000Rp)*, which specialises in Australian imports, is set among spacious grounds.

Places to Stay – Mid-Range
South of Senggigi At the rear of the bakery, **Cafe Wayan Lombok Homestay** *(☎ 693098; rooms 200,000Rp)* has four light, airy bungalows, decorated with *ikat* bedspreads, and set in a pleasant garden setting.

Batu Bolong Cottages & Restaurant *(☎ 693065, fax 693198; inland bungalows 55,000-150,000Rp, beachside bungalows 200,000Rp)*, a peaceful, hassle-free option, has spacious and nicely furnished bungalows on both the beach and inland side of the road – the more expensive rooms have hot water, TV and air-con. Beachside rooms have lovely, unhindered ocean views.

Senggigi The central **Hotel Dharmarie Senggigi** *(☎ 693050; e darmarie@mataram.wasantara.net.id; rooms 200,000-250,000Rp)* has spacious villas set beside a wide lawn that goes down to the beach. With air-con and hot water, it's comfortable and good value. The only downside is that it doesn't have a pool.

Graha Beach Hotel *(☎ 693101, fax 693400; garden & sea view rooms 250,000-300,000Rp, poolside rooms 400,000-500,000Rp)* has its front office, main **restaurant** *(dishes 15,000-60,000Rp)*, large swimming pool and charmless poolside rooms on the inland side of the road, and its better (and less expensive) rooms and beachfront restaurant on the other side. Although the peace may be shattered by local hawkers on the beachside. Guests can use the waterslide for half-price.

With a perfect beachfront location, **Mascot Berugaq Elen Cottages** *(☎ 693365, fax 693236; bungalows US$35-40)* have rooms with air-con, TV, telephone and hot water.

North of Senggigi Worth considering for top-end comforts at mid-range prices, the **Holiday Inn Resort** (☎ 693444, fax 693092; W www.holiday-inn.com; rooms from US$30-250) offers a wide range of room prices.

Puri Mas Hotel (☎/fax 693023; W www .purimasgroup.com; singles US$25-55, doubles US$30-60, villas US$75-165), next door to the Santai Beach Inn, is small but stylish, with attractively decorated, Balinese-style bungalows surrounded by trees and shrubs. All rooms have air-con and hot water, and there is a pool.

Places to Stay – Top-End

Senggigi has quite a few luxury hotels, and big discounts are often available.

Senggigi The first big 'international standard' hotel built at Senggigi, **Senggigi Beach Hotel** (☎ 693210, fax 693200; W www.seng gigibeach.aerowisata.com; Jl Pantai; rooms US$80-160) features thatched cottages built right on the headland. It has a beautiful setting, lovely garden, swimming pool, tennis courts and other mod cons. Breakfast is not included. There is also a **Mandara Spa** here.

Pool Villa Club (☎ 693210, fax 693448; W www.poolvillaclub.aerowisata.com; villas US$380), designed by a French architect and ideal for honeymooners, is a small cluster of luxury two-storey villas, featuring sweeping balcony views, a lagoon pool, tennis courts and satellite TV. There's incredible attention to detail, including espresso machines in each villa.

A handsome luxury hotel in a central location, **Intan Lombok Village** (☎ 693090, fax 693185; W www.intanhotels.com; rooms US$133-157) has friendly staff and a wonderful snaking beachfront pool that easily rivals the best in Bali.

Sheraton Senggigi Beach Resort (☎ 693333, fax 693241; W www.sheraton.com; rooms US$80-200), an obvious five-star option, has a children's playground.

North of Senggigi A boutique beach resort, **Alang Alang** (☎ 693518, fax 693194; rooms US$110) has gorgeously decorated bungalows and delightful outdoor bathrooms. The pool is right on the beach in a dreamy tropical setting.

Continuing north along the coast, a few upmarket options offer character and style.

Hotel Nusa Bunga (☎ 693035, fax 693036; W www.nusabunga.com; Jl Raya Senggigi; bungalow singles/doubles US$40/45), a well-run place, is one of the better ones. It has a splendid, idyllic beachfront position, a pool and thatched bungalows in a pretty garden.

Places to Eat

Senggigi's main strip has wall-to-wall restaurants, although the quality can be varied. Beachside dining is an option at places like Sunshine and Kafe Alberto, especially in the evening when you can enjoy fiery sunsets and cool sea breezes, although beach hawkers sometimes detract from the enjoyment.

Quite a few restaurants provide their customers with free transport, so it's worth phoning first.

South of Senggigi With a terrific seaside outlook, **Kafe Alberto** (☎ 693313; dishes 26,000-40,000Rp) serves pizzas after 6pm and local Indo-Chinese fare otherwise. Lombok music and dance performances are held on Thursday night. Bike hire is also available.

Cafe Wayan & Bakery (☎ 693098, dishes 23,000-30,000Rp) is the sister to cafés in Ubud and Gili Trawangan. The fresh baked breads, cakes, croissants, and tagliatelle for the various pasta dishes, are homemade here. The yummy cakes are around 7500Rp. There's a homestay here too.

Senggigi For inexpensive eating, try the **food stalls** opposite the Pacific Supermarket. The beach-view restaurant at **Intan Lombok Village** is worth a splurge for its rijstaffel (literally, 'rice table'), a classic Dutch-Indonesian banquet.

The Sheraton Senggigi has three restaurants, including a poolside restaurant, and the **Spice Market** (dishes 52,000-145,000Rp), which is open for dinner only. It features some great seafood dishes such as pepes udang (prawns wrapped in banana leaf with candlenut sauce). A rotating set menu, offering choices such as rijstaffel (145,000Rp), is also available nightly.

Sunshine Restaurant (dishes 10,000-50,000Rp) offers the standard range of Indonesian and Chinese dishes, as well as less tempting Western options. You can sit under a tin roof indoors, or if you're able to withstand the beach sellers offering watches, sit outside for a great sea view.

Bumbu Cafe *(dishes 15,000-30,000Rp)* is a low-key place on the main strip that features a delicious range of Thai and Indonesian dishes.

Bayan Restaurant *(☎ 693616; dishes 20,000-145,000Rp)* is a thatch-roofed affair, which swelters under the hot afternoon sun, but is more comfortable in the evening, with live bands every night after 8pm.

Warung Senang *(dishes 5500–18,500Rp)* is a small eatery in the Pacific Supermarket complex. It serves quite good versions of the usual Indonesian dishes, with some Lombok staples.

Taman *(☎ 693482; dishes 20,000-26,000Rp)* is a stylistically overwrought branch of the older, dated and forgettable Taman Senggigi, and has a bar, pool table and comfy couches (sit at the bar only if you enjoy discomfort!). Mexican food is on offer, but if you really feel like you need some reminder of Western life, Australian 'surf and turf' is 51,000Rp.

With candle-lit tables and a relaxed ambience, **Asmara** *(☎ 693619; dishes 18,000-48,000Rp)* features several Lombok dishes, including *gulai lemak*, a beef curry, as well as a range of modern international dishes. There's also a kids' play area upstairs. This is probably the best restaurant you'll find in Senggigi outside of the top-end hotels.

Lina Cottages Restaurant *(mains 15,000-40,000Rp)*, a boisterous place, has a classic seaside setting, and cheap beers during happy hour. Seafood dishes are the best bet here.

North of Senggigi The restaurant at **Windy Cottages** is in an open-sided pavilion facing the sea; a trip up here for lunch makes a lovely outing.

Entertainment

Senggigi has about the only nightlife on Lombok (apart from Gili Trawangan) – but it's mostly pretty low-key, especially when there are few tourists in town. On Saturday night, the nightspots fill up with young people from the Mataram area.

The Local bands do passable rock and reggae music with an Indonesian flavour. Restaurants such as **Kafe Alberto**, **Bayan Restaurant** and **Taman** often have live, mostly acoustic, music. The main venue **Club Tropicana** *(☎ 693432; cover charge 30,000Rp)* is a Mediterranean-style monstrosity that dominates the main street. **Down Under Pub**, under the Princess of Lombok, has pool tables, while **Marley's Club** has cheap beer and live reggae bands and karaoke nightly, with pool tables and football on TV upstairs. Happy hour is from 7pm to 10pm.

For a more low-key evening, head to **Bumi Gora Rice Terrace Bar** at the Senggigi Beach Hotel.

Shopping

The **Pacific Supermarket** was undergoing renovations at the time of research, with a general store operating in its place. The **Pasar Seni art market** was all but destroyed in early 2002 after a fire started in an adjacent restaurant, but a few plucky stallholders remain. The **Senggigi Square shopping centre** has a boutique and some craft shops, and the **Sheraton** also has a shopping arcade.

Gallery Puri Intan *(☎ 693666)* has a wide range of Lombok pottery, and if you have the time and interest, it's worth making a day trip to the **craft and antique shops** in Ampenan, the huge **market** at Bertais or the small **villages** in central Lombok, which specialise in various handicrafts.

Getting There & Away

Bemo Regular bemos travel between Senggigi and the Kebon Roek terminal in Ampenan (1000Rp), and usually continue north as far as Pemenang or Bayan. Don't be surprised if you are overcharged a little on any bemo going to/from Senggigi.

Boat See Perama *(☎ 693007)* for several daily bus/ferry connections between Senggigi and the main tourist centres on Bali: eg, Kuta (105,000Rp) and Ubud (95,000Rp); and on Lombok: eg, Bangsal (25,000Rp) and Kuta (50,000Rp).

Gili Islands Perama operates small boats from Senggigi to the Gili islands at 9am and 3pm daily (40,000Rp, one to 1½ hours). On the flipside, Perama isn't allowed to run boats directly from the Gili islands to Senggigi, though it can provide 'through' tickets on this route using a boat to Bangsal and a bus to Senggigi.

Perama buses also go from Senggigi to Bangsal (25,000Rp), but from there you have to purchase your own boat ticket to the islands.

Catamaran The *Bounty,* a fast, modern catamaran, sails daily from Benoa harbour (Bali) and stops at Teluk Nare (near Bangsal) in Lombok, from where passengers can be bussed to central Senggigi. It also stops at Gili Meno.

See the Lombok entry under the Boat section in the Getting Around chapter for more information.

Getting Around

Taxis regularly ply the main road looking for customers – **Lombok Taksi** (☎ 627000) is reliable. A prepaid taxi from the airport to Senggigi costs 15,000Rp.

To get to/from the airport by public transport, get a connection at Kebon Roek terminal in Ampenan.

The roads south and north of Senggigi are perfect for cycling – **Kafe Alberto** rents bicycles for 15,000/25,000Rp for a half/full day.

If you're renting, **Sheraton Senggigi Beach Resort** (☎ 693333) is an agent for Trac Astra Rent-a-Car, although expect to pay expensive rates. For informal car and motorcycle hire, ask at your hotel.

South Lombok

☎ 0370

South Lombok is drier than the rest of the island and more sparsely populated, with fewer roads and limited public transport. Many tourists visit craft villages on day trips from west Lombok, while others want to kick back at Kuta Beach, a much more serene beach area than Kuta on Bali. If you have your own transport you can explore remote villages and sections of coast with stunning scenery, while surfers charter bemos and boats to visit some excellent surf spots.

PRAYA

This is the main town in the southwest. It's quite attractive, with spacious gardens, tree-lined streets, a few old Dutch buildings and no tourists. The bemo terminal, on the northwestern side of town, is the transport hub for the area, and the town is well connected to Mataram and Kuta. If you need to stay here, **Dienda Hayu Hotel** (☎ 654319; *Jl Untung Surapati 28; economy rooms 40,000Rp, VIP rooms with air-con 60,000Rp*), just up from the market, is clean and comfortable.

AROUND PRAYA

Several of the villages around Praya are noted for different handicrafts. Most of the villages are close to main roads from Praya so you can reach them by public transport, often a combination of bemo and *cidomo.* Bemos are more frequent in the morning. If you want to explore several villages, and buy lots of things, it's useful to have your own transport. Several small back roads wind through the hills to join the main east–west road, enabling a very pretty tour through central Lombok. Most of these places are included in organised tours of the region.

Sukarara

Billed as a 'traditional weaving centre', Sukarara doesn't look very traditional. Much of the main street is given over to commercial craft shops, so it's pretty touristy, but it's still worth a visit to see the various styles of ikat and *songket* (silver or gold-threaded cloth) weaving.

Looms are set up outside workshops along the main street and sarongs hang in bright bands. Typically, there are attractive young women working out the front, in traditional black costumes. More women work inside, often wearing jeans and watching TV as they work, but most of the material is actually made in homes in surrounding villages. Bigger showrooms have professional salespeople who can be informative but also very persuasive. These places are geared to tour groups and have a good range, but charge higher prices.

Get a bemo along the main road to Puyung (where a huge **market** is held every Sunday). From there, hire a *cidomo* or walk the 2km to Sukarara.

Penujak

Penujak is noted for its traditional *gerabah* pottery, which is made from local clay using the simplest of techniques. A New Zealand aid project helped develop this craft into a cottage industry, and pottery from Penujak and several other small villages is now sold in other tourist centres on Lombok and Bali, and exported worldwide.

The elegant pots range in size up to 1m high. There are also various kitchen vessels and decorative figurines, usually in the shape of animals. The traditional pottery has a rich terracotta colour, and is hand-burnished to a

LOMBOK

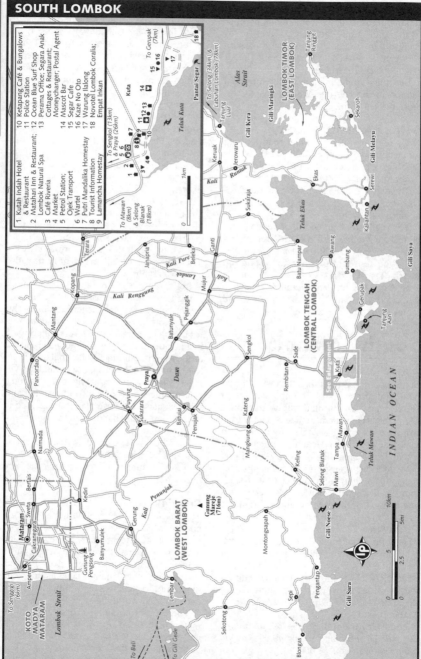

SOUTH LOMBOK

1 Kutah Indah Hotel
   & Restaurant
2 Matahari Inn & Restaurant;
   Lombok Natural Spa
3 Café Riveria
4 Market
5 Petrol Station;
   Ojek Transport
6 Wartel
7 Putri Mandalika Homestay
8 Tourist Information
9 Lamancha Homestay

10 Ketapang Café & Bungalows
11 Police Station
12 Ocean Blue Surf Shop
13 Perama Office; Segara Anak
    Cottages & Restaurant;
    Moneychanger; Postal Agent
14 Mascot Bar
15 Segar Cafe
16 Kaze No Oto
17 Warung Ilalong
18 Novotel Lombok Coralia;
    Empat Inkan

lovely soft sheen. Some of the new designs have bold patterns and bright colours – that's marketing!

Penujak is on the main road from Praya to the south coast; any bemo to Sengkol or Kuta will drop you off.

Pejanggik

This village is known for traditional **weaving**, but it's much more low-key than Sukarara. There are a few workshops near the main road and just off to the south, but you'll have to stop, look and listen for the clack-clack of the looms to find them.

Beleka

The main products of this village, to the north of the main road at Ganti, are **basketware**, **mats** and **boxes** made from natural fibres, such as rattan, grass, palm leaf and bamboo. Showrooms along the main road display and sell some fine examples of this quality work – it's strong, simple and beautifully made.

Rembitan & Sade

The area from Sengkol down to Kuta Beach is a centre of traditional Sasak culture. Regular bemos on this route pass Rembitan and Sade, particularly in the morning, so you can get off at either village and flag down another bemo when you are ready to move on. Donations are requested at both villages.

Rembitan is on a hill just west of the main road. It's a slightly sanitised Sasak village, but is nevertheless an authentic cluster of thatched houses and *lumbung*, surrounded by a wooden fence. On top of the hill is **Masjid Kuno**, an old thatched-roof mosque.

A little further south is Sade. It's another 'traditional' village, which some say was constructed purely for tourists, but it may have merely been an extensive renovation. It has concrete footpaths, and informative guides who'll tell you about Sasak houses and village life. Handicrafts and souvenirs are available, but you don't get a hard sell.

KUTA

The best known place on the south coast is Lombok's Kuta (sometimes spelt 'Kute'), a magnificent although deserted stretch of white sand and turquoise sea with rugged hills rising around it. It has far fewer tourists or facilities than Senggigi, and retains a rural

Nyale Fishing Festival

On the 19th day of the 10th month in the Sasak calendar (generally February or March) thousands of Sasak gather on the beach at Kuta. When night falls, fires are built and young people sit around competing with each other in rhyming couplets called *pantun*. At dawn the next day, the first seaworms for the season are caught as they surface for their reproductive season. After that, it's time for teenagers to have fun (and perhaps commence their own reproductive cycle). In a colourful procession, they sail out to sea – in different boats – and chase one another with lots of noise and laughter. This commemorates the legend of a beautiful princess, who went out to sea and drowned herself rather than choose between her many admirers – her long hair was transformed into the worm-like fish the Sasak call *nyale*. *Nyale* fish are eaten raw or grilled, and are believed to have aphrodisiac properties. A good catch is a sign that the rice harvest will also be good.

feel, with water buffalo grazing in the streets of the main losmen area. There were big plans in the 1990s to develop the whole southern coast with luxury hotels; predictably, however, many of the companies involved were associated with the Soeharto clan, and the demise of the Soeharto regime has left these schemes on hold.

The main attractions are the surrounding surf beats and craft villages. If these don't interest you don't go out of your way to come to laze on the beach here – the local beach sellers (often kids selling textiles and coconuts) are extremely annoying and often quite persistent.

The best time to visit is in February or March, when crowds flock here for the *nyale* fishing celebration (see the boxed text 'Nyale Fishing Festival'). All the accommodation fills up and many people sleep on the beach.

Information

Several places **exchange money** and travellers cheques, including Kutah Indah, Segara Anak Cottages and the privately run **Tourist Information** (☎ 655269). Segara Anak Cottages is also a **postal agency** and has **Internet access** for 500Rp. The Tourist Information office also sells *Bounty* tickets and organises tours of the area for 125,000Rp. There's a **minimarket** by the **wartel**.

The local **market** fires up on Sunday and Wednesday.

There have been readers' reports of female tourists in Kuta being hassled and even spied on. Beware of guys who hang around budget hotels and restaurants, and check your room for peep-holes.

Surfing
Plenty of good waves break on the reefs around here. The bay in front of Kuta has a left-hander on the west side, and the reefs east of Tanjung Aan also have lefts and rights. Local boatmen will take you out for a negotiable fee. Go about 7km east of Kuta to the fishing village of Gerupak, where you can get a local fishing boat to the breaks in the bay and at the entrance to Teluk Gerupak. (Readers' letters, however, have reported that the water at Gerupak is polluted by sewerage and that surfers often contract eye infections here.) There are more breaks further east and west, but nearly all require a boat, which you can charter for a negotiable 200,000Rp per day.

The **Ocean Blue** surf shop does ding repairs and rents surfboards and boogie boards.

Massage & Spas
Lombok Natural Spa (☎ 654832; open 10am to 8pm) at the Matahari Hotel is well worth the 150,000Rp for an hour of relaxation in the airy, high-ceilinged, thatched cottage near the hotel's pool. There is also a **Mandara Spa** (☎ 653333) at the Novotel Coralia.

Places to Stay – Budget
There are plenty of budget options in Kuta, but with very few tourists around, many losmen have fallen into disrepair.

Kutah Indah Hotel (☎ 653781, fax 654628; rooms 100,000Rp, with air-con 130,000Rp, with TV & hot water 185,000Rp) offers clean, not especially attractive rooms. The 'superior' bungalows with hot water and TV are looking pretty run-down, while the cheaper rooms are better value. The swimming pool is surrounded by lawn and coconut trees. Free transport to local beaches and surf spots is a major attraction.

Lamancha Homestay (☎/fax 655186; singles/doubles 30,000/40,000Rp, breakfast included), closest to the main road, is friendly, family-run and a short walk from the sea. It's excellent value, with a handful of clean, well-maintained rooms.

Putri Mandalika Homestay (☎ 655342; singles/doubles 25,000/30,000Rp, breakfast included) has five clean rooms, which come with mosquito nets and squat toilets.

Ketapang Café & Bungalows (☎ 655194; bungalow singles/doubles 25,000/30,000Rp) has standard thatched-roof beach bungalows, which are run-down but adequate.

In a good central location, **Segara Anak Cottages** (☎ 654834; singles/doubles 30,000/40,000Rp) is about the biggest budget place. The rooms are run-down and very basic, but clean, though security is not good – check window locks before you take a room. The **restaurant** has a long list of choices, including (pizza 10,500-35,000Rp). Perama drops off here.

Places to Stay – Mid-Range & Top End
There are limited, though good, options in this category.

Matahari Inn (☎ 654832, fax 655909; rooms 150,000Rp, with hot water & air-con 200,000-300,000Rp), a popular and appealing place, has expansive leafy grounds and a pool. The pleasant rooms have carved wooden furniture, artwork on the walls, modern bathrooms and shady balconies furnished with cane chairs. There is free transport to Tanjung Aan and surfing information is updated daily.

Novotel Lombok Coralia (☎ 653333, fax 653555; w www.novotel-lombok.com; deluxe rooms US$130, with terrace US$150, villas US$250) is a luxurious place with eclectic, pseudo-primitive architecture. It faces a superb beach and a picture-perfect little bay. Children are welcome and are also well catered for. There are activities for guests throughout the day.

Places to Eat & Drink
There are a few scattered warung on the beach road heading east, including **Warung Ilalong** (dishes 5000-20,000Rp), which serves Indonesian dishes, including *kelapa muda* (young coconut juice with ice) as well as Sasak dishes. **Segar Cafe** (dishes 5000-10,000Rp), nearby, has a simple Indonesian menu, and very cheap juices (2500Rp).

Cafe Riviera (*dishes 10,000-30,000Rp*), near the Matahari Inn, is a popular travellers' café serving the usual range of jaffles, Indonesian and seafood dishes, including lobster (ordered one day before). The downside is that you'll probably be sharing a table with a dozen chatty *songket* sellers.

Kutah Indah (*dishes 24,000-39,000Rp*) has a breezy, open-plan restaurant, and **Matahari Inn** (*dishes 15,000-45,000Rp*) has Indonesian dishes, pizza and pasta. Happy hour is from 4pm to 7pm, when a Bintang is 12,000Rp.

Empat Inkan (*dishes 65,000-175,000Rp*) at the Novotel Coralia has a small, simple menu with fresh seafood a speciality, and also an extensive wine list. Although a long way from most other places to stay, the hotel also has a popular happy hour from 6pm to 7pm, when it offers free seafood and fresh nuts.

Mascot Bar is really just a hut in a cow field, but it's the only pub in town.

Getting There & Away
To reach Kuta from Mandalika terminal in Mataram, you'll have to go first to Praya (2500Rp), then to Sengkol (2000Rp) and finally to Kuta (2000Rp). Travel early or you may get stuck and have to charter a vehicle some of the way.

Bemos also go east of Kuta to Awang and Tanjung Aan (2000Rp), and west to Selong Blanak. **Perama** (☎ 654846), based at Segara Anak Cottages, has one tourist shuttle bus per day to Mataram (50,000Rp) and Bangsal (25,000Rp).

Getting Around
Ojeks congregate around the main intersection as you enter Kuta. There's also a petrol station here.

Putri Mandalika Homestay (☎ 655342) has motorbikes available for rent from 25,000Rp to 30,000Rp. The **Tourist Information** can arrange motorbike (35,000Rp) and Kijang (175,000Rp) rental. You can charter bemos to nearby beaches and surf spots.

EAST OF KUTA
Quite good roads go around the coast to the east, passing a series of beautiful bays punctuated by headlands. There's some public transport, but you will see more with your own wheels – a mountain bike would be good (bring your own).

Pantai Segar is about 2km east around the first headland. You can easily walk there by going past the Novotel and following the track.

The road goes inland east of Kuta, but after about 3km a side road swings south to **Tanjung Aan**, a promontory that overlooks the brilliant **Aan Beach**, with its very fine, powdery white sand. The area was slated for upmarket resorts. This road continues another 2km to the fishing village of **Gerupak**, where there's a **market** on Tuesday. From there you can get a boat to the surf breaks in the bay, or across to **Bumbang** on the other side.

Alternatively, you can branch north at the Tanjung Aan turn-off and go to **Awang**, a fishing village with a sideline in seaweed harvesting. You could get a boat from here across to **Ekas** and some of the other not-so-secret surf spots in this bay.

WEST OF KUTA
The road west of Kuta goes past fine beaches at **Mawan**, **Tampa** and **Mawi** (readers report that you must pay locals to park your car here, or they become aggressive), but you have to detour to find them – they all have good surf in the right conditions. The road doesn't follow the coast closely, but you'll catch regular and spectacular ocean vistas.

The road is sealed as far as **Selong Blanak**, which is a lovely sandy bay, but the tourist lodgings here have closed down.

The road from Selong Blanak north to Penujak is rough but passable. To see more of the coast, take the turn-off at Keling, and go generally west through pleasant forested hills to Montongsapah. From there you swing back to the south, and get a brilliant **ocean view** as you descend to Pengantap.

From Pengantap, the road climbs across a headland and descends to another superb bay, which it follows for about 1km. Keep your eyes peeled for the turn-off west to Blongas, which is a very steep, rough and winding road with breathtaking scenery. There are some good places for **surfing** and **diving**, but you'll need to charter a boat to find them.

This is as far west as you can go on this road – return to the junction and turn north to Sekotong (by another scenic road) and on to Lembar. For information on the area west of Sekotong, see the West Lombok section.

This trip from Kuta around to Lembar is excellent, but it's pretty rugged, especially the detour to Blongas. The best option is to go by motorcycle, but only if you're a competent rider – in places it may be too steep, narrow and rutted even for a little Suzuki Jimny jeep. The distance is not great (less than 100km), but allow plenty of time and don't try it in the wet season.

Warning
Tourists have been threatened and robbed on the back roads of South Lombok. Don't leave your vehicle unattended – you can usually find someone to watch it for a small payment.

Gili Islands

☎ 0370

Off the northwestern coast of Lombok are three small, coral-fringed islands – Gili Air, Gili Meno and Gili Trawangan – each with white sandy beaches, clear water, colourful fish and the best snorkelling on Lombok. Although they are known to travellers as the Gili islands, *gili* actually means 'island', so this is not a local name. There's lots of other *gilis* around the coast of Lombok.

Many years ago, descendants of Bugis immigrants were granted leases to establish coconut plantations on the islands, settling first on Gili Air and then moving to the other islands. The economic activities expanded to include fishing, raising livestock, and growing corn, tapioca and peanuts. The first tourists came to the Gilis on day trips, but then began staying for longer periods in local homes. Many of the people on the islands soon found that the most profitable activity was 'picking white coconuts' – providing services to tourists.

Today the islands are hugely popular with young backpackers, who come for the simple pleasures of sun, scuba diving and socialising (with beer in hand). Accommodation is inexpensive, and the absence of cars and motorcycles adds to the pleasure of staying on the Gilis. Beach sellers are present but aren't in your face like elsewhere on Lombok.

Information
Money There are no banks on the Gili islands and moneychanger exchange rates are woeful. Credit-card cash advances are

Warning
Be aware that the waters surrounding the Gilis are subject to strong currents and rough water. Do not attempt to swim between the islands – travellers have drowned doing so.

available through many dive operators, although a 10% commission is generally charged. It's best to bring as much rupiah with you as you think you'll need.

Dangers & Annoyances/Security There are no police on any of the Gilis. Report any theft, assault or other significant problems to the island *kepala* (village head), or, if you're on Gili Trawangan, to Satgas, the community police organisation that supports the *kepala*. Both the *kepala* and Satgas have offices on Gili Trawangan, 40m from the main, shore-hugging road, in Jl Kaswari. Satgas uses its network and knowledge of the island community to resolve any problems, find lost or stolen property, or the culprit(s) of any wrongs. Satgas also staffs the boats that patrol the waters of all three Gili islands to ensure that damaging reef fishing practices of the past are not continued.

Some women have experienced sexual harassment, and even assault, while on Gili Trawangan. Women readers have reported being assaulted at night while using outdoor toilets at restaurants. Be careful and try to stay in pairs at night.

Jellyfish When strong winds blow from the mainland jellyfish are common, and they can leave a painful rash.

Diving & Snorkelling
Some of the coral around the islands is good for snorkelling (despite the damage of dynamite fishing); probably the best area is off the northwest coast of Gili Trawangan. Many snorkelling areas can be reached from the shore, or you can leave the dive operators to the divers and charter a boat – the boatman will know the best snorkelling spots and will probably settle on a price of 40,000Rp to 80,000Rp for a half-day (check that your boatman will stay in the boat to cover you should you run in to difficulty while you're in the water). Mask/snorkel/fin sets can be rented on the islands for about

10,000Rp to 20,000Rp per day. Always ask a boatman or a dive centre about the conditions and currents in the area you want to snorkel, as currents can be extremely strong at times, leading directly out to the open sea.

Unfortunately, many visitors are adding to the already damaged reefs by standing and walking on the reefs while snorkelling. Perfectly formed corals are easily broken and take years to recover. For scuba divers, the visibility is fair to good (best in the dry season), and there are some very good coral reefs accessible by boat. Marine life includes (harmless) sharks, turtles, giant clams and rays. A particularly interesting attraction is the blue coral, with an almost luminous colouring.

The best scuba diving operations are on Gili Air and Gili Trawangan. The price for a day trip with two dives is around US$45, including equipment. A PADI open-water course is about US$275 to US$300.

Accommodation

Some mid-range places have opened, but the Gili islands' standard is still a plain little bamboo bungalow on stilts, with a thatched roof, a small veranda out the front and a concrete bathroom block at the back. Inside, there will be one or two beds with mosquito nets (often with holes in them!). In the high season, accommodation can be hard to find.

Touts often meet boats as they land, and they can be quick to take your luggage, plus you, to the place of *their* choice. If you want to stay in a particular place, don't let a tout convince you that it's full, expensive, closed or doesn't exist.

Getting There & Away

You can reach the Gilis by a Perama boat service from Senggigi or by Bounty Cruises from Bali (see the Lombok entry under Boat in the Getting Around chapter). The standard route, though, is by bus to Pemenang, and from there it's only a 1km walk or a 2000Rp *cidomo* ride to Bangsal, from where you take a boat (it's not necessary to purchase a return ticket) to the island of your choice. (Note that buses do not travel all the way to the ferry terminal at Bangsal.) You may have to wait in Bangsal for a boat, but there are shops, food stalls and moneychangers. Bangsal, however, has become notorious in the last few years for the hassle that travellers

receive – prepare to be pestered to buy from hawkers and shops by the terminal, and don't believe stories about not being able to buy goods such as cigarettes on the island.

Coming from the Gilis, the boat pulls up on the beach at Bangsal, and you get a *cidomo* or walk the 1km to Pemenang. There you can catch a bemo on the main road (Jl Raya Tanjung) south to Mataram, or northeast around the coast. Alternatively, organise a private car outside the terminal area to Mataram, Senggigi or the airport (70,000Rp), Lembar (95,000Rp), Senaru (150,000Rp) or Kuta (200,000Rp).

If you get stuck overnight in Bangsal, the **Taman Sari Restaurant & Homestay** (☎ 626295; singles/doubles 5,000/30,000Rp, with fan 30,000/50,000Rp), 500m from the seafront, opposite the parking area, has clean, basic rooms. It also gives tourist information and has Internet access for 300Rp per minute.

Tourist Shuttle Bus Perama doesn't sell tickets *to* the Gili islands as such, but has a shuttle bus going (almost) to Bangsal every morning from Mataram (25,000Rp), Senggigi (25,000Rp) and other tourist centres, usually via the Pusuk Pass. The bus arrives at the big car park on the Bangsal-Pemeneng road. You'll have to walk or take a *cidomo* the last 500m from there, and buy your own boat ticket at the Koperasi building. Other tourist buses provide a similar service.

Perama does sell tickets *from* the Gili islands, including the shuttle boat to Bangsal and a connecting bus to Mataram, Senggigi, Kuta, Tetebatu or Lembar harbour.

Boat Small local boats with bamboo outriggers ferry people and supplies to the islands from the beach at Bangsal – be ready to wade out with your luggage (anyone who helps with your stuff will expect to be paid). Sometimes the weather can be rough, passengers and luggage get soaked, and landing can be difficult.

The Koperasi Angkutan Laut (Sea Transport Cooperative) is the boat owners' cartel, and it monopolises public transport between Bangsal and the Gili islands. Boat tickets are sold at a desk in the terminal office, a prominent white building on the beach, with details of services and prices typed on a faded inconspicuous note stuck to the door.

Cheapest are the 'public boats', which cost 2500Rp to Gili Air, 2700Rp to Gili Meno and 3000Rp to Gili Trawangan. The catch is, they don't leave until they have a full boat load – it's a matter of sitting and waiting until 16 people buy tickets to the same island. Try to get to Bangsal by 9.30am or 10am, as most boats go in the morning.

Scheduled 'shuttle boat' services leave at 8.30am and 4.30pm, and cost 7000Rp to Gili Air, 10,000Rp to Gili Meno and 10,000Rp to Gili Trawangan. Shuttle boats to Bangsal leave the islands at 10am or 4.30pm.

To charter a whole boat from Bangsal costs 55,000Rp to Gili Air, 65,000Rp to Gili Meno and 70,000Rp to Gili Trawangan.

Perama operates small boats from Senggigi to the Gili islands at 9am and 3pm daily (40,000Rp, 90 minutes to two hours). You may also be able to charter a boat to the Gilis from near the Senggigi Beach Hotel. Perama boats and charter boats can't take passengers from the Gili islands to Senggigi, unless they are Koperasi boats.

Catamaran The *Bounty*, a fast, modern catamaran, arrives from Benoa harbour (Bali), via Nusa Lembongan, docking at a jetty by Bounty Beach Bungalows on Gili Meno. For more information see the Getting There and Away chapter. Local boats can ferry passengers to the other two islands.

Getting Around
Regular and reliable 'island hopping' boats allow people staying on one island to visit the others without going to Bangsal and back again. Check times (generally once in the morning and afternoon) and prices with the local Koperasi. Charter boats (or private 'island hopping') can also be organised through the Koperasi.

On the islands themselves, *cidomos* trot around the tracks (a negotiable 5000Rp per person is the usual charge for a short trip for tourists). But be aware that you should be fair to the horse as well as to the driver, especially on the sandy tracks – Western bodies and large baggage make for heavy loads and hard horse-work. Bicycles are also available to hire for around 10,000Rp to 15,000Rp per day, but the main mode of transport is walking – although a torch can come in handy when walking at night.

GILI AIR
Gili Air is the closest island to the mainland and has the largest permanent population (about 1000). There are beaches around most of the island, but some are not suitable for swimming because they are shallow, with a sharp coral bottom. Because the hotels and restaurants are so scattered, the island has a pleasant, rural character, and is a delight to wander around. Gili Air is the kind of place travellers intend to stay for a few days but instead stay for weeks. There are plenty of other people, but if you stay in one of the more isolated losmen, socialising is optional.

Orientation & Information
It is surprisingly easy to become disoriented on the network of tracks across the island. The simplest option is to follow the coast. Boats stop at the southern end of the island, near (but not at) the jetty. The Koperasi boat operators have an office next to the jetty.

The **Perama office** (☎ 637816) and **wartel**, which also has Internet access (550Rp per minute), are near the Gili Indah Hotel. Coconut Cottages, Gili Air Santai and Ozzy's Shop offer **Internet access** (500Rp per minute). Pondok Gili Air Cafe runs a small **book exchange**. Hany Shop, opposite the path to Gili Air Santai, also has a book exchange, although most titles are in German. Ozzy's Shop, Pondok Gili Air Cafe and Safari Cottages sell refills of filtered water.

Gili Air has a central generator supplying the whole island. It is unreliable, but power is usually available from about 6pm to noon. The better hotels have their own generators, and have power all the time.

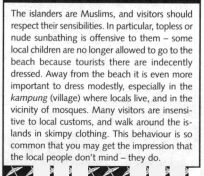

Avoiding Offence

The islanders are Muslims, and visitors should respect their sensibilities. In particular, topless or nude sunbathing is offensive to them – some local children are no longer allowed to go to the beach because tourists there are indecently dressed. Away from the beach it is even more important to dress modestly, especially in the *kampung* (village) where locals live, and in the vicinity of mosques. Many visitors are insensitive to local customs, and walk around the islands in skimpy clothing. This behaviour is so common that you may get the impression that the local people don't mind – they do.

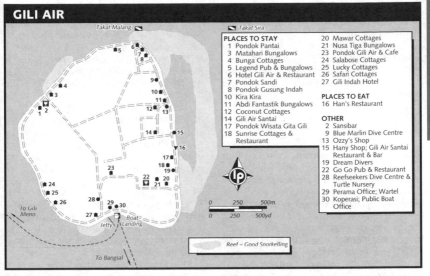

GILI AIR

Takat Malang *Takat Sira*

PLACES TO STAY
1 Pondok Pantai
3 Matahari Bungalows
4 Bunga Cottages
5 Legend Pub & Bungalows
6 Hotel Gili Air & Restaurant
7 Pondok Sandi
8 Pondok Gusung Indah
10 Kira Kira
11 Abdi Fantastik Bungalows
12 Coconut Cottages
14 Gili Air Santai
17 Pondok Wisata Gita Gili
18 Sunrise Cottages & Restaurant

20 Mawar Cottages
21 Nusa Tiga Bungalows
23 Pondok Gili Air & Cafe
24 Salabose Cottages
25 Lucky Cottages
26 Safari Cottages
27 Gili Indah Hotel

PLACES TO EAT
16 Han's Restaurant

OTHER
2 Sansibar
9 Blue Marlin Dive Centre
13 Ozzy's Shop
15 Hany Shop; Gili Air Santai Restaurant & Bar
19 Dream Divers
22 Go Go Pub & Restaurant
28 Reefseekers Dive Centre & Turtle Nursery
29 Perama Office; Wartel
30 Koperasi; Public Boat Office

To Gili Meno

Boat Landing
Jetty

To Bangsal

Reef – Good Snorkelling

0   250   500m
0   250   500yd

Activities

Boat Trips Glass-bottom boat tours to areas all around the three islands are available from **Ozzy's Shop** (☎ 622179) from 9.30am to 3pm. A minimum of six people is required, at 35,000Rp per person including snorkelling gear, and bookings can be made through any hotel on the island.

Diving & Snorkelling There is quite good snorkelling off the eastern and northern sides of the island and **Ozzy's Shop** can rent you gear for 10,000Rp. There is also excellent scuba diving within a short boat ride, with lots of reef sharks and underwater canyons. Recommended dive operators include the following.

Blue Marlin Dive Centre (☎ 634387; **w** www.diveindo.com) All woman dive outfit, also based on Trawangan. It also organises live-aboards to other Nusa Tenggara islands.

Dream Divers (☎ 634547; **w** www.dreamdivers.com) A popular German-run outfit.

Reefseekers Dive Centre & Turtle Nursery (☎ 641008, fax 641005; **w** ww.reefseekers.net) Small company with a strong commitment to conserving the marine environment – turtle eggs bought from public markets are hatched and raised here, and hundreds have now been released into the sea, so these endangered animals are often seen around the Gili islands. Donations are accepted. It also has a dive centre on Flores.

Places to Stay

A few places are on the northeast corner of the island where the best beaches are. There's another cluster in the south, near the boat landing area, and a few on the west side, where the beach is virtually nonexistent.

Places to Stay – Budget

Pondok Legenda (☎ 0812 376 4552; singles 20,000-35,000Rp, doubles 40,000-85,000Rp) has bungalows both at the rear and by the beachfront. All are pleasant, well-maintained and clean, but can be noisy on the nights when the bar fires up.

Pondok Sandi (singles 30,000-70,000Rp, doubles 40,000-90,000Rp) faces a great stretch of beach. The rooms are basic, but the more expensive ones are larger. The café (dishes 9000-20,000Rp) serves traditional Sasak food. **Pondok Gusung Indah** (singles 40,000-40,000Rp, doubles 50,000-70,000Rp) and its café (dishes 8000-20,000Rp) are next door.

Kira Kira (☎ 641021; **e** kirakira@mataram.wasantara.net.id; singles/doubles 95,000/110,000Rp), 50m down a path through the coconut palms, has a peaceful ambience. The five bungalows are set in a lush garden and have lovely rooms, bamboo floors and overhead fans. The **restaurant** (dishes 8000-28,000Rp; open 7am-noon, 1pm-5pm, 7pm-9pm, daily) features Japanese staples (one of the owners is Japanese) such as tempura, as well as a small selection of Indonesian and Western dishes.

Coconut Cottages (☎ 635365; W www .coconuts-giliair.com; bungalows 70,000-150,000Rp), near the east coast and slightly inland, offers a range of rooms, from simple bamboo bungalows to comfortable bungalows with modern bathrooms, hot water and ceiling fans. The bungalows are set in a lush flowering garden.

Gili Air Santai (☎ 641022; singles/doubles 80,000/100,000Rp), not far from Coconut Cottages, has good-sized bungalows, basic interiors and modern bathrooms. The balconies face a coconut grove and garden of red hibiscus. Internet access is available.

Other options nearby are **Abdi Fantastik Bungalows** (☎ 622179; bungalows 80,000-100,000Rp), **Pondok Gita Gili** (rooms 40,000-50,000Rp), **Pino Cottages** (singles/doubles 30,000/50,000Rp), **Mawar Cottage** (bungalows 50,000Rp), **Nusa Tiga Bungalows** (singles/doubles 40,000/50,000Rp), with pleasant thatched bungalows, and the friendly **Pondok Gili Air** (singles/doubles 40,000/60,000Rp), which has a great café.

Behind the Dream Divers centre, **Sunrise Cottages & Restaurant** (☎ 642370; singles/ doubles 100,000/150,000Rp, family bungalow 200,000Rp), has very well-maintained two-storey lumbung-style bungalows with chill-out areas on the lower floor. Some are suitable for families.

On the southwest coast, **Lucky Cottages** (singles/doubles 50,000/70,000Rp) has basic, clean bungalows that have day beds on the balconies.

Safari Cottages (bungalows 60,000/70,000Rp) has very clean, creatively decorated bungalows. It also has a hip little **café** (dishes 10,000-15,000Rp), which is a great place to hang, with hammocks and comfy cane chairs. **Salabose Cottages** (singles 25,000-50,000Rp, doubles 30,000-80,000Rp), nearby, is OK.

On the far northwest coast you'll find **Pondok Pantai** (rooms 30,000-40,000Rp), set well back from the beach, but with uninterrupted views, has basic rooms, **Bunga Cottages** (rooms 25,000-30,000Rp; open Aug-Jan only) has 10 thatch-roofed cottages in a row, and **Matahari Bungalows** (singles 25,000-35,000Rp, doubles 35,000-50,000Rp) has hammocks on the balconies.

Places to Stay – Mid-Range

The biggest place on Gili Air is **Gili Indah Hotel** (☎/fax 637328; W www.mataram.wasan tara.net.id/gili; bungalow US$15, with seaview US$25, with air-con & hot water US$35). It features a variety of bungalows in a big garden facing the beach. The seaview rooms are the best.

Hotel Gili Air (☎/fax 634435; W www .hotelgiliair.com; bungalow singles/doubles US$25/30, with hot water, TV & air-con US$35/40), on the nicer, northern end of the island, offers decent bungalows in a large garden facing a pool and the beach.

Places to Eat

Most places to stay (and some dive centres) have picturesque, simple beachfront restaurants serving inexpensive Western, Chinese and Indonesian food. Stand out options include the following.

Blue Marlin Dive Centre (dishes 15,000-35,000Rp) has a great range of dishes, including fresh fish and even comfort food like baked beans.

Sunrise Cottages (dishes 13,000-50,000Rp) is recommended by locals and offers a large range, including steaks, baguettes, salads and pasta. It also has a small Indonesian menu.

Abdi Fantastik (dishes 6000-20,000Rp) serves genuine Sasak cuisine, such as ikan masak kuning (fish soup spiced with ginger) and tumpi tumpi (fritters), as well as a small Western menu.

Coconut Cottages (dishes 8000-23,000Rp) in a pleasant, shady garden setting serves authentic dishes, such as green papaya soup with coconut milk. It also holds a buffet once a week (35,000Rp).

Gili Air Santai Restaurant & Bar (dishes 8000-35,000Rp), next door to Hany Shop, is a nice spot for a beer and a snack overlooking the beach.

Pondok Gili Air Cafe (dishes 10,000-12,500Rp; open 8.30am-2.30pm & 6pm-late; closed Mon & Thur in the low season) has a mixed veggie Indonesian and Western menu, including lassi and even eggs and beans. Wednesday night is a theme night featuring burritos or Indian dishes, and freshly baked European-style cake is available on Sunday. Book a day in advance for a Sasak dinner.

Han's Restaurant (dishes 10,000-35,000Rp) is known for its pizzas and has a picturesque beachside position.

Entertainment

Nightlife is fairly tame, but **Pondok Legenda** has a 'party' every Wednesday night, featuring reggae music (of course) and an all-you-can eat buffet for 30,000Rp. On other nights, happy hour is between 5pm and 7pm, and the **restaurant** *(dishes 10,000-20,000Rp, plus fresh fish)* serves Indonesian dishes (order lobster and prawns the day before). **Go Go Pub** claims to get going on a Saturday night from around 10.30pm and plays dance music (it even has a disco ball).

Sansibar is a cool, little, out-of-the-way bar, which is great for sipping a drink or two and watching the sunset, or playing a game of boule. It opens in the afternoon from around 3pm.

Getting Around

Walking is the usual form of transport, but at night the beach path can be difficult to navigate in the dark, so ask if your hotel can give you a lantern. *Cidomo* is another option. **Ozzy's Shop** rents decent bicycles for 10,000Rp to 15,000Rp per day.

GILI MENO

Gili Meno, the middle island, has the smallest permanent population of around 300 very friendly local people. It is the quietest island with the fewest tourists. The beach on the east coast is picturesque, and most of the accommodation and facilities are concentrated here. Inland are scattered houses, coconut plantations and a shallow lake that produces salt in the dry season.

The new *Bounty* fast catamaran service from Bali has its terminus on the west coast of Gili Meno, by Bounty Beach Bungalows.

Orientation & Information

You can **exchange money** at various points on the island, including the Gazebo, Bounty Beach Bungalows and Kontiki Meno Bungalows, and make telephone calls at the **wartel** near the boat landing. Only basic supplies are available on the island, so stock up on anything else you may need. Electricity was due to arrive on the island in mid-2002. There's limited fresh water on Gili Meno and the bathing water is brackish. **Right On Bookshop**, behind Jali Café, has a small selection and charges 20,000Rp to exchange books.

Gili Meno Bird Park

Taman Burung *(W www.balipvbgroup.com; adult/child 25,000/12,500Rp; open 9am-5pm daily)* has an impressive and well cared for collection of colourful, exotic species from the Australasian region. A great photo opportunity is available alongside a majestic black cockatoo and four multi-coloured macaws.

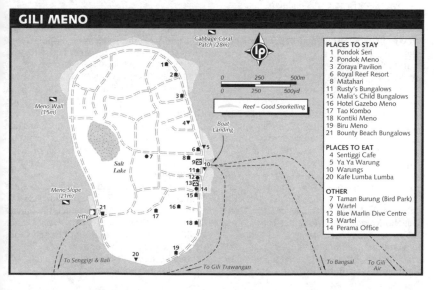

GILI MENO

Cabbage Coral Patch (28m)

Meno Wall (15m)

Reef – Good Snorkelling

Boat Landing

Salt Lake

Meno Slope (21m)

Jetty

0   250   500m
0   250   500yd

To Senggigi & Bali

To Gili Trawangan

To Bangsal

To Gili Air

PLACES TO STAY
1 Pondok Seri
2 Pondok Meno
3 Zoraya Pavilion
6 Royal Reef Resort
8 Matahari
11 Rusty's Bungalows
15 Malia's Child Bungalows
16 Hotel Gazebo Meno
17 Tao Kombo
18 Kontiki Meno
19 Biru Meno
21 Bounty Beach Bungalows

PLACES TO EAT
4 Sentiggi Cafe
5 Ya Ya Warung
10 Warungs
20 Kafe Lumba Lumba

OTHER
7 Taman Burung (Bird Park)
9 Wartel
12 Blue Marlin Dive Centre
13 Wartel
14 Perama Office

Activities
As on all three Gili islands, **snorkelling** around Gili Meno should be undertaken with caution due to the currents that flow through the narrow channels between the islands. Much of the coral around Gili Meno is dead but areas such as near Gili Meno Wall and to the southeast of the island are reviving. The place to find local boatmen who know the best snorkelling spots around is outside Blue Marlin Dive Centre, near the jetty. Expect to pay a negotiable 50,000Rp per head.

Diving is also an option, with **Blue Marlin Dive Centre** (☎ 634387; W www.diveindo .com), based by the jetty and at Bounty Beach Bungalows.

Places to Stay
Gili Meno has several mid-range options, perhaps because the *Bounty* catamaran brings in well-heeled travellers. The basic places, however, may not have electricity – and this means no fans.

At the northern end of the island, **Pondok Meno** (*bungalows 45,000Rp*) is basic and quiet, with a few simple bungalows.

Pondok Seri (*bungalow 200,000Rp*) is a large two-storey bungalow – with a spacious lounging area upstairs offering water views.

Zoraya Pavilion (*singles/doubles 60,000/ 80,000Rp*) on a picturesque, isolated stretch has a few bungalows facing the water.

Royal Reef Resort (*☎/fax 642340; bunga-lows 150,000Rp*), almost opposite the boat landing, looks like the usual bungalows, but they're better finished and better furnished than most.

Rusty's Bungalows (*bungalow singles/ doubles 40,000/50,000Rp*), a little south of Royal Resort, at the focus of tourist activity, are very basic but quite OK.

Malia's Child Bungalows (*☎ 622007; bungalows from 110,000Rp*) are boxy, def-initely ordinary, but they're across from a great stretch of beach and fill up quickly. Breakfast is not included.

Villa Nautilus (*☎ 642143; W www.villa nautilus.com; rooms US$75*) is new and very swish. It features freshwater hot and cold showers, and air-con. Guests can use Hotel Gazebo Meno's pool. Its café, Bibi's, is at the front of the hotel.

Matahari (*singles/doubles 20,000/ 25,000Rp*) is a worn but cheap place, while the nearby **Jali Bungalow** (*singles/doubles 40,000/80,000Rp*), behind the café, has very clean, nicely furnished bungalows, al-though the garden is sparse.

Tao Kombo (*bungalows 100,000Rp*), down a village path, has *lumbung*-style cottages, featuring cobblestone floors, interesting de-sign and lovely open-air bathrooms.

Hotel Gazebo Meno (*☎/fax 635795; bungalows US$55-60*) has 10 tastefully deco-rated Balinese-style bungalows, set back among the trees, all with air-con. Breakfast is not included. Avoid staying in the bunga-lows near the generator.

South of Hotel Gazebo Meno, **Kontiki Meno** (*☎ 632824; bungalow singles/doubles 25,000/30,000Rp, bungalow 100,000Rp*) is also the Perama office, and has clean, basic rooms, some with air-con and day beds.

Further south, **Biru Meno** (*bungalows 50,000Rp*) has cute little bungalows. **Kafe Lumba Lumba** (*bungalows 100,000Rp*) has Dutch-style bungalows decorated in a chintzy manner, but they're reasonably well maintained and have fridges.

Bounty Beach Bungalows (*☎ 649090, fax 641177; e gilimeno@indo.net.id; rooms US$45-55*), on the west coast, by the jetty where the *Bounty* catamaran docks, is a mid-range option, where rooms have air-con, phones and minibars, and there's a pool. It's pleasant, but the grounds are a lit-tle run-down.

Places to Eat & Drink
Ya Ya Warung (*dishes 45000-10,000Rp*) sets up nightly by the waterfront. Popular with locals, long tables are decorated with red lanterns and the atmosphere is festive.

Rusty's (*dishes 7500-28,000Rp*), nearby, is known for its fresh seafood, such as whole barracuda smothered in garlic sauce (25,000Rp).

Jali Café (*dishes 3000-7000Rp*) is a laid-back little spot with barugas facing the water.

Sentigi Café (*dishes 5000-6000Rp*) has a small menu featuring simple dishes, such as *tumpi tumpi*.

At the southern end of the island, **Kafe Lumba Lumba**, with Indonesian and Padang-style food is a fine place to see the sunset behind Gunung Agung. An even longer walk will bring you to **Bounty Beach Club**, which is a reasonable option.

Tao Kombo calls itself a music bar, and its food is recommended.

GILI TRAWANGAN

The largest island, Trawangan has the most visitors and the most facilities, and continues to build on its reputation as the 'party island'. It is, in fact, the smallest island in the world to have an Irish pub – believe it or not. At night the paved esplanade south of the jetty fills with travellers heading to their favoured restaurant and bar for the evening.

The island is about 3km long and 2km wide, and has a local population of about 800, not counting the substantial number of workers from other parts of Indonesia and overseas.

Orientation & Information

Boats pull up on the beach just north of the jetty. The nicest beaches, and a long row of warung, are north of here, while most of the tourist facilities, restaurants and the better hotels are to the south. There are a few places to stay at other points around the coast – they're quiet, but far from most of the action.

Several places will exchange money or travellers cheques, at lower rates than on the mainland. The *Pasar Seni* (Art Market) has a **postal agent** and shops selling most things you'll need, including second-hand books. The **Perama office** and a **wartel** are a little north of the jetty. **Bulan Cybercafe** is inland from the tourist strip and charges 400Rp per minute, as does **Paradise Internet**. **Melati Mini-market** is by Melati cottages. Pondok Lita, in the village, has a **laundry service**. A **doctor** visits Villa Ombok between 10am and 3pm on Tuesday, Thursday and Saturday.

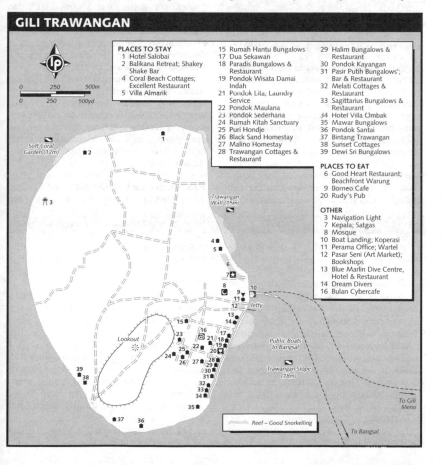

GILI TRAWANGAN

PLACES TO STAY
1 Hotel Salobai
2 Balikana Retreat; Shakey Shake Bar
4 Coral Beach Cottages; Excellent Restaurant
5 Villa Almarik
15 Rumah Hantu Bungalows
17 Dua Sekawan
18 Paradis Bungalows & Restaurant
19 Pondok Wisata Damai Indah
21 Pondok Lita, Laundry Service
22 Pondok Maulana
23 Pondok Sederhana
24 Rumah Kitah Sanctuary
25 Puri Hondje
26 Black Sand Homestay
27 Malino Homestay
28 Trawangan Cottages & Restaurant
29 Halim Bungalows & Restaurant
30 Pondok Kayangan
31 Pasir Putih Bungalows'; Bar & Restaurant
32 Melati Cottages & Restaurant
33 Sagittarius Bungalows & Restaurant
34 Hotel Villa Ombak
35 Mawar Bungalows
36 Pondok Santai
37 Bintang Trawangan
38 Sunset Cottages
39 Dewi Sri Bungalows

PLACES TO EAT
6 Good Heart Restaurant; Beachfront Warung
9 Borneo Cafe
20 Rudy's Pub

OTHER
3 Navigation Light
7 Kepala; Satgas
8 Mosque
10 Boat Landing; Koperasi
11 Perama Office; Wartel
12 Pasar Seni (Art Market); Bookshops
13 Blue Marlin Dive Centre, Hotel & Restaurant
14 Dream Divers
16 Bulan Cybercafe

Soft Coral Garden (12m)

Trawangan Wall (15m)

Trawangan Slope (18m)

Lookout

Public Boats to Bangsal

Jetty

Reef – Good Snorkelling

To Gili Meno

To Bangsal

0   250   500m
0   250   500yd

LOMBOK

Activities
Boat Trips Four-hour trips on glass-bottom boats to the other two islands are sold at various shops-cum-travel agencies (35,000Rp per person). Regular boats can be chartered for a negotiable 200,000Rp per day – find some other passengers to share the cost with you.

Diving Some excellent scuba diving sites are within a short boat ride, especially off Trawangan's west coast. Dive operators on the tourist strip arrange trips and courses – several have attractive pools for introductory dive training.

Recommended dive centres include the following.

Blue Marlin Dive Centre (☎ 632424, fax 642286; |e| bmdc@mataram.wasantara.net.id)
Dream Divers (☎ 634496; |e| dreamdivers@ mataram.wasantara.net.id)
Manta Dive (☎ 0370-643649; |w| www.manta -dive.com)
Villa Ombak Diving Academy (☎ 638531, fax 642337; |e| gilidive@mataram.wasantara.net.id)

Snorkelling The best area for snorkelling is off the northeastern coast. There is coral around most of the island, but much of the reef on the eastern side has been damaged. Beware of strong currents on the eastern side, between Trawangan and Meno. Snorkelling gear can be hired for around 10,000Rp per day from shacks near the boat landing.

Walking You can walk around the whole island in two-or-so pleasant hours. From the hill in the southwestern corner you'll see fine views of Bali's Gunung Agung, especially at sunset. Sunrise over Gunung Rinjani is also impressive. On the far side of the hill behind the Dewi Sri Bungalows, look for the remains of an old **Japanese gun**.

Places to Stay
During the high season it can sometimes be difficult to find a room.

Places to Stay – Budget
The cheapest and often the best places are away from the beach, in the village, including **Rumah Hantu Bungalows** *(bungalows 50,000Rp)*, which has a great atmosphere. Rooms are clean and simple, and the grounds are leafy.

Rumah Kita Sanctuary *(singles/doubles 40,000/60,000Rp)* is set in a Balinese-style garden and the thatch-roofed cottages are decorated with the owner's artwork.

Other decent options in the village include **Malino Homestay** *(singles/doubles 60,000/ 80,000Rp)*; **Pondok Iwan** *(singles/doubles 30,000/45,000Rp)*; **Pondok Maulana** *(singles/ doubles 80,000/100,000Rp)*; the relaxed and kinda funky **Black Sand Homestay** *(☎ 0812 376 8547; singles/doubles 50,000/80,000Rp)*; **Pondok Sederhana** *(☎ 0812 376 4629; singles/doubles 80,000/100,000Rp)*, a nice, friendly, spotlessly clean place; and **Pondok Lita** *(☎ 0812 376 4443; singles/doubles*

The Gili Eco Trust

The Gili Eco Trust was set up in 2000 as a partnership between the foreign-owned dive centre operators and the Gili Trawangan community. The aim is to improve the reefs and island environments through a number of negotiated projects.

The initial project has been to work with local fishing people to agree to fishing exclusion zones, within which some fishing techniques that yield large catches but damage coral have been banned. Much of the coral around the Gili islands have been damaged by recent El Nino events, bomb fishing and careless boat anchoring. Some coral have started the long-term process of rebuilding, and the no-fishing zones are one attempt to protect and encourage this regrowth.

Planned projects include improving the waste disposal and recycling facilities of the island, working with a local coordinating organisation, SATGAS, and to improve lighting in some parts of the island to increase night safety for tourists, especially women.

The trust is currently funded by all divers on the island who pay a 20,000Rp fee to the first Gili Trawangan dive centre they dive with.

When the trust has proven a medium-term success on Gili Trawangan, it may be introduced to the two other islands in this Gili group.

Not What Was Planned

When Gili Trawangan began to attract large numbers of visitors, it also attracted the attention of big business interests from Java. Lombok government officials dreamed of upmarket resorts, and decided to reorganise the land leases on the island.

The plan was to move all the budget bungalows from the northeast beachfront, to make way for grandiose golf courses and four-star hotels. There was negotiation and compensation, but some still refused to move. In 1992, after repeated requests, the authorities ordered the army in, and soldiers closed the bungalows by the simple but effective means of cutting the supporting posts with chainsaws.

All these small businesses were moved to narrow allotments at the south end of the island. Then, a fire in 1993 destroyed some 16 bungalows, and a ruling required new buildings be made of brick, tile and concrete. A rash of charmless concrete boxes ensued, cramped together as closely as possible, without any coherent architecture.

The grand hotel never happened, halted by local resistance and national crisis, so desolate fields face some of the best northern beaches. Meanwhile, the south end of the island has a pleasant paved esplanade, and attracts budget tourists with its stimulating mix of small hotels, restaurants, street stalls and dive schools. It's not perfect, and it's not finished, but it's idiosyncratic and eclectic, and it's better economics than another empty, upmarket resort.

100,000/150,000Rp), which is set around a small garden.

Other options are the Gili-standard bamboo bungalows on the beaches away from the main tourist strip. It will cost at least 5000Rp by *cidomo* to reach these.

Dewi Sri Bungalows *(singles 25,000-50,000Rp, doubles 40,000-75,000Rp)*, on the southwest coast and a 20-minute walk from the harbour, is well away from everything and is almost charming.

If you're after no-frills, **Sunset Cottages** *(singles/doubles 45,000/50,000Rp)* is basic.

At the south end of the island, **Pondok Santi** *(singles/doubles/triples 40,000/50,000/75,000Rp)*, a relaxed place, is on a lovely stretch of coconut-palm filled land.

Bintang Trawangan *(bungalows 50,000-60,000Rp)* has clean but quite basic stone bungalows.

Along the tourist strip there are clean but unmemorable places, including **Paradise Bungalows** *(bungalows 50,000-80,000Rp)*, **Pondok Wisata Damai Indah** *(bungalows 50,000-80,000Rp)*, **Halim Bungalows** *(singles/doubles 50,000/75,000Rp)*, **Melati Cottages** *(rooms 50,000/70,000Rp)*, **Sagittarius Bungalows** *(singles/doubles 50,000/70,000Rp)*, set in a spacious garden, and the very basic **Mawar Bungalows** *(singles/doubles 20,000/25,000Rp)*, where breakfast is not included.

Gili Trawangan Cottages *(☎ 623582; rooms 100,000Rp, with air-con 150,000Rp)* is lacking in atmosphere, but clean and well maintained.

Pondok Kayangan *(☎ 637932; singles/doubles 100,000/150,000Rp, with air-con 150,000/200,000Rp)* is relatively charmless, but is quiet for this location.

Frenchles *(rooms 100,000Rp)*, next door to Dream Divers, is a new place. In a convenient location, the small brick bungalows have balcony hammocks.

Places to Stay – Mid-Range

In the village, **Puri Hondje** *(bungalows US$15/25)* has only two rooms, but is modern and Balinese in style. Floors are cobblestone, there is air-con, lovely outdoor bathrooms and a small pond in the garden.

Blue Marlin *(☎ 632424; singles/doubles US$35/40)* has functional, modern air-con rooms without water views, but the hot water is reliable.

Dream Divers *(☎ 624496; rooms US$25, with air-con & hot water US$35)* has nicely decorated lime-washed rooms with a comfortable ambience and open-air bathrooms.

Balikana Retreat *(☎ 622386; W www.balikanaretreat.com; rooms US$25-35)*, a romantic hideaway in an isolated spot, has loft-style bungalows featuring sunset balcony views, freshwater showers and modern bathrooms. The water directly in front is a great snorkelling spot.

Hotel Salobai *(☎ 643152, fax 643151; rooms US$50, with air-con US$60-70)* is an unusual place that can't be missed – it has a concrete ship (the hotel's restaurant) built on a massive scale in the grounds facing the ocean. Rooms are comfortable and the more expensive ones have TV. The restaurant has great views from the 'top deck', and Chinese and Western food is on offer.

Places to Stay – Top End

Hotel Villa Ombak (☎ 642336, fax 642337; W www.hotel.ombak.com; rooms US$68-85), Trawangan's first top-end option, offers nicely decorated *lumbung*-style rooms and bungalows, set around an ocean view swimming pool. All rooms have air-con with satellite TV, minibar and telephone, and the bungalows have spacious open-air bathrooms. Non-guests can use the pool for 25,000Rp. There's also a **massage spa** here.

Villa Almarik (☎/fax 638520; W www .almarik-lombok.com; rooms $150) has flowering bougainvillea through the grounds and by the pool. The high-roofed bungalows have stylish interiors, hot water, TV and big bathrooms facing a small private garden.

Places to Eat & Drink

Seafood is excellent at most Trawangan restaurants – quite a few display fresh fish on a sidewalk table, and you have a choice of fried, steamed or barbecued. The cheapest places for a meal and drink during the day and early evening are the various makeshift **warung** along the beach, north of the boat landing.

Cafe Wayan & Bakery (*dishes 15,000-35,000Rp*) has a range of Indonesian dishes, breads and pastries, and **Good Heart Restaurant** (*dishes 15,000-30,000Rp*) is recommended by locals.

Dream Divers (*dishes 12,000-31,000Rp*) serves club sandwiches, steaks, pasta and

Indonesian dishes, although the Hangover Breakfast is disappointing, even without a hangover! The café at **Blue Marlin** is also worth a try.

Manta Dive Cafe (*dishes 15,000-40,000Rp*) is an open-air place seamlessly adjoining the Manta Dive Centre. You can sit in a large shady *beruga* or swing in hammocks. The sesame and teriyaki tuna steak for around 25,000Rp is a good bet.

Kantin & Warung Kopi Melanie (☎ 629993; *dishes 4000-7000Rp*) is a small place in the village, with tables under a towering tree and roosters running around. It has lots of satay dishes on offer.

Hotel Villa Ombak (*dishes 25,000-60,000Rp*) offers a mix of international and Asian cuisine, sandwiches, pastas and steaks.

Villa Almarik (☎ 638520; *dishes 21,000-37,000Rp*) has a restaurant overlooking the pool, and offers seafood and simple pasta options.

The **Shakey Shake Bar** (☎ 622386; *dishes 10,000-12,500Rp*) at Balikana Retreat offers smoothies, lassis and milkshakes. The **restaurant** (*dishes 20,000-35,000Rp*) here will also pick-up and drop off by *cidomo*. Call to reserve a place.

Entertainment

In the high season there's a party every night, often with live music – the venue rotates between **Villa Ombak**, **Rudy's Pub**, **Excellent Restaurant** and **Blue Marlin**.

Tir Na Nog, an Irish bar & restaurant, advertises itself with the pithy saying 'Get pissed always solution'. It has a good vibe and is a popular spot to warm up for the night ahead. It also has a large screen showing sports events and films. Its **restaurant** (*dishes 14,000-35,000Rp*) serves Australian steaks and Irish stew among other dishes.

Language

WHO SPEAKS WHAT?
Bali

The indigenous language, Bahasa Bali, is a spoken language with various forms based on traditional caste distinctions. The average traveller needn't worry about learning Balinese, but it can be fun to pick up a few words. For practical purposes, it's easier to concentrate your efforts on learning Bahasa Indonesia.

Bahasa Indonesia is the national language, used in the education system and for all legal and administrative purposes. It's becoming more and more widely used, partly because of its official language status and partly because it allows the many non-Balinese now living and working on Bali to communicate – and avoid the intricacies of the caste system.

A good phrasebook is a wise investment, particularly if you plan to go off the beaten track. Lonely Planet's *Indonesian phrasebook* is a concise and handy introduction to the language. Available at a few bookshops on Bali is the *Bali Pocket Dictionary*, which lists grammar and vocabulary in English, Indonesian and low, polite and high level Balinese.

English is common in the tourist areas, and is usually spoken very well. Many Balinese in the tourist industry also have a smattering (or more) of German, Japanese, French and/or Italian. A few older people speak Dutch and are often keen to practice it, but if you want to travel in remote areas, and communicate with people who aren't in the tourist business, it's a good idea to learn some Bahasa Indonesia.

Lombok

Most people on Lombok are bilingual, and speak their own indigenous language (Sasak), as well as Bahasa Indonesia, which they are taught at school and use as their formal and official mode of communication. Apart from those working in the tourist industry, few people on Lombok speak English, and this includes police and other officials. English is becoming more widely spoken, but is still rare outside the main towns and tourist centres.

BAHASA BALI

The national language of Indonesia, Bahasa Indonesia, is widely used on Bali, but it isn't Balinese.

Balinese, or Bahasa Bali, is another language entirely. It has a completely different vocabulary and grammar, and the rules governing its use are much more complex. It's a difficult language for a foreigner to come to grips with. Firstly, it isn't a written language, so there's no definitive guide to its grammar or vocabulary, and there is considerable variation in usage from one part of the island to another. Bahasa Bali isn't taught in schools either, and dictionaries and grammars that do exist are attempts to document current or historical usage, rather than set down rules for correct syntax or pronunciation.

Balinese is greatly complicated by its caste influences. In effect, different vocabularies and grammatical structures are used, depending on the relative social position of the speaker, the person being spoken to and the person being spoken about. Even traditional usage has always been somewhat arbitrary, because of the intricacies of the caste system.

The various forms of the language (or languages) and their respective uses are categorised as follows:

Basa Lumrah, also called *Biasa* or *Ketah*, is used when talking to people of the same caste or level, and between friends and family. It is an old language of mixed origin, with words drawn from Malayan, Polynesian and Australasian sources.

Basa Sor, or *Rendah*, is used when talking with people of a lower caste, or to people who are non caste.

Basa Alus is used among educated people, and is derived from the Hindu-Javanese court languages of the 10th century.

Basa Madia, or *Midah*, a mixture of Basa Lumrah and Basa Alus, is used as a polite language for speaking to or about strangers, or people to whom one wishes to show respect.

Basa Singgih, virtually a separate language, is used to address persons of high caste, particularly in formal and religious contexts. Even the Balinese are not always fluent in this language. It is based on the ancient Hindu Kawi language, and can be written using a script that resembles Sanskrit, as seen in the *lontar* (palm) books where it's inscribed on strips of leaf (see the 'Gedong Kirtya Library' section and the 'Lontar Books' boxed text in the North Bali chapter). Written Basa Singgih is also seen on the signs that welcome you to, and farewell you from, most villages on Bali.

The different vocabularies only exist for about 1000 basic words, mostly words relating to people and their actions. Other words (in fact, an increasing proportion of the modern vocabulary), are the same regardless of relative caste levels.

Usage is also changing with the decline of the traditional caste system and modern tendencies towards democratisation and social equality. It is now common practice to describe the language in terms of only three forms:

Low Balinese, or *Ia*, equivalent to Basa Lumrah, is used between friends and family, and also when speaking with persons of equal or lower caste, or about oneself.
Polite Balinese, or *Ipun*, the equivalent of Basa Madia, is used for speaking to superiors or strangers, and is becoming more widespread as a sort of common language that isn't so closely linked to caste.
High Balinese, or *Ida*, a mixture of Basa Alus and Basa Singgih, is used to indicate respect for the person being addressed or the person being spoken about.

The polite and high forms of the language frequently use the same word, while the low form often uses the same word as Bahasa Indonesia. The polite form, Basa Madia or Midah, is being used as a more egalitarian language, often combined with Bahasa Indonesia to avoid the risk of embarrassment in case the correct caste distinctions aren't made.

So how does one Balinese know at which level to address another? Well, initially, a conversation between two strangers would commence in the high language. At some point the question of caste would be asked and then the level adjusted accordingly. However, among friends a conversation is likely to be carried on in low Balinese, no matter what the caste of the speakers may be.

Bahasa Bali uses very few greetings and civilities on an everyday basis. There are no equivalents for 'please' and 'thank you'. Nor is there a usage that translates as 'good morning' or 'good evening', although the low Balinese *kenken kebara?* (How are you?/How's it going?) is sometimes used. More common is *lunga kija?*, which literally means 'where are you going?' (in low, polite and high Balinese).

Some other Balinese expressions that a visitor might encounter are listed in low, polite and high forms in the 'Choose Your Words Carefully' boxed text. Some of them may also occur in place names.

Choose Your Words Carefully!

English	Indonesian	Low Balinese	Polite Balinese	High Balinese
yes	ya	nggih, saja	inggih, patut	patut
no	tidak	sing, tuara	tan	nenten, tan wenten
good, well	bagus, baik	melah	becik	becik
bad	jelek	jele, corah	corah	kaon, durmaga
sleep	tidur	pules	sirep sare	makolem
eat	makan	madaar, neda	ngajeng, nunas	ngrayunang
this/these	ini	ne	niki, puniki	puniki
that/those	itu	ento	punika	punika
big	besar	gede	ageng	agung
small	kecil	cenik, cerik	alit	alit
water	air	yeh	toya	tirta
stone	batu	watu	watu	batu
north	utara	kaja	kaler	lor
south	selatan	kelod	kelod	kidul
east	timur	kangin	kangin	wetan
west	barat	kauh	kulon	kulon

Try to pronounce them as you would a Bahasa Indonesia word of the same spelling; they are written on that basis. The Indonesian equivalents are are also provided for comparison.

BAHASA INDONESIA

Like any language, Indonesian has a simplified colloquial form and a more developed literary form. It's among the easiest of all spoken languages to learn – there are no tenses, plurals or genders and, even better, it's easy to pronounce.

Apart from ease of learning, there's another very good reason for trying to pick up at least a handful of Indonesian words and phrases: few people are as delighted with visitors learning their language as Indonesians. They won't criticise you if you mangle your pronunciation or tangle your grammar. They make you feel like you're an expert even if you only know a dozen or so words. Bargaining also seems a whole lot easier and more natural when you do it in their language.

Written Indonesian can be idiosyncratic, however, and there are often inconsistent spellings of place names. Compound names are written as one word or two, eg, Airsanih or Air Sanih, Padangbai or Padang Bai. Words starting with 'Ker' sometimes lose the 'e', as in Kerobokan/Krobokan.

In addition, some Dutch variant spellings remain in common use. These tend to occur in business names, with 'tj' instead of the modern 'c' (as in Tjampuhan/Campuan), and 'oe' instead of 'u' (as in Soekarno/Sukarno).

Pronunciation

Most letters have a pronunciation more or less the same as their English counterparts. Nearly all the syllables carry equal emphasis, but a good approximation is to stress the second to last syllable.

The main exception to the rule is the unstressed **e** in words such as *besar* (big), pronounced 'be-**sarr**'.

a	as in 'father'
e	as in 'bet' when unstressed, although sometimes hardly pronounced at all, as in the greeting *selamat,* which sounds like 'slamat' if said quickly. When stressed **e** is like the 'a' in

'may', as in *becak* (rickshaw), pronounced 'baycha'. There's no general rule as to when the 'e' is stressed or unstressed.

i	as in 'unique'
o	as in 'hot'
u	as in 'put'
ai	as in 'Thai'
au	as the 'ow' in 'cow'
ua	as 'w' when at the start of a word, eg, *uang* (money), pronounced 'wong'
c	as the 'ch' in 'chair'
g	as in 'get'
ng	as the 'ng' in 'sing'
ngg	as the 'ng' in 'anger'
j	as in 'John'
r	slightly trilled, as in Spanish 'r'
h	a little stronger than the 'h' in 'her'; almost silent at the end of a word
k	like English 'k', except at the end of a word when it's more like a closing of the throat with no sound released, eg, *tidak* (no/not), pronounced 'tee-da'
ny	as the 'ny' in canyon

Addressing People

Pronouns, particularly 'you', are rarely used in Indonesian. When speaking to an older man (or anyone old enough to be a father), it's common to call them *bapak* (father) or simply *pak*. Similarly, an older woman is *ibu* (mother) or simply *bu. Tuan* is a respectful term, like 'sir'. *Nyonya* is the equivalent for a married woman, and *nona* for an unmarried woman. *Anda* is the egalitarian form designed to overcome the plethora of words for the second person.

To indicate negation, *tidak* is used with verbs, adjectives and adverbs; *bukan* with nouns and pronouns.

Greetings & Civilities

Welcome.	*Selamat datang.*
Good morning. (before 11 am)	*Selamat pagi.*
Good day. (11 am to 3 pm)	*Selamat siang.*
Good day. (3 to 7 pm)	*Selamat sore.*
Good evening. (after dark)	*Selamat malam.*
Good night. (to someone going to bed)	*Selamat tidur.*
Goodbye. (to person staying)	*Selamat tinggal.*

Goodbye.   *Selamat jalan.*
  (to person going)
Please.   *Tolong.*
  (asking for help)
Please.   *Silahkan.*
  (giving permission)
Thank you (very   *Terima kasih (banyak).*
  much).
You're welcome.   *Kembali.*
Sorry.   *Ma'af.*
Excuse me.   *Permisi.*
How are you?   *Apa kabar?*
I'm fine.   *Kabar baik.*
What's your   *Siapa nama*
  name?   *anda?*
My name is ...   *Nama saya ...*
Are you married?   *Sudah kawin?*
Not yet.   *Belum.*
How old are you?   *Berapa umur anda?*
I'm ... years old.   *Umur saya ... tahun.*

Useful Phrases
Yes.   *Ya.*
No. (not)   *Tidak.*
No. (negative)   *Bukan.*
Maybe.   *Mungkin.*
Good.   *Bagus.*
Good, fine, OK.   *Baik.*

Language Difficulties
I (don't) understand. *Saya (tidak) mengerti.*
Do you speak   *Bisa berbicara bahasa*
  English?   *Inggris?*
I can only speak a   *Saya hanya bisa*
  little (Indonesian). *berbicara (bahasa*
     Indonesia) sedikit.
Please write that   *Tolong tuliskan kata*
  word down.   *itu.*

Getting Around
I want to go to ...   *Saya mau ke ...*
Where is ...?   *Di mana ...?*
How many   *Berapa kilometre?*
  kilometres?

What time does   *Jam berapa ...*
the ... leave?   *berangkat?*
  boat/ship   *kapal*
  bus   *bis*
  plane   *kapal terbang*
  train   *kereta api*

Where can I hire   *Dimana saya bisa*
a ...?   *sewa ...?*
  bicycle   *sepeda*
  motorcycle   *sepeda motor*

station   *stasiun* or *terminal*
ticket   *karcis*

Directions
Which way?   *Ke mana?*
Go straight ahead.   *Jalan terus.*
Turn left/right.   *Belok kiri/kanan.*
Stop!   *Berhenti!*

here/there/   *di sini/situ/sana*
  over there
north   *utara*
south   *selatan*
east   *timur*
west   *barat*

Accommodation
Is there a room   *Ada kamar kosong?*
  available?
How much is it   *Berapa harganya*
  per day?   *sehari?*
Is breakfast   *Apakah harganya*
  included?   *termasuk makan*
     pagi/sarapan?

one night   *satu malam*
one person   *satu orang*
bed   *tempat tidur*
room   *kamar*
bathroom   *kamar mandi*
soap   *sabun*

Around Town
bank   *bank*
immigration   *imigrasi*
market   *pasar*
police station   *kantor polisi*
post office   *kantor pos*
public telephone   *telepon umum*
public toilet   *WC* ('way say')

What ... is this?   *Ini ... apa?*
  street   *jalan*
  town   *kota*
  village   *desa*

What time does it   *Jam berapa*
  open/close?   *buka/tutup?*
May I take photos?   *Boleh saya ambil foto?*

Food & Shopping
What is this?   *Apa ini?*
How much does   *Berapa (harga)?*
  it cost?
expensive   *mahal*

Emergencies

Help!	*Tolong!*
Fire!	*Kebakaran!*
Call a doctor!	*Panggillah dokter!*
Call an ambulance!	*Panggillah ambulin!*
I'm ill.	*Saya sakit.*
I'm allergic to ...	*Saya alergi ...*
Where are the toilets?	*Dimana WC?*
I'm lost.	*Saya kesasar.*
doctor	*dokter*
hospital	*rumah sakit*
chemist/pharmacy	*apotik*

this/that	*ini/itu*
big	*besar*
small	*kecil*

food stall	*warung*
restaurant	*rumah makan*
I can't eat meat.	*Saya tidak boleh makan daging.*
without meat	*tanpa daging*
Another/One more.	*Satu lagi.*

Time

When?	*Kapan?*
What time?	*Jam berapa?*
How many hours?	*Berapa jam?*
7 o'clock	*jam/tujuh*
five hours	*lima jam*
yesterday	*kemarin*
tomorrow	*besok*
hour	*jam*
day	*hari*
week	*minggu*
month	*bulan*
year	*tahun*

Monday	*hari Senen*
Tuesday	*hari Selasa*
Wednesday	*hari Rabu*
Thursday	*hari Kamis*
Friday	*hari Jum'at*
Saturday	*hari Sabtu*
Sunday	*hari Minggu*

Numbers

1	*satu*
2	*dua*
3	*tiga*
4	*empat*
5	*lima*
6	*enam*
7	*tujuh*
8	*delapan*
9	*sembilan*
10	*sepuluh*

A half is *setengah*, which is pronounced 'stenger', eg, *stenger kilo* (half a kilo). 'Approximately' is *kira-kira*. After the numbers one to 10, the 'teens' are *belas*, the 'tens' are *puluh*, the 'hundreds' are *ratus*, the 'thousands' are *ribu* and 'millions' are *juta* – but as a prefix *satu* (one) becomes 'se', eg, *se-ratus* (one hundred). Thus:

11	*sebelas*
12	*duabelas*
13	*tigabelas*
20	*dua puluh*
21	*dua puluh satu*
25	*dua puluh lima*
30	*tiga puluh*
99	*sembilan puluh sembilan*
100	*seratus*
150	*seratus limapuluh*
200	*dua ratus*
888	*delapan ratus delapan puluh delapan*
1000	*seribu*

one million	*sejuta*

Glossary

GENERAL TERMS

ABRI – Angkatan Bersenjata Republik Indonesia; Indonesia's armed forces

adat – tradition, customs and manners

adi kaka – birth ritual

angklung – portable form of the *gamelan*

angkutan kota – literally, 'city transport', and is the official name for the ubiquitous *bemo*

arja – refined operatic form of Balinese theatre

Arjuna – a hero of the *Mahabharata* epic and a popular temple gate guardian image

badawang – the mythological 'world turtle'

bahasa – language; Bahasa Indonesia is the national language of Indonesia

bale – an open-sided pavilion with a steeply pitched thatched roof

bale banjar – communal meeting place of a *banjar*; a house for meetings and *gamelan* practice

bale gede – reception room or guesthouse in the home of a wealthy Balinese

bale kambang – floating pavilion; a building surrounded by a moat

bale tani – family house; see also *serambi*

Bali Aga – the 'original' Balinese

balian – see *dukun*

banci – a less polite term for *waria,* a female impersonator

banjar – local division of a village consisting of all the married adult males

banyan – a type of ficus tree, often considered holy; see *waringin*

bapak – father; also a polite form of address to any older man; also *pak*

Baris – warrior dance

Barong – mythical lion-dog creature

Barong Landung – literally, 'tall *Barong*'

Barong Tengkok – portable *gamelan* used for wedding processions and circumcision ceremonies on Lombok

Batara – title used to address a deceased spirit, particularly that of an important person

batik – process of colouring fabric by coating part of the cloth with wax, then dyeing it and melting the wax out; the waxed part is not coloured, and repeated waxing and dyeing builds up a pattern

Bedaulu, Dalem – legendary last ruler of the Pejeng dynasty

bejak – bicycle rickshaw, no longer used on Bali or Lombok

bemo – popular local transport on Bali and Lombok, traditionally a small pick-up truck with a bench seat down each side in the back; small minibuses are now also commonly used

bensin – petrol (gasoline)

beruga – communal meeting hall on Bali; open-sided pavilion on Lombok

bhoma – fierce-looking guardian spirit represented in many temples

Bima Suarga – a hero of the *Mahabharata* epic

bioskop – cinema

Boma – son of the earth, a temple guardian figure

Brahma – the creator, one of the trinity of Hindu gods

Brahmana – the caste of priests and highest of the Balinese castes; although all priests are Brahmanas, not all Brahmanas are priests

bu – shortened form of *ibu* (mother)

buang au – naming ritual

bukit – hill; also the name of the southern peninsula of Bali

bupati – government official in charge of a *kabupaten* (district)

camat – government official in charge of a *kecamatan* (subdistrict)

candi – shrine, originally of Javanese design; also known as *prasada*

candi bentar – gateway entrance to a temple

caste – hereditary classes into which Hindu society is divided. There are four castes: three branches of the 'nobility' (*Brahmana*, *Ksatriyasa* and *Wesia*), and the common people (*Sudra*).

catur yoga – ancient manuscript on religion and cosmology

cidomo – pony cart with car wheels on Lombok

dalang – puppet master and storyteller in a *wayang kulit* performance

danau – lake

desa – village

dewa – deity or supernatural spirit
dewi – goddess
Dewi Danau – goddess of the lakes
Dewi Sri – goddess of rice
dokar – pony cart; known as a *cidomo* on Lombok
dukun – 'witch doctor'; faith healer and herbal doctor
Durga – goddess of death and destruction, and consort of Shiva
Dwarpala – guardian figure who keeps evil spirits at bay in temples

endek – elegant fabric, like *songket*, but the weft threads are predyed

Gajah Mada – famous Majapahit prime minister who defeated the last great king of Bali and extended Majapahit power over the island
Galungan – great Balinese festival, an annual event in the 210-day Balinese *wuku* calendar
gamelan – traditional Balinese orchestra, with mostly percussion instruments like large xylophones and gongs
Ganesha – Shiva's elephant-headed son
gang – alley or footpath
Garuda – mythical man-bird creature, the vehicle of Vishnu, a modern symbol of Indonesia and the name of the national airline
gedong – shrine
gendong – street vendors who sell *jamu,* said to be a cure-all tonic
gili – small island (Lombok)
goa – cave; also spelt *gua*
gringsing – rare double *ikat* woven cloth
gua – cave; also spelt *goa*
gunung – mountain
gunung api – volcano
gusti – polite title for members of the *Wesia* caste

Hanuman – monkey god who plays a major part in the *Ramayana*
harga biasa – standard price
harga turis – inflated price for tourists
homestay – small, family-run *losmen*

ibu – mother; also polite form of address to any older woman
Ida Bagus – honourable title for a male *Brahmana*
iders-iders – long painted scrolls used as temple decorations

ikat – cloth where a pattern is produced by dyeing the individual threads before weaving; see also *gringsing*
Indra – king of the gods

jalak putih – local name for Bali starling
jalan – road or street; abbreviated to *Jl*
jalan jalan – to walk around
jamu – a cure-all tonic; see also *gendong*
jidur – large cylindrical drums played throughout Lombok
Jimny – small jeep-like Suzuki vehicle; the usual type of rental car
Jl – *jalan*; road or street
jukung – see *prahu*

kabupaten – administrative districts (known as regencies during Dutch rule)
kain – a length of material wrapped tightly around the hips and waist, over a sarong
kaja – in the direction of the mountains; see also *kelod*
kala – demonic face often seen over temple gateways
kampung – village or neighbourhood
kantor – office
Kawi – classical Javanese, the language of poetry
kebaya – Chinese, long-sleeved blouse with low neckline and embroidered edges
Kebo Iwa – legendary giant credited with the creation of several of Bali's oldest stone monuments
Kecak – traditional Balinese dance, which tells a tale from the *Ramayana* about Prince Rama and Princess Siwi
kecamatan – subdistrict
kelod – opposite of *kaja;* the direction away from the mountains and towards the sea
kemban – woman's breast-cloth
kepala desa – village head
kepeng – old Chinese coins with a hole in the centre
ketupat – kind of sticky rice cooked in a banana leaf
kota – city
kretek – Indonesian clove cigarettes
kris – traditional dagger
Ksatriyasa – second Balinese caste
kulkul – hollow tree-trunk drum used to sound a warning or call meetings

labuhan – harbour; also called *pelabuhan*
lambung – long black sarongs worn by *Sasak* women; see also *sabuk*

langse – rectangular decorative hangings used in palaces or temples

Legong – classic Balinese dance

legong – young girls who perform the *Legong*

leyak – evil spirit that can assume fantastic forms by the use of black magic

lontar – type of palm tree

losmen – small Balinese hotel, often family-run

lulur – body mask

lumbung – rice barn with a round roof; an architectural symbol of Lombok

Mahabharata – one of the great Hindu holy books, the epic poem tells of the battle between the Pandavas and the Korawas

main ski – surfing

Majapahit – last great Hindu dynasty on Java

makan Padang – Padang food

mandi – Indonesian 'bath' consisting of a large water tank from which you ladle cold water over yourself

manusa yadnya – ceremonies which mark the various stages of Balinese life from before birth to after cremation

mapadik – marriage by request, as opposed to *ngrorod*

mekepung – traditional water buffalo races

meru – multiroofed shrines in Balinese temples; the name comes from the Hindu holy mountain Mahameru

naga – mythical snake-like creature

nasi – cooked rice

ngrorod – marriage by elopement; see also *mapadik*

nusa – island; also called *pulau*

Nusa Tenggara Barat (NTB) – West Nusa Tenggara; a province of Indonesia comprising the islands of Lombok and Sumbawa

nyale – worm-like fish caught off Kuta Beach, Lombok

Nyepi – major annual festival in the Hindu *saka* calendar, this is a day of complete stillness after a night of chasing out evil spirits

nyunatang – circumcision

odalan – Balinese 'temple birthday' festival held in every temple annually (according to the *wuku* calendar, ie, once every 210 days)

ojek – motorcycle that carries paying pillion passengers

padi – growing rice plant

padmasana – temple shrine resembling a vacant chair; a throne for the supreme god Sanghyang Widhi in the manifestation of Siwa Raditya

paduraksa – covered gateway to a temple

paibon – shrine in a state temple for the royal ancestors

pak – father; shortened form of *bapak*

palinggihs – temple shrines consisting of a simple little throne

pandanus – palm plant used in weaving mats etc

pande – blacksmiths; they are treated somewhat like a caste in their own right

pantai – beach

pantun – ancient Malay poetical verse in rhyming couplets

pasar – market

pasar malam – night market

pedanda – high priest

pekembar – umpire or referee in the traditional *Sasak* trial of strength known as *peresehan*

pelabuhan – harbour; also called *labuhan*

Pelni – the national shipping line

Pendet – formal offering dance performed at temple festivals

penjor – long bamboo pole with decorated end, arched over the road or pathway during festivals or ceremonies

perbekel – government official in charge of a *desa* (village)

peresehan – one-to-one physical contest peculiar to Lombok, in which two men fight each other armed with a small leather shield and a long rattan staff

plus plus – a combined tax and service charge of 21% added by mid-range and top-end accommodation and restaurants

Polda – Polisi Daerah; a regional police station

prahu – traditional Indonesian boat with outriggers

prasada – shrine; see also *candi*

pratima – figure of a god used as a 'stand-in' for the actual god's presence during a ceremony

pria – man; male

propinsi – province; Indonesia has 27 propinsi; Bali is a propinsi, Lombok and its neighbouring island of Sumbawa comprise propinsi Nusa Tenggara Barat

puasa – to fast, or a fast

pulau – island; also called *nusa*

punggawa – chief, or commander

puputan – warrior's fight to the death; an honourable but suicidal option when faced with an unbeatable enemy

pura – temple

pura dalem – temple of the dead

pura desa – temple of the village for everyday functions

pura puseh – temple of the village founders or fathers, honouring the village's origins

pura subak – temple of the rice growers' association

puri – palace

puskesmas – community health centre

rajah – lord or prince

Raksa – guardian figure who keeps evil spirits at bay in temples

Ramadan – Muslim month of fasting

Ramayana – one of the great Hindu holy books, from which stories form the keystone of many Balinese dances and tales

Rangda – widow-witch who represents evil in Balinese theatre and dance

rebab bowed lute

RRI – Radio Republik Indonesia; Indonesia's national radio broadcaster

RSU or **RSUP** – Rumah Sakit Umum or Rumah Sakit Umum Propinsi; a public hospital or provincial public hospital

rumah makan – restaurant; literally, 'eating place'

sabuk – 4m-long scarf that holds the *lambung* in place

sadkahyangan – most sacred temples or 'world sanctuaries'

saka – Balinese calendar which is based on the lunar cycle; see also *wuku*

Sanghyang – trance dance in which the dancers impersonate a local village god

Sanghyang Widi – Balinese supreme being

Sasak – native of Lombok; also the language

sawah – individual rice field; see also *subak*

selandong – traditional scarf

selat – strait

serambi – open veranda on a *bale tani,* the traditional Lombok family house

Shiva – the creator and destroyer; one of the three great Hindu gods

sirih – betel nut, chewed as a mild narcotic

songket – silver or gold-threaded cloth, hand-woven using a floating weft technique

sorong serah – marriage ceremony

subak – village association that organises rice terraces and shares out water for irrigation

Sudra – common caste to which the majority of Balinese belong

sungai – river

taksu – divine interpreter for the gods

tanjung – cape or point

tektekan – ceremonial procession

teluk – gulf or bay

transmigrasi – government program of transmigration

Trisakti – 'three-in-one' or trinity of Hindu gods: Brahma, Shiva and Vishnu

tugu – lord of the ground

TU – Telepon Umum; a public telephone

Vishnu – the preserver; one of the three great Hindu gods

wanita – woman; female

wantilan – large *bale* pavilion used for meetings, performances and cockfights

waria – female impersonator, transvestite or transgendered; combination of the words *wanita* and *pria*; see also *banci*

waringin – banyan tree; large shady tree with drooping branches, which root to produce new trees

warnet – *warung* Internet

wartel – public telephone office; contraction of *warung telekomunikasi*

warung – food stall

wayang kulit – leather puppet used in shadow puppet plays

wayang wong – masked drama playing scenes from the *Ramayana*

Wektu Telu – religion peculiar to Lombok, which originated in Bayan and combines many tenets of Islam and aspects of other faiths

Wesia – military caste and most numerous of the Balinese noble castes

WIB – Waktu Indonesia Barat; West Indonesia Time

wihara – monastery

WIT – Waktu Indonesia Tengah; Central Indonesia Time

wuku – Balinese calendar made up of 10 different weeks, between one and 10 days long, all running concurrently; see also *saka*

yeh – water; also river

CULINARY TERMS

air jeruk – lemon or orange juice
air minum – drinking water
apam – pancake filled with nuts and sprinkled with sugar
arak – colourless, distilled palm wine; the local firewater
asam manis – sweet and sour
avocat – avocado
ayam – chicken

babi – pork
bakmi goreng – fried noodles
bakso – meat balls
bakso ayam – chicken soup with noodles and meatballs
blimbing – starfruit; a cool, crispy, watery tasting fruit
brem – rice wine
bumbu – a hot spice

cap cai – mix of fried vegetables, sometimes with meat

daftar makanan – food menu
daging – beef
dingin – cold
durian – large green fruit with a hard, spiky exterior and a horrific stench

es buah – combination of crushed ice, condensed milk, shaved coconut, syrup, jelly and fruit
es campur – ice with fruit salad

fu yung hai –sweet-and-sour omelette

gado gado – dish of steamed bean sprouts with various vegetables and a spicy peanut sauce
garam – salt
gula – sugar

ikan – fish
ikan belut – eel
jambu – guava
jeruk – citrus fruit

kaki lima – food cart
kare – curry
kentang – potato
kepiting – crab
kodok – frog
krupuk – prawn crackers

lontong – rice steamed in a banana leaf

manggu – mango
mangosteen – small purple-brown fruit with pure-white segments
manis – sweet
mentega – butter
mie goreng – fried noodles, sometimes with vegetables, sometimes with meat
mie kuah – noodle soup

nanas – pineapple
nangka – jackfruit; yellow-green fruit that can weigh over 20kg
nasi campur – steamed rice topped with a little bit of everything
nasi goreng – fried rice
nasi putih – white rice, usually plain, and either boiled or steamed

opor ayam – chicken pieces cooked in coconut milk

pahat – literally means 'bitter', but is used to indicate 'no sugar' in tea or coffee
panas – hot (temperature)
pedas – hot (spicy)
pisang – bananas
pisang goreng – fried banana fritters
pisang molen – deep-fried bananas

rambutan – bright red fruit covered in soft, hairy spines; closely related to the lychee
rijstaffel – Dutch for 'rice table'; buffet of individual dishes with rice
rumah makan – restaurant

sambal – hot, spicy chilli sauce
satay – tiny kebabs of various types of meat served with a spicy peanut sauce
sawo – fruit resembling a potato, with a pear-like flavour
sayur – vegetable
sirsak – soursop; also spelt 'zurzat'
soto – soup; usually fairly spicy
stroop – cordial
susu – milk

teh – tea
telur – egg
tuak – palm beer/wine

udang – prawn
udang karang – lobster

Thanks

Many thanks to the travellers who used the last edition and wrote to us with helpful hints, useful advice and interesting anecdotes. Your names follow.

Donovan Abbott, Palmer Acheson, Wayne Adams, Aryaperwira Adileksana, Jaya Aguilar, Norman Alcuri, Froukje Algera, Priscilla Anson, Marc Arends, Philip Asher, Tim Ashton, Chris Bain, Louis Balme, Angelica Baltus, Gavin Bateman, Lynne Bateman, A Battisti, Suzanne Becker, Gina Behrens, Maria & Tony Benfield, Edith Berger, Helena Bergqvist, Marinus & Jeanette Bergsma, Jerry Berowne, Walter Bertschinger, Ken Bilney, Annie & Norman Bilton, Jacob Binnema, Diane Blanckensee, Marc Bone, Nyki Bonnet, Mattijs Bouma, Rachel Brakke, Eric Branckaert, Viv Braznell, Siobhan Breslin, Kate Brinton, M Brock, Michael & Wendy Brook, Dick & Tracy Brown, Steve Brown, Ulrike Bruckmann, Debbie Bruk, Hannah Buchanan-Smith, Eny Anggraini Buchary, Renee Buffery, Dan Butler, Guy Butterworth.

Beth Cain, Roger Campbell, Alex Carr, Simon Carr-Smith, Denis Cassell, Rosetta Cassini, K M Chow, James Close, Doug Cluer, Jayne Coates, Jonathan Copeland, Joseph Copeland, Dan Coplan, Malcolm Corry, Louise Cote, Peter J Cox, Roby Cran, Nick Czap, Ake Dahllof, Mike Dannatt, Claire Davies, Kathleen Davison, Maxine de Burnay, Stijn de Geus, Toos & Ed de Haan, Aafke de Jong, Lucy de Rijk, Randall de Rijk, Christopher de Silva, Veronique Deblaton, Ian Dempsey, Craig Dicker, Jens Die Kulbes, Karen Dimattina, Francesco Diodato, Manta Dive, Nicole Dolenz, Nicoline Dolman, Bonno & Renate Domke, Jeremy Dowdeswell, Jeremy & Diana Dowdeswell, Sharon Drinkwine, T Duym.

Andrea Eaton, Rick Eaton, Pandora Edmiston, Agneta Ehn, Kristin Eichhorn, Howard Elias, Barnaby Ellis, Brian Ellis, Roger Elvins, Delmasi Emanuele, Rea Erne, Chris Esmond, John Fairholm, Dewi Feehily, Luci Ferspal, Rachael Fewster, Melanie Finlayson, Stanley Finn, Deanna Finnman, Willem Fisher, Janis Fleming, Valerie Fong, Kate & Steve Foskey, Diodato Francesco, Sarah Franklin, Louise Frear, Giselle Fredette, Mike Galvin, Russell Garbutt, Neville Garner, Scott Garner, Ronald Garrett, Tim Gay, Nick Geyman, Dave Goldberg, Natalie Goldstein, Joanne Golton, Vida Goodvach, Del Greger, Dale Grewcock, Michael Griffin, Danielle Grimmon, Marcel & Sytske Groeneweg, Suzie Gruber, Gaetan Guilhon, Mutlu Gunay.

Robert Haines, B N Hall, Kenneth Hall, Rob Hall, Maeve Halpin, Alicia Halton, Candida Hardenberg, Leanne & Nigel Hardie, Barry Harley, Robert Hart, Oliver Harwood, Sharon Hayne, Allan Healy, Phil Heffernan, Albert & Maria Hell, K M Hempfing, Jason Henchman, Andrew Hennessy, Johan Hensen, Keith Hepburn, Monika & Gerald Heschl, Paul Heslop, Bianca Heuckeroth, Philippe Heurtault, Barbara Higgs, Jessica Hilliard, Lol Hind, S Hipperson, Karina Ho, Martina Hochfilzer, Maurice Hoeneveld, Martine Hofstede, Siri Holm, Emma Holmbro, Natalie Hooton, Suzy Howell, Laura Hughes, Rhidian Hughes, Victoria Hume, Rick Hunt, Geoff Hutcheison, Elaine Inns, Ari Iso-Rautio, Wiebrand H Jager, Bill Jarrell, Janaka Jayasingha, Harriet Joao, Komang John, Isabelle Johnson, Robin Johnson, Andy Jones, Mike Jones, Ronaele Jones, Wally Jones.

Alex Ka, Dave Kavanagh, Patrick Kavanagh, Adeline Kee, Colum Keelaghan, Susan Kelso, Jeltsje Kemerink, Pam Kerslake, Joy Kitch, Joop & Ineke Kleijwegt, Jessica Kleiman, Nicole Kleinschmidt, Holger Knoedler, Stefanie Komar, Nynke Koopen, Wim Kuijper, Die Kulbes, Peter Kunkel, Birgit Kurz, Jean Kwok, Michelle Lamming, Peter Lange, Dimitri Lanssens, Klaus Latta, Tom & Becky Lau, Marije Laverman, Ian J Lean, Marylise Lefort, Robert Lehrmitt, Mikelson Leong, Chris Lewis, Nancy & Brett May Licciardello, Judy Lief, Joanne Lillie, Monica Lindvall, Christie & Wiley Long, Sybille Luegenbiehl, Stephen Lyons, Stephanie Machlin, Meelik Mallene, Tomas Maltby, Lee Marsdon, Peter Martin, Sue Mather, Peter Mayes, Sue McArthur, June & Ian McCormack, Dirk McCormick, Craig McDonald, Bob McGuigan, Garry McKellar-James, Laurent CCI Meurthe & Moselle, Thierry Michel, Annie Millard, Emma Mills, Misha Milosavljevic, Glenn Miscall, Theresa Montalan, Joe Montalto, Jose Moreno, Melissa Morris, Sharon Morrison, Gebnard Moser, Cathy Muir, Sanneke Mulderink.

Yermia Nahor T, Stuart Neilson, Paul Nevulis, Dana Nibby, Helen Nicolle, Benny Nielsen, Kay Nolte, Mr & Mrs Noyelle, Sahabuddin Nur, Camilla Nygren, James Oehlcke, Mike Ogden, Ellen Hoog, Michael Oppel, Alison Osborne, Jackie O'Toole, Liliana Paggiaro, Linton Parker, Juliette Parrish, Adam Parsons, Jim Parsons, Jon Pauwels, Angela Peebles, Gill Pereira, Gualberto Perez, Ewa Pettersson, John & Hilary Phillips, Jan Pitts, Nina Pool, Kira Posewitz, Vicky Preston, Herman Prust, Anika Psaila Savona, Sia Suk Pying,

Lesley Queripel, Ingo Rammer, Leah Rasmussen, Tony Reed, Daniel Reeve, Kate Reeves, Anne Reis, Emily Richardson, Jeanette Ridge, lloyd Ridley, Richard Rietvelt, John D Robertson, Debra & Howard Robinson, Peter Roskilly, Karl Roth, Esma Rubini, Christel Ruijs, Regan Russell, Daune Ruth-Heffelbower.

Massimo Sacco, Carl F Salans, Urmimala Sarkar, Kathrin Sattmann, Robert Scanlon, Oliver Scemama, Jack & Joan Schafer, Dimitri Schellings, C Schipper, Mahendra Schmaehling, Martin Schmidt, Emile Schra, Joan Schutte, Stephanie Schwark, Kate Scott, Dee Scully, James Sheppard, Dana Shields, Shawn Slater, Matthew Smedley, Sammy Smedley, Brad Smith, Dr Joel Smith, Emily Smith, Reuben Smith, Heidi Soonae, Susan Spilman, Kirsten Staughan, Robert Steadman, Jorg W Steinhauer, Mareike & Lena Steinmann, Rebecca Stenn, Jill & John Stephenson, Jessica Stevens, Philippa Stevens, Sandra Stevenson, Brian Stewart, Laird Stiegler, Saskia Stokkermans, Phil Storey, Betsy Stumme, Jamie Sturt, Gregory Supple, Rachel Symes, Holy Taylor, Tom Templeton, Lannie Thielen, Lorne Thompson, Martijn Tiet, Catherine Topp, Francisco Trocado, Dylan Tromp, Neil Trudgen, Christoph Tschirky, Stephen Tuff, Anne Tundell, Alexia & Paul Turner.

Andy Unger, Jez Upton, Huib & Annemarie van de Kerk, Anton van den Broecke, Edward van den Elshout, Caroline & Herman van den Wall Bake, Jusus van der meer, Thomas van der Vliet, Rosalyn van Esch, Edwin van Holsteijn, Brenda van Lier, M van Wier, Desiree van zomeren, Inge van Zuuren, Anna Vandepol, Jane Venter, Brian Veprek, Raymond Vermeulen, Peter Verschuuren, Lena Marie Vestli, Pieternal Vollaard, Kai Vonk, Astrid Waack, Simon Waldvogel, Karen Walters, Marilyn Ware, Jeff Waters, Rod Waters, Sue Waters, Wendy Watson, Jane Weber, Jessie Wee, Jay Weissman, Erin Westerhout, Ron Westerhout, Heidi Westerlund, Robert & Benedicte White, Laura Wickens, Justine Williams, Liz Williams, Paul Williamson, Phil Wilson, Tom Wilson, Till Winkelmann, Mell Winnith, Roger Windsor, Mandy Wolthuis, W C Wong, Sue Wragg, Graeme Wright, Kent Wyllie, Caroline Yeh-Garner, Mike Yough, Gordon & Miriam Zittel, Neb Zurkic.

LONELY PLANET

You already know that Lonely Planet produces more than this one guidebook, but you might not be aware of the other products we have on this region. Here is a selection of titles that you may want to check out as well:

Healthy Travel Asia & India
ISBN 1 86450 051 4
US$5.95 • UK£3.99

South-East Asia phrasebook
ISBN 0 86442 435 3
US$8.95 • UK£5.99

Indonesia
ISBN 0 86442 690 9
US$25.95 • UK£15.99

World Food Indonesia
ISBN 1 74059 009 0
US$13.99 • UK£8.99

Diving & Snorkeling Bali & Lombok
ISBN 1 86450 129 4
US$16.99 • UK£10.99

South-East Asia on a shoestring
ISBN 1 86450 158 8
US$21.99 • UK£12.99

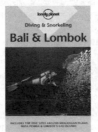

Read This First: Asia & India
ISBN 1 86450 049 2
US$14.95 • UK£8.99

Available wherever books are sold

LONELY PLANET

Guides by Region

Lonely Planet is known worldwide for publishing practical, reliable and no-nonsense travel information in our guides and on our Web site. The Lonely Planet list covers just about every accessible part of the world. Currently there are 16 series: Travel guides, Shoestring guides, Condensed guides, Phrasebooks, Read This First, Healthy Travel, Walking guides, Cycling guides, Watching Wildlife guides, Pisces Diving & Snorkeling guides, City Maps, Road Atlases, Out to Eat, World Food, Journeys travel literature and Pictorials.

AFRICA Africa on a shoestring • Botswana • Cairo • Cairo City Map • Cape Town • Cape Town City Map • East Africa • Egypt • Egyptian Arabic phrasebook • Ethiopia, Eritrea & Djibouti • Ethiopian Amharic phrasebook • The Gambia & Senegal • Healthy Travel Africa • Kenya • Malawi • Morocco • Moroccan Arabic phrasebook • Mozambique • Namibia • Read This First: Africa • South Africa, Lesotho & Swaziland • Southern Africa • Southern Africa Road Atlas • Swahili phrasebook • Tanzania, Zanzibar & Pemba • Trekking in East Africa • Tunisia • Watching Wildlife East Africa • Watching Wildlife Southern Africa • West Africa • World Food Morocco • Zambia • Zimbabwe, Botswana & Namibia
Travel Literature: Mali Blues: Traveling to an African Beat • The Rainbird: A Central African Journey • Songs to an African Sunset: A Zimbabwean Story

AUSTRALIA & THE PACIFIC Aboriginal Australia & the Torres Strait Islands •Auckland • Australia • Australian phrasebook • Australia Road Atlas • Cycling Australia • Cycling New Zealand • Fiji • Fijian phrasebook • Healthy Travel Australia, NZ & the Pacific • Islands of Australia's Great Barrier Reef • Melbourne • Melbourne City Map • Micronesia • New Caledonia • New South Wales • New Zealand • Northern Territory • Outback Australia • Out to Eat – Melbourne • Out to Eat – Sydney • Papua New Guinea • Pidgin phrasebook • Queensland • Rarotonga & the Cook Islands • Samoa • Solomon Islands • South Australia • South Pacific • South Pacific phrasebook • Sydney • Sydney City Map • Sydney Condensed • Tahiti & French Polynesia • Tasmania • Tonga • Tramping in New Zealand • Vanuatu • Victoria • Walking in Australia • Watching Wildlife Australia • Western Australia
Travel Literature: Islands in the Clouds: Travels in the Highlands of New Guinea • Kiwi Tracks: A New Zealand Journey • Sean & David's Long Drive

CENTRAL AMERICA & THE CARIBBEAN Bahamas, Turks & Caicos • Baja California • Belize, Guatemala & Yucatán • Bermuda • Central America on a shoestring • Costa Rica • Costa Rica Spanish phrasebook • Cuba • Cycling Cuba • Dominican Republic & Haiti • Eastern Caribbean • Guatemala • Havana • Healthy Travel Central & South America • Jamaica • Mexico • Mexico City • Panama • Puerto Rico • Read This First: Central & South America • Virgin Islands • World Food Caribbean • World Food Mexico • Yucatán
Travel Literature: Green Dreams: Travels in Central America

EUROPE Amsterdam • Amsterdam City Map • Amsterdam Condensed • Andalucía • Athens • Austria • Baltic States phrasebook • Barcelona • Barcelona City Map • Belgium & Luxembourg • Berlin • Berlin City Map • Britain • British phrasebook • Brussels, Bruges & Antwerp • Brussels City Map • Budapest • Budapest City Map • Canary Islands • Catalunya & the Costa Brava • Central Europe • Central Europe phrasebook • Copenhagen • Corfu & the Ionians • Corsica • Crete • Crete Condensed • Croatia • Cycling Britain • Cycling France • Cyprus • Czech & Slovak Republics • Czech phrasebook • Denmark • Dublin • Dublin City Map • Dublin Condensed • Eastern Europe • Eastern Europe phrasebook • Edinburgh • Edinburgh City Map • England • Estonia, Latvia & Lithuania • Europe on a shoestring • Europe phrasebook • Finland • Florence • Florence City Map • France • Frankfurt City Map • Frankfurt Condensed • French phrasebook • Georgia, Armenia & Azerbaijan • Germany • German phrasebook • Greece • Greek Islands • Greek phrasebook • Hungary • Iceland, Greenland & the Faroe Islands • Ireland • Italian phrasebook • Italy • Kraków • Lisbon • The Loire • London • London City Map • London Condensed • Madrid • Madrid City Map • Malta • Mediterranean Europe • Milan, Turin & Genoa • Moscow • Munich • Netherlands • Normandy • Norway • Out to Eat – London • Out to Eat – Paris • Paris • Paris City Map • Paris Condensed • Poland • Polish phrasebook • Portugal • Portuguese phrasebook • Prague • Prague City Map • Provence & the Côte d'Azur • Read This First: Europe • Rhodes & the Dodecanese • Romania & Moldova • Rome • Rome City Map • Rome Condensed • Russia, Ukraine & Belarus • Russian phrasebook • Scandinavian & Baltic Europe • Scandinavian phrasebook • Scotland • Sicily • Slovenia • South-West France • Spain • Spanish phrasebook • Stockholm • St Petersburg • St Petersburg City Map • Sweden • Switzerland • Tuscany • Ukrainian phrasebook • Venice • Vienna • Wales • Walking in Britain • Walking in France • Walking in Ireland • Walking in Italy • Walking in Scotland • Walking in Spain • Walking in Switzerland • Western Europe • World Food France • World Food Greece • World Food Ireland • World Food Italy • World Food Spain **Travel Literature:** After Yugoslavia • Love and War in the Apennines • The Olive Grove: Travels in Greece • On the Shores of the Mediterranean • Round Ireland in Low Gear • A Small Place in Italy

LONELY PLANET

Mail Order

Lonely Planet products are distributed worldwide. They are also available by mail order from Lonely Planet, so if you have difficulty finding a title please write to us. North and South American residents should write to 150 Linden St, Oakland, CA 94607, USA; European and African residents should write to 10a Spring Place, London NW5 3BH, UK; and residents of other countries to Locked Bag 1, Footscray, Victoria 3011, Australia.

INDIAN SUBCONTINENT & THE INDIAN OCEAN Bangladesh • Bengali phrasebook • Bhutan • Delhi • Goa • Healthy Travel Asia & India • Hindi & Urdu phrasebook • India • India & Bangladesh City Map • Indian Himalaya • Karakoram Highway • Kathmandu City Map • Kerala • Madagascar • Maldives • Mauritius, Réunion & Seychelles • Mumbai (Bombay) • Nepal • Nepali phrasebook • North India • Pakistan • Rajasthan • Read This First: Asia & India • South India • Sri Lanka • Sri Lanka phrasebook • Tibet • Tibetan phrasebook • Trekking in the Indian Himalaya • Trekking in the Karakoram & Hindukush • Trekking in the Nepal Himalaya • World Food India **Travel Literature**: The Age of Kali: Indian Travels and Encounters • Hello Goodnight: A Life of Goa • In Rajasthan • Maverick in Madagascar • A Season in Heaven: True Tales from the Road to Kathmandu • Shopping for Buddhas • A Short Walk in the Hindu Kush • Slowly Down the Ganges

MIDDLE EAST & CENTRAL ASIA Bahrain, Kuwait & Qatar • Central Asia • Central Asia phrasebook • Dubai • Farsi (Persian) phrasebook • Hebrew phrasebook • Iran • Israel & the Palestinian Territories • Istanbul • Istanbul City Map • Istanbul to Cairo • Istanbul to Kathmandu • Jerusalem • Jerusalem City Map • Jordan • Lebanon • Middle East • Oman & the United Arab Emirates • Syria • Turkey • Turkish phrasebook • World Food Turkey • Yemen **Travel Literature**: Black on Black: Iran Revisited • Breaking Ranks: Turbulent Travels in the Promised Land • The Gates of Damascus • Kingdom of the Film Stars: Journey into Jordan

NORTH AMERICA Alaska • Boston • Boston City Map • Boston Condensed • British Columbia • California & Nevada • California Condensed • Canada • Chicago • Chicago City Map • Chicago Condensed • Florida • Georgia & the Carolinas • Great Lakes • Hawaii • Hiking in Alaska • Hiking in the USA • Honolulu & Oahu City Map • Las Vegas • Los Angeles • Los Angeles City Map • Louisiana & the Deep South • Miami • Miami City Map • Montreal • New England • New Orleans • New Orleans City Map • New York City • New York City City Map • New York City Condensed • New York, New Jersey & Pennsylvania • Oahu • Out to Eat – San Francisco • Pacific Northwest • Rocky Mountains • San Diego & Tijuana • San Francisco • San Francisco City Map • Seattle • Seattle City Map • Southwest • Texas • Toronto • USA • USA phrasebook • Vancouver • Vancouver City Map • Virginia & the Capital Region • Washington, DC • Washington, DC City Map • World Food New Orleans **Travel Literature**: Caught Inside: A Surfer's Year on the California Coast • Drive Thru America

NORTH-EAST ASIA Beijing • Beijing City Map • Cantonese phrasebook • China • Hiking in Japan • Hong Kong & Macau • Hong Kong City Map • Hong Kong Condensed • Japan • Japanese phrasebook • Korea • Korean phrasebook • Kyoto • Mandarin phrasebook • Mongolia • Mongolian phrasebook • Seoul • Shanghai • South-West China • Taiwan • Tokyo • Tokyo Condensed • World Food Hong Kong • World Food Japan **Travel Literature**: In Xanadu: A Quest • Lost Japan

SOUTH AMERICA Argentina, Uruguay & Paraguay • Bolivia • Brazil • Brazilian phrasebook • Buenos Aires • Buenos Aires City Map • Chile & Easter Island • Colombia • Ecuador & the Galapagos Islands • Healthy Travel Central & South America • Latin American Spanish phrasebook • Peru • Quechua phrasebook • Read This First: Central & South America • Rio de Janeiro • Rio de Janeiro City Map • Santiago de Chile • South America on a shoestring • Trekking in the Patagonian Andes • Venezuela **Travel Literature**: Full Circle: A South American Journey

SOUTH-EAST ASIA Bali & Lombok • Bangkok • Bangkok City Map • Burmese phrasebook • Cambodia • Cycling Vietnam, Laos & Cambodia • East Timor phrasebook • Hanoi • Healthy Travel Asia & India • Hill Tribes phrasebook • Ho Chi Minh City (Saigon) • Indonesia • Indonesian phrasebook • Indonesia's Eastern Islands • Java • Lao phrasebook • Laos • Malay phrasebook • Malaysia, Singapore & Brunei • Myanmar (Burma) • Philippines • Pilipino (Tagalog) phrasebook • Read This First: Asia & India • Singapore • Singapore City Map • South-East Asia on a shoestring • South-East Asia phrasebook • Thailand • Thailand's Islands & Beaches • Thailand, Vietnam, Laos & Cambodia Road Atlas • Thai phrasebook • Vietnam • Vietnamese phrasebook • World Food Indonesia • World Food Thailand • World Food Vietnam

ALSO AVAILABLE: Antarctica • The Arctic • The Blue Man: Tales of Travel, Love and Coffee • Brief Encounters: Stories of Love, Sex & Travel • Buddhist Stupas in Asia: The Shape of Perfection • Chasing Rickshaws • The Last Grain Race • Lonely Planet ... On the Edge: Adventurous Escapades from Around the World • Lonely Planet Unpacked • Lonely Planet Unpacked Again • Not the Only Planet: Science Fiction Travel Stories • Ports of Call: A Journey by Sea • Sacred India • Travel Photography: A Guide to Taking Better Pictures • Travel with Children • Tuvalu: Portrait of an Island Nation

Index

Abbreviations

L – Lombok

Text

Bold indicates maps.

Bold indicates maps.

Boxed Text

MAP LEGEND

CITY ROUTES

Freeway	Freeway	====	Unsealed Road
Highway	Primary Road		One Way Street
Road	Secondary Road		Pedestrian Street
Street	Street	⊓⊓⊓⊓⊓	Stepped Street
Lane	Lane	⌣)-	Pass, Tunnel
	On/Off Ramp		Footbridge

REGIONAL ROUTES

	Tollway, Freeway
	Primary Road
	Secondary Road
	Minor Road

BOUNDARIES

	International
	District
⊥⊥⊥⊥	Cliff/Escarpment
	Fortified Wall

HYDROGRAPHY

	River, Creek		Dry Lake, Salt Lake
	Canal	⊙ ~~→	Spring, Rapids
	Lake	⊛ ⇥⇥	Waterfalls

TRANSPORT ROUTES & STATIONS

---O--	Train	-----🔲	Ferry
	Underground Train	-----	Walking Trail
—Ⓜ	Metro	....	Walking Tour
	Tramway		Path
⊢⊣⊢⊣	Cable Car, Chairlift		Pier or Jetty

AREA FEATURES

	Building		Market		Beach		Campus

⊛	Park, Gardens		Sports Ground	+ + +	Cemetery		Plaza

POPULATION SYMBOLS

✪ CAPITAL	National Capital	● CITY	City	● Village	Village
◉ CAPITAL	Provincial Capital	● Town	Town		Urban Area

MAP SYMBOLS

▪	Place to Stay	▼	Place to Eat	●	Point of Interest

✈	Airport	🛂	Embassy	🏛 🏛 Museum, Palace (Puri)	⚓ 🏄	Surfing, Swimming
⑤	Bank	❾	Golf Course	⬛	National Park	☎	Telephone
🐦	Bird Sanctuary/Zoo	⊕	Hospital	🅿 ⊙ Parking, Petrol	⚑ ⚑	Temple, Meru
🚌 🚏	Bus Terminal/Stop	🖥	Internet Cafe	🚔 ✉ Police, Post Office	🏯	Temple (Mahayama)
⛺ ⌂	Camping Area, Cave	⚿ ☀ Lighthouse, Lookout	🍺	Pub or Bar	❶	Tourist Information
✚	Church	⚑ ☪ Monument, Mosque	🏚 ⚓ Ruin, Shipwreck	▣	Tomb
🤿 ⊙	Diving, Snorkelling	▲	Mountain	🛒	Shopping Centre	🚉	Transport

Note: not all symbols displayed above appear in this book

LONELY PLANET OFFICES

Australia
Locked Bag 1, Footscray, Victoria 3011
☎ 03 8379 8000 fax 03 8379 8111
email: talk2us@lonelyplanet.com.au

UK
10a Spring Place, London NW5 3BH
☎ 020 7428 4800 fax 020 7428 4828
email: go@lonelyplanet.co.uk

USA
150 Linden St, Oakland, CA 94607
☎ 510 893 8555 TOLL FREE: 800 275 8555
fax 510 893 8572
email: info@lonelyplanet.com

France
1 rue du Dahomey, 75011 Paris
☎ 01 55 25 33 00 fax 01 55 25 33 01
email: bip@lonelyplanet.fr
www.lonelyplanet.fr

World Wide Web: www.lonelyplanet.com *or* AOL keyword: lp
Lonely Planet Images: www.lonelyplanetimages.com